Drama
An Introduction

Robert DiYanni

Boston   Burr Ridge, IL   Dubuque, IA   Madison, WI
New York   San Francisco   St. Louis
Bangkok Bogotá Caracas Lisbon London   Madrid Mexico City
Milan   New Delhi   Seoul   Singapore   Sydney   Taipei   Toronto

McGraw-Hill Higher Education

A Division of The McGraw-Hill Companies

DRAMA: AN INTRODUCTION

This book is printed on acid-free paper.

1 2 3 4 5 6 7 8 9 0 KPH/KPH 9 0 4 3 2 1 0 9

ISBN 0-07-229507-4 (combined volume)
ISBN 0-07-229509-0 (fiction)
ISBN 0-07-229510-4 (poetry)
ISBN 0-07-229511-2 (drama)

Cover image: *Peterson, Margaret, Three Women
(1938, egg tempera on wood), The Oakland Museum of California*
Editorial director: *Phillip A. Butcher*
Sponsoring editor: *Sarah Touborg Moyers*
Developmental editor: *Alexis Walker*
Editorial assistant: *Bennett Morrison*
Project manager: *Margaret Rathke*
Manager, new book production: *Melonie Salvati*
Designer: *Kiera Cunningham*
Senior photo research coordinator: *Keri Johnson*
Supplement coordinator: *Marc Mattson*
Compositor: *GAC Indianapolis*
Typeface: *10.5/12 Bembo*
Printer: *Quebecor Printing Book Group/Hawkins*

Library of Congress has cataloged an earlier edition as follows:

DiYanni, Robert.
    Literature: reading fiction, poetry, and drama / Robert DiYanni.
    — Compact ed.
        p.   cm.
    Includes index.
        ISBN 0-07-229507-4 (combined). — ISBN 0-07-229509-0 (fiction). —
    ISBN 0-07-229510-4 (poetry). — ISBN 0-07-229511-2 (drama)
        1. Literature.   2. Literature—Collections.   I. Title.
PN49.D53   2000
808—dc21   99-14165
                                                                                                      CIP

www.mhhe.com

About the Author

Robert DiYanni is Professor of English at Pace University, Pleasantville, New York, where he teaches courses in literature, writing, and humanities. He has also taught at Queens College of the City University of New York, at New York University in the Graduate Rhetoric Program, and most recently in the Expository Writing Program at Harvard University. He received his B.A. from Rutgers University (1968) and his Ph.D. from the City University of New York (1976).

Professor DiYanni has written articles and reviews on various aspects of literature, composition, and pedagogy. His books include *The McGraw-Hill Book of Poetry; Women's Voices; Like Season'd Timber: New Essays on George Herbert;* and *Modern American Poets: Their Voices and Visions* (a text to accompany the Public Broadcasting Television series that aired in 1988). With Kraft Rompf, he edited *The McGraw-Hill Book of Poetry* (1993) and *The McGraw-Hill Book of Fiction* (1995). With Janetta Benton he wrote *Arts & Culture: An Introduction to the Humanities* (1998).

For my colleagues,
who have made the reading
and teaching of drama an
ever-increasing pleasure

Contents

Preface

Drama: An Introduction presents an approach to plays that emphasizes reading as an active enterprise involving thought and feeling. It encourages students to value their emotional reactions and their previous experience with life and with language. Students are introduced to interpretation through illustrated discussions of the elements of drama. They are invited to consider why they respond as they do and how their responses change during subsequent readings of a play; they are asked, in short, to relate their experience in reading plays to their experience in living. They are encouraged to see dramatic literature as a significant reflection of life and an imaginative extension of its possibilities.

From first page to last, *Drama* is designed to involve students in the twin acts of reading and analysis. The genre of drama is introduced by a three-part explanatory overview of the reading process. The introduction is organized around the approach to texts outlined in Robert Scholes's *Textual Power* (Yale University Press, 1985), modified and adapted to my own approach to teaching literature. Scholes identifies three aspects of literary response: reading, interpretation, and criticism. The three-part structure of the introduction breaks down as follows:

the experience of drama
the interpretation of drama
the evaluation of drama

Our *experience* of drama concerns our impressions of a work, especially our subjective impressions and emotional responses. *Interpretation* involves intellectual and analytical thinking. And the *evaluation* of drama involves an assessment of aesthetic distinction along with a consideration of a work's social, moral, and cultural values.

Paralleling this schema for the introductory discussion is a similarly organized introduction to writing about drama. This chapter describes how to
apply and adapt the approaches presented in the drama introduction. The writing chapter includes examples of student writing, sample topics, documentation procedures, and a general review of the writing process.

For the introduction to drama, I have also provided a separate illustration of
the "act of reading": a set of questions in response to the opening scene of Lady
Gregory's *The Rising of the Moon* that suggest specific strategies for the critical
reading of dramatic literature.

In addition to emphasizing the subjective, analytical, and evaluative aspects
of reading plays, *Drama* introduces the traditional elements, such as plot, character, and setting, through discussions tied to specific works. Throughout these
discussions, students are asked to return to certain plays and reconsider them
from different perspectives.

A word about the choice of plays. The classic and contemporary selections
reflect a wide range of styles, voices, subjects, and points of view. Complex and
challenging works appear alongside more readily approachable and accessible
ones. *Drama,* moreover, contains both in sufficient variety for instructors to assign the more accessible ones for students to read and write about on their
own, while reserving the more ambitious selections for class discussion.

This edition of *Drama: An Introduction* is based on the fourth edition of *Literature*. The following features should be highlighted:

- Writing instruction includes a chapter on Writing about Drama and another
  on Writing with Sources.
- Works are provided with dates of publication or performance.
- The works of two dramatists are highlighted and contextualized. Multiple selections are included for Sophocles and Shakespeare and are accompanied by
  an extensive biocritical introduction and critical perspectives written by literary scholars.
- An extensive chapter on Critical Perspectives has been included, in which
  the major schools of literary theory are described and illustrated. Guiding
  questions and brief bibliographies augment the application of ten critical
  approaches.

This book represents the cooperative efforts of a number of people. This sin-
gle-genre spinoff owes its existence ultimately to Steve Pensinger, who encouraged me to develop the first edition of the four-genre full-size book,
Literature: Reading Fiction, Poetry, Drama, and the Essay, the predecessor of
the newly published compact edition. For both this book and for the compact edition of *Literature,* its parent, I have had the pleasure of working with
McGraw-Hill colleagues Sarah Moyers, English editor; Alexis Walker, developmental editor; and Maggie Bogovich, project manager. Each provided
me with the kind of high-quality professional assistance I have come to expect from McGraw-Hill. It continues to be a pleasure to work with them and
with their publishing colleagues.

I have had the additional pleasure of working with Professor Tom Kitts of St. John's University. Professor Kitts has written a practical and graceful instructor's manual, which serves as a rich and rewarding source of practical and provocative classroom applications.

Finally, I want to thank my wife, Mary, whose loving assistance enabled me to complete this book on schedule.

ROBERT DIYANNI

CHAPTER ONE

Reading Plays

Drama, unlike the other literary genres, is a staged art. Plays are written to be performed by actors before an audience. But the plays we wish to see are not always performed. We might have to wait years, for example, to see a production of Sophocles' *Oedipus Rex* or Arthur Miller's *Death of a Salesman*. We simply might never have an opportunity to see certain plays. A reasonable alternative is to read them with attention to both their theatrical and literary dimensions.

THE EXPERIENCE OF DRAMA

As a literary genre, drama has affinities with fiction and poetry. Like fiction, drama possesses a narrative dimension: a play often narrates a story in the form of a plot. Like fiction, drama relies on dialogue and description, which takes the form of *stage directions,* lines describing characters, scenes, or actions with clues to production. Unlike fiction, however, in which a narrator often mediates between us and the story, there is no such authorial presence in drama. Instead, we hear the words of the characters directly.

Although drama is most like fiction, it shares features with poetry as well. Plays may, in fact, be written in verse: Shakespeare wrote in *blank verse* (unrhymed iambic pentameter), Molière in rhymed couplets. Plays, like lyric poems, are also overheard: we listen to characters expressing their concerns as if there were no audience present. Poems also contain dramatic elements. The dramatic lyrics and monologues of Robert Browning and some of the poems of John Donne portray characters speaking and listening to one another.

Plays may be vehicles of persuasion. Henrik Ibsen and Bernard Shaw frequently used the stage to dramatize ideas and issues. For most of his plays Shaw wrote prefaces in which he discussed the plays' dominant ideas. In drama, ideas possess more primacy than they do in poetry and fiction, something to which critics of the genre testify. Aristotle, for example, made *thought* one of his six elements of drama; Eric Bentley, a modern critic, entitled one of his books *The Playwright as Thinker.*

But if we look exclusively to the literary aspects of drama, to its poetic and fictional elements, and to its dramatization of ideas, we may fail to appreciate its uniquely theatrical idiom. To gain this appreciation we should read drama with special attention to its performance elements. We can try to hear the voices of characters, and imagine tones and inflections. We can try to see mentally how characters look, where they stand in relation to one another, how they move and gesture. We can read, in short, as armchair directors and as aspiring actors and actresses considering the physical and practical realities of performance.

In doing so we will enrich our experience of the plays we read. Our experience of drama includes more than an intellectual understanding of the ideas particular plays may dramatize. It also includes our emotional reactions to plots and our responses to the interaction of the characters. It encompasses our vision of their dramatic worlds, and it is affected by our changing perceptions and feelings as we read. Our experience of reading drama involves more than a rational and analytic understanding of the text. More inclusive, more integrated, and more imaginative, that experience includes feelings as well as thought, emotional apprehension as well as intellectual comprehension.

As active readers of drama we will bring a special awareness of the ways the written text of a play (its *script*) suggests possibilities for performance. To suggest how we might do this, we include excerpts from three plays, each accompanied by notes and comments. As you read the first excerpt, the opening scene of Henrik Ibsen's *A Doll House,* consider what the stage directions and cast of characters reveal about the world of the play.

CHARACTERS

TORVALD HELMER, *A LAWYER*
NORA, *HIS WIFE*
DR. RANK
MRS. LINDE
NILS KROGSTAD, *A BANK CLERK*
THE HELMERS' THREE SMALL CHILDREN
ANNE-MARIE, *THEIR NURSE*
HELENE, *A MAID*
A DELIVERY BOY

The action takes place in HELMER'S *residence.*

ACT I

A comfortable room, tastefully but not expensively furnished. A door to the right in the back wall leads to the entryway, another to the left leads to HELMER'S *study. Between these doors, a piano. Midway in the left-hand wall a door, and further back a window. Near the window a round table with an armchair and a small sofa. In the right-hand wall, toward the rear a door, and nearer the foreground a porcelain stove with two armchairs and a rocking chair beside it. Between the stove and the side door, a small table. Engravings on the walls. An etagére with china figures and other small art objects; a small bookcase with richly bound books; the floor carpeted; a fire burning in the stove. It is a winter day.*

A bell rings in the entryway; shortly after we hear the door being unlocked. NORA *comes into the room, humming happily to herself; she is wearing street clothes and carries an armload of packages, which she puts down on the table to the right. She has left the hall door open; and through it a* DELIVERY BOY *is seen, holding a Christmas tree and a basket which he gives to the* MAID *who let them in.*

NORA: Hide the tree well, Helene. The children mustn't get a glimpse of it till this evening, after it's trimmed. (*To the* DELIVERY BOY, *taking out her purse*) How much?

DELIVERY BOY: Fifty, ma'am.

NORA: There's a crown. No, keep the change. (*The* BOY *thanks her and leaves.* NORA *shuts the door. She laughs softly to herself while taking off her street things. Drawing a bag of macaroons from her pocket, she eats a couple, then steals over and listens at her husband's study door.*) Yes, he's home. (*Hums again as she moves to the table, right.*)

HELMER (*from the study*): Is that my little lark twittering out there?

NORA (*busy opening some packages*): Yes, it is.

HELMER: Is that my squirrel rummaging around?

NORA: Yes!

HELMER: When did my squirrel get in?

NORA: Just now. (*Putting the macaroon bag in her pocket and wiping her mouth*) Do come in, Torvald, and see what I've bought.

HELMER: Can't be disturbed. (*After a moment he opens the door and peers in, pen in hand.*) Bought, you say? All that there? Has the little spendthrift been out throwing money around again?

NORA: Oh, but Torvald, this year we really should let ourselves go a bit. It's the first Christmas we haven't had to economize.

HELMER: But you know we can't go squandering.

NORA: Oh yes, Torvald, we can squander a little now. Can't we? Just a tiny, wee bit. Now that you've got a big salary and are going to make piles and piles of money.

HELMER: Yes—starting New Year's. But then it's a full three months till the raise comes through.

NORA: Pooh! We can borrow that long.

HELMER: Nora! (*Goes over and playfully takes her by the ear*) Are your scatterbrains off again? What if today I borrowed a thousand crowns, and you squandered them over Christmas week, and then on New Year's Eve a roof tile fell on my head, and I lay there—

NORA (*putting her hand on his mouth*): Oh! Don't say such things!

HELMER: Yes, but what if it happened—then what?

NORA: If anything so awful happened, then it just wouldn't matter if I had debts or not.

HELMER: Well, but the people I'd borrowed from?

NORA: Them? Who cares about them! They're strangers.

HELMER: Nora, Nora, how like a woman! No, but seriously, Nora, you know what I think about that. No debts! Never borrow! Something of freedom's lost—and something of beauty, too—from a home that's founded on borrowing and debt. We've made a brave stand up to now, the two of us; and we'll go right on like that the little while we have to.

NORA (*going toward the stove*):   Yes, whatever you say, Torvald.

HELMER (*following her*):   Now, now, the little lark's wings mustn't droop. Come on, don't be a sulky squirrel. (*Taking out his wallet*) Nora, guess what I have here.

NORA (*turning quickly*):   Money!

HELMER: There, see. (*Hands her some notes*) Good grief, I know how costs go up in a house at Christmastime.

NORA: Ten—twenty—thirty—forty. Oh, thank you, Torvald; I can manage no end on this.

HELMER: You really will have to.

NORA: Oh yes, I promise I will! But come here so I can show you everything I bought. And so cheap! Look, new clothes for Ivar here—and a sword. Here a horse and a trumpet for Bob. And a doll and a doll's bed here for Emmy; they're nothing much, but she'll tear them to bits in no time anyway. And here I have dress material and handkerchiefs for the maids. Old Anne-Marie really deserves something more.

HELMER: And what's in that package there?

NORA (*with a cry*):   Torvald, no! You can't see that till tonight!

HELMER: I see. But tell me now, you little prodigal, what have you thought of for yourself?

NORA: For myself? Oh, I don't want anything at all.

HELMER: Of course you do. Tell me just what—within reason—you'd most like to have.

NORA: I honestly don't know. Oh, listen, Torvald—

HELMER: Well?

NORA (*fumbling at his coat buttons, without looking at him*):   If you want to give me something, then maybe you could—you could—

HELMER: Come on, out with it.

NORA (*hurriedly*):   You could give me money, Torvald. No more than you think you can spare, then one of these days I'll buy something with it.

HELMER: But Nora—

NORA: Oh, please, Torvald darling, do that! I beg you, please. Then I could hang the bills in pretty gilt paper on the Christmas tree. Wouldn't that be fun?

HELMER: What are those little birds called that always fly through their fortunes?

NORA: Oh yes, spendthrifts; I know all that. But let's do as I say, Torvald; then I'll have time to decide what I really need most. That's very sensible, isn't it?

HELMER (*smiling*):   Yes, very—that is, if you actually hung onto the money I give you, and you actually used it to buy yourself something, But it goes for the house and for all sorts of foolish things, and then I only have to lay out some more.

NORA: Oh, but Torvald—

HELMER: Don't deny it, my dear little Nora. (*Putting his arm around her waist*) Spendthrifts are sweet, but they use up a frightful amount of money. It's incredible what it costs a man to feed such birds.

NORA: Oh, how can you say that! Really, I save everything I can.

HELMER (*laughing*):   Yes, that's the truth. Everything you can. But that's nothing at all.

NORA (*humming, with a smile of quiet satisfaction*):   Hm, if you only knew what expenses we larks and squirrels have, Torvald.

HELMER: You're an odd little one. Exactly the way your father was. You're never at a loss for scaring up money; but the moment you have it, it runs right out through your fingers; you never know what you've done with it. Well, one takes you as you are. It's deep in your blood. Yes, these things are hereditary, Nora.

NORA: Ah, I could wish I'd inherited many of Papa's qualities.

HELMER: And I couldn't wish you anything but just what you are, my sweet little lark. But wait; it seems to me you have a very—what should I call it?—a very suspicious look today—

NORA: I do?

HELMER: You certainly do. Look me straight in the eye.

NORA (looking at him):   Well?

HELMER (*shaking an admonitory finger*):   Surely my sweet tooth hasn't been running riot in town today, has she?

NORA: No. Why do you imagine that?

HELMER: My sweet tooth really didn't make a little detour through the confectioner's?

NORA: No, I assure you, Torvald—

HELMER: Hasn't nibbled some pastry?

NORA: No, not at all.

HELMER: Not even munched a macaroon or two?

NORA: No, Torvald, I assure you, really—

HELMER: There, there now. Of course I'm only joking.

NORA (*going to the table, right*):   You know I could never think of going against you.

HELMER: No, I understand that; and you *have* given me your word. (*Going over to her*) Well, you keep your little Christmas secrets to yourself, Nora darling. I expect they'll come to light this evening, when the tree is lit.

NORA: Did you remember to ask Dr. Rank?

HELMER: No. But there's no need for that; it's assumed he'll be dining with us. All the same, I'll ask him when he stops by here this morning. I've ordered some fine wine. Nora, you can't imagine how I'm looking forward to this evening.

NORA: So am I. And what fun for the children, Torvald!

HELMER: Ah, it's so gratifying to know that one's gotten a safe, secure job, and with a comfortable salary. It's a great satisfaction, isn't it?

NORA: Oh, it's wonderful!

HELMER: Remember last Christmas? Three whole weeks before, you shut yourself in every evening till long after midnight, making flowers for the Christmas tree, and all the other decorations to surprise us. Ugh, that was the dullest time I've ever lived through.

NORA: It wasn't at all dull for me.

HELMER (*smiling*): But the outcome *was* pretty sorry, Nora.

NORA: Oh, don't tease me with that again. How could I help it that the cat came in and tore everything to shreds.

HELMER: No, poor thing, you certainly couldn't. You wanted so much to please us all, and that's what counts. But it's just as well that the hard times are past.

NORA: Yes, it's really wonderful.

HELMER: Now I don't have to sit here alone, boring myself, and you don't have to tire your precious eyes and your fair little delicate hands—

NORA (*clapping her hands*): No, is it really true, Torvald, I don't have to? Oh, how wonderfully lovely to hear! (*Taking his arm*) Now I'll tell you just how I've thought we should plan things. Right after Christmas—(*The doorbell rings.*) Oh, the bell. (*Straightening the room up a bit*) Somebody would have to come. What a bore!

HELMER: I'm not at home to visitors, don't forget.

MAID (*from the hall doorway*): Ma'am, a lady to see you—

NORA: All right, let her come in.

MAID (*to* HELMER): And the doctor's just come too.

HELMER: Did he go right to my study?

MAID: Yes, he did.

The first thing we notice is the title: *A Doll House.* Does Ibsen alert us to a central concern of the play with this provocative title? Is it literal or symbolic? As we read the opening scene we test our preliminary sense of the title's implications. As we watch the relationship between Nora and Torvald unfold, we consider what the title suggests about their marriage.

Beneath the title is a list of characters. It's worth pausing over, for a playwright may signal important relationships there. Although only the husband-and-wife relationship of Torvald and Nora is signaled in Ibsen's list, we gain a sense of the play's social milieu from it. We notice that Torvald Helmer is a lawyer and Nils Krogstad a bank clerk, and that another woman and a doctor appear (in addition to minor figures such as a nurse and delivery boy).

We may pass quickly over these details before getting to the script. The first sentences set the scene we must keep in our mind's eye. The italicized words are stage directions (notes to the reader that establish the play's social context). Ibsen's opening stage directions describe the living room of a middle-class family with its piano, books, and pictures. The room represents a familiar world for many readers both in its realistic detail and its bourgeois domesticity.

The manner of Nora's arrival with her packages, the Christmas tree, and basket create an impression of the gaiety typically associated with the Christmas season. The playful quality of Nora's first words—about hiding the Christmas tree—reinforce our sense of this lightheartedness.

As we watch the initial incidents unfold, we begin making inferences and drawing tentative conclusions about the characters. We may wonder, for example, about the large tip Nora gives the delivery boy. Is it a sign of generosity or of extravagance? Does it reflect her state of mind? Does it reveal an inadequate attentiveness to money? Such questions occur almost unconsciously as we read, and the provisional answers we arrive at will be modified, strengthened, or abandoned as we read further.

After the exchange with the delivery boy, Nora hums softly to herself. Eating a few macaroons, she tiptoes stealthily to the closed door of her husband's study. Whatever our sense of these opening moments, the brief series of actions forms a prologue to the first major action of the play, Nora's conversation with Torvald. It is here that we gain our sense of Torvald, particularly of his concern for Nora's spending habits, which may unsettle our previous expectations about Nora's tip as an instance of generosity. We become alert.

Perhaps even stronger is our response to Torvald's pet names for Nora. He calls her "little lark" and "my squirrel," and repeatedly uses diminutives and possessives in addressing her. He also teases her, calling her "the little spendthrift," then gives her the money she wants. In a few swift strokes of dialogue and action, Ibsen shows us how seriously Torvald takes himself and how patronizingly he treats his wife.

Nora seems to accept the role Torvald assigns her. She submits to his teasing, accepts his explanations, and responds with childlike enthusiasm. Their gestures bear out the implications of the dialogue: Torvald pulls her ear, Nora clamps her hand over his mouth, plays flirtatiously with Torvald's coat buttons, claps her hands, and twice walks away from him—presumably knowing that he will follow. Torvald seems to enjoy the game as much as Nora. He follows her, probably not realizing that she is leading him and that he is responding as she wants him to.

When we see Torvald wag his finger at Nora and accuse her of eating sweets, we may sense that he doesn't really believe his accusation; he says as much almost immediately. But we, of course, know something that he does not: that Nora has indeed been eating macaroons. And we may suspect that there are other things about her that Torvald does not know from her previous remark, "Hm. If you only knew what expenses we larks and squirrels have, Torvald."

This dialogue is worth considering a bit further. Essentially, Ibsen has Torvald repeat his suspicious question and Nora deny that she has eaten sweets four times. The game that they make of this suggests that it is a familiar ritual. The action seems humorous partly because Torvald's accusations become increasingly accurate while he seems to remain unaware of their truth. Ibsen treats him ironically; there is a discrepancy between his view of himself and our view of him. How do we respond to his presumption and complacency? How do we evaluate his position as master of his house? And how might we sum up Torvald's attitude toward women?

THE INTERPRETATION OF DRAMA

In our discussion of the opening scene of *A Doll House,* we have focused on our experience of the developing action, on our impression of its two central characters, and on our attitudes toward them. Implicit in this discussion, however, was also an inevitable movement in the direction of interpretation. The questions we raised, the details we observed, and the hypotheses we entertained are all aspects of interpretation.

As we read the opening scene of *A Doll House,* observing the action and listening in on the dialogue, we have been drawing tentative conclusions about the characters and their relationship. Our curiosity has been aroused by dialogue, by action, and by the arrival of additional characters. Subsequent dialogue and action will either confirm our initial impressions or dispel them. We are left at the end of this first scene with a sense of uncertainty. While we don't know that this is not a happy household, neither do we know that it is. We have become alerted to possible problems involving matters of money and of secrecy. And we have been prepared to attend to the developing action as the scene changes and new characters appear. When we read the entire play later in this book, we will discover if our inferences are accurate and our suspicions justified.

Interpretation is a series of intellectual and analytical mental acts that lead to a conclusion about the play's meaning and significance. We can isolate four aspects of interpretation that we perform almost automatically. First, we observe details of speech, setting, and action. Second, we connect these details into patterns; we relate them so they begin to make sense to us. Third, we draw inferences—educated guesses or hypotheses—based on these connections. Finally, we formulate from our inferences a consistent and coherent interpretation of the play.

In reading (or viewing) any play, it is important to distinguish between our experience of a play and our interpretation of it. Our experience concerns our direct apprehension of the ongoing performance either on stage or in our mind's eye; interpretation concerns our comprehension of the work after we have finished reading or seeing it performed. Our experience of a play involves our emotions and subjective impressions of the play's dramatic action. Our interpretation of a play involves our ideas and thoughts about the meaning of that action. Our experience of a play is private, personal, and subjective: we discover how it entertains, moves, pleases, frustrates, or otherwise affects us. Our interpretation, though based on our experience, moves outward from it toward a set of more public and objective considerations. In interpreting a play, we try to discover what it might mean for others as well. We ask ourselves not so much: "How do I respond to the speech and actions of the characters?" but instead "What do their speech and actions signify; what do they mean?"

In answering the last question about Ibsen's *A Doll House,* we move beyond our personal response to consider what the play and its characters "say" or suggest more generally. Although it is not possible to understand a play's meaning without viewing or reading it in its entirety, we can nonetheless offer some interpretive possibilities from reading its opening scene alone. We might say, for example, that Ibsen's play appears to be about the relations between the sexes, especially the marital relationship. What *A Doll House* suggests, finally, about that relationship remains best determined by considering the play's final act.

From the opening scene we might surmise that the play is about more than marriage, however. There are hints in the first scene that *A Doll House* will have something to say about moral issues, particularly concerning money and secrecy. There are also hints that the play will concern itself with issues of character, not so much about how people behave, but why they behave as they do, and about who they really are and what they might become.

THE EVALUATION OF DRAMA

Our discussion of the scene from *A Doll House* focused explicitly on our experience of the play and on our acts of interpretation. And although we separated these discussions to identify more precisely each aspect of reading drama, our experience and interpretation of plays actually occur simultaneously; the two aspects of reading reinforce each other. But there is a third dimension to our reading of drama—evaluation—which was implicit in our previous discussions. Our comments about *A Doll House* raised questions about the values displayed in the characters' speech and actions.

What do we mean by the values displayed in a play? Generally speaking, we mean such things as cultural attitudes, moral dispositions, religious beliefs, and social norms. In considering such values as they emerge from our reading of any play, we should be careful to distinguish between the attitudes and dispositions of individual characters and those of the play (those of the author). We should also be aware of how our social and cultural perspectives may differ in important ways from the social norms and cultural attitudes of earlier times. To acknowledge how our individual way of responding to a play is influenced by gender, race, and ethnicity, as well as religious and cultural identity, is important in assessing its worth both for ourselves and for others. Since the values a play's characters display typically constitute an important focus of dramatic interest, our perception of the characters' values will affect to a considerable degree our own experience, interpretation, and evaluation of the overall work.

Further complicating our evaluation of a play is the extent to which we appreciate and enjoy its literary and theatrical artistry. For example, we may admire the way playwrights structure plots, largely by dangling before us a series of temporarily unanswered questions. We may find merit in portrayals of characters or the symbolic use of costume and setting. We may be affected by the language of the play, both in long speeches and in briefer exchanges of dialogue. We may derive aesthetic pleasure from these and many other exhibitions of stagecraft. And the enjoyment we derive, coupled with our assessment of what we understand as the playwright's central values or controlling idea, constitute the basis for our evaluation.

So the evaluation of any play is tied to our interpretation of it. But our interpretation is affected by our perception of the moral and cultural values it exhibits. In identifying the play's central concerns and in deciding which values are endorsed by the playwright, we shift back and forth between interpretation and evaluation. We do not first interpret the play and then evaluate it; we perform the two acts together. We evaluate and interpret a play, moreover, in conjunction with a subjective and immediate response to our experience of it. We can say, then, that each aspect of reading (experience, interpretation, evaluation) affects the other, and that the three aspects of reading drama taken together define our "reading" of any play.

Consider for a moment the way our values shape our interpretation and evaluation. If we see Ibsen's Torvald as an admirable figure, one whose treatment of his wife is appropriate and commendable, we will regard his behavior differently than if we see him as a fool who is manipulated by his wife. Our perspective on Torvald's character and on Nora's will be influenced partly by our gender. Women may be even more affected by Nora's game playing than by Torvald's male chauvinism. Additional influences on our perceptions of *A Doll House* include our cultural background, our experiences as a member of a family, our religious beliefs, and our ethnic traditions as they relate to marriage and the norms governing the relationship between husbands and wives.

Our aesthetic evaluation of *A Doll House* will be based on these and similar observations about the characters and our understanding of the author's view of them. Our evaluation will be affected by how relevant we find the central concerns of the play. (And what we find relevant at one time we may find irrelevant at another—and vice versa.) Our evaluation will also be influenced by our experience in reading and seeing other plays. Aesthetic evaluation thus involves comparing the literary and theatrical artistry of one play with the stagecraft of others. Without considerable experience with drama, judgments about a play's aesthetic merit need to be made with caution. But we must begin somewhere. Evaluation is inevitable, and we cannot avoid judging the plays we read, any more than we can avoid judging the people we meet.

The scene from Sophocles' *Antigonê* that follows provides an immediate opportunity to test these ideas. In reading the entire play later, we can consider how the characters' competing values, as evidenced in the excerpt, serve as the central conflict in the play. Scene II begins at the point where Antigonê, the daughter of Oedipus, has been taken into custody for violating an edict of Creon, King of Thebes. The edict concerns Antigonê's brother, Polyneicês, who was killed in a battle while fighting against Thebes. Creon has forbidden Polyneicês' burial; Antigonê has buried him.

SCENE II

(Reenter SENTRY *leading* ANTIGONÊ*)*

CHORAGOS: What does this mean? Surely this captive woman
   Is the Princess, Antigonê. Why should she be taken?
SENTRY: Here is the one who did it! We caught her
   In the very act of burying him.—Where is Creon?
CHORAGOS: Just coming from the house.

(Enter CREON, *center.)*

CREON: What has happened?   5
   Why have you come back so soon?
SENTRY *(expansively)*:   O King,
   A man should never be too sure of anything:
   I would have sworn
   That you'd not see me here again: your anger

Frightened me so, and the things you threatened me with; 10
But how could I tell then
That I'd be able to solve the case so soon?
No dice-throwing this time: I was only too glad to come!
Here is this woman. She is the guilty one:
We found her trying to bury him. 15
Take her, then; question her; judge her as you will.
I am through with the whole thing now, and glad of it.

CREON: But this is Antigonê! Why have you brought her here?
SENTRY: She was burying him, I tell you!
CREON (*severely*):   Is this the truth?
SENTRY: I saw her with my own eyes. Can I say more? 20
CREON: The details: come, tell me quickly!
SENTRY: It was like this:
After those terrible threats of yours, King,
We went back and brushed the dust away from the body.
The flesh was soft by now, and stinking,
So we sat on a hill to windward and kept guard. 25
No napping this time! We kept each other awake.
But nothing happened until the white round sun
Whirled in the center of the round sky over us:
Then, suddenly,
A storm of dust roared up from the earth, and the sky 30
Went out, the plain vanished with all its trees
In the stinging dark. We closed our eyes and endured it.
The whirlwind lasted a long time, but it passed;
And then we looked, and there was Antigonê!
I have seen 35
A mother bird come back to a stripped nest, heard
Her crying bitterly a broken note or two
For the young ones stolen. Just so, when this girl
Found the bare corpse, and all her love's work wasted,
She wept, and cried on heaven to damn the hands 40
That had done this thing.
                    And then she brought more dust
And sprinkled wine three times for her brother's ghost.
We ran and took her at once. She was not afraid,
Not even when we charged her with what she had done.
She denied nothing.
                    And this was a comfort to me, 45
And some uneasiness: for it is a good thing
To escape from death, but it is no great pleasure
To bring death to a friend.
                    Yet I always say
There is nothing so comfortable as your own safe skin!
CREON (*slowly, dangerously*):   And you, Antigonê, 50
You with your head hanging,—do you confess this thing?

ANTIGONÊ: I do. I deny nothing.
CREON (*to* SENTRY):   You may go.

                    (*Exit* SENTRY.)

(*To* ANTIGONÊ.) Tell me, tell me briefly:
Had you heard my proclamation touching this matter?
ANTIGONÊ: It was public. Could I help hearing it?   55
CREON: And yet you dared defy the law.
ANTIGONÊ: I dared.
    It was not God's proclamation. That final Justice
    That rules the world below makes no such laws.

Your edict, King, was strong,
But all your strength is weakness itself against   60
The immortal unrecorded laws of God.
They are not merely now: they were, and shall be,
Operative for ever, beyond man utterly.

I knew I must die, even without your decree:
I am only mortal. And if I must die   65
Now, before it is my time to die,
Surely this is no hardship: can anyone
Living, as I live, with evil all about me,
Think Death less than a friend? This death of mine
Is of no importance; but if I had left my brother   70
Lying in death unburied, I should have suffered.
Now I do not.

                    You smile at me. Ah Creon,
    Think me a fool, if you like; but it may well be
    That a fool convicts me of folly.
CHORAGOS: Like father, like daughter: both headstrong, deaf to reason!   75
    She has never learned to yield:
CREON: She has much to learn.
    The inflexible heart breaks first, the toughest iron
    Cracks first, and the wildest horses bend their necks
    At the pull of the smallest curb.
                                        Pride? In a slave?
    This girl is guilty of a double insolence,   80
    Breaking the given laws and boasting of it.
    Who is the man here,
    She or I, if this crime goes unpunished?
    Sister's child, or more than sister's child,
    Or closer yet in blood—she and her sister   85
    Win bitter death for this!

                    (*To* SERVANTS.)

Go, some of you,
Arrest Ismenê. I accuse her equally.
Bring her: you will find her sniffling in the house there.
Her mind's a traitor: crimes kept in the dark
Cry for light, and the guardian brain shudders; 90
But how much worse than this
Is brazen boasting of barefaced anarchy!
ANTIGONÊ: Creon, what more do you want than my death?
CREON: Nothing.
That gives me everything.
ANTIGONÊ: Then I beg you: kill me.
This talking is a great weariness: your words 95
Are distasteful to me, and I am sure that mine
Seem so to you. And yet they should not seem so:
I should have praise and honor for what I have done.
All these men here would praise me
Were their lips not frozen shut with fear of you. 100
(*Bitterly.*) Ah the good fortune of kings,
Licensed to say and do whatever they please!
CREON: You are alone here in that opinion.
ANTIGONÊ: No, they are with me. But they keep their tongues in leash.
CREON: Maybe. But you are guilty, and they are not. 105
ANTIGONÊ: There is no guilt in reverence for the dead.
CREON: But Eteoclês—was he not your brother too?
ANTIGONÊ: My brother too.
CREON: And you insult his memory?
ANTIGONÊ (*softly*): The dead man would not say that I insult it.
CREON: He would: for you honor a traitor as much as him. 110
ANTIGONÊ: His own brother, traitor or not, and equal in blood.
CREON: He made war on his country. Eteoclês defended it.
ANTIGONÊ: Nevertheless, there are honors due all the dead.
CREON: But not the same for the wicked as for the just.
ANTIGONÊ: Ah Creon, Creon, 115
Which of us can say what the gods hold wicked?
CREON: An enemy is an enemy, even dead.
ANTIGONÊ: It is my nature to join in love, not hate.
CREON (*finally losing patience*): Go join them then; if you must have your
love, Find it in hell! 120
CHORAGOS: But see, Ismenê comes:

(*Enter* ISMENÊ, *guarded.*)

Those tears are sisterly, the cloud
That shadows her eyes rains down gentle sorrow.
CREON: You too, Ismenê,
Snake in my ordered house, sucking my blood
Stealthily—and all the time I never knew 125
That these two sisters were aiming at my throne!

                                                     Ismenê,
Do you confess your share in this crime, or deny it?
Answer me.
ISMENÊ: Yes, if she will let me say so. I am guilty.   130
ANTIGONÊ (*coldly*):   No, Ismenê. You have no right to say so.
You would not help me, and I will not have you help me.
ISMENÊ: But now I know what you meant; and I am here
To join you, to take my share of punishment.
ANTIGONÊ: The dead man and the gods who rule the dead   135
Know whose act this was. Words are not friends.
ISMENÊ: Do you refuse me, Antigonê? I want to die with you:
I too have a duty that I must discharge to the dead.
ANTIGONÊ: You shall not lessen my death by sharing it.
ISMENÊ: What do I care for life when you are dead?   140
ANTIGONÊ: Ask Creon. You're always hanging on his opinions.
ISMENÊ: You are laughing at me. Why, Antigonê?
ANTIGONÊ: It's a joyless laughter, Ismenê.
ISMENÊ: But can I do nothing?
ANTIGONÊ: Yes. Save yourself. I shall not envy you.
There are those who will praise you; I shall have honor, too.   145
ISMENÊ: But we are equally guilty!
ANTIGONÊ: No more, Ismenê.
You are alive, but I belong to Death.
CREON (*to the* CHORUS):   Gentlemen, I beg you to observe these girls:
One has just now lost her mind; the other,
It seems, has never had a mind at all.   150
ISMENÊ: Grief teaches the steadiest minds to waver, King.
CREON: Yours certainly did, when you assumed guilt with the guilty!
ISMENÊ: But how could I go on living without her?
CREON: You are.
She is already dead.
ISMENÊ: But your own son's bride!
CREON: There are places enough for him to push his plow.   155
I want no wicked women for my sons!
ISMENÊ: O dearest Haimon, how your father wrongs you!
CREON: I've had enough of your childish talk of marriage!
CHORAGOS: Do you really intend to steal this girl from your son?
CREON: No; Death will do that for me.
CHORAGOS: Then she must die?   160
CREON (*ironically*):   You dazzle me.
                            —But enough of this talk!
(*To* GUARDS.) You, there, take them away and guard them well:
For they are but women, and even brave men run
When they see Death coming.

(*Exeunt* ISMENÊ, ANTIGONÊ, *and* GUARDS.)

   In this scene we witness a developing conflict between Creon and Antigonê,
one that is more than a clash of two stubborn wills. Opposing views of propriety

emerge, along with competing moral values and contrasting attitudes toward political authority. What are we to make of these attitudes and these arguments? How does our sense of their tone and manner affect our perception and evaluation of the substance of their speech and action? Whose values do you think should take precedence, and why? And finally, how highly do we rate the literary and theatrical qualities of the text? As a portion of a work of art, how successfully does it achieve its artistic and dramatic aims?

THE ACT OF READING DRAMA

To read drama actively, it is helpful to read with a pen in hand and to make notes in the margins. Here we illustrate a variation on that approach to active reading: asking questions of the play as we read it. Our questions will range over various concerns we have in reading, including evaluation, interpretation, and our experience of the text, as well as how to bring its theatrical and performance qualities to life in our minds.

To this end, we consider the opening scene of Isabella Augusta Persse, Lady Gregory's *The Rising of the Moon.*

Scene: Side of a quay in a seaport town. Some posts and chains. A large barrel. Enter three policemen. Moonlight.

SERGEANT, *who is older than the others, crosses the stage to right and looks down steps. The others put down a pastepot and unroll a bundle of placards.*

POLICEMAN B: I think this would be a good place to put up a notice. (*He points to barrel.*)

POLICEMAN X: Better ask him. (*Calls to* SERGEANT) Will this be a good place for a placard? (*No answer.*)

POLICEMAN B: Will we put up a notice here on the barrel? (*No answer.*)

SERGEANT: There's a flight of steps here that leads to the water. This is a place that should be minded well. If he got down here, his friends might have a boat to meet him; they might send it in here from outside.

POLICEMAN B: Would the barrel be a good place to put a notice up?

SERGEANT: It might; you can put it there.

(They paste the notice up.)

SERGEANT (*reading it*):   Dark hair—dark eyes, smooth face, height five feet five—there's not much to take hold of in that—It's a pity I had no chance of seeing him before he broke out of gaol. They say he's a wonder, that it's he makes all the plans for the whole organization. There isn't another man in Ireland would have broken gaol the way he did. He must have some friends among the gaolers.

POLICEMAN B: A hundred pounds is little enough for the Government to offer for him. You may be sure any man in the force that takes him will get promotion.

SERGEANT: I'll mind this place myself. I wouldn't wonder at all if he came this way. He might come slipping along there (*points to side of quay*), and his friends might be waiting for him there (*points down steps*), and once he got away it's little chance we'd have of finding him; it's maybe under a load of kelp he'd be in a fishing boat, and not one to help a married man that wants it to the reward.

POLICEMAN X: And if we get him itself, nothing but abuse on our heads for it from the people, and maybe from our own relations.

SERGEANT: Well, we have to do our duty in the force. Haven't we the whole country depending on us to keep law and order? It's those that are down would be up and those that are up would be down, if it wasn't for us. Well, hurry on, you have plenty of other places to placard yet, and come back here then to me. You can take the lantern. Don't be too long now. It's very lonesome here with nothing but the moon.

POLICEMAN B: It's a pity we can't stop with you. The Government should have brought more police into the town, with *him* in gaol, and at assize time too. Well, good luck to your watch. (*They go out.*)

SERGEANT (*walks up and down once or twice and looks at placard*):   A hundred pounds and promotion sure. There must be a great deal of spending in a hundred pounds. It's a pity some honest man not to be the better of that.

(*A ragged man appears at left and tries to slip past.* SERGEANT *suddenly turns.*)

Here is a list of questions we might generate during an active interrogation of the text.

1. What are the implications of the title, "The Rising of the Moon"? How is the title related to the suggested lighting? How important will the moon and the moonlight become?
2. Why don't the policemen have names? Of what importance are their repeated questions and the sergeant's distracted answer?
3. Why does the sergeant say that "it's a pity" he didn't see the criminal before his escape from jail? Is it simply that the sergeant would know what the man looked like and thus could recognize him more easily?
4. How does Lady Gregory draw us into the play? How does she engage our interest in these characters and their situation?
5. How important will the theme of duty become? Is it significant that the sergeant introduces this topic?
6. How effective theatrically is the sergeant's pointing to the quay and steps as he imagines the escaped man coming past where he stands?
7. Where in fact do the sergeant and his men stand on stage? How are they dressed? And where is the barrel placed?
8. As each character speaks, how does he gesture? At whom does he look? Where is he positioned in relation to the others?
9. How important to the play's action and idea are the props—the barrel, placards, and lantern? What other props will become important?
10. Of what significance is policeman X's comment about getting abuse from the people and his relatives for capturing the escaped convict?
11. How important are the sergeant's references to a reward and promotion? His references to the escaped man's friends? Might these references be significant beyond their function in the play's action?
12. Why are certain words and phrases repeated?
13. How helpful are the italicized stage directions in letting us imagine the scene and the action?

14. What do we expect to happen next? How well has the playwright prepared readers/viewers for the sergeant's encounter with the "ragged man"?
15. With whom do our sympathies lie? Why? How do our attitudes about police officers and the concept of the "law" affect our response?

   Asking questions such as these involves us actively in reading the play. Some of these questions can be asked during an initial reading; others may arise during subsequent readings. Writing out a series of questions enables us to focus on aspects of the text we may have overlooked or perhaps noticed only vaguely. Also, interrogating the text can lead us to an interpretation that is thoroughly grounded in careful observation. The answers to our questions provide the authoritative basis for an interpretation worthy of consideration by other readers.

CHAPTER TWO

Types of Drama

Some plays elicit laughter, others evoke tears. Some are comic, others tragic, still others a mixture of both. The two major dramatic modes, *tragedy* and *comedy*, have been represented traditionally by contrasting masks, one sorrowful, the other joyful. The masks represent more than different types of plays: they also stand for contrasting ways of looking at the world, aptly summarized in Horace Walpole's remark, "the world is a comedy to those who think and a tragedy to those who feel."

The comic view celebrates life and affirms it; it is typically joyous and festive. The tragic view highlights life's sorrows; it is typically brooding and solemn. Tragic plays end unhappily, often with the death of the hero; comedies usually end happily, often with a celebration such as a marriage. Both comedy and tragedy contain changes of fortune, with the fortunes of comic characters turning from bad to good and those of tragic characters from good to bad.

TRAGEDY

In the *Poetics,* Aristotle described *tragedy* as "an imitation of an action that is serious, complete in itself, and of a certain magnitude." This definition suggests that tragedies are solemn plays concerned with grave human actions and their consequences. The action of a tragedy is complete—it possesses a beginning, a middle, and an end. Elsewhere in the *Poetics,* Aristotle notes that the incidents of a tragedy must be causally connected. The events have to be logically related, one growing naturally out of another, each leading to the inevitable catastrophe, usually the downfall of the hero.

Some readers of tragedy have suggested that, according to Aristotle, the catastrophe results from a flaw in the character of the hero. Others have contended that the hero's tragic flaw results from fate or coincidence, from circumstances beyond the hero's control. A third view proposes that tragedy results from an error of judgment committed by the hero, one that may or may not have as its source a weakness in character. Typically, tragic protagonists make mistakes: they misjudge other characters, they misinterpret events, and they confuse appearance with reality. Shakespeare's Othello, for example, mistakes Iago for an honest, loving friend; and he mistakes his faithful wife, Desdemona, for an adultress. Sophocles' Oedipus mistakes his own identity and misconstrues his destiny. The misfortune and catastrophes of tragedy are frequently precipitated by errors of judgment; mistaken perceptions lead to misdirected actions that eventually result in catastrophe.

Tragic heroes such as Oedipus and Othello are grand, noble characters. They are men, as Aristotle says, "of high estate," who enjoy "great reputation and prosperity." Tragic heroes, in short, are privileged, exalted personages who have earned their high repute and status by heroic exploit (Othello), by intelligence (Oedipus), or by their inherent nobility (Othello and Oedipus). Their tragedy resides in a fall from glory that crushes not only the tragic hero himself but other related characters as well. Othello's tragedy includes his wife and his faithful lieutenant, Cassio. Oedipus' tragedy extends to his entire family, including his wife-mother, his two sons, his daughters, and his brother-in-law, Creon, and his family. Greek tragedy, typically, involves the destruction and downfall of an entire house or family, reaching across generations. The catastrophe of Shakespearean tragedy is usually not as extensive.

An essential element of the tragic hero's experience is a *recognition* of what has happened to him. Frequently this takes the form of the hero discovering something previously unknown or something he knew but misconstrued. According to Aristotle, the tragic hero's recognition (or discovery) is often allied with a reversal of his expectations. Such an ironic reversal occurs in *Oedipus Rex* when the messenger's speech unsettles rather than reassures Oedipus about who he is and what he has done. Once the reversal and discovery occur, tragic plots move swiftly to their conclusions.

We may consider why, amid such suffering and catastrophe, tragedies are not depressing. Aristotle suggested that the pity and fear aroused in the audience are purged or released and the audience experiences a cleansing of those emotions and a sense of relief that the action is over. Perhaps tragedy represents for us the ultimate downfall we will all experience in death: we watch in fascination and awe a dramatic reminder of our own inevitable mortality. Or perhaps we are somehow exalted in witnessing the high human aspiration and the noble conception of human character embodied in tragic heroes like Oedipus and Othello.

COMEDY

Some of the same dramatic elements we find in tragedy occur in comedy as well. Discovery scenes and consequent reversals of fortune, for example, occur in both. So too do misperceptions and errors of judgment, exhibitions of human weakness and failure. But in comedy the reversals and errors lead not to calamity as they do in tragedy, but to prosperity and happiness. Comic heroes

are usually ordinary people; they are less grand, less noble than tragic protagonists. Moreover, comic characters are frequently one-dimensional to the extent
that many are stereotypes: the braggart, for example, or the hypocrite, the unfaithful wife, the cuckold, the ardent young lovers.

If comic characters are frequently predictable in their behavior, comic plots
are not: they thrive on the surprise of the unexpected and on improbability.
Cinderella stories like these are the staples of comedy: an impoverished student
inherits a fortune; a beggar turns out to be a prince; a wife (or husband or
child) presumed dead turns up alive and well; the war (between nations, classes,
families, the sexes) ends, the two sides are reconciled and everybody lives happily ever after. But whether the incongruities of comedy exist between a character's speech and actions, between what we expect the characters to be and
what they show themselves to be, or between how they think of themselves
and how we see them, things work out in the end.

The happy endings of comedies are not always happy for all the characters
involved. This marks one of the significant differences between the two major
types of comedy: *satiric* and *romantic* comedy. Though much of what we have
said so far about comedy applies to both types, it applies more extensively to
romantic than to satiric comedy, or satire. *Satire* exposes human folly, criticizes
human conduct, and aims to correct it. Ridiculing the weaknesses of human
nature, satiric comedy shows us the low level to which human behavior can
sink. Molière's *Tartuffe* is such a satiric comedy; it exposes religious hypocrisy,
castigates folly, and ultimately celebrates virtue. Although things may work out
well in the end for most of the characters, the play contains some harsh moments and a bitter ending for at least one character.

Romantic comedy, on the other hand, portrays characters gently, even generously; its spirit is more tolerant and its tone more genial. Whatever adversities the heroes and heroines of romantic comedy must overcome, the tone is
typically devoid of rancor and bitterness. The humor of romantic comedy is
more sympathetic than corrective, and it intends more to entertain than instruct, to delight than ridicule.

Because of such differences, our approaches to reading satire and romance
should be different. When we read satiric comedies such as Shaw's *Arms and the
Man,* we should identify the object of the dramatist's criticism and determine
why the behavior of certain characters is objectionable. In reading romantic
comedies, such as Shakespeare's *A Midsummer Night's Dream,* we are invited
simply to enjoy the raveling and unraveling of plot as the protagonists are led
to the inevitable happy ending.

These distinctions, however, are useful only as they help us gauge a play's
prevailing characteristics. They should serve as guidelines to prevailing tenden-
cies rather than as rigid descriptions of dramatic types. Frequently romantic
comedies may contain elements of satire and satiric comedies elements of
romance.

CHAPTER THREE

Elements of Drama

The elements of drama include plot, character, dialogue, staging, and theme. Our discussions of each of these elements individually allows us to highlight the characteristic features of drama in a convenient way. We should remember, however, that analysis of any single element of drama (plot, for example) should not blind us to its function in conjunction with such other elements as character. Ultimately any analysis we engage in must be followed by an act of synthesis in which we bring a number of elements of the play into relationship with one another.

PLOT

Plot is the structure of a play's action. Although it encompasses what happens in a play, plot is more than the sum of its incidents. Plot is the order of the incidents, their arrangement and form. Following Aristotle, we can distinguish between all the little actions or incidents that make up a play and the single *action* that unifies them. It is this unified structure of incidents (or little actions) Aristotle calls *action* and we call *plot*.

Traditional plot structure consists of an *exposition,* presentation of background information necessary for the development of the plot; *rising action,* a set of conflicts and crises; *climax,* the play's most decisive crisis; *falling action,* a follow–up that moves toward the play's resolution or *denouement* (French for the untying of a knot).

The plot of a realistic drama can be diagrammed in the following manner:

Crisis
Turning point or climax

Complication(s)

Falling action

Resolution

Exposition

(denouement)

Whether playwrights use a traditional plot structure or vary the formula, they control our expectations about what is happening through plot. They decide when to present action and information, what to reveal and what to conceal. By the arrangement of incidents, a dramatist may create suspense, evoke laughter, cause anxiety, or elicit surprise. One of our main sources of pleasure in plot is surprise, whether we are shown something we didn't expect or whether we see *how* something will happen even when we may know *what* will happen. Frequently surprise follows suspense—fulfilling our need to find out what will happen as we wait for a resolution of a play's action.

Suspense is created by conflict. Drama is essentially the development and resolution of conflicts. Each of the scenes excerpted in Chapter One, Reading Plays, contains conflict. The conflict in Sophocles' *Antigonê* is overt and explicit. It occurs relentlessly in the play's dialogue and action. In the opening scene of Ibsen's *A Doll House* the conflict is implicit, at least initially. As the play develops, we see that Nora's conflict is less an opposition to Torvald than a conflict within herself.

Besides looking at how instances of conflict are structured into plot in these scenes, we must also consider what each contributes to the plot of the play overall. What, for example, in Sophocles' *Oedipus Rex* does Oedipus's debate with Teiresias lead up to? How is the opening scene of *A Doll House* related to its developing action, its concluding scene, its themes?

When we examine the plot of any play, we should be concerned with its developing action, the play in motion, and its completed action, the play at rest. By remaining attentive to what happens to us as we read and by highlighting the arrangement of scenes, we alert ourselves to the play as a performance. When we detach ourselves from the play to study its construction, the relationship among its parts, we study and appreciate the play as literature. Drama is both theater and literature. Study of plot can enrich our experience of each.

CHARACTER

If plot is the skeletal framework of a play, character is its vital center. Characters bring plays to life. First and last we become absorbed in the characters: how they look and what their appearance tells us about them; what they say and what their manner of saying expresses; what they do and how their actions reveal who they are and what they represent. We may come to know them and respond to them in ways we come to know and respond to actual people, all the while realizing that characters are literary imitations of human beings.

But even though the characters in plays are not real people, their human dimension is impossible to ignore since actors portray them, and their human qualities are perhaps their most engaging feature. It is, indeed, their *human* aspect that attracts us to the characters of drama, not their symbolic significance. When we see characters engaged in significant human action, we examine their words and deeds. We make sense of them by relying on models of human behavior and by applying standards of conduct derived from our everyday experience; we assess their motives and evaluate their behavior in accordance with psychological probability. It is nearly impossible not to.

Nonetheless, it is helpful to remain mindful of the distinction between dramatic characters and actual people so that we do not always expect them to behave realistically. Nor should we expect playwrights to tell us everything about them. They will tell us only what we need to know. If it is not important for us to know Nora's age or Torvald's height, the playwrights won't bother us with such information. Dramatists reveal only what is relevant to their dramatic purposes.

Drama lives in the encounter of characters, for its action is interaction. Its essence is human relationships, the things men and women say and do to each other. Dramatic characters come together and affect each other, making things happen by coming into conflict. It is in conflict that characters reveal themselves and advance the plot.

DIALOGUE

Ezra Pound, the modern American poet, once described drama as "persons moving about on a stage using words"—in short, people talking. Listening to their talk we hear identifiable, individual voices. In their presence we encounter persons, for dialogue inevitably brings us back to character, drama's human center. And though dialogue in plays typically has three major functions—to advance the plot, to establish setting (the time and place of the action), and to reveal character, its most important and consistent function is the revelation of character.

Our examples come from Act IV, Scene III of Shakespeare's *Othello*. Consider first the following conversation between Desdemona (wife of the military hero Othello) and Emilia (maid to Desdemona and wife of Othello's lieutenant, Iago). They are talking about adultery:

DESDEMONA: Dost thou in conscience think, tell me, Emilia,
That there be women do abuse their husbands
In such gross kind?

EMILIA: There be some such, no question.

DESDEMONA: Wouldst thou do such a deed for all the world?
EMILIA: Why, would not you?
DESDEMONA: No, by this heavenly light!
EMILIA: Nor I either by this heavenly light.
       I might do't as well i'the dark.
DESDEMONA: Wouldst thou do such a deed for all the world?
EMILIA: The world's a huge thing; it is a great price for a small vice.
DESDEMONA: In troth, I think thou wouldst not.
EMILIA: In troth, I think I should; and undo't when I had done. Marry, I would not do such a thing for a joint-ring, nor for measures of lawn, nor gowns, petticoats, nor caps, nor any petty exhibition, but for all the whole world? Why, who would not make her husband a cuckold to make a monarch? I should venture purgatory for't.
DESDEMONA: Beshrew me if I would do such a wrong for the whole world.
EMILIA: Why, the wrong is but a wrong i'th'world; and having the world for your labor, 'tis a wrong in your own world, and you might quickly make it right.
DESDEMONA: I do not think there is any such woman.

In this dialogue we not only see and hear evidence of a radical difference of values, but we also observe a striking difference of character. Desdemona's innocence is underscored by her unwillingness to be unfaithful to her husband; her naiveté, by her inability to believe in any woman's infidelity. Emilia is willing to compromise her virtue and finds enough practical reasons to assure herself of its correctness. Her joking tone and bluntness also contrast with Desdemona's solemnity and inability to name directly what she is referring to: adultery.

And now listen to Iago working on Desdemona's father, Brabantio, to tell him about his daughter's elopement with Othello (Act I, Scene I):

> Zounds, sir y'are robbed! For shame. Put on your gown!
> Your heart is burst, you have lost half your soul.
> Even now, now, very now, an old black ram
> Is tupping your white ewe. Arise, arise!
> Awake the snorting citizens with the bell,
> Or else the devil will make a grandsire of you.
>
>   . . .
>
> I am one sir, that comes to tell you your daughter
> and the Moor are making the beast with two backs.

Iago's language reveals his coarseness; he crudely reduces sexual love to animal copulation. It also shows his ability to make things happen: he has infuriated Brabantio. The remainder of the scene shows the consequences of his speech, its power to inspire action. Iago is thus revealed as both an instigator and a man of crude sensibilities.

His language is cast in a similar mold in Act II, Scene I, when he tries to convince Roderigo, a rejected suitor of Desdemona, that Desdemona will tire of Othello and turn to someone else for sexual satisfaction. Notice how Iago's words stress the carnality of sex and reveal his violent imagination:

> Her eye must be fed. And what delight
> shall she have to look on the devil? When the
> blood is made dull with the act of sport, there
> should be a game to inflame it and to give
> satiety a fresh appetite, loveliness in favor,
> sympathy in years, manners, and beauties; all
> which the Moor is defective in. Now for want of
> these required conveniences, her delicate tenderness will find
> itself abused, begin to heave the gorge, disrelish and
> abhor the Moor. Very nature will instruct her in it
> and compel her to some second choice. . . .

Othello's language, like Iago's, reveals his character and his decline from a courageous and confident leader to a jealous lover distracted to madness by Iago's insinuations about his wife's infidelity. The elegance and control, even the exaltation of his early speeches, give way to the crude degradation of his later remarks. Here is Othello in Act I, Scene II, responding to a search party out to find him:

> Hold your hands,
> Both you of my inclining and the rest,
> Were it my cue to fight, I should have known it
> Without a prompter. Whither will you that I go
> To answer this your charge?

The language of this speech is formal, stately, and controlled. It bespeaks a man in command of himself, one who assumes authority naturally and easily.

In Act I, Scene III, Othello speaks to the political authorities and to Brabantio, Desdemona's enraged father:

> Most potent, grave, and reverend signiors,
> My very noble and approved good masters,
> That I have ta'en away this old man's daughter,
> It is most true; true I have married her.
> The very head and front of my offending
> Hath this extent, no more. . . .

From these few lines alone we can sense Othello's stature, his dignity, his self-confidence, and his courtesy. Coupled with other passages from the first two acts of the play, we come away impressed with Othello's gravity and grandeur. His language in large part accounts for our sympathetic response to him, for our admiration, not only for his military exploits, but for his measure of control, poise, and equanimity.

By the middle of Act III, however, this view of Othello is no longer tenable. Othello is reduced by Iago to an incoherent babbler, to a man at odds with himself, one who has lost his equilibrium. In Act IV, Scene I, we see the Othello Iago has created by suggesting that Desdemona has been unchaste with Othello's lieutenant, Michael Cassio:

OTHELLO: Lie with her? Lie on her?—We say lie on her when they belie her—Lie with her! Zounds, that's fulsome. Handkerchief—confession—handkerchief—To confess, and be hanged for his labor—first to be hanged, and then to confess! I tremble at it. . . . It is not words that shake me thus.—Pish! Noses, ears, and lips? Is't possible?—Confess?— Handkerchief?—O devil.

In the language of both Iago and Othello we see meaning enacted as well as expressed. The verbal dimension of their dialogue is reinforced by action, gesture, movement. We can observe in these brief excerpts and throughout the play not only how language reveals character, advances the action, and establishes the setting, but how it also makes things happen and in effect itself becomes action.

STAGING

By *staging* we have in mind the spectacle a play presents in performance, its visual detail. This includes such things as the positions of actors onstage (sometimes referred to as *blocking*), their nonverbal gestures and movements (also called *stage business*), the scenic background, the props and costumes, lighting, and sound effects.

Though often taken for granted, costumes can reveal the characters beneath them. Ibsen's Nora changes costumes more than once. She appears by turns in ordinary clothing, in a multicolored shawl, in a dancing costume, and in a black shawl. Each costume change expresses a change in Nora's feelings.

Besides costume, any physical object that appears in a play has the potential to become an important dramatic symbol. The Christmas tree, which stands throughout Ibsen's *A Doll House,* is an ironic visual counterpart to the play's unfolding action. More dramatic perhaps and more central to plot is the handkerchief in *Othello.* Having its own history, which we learn when Desdemona wipes Othello's brow, the handkerchief becomes a crucial dramatic object, one that offers Othello the "ocular proof" he requires to condemn Desdemona as an adulterer.

From costumes and objects, we turn to sound. Ibsen uses sound effectively in *A Doll House* when he asks for music to accompany Nora's frenzied dancing as she attempts to delay Torvald's discovery of Krogstad's letter. In this same scene Ibsen also uses sound to heighten suspense as he has Torvald open the mailbox off-stage: we hear but don't see the mailbox click open.

A playwright's stage directions will sometimes help us see and hear things like these as we read. But with or without stage directions, we have to use our aural as well as our visual imagination. An increased imaginative alertness to the sights and sounds of a play, while no substitute for direct physical apprehension, can nonetheless help us approximate the experience of a dramatic performance. It can also enhance our appreciation of the dramatist's craftsmanship and increase our understanding of the play.

THEME

From plot, character, dialogue, and staging we derive a sense of the play's meaning or significance. An abstraction of this meaning is its central idea or *theme*. It is often helpful to try to express the theme of a play in a carefully worded sentence or two, but we should be aware, however, that any summary statement of a complex work of art is bound to be limited and limiting.

Nonetheless as readers we reach for theme as a way of organizing our responses to a play. At the same time we also let the work modify and alter our notion of its theme. We work back and forth between its details (of dialogue, gesture, and movement, for example) and our conception of their significance. As we notice details and connect them, as we discover and remember, our sense of the play's theme changes. It may change in such a way that we end up, provisionally at least, seeing the play's theme as ambiguous (suggesting contradictory or opposite ideas simultaneously with a resulting uncertainty and indefiniteness about its meaning). And of course there is the very good chance that a play will include more than one theme.

Perhaps we can best approach consideration of a play's theme by noting the dialogue of its characters, who frequently represent conflicting ideals and viewpoints. Some plays, for example, Sophocles' *Antigonê,* can certainly be approached this way. Antigonê herself, for example, represents a commitment to a religious ideal ineluctably in conflict with the political idea that Creon stands for. In her debate with Creon, Antigonê appeals to higher laws, religious and spiritual principles that require burial of the dead, especially if the dead are relatives. Because Antigonê acts in violation of Creon's edict, and since Creon as king represents the supreme authority of the state, she can be seen to pit God's law against man's. Another way of saying this is to note that she values a religious obligation more than a legal code. Still another is to see it as a conflict between two kinds of duty: duty to the state and duty to one's family. Legal obligation conflicts with moral responsibility; public duty collides with private conscience.

We have stated that Antigonê and Creon represent two different positions, two conflicting ideals. We make such a generalization, confident that we are not violating the play because the speeches of both characters refer directly to the ideals that motivate them. If we elaborate, however, we will have to qualify the view of their conflict suggested so far for two reasons. This paradigm is too neat: it ignores aspects of Antigonê's and Creon's motivation and character, and it also reduces the play as a whole to this conflict of values.

Because Greek tragedy typically enacts a reconciliation of the human and divine orders, Antigonê's appeal must be seen as an attempt to make that reconciliation and Creon's refusal as a denial of it. Thus, her appeal is not only personal—based on family honor—but is much more inclusive, far more so than Creon's reasons of state. To express this as a theme we might say that in the conflict between two goods, one divinely based (Antigonê's) and one humanly based (Creon's) the higher good should prevail.

We have been using Sophocles' drama to suggest that it is both natural and necessary to generalize from a play's action and dialogue to an idea it embodies. But we have also noted that to reduce the play's thought to a satisfactorily inclusive statement of theme is no easy matter. At best such a statement offers an approximation of a play's meaning, one that clarifies and illuminates our experience. At worst it oversimplifies the play, distorting its significance and impoverishing our experience of it.

CHAPTER FOUR

Writing about Drama

REASONS FOR WRITING ABOUT DRAMA

Why write about drama? One reason is to find out what you think about a play that interests you. Another is to induce yourself to read a play you have heard about or that you like more carefully. You may write about a work of drama because it engages you, and you may wish to celebrate it or to argue with its implied ideas and values. Still another reason is that you may simply be required to do so as a course assignment.

Whatever your reasons for writing about drama, a number of things happen when you do. First, in writing about a play you tend to read it more attentively, noticing things you might overlook in a more casual reading. Second, since writing stimulates thinking, when you write about drama you find yourself thinking more about what a particular work means and why you respond to it as you do. And third, you begin to acquire power over the works you write about, making them part of your experience and more meaningful to you.

INFORMAL WAYS OF WRITING ABOUT DRAMA

When you write about a play, you may write for yourself or you may write for others. Writing for yourself, to discover what you think, often takes casual forms such as annotation and freewriting. These less formal kinds of writing are useful for helping you focus on your reading of plays. They are helpful in studying for tests about drama. They can also serve as preliminary forms of writing when you write more formal essays and papers.

Annotation

When you annotate a text, you make notes about it, usually in the margins or at the top and bottom of pages—or both. Annotations can also be made within the text, as underlined words, circled phrases, or bracketed sentences or paragraphs. Annotations may also assume the form of arrows, question marks, and various other marks.

Annotating a literary work offers a convenient and relatively painless way to begin writing about it. Annotating can get you started zeroing in on what you think interesting or important. You can also annotate to signal details that puzzle or disconcert you.

Your markings serve to focus your attention and clarify your understanding of a story or novel. Your annotations can save you time in rereading or studying a work. And they can also be used when you write a more formal paper.

Annotations for the following scene illustrate the process.

The following excerpt from *Antigonê* begins at the point where Antigonê has been taken into custody for violating an edict of Creon, king of Thebes. Creon's edict concerns Antigonê's brother, Polyneicês, who was killed in a battle while fighting against Thebes. Creon has forbidden Polyneicês' burial, but in violation of the edict Antigonê has buried him.

CREON (*to* SENTRY):   You may go.

(*Exit* SENTRY.)

(*To* ANTIGONÊ):   Tell me, tell me briefly:
  Had you heard my proclamation touching this matter?
ANTIGONÊ: It was public. Could I help hearing it?
CREON: And yet you dared defy the law.
ANTIGONÊ: I dared.
  It was not God's proclamation. That final Justice
  That rules the world below makes no such laws.

  Your edict, King, was strong,
  But all your strength is weakness itself against
  The immortal unrecorded laws of God.
  They are not merely now: they were, and shall be,
  Operative for ever, beyond man utterly.

  I knew I must die, even without your decree:
  I am only mortal. And if I must die
  Now, before it is my time to die,
  Surely this is no hardship: can anyone
  Living, as I live, with evil all about me,
  Think Death less than a friend? This death of mine
  is of no importance; but if I had left my brother
  lying in death unburied, I should have suffered.
  Now I do not.
        You smile at me. Ah Creon,
  Think me a fool, if you like; but it may well be

Marginal annotations:

Creon can't believe that she would disobey—hence his question.

He sees himself as "the law."

Antigonê identifies conflict: God/man divine/human

Is she a bit too eager to die?

implicit stage direction: "You smile . . ."

That a fool convicts me of folly.
CHORAGOS: Like father, like daughter:
  both headstrong, deaf to reason!
  She has never learned to yield:
CREON: She has much to learn.
  The inflexible heart breaks first, the toughest iron
  Cracks first, and the wildest horses bend their necks
  At the pull of the smallest curb.
                    Pride? In a slave?
  This girl is guilty of a double insolence.
  Breaking the given laws and boasting of it.
  Who is the man here,
  She or I, if this crime goes unpunished?
  Sister's child, or more than sister's child,
  Or closer yet in blood—she and her sister
  Win bitter death for this!

                (*To* SERVANTS)

          Go, some of you.
  Arrest Ismenê. I accuse her equally.
  Bring her: you will find her sniffling in the house there.
  Her mind's a traitor: crimes kept in the dark
  Cry for light, and the guardian brain shudders;
  But how much worse than this
  Is brazen boasting of barefaced anarchy!
ANTIGONÊ: Creon, what more do you want than my death?
CREON: Nothing.
  That gives me everything.
ANTIGONÊ: Then I beg you: kill me.
  This talking is a great weariness: your words
  Are distasteful to me, and I am sure that mine
  Seem so to you. And yet they should not seem so:
  I should have praise and honor for what I have done.
  All these men here would praise me
  Were their lips not frozen shut with fear of you.
  (*Bitterly*) Ah the good fortune of kings.
  Licensed to say and do whatever they please!
CREON: You are alone here in that opinion.
ANTIGONÊ: No, they are with me. But they
  keep their tongues in leash.
CREON: Maybe. But you are guilty, and they are not.
ANTIGONÊ: There is no guilt in reverence for the dead.
CREON: But Eteoclês—was he not your brother too?
ANTIGONÊ: My brother too.
CREON: And you insult his memory?
ANTIGONÊ (*softly*):   The dead man would not say that I insult it.
CREON: He would: for you honor a traitor as much as him.
ANTIGONÊ: His own brother, traitor or not, and equal in blood.
CREON: He made war on his country. Eteoclês defended it.
ANTIGONÊ: Nevertheless, there are honors due all the dead.
CREON: But not the same for the wicked as for the just.

Margin annotations:

How important is this choral comment?

images: iron, horses

conflict: man/woman
age/youth

Why does Creon accuse Ismenê?

Anarchy? Is Creon a bit paranoid?

She knows how to fight back.

image: dogs on a leash held in check by fear

a complication: the other brother, Eteoclês

tempo: pace picks up here with rapid-fire dialogue exchange

buildup of intensity

ANTIGONÊ: Ah Creon, Creon,
   Which of us can say what the gods hold wicked?
CREON: An enemy is an enemy, even dead.
ANTIGONÊ: It is my nature to join in love, not hate.
CREON (*finally losing patience*):   Go join them then;
   if you must have your love. Find it in hell!

Double-Column Notebook

Another way of writing for yourself, informally, is to use the double-column notebook. To create a double-column notebook, divide a page in half vertically (or open a notebook so that you face two blank pages side by side). On one side *take* notes, summarizing the scene's situation, action, and ideas. On the other side, the responding side, *make* notes, recording your thinking about what you summarized on the opposite side. On the responding side, ask questions; speculate; make connections.

   Here is an example of a double-column notebook for the excerpt from *Antigonê* annotated above. Notice how the entries in the double-column notebook are more detailed, and written in a more formal style, than the annotations shown with the excerpt.

Summary and Observations

Creon's language is formal, even self-important. He sounds like, or tries to sound like, a king.

Part of Creon's anger stems from Antigonê's rebellion against *him,* against *his* law. Part derives from her seeming disregard for the law of the land more generally.

Antigonê's view seems to be that since Creon's law was a bad one, she shouldn't obey it. And even further, that she has a responsibility to disobey it since the gods require that family members honor their dead. She points out that her burial of her brother was necessary for her own peace of mind.

Antigonê at one point angers Creon by reminding him that he is not almighty. She attempts to put him in his place, to remind him that his rule has limits. He doesn't like that. Nor does he like her suggestion that it is better to die than to obey an unjust law or live in a corrupt society.

Creon, of course, sees her act of rebellion and her disrespectful attitude toward him as king as the cause of societal corruption.

Responses and Reactions

Creon is unpalatable here. He's pompous and arrogant. Yet to some extent he seems justified in being angry. What's interesting here is why Creon reacts so strongly to the violation of his edict. It probably has something to do with his recent acquisition of power. He is very likely more than a little insecure in his new position. He must feel the need to assert himself and establish his authority. Suppose he ignores Antigonê's action. What will people think of him? Won't they see him as weak?

Antigonê's point has merit. She has to do what she has to do.

Antigonê seems the more likeable of the two.

Antigonê enjoys pulling Creon down a peg. Her tone does sound insulting. She almost seems to enjoy thinking of herself as a martyr for a cause. Isn't she a bit theatrical here, relishing her role and the image she projects as much as, or even more than, the idea and point of view she stands up for?

Doesn't Creon overreact here in seeing Antigonê's action as an example of "anarchy"? And doesn't he also overreact in assuming that Ismenê is also guilty? He assumes things without testing them.

During the course of their dialogue (more a confrontation or debate than a conversation), they insult each other. Creon calls Antigonê stubborn; Antigonê calls Creon a fool.

As in any good fight, the antagonists really do try to hurt each other.

It's an enjoyable verbal battle—for us readers.

Creon's long speech parallels and answers Antigonê's. Once the two positions have been established, we watch and listen as the dialogue speeds up as Antigonê and Creon trade arguments and insults.

Even though the dialogue is somewhat stylized and conventional, it is beautifully arranged for maximum punch and counterpunch.

Throughout this taut scene both characters seem tense and angry. They neither like nor respect each other.

The effect overall is of tension building to the point of explosion.

FORMAL WAYS OF WRITING ABOUT DRAMA

Among the more common formal ways of writing about drama is analysis. In writing an analytical essay about a play or a scene from a play, your goal is to explain how one or more particular aspects or issues in the work or the scene contributes to its overall meaning. You might analyze the dialogue in a scene from Ibsen's *A Doll House* or Lady Gregory's *The Rising of the Moon*. Your goal would be to explain what the verbal exchanges between characters contribute to the play's meaning and to its effect on the audience. You might analyze the imagery of Sophocles' *Oedipus the King* or Shakespeare's *Othello* to see what that imagery suggests about a character's perspective or the author's attitude toward the characters or the action. Or you might analyze the plot or staging of Glaspell's *Trifles* to see how the playwright's manipulation of action creates tension and conflict, humor and irony. (See these plays and others that we discuss reproduced in the chapters that follow.)

In addition to analyzing these and other dramatic elements in a play, you might also compare two plays or scenes, perhaps by focusing on their use of stage directions, lighting, or other theatrical effects. Or, instead of focusing on literary elements per se, you might write to see how a particular critical perspective (see Chapter Nine) illuminates a play. For example, you might consider the ways reader response criticism or new historicism contributes to your understanding of Hansberry's *A Raisin in the Sun*.

The following student papers analyze significant aspects of *Hamlet* and *Antigonê* respectively. In the first paper, the writer examines the character Hamlet's internal conflicts and then explains how they are resolved in the play. In the second paper, the writer analyzes the character Antigonê's conflict between her duty to the law of the state and her obligation to honor her dead brother by burying him.

Student Papers on Drama

Carolyn Kaparini
Prof. Eisenstadt

Hamlet's Conflict Resolved

In Shakespearean tragedies, characters often are confronted
with problems they must resolve. *The Tragedy of Hamlet, Prince
of Denmark* is one tragedy that reveals a tormented hero who
suffers greatly during the course of the play. Hamlet, the
tragic hero, must resolve many conflicts, which include
confusion and anger at his mother's hasty remarriage, horror
at the ghost's request to avenge the murder of his father, and
a general disgust with life as he contemplates suicide. Before
he can accept the responsibility of setting his world aright,
Hamlet must resolve his internal conflicts.

The first dilemma Hamlet must resolve results from the loss
of his father. Hamlet is first seen dressed in black as he
mourns the death of King Hamlet, his father. Hamlet cannot
understand why no one besides himself and Horatio continues to
grieve for Hamlet's father. What is even more upsetting to
Hamlet is that the court is celebrating the coronation of
Claudius and his royal marriage to Hamlet's mother, Queen
Gertrude. Hamlet is especially infuriated with his mother, who
he thinks has not mourned her husband's death sufficiently. In
an important soliloquy in Act I, scene ii, Hamlet complains
that even a beast "would have mourned longer" than his mother
did. And he reveals his disgust with both her and Claudius
when he calls their hasty marriage both "wicked" and
"incestuous." Throughout the play, Hamlet will continue to
find their marriage itself and its hasty occurrence after his
father's death consistently painful to think about.

A second internal conflict with which Hamlet deals is the
problem presented by the ghost. When Hamlet first encounters
the ghost he asks whether the ghost is "a spirit of health or
goblin damned." Before anything else, Hamlet has to resolve
the problem of the ghost's good or evil nature, of whether he
can trust the ghost to be honest and truthful. Once he decides
that the ghost really is the spirit of his dead father, Hamlet
faces an even greater problem: to act on the command the ghost
gives him to avenge the foul murder committed by Claudius.
Hamlet is appalled by the story the ghost of his father tells
about how Claudius murdered him to acquire first his crown and

then his queen. The absolute evil of Claudius's actions and Hamlet's disgust with his mother's behavior lead him to recognize that "something's rotten in the state of Denmark." Hamlet describes his predicament in the following lines:

> The time is out of joint. O cursed spite,
> That ever I was born to set it right.

Before Hamlet can set things right, however, he has to come to terms with the world of destructive evil that Claudius's act typifies.

Hamlet's greatest conflict occurs as a result of his indecision over what to do about his mother and how to avenge his father's murder. Even though these both distress him greatly, he suffers from a deeper and more pervasive disgust with life. Because of Claudius's crime, he sees evil all around him, especially at court. Because of his mother's actions, he thinks of all women as sinful, even the innocent Ophelia. He expresses his general dissatisfaction with life many times. On one occasion right after describing man as "noble" and a "paragon," after comparing him with angels and gods, Hamlet says "and yet to me, what is this quintessence of dust? Man delights not me." Later, he considers the question of whether it is better to live or to die:

> To be, or not to be: that is the question:
> Whether 'tis nobler in the mind to suffer
> The slings and arrows of outrageous fortune,
> Or to take arms against a sea of troubles,
> And by opposing end them.

These and many other lines in the play reveal Hamlet disappointed with the injustice and cruelty of life. His anger and frustration lead him to think constantly about death and to make plans to avenge his father's death. But he does not act. Instead he thinks and delays acting.

Hamlet perceives how difficult his task really is. Perhaps that is why it takes him so long to act. He is also seriously depressed by the state of affairs in Denmark. One turning point comes when Hamlet decides to confront his mother. He unleashes his anger and criticizes her severely for marrying Claudius. He also urges her not to sleep with the king. Another turning point occurs, when upon discovering Claudius's plot to have him murdered, Hamlet substitutes another letter ensuring the deaths of Rosencrantz and Guildenstern. In addition, during Hamlet's time away from the court when he is captured by pirates and then released to make his way home, he seems to have changed. When he reappears in Act V, Hamlet is more accepting of what fate or God has in store for him. Even though he does not yet know of the treachery that Laertes and Claudius have planned for him, he is determined to do what is necessary and to accept the consequences.

One important indication of this change of attitude occurs when he holds the skull of Yorick and he talks about the inevitability of death. He describes how death comes to all people, the great and important as well as the common people. All are equal when their bodies have decayed and their souls have departed. In addition, Hamlet recognizes that, as he tells Horatio, "there's a divinity that shapes our ends," regardless of what we prepare for ourselves. This recognition of a divine power governing the lives of men is acknowledged in another speech that reveals that Hamlet has learned from his suffering. It suggests that he has mentally resolved his internal conflicts. He says to Horatio:

> There is special providence in the fall of a
> sparrow. If it be now, 'tis not to come; if it
> be not to come, it will be now; if it be not
> now, yet it will come. The readiness is all.
> Since no man of aught he leaves knows, what is't
> to leave betimes? Let be.

In the play's final scene, Hamlet settles the score with Claudius by stabbing him with his sword. He has already resolved his argument with his mother, and the treacherous drink Claudius had prepared for Hamlet does the rest. After Hamlet and Laertes, Gertrude and Claudius die, Horatio is left to explain what really happened and what Hamlet himself was really like. It is left to Fortinbras to restore order to the disorder of Denmark. Even though Hamlet alone could not set his world aright, he had found his own peace and resolved his internal conflicts.

Alayna Phieffer
Dr. Kitts
12/10/96

   Antigonê: A Struggle between Human and Divine Powers

   In *Antigonê* by Sophocles there are several ways to interpret
the conflict between Creon and Antigonê. Perhaps the most
widely accepted interpretation is that their conflict
represents a struggle between state and individual. This
reading is valid but it is also shallow; if looked into
deeper, we can see that the struggle in this play lies between
earthly and divine powers.
   Creon represents a tyrannical rule that makes no allowances
for the unwritten laws, spiritual in nature, which so often
guide humans to act. He is so consumed with ruling the state
and so intoxicated with the power he possesses that he is
unable to comprehend the motives behind Antigonê's burial of
her brother Polyneicês. This can be seen in the first
encounter between Antigonê and Creon.

      Creon: And yet you dared defy the law.
      Antigonê: I dared.
        It was not God's proclamation. That final Justice
        That rules the world below makes no such law.

        Your edict, King, was strong,
        But all your strength is weakness itself against
        The immortal unrecorded laws of God.
        They are not merely now: they were, and shall be,
        Operative for ever, beyond man utterly.

                      . . . but if I had left my brother
        Lying in death unburied, I should have suffered.
        Now I do not.   (II, 56-70)

This conversation immediately establishes Antigonê's ideal; to
her, divine law is more powerful and right than any law
decreed by the state. Creon, to save face and maintain order,
sticks to his decree and sentences her to death.
   This conflict of harsh state laws with one's inner duty
goes still deeper, and it is clear that the gods are on
Antigonê's side. It seems best to look at what Antigonê and
others say about divine intervention and their actions
concerning it. The first evidence that the gods are involved

can be seen in the double burial. Antigonê is apprehended
when she goes to her brother's body, but just before this we
are told by the Sentry that someone has buried the body of
Polyneicês. He states that there are no signs of human
involvement, no wheel tracks or any sign of animals present;
the body is covered with a light dusting. We can perceive
this statement to be true; otherwise why would Sophocles have
included it? Why did Antigonê then go back to her brother for
a second time? Perhaps the answer lies in a statement made by
the chorus-leader: "I have been wondering, King: can it be
that the gods have done this?" (I, 99).

The watchman's actions, upon entering the palace, are
revealing. He twists and turns as though he is afraid that
Creon will not believe him; after all, he cannot understand it
himself. If the body had been buried deep in the ground, one
could argue that this is evidence that it was done by man, but
the light dusting of the body implies something more.

Another piece of evidence to support God's involvement in
this play's action is apparent in the first conversation
between Antigonê and Ismenê. Antigonê says "Creon is not
strong enough to stand in my way" (Prologue, 35). And later
after Ismenê says how dangerous it is to go against authority,
Antigonê responds:

                    If that is what you think,
    I should not want you, even if you asked to come.
    You have made your choice, you can be what you want to be.
    But I will bury him; and if I must die,
    I say that this crime is holy: I shall lie down
    With him in death, and I shall be as dear
    To him as he is to me.
                    It is the dead,
    Not the living, who make the longest demands:
    We die for ever . . .
                    You may do as you like,
    Since apparently the laws of the gods mean nothing to you.
                                        (Prologue, 52-61)

Antigonê is saying that she is acting in accordance with the
will of the gods; divine law will always surpass any human
laws.

Later, she tells Creon that it was not the words of the gods
that she disobeyed, but it was their word that led her to act.
This idea is common in Greek tragedy. When characters like
Antigonê act in ways fundamentally necessary in human life, or
out of a place deep within themselves, they are said to be
working with the gods, and this becomes so sacred that not
even written law could stop them.

As Antigonê is about to be buried alive, she realizes that no one understands her. Still she feels that she was obeying a divine law, even though now the gods seem to have nothing to do with her and have made no attempt to save her. But still she maintains her deep belief that she had to do it, and says that she had no choice:

> Thebes, and you my fathers' gods,
> And rulers of Thebes, you see me now, the last
> Unhappy daughter of a line of kings,
> Your kings, led away to death. You will remember
> What things I suffer, and at what men's hands,
> Because I would not transgress the laws of heaven.
>
> (IV, 75-80)

To her, the laws of heaven must guide our lives and they must always be obeyed no matter the consequence.

Finally we see the divine hand in prophecy, most obviously in the tragic destiny of Oedipus. His tragedy is sorrowfully left behind to his descendants. Tragedy must fall upon Antigonê as it fell upon her brothers. When she decides to bury Polyneicês, it is indeed an act of freewill, but one cannot disclaim the necessity of this action by fate—a tragic, inherited curse.

Teiresias may help Creon decide to amend his law, but he also serves a deeper purpose. Prophecy delivered by the gods implies law. Creon, by refusing to bury Polyneicês, has gone against the gods. Teiresias makes Creon's offense to the gods clear. He tells of evil omens that he has witnessed, like the fighting birds and the fat not catching on fire. These incidents portend Creon's tragic destiny. His conflicts are now with both upper and nether gods.

Creon's actions lead him into a world of suffering; for although he recognizes his mistakes and tries to correct them, he is too late. After taking care of Polyneicês's remains, he hurries to Antigonê's tomb only to find his son and Antigonê dead. Upon hearing the news of her son, his wife kills herself. This leaves Creon in a world full of despair. With his son and wife dead he is left to suffer and remember that universal laws are more powerful than any he may ever decree.

The idea that runs throughout this play is that there will always be certain forces and absolutes in life that must be respected, and essentially will be because they are divine in nature. When individuals do not look past the apparent causes and fail to see the divine implications, they may work against these laws. If the laws are offended, the wrath will be felt, not necessarily from supernatural powers, but in the actions and reactions of people who are strong enough or desperate

enough to follow their own hearts and live by their ideals.
Life on earth produces no human laws that are unbreakable. The
only way to be sure of not wreaking this havoc upon oneself is
to understand and respect the gods. By doing so one
demonstrates respect for humanity as well.

QUESTIONS FOR WRITING ABOUT DRAMA

In writing about the elements of drama, the following questions can help you
focus your thinking and prepare yourself for writing analytical essays and papers. Use the questions as a checklist to guide you to important aspects of any
play you read.

Plot

1. How does the playwright order the incidents of the play? What is the effect of this
   arrangement of incidents?
2. What is the central conflict of the play? What subsidiary conflicts are related to it?
3. Where is the play's climax? How is that climax prepared for dramatically? With
   what effects?

Character

4. To what extent are the play's characters—its *dramatis personae*—similar to actual
   people? In what ways are the play's characters different from actual people?
5. Using the characters' actions and speech, how would you evaluate their behavior?
   How are the characters related to one another dramatically and in other ways?
6. What function does each of the minor characters serve? If there is a chorus, what
   are its functions?

Dialogue

7. How would you characterize the voices of the various characters? How do you
   imagine them sounding in each of their major soliloquies or exchanges with other
   characters?
8. How does the dialogue advance the plot of the play? How does the dialogue establish setting?
9. How does the dialogue reveal character and motivation? Which particular
   speeches or other verbal exchanges are especially important for revealing character? Why?

Staging

10. What information is explicitly provided or implicitly suggested about how the play's characters are costumed? Do they change costumes at any point? Why? To what extent might such costume changes signal changes in attitude, behavior, or state of mind?
11. What objects or props in the play are emphasized? Which carry symbolic weight? How do you know?
12. What kinds of stage directions are provided? How do they help you understand the action? What do they contribute to your understanding of the characters?
13. How does the setting of the play contribute to its mood and theme? What do lighting and the use of sound contribute to the play's overall effects?

Theme

14. What is the central theme of the play? What subsidiary or ancillary themes support or accompany it?
15. How does your analysis of the elements of drama help you understand a play's theme?
16. Does the playwright convey the theme directly or indirectly? Can you identify one or more key passages in which the theme is made explicit? Or do you have to infer the theme from the implications of the play's dialogue and action, setting, staging, and character relationships?

Critical Perspectives

17. Among the critical perspectives you might bring to bear on the play, which one(s) seem(s) particularly useful for interpreting it? Why?
18. To what extent can you base your interpretation of the play on its language and details alone? To what extent is outside information about historical and biographical context necessary or helpful in understanding it?
19. To what extent does the play confirm or support your personal beliefs and values? To what extent is it in conflict with those beliefs and values? To what extent do your values and personal dispositions affect or influence your interpretation?
20. How do you imagine seeing the play staged would enhance your understanding, increase your emotional response, or otherwise alter your perception of the play?

QUESTIONS FOR IN-DEPTH READING

1. What general or overall thematic connections can you make between different works?
2. What stylistic similarities do you notice between and among different works?
3. How do the works differ in emphasis, tone, and style?

4. Once you have identified a writer's major preoccupations, place each work on a spectrum or a grid that represents the range of the writer's concerns.

5. What connections and disjunctions do you find among the following literary elements as they are embodied in different plays by the same writer?
   (a) plot and structure
   (b) character and characterization
   (c) dialogue and monologue
   (d) staging and setting
   (e) theme and thought

6. To what extent are your responses to and perceptions of different works by the same writer shared by others—by critics, by classmates, and by the writers themselves?

7. What relationships and differences do you see between the work of one writer and that of another who shares similar thematic interests, stylistic proclivities, or cultural, religious, or social values?

8. Which of the critical perspectives (see Chapter Nine) seem most useful as analytical tools for approaching the body of work of particular writers?

Suggestions for Writing
The Experience of Drama

1. Write a paper in which you recount your experience of reading a particular play or series of plays by the same author. You may want to compare your initial experience with your experience in later readings.

2. Write a paper comparing your experience reading a play with your experience witnessing a performance of it.

3. Discuss your changing perception or understanding of a particular play. Indicate how you felt about the play initially and what made you change your way of responding to it.

4. Relate the action or situation of a play to your own experience. Explain how the play is relevant to your situation, and comment on how reading and thinking about it may have helped you see your own life and experience more clearly.

5. Compare reading a play with watching a film of a performance or a film based on a play. For a filmed performance of a play, consider watching the videocassette of Arthur Miller's *Death of a Salesman,* starring Dustin Hoffman. For a film based on a play, consider viewing the movie version of Hansberry's *A Raisin in the Sun,* starring Sidney Poitier.

The Interpretation of Drama

6. Describe and characterize a single character from any play. Present a sketch of the character by referring to the language of his or her speeches and to the playwright's use of costume and stage directions.
7. Analyze a character at the moment he or she is making an important decision. Identify the situation, explain the reasons for the character's decision, and speculate about the possible consequences. Some possibilities: Nora in *A Doll House,* Antigonê in *Antigonê,* Othello in *Othello,* the Sergeant in *The Rising of the Moon.*
8. Explicate the opening dialogue of any play. Explain the significance of the opening section in setting the tone, establishing thematic preoccupations, and preparing us for what follows.
9. Select two or three brief passages that appear to be significant in their implications. They may be descriptive passages or dialogue. Establish the connections between one passage and the others, and explain their cumulative significance.
10. Analyze the closing dialogue of any play. Explain the significance of the ending and comment on its appropriateness.
11. Analyze the imagery of a play. Consider how particular kinds of language serve to advance the play's theme(s) or to reveal its characters. Some possibilities: political and natural images in Sophocles' *Antigonê;* animal imagery in *Othello;* images of dream and illusion in Arthur Miller's *Death of a Salesman.*
12. Analyze the ironic dimensions of any play. Consider how the playwright uses irony in the plot, dialogue, and/or setting. Some possibilities: *Oedipus Rex, Antigonê, Trifles.*
13. Explain the symbolic implications of any props used in the play. Consider the dramatic functions of the objects and their resonance as symbols. Some possibilities: the handkerchief in *Othello;* the Christmas tree in *A Doll House;* the balloons in *Andre's Mother.*
14. Analyze the structure of any play. Consider its major parts or sections—its acts and scenes. Explain what each contributes to the whole and how the parts fit together into a unified whole.
15. Analyze the plot of a play. Comment on the way it illustrates or deviates from the classic plot structure.
16. Analyze the setting of a play. Consider both time and place. Also consider small-scale aspects of setting, such as whether the action occurs indoors or out. Notice the descriptive details about the setting, whether the setting changes, and whether the action occurs in one time or place.
17. Analyze a character from any play. Evaluate the character, offering reasons and evidence for your views. Consider what the character does, says, does not do or say—and why. Note also what other characters say about him or her, and how they respond in action. Consider whether the character changes during the course of the play and what that possible change (or lack thereof) may signify.

18. Discuss any character relationship. Consider how the characters affect each other. Explain the nature of their relationship and speculate on its probable future.

The Evaluation of Drama

19. Evaluate a play from the point of view of its merit or excellence—or lack thereof. Explain why you consider it to be a successful or unsuccessful play.
20. Do a comparative evaluation of the merit of any two plays. Explain what they share, how they differ, and why one is more impressive or effective than the other.
21. Discuss the values exemplified by the characters in any play. Identify those values, relate them to your own, and comment on their significance. You may also wish to discuss the author's point of view as you see it reflected in the play.
22. Write a review of the performance of a play. Consider the staging and lighting of the performance, the costumes, the set design, and the sound effects.
23. Write a review of a play's performance concentrating on the acting. Consider how well the actors and actresses delivered their lines, how well they worked together and how well they communicated emotions and ideas.
24. Write a review of a film, concentrating on its theatrical characteristics and qualities.

To Research or Imagine

25. Develop an alternative ending for any play, changing the outcome in whatever way you deem appropriate. Be prepared to defend your alternative ending as a reasonable possibility. Consider why the author chose to end the play as he or she did.
26. Try your hand at writing a scene from a play. Invent a scenario, create a couple of characters, and start them talking and acting.
27. Read a few letters or essays written by a dramatist. Consider what light they shed on your reading of the play(s).
28. Read a full-scale biography of a dramatist. Write a paper explaining how the author's life is or is not reflected in his work.
29. Discuss how a particular playwright reflects or rebels against important social, political, moral, or cultural issues of his or her time.
30. Read a critical study of a writer's plays. Write a paper explaining how the book aids your understanding or enhances your enjoyment of the play(s).

CHAPTER FIVE

The Greek Theater: Sophocles in Context

Greek drama developed from celebrations honoring Dionysus, the Greek god of wine and fertility. These celebrations included choric dancing as part of the religious ritual. It is possible that the leader of the chorus (the *choragos*) may have engaged the rest of the chorus in responsive chanting. Legend suggests that the poet Thespis introduced a speaker who, detached from the chorus, engaged in dialogue with it. At that point drama was born. A second actor was added by Aeschylus (524–456 B.C.) and a third by Sophocles (496?–406 B.C.). In Greek drama no more than three characters appeared onstage together at one time, although it was common for actors to double and triple parts, changing masks for their multiple roles.

Greek plays were performed in huge outdoor amphitheaters capable of seating upwards of fourteen thousand people. Members of the audience were seated in tiers that sloped up hillsides where the theaters were built; the hills echoed the sound of the actors' voices. The actors wore masks that amplified their voices in the manner of megaphones. The masks were large, and with the elevated shoes sometimes worn by the actors, they projected the characters as larger-than-life figures. The masks and elevated shoes restricted what the actors could do and what the dramatist could expect of them. Subtle nuances of voice, of facial expression, and of gesture were impossible. The playwright's language rather than his stage business conveyed nuances of meaning and feeling.

The plays were performed on an elevated platform. Behind the acting area was a scene building *(skene)* that functioned both as dressing room and as scenic background, and below the stage was the *orchestra* or dancing place for the chorus. Standing between the actors and the audience, the chorus represented the common or communal viewpoint. Its leader, the choragos, sometimes engaged the chorus in dialogue with the other characters, and sometimes the choragos engaged in dialogue with the chorus itself.

An important function of the chorus was to mark the divisions between the scenes of a play, when the chorus would dance and chant poetry. Lyric rather than dramatic in form, these choral interludes sometimes commented on the action, sometimes generalized from it. They remained in Greek drama as vestiges of its origins in religious ritual. For modern readers these choric interludes pace the play, affording respite from the gradually intensifying action, and allowing time to ponder its implications.

The scenes of Greek plays usually consist of two, sometimes three characters with the third usually acting as an observer who occasionally comments on the debate occurring between the other two characters. Sometimes most of a scene is given over to a debate between two characters, as, for example, in Scene III of *Antigonê* with Haimon challenging Creon, his father, or Scene I of *Oedipus Rex* in which Oedipus argues with Teiresias. Some scenes, such as Scene II of *Antigonê,* include debates between Creon-Antigonê, Antigonê-Ismenê, Ismenê-Creon, and Creon-Choragos. The debates typically begin with leisurely speeches in which each character sets forth a position. The speeches are followed by rapid-fire dialogue *(stichomythia)* that brings the characters' antagonisms to a climax. This pattern is repeated throughout the play in something like a theme with variations, each scene usually developing a conflict. The accumulation of conflicts advances the action, leading to the inevitable tragic catastrophe.

Brevity is a characteristic of Greek tragedy: the plays are short with most having a playing time of roughly ninety minutes. Greek dramatists based their plays on myths that were familiar to the audience, which reduced the amount of time allotted for exposition. The plays also have a musical dimension, which, combined with the dancing and chanting of the chorus, increased the emotional impact of the ancient performances.

Of the three great Greek tragic dramatists, Sophocles is perhaps the most widely read today. Unlike his forebear Aeschylus, Sophocles focused his plays on human rather than religious concerns. As theater historian Peter Arnott has noted, he wrote "for a generation whose religious faith was waning."★ His most famous plays center on a crisis and portray characters under duress. *Antigonê,* which takes place in Thebes, a city prostrated by war, turns on the difficult decisions both Antigonê and Creon must make. In *Oedipus Rex,* set against a background of the plague-stricken city of Thebes, Sophocles examines the behavior of Oedipus, who has been destined to murder his father and marry his mother. Though the two tragedies differ in the way their calamities ensue, both raise questions about inescapable human problems and portray characters confronting them with dignity and courage.

The following chart clarifies the relationships among the Theban royal families:

★Peter Arnott, *The Theatre in Its Time* (Boston: Little, Brown, 1981), page 51.

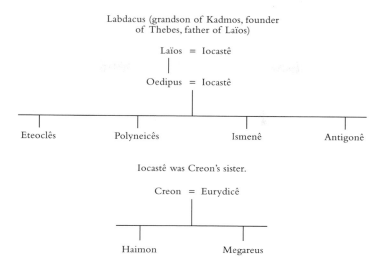

The Athenian audience that watched performances of *Oedipus Tyrannus* (the original Greek title of the play) would have been familiar with Oedipus's story from sources as early as Homer's *Odyssey*. They would have known, for example, that Oedipus was fated to kill his father and marry his mother, and that to prevent this from happening, the infant Oedipus was given up by his parents, King Laius and Queen Jocasta, and left in the wilderness to die. This plan went awry when Oedipus was taken by a shepherd to Corinth, where he was adopted by a childless couple, King Polybus and Queen Merope. The Athenian audience would also have been aware of the reason for Oedipus's clubfoot (his feet had been pinned together as an infant). They would have known too of how upon hearing the oracle pronounce his grisly fate, Oedipus had left Corinth, where he had been raised as a prince, thinking that he had to get as far away as he could from Polybus and Merope, who he assumed were his biological parents. For the Athenian audience, then, and for later audiences who know the Oedipus story, the play's power resides less in the surprising twists and turns of its plot than in its relentless tragic action.

Oedipus Rex begins at the point when Thebes is undergoing a series of catastrophes, most important of which is a devastating plague. Prior to this series of events, Oedipus had saved Thebes from the Sphinx, a winged creature with the body of a lion and the head of a woman. The Sphinx had terrorized the city by devouring anyone who crossed its path and who was unable to answer its riddle correctly: What goes on four legs in the morning, two legs in the afternoon, and three legs in the evening? Oedipus solved the riddle by answering "Man." After he slew the Sphinx, he was given in reward the kingship of Thebes and the hand of its recently widowed queen, Jocasta. Unknown to Oedipus, but known to the Athenian audience, was the fact that Jocasta was his mother and that her recently slain husband, Laius, had been killed by Oedipus himself (who of course did not know who Laius really was). All this and more Oedipus soon discovers.

INTRODUCTION TO SOPHOCLES

[c. 496–406 B.C.]

The ancient Greek tragic dramatist Sophocles lived during the Athenian Golden Age, when the military power, artistic glory, and philosophical achievements of Athens were at their zenith. The most generally admired of the ancient Greek dramatists, Sophocles was also acknowledged for his musical skill and his handsome appearance.

Sophocles also held political and military positions. He served, for example, as a general with the Athenian statesman Pericles and was a commissioner of the Athenian empire. He was also a priest of Asclepius, the Greek god of healing and medicine. It is for his plays, however, that Sophocles is best known and most widely admired.

Sophocles wrote more than one hundred plays, only seven of which have survived. Many of his plays were entered in competition with plays by other Greek tragic dramatists, including Aeschylus and Euripides, whose work Sophocles surpassed on at least twenty occasions. More conservative than the other Greek dramatists who were his contemporaries, Sophocles emphasized the individual's uncompromising search for truth, which is evident in both his plays *Oedipus Rex* and *Antigonê*.

Oedipus Rex

AN ENGLISH VERSION BY DUDLEY FITTS AND ROBERT FITZGERALD

CHARACTERS

OEDIPUS
A PRIEST
CREON
TEIRESIAS
IOCASTÊ
MESSENGER
SHEPHERD OF LAÏOS
SECOND MESSENGER
CHORUS OF THEBAN ELDERS

Scene. *Before the palace of* OEDIPUS, *King of Thebes. A central door and two lateral doors open onto a platform which runs the length of the façade. On the platform, right and left, are altars; and three steps lead down into the "orchestra," or chorus-ground. At the beginning of the action these steps are crowded by* SUPPLIANTS *who have brought branches and chaplets of olive leaves and who lie in various attitudes of despair.* OEDIPUS *enters.*

PROLOGUE

OEDIPUS: My children, generations of the living
   In the line of Kadmos,° nursed at his ancient hearth:
   Why have you strewn yourselves before these altars
   In supplication, with your boughs and garlands?
   The breath of incense rises from the city   5
   With a sound of prayer and lamentation.
                          Children,
   I would not have you speak through messengers,
   And therefore I have come myself to hear you—
   I, Oedipus, who bear the famous name.
   (*To a* PRIEST.) You, there, since you are eldest in the company,   10
   Speak for them all, tell me what preys upon you,
   Whether you come in dread, or crave some blessing:
   Tell me, and never doubt that I will help you
   In every way I can; I should be heartless
   Were I not moved to find you suppliant here.   15
PRIEST: Great Oedipus, O powerful King of Thebes!
   You see how all the ages of our people
   Cling to your altar steps: here are boys
   Who can barely stand alone, and here are priests
   By weight of age, as I am a priest of God,   20
   And young men chosen from those yet unmarried;
   As for the others, all that multitude,
   They wait with olive chaplets in the squares,
   At the two shrines of Pallas,° and where Apollo°
   Speaks in the glowing embers.
                    Your own eyes   25
   Must tell you: Thebes is in her extremity
   And cannot lift her head from the surge of death.
   A rust consumes the buds and fruits of the earth;
   The herds are sick; children die unborn,
   And labor is vain. The god of plague and pyre   30
   Raids like detestable lightning through the city,
   And all the house of Kadmos is laid waste,
   All emptied, and all darkened: Death alone
   Battens upon the misery of Thebes.
   You are not one of the immortal gods, we know;   35
   Yet we have come to you to make our prayer
   As to the man of all men best in adversity
   And wisest in the ways of God. You saved us
   From the Sphinx,° that flinty singer, and the tribute

2**Kadmos** *legendary founder of Thebes.*   24**Pallas** *Athena, goddess of wisdom.*   24**Apollo** *god of poetry and prophecy.*   39**the Sphinx** *a monster with a lion's body, birds' wings, and woman's face.*

We paid to her so long; yet you were never   40
Better informed than we, nor could we teach you:
It was some god breathed in you to set us free.

Therefore, O mighty King, we turn to you:
Find us our safety, find us a remedy,
Whether by counsel of the gods or the men.   45
A king of wisdom tested in the past
Can act in a time of troubles, and act well.
Noblest of men, restore
Life to your city! Think how all men call you
Liberator for your triumph long ago;   50
Ah, when your years of kingship are remembered,
Let them not say *We rose, but later fell—*
Keep the State from going down in the storm!
Once, years ago, with happy augury,
You brought us fortune; be the same again!   55
No man questions your power to rule the land:
But rule over men, not over a dead city!
Ships are only hulls, citadels are nothing,
When no life moves in the empty passageways.
OEDIPUS: Poor children! You may be sure I know   60
    All that you longed for in your coming here.
    I know that you are deathly sick; and yet,
    Sick as you are, not one is as sick as I.
    Each of you suffers in himself alone
    His anguish, not another's; but my spirit   65
    Groans for the city, for myself, for you.

    I was not sleeping, you are not waking me.
    No, I have been in tears for a long while
    And in my restless thought walked many ways.
    In all my search, I found one helpful course,   70
    And that I have taken: I have sent Creon,
    Son of Menoikeus, brother of the Queen,
    To Delphi, Apollo's place of revelation,
    To learn there, if he can,
    What act or pledge of mine may save the city.   75
    I have counted the days, and now, this very day,
    I am troubled, for he has overstayed his time.
    What is he doing? He has been gone too long.
    Yet whenever he comes back, I should do ill
    To scant whatever hint the god may give.   80
PRIEST: It is a timely promise. At this instant
    They tell me Creon is here.
OEDIPUS: O Lord Apollo!
    May his news be fair as his face is radiant!
PRIEST: It could not be otherwise: he is crowned with bay,

The chaplet is thick with berries.

OEDIPUS: We shall soon know;   85
 He is near enough to hear us now.

Enter CREON.

                          O Prince:
 Brother: son of Menoikeus:
 What answer do you bring us from the god?

CREON: It is favorable. I can tell you, great afflictions
 Will turn out well, if they are taken well.   90

OEDIPUS: What was the oracle? These vague words
 Leave me still hanging between hope and fear.

CREON: Is it your pleasure to hear me with all these
 Gathered around us? I am prepared to speak,
 But should we not go in?

OEDIPUS: Let them all hear it.   95
 It is for them I suffer, more than myself.

CREON: Then I will tell you what I heard at Delphi.

 In plain words
 The god commands us to expel from the land of Thebes
 An old defilement that it seems we shelter.   100
 It is a deathly thing, beyond expiation.
 We must not let it feed upon us longer.

OEDIPUS: What defilement? How shall we rid ourselves of it?

CREON: By exile or death, blood for blood. It was
 Murder that brought the plague-wind on the city.   105

OEDIPUS: Murder of whom? Surely the god has named him?

CREON: My lord: long ago Laïos was our king,
 Before you came to govern us.

OEDIPUS: I know;
 I learned of him from others; I never saw him.

CREON: He was murdered; and Apollo commands us now   110
 To take revenge upon whoever killed him.

OEDIPUS: Upon whom? Where are they? Where shall we find a clue
 To solve that crime, after so many years?

CREON: Here in this land, he said.
                          If we make enquiry,
 We may touch things that otherwise escape us.   115

OEDIPUS: Tell me: Was Laïos murdered in his house,
 Or in the fields, or in some foreign country?

CREON: He said he planned to make a pilgrimage.
 He did not come home again.

OEDIPUS: And was there no one,
 No witness, no companion, to tell what happened?   120

CREON: They were all killed but one, and he got away
 So frightened that he could remember one thing only.

OEDIPUS: What was that one thing? One may be the key

To everything, if we resolve to use it.
CREON: He said that a band of highwaymen attacked them,   125
    Outnumbered them, and overwhelmed the King.
OEDIPUS: Strange, that a highwayman should be so daring—
    Unless some faction here bribed him to do it.
CREON: We thought of that. But after Laïos' death
    New troubles arose and we had no avenger.   130
OEDIPUS: What troubles could prevent your hunting down the killers?
CREON: The riddling Sphinx's song
    Made us deaf to all mysteries but her own.
OEDIPUS: Then once more I must bring what is dark to light.
    It is most fitting that Apollo shows,   135
    As you do, this compunction for the dead.
    You shall see how I stand by you, as I should,
    To avenge the city and the city's god,
    And not as though it were for some distant friend,
    But for my own sake, to be rid of evil.   140
    Whoever killed King Laïos might—who knows?—
    Decide at any moment to kill me as well.
    By avenging the murdered king I protect myself.
    Come, then, my children: leave the altar steps,
    Lift up your olive boughs!
            One of you go   145
    And summon the people of Kadmos to gather here.
    I will do all that I can; you may tell them that.

                    (*Exit a* PAGE.)

    So, with the help of God,
    We shall be saved—or else indeed we are lost.
PRIEST: Let us rise, children. It was for this we came,   150
    And now the King has promised it himself.
    Phoibos° has sent us an oracle; may he descend
    Himself to save us and drive out the plague.

    Exeunt OEDIPUS *and* CREON *into the palace by the central door. The* PRIEST *and the*
    SUPPLIANTS *disperse right and left. After a short pause the* CHORUS *enters the orchestra.*

                    PÁRODOS°

Strophe 1

CHORUS: What is God singing in his profound
    Delphi of gold and shadow?

---

[152]**Phoibos**   *Phoebus Apollo, the sun god.*   **Párodos**   *sung as the chorus enters the stage area. Presumably they sang the strophe while dancing from right to left and the antistrophe as they reversed direction.*

What oracle for Thebes, the sunwhipped city?
Fear unjoints me, the roots of my heart tremble.
Now I remember, O Healer, your power, and wonder;   5
Will you send doom like a sudden cloud, or weave it
Like nightfall of the past?
Speak, speak to us, issue of holy sound:
Dearest to our expectancy: be tender!

Antistrophe 1

Let me pray to Athenê, the immortal daughter of Zeus,   10
And to Artemis her sister
Who keeps her famous throne in the market ring,
And to Apollo, bowman at the far butts of heaven—

O gods, descend! Like three streams leap against
The fires of our grief, the fires of darkness;   15
Be swift to bring us rest!

As in the old time from the brilliant house
Of air you stepped to save us, come again!

Strophe 2

Now our afflictions have no end,
Now all our stricken host lies down   20
And no man fights off death with his mind;

The noble plowland bears no grain,
And groaning mothers cannot bear—

See, how our lives like birds take wing.
Like sparks that fly when a fire soars,   25
To the shore of the god of evening.

Antistrophe 2

The plague burns on, it is pitiless,
Though pallid children laden with death
Lie unwept in the stony ways,
And old gray women by every path   30

Flock to the strand about the altars
There to strike their breasts and cry
Worship of Phoibos in wailing prayers:
Be kind, God's golden child!

Strophe 3

There are no swords in this attack by fire,   35
No shields, but we are ringed with cries.
Send the besieger plunging from our homes
Into the vast sea-room of the Atlantic
Or into the waves that foam eastward of Thrace—
For the day ravages what the night spares—   40

Destroy our enemy, lord of the thunder!
Let him be riven by lightning from heaven!

Antistrophe 3

Phoibos Apollo, stretch the sun's bowstring,
That golden cord, until it sing for us,
Flashing arrows in heaven!
                    Artemis,° Huntress,   45
Race with flaring lights upon our mountains!
O scarlet god, O golden-banded brow,
O Theban Bacchos° in a storm of Maenads,°

                    Enter OEDIPUS, *center.*

Whirl upon Death, that all the Undying hate!
Come with blinding cressets, come in joy!   50

SCENE I

OEDIPUS: Is this your prayer? It may be answered. Come,
Listen to me, act as the crisis demands,
And you shall have relief from all these evils.

    Until now I was a stranger to this tale,
As I had been a stranger to the crime.   5
Could I track down the murderer without a clue?
But now, friends,
As one who became a citizen after the murder,
I make this proclamation to all Thebans:
If any man knows by whose hand Laïos, son of Labdakos,   10
Met his death, I direct that man to tell me everything,
No matter what he fears for having so long withheld it.
Let it stand as promised that no further trouble

---

[45] **Artemis**   *goddess of hunting and chastity.*   [48] **Bacchos . . . Maenads**   *god of wine and revelry with his at-*
tendants.

Will come to him, but he may leave the land in safety.
Moreover: If anyone knows the murderer to be foreign, 15
Let him not keep silent: he shall have his reward from me.
However, if he does conceal it; if any man
Fearing for his friend or for himself disobeys this edict,
Hear what I propose to do:

I solemnly forbid the people of this country, 20
Where power and throne are mine, ever to receive that man
Or speak to him, no matter who he is, or let him
Join in sacrifice, lustration, or in prayer.
I decree that he be driven from every house,

Being, as he is, corruption itself to us: the Delphic 25
Voice of Zeus has pronounced this revelation.
Thus I associate myself with the oracle
And take the side of the murdered king.

As for the criminal, I pray to God—
Whether it be a lurking thief, or one of a number— 30
I pray that that man's life be consumed in evil and
    wretchedness.
And as for me, this curse applies no less
If it should turn out that the culprit is my guest here,
Sharing my hearth.
           You have heard the penalty.
I lay it on you now to attend to this 35
For my sake, for Apollo's, for the sick
Sterile city that heaven has abandoned.
Suppose the oracle had given you no command:
Should this defilement go uncleansed for ever?
You should have found the murderer: your king, 40
A noble king, had been destroyed!
           Now I,
Having the power that he held before me,
Having his bed, begetting children there
Upon his wife, as he would have, had he lived—
Their son would have been my children's brother, 45
If Laïos had had luck in fatherhood!
(But surely ill luck rushed upon his reign)—
I say I take the son's part, just as though
I were his son, to press the fight for him
And see it won! I'll find the hand that brought 50
Death to Labdakos' and Polydoros' child,
Heir of Kadmos' and Agenor's line.
And as for those who fail me,
May the gods deny them the fruit of the earth,

Fruit of the womb, and may they rot utterly!   55
Let them be wretched as we are wretched, and worse!
For you, for loyal Thebans, and for all
Who find my actions right, I pray the favor
Of justice, and of all the immortal gods.
CHORAGOS: Since I am under oath, my lord, I swear   60
   I did not do the murder, I cannot name
   The murderer. Might not the oracle
   That has ordained the search tell where to find him?
OEDIPUS: An honest question. But no man in the world
   Can make the gods do more than the gods will.   65
CHORAGOS: There is one last expedient—
OEDIPUS: Tell me what it is.
   Though it seem slight, you must not hold it back.
CHORAGOS: A lord clairvoyant to the lord Apollo,
   As we all know, is the skilled Teiresias.
   One might learn much about this from him, Oedipus.   70
OEDIPUS: I am not wasting time:
   Creon spoke of this, and I have sent for him—
   Twice, in fact; it is strange that he is not here.
CHORAGOS: The other matter—that old report—seems useless.
OEDIPUS: Tell me. I am interested in all reports.   75
CHORAGOS: The King was said to have been killed by highwaymen.
OEDIPUS: I know. But we have no witnesses to that.
CHORAGOS: If the killer can feel a particle of dread,
   Your curse will bring him out of hiding!
OEDIPUS: No.
   The man who dared that act will fear no curse.   80

Enter the blind seer TEIRESIAS, *led by a* PAGE.

CHORAGOS: But there is one man who may detect the criminal.
   This is Teiresias, this is the holy prophet
   In whom, alone of all men, truth was born.
OEDIPUS: Teiresias: seer: student of mysteries,
   Of all that's taught and all that no man tells,   85
   Secrets of Heaven and secrets of the earth:
   Blind though you are, you know the city lies
   Sick with plague; and from this plague, my lord,
   We find that you alone can guard or save us.

   Possibly you did not hear the messengers?   90
   Apollo, when we sent to him,
   Sent us back word that this great pestilence
   Would lift, but only if we established clearly
   The identity of those who murdered Laïos.
   They must be killed or exiled.
             Can you use   95

Birdflight or any art of divination
To purify yourself, and Thebes, and me
From this contagion? We are in your hands.
There is no fairer duty
Than that of helping others in distress. 100
TEIRESIAS: How dreadful knowledge of the truth can be
    When there's no help in truth! I knew this well,
    But did not act on it: else I should not have come.
OEDIPUS: What is troubling you? Why are your eyes so cold?
TEIRESIAS: Let me go home. Bear your own fate, and I'll 105
    Bear mine. It is better so: trust what I say.
OEDIPUS: What you say is ungracious and unhelpful
    To your native country. Do not refuse to speak.
TEIRESIAS: When it comes to speech, your own is neither temperate
    Nor opportune. I wish to be more prudent. 110
OEDIPUS: In God's name, we all beg you—
TEIRESIAS: You are all ignorant.
    No; I will never tell you what I know.
    Now it is my misery; then, it would be yours.
OEDIPUS: What! You do know something, and will not tell us?
    You would betray us all and wreck the State? 115
TEIRESIAS: I do not intend to torture myself, or you.
    Why persist in asking? You will not persuade me.
OEDIPUS: What a wicked old man you are! You'd try a stone's
    Patience! Out with it! Have you no feeling at all?
TEIRESIAS: You call me unfeeling. If you could only see 120
    The nature of your own feelings . . .
OEDIPUS: Why,
    Who would not feel as I do? Who could endure
    Your arrogance toward the city?
TEIRESIAS: What does it matter!
    Whether I speak or not, it is bound to come.
OEDIPUS: Then, if "it" is bound to come, you are bound
    to tell me. 125
TEIRESIAS: No, I will not go on. Rage as you please.
OEDIPUS: Rage? Why not!
                And I'll tell you what I think:
    You planned it, you had it done, you all but
    Killed him with your own hands: if you had eyes,
    I'd say the crime was yours, and yours alone. 130
TEIRESIAS: So? I charge you, then,
    Abide by the proclamation you have made:
    From this day forth
    Never speak again to these men or to me;
    You yourself are the pollution of this country. 135
OEDIPUS: You dare say that! Can you possibly think you have
    Some way of going free, after such insolence?

TEIRESIAS: I have gone free. It is the truth sustains me.

OEDIPUS: Who taught you shamelessness? It was not your craft.

TEIRESIAS: You did. You made me speak. I did not want to.   140

OEDIPUS: Speak what? Let me hear it again more clearly.

TEIRESIAS: Was it not clear before? Are you tempting me?

OEDIPUS: I did not understand it. Say it again.

TEIRESIAS: I say that you are the murderer whom you seek.

OEDIPUS: Now twice you have spat out infamy. You'll
          pay for it!   145

TEIRESIAS: Would you care for more? Do you wish to be really angry?

OEDIPUS: Say what you will. Whatever you say is worthless.

TEIRESIAS: I say you live in hideous shame with those
    Most dear to you. You cannot see the evil.

OEDIPUS: It seems you can go on mouthing like this for ever.   150

TEIRESIAS: I can, if there is power in truth.

OEDIPUS: There is:
    But not for you, not for you,
    You sightless, witless, senseless, mad old man!

TEIRESIAS: You are the madman. There is no one here
    Who will not curse you soon, as you curse me.   155

OEDIPUS: You child of endless night! You cannot hurt me
    Or any other man who sees the sun.

TEIRESIAS: True: it is not from me your fate will come.
    That lies within Apollo's competence,
    As it is his concern.

OEDIPUS: Tell me: 160
    Are you speaking for Creon, or for yourself?

TEIRESIAS: Creon is no threat. You weave your own doom.

OEDIPUS: Wealth, power, craft of statesmanship!
    Kingly position, everywhere admired!
    What savage envy is stored up against these,   165
    If Creon, whom I trusted, Creon my friend,
    For this great office which the city once
    Put in my hands unsought—if for this power
    Creon desires in secret to destroy me!
    He has brought this decrepit fortune-teller, this   170
    Collector of dirty pennies, this prophet fraud—
    Why, he is no more clairvoyant than I am!
                              Tell us:
    Has your mystic mummery ever approached the truth?
    When that hellcat the Sphinx was performing here,
    What help were you to these people?   175
    Her magic was not for the first man who came along:
    It demanded a real exorcist. Your birds—
    What good were they? or the gods, for the matter of that?
    But I came by,
    Oedipus, the simple man, who knows nothing—   180

I thought it out for myself, no birds helped me!
And this is the man you think you can destroy,
That you may be close to Creon when he's king!
Well, you and your friend Creon, it seems to me,
Will suffer most. If you were not an old man,   185
You would have paid already for your plot.
CHORAGOS: We cannot see that his words or yours
Have been spoken except in anger, Oedipus,
And of anger we have no need. How can God's will
Be accomplished best? That is what most concerns us.   190
TEIRESIAS: You are a king. But where argument's concerned
I am your man, as much a king as you.
I am not your servant, but Apollo's.
I have no need of Creon to speak for me.

Listen to me. You mock my blindness, do you?   195
But I say that you, with both your eyes, are blind:
You cannot see the wretchedness of your life,
Nor in whose house you live, no, nor with whom.
Who are your father and mother? Can you tell me?
You do not even know the blind wrongs   200
That you have done them, on earth and in the world below.
But the double lash of your parents' curse will whip you
Out of this land some day, with only night
Upon your precious eyes.
Your cries then—where will they not be heard?   205
What fastness of Kithairon will not echo them?
And that bridal-descant of yours—you'll know it then,
The song they sang when you came here to Thebes
And found your misguided berthing.
All this, and more, that you cannot guess at now,   210
Will bring you to yourself among your children.
Be angry, then. Curse Creon. Curse my words.
I tell you, no man that walks upon the earth
Shall be rooted out more horribly than you.
OEDIPUS: Am I to bear this from him?—Damnation   215
    Take you! Out of this place! Out of my sight!
TEIRESIAS: I would not have come at all if you had not asked me.
OEDIPUS: Could I have told that you'd talk nonsense, that
    You'd come here to make a fool of yourself, and of me?
TEIRESIAS: A fool? Your parents thought me sane enough.   220
OEDIPUS: My parents again!—Wait: who were my parents?
TEIRESIAS: This day will give you a father, and break your heart.
OEDIPUS: Your infantile riddles! Your damned abracadabra!
TEIRESIAS: You were a great man once at solving riddles.
OEDIPUS: Mock me with that if you like; you will find it true.   225
TEIRESIAS: It was true enough. It brought about your ruin.

OEDIPUS: But if it saved this town?

TEIRESIAS (*to the* PAGE): Boy, give me your hand.

OEDIPUS: Yes, boy; lead him away.

                    —While you are here

  We can do nothing. Go; leave us in peace.

TEIRESIAS: I will go when I have said what I have to say.   230

  How can you hurt me? And I tell you again:

  The man you have been looking for all this time,

  The damned man, the murderer of Laïos,

  That man is in Thebes. To your mind he is foreignborn,

  But it will soon be shown that he is a Theban,   235

  A revelation that will fail to please.

               A blind man,

  Who has his eyes now; a penniless man, who is rich now;

  And he will go tapping the strange earth with his staff;

  To the children with whom he lives now he will be

  Brother and father—the very same; to her   240

  Who bore him, son and husband—the very same

  Who came to his father's bed, wet with his father's blood.

  Enough. Go think that over.

  If later you find error in what I have said,

  You may say that I have no skill in prophecy.   245

       Exit TEIRESIAS, *led by his* PAGE. OEDIPUS *goes into the palace.*

ODE I°

Strophe 1

CHORUS: The Delphic stone of prophecies

  Remembers ancient regicide

  And a still bloody hand.

  That killer's hour of flight has come.

  He must be stronger than riderless   5

  Coursers of untiring wind,

  For the son of Zeus° armed with his father's thunder

  Leaps in lightning after him;

  And the Furies° follow him, the sad Furies.

Antistrophe 1

  Holy Parnossos' peak of snow   10

  Flashes and blinds that secret man,

  That all shall hunt him down:

  Though he may roam the forest shade

---

ode *a poetic song sung by the chorus.*   [7]**son of Zeus** *Apollo.*   [9]**the Furies** *three women spirits who punished evildoers.*

Like a bull gone wild from pasture
To rage through glooms of stone. 15
Doom comes down on him; flight will not avail him;
For the world's heart calls him desolate,
And the immortal Furies follow, for ever follow.

Strophe 2

But now a wilder thing is heard
From the old man skilled at hearing Fate in the
    wingbeat of a bird. 20
Bewildered as a blown bird, my soul hovers and cannot find
Foothold in this debate, or any reason or rest of mind.
But no man ever brought—none can bring
Proof of strife between Thebes' royal house,
Labdakos' line,° and the son of Polybos;° 25
And never until now has any man brought word
Of Laïos' dark death staining Oedipus the King.

Antistrophe 2

Divine Zeus and Apollo hold
Perfect intelligence alone of all tales ever told;
And well though this diviner works, he works in his own night; 30
No man can judge that rough unknown or trust in second sight,
For wisdom changes hands among the wise.
Shall I believe my great lord criminal
At a raging word that a blind old man let fall?
I saw him, when the carrion woman faced him of old, 35
Prove his heroic mind! These evil words are lies.

SCENE II

CREON: Men of Thebes:
I am told that heavy accusations
Have been brought against me by King Oedipus.
I am not the kind of man to bear this tamely.

If in these present difficulties 5
He holds me accountable for any harm to him
Through anything I have said or done—why, then,
I do not value life in this dishonor.
It is not as though this rumor touched upon
Some private indiscretion. The matter is grave. 10
The fact is that I am being called disloyal
To the State, to my fellow citizens, to my friends.

---

[25] **Labdakos' line**   *his descendants.*   [25] **Polybos**   *King of Corinth who adopted Oedipus as an infant.*

CHORAGOS: He may have spoken in anger, not from his mind.
CREON: But did you not hear him say I was the one
   Who seduced the old prophet into lying?   15
CHORAGOS: The thing was said; I do not know how seriously.
CREON: But you were watching him! Were his eyes steady?
   Did he look like a man in his right mind?
CHORAGOS: I do not know.
   I cannot judge the behavior of great men.
   But here is the King himself.

Enter OEDIPUS.

OEDIPUS: So you dared come back.   20
   Why? How brazen of you to come to my house,
   You murderer!
          Do you think I do not know
   That you plotted to kill me, plotted to steal my throne?
   Tell me, in God's name: am I coward, a fool,
   That you should dream you could accomplish this?   25
   A fool who could not see your slippery game?
   A coward, not to fight back when I saw it?
   You are the fool, Creon, are you not? hoping
   Without support or friends to get a throne?
   Thrones may be won or bought: you could do neither.   30
CREON: Now listen to me. You have talked; let me talk, too.
   You cannot judge unless you know the facts.
OEDIPUS: You speak well: there is one fact; but I find it hard
   To learn from the deadliest enemy I have.
CREON: That above all I must dispute with you.   35
OEDIPUS: That above all I will not hear you deny.
CREON: If you think there is anything good in being stubborn
   Against all reason, then I say you are wrong.
OEDIPUS: If you think a man can sin against his own kind
   And not be punished for it, I say you are mad.   40
CREON: I agree. But tell me: what have I done to you?
OEDIPUS: You advised me to send for that wizard, did you not?
CREON: I did. I should do it again.
OEDIPUS: Very well. Now tell me:
   How long has it been since Laïos—
CREON: What of Laïos?
OEDIPUS: Since he vanished in that onset by the road?   45
CREON: It was long ago, a long time.
OEDIPUS: And this prophet,
   Was he practicing here then?
CREON: He was; and with honor, as now.
OEDIPUS: Did he speak of me at that time?
CREON: He never did;
   At least, not when I was present.

OEDIPUS: But . . . the enquiry?
  I suppose you held one?
CREON: We did, but we learned nothing.   50
OEDIPUS: Why did the prophet not speak against me then?
CREON: I do not know; and I am the kind of man
  Who holds his tongue when he has no facts to go on.
OEDIPUS: There's one fact that you know, and you could tell it.
CREON: What fact is that? If I know it, you shall have it.   55
OEDIPUS: If he were not involved with you, he could not say
  That it was I who murdered Laïos.
CREON: If he says that, you are the one that knows it!—
  But now it is my turn to question you.
OEDIPUS: Put your questions. I am no murderer.   60
CREON: First, then: You married my sister?
OEDIPUS: I married your sister.
CREON: And you rule the kingdom equally with her?
OEDIPUS: Everything that she wants she has from me.
CREON: And I am the third, equal to both of you?
OEDIPUS: That is why I call you a bad friend.   65
CREON: No. Reason it out, as I have done.
  Think of this first. Would any sane man prefer
  Power, with all a king's anxieties,
  To that same power and the grace of sleep?
  Certainly not I.   70
  I have never longed for the king's power—only his rights.
  Would any wise man differ from me in this?
  As matters stand, I have my way in everything
  With your consent, and no responsibilities.
  If I were king, I should be a slave to policy.   75
  How could I desire a scepter more
  Than what is now mine—untroubled influence?
  No, I have not gone mad; I need no honors,
  Except those with the perquisites I have now.
  I am welcome everywhere; every man salutes me,   80
  And those who want your favor seek my ear,
  Since I know how to manage what they ask.
  Should I exchange this ease for that anxiety?
  Besides, no sober mind is treasonable.
  I hate anarchy   85
  And never would deal with any man who likes it.

  Test what I have said. Go to the priestess
  At Delphi, ask if I quoted her correctly.
  And as for this other thing: if I am found
  Guilty of treason with Teiresias,   90
  Then sentence me to death! You have my word
  It is a sentence I should cast my vote for—

But not without evidence!
                    You do wrong
When you take good men for bad, bad men for good.
A true friend thrown aside—why, life itself   95
Is not more precious!
                    In time you will know this well:
For time, and time alone, will show the just man,
Though scoundrels are discovered in a day.
CHORAGOS: This is well said, and a prudent man would ponder it.
   Judgments too quickly formed are dangerous.   100
OEDIPUS: But is he not quick in his duplicity?
   And shall I not be quick to parry him?
   Would you have me stand still, hold my peace, and let
   This man win everything, through my inaction?
CREON: And you want—what is it, then? To banish me?   105
OEDIPUS: No, not exile. It is your death I want,
   So that all the world may see what treason means.
CREON: You will persist, then? You will not believe me?
OEDIPUS: How can I believe you?
CREON: Then you are a fool.
OEDIPUS: To save myself?
CREON: In justice, think of me.   110
OEDIPUS: You are evil incarnate.
CREON: But suppose that you are wrong?
OEDIPUS: Still I must rule.
CREON: But not if you rule badly.
OEDIPUS: O city, city!
CREON: It is my city, too!
CHORAGOS: Now, my lords, be still. I see the Queen,
   Iocastê, coming from her palace chambers;   115
   And it is time she came, for the sake of you both.
   This dreadful quarrel can be resolved through her.

                    Enter IOCASTÊ.

IOCASTÊ: Poor foolish men, what wicked din is this?
   With Thebes sick to death, is it not shameful
   That you should rake some private quarrel up?   120

                    (*To* OEDIPUS.)

Come into the house.
                    —And you, Creon, go now:
   Let us have no more of this tumult over nothing.
CREON: Nothing? No, sister: what your husband plans for me
   Is one of two great evils: exile or death.
OEDIPUS: He is right.
                    Why, woman, I have caught him squarely   125
   Plotting against my life.

CREON: No! Let me die
   Accurst if ever I have wished you harm!
IOCASTÊ: Ah, believe it, Oedipus!
   In the name of the gods, respect this oath of his
   For my sake, for the sake of these people here!   130

Strophe 1

CHORAGOS: Open your mind to her, my lord. Be ruled by her, I beg you!
OEDIPUS: What would you have me do?
CHORAGOS: Respect Creon's word. He has never spoken like a fool,
   And now he has sworn an oath.
OEDIPUS: You know what you ask?
CHORAGOS: I do.
OEDIPUS: Speak on, then.
CHORAGOS: A friend so sworn should not be baited so,   135
   In blind malice, and without final proof.
OEDIPUS: You are aware, I hope, that what you say
   Means death for me, or exile at the least.

Strophe 2

CHORAGOS: No, I swear by Helios, first in Heaven!
   May I die friendless and accurst,   140
   The worst of deaths, if ever I meant that!
      It is the withering fields
         That hurt my sick heart:
   Must we bear all these ills,
        And now your bad blood as well?   145
OEDIPUS: Then let him go. And let me die, if I must,
   Or be driven by him in shame from the land of Thebes.
   It is your unhappiness, and not his talk,
   That touches me.
        As for him—
   Wherever he is, I will hate him as long as I live.   150
CREON: Ugly in yielding, as you were ugly in rage!
   Natures like yours chiefly torment themselves.
OEDIPUS: Can you not go? Can you not leave me?
CREON: I can.
   You do not know me; but the city knows me,
   And in its eyes I am just, if not in yours.   155

(*Exit* CREON.)

Antistrophe 1

CHORAGOS: Lady Iocastê, did you not ask the King
   to go to his chambers?

IOCASTÊ: First tell me what has happened.

CHORAGOS: There was suspicion without evidence; yet it rankled
    As even false charges will.

IOCASTÊ: On both sides?

CHORAGOS: On both.

IOCASTÊ: But what was said?

CHORAGOS: Oh let it rest, let it be done with!   160
    Have we not suffered enough?

OEDIPUS: You see to what your decency has brought you:
    You have made difficulties where my heart saw none.

Antistrophe 2

CHORAGOS: Oedipus, it is not once only I have told you—
    You must know I should count myself unwise   165
    To the point of madness, should I now forsake you—
        You, under whose hand,
            In the storm of another time,
        Our dear land sailed out free.
            But now stand fast at the helm!   170

IOCASTÊ: In God's name, Oedipus, inform your wife as well:
    Why are you so set in this hard anger?

OEDIPUS: I will tell you, for none of these men deserves
    My confidence as you do. It is Creon's work,
    His treachery, his plotting against me.   175

IOCASTÊ: Go on, if you can make this clear to me.

OEDIPUS: He charges me with the murder of Laïos.

IOCASTÊ: Has he some knowledge? Or does he speak from hearsay?

OEDIPUS: He would not commit himself to such a charge,
    But he has brought in that damnable soothsayer   180
    To tell his story.

IOCASTÊ: Set your mind at rest.
    If it is a question of soothsayers, I tell you
    That you will find no man whose craft gives knowledge
    Of the unknowable.
            Here is my proof:

An oracle was reported to Laïos once   185
(I will not say from Phoibos himself, but from
His appointed ministers, at any rate)
That his doom would be death at the hands of his own son—
His son, born of his flesh and of mine!

Now, you remember the story: Laïos was killed   190
By marauding strangers where three highways meet;
But his child had not been three days in this world

Before the King had pierced the baby's ankles
And left him to die on a lonely mountainside.

Thus, Apollo never caused that child   195
To kill his father, and it was not Laïos' fate
To die at the hands of his son, as he had feared.
This is what prophets and prophecies are worth!
Have no dread of them.
               It is God himself
Who can show us what he wills, in his own way.   200
OEDIPUS: How strange a shadowy memory crossed my mind,
  Just now while you were speaking; it chilled my heart.
IOCASTÊ: What do you mean? What memory do you speak of?
OEDIPUS: If I understand you, Laïos was killed
  At a place where three roads meet.
IOCASTÊ: So it was said;   205
  We have no later story.
OEDIPUS: Where did it happen?
IOCASTÊ: Phokis, it is called: at a place where the Theban Way
  Divides into the roads towards Delphi and Daulia.
OEDIPUS: When?
IOCASTÊ: We had the news not long before you came
  And proved the right to your succession here.   210
OEDIPUS: Ah, what net has God been weaving for me?
IOCASTÊ: Oedipus! Why does this trouble you?
OEDIPUS: Do not ask me yet.
  First, tell me how Laïos looked, and tell me
  How old he was.
IOCASTÊ: He was tall, his hair just touched
  With white; his form was not unlike your own.   215
OEDIPUS: I think that I myself may be accurst
  By my own ignorant edict.
IOCASTÊ: You speak strangely.
  It makes me tremble to look at you, my King.
OEDIPUS: I am not sure that the blind man cannot see.
  But I should know better if you were to tell me—   220
IOCASTÊ: Anything—though I dread to hear you ask it.
OEDIPUS: Was the King lightly escorted, or did he ride
  With a large company, as a ruler should?
IOCASTÊ: There were five men with him in all: one was a herald;
  And a single chariot, which he was driving.   225
OEDIPUS: Alas, that makes it plain enough!
                     But who—
  Who told you how it happened?
IOCASTÊ: A household servant,
  The only one to escape.
OEDIPUS: And is he still

A servant of ours?
IOCASTÊ: No; for when he came back at last
And found you enthroned in the place of the dead king,   230
He came to me, touched my hand with his, and begged
That I would send him away to the frontier district
Where only the shepherds go—
As far away from the city as I could send him.
I granted his prayer; for although the man was a slave,   235
He had earned more than this favor at my hands.
OEDIPUS: Can he be called back quickly?
IOCASTÊ: Easily.
    But why?
OEDIPUS: I have taken too much upon myself
    Without enquiry; therefore I wish to consult him.
IOCASTÊ: Then he shall come.
                          But am I not one also   240
    To whom you might confide these fears of yours!
OEDIPUS: That is your right; it will not be denied you,
    Now least of all; for I have reached a pitch
    Of wild foreboding. Is there anyone
    To whom I should sooner speak?   245
    Polybos of Corinth is my father.
    My mother is a Dorian: Meropê.
    I grew up chief among the men of Corinth
    Until a strange thing happened—
    Not worth my passion, it may be, but strange.   250

    At a feast, a drunken man maundering in his cups
    Cries out that I am not my father's son!
    I contained myself that night, though I felt anger
    And a sinking heart. The next day I visited
    My father and mother, and questioned them. They stormed,   255
    Calling it all the slanderous rant of a fool;
    And this relieved me. Yet the suspicion
    Remained always aching in my mind;
    I knew there was talk; I could not rest;
    And finally, saying nothing to my parents,   260
    I went to the shrine at Delphi.
    The god dismissed my question without reply;
    He spoke of other things.
                          Some were clear,
    Full of wretchedness, dreadful, unbearable:
    As, that I should lie with my own mother, breed   265
    Children from whom all men would turn their eyes;
    And that I should be my father's murderer.

    I heard all this, and fled. And from that day
    Corinth to me was only in the stars

Descending in that quarter of the sky,   270
As I wandered farther and farther on my way
To a land where I should never see the evil
Sung by the oracle. And I came to this country
Where, so you say, King Laïos was killed.
I will tell you all that happened there, my lady.   275

There were three highways
Coming together at a place I passed;
And there a herald came towards me, and a chariot
Drawn by horses, with a man such as you describe
Seated in it. The groom leading the horses   280
Forced me off the road at his lord's command;
But as this charioteer lurched over towards me
I struck him in my rage. The old man saw me
And brought his double goad down upon my head
As I came abreast.

     He was paid back, and more!   285
Swinging my club in this right hand I knocked him
Out of his car, and he rolled on the ground.

         I killed him.

I killed them all.
Now if that stranger and Laïos were—kin,
Where is a man more miserable than I?   290
More hated by the gods? Citizen and alien alike
Must never shelter me or speak to me—
I must be shunned by all.

     And I myself
Pronounced this malediction upon myself!

Think of it: I have touched you with these hands,   295
These hands that killed your husband. What defilement!

Am I all evil, then? It must be so,
Since I must flee from Thebes, yet never again
See my own countrymen, my own country,
For fear of joining my mother in marriage   300
And killing Polybos, my father.

     Ah,
If I was created so, born to this fate,
Who could deny the savagery of God?

O holy majesty of heavenly powers!
May I never see that day! Never!   305
Rather let me vanish from the race of men
Than know the abomination destined me!
CHORAGOS: We too, my lord, have felt dismay at this.

But there is hope: you have yet to hear the shepherd.
OEDIPUS: Indeed, I fear no other hope is left me.   310
IOCASTÊ: What do you hope from him when he comes?
OEDIPUS: This much:
   If his account of the murder tallies with yours,
   Then I am cleared.
IOCASTÊ: What was it that I said
   Of such importance?
OEDIPUS: Why, "marauders," you said,
   Killed the King, according to this man's story.   315
   If he maintains that still, if there were several,
   Clearly the guilt is not mine: I was alone.
   But if he says one man, singlehanded, did it,
   Then the evidence all points to me.
IOCASTÊ: You may be sure that he said there were several;   320
   And can he call back that story now? He cannot.
   The whole city heard it as plainly as I.
   But suppose he alters some detail of it:
   He cannot ever show that Laïos' death
   Fulfilled the oracle: for Apollo said   325
   My child was doomed to kill him; and my child—
   Poor baby!—it was my child that died first.

   No. From now on, where oracles are concerned,
   I would not waste a second thought on any.
OEDIPUS: You may be right.
                             But come: let someone go   330
   For the shepherd at once. This matter must be settled.
IOCASTÊ: I will send for him.
   I would not wish to cross you in anything,
   And surely not in this.—Let us go in.

                   Exeunt into the palace.

ODE II

Strophe 1

CHORUS: Let me be reverent in the ways of right,
   Lowly the paths I journey on;
   Let all my words and actions keep
   The laws of the pure universe
   From highest Heaven handed down.   5
   For Heaven is their bright nurse,
   Those generations of the realms of light;
   Ah, never of mortal kind were they begot,

Nor are they slaves of memory, lost in sleep:
Their Father is greater than Time, and ages not. 10

Antistrophe 1

The tyrant is a child of Pride
Who drinks from his great sickening cup
Recklessness and vanity,
Until from his high crest headlong
He plummets to the dust of hope. 15
That strong man is not strong.
But let no fair ambition be denied;
May God protect the wrestler for the State
In government, in comely policy,
Who will fear God, and on His ordinance wait. 20

Strophe 2

Haughtiness and the high hand of disdain
Tempt and outrage God's holy law;
And any mortal who dares hold
No immortal Power in awe
Will be caught up in a net of pain: 25
The price for which his levity is sold.
Let each man take due earnings, then,
And keep his hands from holy things,
And from blasphemy stand apart—
Else the crackling blast of heaven 30
Blows on his head, and on his desperate heart;
Though fools will honor impious men,
In their cities no tragic poet sings.

Antistrophe 2

Shall we lose faith in Delphi's obscurities,
We who have heard the world's core 35
Discredited, and the sacred wood
Of Zeus at Elis praised no more?
The deeds and the strange prophecies
Must make a pattern yet to be understood.
Zeus, if indeed you are lord of all, 40
Throned in light over night and day,
Mirror this in your endless mind:
Our masters call the oracle
Words on the wind, and the Delphic vision blind!
Their hearts no longer know Apollo, 45
And reverence for the gods has died away.

SCENE III

Enter IOCASTÊ.

IOCASTÊ: Princes of Thebes, it has occurred to me
  To visit the altars of the gods, bearing
  These branches as a suppliant, and this incense.
  Our King is not himself: his noble soul
  Is overwrought with fantasies of dread,   5
  Else he would consider
  The new prophecies in the light of the old.
  He will listen to any voice that speaks disaster,
  And my advice goes for nothing.

                She approaches the altar, right.

                      To you, then, Apollo,
  Lycean lord, since you are nearest, I turn in prayer.   10
  Receive these offerings, and grant us deliverance
  From defilement. Our hearts are heavy with fear
  When we see our leader distracted, as helpless sailors
  Are terrified by the confusion of their helmsman.

                Enter MESSENGER.

MESSENGER: Friends, no doubt you can direct me: 15
  Where shall I find the house of Oedipus,
  Or, better still, where is the King himself?
CHORAGOS: It is this very place, stranger; he is inside.
  This is his wife and mother of his children.
MESSENGER: I wish her happiness in a happy house,   20
  Blest in all the fulfillment of her marriage.
IOCASTÊ: I wish as much for you: your courtesy
  Deserves a like good fortune. But now, tell me:
  Why have you come? What have you to say to us?
MESSENGER: Good news, my lady, for your house and your husband.   25
IOCASTÊ: What news? Who sent you here?
MESSENGER: I am from Corinth.
  The news I bring ought to mean joy for you,
  Though it may be you will find some grief in it.
IOCASTÊ: What is it? How can it touch us in both ways?
MESSENGER: The people of Corinth, they say,   30
  Intend to call Oedipus to be their king.
IOCASTÊ: But old Polybos—is he not reigning still?
MESSENGER: No. Death holds him in his sepulchre.
IOCASTÊ: What are you saying? Polybos is dead?
MESSENGER: If I am not telling the truth, may I die myself.   35
IOCASTÊ (*to a* MAIDSERVANT): Go in, go quickly; tell this to your master.

O riddlers of God's will, where are you now!
This was the man whom Oedipus, long ago,
Feared so, fled so, in dread of destroying him—
But it was another fate by which he died.   40

Enter OEDIPUS, *center.*

OEDIPUS: Dearest Iocastê, why have you sent for me?
IOCASTÊ: Listen to what this man says, and then tell me
    What has become of the solemn prophecies.
OEDIPUS: Who is this man? What is his news for me?
IOCASTÊ: He has come from Corinth to announce your father's death!   45
OEDIPUS: Is it true, stranger? Tell me in your own words.
MESSENGER: I cannot say it more clearly: the King is dead.
OEDIPUS: Was it by treason? Or by an attack of illness?
MESSENGER: A little thing brings old men to their rest.
OEDIPUS: It was sickness, then?
MESSENGER: Yes, and his many years.   50
OEDIPUS: Ah!
    Why should a man respect the Pythian hearth,° or
    Give heed to the birds that jangle above his head?
    They prophesied that I should kill Polybos,
    Kill my own father; but he is dead and buried,   55
    And I am here—I never touched him, never,
    Unless he died in grief for my departure,
    And thus, in a sense, through me. No. Polybos
    Has packed the oracles off with him underground.
    They are empty words.
IOCASTÊ: Had I not told you so?   60
OEDIPUS: You had; it was my faint heart that betrayed me.
IOCASTÊ: From now on never think of those things again.
OEDIPUS: And yet—must I not fear my mother's bed?
IOCASTÊ: Why should anyone in this world be afraid,
    Since Fate rules us and nothing can be foreseen?   65
    A man should live only for the present day.
    Have no more fear of sleeping with your mother:
    How many men, in dreams, have lain with their mothers!
    No reasonable man is troubled by such things.
OEDIPUS: That is true; only—   70
    If only my mother were not still alive!
    But she is alive. I cannot help my dread.
IOCASTÊ: Yet this news of your father's death is wonderful.
OEDIPUS: Wonderful. But I fear the living woman.
MESSENGER: Tell me, who is this woman that you fear?   75
OEDIPUS: It is Meropê, man; the wife of King Polybos.
MESSENGER: Meropê? Why should you be afraid of her?

---

[52] **Pythian hearth**   *Delphi, also called Pytho because a large dragon, the Python, had guarded the chasm at Delphi until Apollo killed it and established his oracle on the site.*

OEDIPUS: An oracle of the gods, a dreadful saying.

MESSENGER: Can you tell me about it or are you sworn to silence?

OEDIPUS: I can tell you, and I will.   80

    Apollo said through his prophet that I was the man

    Who should marry his own mother, shed his father's blood

    With his own hands. And so, for all these years

    I have kept clear of Corinth, and no harm has come—

    Though it would have been sweet to see my parents again.   85

MESSENGER: And is this the fear that drove you out of Corinth?

OEDIPUS: Would you have me kill my father?

MESSENGER: As for that

    You must be reassured by the news I gave you.

OEDIPUS: If you could reassure me, I would reward you.

MESSENGER: I had that in mind, I will confess: I thought   90

    I could count on you when you returned to Corinth.

OEDIPUS: No: I will never go near my parents again.

MESSENGER: Ah, son, you still do not know what you are doing—

OEDIPUS: What do you mean? In the name of God tell me!

MESSENGER:—If these are your reasons for not going home.   95

OEDIPUS: I tell you, I fear the oracle may come true.

MESSENGER: And guilt may come upon you through your parents?

OEDIPUS: That is the dread that is always in my heart.

MESSENGER: Can you not see that all your fears are groundless?

OEDIPUS: How can you say that? They are my parents, surely?   100

MESSENGER: Polybos was not your father.

OEDIPUS: Not my father?

MESSENGER: No more your father than the man speaking to you.

OEDIPUS: But you are nothing to me!

MESSENGER: Neither was he.

OEDIPUS: Then why did he call me son?

MESSENGER: I will tell you:

    Long ago he had you from my hands, as a gift.   105

OEDIPUS: Then how could he love me so, if I was not his?

MESSENGER: He had no children, and his heart turned to you.

OEDIPUS: What of you? Did you buy me? Did you find me by chance?

MESSENGER: I came upon you in the crooked pass of Kithairon.

OEDIPUS: And what were you doing there?

MESSENGER: Tending my flocks.   110

OEDIPUS: A wandering shepherd?

MESSENGER: But your savior, son, that day.

OEDIPUS: From what did you save me?

MESSENGER: Your ankles should tell you that.

OEDIPUS: Ah, stranger, why do you speak of that childhood pain?

MESSENGER: I cut the bonds that tied your ankles together.

OEDIPUS: I have had the mark as long as I can remember.   115

MESSENGER: That was why you were given the name you bear.°

---

¹¹⁶**name you bear**   *"Oedipus" means "swollen-foot."*

OEDIPUS: God! Was it my father or my mother who did it?
Tell me!
MESSENGER: I do not know. The man who gave you to me   120
Can tell you better than I.
OEDIPUS: It was not you that found me, but another?
MESSENGER: It was another shepherd gave you to me.
OEDIPUS: Who was he? Can you tell me who he was?
MESSENGER: I think he was said to be one of Laïos' people.
OEDIPUS: You mean the Laïos who was king here years ago?   125
MESSENGER: Yes; King Laïos; and the man was one of his herdsmen.
OEDIPUS: Is he still alive? Can I see him?
MESSENGER: These men here
Know best about such things.
OEDIPUS: Does anyone here
Know this shepherd that he is talking about?
Have you seen him in the fields, or in the town?   130
If you have, tell me. It is time things were made plain.
CHORAGOS: I think the man he means is that same shepherd
You have already asked to see. Iocastê perhaps
Could tell you something.
OEDIPUS: Do you know anything
About him, Lady? Is he the man we have summoned?   135
Is that the man this shepherd means?
IOCASTÊ: Why think of him?
Forget this herdsman. Forget it all.
This talk is a waste of time.
OEDIPUS: How can you say that,
When the clues to my true birth are in my hands?
IOCASTÊ: For God's love, let us have no more questioning!   140
Is your life nothing to you?
My own is pain enough for me to bear.
OEDIPUS: You need not worry. Suppose my mother a slave,
And born of slaves: no baseness can touch you.
IOCASTÊ: Listen to me, I beg you: do not do this thing!   145
OEDIPUS: I will not listen; the truth must be made known.
IOCASTÊ: Everything that I say is for your own good!
OEDIPUS: My own good
Snaps my patience, then: I want none of it.
IOCASTÊ: You are fatally wrong! May you never learn who you are!
OEDIPUS: Go, one of you, and bring the shepherd here.   150
Let us leave this woman to brag of her royal name.
IOCASTÊ: Ah, miserable!
That is the only word I have for you now.
That is the only word I can ever have.

Exit into the palace.

CHORAGOS: Why has she left us, Oedipus? Why has she gone   155
In such a passion of sorrow? I fear this silence:

Something dreadful may come of it.

OEDIPUS: Let it come!

However base my birth, I must know about it.
The Queen, like a woman, is perhaps ashamed
To think of my low origin. But I   160
Am a child of luck; I cannot be dishonored.
Luck is my mother; the passing months, my brothers,
Have seen me rich and poor.

                   If this is so,
How could I wish that I were someone else?
How could I not be glad to know my birth?   165

ODE III

Strophe

CHORUS: If ever the coming time were known
    To my heart's pondering,
    Kithairon, now by Heaven I see the torches
    At the festival of the next full moon,
    And see the dance, and hear the choir sing   5
    A grace to your gentle shade:
    Mountain where Oedipus was found,
    O mountain guard of a noble race!
    May the god who heals us lend his aid,
    And let that glory come to pass   10
    For our king's cradling-ground.

Antistrophe

    Of the nymphs that flower beyond the years,
    Who bore you, royal child,
    To Pan of the hills or the timberline Apollo,
    Cold in delight where the upland clears,   15
    Or Hermês for whom Kyllenê's heights° are piled?
    Or flushed as evening cloud,
    Great Dionysos, roamer of mountains,
    He—was it he who found you there,
    And caught you up in his own proud   20
    Arms from the sweet god-ravisher
    Who laughed by the Muses' fountains?

SCENE IV

OEDIPUS: Sirs: though I do not know the man,
    I think I see him coming, this shepherd we want:

---

[16]**Kyllenê's heights**   *holy mountain, birthplace of Hermes, messenger of the gods.*

He is old, like our friend here, and the men
Bringing him seem to be servants of my house.
But you can tell, if you have ever seen him. 5

Enter SHEPHERD *escorted by servants.*

CHORAGOS: I know him, he was Laïos' man. You can trust him.
OEDIPUS: Tell me first, you from Corinth: is this the shepherd
   We were discussing?
MESSENGER: This is the very man.
OEDIPUS (*to* SHEPHERD): Come here. No, look at me. You must answer
   Everything I ask.—You belonged to Laïos? 10
SHEPHERD: Yes: born his slave, brought up in his house.
OEDIPUS: Tell me: what kind of work did you do for him?
SHEPHERD: I was a shepherd of his, most of my life.
OEDIPUS: Where mainly did you go for pasturage?
SHEPHERD: Sometimes Kithairon, sometimes the hills near-by. 15
OEDIPUS: Do you remember ever seeing this man out there?
SHEPHERD: What would he be doing there? This man?
OEDIPUS: This man standing here. Have you ever seen him before?
SHEPHERD: No. At least, not to my recollection.
MESSENGER: And that is not strange, my lord. But I'll refresh 20
   His memory: he must remember when we two
   Spent three whole seasons together, March to September,
   On Kithairon or thereabouts. He had two flocks;
   I had one. Each autumn I'd drive mine home
   And he would go back with his to Laïos' sheepfold.— 25
   Is this not true, just as I have described it?
SHEPHERD: True, yes; but it was all so long ago.
MESSENGER: Well, then: do you remember, back in those days
   That you gave me a baby boy to bring up as my own?
SHEPHERD: What if I did? What are you trying to say? 30
MESSENGER: King Oedipus was once that little child.
SHEPHERD: Damn you, hold your tongue!
OEDIPUS: No more of that!
   It is your tongue needs watching, not this man's.
SHEPHERD: My King, my Master, what is it I have done wrong?
OEDIPUS: You have not answered his question about the boy. 35
SHEPHERD: He does not know . . . He is only making trouble . . .
OEDIPUS: Come, speak plainly, or it will go hard with you.
SHEPHERD: In God's name, do not torture an old man!
OEDIPUS: Come here, one of you; bind his arms behind him.
SHEPHERD: Unhappy king! What more do you wish to learn? 40
OEDIPUS: Did you give this man the child he speaks of?
SHEPHERD: I did.
   And I would to God I had died that very day.
OEDIPUS: You will die now unless you speak the truth.
SHEPHERD: Yet if I speak the truth, I am worse than dead.
OEDIPUS: Very well; since you insist upon delaying— 45

SHEPHERD: No! I have told you already that I gave him the boy.

OEDIPUS: Where did you get him? From your house?
     From somewhere else?

SHEPHERD: Not from mine, no. A man gave him to me.

OEDIPUS: Is that man here? Do you know whose slave he was?

SHEPHERD: For God's love, my King, do not ask me any more!   50

OEDIPUS: You are a dead man if I have to ask you again.

SHEPHERD: Then . . . Then the child was from the palace of Laïos.

OEDIPUS: A slave child? or a child of his own line?

SHEPHERD: Ah, I am on the brink of dreadful speech!

OEDIPUS: And I of dreadful hearing. Yet I must hear.   55

SHEPHERD: If you must be told, then . . .
                         They said it was Laïos' child,
     But it is your wife who can tell you about that.

OEDIPUS: My wife!—Did she give it to you?

SHEPHERD: My lord, she did.

OEDIPUS: Do you know why?

SHEPHERD: I was told to get rid of it.

OEDIPUS: An unspeakable mother!

SHEPHERD: There had been prophecies . . .   60

OEDIPUS: Tell me.

SHEPHERD: It was said that the boy would kill his own father.

OEDIPUS: Then why did you give him over to this old man?

SHEPHERD: I pitied the baby, my King.
     And I thought that this man would take him far away
     To his own country.
                         He saved him—but for what a fate!   65
     For if you are what this man says you are,
     No man living is more wretched than Oedipus.

OEDIPUS: Ah God!
     It was true!
          All the prophecies!
                    —Now,
     O Light, may I look on you for the last time!   70
     I, Oedipus,
     Oedipus, damned in his birth, in his marriage damned,
     Damned in the blood he shed with his own hand!

                    He rushes into the palace.

                         ODE IV

Strophe 1

CHORUS: Alas for the seed of men.
     What measure shall I give these generations

That breathe on the void and are void
And exist and do not exist?

Who bears more weight of joy 5
Than mass of sunlight shifting in images,
Or who shall make his thought stay on
That down time drifts away?

Your splendor is all fallen.

O naked brow of wrath and tears, 10
O change of Oedipus!
I who saw your days call no man blest—
Your great days like ghósts góne.

Antistrophe 1

That mind was a strong bow.
Deep, how deep you drew it then, hard archer, 15
At a dim fearful range,
And brought dear glory down!

You overcame the stranger—
The virgin with her hooking lion claws—
And though death sang, stood like a tower 20
To make pale Thebes take heart.

Fortress against our sorrow!

Divine king, giver of laws,
Majestic Oedipus!
No prince in Thebes had ever such renown, 25
No prince won such grace of power.

Strophe 2

And now of all men ever known
Most pitiful is this man's story:
His fortunes are most changed, his state
Fallen to a low slave's 30
Ground under bitter fate.

O Oedipus, most royal one!
The great door that expelled you to the light
Gave at night—ah, gave night to your glory:
As to the father, to the fathering son. 35

All understood too late.

How could that queen whom Laïos won,
The garden that he harrowed at his height,
Be silent when that act was done?

Antistrophe 2

But all eyes fail before time's eye,   40
All actions come to justice there.
Though never willed, though far down the deep past,
Your bed, your dread sirings,
Are brought to book at last.
Child by Laïos doomed to die,   45
Then doomed to lose that fortunate little death,
Would God you never took breath in this air
That with my wailing lips I take to cry:

For I weep the world's outcast.

I was blind, and now I can tell why: 50
Asleep, for you had given ease of breath
To Thebes, while the false years went by.

EXODOS

Enter, from the palace, SECOND MESSENGER.

SECOND MESSENGER: Elders of Thebes, most honored in this land,
    What horrors are yours to see and hear, what weight
    Of sorrow to be endured, if, true to your birth,
    You venerate the line of Labdakos!
    I think neither Istros nor Phasis, those great rivers,   5
    Could purify this place of the corruption
    It shelters now, or soon must bring to light—
    Evil not done unconsciously, but willed.

    The greatest griefs are those we cause ourselves.
CHORAGOS: Surely, friend, we have grief enough already;   10
    What new sorrow do you mean?
SECOND MESSENGER: The Queen is dead.
CHORAGOS: Iocastê? Dead? But at whose hand?
SECOND MESSENGER: Her own.
    The full horror of what happened you cannot know,
    For you did not see it; but I, who did, will tell you
    As clearly as I can how she met her death.   15

When she had left us,
In passionate silence, passing through the court,
She ran to her apartment in the house,
Her hair clutched by the fingers of both hands.
She closed the doors behind her; then, by that bed   20
Where long ago the fatal son was conceived—
That son who should bring about his father's death—
We heard her call upon Laïos, dead so many years,
And heard her wail for the double fruit of her marriage,
A husband by her husband, children by her child.   25

Exactly how she died I do not know:
For Oedipus burst in moaning and would not let us
Keep vigil to the end: it was by him
As he stormed about the room that our eyes were caught.
From one to another of us he went, begging a sword,   30
Cursing the wife who was not his wife, the mother
Whose womb had carried his own children and himself.
I do not know: it was none of us aided him,
But surely one of the gods was in control!
For with a dreadful cry   35
He hurled his weight, as though wrenched out of himself,
At the twin doors: the bolts gave, and he rushed in.
And there we saw her hanging, her body swaying
From the cruel cord she had noosed about her neck.
A great sob broke from him heartbreaking to hear,   40
As he loosed the rope and lowered her to the ground.

I would blot out from my mind what happened next!
For the King ripped from her gown the golden brooches
That were her ornament, and raised them, and plunged them down
Straight into his own eyeballs, crying, "No more,   45
No more shall you look on the misery about me,
The horrors of my own doing! Too long you have known
The faces of those whom I should never have seen,
Too long been blind to those for whom I was searching!
From this hour, go in darkness!" And as he spoke,   50
He struck at his eyes—not once, but many times;
And the blood spattered his beard,
Bursting from his ruined sockets like red hail.

So from the unhappiness of two this evil has sprung,
A curse on the man and woman alike. The old   55
Happiness of the house of Labdakos
Was happiness enough: where is it today?
It is all wailing and ruin, disgrace, death—all
The misery of mankind that has a name—

And it is wholly and for ever theirs.   60
CHORAGOS: Is he in agony still? Is there no rest for him?
SECOND MESSENGER: He is calling for someone to lead him to the gates
    So that all the children of Kadmos may look upon
    His father's murderer, his mother's—no,
    I cannot say it!
              And then he will leave Thebes,   65
    Self-exiled, in order that the curse
    Which he himself pronounced may depart from the house.
    He is weak, and there is none to lead him,
    So terrible is his suffering.
        But you will see:
    Look, the doors are opening; in a moment   70
    You will see a thing that would crush a heart of stone.

           The central door is opened; OEDIPUS, *blinded, is led in.*

CHORAGOS: Dreadful indeed for men to see.
    Never have my own eyes
    Looked on a sight so full of fear.

    Oedipus!   75
    What madness came upon you, what daemon
    Leaped on your life with heavier
    Punishment than a mortal man can bear?
    No: I cannot even
    Look at you, poor ruined one.   80
    And I would speak, question, ponder,
    If I were able. No.
    You make me shudder.
OEDIPUS: God. God.
    Is there a sorrow greater?   85
    Where shall I find harbor in this world?
    My voice is hurled far on a dark wind.
    What has God done to me?
CHORAGOS: Too terrible to think of, or to see.

Strophe 1

OEDIPUS: O cloud of night,   90
    Never to be turned away: night coming on,
    I cannot tell how: night like a shroud!
    My fair winds brought me here.
                Oh God. Again
    The pain of the spikes where I had sight,
    The flooding pain   95
    Of memory, never to be gouged out.
CHORAGOS: This is not strange.

You suffer it all twice over, remorse in pain,
Pain in remorse.

Antistrophe 1

OEDIPUS: Ah dear friend   100
  Are you faithful even yet, you alone?
  Are you still standing near me, will you stay here,
  Patient, to care for the blind?
                          The blind man!
  Yet even blind I know who it is attends me,
  By the voice's tone—   105
  Though my new darkness hide the comforter.
CHORAGOS: Oh fearful act!
  What god was it drove you to rake black
  Night across your eyes?

Strophe 2

OEDIPUS: Apollo. Apollo. Dear   110
  Children, the god was Apollo.
  He brought my sick, sick fate upon me.
  But the blinding hand was my own!
  How could I bear to see
  When all my sight was horror everywhere?   115
CHORAGOS: Everywhere; that is true.
OEDIPUS: And now what is left?
  Images? Love? A greeting even,
  Sweet to the senses? Is there anything?
  Ah, no, friends: lead me away.   120
  Lead me away from Thebes.
                          Lead the great wreck
  And hell of Oedipus, whom the gods hate.
CHORAGOS: Your fate is clear, you are not blind to that.
  Would God you had never found it out!

Antistrophe 2

OEDIPUS: Death take the man who unbound   125
  My feet on that hillside
  And delivered me from death to life! What life?
  If only I had died,
  This weight of monstrous doom
  Could not have dragged me and my darlings down.   130
CHORAGOS: I would have wished the same.
OEDIPUS: Oh never to have come here
  With my father's blood upon me! Never

To have been the man they call his mother's husband!   135
Oh accurst! Oh child of evil,
To have entered that wretched bed—
                              the selfsame one!
More primal than sin itself, this fell to me.
CHORAGOS: I do not know how I can answer you.
You were better dead than alive and blind.
OEDIPUS: Do not counsel me any more. This punishment   140
That I have laid upon myself is just.
If I had eyes,
I do not know how I could bear the sight
Of my father, when I came to the house of Death,
Or my mother: for I have sinned against them both   145
So vilely that I could not make my peace
By strangling my own life.
                              Or do you think my children,
Born as they were born, would be sweet to my eyes?
Ah never, never! Nor this town with its high walls,
Nor the holy images of the gods.
                              For I,   150
Thrice miserable—Oedipus, noblest of all the line
Of Kadmos, have condemned myself to enjoy
These things no more, by my own malediction
Expelling that man whom the gods declared
To be a defilement in the house of Laïos.   155
After exposing the rankness of my own guilt,
How could I look men frankly in the eyes?
No, I swear it,
If I could have stifled my hearing at its source,
I would have done it and made all this body   160
A tight cell of misery, blank to light and sound:
So I should have been safe in a dark agony
Beyond all recollection.
                              Ah Kithairon!
Why did you shelter me? When I was cast upon you,
Why did I not die? Then I should never   165
Have shown the world my execrable birth.

Ah Polybos! Corinth, city that I believed
The ancient seat of my ancestors: how fair
I seemed, your child! And all the while this evil
Was cancerous within me!
                              For I am sick   170
In my daily life, sick in my origin.

O three roads, dark ravine, woodland and way
Where three roads met you, drinking my father's blood,

My own blood, spilled by my own hand: can you remember
The unspeakable things I did there, and the things   175
I went on from there to do?

                  O marriage, marriage!
The act that engendered me, and again the act
Performed by the son in the same bed—

                       Ah, the net
Of incest, mingling fathers, brothers, sons,
With brides, wives, mothers: the last evil   180
That can be known by men: no tongue can say
How evil!

       No. For the love of God, conceal me
Somewhere far from Thebes; or kill me; or hurl me
Into the sea, away from men's eyes for ever.
Come, lead me. You need not fear to touch me.   185
Of all men, I alone can bear this guilt.

Enter CREON.

CHORAGOS: We are not the ones to decide; but Creon here
   May fitly judge of what you ask. He only
   Is left to protect the city in your place.
OEDIPUS: Alas, how can I speak to him? What right have I   190
   To beg his courtesy whom I have deeply wronged?
CREON: I have not come to mock you, Oedipus,
   Or to reproach you, either.

(*To* ATTENDANTS.)

            —You, standing there:
If you have lost all respect for man's dignity,
At least respect the flame of Lord Helios: 195
Do not allow this pollution to show itself
Openly here, an affront to the earth
And Heaven's rain and the light of day. No, take him
Into the house as quickly as you can.
For it is proper   200
That only the close kindred see his grief.
OEDIPUS: I pray you in God's name, since your courtesy
   Ignores my dark expectation, visiting
   With mercy this man of all men most execrable:
   Give me what I ask—for your good, not for mine.   205
CREON: And what is it that you would have me do?
OEDIPUS: Drive me out of this country as quickly as may be
   To a place where no human voice can ever greet me.
CREON: I should have done that before now—only,
   God's will had not been wholly revealed to me.   210
OEDIPUS: But his command is plain: the parricide
   Must be destroyed. I am that evil man.

CREON: That is the sense of it, yes; but as things are,
    We had best discover clearly what is to be done.
OEDIPUS: You would learn more about a man like me?   215
CREON: You are ready now to listen to the god.
OEDIPUS: I will listen. But it is to you
    That I must turn for help. I beg you, hear me.

    The woman in there—
    Give her whatever funeral you think proper: 220
    She is your sister.
                —But let me go, Creon!
    Let me purge my father's Thebes of the pollution
    Of my living here, and go out to the wild hills,
    To Kithairon, that has won such fame with me,
    The tomb my mother and father appointed for me,   225
    And let me die there, as they willed I should.
    And yet I know
    Death will not ever come to me through sickness
    Or in any natural way: I have been preserved
    For some unthinkable fate. But let that be.   230
    As for my sons, you need not care for them.
    They are men, they will find some way to live.
    But my poor daughters, who have shared my table,
    Who never before have been parted from their father—
    Take care of them, Creon; do this for me.   235
    And will you let me touch them with my hands
    A last time, and let us weep together?
    Be kind, my lord,
    Great prince, be kind!
                Could I but touch them,
    They would be mine again, as when I had my eyes.   240

           Enter ANTIGONÊ *and* ISMENÊ, *attended.*

    Ah, God!
    Is it my dearest children I hear weeping?
    Has Creon pitied me and sent my daughters?
CREON: Yes, Oedipus: I knew that they were dear to you
    In the old days, and know you must love them still.   245
OEDIPUS: May God bless you for this—and be a friendlier
    Guardian to you than he has been to me!

    Children, where are you?
    Come quickly to my hands: they are your brother's—
    Hands that have brought your father's once clear eyes   250
    To this way of seeing—
                Ah dearest ones,
    I had neither sight nor knowledge then, your father

By the woman who was the source of his own life!
And I weep for you—having no strength to see you—,
I weep for you when I think of the bitterness   255
That men will visit upon you all your lives.
What homes, what festivals can you attend
Without being forced to depart again in tears?
And when you come to marriageable age,
Where is the man, my daughters, who would dare   260
Risk the bane that lies on all my children?
Is there any evil wanting? Your father killed
His father; sowed the womb of her who bore him;
Engendered you at the fount of his own existence!
That is what they will say of you.
                                      Then, whom   265
Can you ever marry? There are no bridegrooms for you,
And your lives must wither away in sterile dreaming.
O Creon, son of Menoikeus!
You are the only father my daughters have,
Since we, their parents, are both of us gone for ever.   270
They are your own blood: you will not let them
Fall into beggary and loneliness;
You will keep them from the miseries that are mine!
Take pity on them; see, they are only children,
Friendless except for you. Promise me this,   275
Great Prince, and give me your hand in token of it.

CREON *clasps his right hand.*

Children:
I could say much, if you could understand me,
But as it is, I have only this prayer for you:
Live where you can, be as happy as you can—   280
Happier, please God, than God has made your father!
CREON: Enough. You have wept enough. Now go within.
OEDIPUS: I must; but it is hard.
CREON: Time eases all things.
OEDIPUS: But you must promise—
CREON: Say what you desire.
OEDIPUS: Send me from Thebes!
CREON: God grant that I may!   285
OEDIPUS: But since God hates me . . .
CREON: No, he will grant your wish.
OEDIPUS: You promise?
CREON: I cannot speak beyond my knowledge.
OEDIPUS: Then lead me in.
CREON: Come now, and leave your children.
OEDIPUS: No! Do not take them from me!
CREON: Think no longer

That you are in command here, but rather think   290
How, when you were, you served your own destruction.

Exeunt into the house all but the CHORUS; *the* CHORAGOS *chants directly to the audience.*

CHORAGOS: Men of Thebes: look upon Oedipus.
    This is the king who solved the famous riddle
    And towered up, most powerful of men
    No mortal eyes but looked on him with envy.   295
    Yet in the end ruin swept over him.

    Let every man in mankind's frailty
    Consider his last day; and let none
    Presume on his good fortune until he find
    Life, at his death, a memory without pain.   300

(c. 430 B.C.)

QUESTIONS FOR REFLECTION

Experience

1. Describe your experience of reading *Oedipus Rex*. Were you surprised? Baffled? Horrified—at any point? If so, where and why?

Interpretation

2. What makes Oedipus a tragic hero? What makes his predicament fascinating rather than merely horrifying? Account for the continued appeal of the play.
3. Identify and explain the different types of irony in *Oedipus Rex*.
4. How is the imagery of light and darkness employed throughout the play? How is it related to Oedipus' blindness?
5. What roles do the chorus and choragos assume? Compare their functions in the beginning, middle, and end of the play.
6. Rather than dramatize on stage the shocking and horrible events in which the play culminates, Sophocles has them occur offstage, and we learn about them through a messenger's report. What are the limitations and advantages of such a method?
7. Iocastê appears a number of times, but she has little to say. What is she like? How much do we know about her—especially her thoughts and feelings?

Evaluation

8. Evaluate Oedipus's actions. Is he to blame for what happens? Account for his change of attitude and manner by comparing his speech and behavior in the opening and closing scenes.

Readers will be able to understand *Antigonê* more fully if they understand the background of Polyneicês' death. After Oedipus exiled himself from

Thebes (see the conclusion of *Oedipus Rex*), his two sons, Eteoclês and Polyneicês, shared the rule of Thebes. Although they originally agreed to reign in alternate years, Eteoclês refused to step down when his allotted time had passed.
Polyneicês, with the help of the king of Argos, attempted to remove Eteoclês
from the throne. In the attack on Thebes, the brothers killed one another.
Creon assumed the throne and declared that Eteoclês should be buried with
full honors. Because Polyneicês had attacked his native city, his body was to be
shamefully left lying where he fell.

The stage directions for *Antigonê* are simple, stating that the play begins at
dawn in front of the palace in Thebes. Antigonê and Ismenê enter from the
palace, engaged in a conversation that clearly establishes their relationship and
the conflicts between them. Tension builds slowly; Antigonê and Creon do not
come face to face until Scene II, with the clash between law (represented by
Creon) and justice (represented by Antigonê) constituting one of the play's
primary themes.

Antigonê

AN ENGLISH VERSION BY DUDLEY FITTS AND ROBERT FITZGERALD

CHARACTERS

ANTIGONÊ

ISMENÊ

EURYDICÊ

CREON

HAIMON

TEIRESIAS

A SENTRY

A MESSENGER

CHORUS

Scene. *Before the palace of* CREON, *King of Thebes. A central double door, and two lateral doors.*
A platform extends the length of the façade, and from this platform three steps lead down into the
"orchestra," or chorus-ground.
Time. *Dawn of the day after the repulse of the Argive army from the assault on Thebes.*

PROLOGUE

ANTIGONÊ *and* ISMENÊ *enter from the central door of the palace.*

ANTIGONÊ: Ismenê, dear sister,
  You would think that we had already suffered enough

For the curse on Oedipus.°
I cannot imagine any grief
That you and I have not gone through. And now—   5
Have they told you of the new decree of our King Creon?
ISMENÊ: I have heard nothing: I know
    That two sisters lost two brothers, a double death
    In a single hour; and I know that the Argive army
    Fled in the night; but beyond this, nothing.   10
ANTIGONÊ: I thought so. And that is why I wanted you
    To come out here with me. There is something we must do.
ISMENÊ: Why do you speak so strangely?
ANTIGONÊ: Listen, Ismenê:
    Creon buried our brother Eteoclês   15
    With military honors, gave him a soldier's funeral,
    And it was right that he should; but Polyneicês,
    Who fought as bravely and died as miserably—
    They say that Creon has sworn
    No one shall bury him, no one mourn for him,   20
    But his body must lie in the fields, a sweet treasure
    For carrion birds to find as they search for food.
    That is what they say, and our good Creon is coming here
    To announce it publicly; and the penalty—
    Stoning to death in the public square!
                                        There it is,   25
    And now you can prove what you are:
    A true sister, or a traitor to your family.
ISMENÊ: Antigonê, you are mad! What could I possibly do?
ANTIGONÊ: You must decide whether you will help me or not.
ISMENÊ: I do not understand you. Help you in what?   30
ANTIGONÊ: Ismenê, I am going to bury him. Will you come?
ISMENÊ: Bury him! You have just said the new law forbids it.
ANTIGONÊ: He is my brother. And he is your brother, too.
ISMENÊ: But think of the danger! Think what Creon will do!
ANTIGONÊ: Creon is not strong enough to stand in my way.   35
ISMENÊ: Ah sister!
    Oedipus died, everyone hating him
    For what his own search brought to light, his eyes
    Ripped out by his own hand; and Iocastê died,
    His mother and wife at once: she twisted the cords   40
    That strangled her life; and our two brothers died,
    Each killed by the other's sword. And we are left:
    But oh, Antigonê,
    Think how much more terrible than these

---

³**Oedipus**   *former King of Thebes, father of Antigonê and Ismenê, and of Polyneicês and Eteoclês, their brothers. Oedipus unwittingly killed his father, Laïos, and married his mother, Iocastê. When he learned what he had done, he blinded himself and left Thebes. Eteoclês and Polyneicês quarreled; Polyneicês was defeated but returned to assault Thebes. Both brothers were killed in the battle; Creon ordered that Polyneicês remain unburied.*

Our own death would be if we should go against Creon 45
And do what he has forbidden! We are only women,
We cannot fight with men, Antigonê!
The law is strong, we must give in to the law
In this thing, and in worse. I beg the Dead
To forgive me, but I am helpless: I must yield 50
To those in authority. And I think it is dangerous business
To be always meddling.
ANTIGONÊ: If that is what you think,
I should not want you, even if you asked to come.
You have made your choice, you can be what you want to be.
But I will bury him; and if I must die, 55
I say that this crime is holy: I shall lie down
With him in death, and I shall be as dear
To him as he to me.
              It is the dead,
Not the living, who make the longest demands:
We die for ever . . .
              You may do as you like, 60
Since apparently the laws of the gods mean nothing to you.
ISMENÊ: They mean a great deal to me; but I have no strength
To break laws that were made for the public good.
ANTIGONÊ: That must be your excuse, I suppose. But as for me,
I will bury the brother I love.
ISMENÊ: Antigonê, 65
I am so afraid for you!
ANTIGONÊ: You need not be:
You have yourself to consider, after all.
ISMENÊ: But no one must hear of this, you must tell no one!
I will keep it a secret, I promise!
ANTIGONÊ: O tell it! Tell everyone!
Think how they'll hate you when it all comes out 70
If they learn that you knew about it all the time!
ISMENÊ: So fiery! You should be cold with fear.
ANTIGONÊ: Perhaps. But I am doing only what I must.
ISMENÊ: But can you do it? I say that you cannot.
ANTIGONÊ: Very well: when my strength gives out,
I shall do no more. 75
ISMENÊ: Impossible things should not be tried at all.
ANTIGONÊ: Go away, Ismenê:
I shall be hating you soon, and the dead will too,
For your words are hateful. Leave me my foolish plan:
I am not afraid of the danger; if it means death, 80
It will not be the worst of deaths—death without honor.
ISMENÊ: Go then, if you feel that you must.
You are unwise,
But a loyal friend indeed to those who love you.

Exit into the palace. ANTIGONÊ *goes off, left. Enter the* CHORUS.

PÁRODOS

Strophe 1

CHORUS: Now the long blade of the sun, lying
   Level east to west, touches with glory
   Thebes of the Seven Gates. Open, unlidded
   Eye of golden day! O marching light
   Across the eddy and rush of Dircê's stream,°   5
   Striking the white shields of the enemy
   Thrown headlong backward from the blaze of morning!
CHORAGOS:°   Polyneicês their commander
   Roused them with windy phrases,
   He the wild eagle screaming   10
   Insults above our land,
   His wings their shields of snow,
   His crest their marshalled helms.

Antistrophe 1

CHORUS: Against our seven gates in a yawning ring
   The famished spears came onward in the night;   15
   But before his jaws were sated with our blood,
   Or pinefire took the garland of our towers,
   He was thrown back; and as he turned, great Thebes—
   No tender victim for his noisy power—
   Rose like a dragon behind him, shouting war.   20
CHORAGOS: For God hates utterly
   The bray of bragging tongues;
   And when he beheld their smiling,
   Their swagger of golden helms,
   The frown of his thunder blasted   25
   Their first man from our walls.

Strophe 2

CHORUS: We heard his shout of triumph high in the air
   Turn to a scream; far out in a flaming arc
   He fell with his windy torch, and the earth struck him.
   And others storming in fury no less than his   30
   Found shock of death in the dusty joy of battle.
CHORAGOS: Seven captains at seven gates

---

[5] **Dircê's stream**   *river near Thebes.*   [8] **Choragos**   *leader of the chorus.*

Yielded their clanging arms to the god
That bends the battle-line and breaks it.
These two only, brothers in blood,   35
Face to face in matchless rage,
Mirroring each the other's death,
Clashed in long combat.

Antistrophe 2

CHORUS: But now in the beautiful morning of victory
Let Thebes of the many chariots sing for joy!   40
With hearts for dancing we'll take leave of war:
Our temples shall be sweet with hymns of praise,
And the long nights shall echo with our chorus.

SCENE I

CHORAGOS: But now at last our new King is coming:
Creon of Thebes, Menoikeus' son.
In this auspicious dawn of his reign
What are the new complexities
That shifting Fate has woven for him?   5
What is his counsel? Why has he summoned
The old men to hear him?

> *Enter* CREON *from the palace, center. He addresses the* CHORUS *from the top step.*

CREON: Gentlemen: I have the honor to inform you that our Ship of State, which
recent storms have threatened to destroy, has come safely to harbor at last, guided   10
by the merciful wisdom of Heaven. I have summoned you here this morning
because I know that I can depend upon you: your devotion to King Laïos was
absolute; you never hesitated in your duty to our late ruler Oedipus; and when
Oedipus died, your loyalty was transferred to his children. Unfortunately, as you
know, his two sons, the princes Eteoclês and Polyneicês, have killed each other   15
in battle; and I, as the next in blood, have succeeded to the full power of the
throne.

I am aware, of course, that no Ruler can expect complete loyalty from his
subjects until he has been tested in office. Nevertheless, I say to you at the very
outset that I have nothing but contempt for the kind of Governor who is afraid,   20
for whatever reason, to follow the course that he knows is best for the State; and
as for the man who sets private friendship above the public welfare,—I have no
use for him, either. I call God to witness that if I saw my country headed for
ruin, I should not be afraid to speak out plainly; and I need hardly remind you
that I would never have any dealings with an enemy of the people. No one   25
values friendship more highly than I; but we must remember that friends made
at the risk of wrecking our Ship are not real friends at all.

These are my principles, at any rate, and that is why I have made the following
decision concerning the sons of Oedipus: Eteoclês, who died as a man should die, 30
fighting for his country, is to be buried with full military honors, with all the
ceremony that is usual when the greatest heroes die; but his brother Polyneicês,
who broke his exile to come back with fire and sword against his native city and
the shrines of his fathers' gods, whose one idea was to spill the blood of his blood
and sell his own people into slavery—Polyneicês, I say, is to have no burial: no man 35
is to touch him or say the least prayer for him; he shall lie on the plain, unburied;
and the birds and the scavenging dogs can do with him whatever they like.

This is my command, and you can see the wisdom behind it. As long as I am 40
King, no traitor is going to be honored with the loyal man. But whoever shows
by word and deed that he is on the side of the State,—he shall have my respect
while he is living and my reverence when he is dead.

CHORAGOS: If that is your will, Creon son of Menoikeus,
You have the right to enforce it: we are yours.   45
CREON: That is my will. Take care that you do your part.
CHORAGOS: We are old men: let the younger ones carry it out.
CREON: I do not mean that: the sentries have been appointed.
CHORAGOS: Then what is it that you would have us do?
CREON: You will give no support to whoever breaks this law.   50
CHORAGOS: Only a crazy man is in love with death!
CREON: And death it is; yet money talks, and the wisest
Have sometimes been known to count a few coins too many.

Enter SENTRY *from left.*

SENTRY: I'll not say that I'm out of breath from running, King, because every time
I stopped to think about what I have to tell you, I felt like going back. And all 55
the time a voice kept saying, "You fool, don't you know you're walking straight
into trouble?"; and then another voice: "Yes, but if you let somebody else get the
news to Creon first, it will be even worse than that for you!" But good sense
won out, at least I hope it was good sense, and here I am with a story that makes
no sense at all; but I'll tell it anyhow, because, as they say, what's going to
happen's going to happen and—
CREON: Come to the point. What have you to say?
SENTRY: I did not do it. I did not see who did it. You must not punish me for
what someone else has done.   65
CREON: A comprehensive defense! More effective, perhaps,
If I knew its purpose. Come: what is it?
SENTRY: A dreadful thing . . . I don't know how to put it—
CREON: Out with it!
SENTRY: Well, then;
The dead man—
           Polyneicês—

Pause. The SENTRY *is overcome, fumbles for words.* CREON *waits impassively.*

out there—
           someone,—   70

New dust on the slimy flesh!

Pause. No sign from CREON.

Someone has given it burial that way, and
Gone . . .

Long pause. CREON *finally speaks with deadly control.*

CREON: And the man who dared do this?
SENTRY: I swear I
Do not know! You must believe me!   75
   Listen:
The ground was dry, not a sign of digging, no,
Not a wheeltrack in the dust, no trace of anyone.
It was when they relieved us this morning: and one of them,
The corporal, pointed to it.
                There it was,
The strangest—
         Look: 80
The body, just mounded over with light dust: you see?
Not buried really, but as if they'd covered it
Just enough for the ghost's peace. And no sign
Of dogs or any wild animal that had been there.
And then what a scene there was! Every man of us   85
Accusing the other: we all proved the other man did it,
We all had proof that we could not have done it.
We were ready to take hot iron in our hands,
Walk through fire, swear by all the gods,
It was not I!   90
I do not know who it was, but it was not I!

CREON's *rage has been mounting steadily, but the* SENTRY *is too intent upon his story to
notice it.*

And then, when this came to nothing, someone said
A thing that silenced us and made us stare
Down at the ground: you had to be told the news,
And one of us had to do it! We threw the dice,   95
And the bad luck fell to me. So here I am,
No happier to be here than you are to have me:
Nobody likes the man who brings bad news.
CHORAGOS: I have been wondering, King: can it be that the gods have
   done this?
CREON (*furiously*): Stop!   100
   Must you doddering wrecks
Go out of your heads entirely? "The gods"!
Intolerable!
The gods favor this corpse? Why? How had he served them?
Tried to loot their temples, burn their images,`   105

Yes, and the whole State, and its laws with it!
Is it your senile opinion that the gods love to honor bad men?
A pious thought!—
            No, from the very beginning
There have been those who have whispered together,
Stiff-necked anarchists, putting their heads together,   110
Scheming against me in alleys. These are the men,
And they have bribed my own guard to do this thing.
(*Sententiously.*) Money!
There's nothing in the world so demoralizing as money.
Down go your cities,   115
Homes gone, men gone, honest hearts corrupted,
Crookedness of all kinds, and all for money!

(To SENTRY.*)*

                  But you—!
I swear by God and by the throne of God,
The man who has done this thing shall pay for it!
Find that man, bring him here to me, or your death   120
Will be the least of your problems: I'll string you up
Alive, and there will be certain ways to make you
Discover your employer before you die;
And the process may teach you a lesson you seem to have missed:
The dearest profit is sometimes all too dear: 125
That depends on the source. Do you understand me?
A fortune won is often misfortune.
SENTRY: King, may I speak?
CREON: Your very voice distresses me.
SENTRY: Are you sure that it is my voice, and not your conscience?
CREON: By God, he wants to analyze me now!   130
SENTRY: It is not what I say, but what has been done, that hurts you.
CREON: You talk too much.
SENTRY: Maybe; but I've done nothing.
CREON: Sold your soul for some silver: that's all you've done.
SENTRY: How dreadful it is when the right judge judges wrong!
CREON: Your figures of speech   135
   May entertain you now; but unless you bring me the man,
   You will get little profit from them in the end.

Exit CREON *into the palace.*

SENTRY: "Bring me the man"—!
   I'd like nothing better than bringing him the man!
   But bring him or not, you have seen the last of me here.   140
   At any rate, I am safe!

(*Exit* SENTRY.)

ODE I

Strophe 1

CHORUS: Numberless are the world's wonders, but none
  More wonderful than man; the stormgray sea
  Yields to his prows, the huge crests bear him high;
  Earth, holy and inexhaustible, is graven
  With shining furrows where his plows have gone   5
  Year after year, the timeless labor of stallions.

Antistrophe 1

  The lightboned birds and beasts that cling to cover,
  The lithe fish lighting their reaches of dim water,
  All are taken, tamed in the net of his mind;
  The lion on the hill, the wild horse windy-maned,   10
  Resign to him; and his blunt yoke has broken
  The sultry shoulders of the mountain bull.

Strophe 2

  Words also, and thought as rapid as air,
  He fashions to his good use; statecraft is his,
  And his the skill that deflects the arrows of snow,   15
  The spears of winter rain: from every wind
  He has made himself secure—from all but one:
  In the late wind of death he cannot stand.

Antistrophe 2

  O clear intelligence, force beyond all measure!
  O fate of man, working both good and evil!   20
  When the laws are kept, how proudly his city stands!
  When the laws are broken, what of his city then?
  Never may the anárchic man find rest at my hearth,
  Never be it said that my thoughts are his thoughts.

SCENE II

Reenter SENTRY *leading* ANTIGONÊ.

CHORAGOS: What does this mean? Surely this captive woman
    Is the Princess, Antigonê. Why should she be taken?
SENTRY: Here is the one who did it! We caught her
    In the very act of burying him.—Where is Creon?
CHORAGOS: Just coming from the house.

Enter CREON, *center.*

CREON: What has happened?   5
    Why have you come back so soon?
SENTRY (*expansively*):   O King,
    A man should never be too sure of anything:
    I would have sworn
    That you'd not see me here again: your anger
    Frightened me so, and the things you threatened me with;   10
    But how could I tell then
    That I'd be able to solve the case so soon?
    No dice-throwing this time: I was only too glad to come!
    Here is this woman. She is the guilty one:
    We found her trying to bury him.   15
    Take her, then; question her; judge her as you will.
    I am through with the whole thing now, and glad of it.
CREON: But this is Antigonê! Why have you brought her here?
SENTRY: She was burying him, I tell you!
CREON (*severely*):   Is this the truth?
SENTRY: I saw her with my own eyes. Can I say more?   20
CREON: The details: come, tell me quickly!
SENTRY: It was like this:
    After those terrible threats of yours, King,
    We went back and brushed the dust away from the body.
    The flesh was soft by now, and stinking,
    So we sat on a hill to windward and kept guard.   25
    No napping this time! We kept each other awake.
    But nothing happened until the white round sun
    Whirled in the center of the round sky over us:
    Then, suddenly,
    A storm of dust roared up from the earth, and the sky   30
    Went out, the plain vanished with all its trees
    In the stinging dark. We closed our eyes and endured it.
    The whirlwind lasted a long time, but it passed;
    And then we looked, and there was Antigonê!
    I have seen   35
    A mother bird come back to a stripped nest, heard

Her crying bitterly a broken note or two
For the young ones stolen. Just so, when this girl
Found the bare corpse, and all her love's work wasted,
She wept, and cried on heaven to damn the hands   40
That had done this thing.

                    And then she brought more dust
And sprinkled wine three times for her brother's ghost.

We ran and took her at once. She was not afraid,
Not even when we charged her with what she had done.
She denied nothing.

                 And this was a comfort to me,   45
And some uneasiness: for it is a good thing
To escape from death, but it is no great pleasure
To bring death to a friend.

                Yet I always say
There is nothing so comfortable as your own safe skin!
CREON (*slowly, dangerously*): And you, Antigonê,   50
   You with your head hanging,—do you confess this thing?
ANTIGONÊ: I do. I deny nothing.
CREON (*to* SENTRY):   You may go.

               (*Exit* SENTRY.)

(*To* ANTIGONÊ.) Tell me, tell me briefly:
   Had you heard my proclamation touching this matter?
ANTIGONÊ: It was public. Could I help hearing it?   55
CREON: And yet you dared defy the law.
ANTIGONÊ: I dared.
   It was not God's proclamation. That final Justice
   That rules the world below makes no such laws.

Your edict, King, was strong,
But all your strength is weakness itself against   60
The immortal unrecorded laws of God.
They are not merely now: they were, and shall be,
Operative for ever, beyond man utterly.

I knew I must die, even without your decree:
I am only mortal. And if I must die   65
Now, before it is my time to die,
Surely this is no hardship: can anyone
Living, as I live, with evil all about me,
Think Death less than a friend? This death of mine
Is of no importance; but if I had left my brother   70
Lying in death unburied, I should have suffered.
Now I do not.
         You smile at me. Ah Creon,

Think me a fool, if you like; but it may well be
That a fool convicts me of folly.
CHORAGOS: Like father, like daughter: both headstrong, deaf to reason!   75
    She has never learned to yield:
CREON: She has much to learn.
    The inflexible heart breaks first, the toughest iron
    Cracks first, and the wildest horses bend their necks
    At the pull of the smallest curb.
                                Pride? In a slave?
    This girl is guilty of a double insolence,   80
    Breaking the given laws and boasting of it.
    Who is the man here,
    She or I, if this crime goes unpunished?
    Sister's child, or more than sister's child,
    Or closer yet in blood—she and her sister   85
    Win bitter death for this!

                        (*To* SERVANTS.)

                    Go, some of you,
    Arrest Ismenê. I accuse her equally.
    Bring her: you will find her sniffling in the house there.

    Her mind's a traitor: crimes kept in the dark
    Cry for light, and the guardian brain shudders;   90
    But how much worse than this
    Is brazen boasting of barefaced anarchy!
ANTIGONÊ: Creon, what more do you want than my death?
CREON: Nothing.
    That gives me everything.
ANTIGONÊ: Then I beg you: kill me.
    This talking is a great weariness: your words   95
    Are distasteful to me, and I am sure that mine
    Seem so to you. And yet they should not seem so:
    I should have praise and honor for what I have done.
    All these men here would praise me
    Were their lips not frozen shut with fear of you.   100
    (*Bitterly.*) Ah the good fortune of kings,
    Licensed to say and do whatever they please!
CREON: You are alone here in that opinion.
ANTIGONÊ: No, they are with me. But they keep their tongues in leash.
CREON: Maybe. But you are guilty, and they are not.   105
ANTIGONÊ: There is no guilt in reverence for the dead.
CREON: But Eteoclês—was he not your brother too?
ANTIGONÊ: My brother too.
CREON: And you insult his memory?
ANTIGONÊ (*softly*): The dead man would not say that I insult it.
CREON: He would: for you honor a traitor as much as him.   110

ANTIGONÊ: His own brother, traitor or not, and equal in blood.
CREON: He made war on his country. Eteoclês defended it.
ANTIGONÊ: Nevertheless, there are honors due all the dead.
CREON: But not the same for the wicked as for the just.
ANTIGONÊ: Ah Creon, Creon,   115
    Which of us can say what the gods hold wicked?
CREON: An enemy is an enemy, even dead.
ANTIGONÊ: It is my nature to join in love, not hate.
CREON (*finally losing patience*): Go join them then; if you must have your love,
    Find it in hell!   120
CHORAGOS: But see, Ismenê comes:

Enter ISMENÊ, *guarded.*

    Those tears are sisterly, the cloud
    That shadows her eyes rains down gentle sorrow.
CREON: You too, Ismenê,
    Snake in my ordered house, sucking my blood   125
    Stealthily—and all the time I never knew
    That these two sisters were aiming at my throne!
                                Ismenê,
    Do you confess your share in this crime, or deny it?
    Answer me.
ISMENÊ: Yes, if she will let me say so. I am guilty.   130
ANTIGONE (*coldly*): No, Ismenê. You have no right to say so.
    You would not help me, and I will not have you help me.
ISMENÊ: But now I know what you meant; and I am here
    To join you, to take my share of punishment.
ANTIGONÊ: The dead man and the gods who rule the dead   135
    Know whose act this was. Words are not friends.
ISMENÊ: Do you refuse me, Antigonê? I want to die with you:
    I too have a duty that I must discharge to the dead.
ANTIGONÊ: You shall not lessen my death by sharing it.
ISMENÊ: What do I care for life when you are dead?   140
ANTIGONÊ: Ask Creon. You're always hanging on his opinions.
ISMENÊ: You are laughing at me. Why, Antigonê?
ANTIGONÊ: It's a joyless laughter, Ismenê.
ISMENÊ: But can I do nothing?
ANTIGONÊ: Yes. Save yourself. I shall not envy you.
    There are those who will praise you; I shall have honor, too.   145
ISMENÊ: But we are equally guilty!
ANTIGONÊ: No more, Ismenê.
    You are alive, but I belong to Death.
CREON (*to the* CHORUS): Gentlemen, I beg you to observe these girls:
    One has just now lost her mind; the other,
    It seems, has never had a mind at all.   150
ISMENÊ: Grief teaches the steadiest minds to waver, King.
CREON: Yours certainly did, when you assumed guilt with the guilty!

ISMENÊ: But how could I go on living without her?
CREON: You are.
    She is already dead.
ISMENÊ: But your own son's bride!
CREON: There are places enough for him to push his plow.   155
    I want no wicked women for my sons!
ISMENÊ: O dearest Haimon, how your father wrongs you!
CREON: I've had enough of your childish talk of marriage!
CHORAGOS: Do you really intend to steal this girl from your son?
CREON: No; Death will do that for me.
CHORAGOS: Then she must die?   160
CREON (*ironically*): You dazzle me.
                        —But enough of this talk!
    (*To* GUARDS.) You, there, take them away and guard them well:
    For they are but women, and even brave men run
    When they see Death coming.

                    Exeunt ISMENÊ, ANTIGONÊ, *and* GUARDS.

ODE II

Strophe 1

CHORUS: Fortunate is the man who has never tasted God's vengeance!
    Where once the anger of heaven has struck, that house is shaken
    For ever: damnation rises behind each child
    Like a wave cresting out of the black northeast,
    When the long darkness under sea roars up   5
    And bursts drumming death upon the windwhipped sand.

Antistrophe 1

    I have seen this gathering sorrow from time long past
    Loom upon Oedipus' children: generation from generation
    Takes the compulsive rage of the enemy god.
    So lately this last flower of Oedipus' line   10
    Drank the sunlight! but now a passionate word
    And a handful of dust have closed up all its beauty.

Strophe 2

        What mortal arrogance
        Transcends the wrath of Zeus?
    Sleep cannot lull him nor the effortless long months   15
    Of the timeless gods: but he is young for ever,

And his house is the shining day of high Olympos.
    All that is and shall be,
    And all the past, is his.
No pride on earth is free of the curse of heaven.   20

Antistrophe 2

The straying dreams of men
    May bring them ghosts of joy:
But as they drowse, the waking embers burn them;
Or they walk with fixed eyes, as blind men walk.
But the ancient wisdom speaks for our own time: 25
      Fate works most for woe
      With Folly's fairest show.
Man's little pleasure is the spring of sorrow.

SCENE III

CHORAGOS: But here is Haimon, King, the last of all your sons.
  Is it grief for Antigonê that brings him here,
  And bitterness at being robbed of his bride?

Enter HAIMON.

CREON: We shall soon see, and no need of diviners.
                           —Son,
  You have heard my final judgment on that girl: 5
  Have you come here hating me, or have you come
  With deference and with love, whatever I do?
HAIMON: I am your son, father. You are my guide.
  You make things clear for me, and I obey you.
  No marriage means more to me than your continuing wisdom.   10
CREON: Good. That is the way to behave: subordinate
  Everything else, my son, to your father's will.
  This is what a man prays for, that he may get
  Sons attentive and dutiful in his house,
  Each one hating his father's enemies,   15
  Honoring his father's friends. But if his sons
  Fail him, if they turn out unprofitably,
  What has he fathered but trouble for himself
  And amusement for the malicious?
                  So you are right
  Not to lose your head over this woman.   20
  Your pleasure with her would soon grow cold, Haimon,
  And then you'd have a hellcat in bed and elsewhere.

Let her find her husband in Hell!
Of all the people in this city, only she
Has had contempt for my law and broken it.   25

Do you want me to show myself weak before the people?
Or to break my sworn word? No, and I will not.
The woman dies.
I suppose she'll plead "family ties." Well, let her.
If I permit my own family to rebel,   30
How shall I earn the world's obedience?
Show me the man who keeps his house in hand,
He's fit for public authority.
                              I'll have no dealings
With lawbreakers, critics of the government:
Whoever is chosen to govern should be obeyed—   35
Must be obeyed, in all things, great and small,
Just and unjust! O Haimon,
The man who knows how to obey, and that man only,
Knows how to give commands when the time comes.
You can depend on him, no matter how fast   40
The spears come: he's a good soldier, he'll stick it out.

Anarchy, anarchy! Show me a greater evil!
This is why cities tumble and the great houses rain down,
This is what scatters armies!
No, no: good lives are made so by discipline.   45
We keep the laws then, and the lawmakers,
And no woman shall seduce us. If we must lose,
Let's lose to a man, at least! Is a woman stronger than we?
CHORAGOS: Unless time has rusted my wits,
     What you say, King, is said with point and dignity.   50
HAIMON (*boyishly earnest*): Father:
     Reason is God's crowning gift to man, and you are right
     To warn me against losing mine. I cannot say—
     I hope that I shall never want to say!—that you
     Have reasoned badly. Yet there are other men   55
     Who can reason, too; and their opinions might be helpful.
     You are not in a position to know everything
     That people say or do, or what they feel:
     Your temper terrifies—everyone
     Will tell you only what you like to hear.   60
     But I, at any rate, can listen; and I have heard them
     Muttering and whispering in the dark about this girl.
     They say no woman has ever, so unreasonably,
     Died so shameful a death for a generous act:
     "She covered her brother's body. Is this indecent?   65
     She kept him from dogs and vultures. Is this a crime?

Death?—She should have all the honor that we can give her!"

This is the way they talk out there in the city.

You must believe me:
Nothing is closer to me than your happiness.   70
What could be closer? Must not any son
Value his father's fortune as his father does his?
I beg you, do not be unchangeable:
Do not believe that you alone can be right.
The man who thinks that,   75
The man who maintains that only he has the power
To reason correctly, the gift to speak, the soul—
A man like that, when you know him, turns out empty.

It is not reason never to yield to reason!

In flood time you can see how some trees bend,   80
And because they bend, even their twigs are safe,
While stubborn trees are torn up, roots and all.
And the same thing happens in sailing:
Make your sheet fast, never slacken,—and over you go,
Head over heels and under: and there's your voyage.   85
Forget you are angry! Let yourself be moved!
I know I am young; but please let me say this:
The ideal condition
Would be, I admit, that men should be right by instinct;
But since we are all too likely to go astray,   90
The reasonable thing is to learn from those who can teach.
CHORAGOS: You will do well to listen to him, King,
    If what he says is sensible. And you, Haimon,
    Must listen to your father.—Both speak well.
CREON: You consider it right for a man of my years and experience   95
    To go to school to a boy?
HAIMON: It is not right
    If I am wrong. But if I am young, and right,
    What does my age matter?
CREON: You think it right to stand up for an anarchist?
HAIMON: Not at all. I pay no respect to criminals.   100
CREON: Then she is not a criminal?
HAIMON: The City would deny it, to a man.
CREON: And the City proposes to teach me how to rule?
HAIMON: Ah. Who is it that's talking like a boy now?
CREON: My voice is the one voice giving orders in this City!   105
HAIMON: It is no City if it takes orders from one voice.
CREON: The State is the King!
HAIMON: Yes, if the State is a desert.

Pause.

CREON: This boy, it seems, has sold out to a woman.

HAIMON: If you are a woman: my concern is only for you.

CREON: So? Your "concern"! In a public brawl with your father!   110

HAIMON: How about you, in a public brawl with justice?

CREON: With justice, when all that I do is within my rights?

HAIMON: You have no right to trample on God's right.

CREON (*completely out of control*): Fool, adolescent fool! Taken in
   by a woman!

HAIMON: You'll never see me taken in by anything vile.   115

CREON: Every word you say is for her!

HAIMON (*quietly, darkly*):   And for you.
   And for me. And for the gods under the earth.

CREON: You'll never marry her while she lives.

HAIMON: Then she must die.—But her death will cause another.

CREON: Another?   120
   Have you lost your senses? Is this an open threat?

HAIMON: There is no threat in speaking to emptiness.

CREON: I swear you'll regret this superior tone of yours!
   You are the empty one!

HAIMON: If you were not my father, I'd say you were
      perverse.   125

CREON: You girlstruck fool, don't play at words with me!

HAIMON: I am sorry. You prefer silence.

CREON: Now, by God—!
   I swear, by all the gods in heaven above us,
   You'll watch it, I swear you shall!

(*To the* SERVANTS.)

                    Bring her out!
   Bring the woman out! Let her die before his eyes!   130
   Here, this instant, with her bridegroom beside her!

HAIMON: Not here, no; she will not die here, King.
   And you will never see my face again.
   Go on raving as long as you've a friend to endure you.

(*Exit* HAIMON.)

CHORAGOS: Gone, gone.
   Creon, a young man in a rage is dangerous!   135

CREON: Let him do, or dream to do, more than a man can.
   He shall not save these girls from death.

CHORAGOS: These girls?
   You have sentenced them both?

CREON: No, you are right.
   I will not kill the one whose hands are clean.   140

CHORAGOS: But Antigonê?

CREON (*somberly*):   I will carry her far away
  Out there in the wilderness, and lock her
  Living in a vault of stone. She shall have food,
  As the custom is, to absolve the State of her death.
  And there let her pray to the gods of hell: 145
  They are her only gods:
  Perhaps they will show her an escape from death,
  Or she may learn,
              though late,
  That piety shown the dead is pity in vain.

                      (*Exit* CREON.)

ODE III

Strophe

CHORUS: Love, unconquerable
  Waster of rich men, keeper
  Of warm lights and all-night vigil
  In the soft face of a girl:
  Sea-wanderer, forest-visitor!   5
  Even the pure Immortals cannot escape you,
  And mortal man, in his one day's dusk,
  Trembles before your glory.

Antistrophe

  Surely you swerve upon ruin
  The just man's consenting heart,   10
  As here you have made bright anger
  Strike between father and son—
  And none has conquered but Love!
  A girl's glánce wórking the will of heaven:
  Pleasure to her alone who mocks us,   15
  Merciless Aphroditê.°

SCENE IV

CHORAGOS (*as* ANTIGONÊ *enters guarded*): But I can no longer stand
  in awe of this,
  Nor, seeing what I see, keep back my tears.

---

[16]*Aphroditê*   *goddess of love.*

Here is Antigonê, passing to that chamber
Where all find sleep at last.

Strophe 1

ANTIGONÊ: Look upon me, friends, and pity me   5
    Turning back at the night's edge to say
    Good-by to the sun that shines for me no longer;
    Now sleepy Death
    Summons me down to Acheron,° that cold shore:
    There is no bridesong there, nor any music.   10
CHORUS: Yet not unpraised, not without a kind of honor,
    You walk at last into the underworld;
    Untouched by sickness, broken by no sword.
    What woman has ever found your way to death?

Antistrophe 1

ANTIGONÊ: How often I have heard the story of Niobê,   15
    Tantalos' wretched daughter, how the stone
    Clung fast about her, ivy-close: and they say
    The rain falls endlessly
    And sifting soft snow; her tears are never done.
    I feel the loneliness of her death in mine.   20
CHORUS: But she was born of heaven, and you
    Are woman, woman-born. If her death is yours,
    A mortal woman's, is this not for you
    Glory in our world and in the world beyond?

Strophe 2

ANTIGONÊ: You laugh at me. Ah, friends, friends,   25
    Can you not wait until I am dead? O Thebes,
    O men many-charioted, in love with Fortune,
    Dear springs of Dircê, sacred Theban grove,
    Be witnesses for me, denied all pity,
    Unjustly judged! and think a word of love   30
    For her whose path turns
    Under dark earth, where there are no more tears.
CHORUS: You have passed beyond human daring and come at last
    Into a place of stone where Justice sits.
    I cannot tell   35
    What shape of your father's guilt appears in this.

---

[9]**Acheron**   *a river of the underworld.*

Antistrophe 2

ANTIGONÊ: You have touched it at last: that bridal bed
   Unspeakable, horror of son and mother mingling:
   Their crime, infection of all our family!
   O Oedipus, father and brother!   40
   Your marriage strikes from the grave to murder mine.
   I have been a stranger here in my own land:
   All my life
   The blasphemy of my birth has followed me.
CHORUS: Reverence is a virtue, but strength   45
   Lives in established law: that must prevail.
   You have made your choice,
   Your death is the doing of your conscious hand.

Epode

ANTIGONÊ: Then let me go, since all your words are bitter,
   And the very light of the sun is cold to me.   50
   Lead me to my vigil, where I must have
   Neither love nor lamentation; no song, but silence.

CREON interrupts impatiently.

CREON: If dirges and planned lamentations could put off death,
   Men would be singing for ever.

(To the SERVANTS.)

             Take her, go!
  You know your orders: take her to the vault   55
  And leave her alone there. And if she lives or dies,
  That's her affair, not ours: our hands are clean.
ANTIGONÊ: O tomb, vaulted bride-bed in eternal rock,
  Soon I shall be with my own again
  Where Persephonê° welcomes the thin ghosts underground: 60
  And I shall see my father again, and you, mother,
  And dearest Polyneicês—
              dearest indeed
  To me, since it was my hand
  That washed him clean and poured the ritual wine:
  And my reward is death before my time!   65

  And yet, as men's hearts know, I have done no wrong,
  I have not sinned before God. Or if I have,
  I shall know the truth in death. But if the guilt
  Lies upon Creon who judged me, then, I pray,

---

⁶⁰**Persephonê**   *queen of the underworld.*

May his punishment equal my own.
CHORAGOS: O passionate heart,   70
   Unyielding, tormented still by the same winds!
CREON: Her guards shall have good cause to regret their delaying.
ANTIGONÊ: Ah! That voice is like the voice of death!
CREON: I can give you no reason to think you are mistaken.
ANTIGONÊ: Thebes, and you my fathers' gods,   75
   And rulers of Thebes, you see me now, the last
   Unhappy daughter of a line of kings,
   Your kings, led away to death. You will remember
   What things I suffer, and at what men's hands,
   Because I would not transgress the laws of heaven.   80
   (*To the* GUARDS, *simply.*) Come: let us wait no longer.

(*Exit* ANTIGONÊ, *left, guarded.*)

ODE IV

Strophe 1

CHORUS: All Danaê's beauty was locked away
   In a brazen cell where the sunlight could not come:
   A small room still as any grave, enclosed her.
   Yet she was a princess too,
   And Zeus in a rain of gold poured love upon her.   5
   O child, child,
   No power in wealth or war
   Or tough sea-blackened ships
   Can prevail against untiring Destiny!

Antistrophe 1

   And Dryas' son° also, that furious king,   10
   Bore the god's prisoning anger for his pride:
   Sealed up by Dionysos in deaf stone,
   His madness died among echoes.
   So at the last he learned what dreadful power
   His tongue had mocked: 15
   For he had profaned the revels,
   And fired the wrath of the nine
   Implacable Sisters° that love the sound of the flute.

Strophe 2

   And old men tell a half-remembered tale
   Of horror where a dark ledge splits the sea   20

---

[10]**Dryas' son**   *Lycurgus, King of Thrace.*   [18]**Implacable Sisters**   *the Muses.*

And a double surf beats on the gráy shóres:
How a king's new woman,° sick
With hatred for the queen he had imprisoned,
Ripped out his two sons' eyes with her bloody hands
While grinning Arês° watched the shuttle plunge   25
Four times: four blind wounds crying for revenge,

Antistrophe 2

Crying, tears and blood mingled.—Piteously born,
Those sons whose mother was of heavenly birth!
Her father was the god of the North Wind
And she was cradled by gales,   30
She raced with young colts on the glittering hills
And walked untrammeled in the open light:
But in her marriage deathless Fate found means
To build a tomb like yours for all her joy.

SCENE V

Enter blind TEIRESIAS, *led by a boy. The opening speeches of* TEIRESIAS *should be in singsong contrast to the realistic lines of* CREON.

TEIRESIAS: This is the way the blind man comes, Princes, Princes,
    Lock-step, two heads lit by the eyes of one.
CREON: What new thing have you to tell us, old Teiresias?
TEIRESIAS: I have much to tell you: listen to the prophet, Creon.
CREON: I am not aware that I have ever failed to listen.   5
TEIRESIAS: Then you have done wisely, King, and ruled well.
CREON: I admit my debt to you. But what have you to say?
TEIRESIAS: This, Creon: you stand once more on the edge of fate.
CREON: What do you mean? Your words are a kind of dread.
TEIRESIAS: Listen, Creon: 10
    I was sitting in my chair of augury, at the place
    Where the birds gather about me. They were all a-chatter,
    As is their habit, when suddenly I heard
    A strange note in their jangling, a scream, a
    Whirring fury; I knew that they were fighting,   15
    Tearing each other, dying
    In a whirlwind of wings clashing. And I was afraid.
    I began the rites of burnt-offering at the altar,
    But Hephaistos° failed me: instead of bright flame,
    There was only the sputtering slime of the fat thigh-flesh   20

---

[22]**King's new woman**   *Eidothea, second wife of King Phineas, blinded her stepsons after the King had imprisoned their mother in a cave.*   [25]**Arês**   *god of war.*   [19]**Hephaistos**   *god of fire.*

Melting: the entrails dissolved in gray smoke,
The bare bone burst from the welter. And no blaze!
This was a sign from heaven. My boy described it,
Seeing for me as I see for others.

I tell you, Creon, yourself have brought   25
This new calamity upon us. Our hearths and altars
Are stained with the corruption of dogs and carrion birds
That glut themselves on the corpse of Oedipus' son.
The gods are deaf when we pray to them, their fire
Recoils from our offering, their birds of omen   30
Have no cry of comfort, for they are gorged
With the thick blood of the dead.
                              O my son,
These are no trifles! Think: all men make mistakes,
But a good man yields when he knows his course is wrong,
And repairs the evil. The only crime is pride.   35

Give in to the dead man, then: do not fight with a corpse—
What glory is it to kill a man who is dead?
Think, I beg you:
It is for your own good that I speak as I do.
You should be able to yield for your own good.   40
CREON: It seems that prophets have made me their especial province.
    All my life long
    I have been a kind of butt for the dull arrows
    Of doddering fortune-tellers!
                              No, Teiresias:
    If your birds—if the great eagles of God himself   45
    Should carry him stinking bit by bit to heaven,
    I would not yield. I am not afraid of pollution:
    No man can defile the gods.
                              Do what you will,
    Go into business, make money, speculate
    In India gold or that synthetic gold from Sardis,   50
    Get rich otherwise than by my consent to bury him.
    Teiresias, it is a sorry thing when a wise man
    Sells his wisdom, lets out his words for hire!
TEIRESIAS: Ah Creon! Is there no man left in the world—
CREON: To do what?—Come, let's have the aphorism!   55
TEIRESIAS: No man who knows that wisdom outweighs any wealth?
CREON: As surely as bribes are baser than any baseness.
TEIRESIAS: You are sick, Creon! You are deathly sick!
CREON: As you say: it is not my place to challenge a prophet.
TEIRESIAS: Yet you have said my prophecy is for sale.   60
CREON: The generation of prophets has always loved gold.
TEIRESIAS: The generation of kings has always loved brass.

CREON: You forget yourself! You are speaking to your King.

TEIRESIAS: I know it. You are a king because of me.

CREON: You have a certain skill; but you have sold out. 65

TEIRESIAS: King, you will drive me to words that—

CREON: Say them, say them!
    Only remember: I will not pay you for them.

TEIRESIAS: No, you will find them too costly.

CREON: No doubt. Speak:
    Whatever you say, you will not change my will.

TEIRESIAS: Then take this, and take it to heart! 70
    The time is not far off when you shall pay back
    Corpse for corpse, flesh of your own flesh.
    You have thrust the child of this world into living night,
    You have kept from the gods below the child that is theirs:
    The one in a grave before her death, the other, 75
    Dead, denied the grave. This is your crime:
    And the Furies and the dark gods of Hell
    Are swift with terrible punishment for you.

    Do you want to buy me now, Creon?
    Not many days,
    And your house will be full of men and women weeping, 80
    And curses will be hurled at you from far
    Cities grieving for sons unburied, left to rot
    Before the walls of Thebes.

    These are my arrows, Creon: they are all for you.

    (*To* BOY.) But come, child: lead me home. 85
    Let him waste his fine anger upon younger men.
    Maybe he will learn at last
    To control a wiser tongue in a better head.

               (*Exit* TEIRESIAS.)

CHORAGOS: The old man has gone, King, but his words
    Remain to plague us. I am old, too, 90
    But I cannot remember that he was ever false.

CREON: That is true. . . . It troubles me.
    Oh it is hard to give in! but it is worse
    To risk everything for stubborn pride.

CHORAGOS: Creon: take my advice.

CREON: What shall I do? 95

CHORAGOS: Go quickly: free Antigonê from her vault
    And build a tomb for the body of Polyneicês.

CREON: You would have me do this!

CHORAGOS: Creon, yes!
    And it must be done at once: God moves

Swiftly to cancel the folly of stubborn men.   100
CREON: It is hard to deny the heart! But I
    Will do it: I will not fight with destiny.
CHORAGOS: You must go yourself, you cannot leave it to others.
CREON: I will go.
                —Bring axes, servants:
    Come with me to the tomb. I buried her. I   105
    Will set her free.
                Oh quickly!
    My mind misgives—
    The laws of the gods are mighty, and a man must serve them
    To the last day of his life!

(*Exit* CREON.)

PAEAN°

Strophe 1

CHORAGOS: God of many names
CHORUS: O Iacchos°
                                          son
    of Kadmeian Sémelê°
                        O born of the Thunder!
    Guardian of the West
                        Regent
    of Eleusis' plain
                    O Prince of maenad° Thebes
    and the Dragon Field by rippling Ismenós.°   5

Antistrophe 1

CHORAGOS: God of many names
CHORUS: the flame of torches
        flares on our hills
                        the nymphs of Iacchos
        dance at the spring of Castalia.°
        from the vine-close mountain
                            come ah come in ivy:
        Evohé evohé! sings through the streets of Thebes   10

Paean   *a hymn.*   [1]***Iacchos***   *Bacchos or Dionysos, god of wine and revelry.*   [2]***Sémelê***   *mother of Iacchos,* *consort of Zeus.*   [4]***maenad***   *female worshipper, attendant of Iacchos.*   [5]***Ismenós***   *a river near Thebes where,* *according to legend, dragon's teeth were sown from which sprang the ancestors of Thebes.*   [8]***Castalia***   *a spring on* *Mount Parnasos.*

Strophe 2

CHORAGOS: God of many names
CHORUS: Iacchos of Thebes
     heavenly Child
                    of Sémelê bride of the Thunderer!
     The shadow of plague is upon us:
                                   come
     with clement feet
                        oh come from Parnasos
     down the long slopes
                        across the lamenting water   15

Antistrophe 2

CHORAGOS: Iô Fire! Chorister of the throbbing stars!
     O purest among the voices of the night!
     Thou son of God, blaze for us!
CHORUS: Come with choric rapture of circling Maenads
     Who cry *Iô Iacche!*
                    God of many names!   20

EXODOS

Enter MESSENGER *from left.*

MESSENGER: Men of the line of Kadmos,° you who live
     Near Amphion's citadel,°
                    I cannot say
     Of any condition of human life "This is fixed,
     This is clearly good, or bad." Fate raises up,
     And Fate casts down the happy and unhappy alike: 5
     No man can foretell his Fate.
                         Take the case of Creon:
     Creon was happy once, as I count happiness:
     Victorious in battle, sole governor of the land,
     Fortunate father of children nobly born.
     And now it has all gone from him! Who can say   10
     That a man is still alive when his life's joy fails?
     He is a walking dead man. Grant him rich,
     Let him live like a king in his great house:
     If his pleasure is gone, I would not give

---

[1]**Kadmos**   *sowed the dragon's teeth; founded Thebes.*   [2]**Amphion's citadel**   *Amphion's lyre playing charmed stones to form a wall around Thebes.*

So much as the shadow of smoke for all he owns.   15
CHORAGOS: Your words hint at sorrow: what is your news for us?
MESSENGER: They are dead. The living are guilty of their death.
CHORAGOS: Who is guilty? Who is dead? Speak!
MESSENGER: Haimon.
   Haimon is dead; and the hand that killed him
   Is his own hand.
CHORAGOS: His father's? or his own?   20
MESSENGER: His own, driven mad by the murder his father had done.
CHORAGOS: Teiresias, Teiresias, how clearly you saw it all!
MESSENGER: This is my news: you must draw what conclusions you can
    from it.
CHORAGOS: But look: Eurydicê, our Queen:
   Has she overheard us?   25

Enter EURYDICÊ *from the palace, center.*

EURYDICE: I have heard something, friends:
   As I was unlocking the gate of Pallas' shrine,
   For I needed her help today, I heard a voice
   Telling of some new sorrow. And I fainted
   There at the temple with all my maidens about me.   30
   But speak again: whatever it is, I can bear it:
   Grief and I are no strangers.
MESSENGER: Dearest Lady,
   I will tell you plainly all that I have seen.
   I shall not try to comfort you: what is the use,
   Since comfort could lie only in what is not true?   35
   The truth is always best.
                I went with Creon
   To the outer plain where Polyneicês was lying,
   No friend to pity him, his body shredded by dogs.
   We made our prayers in that place to Hecatê
   And Pluto, that they would be merciful. And we bathed   40
   The corpse with holy water, and we brought
   Fresh-broken branches to burn what was left of it,
   And upon the urn we heaped up a towering barrow
   Of the earth of his own land.
               When we were done, we ran
   To the vault where Antigonê lay on her couch of stone.   45
   One of the servants had gone ahead,
   And while he was yet far off he heard a voice
   Grieving within the chamber, and he came back
   And told Creon. And as the King went closer,
   The air was full of wailing, the words lost,   50
   And he begged us to make all haste. "Am I a prophet?"
   He said, weeping, "And must I walk this road,
   The saddest of all that I have gone before?

My son's voice calls me on. Oh quickly, quickly!
Look through the crevice there, and tell me 55
If it is Haimon, or some deception of the gods!"

We obeyed; and in the cavern's farthest corner
We saw her lying:
She had made a noose of her fine linen veil
And hanged herself. Haimon lay beside her, 60
His arms about her waist, lamenting her,
His love lost under ground, crying out
That his father had stolen her away from him.

When Creon saw him the tears rushed to his eyes
And he called to him: "What have you done, child?
    Speak to me. 65
What are you thinking that makes your eyes so strange?
O my son, my son, I come to you on my knees!"
But Haimon spat in his face. He said not a word,
Staring—
        And suddenly drew his sword
And lunged. Creon shrank back, the blade missed; and the boy, 70
Desperate against himself, drove it half its length
Into his own side, and fell. And as he died
He gathered Antigonê close in his arms again,
Choking, his blood bright red on her white cheek.
And now he lies dead with the dead, and she is his 75
At last, his bride in the house of the dead.

Exit EURYDICÊ *into the palace.*

CHORAGOS: She has left us without a word. What can this mean?
MESSENGER: It troubles me, too; yet she knows what is best,
    Her grief is too great for public lamentation,
    And doubtless she has gone to her chamber to weep 80
    For her dead son, leading her maidens in his dirge.

Pause.

CHORAGOS: It may be so: but I fear this deep silence.
MESSENGER: I will see what she is doing. I will go in.

Exit MESSENGER *into the palace.*

Enter CREON *with attendants, bearing* HAIMON'S *body.*

CHORAGOS: But here is the king himself: oh look at him,
    Bearing his own damnation in his arms. 85
CREON: Nothing you say can touch me any more.
    My own blind heart has brought me
    From darkness to final darkness. Here you see

The father murdering, the murdered son—
And all my civic wisdom!   90
Haimon my son, so young, so young to die,
I was the fool, not you; and you died for me.
CHORAGOS: That is the truth; but you were late in learning it.
CREON: This truth is hard to bear. Surely a god
Has crushed me beneath the hugest weight of heaven,   95
And driven me headlong a barbaric way
To trample out the thing I held most dear.
The pains that men will take to come to pain!

Enter MESSENGER *from the palace.*

MESSENGER: The burden you carry in your hands is heavy,
But it is not all: you will find more in your house.   100
CREON: What burden worse than this shall I find there?
MESSENGER: The Queen is dead.
CREON: O port of death, deaf world,
Is there no pity for me? And you, Angel of evil,
I was dead, and your words are death again.   105
Is it true, boy? Can it be true?
Is my wife dead? Has death bred death?
MESSENGER: You can see for yourself.

The doors are opened and the body of EURYDICÊ *is disclosed within.*

CREON: Oh pity!
All true, all true, and more than I can bear!   110
O my wife, my son!
MESSENGER: She stood before the altar, and her heart
Welcomed the knife her own hand guided,
And a great cry burst from her lips for Megareus dead,
And for Haimon dead, her sons; and her last breath   115
Was a curse for their father, the murderer of her sons.
And she fell, and the dark flowed in through her closing eyes.
CREON: O God, I am sick with fear.
Are there no swords here? Has no one a blow for me?
MESSENGER: Her curse is upon you for the deaths of both.   120
CREON: It is right that it should be. I alone am guilty.
I know it, and I say it. Lead me in,
Quickly, friends.
I have neither life nor substance. Lead me in.
CHORAGOS: You are right, if there can be right in so much wrong.   125
The briefest way is best in a world of sorrow.
CREON: Let it come,
Let death come quickly, and be kind to me.
I would not ever see the sun again.
CHORAGOS: All that will come when it will; but we, meanwhile,   130
Have much to do. Leave the future to itself.
CREON: All my heart was in that prayer!

CHORAGOS: Then do not pray any more: the sky is deaf.
CREON: Lead me away. I have been rash and foolish.
    I have killed my son and my wife.   135
    I look for comfort; my comfort lies here dead.
    Whatever my hands have touched has come to nothing.
    Fate has brought all my pride to a thought of dust.

As CREON *is being led into the house, the* CHORAGOS *advances and speaks directly to the audience.*

CHORAGOS: There is no happiness where there is no wisdom;
    No wisdom but in submission to the gods.   140
    Big words are always punished,
    And proud men in old age learn to be wise.

(*c. 441* B.C.)

QUESTIONS FOR REFLECTION

Experience

1. To what extent can you relate to the dilemma faced by Antigonê? Why?

Interpretation

2. Describe the central problem of the play. Whose rights should assume priority—Creon's to legislate and punish, or Antigonê's to bury her brother? Is there any way to resolve the competing claims of Creon and Antigonê?
3. How does Sophocles characterize Creon and Antigonê? Consider their speeches, actions, and gestures.
4. What is Haimon's role in the play? What does Haimon's dialogue with his father reveal about the two characters?
5. What do Ismenê and Euridycê contribute to the play? How would *Antigonê* differ if either or both were absent?
6. Describe the structure of the play. How is its plot constructed and developed? Explain the focus of each scene. What is the purpose of the poetic odes that punctuate the dramatic action of the play?
7. What is the chorus's role? Single out two important comments made by the chorus and explain their significance.
8. Compare Antigonê's tragedy with Creon's suffering. Which character do you sympathize with most? Why?
9. Compare Creon's actions at the beginning and end of the play. How does he change?

Evaluation

10. Whose values does the play finally seem to endorse? Antigonê's? Creon's? Both? Neither? Explain.

CRITICS ON SOPHOCLES

ARISTOTLE
[*384–322 B.C.*]

The Six Elements of Tragedy

TRANSLATED BY GERALD F. ELSE

from *Poetics: Tragedy*

At present let us deal with tragedy, recovering from what has been said so far the definition of its essential nature, as it was in development. Tragedy, then, is a process of imitating an action which has serious implications, is complete, and possesses magnitude; by means of language which has been made sensuously attractive, with each of its varieties found separately in the parts; enacted by the persons themselves and not presented through narrative; through a course of pity and fear completing the purification of tragic acts which have those emotional characteristics. By "language made sensuously attractive" I mean language that has rhythm and melody, and by "its varieties found separately" I mean the fact that certain parts of the play are carried on through spoken verses alone and others the other way around, through song.

Now first of all, since they perform the imitation through action (by acting it), the adornment of their visual appearance will perforce constitute some part of the making of tragedy; and song-composition and verbal expression also, for those are the media in which they perform the imitation. By "verbal expression" I mean the actual composition of the verses, and by "song-composition" something whose meaning is entirely clear.

Next, since it is an imitation of an action and is enacted by certain people who are performing the action, and since those people must necessarily have certain traits both of character and thought (for it is thanks to these two factors that we speak of people's actions also as having a defined character, and it is in accordance with their actions that all either succeed or fail); and since the imitation of the action is the plot, for by "plot" I mean here the structuring of the events, and by the "characters" that in accordance with which we say that the persons who are acting have a defined moral character, and by "thought" all the passages in which they attempt to prove some thesis or set forth an opinion—it follows of necessity, then, that tragedy as a whole has just six constituent elements, in relation to the essence that makes it a distinct species; and they are plot, characters, verbal expression, thought, visual adornment, and song-composition. For the elements by which they imitate are two (i.e., verbal expression and song-composition), the manner in which they imitate is one (visual adornment), the things they imitate are three (plot, characters, thought), and there is nothing more beyond these. These then are the constituent forms they use.

Simple and Complex Plots

from *Poetics: Tragedy*

Among simple plots and actions the episodic are the worst. By "episodic" plot I mean one in which there is no probability or necessity for the order in which the episodes follow one another. Such structures are composed by the bad poets because they are bad poets, but by the good poets because of the actors: in composing contest pieces for them, and stretching out the plot beyond its capacity, they are forced frequently to dislocate the sequence.

Furthermore, since the tragic imitation is not only of a complete action but also of events that are fearful and pathetic, and these come about best when they come about contrary to one's expectation yet logically, one following from the other; that way they will be more productive of wonder than if they happen merely at random, by chance—because even among chance occurrences the ones people consider most marvelous are those that seem to have come about as if on purpose: for example the way the statue of Mitys at Argos killed the man who had been the cause of Mitys's death, by falling on him while he was attending the festival; it stands to reason, people think, that such things don't happen by chance—so plots of that sort cannot fail to be artistically superior.

Some plots are simple, others are complex; indeed the actions of which the plots are imitations already fall into these two categories. By "simple" action I mean one the development of which being continuous and unified in the manner stated above, the reversal comes without peripety or recognition, and by "complex" action one in which the reversal is continuous but with recognition or peripety or both. And these developments must grow out of the very structure of the plot itself, in such a way that on the basis of what has happened previously this particular outcome follows either by necessity or in accordance with probability; for there is a great difference in whether these events happen because of those or merely after them.

"Peripety" is a shift of what is being undertaken to the opposite in the way previously stated, and that in accordance with probability or necessity as we have just been saying; as for example in the *Oedipus* the man who has come, thinking that he will reassure Oedipus, that is, relieve him of his fear with respect to his mother, by revealing who he once was, brings about the opposite; and in the *Lynceus,* as he (Lynceus) is being led away with every prospect of being executed, and Danaus pursuing him with every prospect of doing the executing, it comes about as a result of the other things that have happened in the play that *he* is executed and Lynceus is saved. And "recognition" is, as indeed the name indicates, a shift from ignorance to awareness, pointing in the direction either of close blood ties or of hostility, of people who have previously been in a clearly marked state of happiness or unhappiness.

The finest recognition is one that happens at the same time as a peripety, as is the case with the one in the *Oedipus*. Naturally, there are also other kinds of recognition: it is possible for one to take place in the prescribed manner in relation to inanimate objects and chance occurrences, and it is possible to recognize whether a person has acted or not acted. But the form that is most integrally a part of the plot, the action, is the one aforesaid; for that kind of recognition combined with peripety will excite either pity or fear (and these are the kinds of action of which tragedy is an imitation according to our definition), because both good and bad fortune will also be most likely to follow that kind of event. Since, further, the recognition is a recognition of persons, some are of one person by the other one only (when it is already known who the "other one" is), but sometimes it is necessary for both persons to go through a recognition, as for example, Iphigenia is recognized by her brother through the sending of the letter, but of him by Iphigenia another recognition is required.

These then are two elements of plot: peripety and recognition; third is the *pathos*. Of these, peripety and recognition have been discussed; a *pathos* is a destructive or painful act, such as deaths on stage, paroxysms of pain, woundings, and all that sort of thing.

SIGMUND FREUD
[1856–1939]

The Oedipus Complex

from The Interpretation of Dreams

The action of the play consists in nothing other than the process of revealing, with cunning delays and ever-mounting excitement—a process that can be likened to the work of a psychoanalysis—that Oedipus himself is the murderer of Laïus, but further that he is the son of the murdered man and of Jocasta. Appalled at the abomination which he has unwittingly perpetrated, Oedipus blinds himself and forsakes his home. The oracle has been fulfilled.

Oedipus Rex is what is known as a tragedy of destiny. Its tragic effect is said to lie in the contrast between the supreme will of the gods and the vain attempts of mankind to escape the evil that threatens them. The lesson which, it is said, the deeply moved spectator should learn from the tragedy is submission to the divine will and realization of his own impotence. Modern dramatists have accordingly tried to achieve a similar tragic effect by weaving the same contrast into a plot invented by themselves. But the spectators have looked on unmoved while a curse or an oracle was fulfilled in spite of all the efforts of some innocent man: later tragedies of destiny have failed in their effect.

If *Oedipus Rex* moves a modern audience no less than it did the contemporary Greek one, the explanation can only be that its effect does not lie in the contrast between destiny and human will, but is to be looked for in the particular nature of the material on which that contrast is exemplified. There must be something which makes a voice within us ready to recognize the compelling force of destiny in the *Oedipus,* while we can dismiss as merely arbitrary such dispositions as are laid down in [Grillparzer's] *Die Ahnfrau* or other modern tragedies of destiny. And a factor of this kind is in fact involved in the story of King Oedipus. His destiny moves us only because it might have been ours—because the oracle laid the same curse upon us before our birth as upon him. It is the fate of all of us, perhaps, to direct our first sexual impulse toward our mother and our first hatred and our first murderous wish against our father. Our dreams convince us that that is so. King Oedipus, who slew his father Laïus and married his mother Jocasta, merely shows us the fulfillment of our own childhood wishes. But, more fortunate than he, we have meanwhile succeeded, in so far as we have not become psychoneurotics, in detaching our sexual impulses from our mothers and in forgetting our jealousy of our fathers. Here is one in whom these primeval wishes of our childhood have been fulfilled, and we shrink back from him with the whole force of the repression by which those wishes have since that time been held down within us. While the poet, as he unravels the past, brings to light the guilt of Oedipus, he is at the same time compelling us to recognize our own inner minds, in which those same impulses, though suppressed, are still to be found. The contrast with which the closing Chorus leaves us confronted—

> . . . Fix on Oedipus your eyes,
> Who resolved the dark enigma, noblest champion and most wise.
> Like a star his envied fortune mounted beaming far and wide:
> Now he sinks in seas of anguish, whelmed beneath a raging tide . . .

—strikes as a warning at ourselves and our pride, at us who since our childhood have grown so wise and so mighty in our own eyes. Like Oedipus, we live in ignorance of these wishes, repugnant to morality, which have been forced upon us by Nature, and after their revelation we may all of us well seek to close our eyes to the scenes of our childhood.

There is an unmistakable indication in the text of Sophocles' tragedy itself that the legend of Oedipus sprang from some primeval dream material which had as its content the distressing disturbance of a child's relation to his parents owing to the first stirrings of sexuality. At a point when Oedipus, though he is not yet enlightened, has begun to feel troubled by his recollection of the oracle, Jocasta consoles him by referring to a dream which many people dream, though, as she thinks, it has no meaning:

> Many a man ere now in dreams hath lain
> With her who bare him. He hath least annoy
> Who with such omens troubleth not his mind.

Today, just as then, many men dream of having sexual relations with their mothers, and speak of the fact with indignation and astonishment. It is clearly the key to the tragedy and the complement to the dream of the dreamer's father being dead. The story of Oedipus is the reaction of the imagination to these two typical dreams. And just as these dreams, when dreamt by adults, are accompanied by feelings of repulsion, so too the legend must include horror and self-punishment. Its further modification originates once again in a misconceived secondary revision of the material, which has sought to exploit it for theological purposes. . . . The attempt to harmonize divine omnipotence with human responsibility must naturally fail in connection with this subject matter just as with any other.

BERNARD KNOX

Sophocles' Oedipus

from *Word and Action*

In an earlier Sophoclean play, *Antigonê,* the chorus sings a hymn to this man the conqueror. "Many are the wonders and terrors, and nothing more wonderful and terrible than man." He has conquered the sea, "this creature goes beyond the white sea pressing forward as the swell crashes about him"; and he has conquered the land, "earth, highest of the gods . . . he wears away with the turning plough." He has mastered not only the elements, sea, and land, but the birds, beasts, and fishes; "through knowledge and technique," sings the chorus, he is yoker of the horse, tamer of the bull. "And he has taught himself speech and thought swift as the wind and attitudes which enable him to live in communities and means to shelter himself from the frost and rain. Full of resources he faces the future, nothing will find him at a loss. Death, it is true, he will not avoid, yet he has thought out ways of escape from desperate diseases. His knowledge, ingenuity and technique are beyond anything that could have been foreseen." These lyrics describe the rise to power of *anthropos tyrannos;* self-taught, he seizes control of his environment, he is master of the elements, the animals, the arts and sciences of civilization. "Full of resources he faces the future"—an apt description of Oedipus at the beginning of our play.

And it is not the only phrase of this ode which is relevant; for Oedipus is connected by the terms he uses, and which are used to and about him, with the whole range of human achievement which has raised man to his present level. All the items of this triumphant catalog recur in the *Oedipus Tyrannos* [*Oedipus Rex*]; the images of the play define him as helmsman, conqueror of the sea, and ploughman, conqueror of the land, as hunter, master of speech and thought, inventor, legislator, physician. Oedipus is faced in the play with an intellectual problem, and as he marshals his intellectual resources to solve it, the language of the play suggests a comparison between Oedipus' methods in the play and the whole range of sciences and techniques which have brought man to mastery, made him *tyrannos* of the world.

Oedipus' problem is apparently simple: "Who is the murderer of Laius?" But as he pursues the answer, the question changes shape. It becomes a different problem: "Who am I?" And the answer to this problem involves the gods as well as man. The answer to the question is not what he expected, it is in fact a reversal, that *peripeteia* which Aristotle speaks of in connection with this play. The state of Oedipus is reversed from "first of men" to "most accursed of men"; his attitude from the proud ἀρκτέον, "I must rule," to the humble πειστέον, "I must obey." "Reversal," says Aristotle, "is a change of the action into the opposite," and one meaning of this much disputed phrase is that the action produces the opposite of the actor's intentions. So Oedipus curses the murderer of Laius and it turns out that he has cursed himself. But this reversal is not confined to the action; it is also the process of all the great images of the play which identify Oedipus as the inventive, critical spirit of his century. As the images unfold, the inquirer turns into the object of inquiry, the hunter into the prey, the doctor into the patient, the investigator into the criminal, the revealer into the thing revealed, the finder into the thing found, the savior into the thing saved ("I was saved, for some dreadful destiny"), the liberator into the thing released ("I released your feet from the bonds which pierced your ankles," says the Corinthian messenger). The accuser becomes the defendant, the ruler the subject, the teacher not only the pupil but also the object lesson, the example—a change of the action into its opposite, from active to passive.

And the two opening images of the *Antigonê* ode recur with hideous effect. Oedipus the helmsman, who steers the ship of state, is seen, in Tiresias' words, as one who "steers his ship into a nameless anchorage," who, in the chorus's words, "shared the same great harbour with his father." And Oedipus the ploughman—"How," asks the chorus, "how could the furrows which your father ploughed bear you in silence for so long?"

This reversal is the movement of the play, parallel in the imagery and the action: it is the overthrow of the *tyrannos,* of man who seized power and thought himself "equated to the gods." The bold metaphor of the priest introduces another of the images which parallel in their development the reversal of the hero and suggest that Oedipus is a figure symbolic of human intelligence and achievement in general. He is not only helmsman, ploughman, inventor, legislator, liberator, revealer, doctor—he is also equator, mathematician, calculator; "equated" is a mathematical term, and it is only one of a whole complex of such terms which present Oedipus in yet a fresh aspect of man *tyrannos.* One of Oedipus' favorite words is "measure," and this is of course a significant metaphor: measure, mensuration, number, calculation—these are among the most important inventions which have brought man to power. Aeschylus' Prometheus, the mythical civilizer of human life, counts number among the foremost of his gifts to man. "And number, too, I invented, outstanding among clever devices." In the river valleys of the East, generations of mensuration and calculation had brought man to an understanding of the movements of the stars and of time: in the histories of his friend Herodotus, Sophocles had read of the calculation and mensuration which had gone into the building of the pyramids. "Measure"—it is Protagoras' word: "Man is the measure of all things." In this play man's measure is taken, his true equation found. The play is full of equations, some of them incomplete, some false; the final equation shows man equated not to the gods but to himself, as Oedipus is finally equated to himself. For there are in the play not one Oedipus but two.

One is the magnificent figure set before us in the opening scenes, *tyrannos,* the man of wealth and power, first of men, the intellect and energy which drive on the search. The other is the object of the search, a shadowy figure who has violated the most fundamental human taboos, an incestuous parricide, "most accursed of men." And even before the one Oedipus finds the other, they are connected and equated in the name which they both bear, Oedipus. Oedipus—Swollen-foot; it emphasizes the physical blemish which scars the body of the splendid *tyrannos,* a defect which he tries to forget but which reminds us of the outcast child this *tyrannos* once was and the outcast man he is soon to be. The second half of the name πουζ, "foot," recurs throughout the play, as a mocking phrase which recalls this other Oedipus. "The Sphinx forced us to look at what was at our feet," says Creon. Tiresias invokes "the dread-footed curse of your father and mother." And the choral odes echo and re-echo with this word. "Let the murderer of Laius set his foot in motion in flight." "The murderer is a man alone with forlorn foot." "The laws of Zeus are high-footed." "The man of pride plunges down into doom where he cannot use his foot."

These mocking repetitions of one-half the name invoke the unknown Oedipus who will be revealed: the equally emphatic repetition of the first half emphasizes the dominant attitude of the man before us.

ADRIAN POOLE

Oedipus and Athens

from *Tragedy: Shakespeare and the Greek Example*

Oedipus is quick to decide and to act; he anticipates advice and suggestion. When the priest hints that he should send to Delphi for help, he has already done so; when the chorus suggests sending for Tiresias, the prophet has already been summoned and is on the way. This swiftness in action is a well-known Athenian quality, one their enemies are well aware of. "They are the only people," say the Corinthians, "who simultaneously hope for and have what they plan, because of their quick fulfillment of decisions." But this action is not rash, it is based on reflection; Oedipus reached the decision to apply to Delphi "groping, laboring over many paths of thought." This too is typically Athenian. "We are unique," says Pericles, "in our combination of the most courageous action and rational discussion of our plans." The Athenians also spoke with pride of the intelligence that informed such discussion: Pericles attributes the Athenian victories over the Persians "not to luck, but to intelligence." And this is the claim of Oedipus, too. "The flight of my own intelligence hit the mark," he says, as he recalls his solution of the riddle of the Sphinx. The riddle has sinister verbal connections with his fate (his name in Greek is *Oidipous,* and *dipous* is the Greek word for "two-footed" in the riddle, not to mention the later prophecy of Tiresias that he would leave Thebes as a blind man, "a stick tapping before him step by step"), but the answer he proposed to the riddle—"Man"—is appropriate for the optimistic picture of man's achievement and potential that the figure of Oedipus represents.

Above all, as we see from the priest's speech in the prologue and the prompt, energetic action Oedipus takes to rescue his subjects from the plague, he is a man dedicated to the interests and the needs of the city. It is this public spirit that drives him on to the discovery of the truth—to reject Creon's hint that the matter should be kept under wraps, to send for Tiresias, to pronounce the curse and sentence of banishment on the murderer of Laius. This spirit was the great civic virtue that Pericles preached—"I would have you fix your eyes every day on the greatness of Athens until you fall in love with her"—and that the enemies of Athens knew they had to reckon with. "In the city's service," say the Corinthians, "they use their bodies as if they did not belong to them."

All this does not necessarily mean that Sophocles' audience drew a conscious parallel between Oedipus and Athens (or even that Sophocles himself did); what is important is that they could have seen in Oedipus a man endowed with the temperament and talents they prized most highly in their own democratic leaders and in their ideal vision of themselves. Oedipus the King is a dramatic embodiment of the creative vigor and intellectual daring of the fifth-century Athenian spirit.

But there is an even greater dimension to this extraordinary dramatic figure. The fifth century in Athens saw the birth of the historical spirit. The past came to be seen no longer as a golden age from which there had been a decline if not a fall, but as a steady progress from primitive barbarism to the high civilization of the city-state. . . .

The figure of Oedipus represents not only the techniques of the transition from savagery to civilization and the political achievements of the newly settled society, but also the temper and methods of the fifth-century intellectual revolution. His speeches are full of words, phrases, and attitudes that link him with the "enlightenment" of Sophocles' own Athens. "I'll bring it all to light," he says; he is like some Protagoras or Democritus dispelling the darkness of ignorance and superstition. He is a questioner, a researcher, a discoverer—the Greek words are those of the sophistic vocabulary. Above all Oedipus is presented to the audience as a symbol of two of the greatest scientific achievements of the age—mathematics and medicine. Mathematical language recurs incessantly in the imagery of the play—such terms as "measure" (*metrein*), "equate" (*isoun*), "define" (*diorizein*)—and at one climactic moment Oedipus expresses as a mathematical axiom his hope that a discrepancy in the evidence will clear him of the charge of Laius's murder: "One can't equal many." This obsessive image, Oedipus the calculator, is one more means of investing the mythical figure with the salient characteristics of the fifth-century achievement, but it is also magnificently functional. For, in his search for truth, he is engaged in a great calculation to determine the measure of man, whom Protagoras called "the measure of all things."

GEORGE STEINER
[*b. 1929*]

Principal Constants of Conflict in Antigonê

from *Antigonê*

It has, I believe, been given to only one literary text to express all the principal constants of conflict in the condition of man. These constants are fivefold: the confrontation of men and of women; of age and of youth; of society and of the individual; of the living and the dead; of men and of god(s). The conflicts which come of these five orders of confrontation are not negotiable. Men and women, old and young, the individual and the community or state, the quick and the dead, mortals and immortals, define themselves in the conflictual process of defining each other. Self-definition and the agonistic recognition of "otherness" (of *l'autre*) across the threatened boundaries of self are indissociable. The polarities of masculinity and of femininity, of aging and of youth, of private autonomy and of social collectivity, of existence and mortality, of the human and the divine, can be crystallized only in adversative terms (whatever the many shades of accommodation between them). To arrive at oneself—the primordial journey—is to come up, polemically, against "the other." The boundary-conditions of the human person are those set by gender, by age, by community, by the cut between life and death, and by the potentials of accepted or denied encounter between the existential and the transcendent.

But "collision" is, of course, a monistic and, therefore, inadequate term. Equally decisive are those categories of reciprocal perception, of grappling with "otherness," that can be defined as erotic, filial, social, ritual, and metaphysical. Men and women, old and young, individual and *communitas,* living and deceased, mortals and gods, meet and mesh in contiguities of love, of kinship, of commonality and group-communion, of caring remembrance, of worship. Sex, the honeycomb of generations and of kinship, the social unit, the presentness of the departed in the weave of the living, the practices of religion, are the modes of enactment of ultimate ontological dualities. In essence, the constants of conflict and of positive intimacy are the same. When man and woman meet, they stand against each other as they stand close. Old and young seek in each other the pain of remembrance and the matching solace of futurity. Anarchic individuation seeks interaction with the compulsions of law, of collective cohesion in the body politic. The dead inhabit the living and, in turn, await their visit. The duel between men and god(s) is the most aggressively amorous known to experience. In the physics of man's being, fission is also fusion. . . .

Creon and Antigonê clash as man and as woman. Creon is a mature, indeed an aging, man; Antigonê's is the virginity of youth. Their fatal debate turns on the nature of the coexistence between private vision and public need, between ego and community. The imperatives of immanence, of the living in the [*polis*], πόλισ, press on Creon; in Antigonê, these imperatives encounter the no less exigent night-throng of the dead. No syllable spoken, no gesture made, in the dialogue of Antigone and Creon but has within it the manifold, perhaps duplicitous, nearness of the gods.

CHAPTER SIX

The Elizabethan Theater: Shakespeare in Context

STAGECRAFT IN THE ELIZABETHAN AGE

The drama of Shakespeare's time, the Elizabethan Age (1558–1603), shares some features with Greek drama. Like the Greek dramatists, Elizabethan playwrights wrote both comedies and tragedies, but the Elizabethans extended the possibilities of each genre. They wrote domestic tragedies, tragedies of character, and revenge tragedies; they contributed comedies of manners and comedies of humors to the earlier romantic and satiric comedies. In Greek and Elizabethan theater, props were few, scenery was simple, and dialogue often indicated changes of locale and time. Elizabethan plays were also written in verse rather than prose.

An Elizabethan playhouse such as the Globe, where many of Shakespeare's plays were staged, had a much smaller seating capacity than the large Greek amphitheaters, which could seat thousands (fifteen thousand at Epidaurus). The Globe could accommodate about twenty-three hundred people, including roughly eight hundred groundlings who, exposed to the elements, stood around the stage. The stage itself projected from an inside wall into their midst. More prosperous spectators sat in one of the three stories that nearly encircled the stage. The vastly smaller size and seating capacity of the Elizabethan theater and the projection of its stage made for a greater intimacy between actors and audience. Though actors still had to project their voices and exaggerate their gestures, they could be heard and seen without the aid of large megaphonic masks and elevated shoes. Elizabethan actors could modulate their voices and vary their pitch, stress, and intonation in ways not suited to the Greek stage. They could also make greater and more subtle use of facial expression and of gesture to enforce their greater verbal and vocal flexibility.

In addition to greater intimacy, the Elizabethan stage also offered more versatility than its Greek counterpart. Although the Greek *skene* building could be used for scenes occuring above the ground, such as a god descending in a machine (*deus ex machina*),★ the Greek stage was really a single-level acting area. Not so the Elizabethan stage, which contained a second-level balcony (from which Brabantio looks out in Act I, scene ii of *Othello*). Besides its balcony, Shakespeare's stage had doors at the back for entrances and exits, a curtained alcove (useful for scenes of intrigue), and a stage floor trapdoor, from which the Ghost ascends in Shakespeare's *Hamlet*. Such a stage was suitable for rapidly shifting scenes and continuous action. Thus, Elizabethan stage conventions did not include divisions between scenes as in Greek drama. The act and scene divisions that appear in *Othello* and *Hamlet* were devised by modern editors.

INTRODUCTION TO SHAKESPEARE

[1564–1616]

William Shakespeare, the most famous English writer, is also among the most popular. His fame and popularity rest on his plays more than on his nondramatic poetry—though his sonnets remain perennially in fashion. What makes Shakespeare such a literary phenomenon? Why are readers so drawn to his work? Here are two simple explanations: (1) his revelation of human character, especially his exploration of complex states of mind and feeling; (2) his explosive and exuberant language, particularly the richness and variety of his metaphors. Both of these literary virtues abound in the sequence of 154 sonnets Shakespeare wrote in the 1590s. Both also consistently appear in his thirty-seven plays, particularly in the soliloquies, those inward meditative speeches of the major characters. The richness of Shakespeare's language is also apparent in the songs he wrote for the plays, especially the songs in the comedies.

Another source of Shakespeare's popularity is his immense quotability. Shakespeare's plays and poems provide a repository of familiar sayings and recognizable quotations. From *Hamlet* alone we glean the following:

In my mind's eye

To the manner born

There are more things in heaven and earth

★A god who resolves the entanglements of a play by his supernatural intervention (literally, a god from the machine) or any artificial device used to resolve a plot.

Hold the mirror up to nature

I must be cruel only to be kind.

Brevity is the soul of wit.

To be or not to be, that is the question.

Neither a borrower nor a lender be.

Something's rotten in the state of Denmark.

What a piece of work is a man.

To reduce Shakespeare's appeal to the fact that he is eminently quotable, however, is to ignore other important dimensions of his popularity. It is, moreover, to get things backward—to put the cart before the horse. Shakespeare is not a great writer because he is quotable; he is quotable because he is a great writer. It is his manipulation of language and his revelation of character that have made him both widely read and deeply revered.

Very little is known with certainty about Shakespeare's life. Scholars, however, have determined the following basic facts. He was born in Stratford-on-Avon in April of 1564. He attended the local grammar school, where he would have studied Latin and perhaps a little Greek. His formal education did not include attendance at the university—in his day either Oxford or Cambridge. Instead, at eighteen, he married Anne Hathaway, who bore three children in as many years, a daughter in 1583 and twins, a boy and girl, in 1585. Shakespeare wrote and acted in plays, for by 1592 he was known in London as both actor and playwright.

Many tributes have been paid to Shakespeare. One, however, stands above the rest: his contemporary Ben Jonson's judgment that "he is not for an age, but for all time."

Othello

Shakespeare's plays generally, and *Othello* in particular, appealed to an audience ranging from the illiterate to the educated: bawdy jokes exist alongside sublime poetry; subtle introspective moments coexist with violence and passion. Shakespeare's language is among the richest and most resourceful ever written (and spoken), and *Othello* testifies to its vitality and exuberance. Written predominantly in blank verse, *Othello* also includes prose passages (many spoken by Iago) and rhymed couplets (which punctuate the ends of some scenes). The play's language is rich in metaphor and images, puns, and other forms of wordplay.

Deriving the story of Othello from a sixteenth-century tale by Giraldi Cinthio, Shakespeare improved the plot, enriched the language, and deepened the characters. *Othello* has been among the most admired of Shakespeare's plays. Part of its attraction is its language, but its characters are perhaps even more immediately compelling: the noble Othello; his gentle and naive Venetian wife, Desdemona; the brilliant, magnetic, and inexplicable Iago; his crude and manipulated wife, Emilia. The play's central concerns—love and trust, good and evil, nobility and debasement—are also universal.

The Tragedy of Othello

THE MOOR OF VENICE

EDITED BY ALVIN KERNAN

CHARACTERS

OTHELLO, *the Moor*
BRABANTIO, *father to Desdemona*
CASSIO, *an honorable lieutenant*
IAGO, *a villain*
RODERIGO, *a gulled gentleman*
DUKE OF VENICE
SENATORS
MONTANO, *Governor of Cyprus*
GENTLEMEN OF CYPRUS
LODOVICO AND GRATIANO, *two noble Venetians*
SAILORS
CLOWN
DESDEMONA, *wife to Othello*
EMILIA, *wife to Iago*
BIANCA, *a courtesan*
(MESSENGER, HERALD, OFFICERS, GENTLEMEN, MUSICIANS, ATTENDANTS)

Scene. *Venice and Cyprus.*

ACT I

Scene I [*Venice. A street.*]

RODERIGO: Tush! Never tell me? I take it much unkindly
　That thou, Iago, who hast had my purse
　As if the strings were thine, shouldst know of this.
IAGO: 'Sblood,° but you'll not hear me! If ever I did dream
　Of such a matter, abhor me.
RODERIGO:　　　　　　　　　Thou told'st me　　　　　　　5
　Thou didst hold him in thy hate.
IAGO:　　　　　　　　　　Despise me

I.i. ⁴·**Sblood** *by God's blood.*

If I do not. Three great ones of the city,
In personal suit to make me his lieutenant,
Off-capped° to him; and, by the faith of man,
I know my price; I am worth no worse a place.   10
But he, as loving his own pride and purposes,
Evades them with a bombast circumstance,°
Horribly stuffed with epithets of war;
Nonsuits° my mediators. For, "Certes," says he,
"I have already chose my officer." And what was he?   15
Forsooth, a great arithmetician,°
One Michael Cassio, a Florentine,
(A fellow almost damned in a fair wife)°
That never set a squadron in the field,
Nor the division of a battle knows   20
More than a spinster; unless the bookish theoric,
Wherein the tonguèd° consuls can propose
As masterly as he. Mere prattle without practice
Is all his soldiership. But he, sir, had th' election;
And I, of whom his eyes had seen the proof   25
At Rhodes, at Cyprus, and on other grounds
Christian and heathen, must be belee'd and calmed
By debitor and creditor. This counter-caster,°
He, in good time, must his lieutenant be,
And I—God bless the mark!—his Moorship's ancient.°   30
RODERIGO: By heaven, I rather would have been his hangman.
IAGO: Why, there's no remedy. 'Tis the curse of service:
Preferment goes by letter and affection,°
And not by old gradation,° where each second
Stood heir to th' first. Now, sir, be judge yourself, 35
Whether I in any just term am affined°
To love the Moor.
RODERIGO: I would not follow him then.
IAGO: O, sir, content you.
I follow him to serve my turn upon him.
We cannot all be masters, nor all masters   40
Cannot be truly followed. You shall mark
Many a duteous and knee-crooking° knave
That, doting on his own obsequious bondage,
Wears out his time, much like his master's ass,

9**Off-capped** *doffed their caps—as a mark of respect.* 12**bombast circumstance** *stuffed, roundabout speech.* 14**Nonsuits** *rejects.* 16**arithmetician** *theorist (rather than practical).* 18**(A . . . wife)** *a much-disputed passage, probably best taken as a general sneer at Cassio as a dandy and a ladies' man. But in the story from which Shakespeare took his plot the counterpart of Cassio is married, and it may be that at the beginning of the play, Shakespeare had decided to keep him married but later changed his mind.* 22**tonguèd** *eloquent.* 28**counter-caster** *i.e., a bookkeeper who casts (reckons up) figures on a counter (abacus).* 30**ancient** *standard-bearer; an under-officer.* 33**letter and affection** *recommendations (from men of power) and personal preference.* 34**old gradation** *seniority.* 36**affined** *bound.* 42**knee-crooking** *bowing.*

For naught but provender; and when he's old, cashiered.   45
Whip me such honest knaves! Others there are
Who, trimmed in forms and visages of duty,
Keep yet their hearts attending on themselves,
And, throwing but shows of service on their lords,
Do well thrive by them, and when they have lined their coats,   50
Do themselves homage. These fellows have some soul;
And such a one do I profess myself. For, sir,
It is as sure as you are Roderigo,
Were I the Moor, I would not be Iago.
In following him, I follow but myself.   55
Heaven is my judge, not I for love and duty,
But seeming so, for my peculiar° end;
For when my outward action doth demonstrate
The native° act and figure of my heart
In complement extern,° 'tis not long after   60
But I will wear my heart upon my sleeve
For daws to peck at; I am not what I am.
RODERIGO: What a full fortune does the thick-lips owe°
    If he can carry't thus!
IAGO: Call up her father,
    Rouse him. Make after him, poison his delight,   65
    Proclaim him in the streets, incense her kinsmen,
    And though he in a fertile climate dwell,
    Plague him with flies; though that his joy be joy,
    Yet throw such chances of vexation on't
    As it may lose some color.   70
RODERIGO: Here is her father's house. I'll call aloud.
IAGO: Do, with like timorous° accent and dire yell
    As when, by night and negligence, the fire
    Is spied in populous cities.
RODERIGO: What, ho, Brabantio! Signior Brabantio, ho!   75
IAGO: Awake! What, ho, Brabantio! Thieves! Thieves!
    Look to your house, your daughter, and your bags!
    Thieves! Thieves!

            BRABANTIO *above*° [*at a window*].

BRABANTIO: What is the reason of this terrible summons?
    What is the matter there?   80
RODERIGO: Signior, is all your family within?
IAGO: Are your doors locked?
BRABANTIO: Why, wherefore ask you this?
IAGO: Zounds, sir, y'are robbed! For shame. Put on your gown!

---

[57]**peculiar** *personal.*   [59]**native** *natural, innate.*   [60]**complement extern** *outward appearance.*   [63]**owe**
own.   [72]**timorous** *frightening.*   [78]**s.d. above** *(i.e., on the small upper stage above and to the rear of the*
main platform stage, which resembled the projecting upper story of an Elizabethan house).

Your heart is burst, you have lost half your soul.
Even now, now, very now, an old black ram   85
Is tupping your white ewe. Arise, arise!
Awake the snorting citizens with the bell,
Or else the devil will make a grandsire of you.
Arise, I say!
BRABANTIO: What, have you lost your wits?
RODERIGO: Most reverend signior, do you know my voice?   90
BRABANTIO: Not I. What are you?
RODERIGO: My name is Roderigo.
BRABANTIO: The worser welcome!
I have charged thee not to haunt about my doors.
In honest plainness thou hast heard me say
My daughter is not for thee; and now, in madness,   95
Being full of supper and distemp'ring draughts,°
Upon malicious knavery dost thou come
To start° my quiet.
RODERIGO: Sir, sir, sir—
BRABANTIO: But thou must needs be sure
My spirits and my place° have in their power   100
To make this bitter to thee.
RODERIGO: Patience, good sir.
BRABANTIO: What tell'st thou me of robbing? This is Venice,
My house is not a grange.°
RODERIGO: Most grave Brabantio,
In simple and pure soul I come to you.

IAGO: Zounds, sir, you are one of those that will not serve God if the devil bid you.
   Because we come to do you service and you think we are ruffians, you'll have
   your daughter covered with a Barbary° horse, you'll have your nephews° neigh
   to you, you'll have coursers for cousins,° and gennets for germans.°
BRABANTIO: What profane wretch art thou?   110
IAGO: I am one, sir, that comes to tell you your daughter and the Moor are making
   the beast with two backs.
BRABANTIO: Thou art a villain.
IAGO: You are—a senator.
BRABANTIO: This thou shalt answer. I know thee, Roderigo.
RODERIGO: Sir, I will answer anything. But I beseech you,   115
If 't be your pleasure and most wise consent,
As partly I find it is, that your fair daughter,
At this odd-even° and dull watch o' th' night,
Transported, with no worse nor better guard

---

⁹⁶*distemp'ring draughts* *unsettling drinks.* ⁹⁸*start* *disrupt.* ¹⁰⁰*place* *rank, i.e., of senator.* ¹⁰³*grange*
isolated house. ¹⁰⁷*Barbary* *Arabian, i.e., Moorish.* ¹⁰⁸*nephews* *i.e., grandsons.* ¹⁰⁸*cousins* *re-*
lations. ¹⁰⁹*gennets for germans* *Spanish horses for blood relatives.* ¹¹⁸*odd-even* *between night and*
morning.

But with a knave of common hire, a gondolier,   120
To the gross clasps of a lascivious Moor—
If this be known to you, and your allowance,
We then have done you bold and saucy wrongs;
But if you know not this, my manners tell me
We have your wrong rebuke. Do not believe   125
That from the sense of all civility°
I thus would play and trifle with your reverence.
Your daughter, if you have not given her leave,
I say again, hath made a gross revolt,
Tying her duty, beauty, wit, and fortunes   130
In an extravagant° and wheeling stranger
Of here and everywhere. Straight satisfy yourself.
If she be in her chamber, or your house,
Let loose on me the justice of the state
For thus deluding you.
BRABANTIO: Strike on the tinder, ho!   135
    Give me a taper! Call up all my people!
    This accident° is not unlike my dream.
    Belief of it oppresses me already.
    Light, I say! Light!   Exit [above].
IAGO: Farewell, for I must leave you.
    It seems not meet, nor wholesome to my place,   140
    To be produced—as, if I stay, I shall—
    Against the Moor. For I do know the State,
    However this may gall him with some check,°
    Cannot with safety cast° him; for he's embarked
    With such loud reason to the Cyprus wars,   145
    Which even now stands in act,° that for their souls
    Another of his fathom° they have none
    To lead their business; in which regard,
    Though I do hate him as I do hell-pains,
    Yet, for necessity of present life,   150
    I must show out a flag and sign of love,
    Which is indeed but sign. That you shall surely find him,
    Lead to the Sagittary° that raisèd search:
    And there will I be with him. So farewell.   [Exit.]

        Enter BRABANTIO [in his nightgown], with SERVANTS and torches.

BRABANTIO: It is too true an evil. Gone she is;   155
    And what's to come of my despisèd time
    Is naught but bitterness. Now, Roderigo,

126*sense of all civility*   *feeling of what is proper.*   131*extravagant*   *vagrant, wandering (Othello is not Vene-*
tian and thus may be considered a wandering soldier of fortune).   137*accident*   *happening.*   143*check*   *re-*
straint.   144*cast*   *dismiss.*   146*stands in act*   *takes place.*   147*fathom*   *ability.*   153*Sagittary*
probably the name of an inn.

Where didst thou see her?—O unhappy girl!—
With the Moor, say'st thou?—Who would be a father?—
How didst thou know 'twas she?—O, she deceives me   160
Past thought!—What said she to you? Get moe° tapers!
Raise all my kindred!—Are they married, think you?

RODERIGO: Truly I think they are.

BRABANTIO: O heaven! How got she out? O treason of the blood!
    Fathers, from hence trust not your daughters' minds   165
    By what you see them act.° Is there not charms
    By which the property° of youth and maidhood
    May be abused? Have you not read, Roderigo,
    Of some such thing?

RODERIGO: Yes, sir, I have indeed.

BRABANTIO: Call up my brother.—O, would you had had her!—   170
    Some one way, some another.—Do you know
    Where we may apprehend her and the Moor?

RODERIGO: I think I can discover him, if you please
    To get good guard and go along with me.

BRABANTIO: Pray you lead on. At every house I'll call;   175
    I may command at most.—Get weapons, ho!
    And raise some special officers of night.—
    On, good Roderigo; I will deserve your pains.°   [*Exeunt.*]

Scene II [*A street.*]

Enter OTHELLO, IAGO, ATTENDANTS *with torches.*

IAGO: Though in the trade of war I have slain men,
    Yet do I hold it very stuff ° o' th' conscience
    To do no contrived murder. I lack iniquity
    Sometime to do me service. Nine or ten times
    I had thought t' have yerked° him here, under the ribs.   5

OTHELLO: 'Tis better as it is.

IAGO: Nay, but he prated,
    And spoke such scurvy and provoking terms
    Against your honor, that with the little godliness I have
    I did full hard forbear him. But I pray you, sir,
    Are you fast married? Be assured of this,   10
    That the magnifico° is much beloved,
    And hath in his effect a voice potential
    As double as the Duke's.° He will divorce you,
    Or put upon you what restraint or grievance
    The law, with all his might to enforce it on,   15

---

[161]**moe** *more.*   [166]**act** *do.*   [167]**property** *true nature.*   [178]**deserve your pains** *be worthy of (and reward) your efforts.*   **I.ii.**   [2]**stuff** *essence.*   [5]**yerked** *stabbed.*   [11]**magnifico** *nobleman.*
[12–13]**hath ... Duke's** *i.e., can be as effective as the Duke.*

Will give him cable.°
OTHELLO: Let him do his spite.
My services which I have done the Signiory°
Shall out-tongue his complaints. 'Tis yet to know°—
Which when I know that boasting is an honor
I shall promulgate—I fetch my life and being   20
From men of royal siege,° and my demerits°
May speak unbonneted to as proud a fortune
As this that I have reached.° For know, Iago,
But that I love the gentle Desdemona,
I would not my unhousèd° free condition   25
Put into circumscription and confine
For the seas' worth. But look, what lights come yond?

Enter CASSIO, *with* [OFFICERS *and*] *torches.*

IAGO: Those are the raisèd father and his friends.
You were best go in.
OTHELLO: Not I. I must be found.
My parts, my title, and my perfect soul°   30
Shall manifest me rightly. Is it they?
IAGO: By Janus, I think no.
OTHELLO: The servants of the Duke? And my lieutenant?
The goodness of the night upon you, friends.
What is the news?
CASSIO: The Duke does greet you, general;   35
And he requires your haste-posthaste appearance
Even on the instant.
OTHELLO: What is the matter, think you?
CASSIO:Something from Cyprus, as I may divine.
It is a business of some heat. The galleys
Have sent a dozen sequent° messengers   40
This very night at one another's heels,
And many of the consuls, raised and met,
Are at the Duke's already. You have been hotly called for.
When, being not at your lodging to be found,
The Senate hath sent about three several° quests   45
To search you out.
OTHELLO: 'Tis well I am found by you.
I will but spend a word here in the house,
And go with you.   [*Exit.*]
CASSIO: Ancient, what makes he here?
IAGO: Faith, he tonight hath boarded a land carack.°

---

¹⁶*cable*   *range, scope.*   ¹⁷**Signiory**   *the rulers of Venice.*   ¹⁸**yet to know**   *unknown as yet.*   ²¹**siege** *rank.*   ²¹**demerits**   *deserts.*   ²²⁻²³**May . . . reached**   *i.e., are the equal of the family I have married into.* ²⁵**unhousèd**   *unconfined.*   ³⁰**perfect soul**   *clear, unflawed conscience.*   ⁴⁰**sequent**   *successive.*   ⁴⁵**several** *separate.*   ⁴⁹**carack**   *treasure ship.*

If it prove lawful prize, he's made forever.　　　　　　　　50
CASSIO: I do not understand.
IAGO:　　　　　　　　　He's married.
CASSIO:　　　　　　　　　　　To who?

[*Enter* OTHELLO.]

IAGO: Marry,° to—Come captain, will you go?
OTHELLO:　　　　　　　　　　Have with you.
CASSIO: Here comes another troop to seek for you.

Enter BRABANTIO, RODERIGO, *with* OFFICERS *and torches.*

IAGO: It is Brabantio. General, be advised.
　　He comes to bad intent.
OTHELLO:　　　　　　　Holla! Stand there!　　　　　55
RODERIGO: Signior, it is the Moor.
BRABANTIO:　　　　　　　Down with him, thief!　　　[*They draw swords.*]
IAGO: You, Roderigo? Come, sir, I am for you.
OTHELLO: Keep up your bright swords, for the dew will rust them.
　　Good signior, you shall more command with years
　　Than with your weapons.　　　　　　　　　60
BRABANTIO: O thou foul thief, where hast thou stowed my daughter?
　　Damned as thou art, thou hast enchanted her!
　　For I'll refer me to all things of sense,°
　　If she in chains of magic were not bound,
　　Whether a maid so tender, fair, and happy,　　　　　65
　　So opposite to marriage that she shunned
　　The wealthy, curlèd darlings of our nation,
　　Would ever have, t'incur a general mock,°
　　Run from her guardage to the sooty bosom
　　Of such a thing as thou—to fear, not to delight.　　　70
　　Judge me the world if 'tis not gross in sense°
　　That thou hast practiced° on her with foul charms,
　　Abused her delicate youth with drugs or minerals
　　That weaken motion.° I'll have't disputed on;
　　'Tis probable, and palpable to thinking.　　　　　75
　　I therefore apprehend and do attach° thee
　　For an abuser of the world, a practicer
　　Of arts inhibited and out of warrant.°
　　Lay hold upon him. If he do resist,
　　Subdue him at his peril.
OTHELLO:　　　　　　　Hold your hands,　　　　80
　　Both you of my inclining and the rest.

Were it my cue to fight, I should have known it
Without a prompter. Whither will you that I go
To answer this your charge?
BRABANTIO: To prison, till fit time
Of law and course of direct session   85
Call thee to answer.
OTHELLO: What if I do obey?
How may the Duke be therewith satisfied,
Whose messengers are here about my side
Upon some present° business of the state
To bring me to him?
OFFICER: 'Tis true, most worthy signior.   90
The Duke's in council, and your noble self
I am sure is sent for.
BRABANTIO: How? The Duke in council?
In this time of the night? Bring him away.
Mine's not an idle cause. The Duke himself,
Or any of my brothers° of the state,   95
Cannot but feel this wrong as 'twere their own;
For if such actions may have passage free,
Bondslaves and pagans shall our statesmen be.   *Exeunt.*

Scene III [A council chamber.]

Enter DUKE, SENATORS, *and* OFFICERS [*set at a table, with lights and* ATTENDANTS].

DUKE: There's no composition° in this news
That gives them credit.°
FIRST SENATOR: Indeed, they are disproportioned.
My letters say a hundred and seven galleys.
DUKE: And mine a hundred forty.
SECOND SENATOR: And mine two hundred.
But though they jump° not on a just accompt°—   5
As in these cases where the aim° reports
'Tis oft with difference—yet do they all confirm
A Turkish fleet, and bearing up to Cyprus.
DUKE: Nay, it is possible enough to judgment.°
I do not so secure me in the error,   10
But the main article I do approve
In fearful sense.°
SAILOR [*Within*]:   What, ho! What, ho! What, ho!

Enter SAILOR.

---

⁸⁹*present* *immediate.*   ⁹⁵*brothers* *i.e., the other senators.*   **I.iii.** ¹*composition agreement.*   ²*gives*
them credit *makes them believable.*   ⁵*jump* *agree.*   ⁵***just accompt*** *exact counting.*   ⁶***aim*** *ap-*
proximation.   ⁹***to judgment*** *when carefully considered.*   ¹⁰⁻¹²***I do . . . sense*** *i.e., just because the num-*
bers disagree in the reports, I do not doubt that the principal information (that the Turkish fleet is out) is fearfully true.

OFFICER: A messenger from the galleys.

DUKE: Now? What's the business?

SAILOR: The Turkish preparation makes for Rhodes.
    So was I bid report here to the State 15
    By Signior Angelo.

DUKE: How say you by this change?

FIRST SENATOR: This cannot be
    By no assay of reason. 'Tis a pageant°
    To keep us in false gaze.° When we consider
    Th' importancy of Cyprus to the Turk, 20
    And let ourselves again but understand
    That, as it more concerns the Turk than Rhodes,
    So may he with more facile question° bear it,
    For that it stands not in such warlike brace,°
    But altogether lacks th' abilities 25
    That Rhodes is dressed in. If we make thought of this,
    We must not think the Turk is so unskillful
    To leave that latest which concerns him first,
    Neglecting an attempt of ease and gain
    To wake and wage a danger profitless. 30

DUKE: Nay, in all confidence he's not for Rhodes.

OFFICER: Here is more news.

Enter a MESSENGER.

MESSENGER: The Ottomites, reverend and gracious,
    Steering with due course toward the isle of Rhodes,
    Have there injointed them with an after° fleet. 35

FIRST SENATOR: Ay, so I thought. How many, as you guess?

MESSENGER: Of thirty sail; and now they do restem
    Their backward course, bearing with frank appearance
    Their purposes toward Cyprus. Signior Montano,
    Your trusty and most valiant servitor, 40
    With his free duty° recommends° you thus,
    And prays you to believe him.

DUKE: 'Tis certain then for Cyprus.
    Marcus Luccicos, is not he in town?

FIRST SENATOR: He's now in Florence. 45

DUKE: Write from us to him; post-posthaste dispatch.

FIRST SENATOR: Here comes Brabantio and the valiant Moor.

Enter BRABANTIO, OTHELLO, CASSIO, IAGO, RODERIGO, *and* OFFICERS.

DUKE: Valiant Othello, we must straight° employ you
    Against the general° enemy Ottoman.

---

[18] *pageant* *show, pretense.*   [19] *in false gaze* *looking the wrong way.*   [23] *facile question* *easy struggle.*
[24] *warlike brace* *"military posture."*   [35] *after* *following.*   [41] *free duty* *unlimited respect.*   [41] *recom-*
mends *informs.*   [48] *straight* *at once.*   [49] *general* *universal.*

[*To* BRABANTIO] I did not see you. Welcome, gentle signior.   50
   We lacked your counsel and your help tonight.
BRABANTIO: So did I yours. Good your grace, pardon me.
   Neither my place, nor aught I heard of business,
   Hath raised me from my bed; nor doth the general care
   Take hold on me; for my particular grief   55
   Is of so floodgate and o'erbearing nature
   That it engluts and swallows other sorrows,
   And it is still itself.
DUKE: Why, what's the matter?
BRABANTIO: My daughter! O, my daughter!
SENATORS: Dead?
BRABANTIO: Ay, to me.
   She is abused, stol'n from me, and corrupted   60
   By spells and medicines bought of mountebanks;
   For nature so prepost'rously to err,
   Being not deficient, blind, or lame of sense,
   Sans° witchcraft could not.
DUKE: Whoe'er he be that in this foul proceeding   65
   Hath thus beguiled your daughter of herself,
   And you of her, the bloody book of law
   You shall yourself read in the bitter letter
   After your own sense; yea, though our proper° son
   Stood in your action.°
BRABANTIO: Humbly I thank your Grace.   70
   Here is the man—this Moor, whom now, it seems,
   Your special mandate for the state affairs
   Hath hither brought.
ALL: We are very sorry for't.
DUKE [*To* OTHELLO]: What in your own part can you say to this?
BRABANTIO: Nothing, but this is so.   75
OTHELLO: Most potent, grave, and reverend signiors,
   My very noble and approved° good masters,
   That I have ta'en away this old man's daughter,
   It is most true; true I have married her.
   The very head and front° of my offending   80
   Hath this extent, no more. Rude am I in my speech,
   And little blessed with the soft phrase of peace.
   For since these arms of mine had seven years' pith°
   Till now some nine moons wasted,° they have used
   Their dearest° action in the tented field;   85
   And little of this great world can I speak
   More than pertains to feats of broils and battle;

---

[64]**Sans** *without.*   [69]**proper** *own.*   [70]**Stood in your action** *were the accused in your suit.*   [77]**approved** *tested, proven by past performance.*   [80]**head and front** *extreme form (front = forehead).*   [83]**pith**
strength.   [84]**wasted** *past.*   [85]**dearest** *most important.*

And therefore little shall I grace my cause
In speaking for myself. Yet, by your gracious patience,
I will a round° unvarnished tale deliver   90
Of my whole course of love—what drugs, what charms,
What conjuration, and what mighty magic,
For such proceeding I am charged withal,
I won his daughter—
BRABANTIO: A maiden never bold,
Of spirit so still and quiet that her motion   95
Blushed at herself,° and she, in spite of nature,
Of years, of country, credit, everything,
To fall in love with what she feared to look on!
It is a judgment maimed and most imperfect
That will confess perfection so could err   100
Against all rules of nature, and must be driven
To find out practices of cunning hell
Why this should be. I therefore vouch again
That with some mixtures pow'rful o'er the blood,
Or with some dram, conjured to this effect,   105
He wrought upon her.
DUKE: To vouch this is no proof,
Without more wider and more overt test
Than these thin habits° and poor likelihoods
Of modern° seeming do prefer against him.
FIRST SENATOR: But, Othello, speak.   110
Did you by indirect and forcèd courses
Subdue and poison this young maid's affections?
Or came it by request, and such fair question°
As soul to soul affordeth?
OTHELLO: I do beseech you,
Send for the lady to the Sagittary   115
And let her speak of me before her father.
If you do find me foul in her report,
The trust, the office, I do hold of you
Not only take away, but let your sentence
Even fall upon my life.
DUKE: Fetch Desdemona hither.   120
OTHELLO: Ancient, conduct them; you best know the place.

[*Exit* IAGO, *with two or three* ATTENDANTS.]

And till she come, as truly as to heaven
I do confess the vices of my blood,
So justly to your grave ears I'll present
How I did thrive in this fair lady's love,   125

---

⁹⁰**round** *blunt.*   ⁹⁵⁻⁹⁶**her motion/Blushed at herself** *i.e., she was so modest that she blushed at every thought (and movement).*   ¹⁰⁸**habits** *clothing.*   ¹⁰⁹**modern** *trivial.*   ¹¹³**question** *discussion.*

And she in mine.
DUKE: Say it, Othello.
OTHELLO: Her father loved me; oft invited me;
Still° questioned me the story of my life
From year to year, the battle, sieges, fortune
That I have passed.   130
I ran it through, even from my boyish days
To th' very moment that he bade me tell it.
Wherein I spoke of most disastrous chances,
Of moving accidents by flood and field,
Of hairbreadth scapes i' th' imminent° deadly breach,   135
Of being taken by the insolent foe
And sold to slavery, of my redemption thence
And portance° in my travel's history,
Wherein of anters° vast and deserts idle,°
Rough quarries, rocks, and hills whose heads touch heaven,   140
It was my hint to speak. Such was my process.
And of the Cannibals that each other eat,
The Anthropophagi,° and men whose heads
Grew beneath their shoulders. These things to hear
Would Desdemona seriously incline;   145
But still the house affairs would draw her thence;
Which ever as she could with haste dispatch,
She'd come again, and with a greedy ear
Devour up my discourse. Which I observing,
Took once a pliant hour, and found good means   150
To draw from her a prayer of earnest heart
That I would all my pilgrimage dilate,°
Whereof by parcels she had something heard,
But not intentively.° I did consent,
And often did beguile her of her tears   155
When I did speak of some distressful stroke
That my youth suffered. My story being done,
She gave me for my pains a world of kisses.
She swore in faith 'twas strange, 'twas passing° strange;
'Twas pitiful, 'twas wondrous pitiful.   160
She wished she had not heard it; yet she wished
That heaven had made her such a man. She thanked me,
And bade me, if I had a friend that loved her,
I should but teach him how to tell my story,
And that would woo her. Upon this hint I spake.   165
She loved me for the dangers I had passed,
And I loved her that she did pity them.

128**Still** *regularly.*   135**imminent** *threatening.*   138**portance** *manner of acting.*   139**anters** *caves.*
139**idle** *empty, sterile.*   143**Anthropophagi** *maneaters.*   152**dilate** *relate in full.*   154**intentively**
at length and in sequence.   159**passing** *surpassing.*

This only is the witchcraft I have used.
Here comes the lady. Let her witness it.

Enter DESDEMONA, IAGO, ATTENDANTS.

DUKE: I think this tale would win my daughter too.   170
    Good Brabantio, take up this mangled matter at the best.°
    Men do their broken weapons rather use
    Than their bare hands.
BRABANTIO: I pray you hear her speak.
    If she confess that she was half the wooer,
    Destruction on my head if my bad blame   175
    Light on the man. Come hither, gentle mistress.
    Do you perceive in all this noble company
    Where most you owe obedience?
DESDEMONA: My noble father,
    I do perceive here a divided duty.
    To you I am bound for life and education;   180
    My life and education both do learn me
    How to respect you. You are the lord of duty,
    I am hitherto your daughter. But here's my husband,
    And so much duty as my mother showed
    To you, preferring you before her father,   185
    So much I challenge° that I may profess
    Due to the Moor my lord.
BRABANTIO: God be with you. I have done.
    Please it your Grace, on to the state affairs.
    I had rather to adopt a child than get° it.
    Come hither, Moor.   190
    I here do give thee that with all my heart
    Which, but thou hast already, with all my heart
    I would keep from thee. For your sake,° jewel,
    I am glad at soul I have no other child,
    For thy escape would teach me tyranny,   195
    To hang clogs on them. I have done, my lord.
DUKE: Let me speak like yourself and lay a sentence°
    Which, as a grise° or step, may help these lovers.
    When remedies are past, the griefs are ended
    By seeing the worst, which late on hopes depended.°   200
    To mourn a mischief that is past and gone
    Is the next° way to draw new mischief on.
    What cannot be preserved when fortune takes,
    Patience her injury a mock'ry makes.
    The robbed that smiles, steals something from the thief;   205

---

[171]**take . . . best**   *i.e., make the best of this disaster.*   [186]**challenge**   *claim as right.*   [189]**get**   *beget.*
[193]**For your sake**   *because of you.*   [197]**lay a sentence**   *provide a maxim.*   [198]**grise**   *step.*   [200]**late**
on hopes depended   *was supported by hope (of a better outcome) until lately.*   [202]**next**   *closest, surest.*

He robs himself that spends a bootless° grief.
BRABANTIO: So let the Turk of Cyprus us beguile:
    We lose it not so long as we can smile.
    He bears the sentence well that nothing bears
    But the free comfort which from thence he hears;   210
    But he bears both the sentence and the sorrow
    That to pay grief must of poor patience borrow.
    These sentences, to sugar, or to gall,
    Being strong on both sides, are equivocal.
    But words are words. I never yet did hear   215
    That the bruisèd heart was piercèd° through the ear.
    I humbly beseech you, proceed to th' affairs of state.
DUKE: The Turk with a most mighty preparation makes for Cyprus. Othello, the
    fortitude° of the place is best known to you; and though we have there a
    substitute° of most allowed sufficiency,° yet opinion, a more sovereign mistress 220
    of effects, throws a more safer voice on you.° You must therefore be content to
    slubber° the gloss of your new fortunes with this more stubborn and
    boisterous° expedition.
OTHELLO: The tyrant Custom, most grave senators,
    Hath made the flinty and steel couch of war   225
    My thrice-driven° bed of down. I do agnize°
    A natural and prompt alacrity
    I find in hardness and do undertake
    These present wars against the Ottomites.
    Most humbly, therefore, bending to your state,   230
    I crave fit disposition for my wife,
    Due reference of place, and exhibition,°
    With such accommodation and besort
    As levels with° her breeding.
DUKE: Why, at her father's.
BRABANTIO: I will not have it so.
OTHELLO: Nor I.   235
DESDEMONA: Nor would I there reside,
    To put my father in impatient thoughts
    By being in his eye. Most gracious Duke,
    To my unfolding° lend your prosperous° ear,
    And let me find a charter° in your voice,   240
    T' assist my simpleness.

206*bootless* valueless.   216*piercèd* (some editors emend to piecèd, i.e., "healed." But piercèd makes good
sense: Brabantio is saying in effect that his heart cannot be further hurt [pierced] by the indignity of the useless, conventional advice the Duke offers him. Piercèd can also mean, however, "lanced" in the medical sense, and would then mean
"treated").   219*fortitude* fortification.   220*substitute* viceroy.   220*most allowed sufficiency* generally acknowledged capability.   220-221*opinion. . . you* i.e., the general opinion, which finally controls affairs,
is that you would be the best man in this situation.   222*slubber* besmear.   223*stubborn and boisterous*
rough and violent.   226*thrice-driven* i.e., softest.   226*agnize* known in myself.   232*exhibition*
grant of funds.   234*levels with* is suitable to.   239*unfolding* explanation.   239*prosperous* favoring.
240*charter* permission.

DUKE: What would you, Desdemona?

DESDEMONA: That I love the Moor to live with him,
My downright violence, and storm of fortunes,
May trumpet to the world. My heart's subdued
Even to the very quality of my lord.° 245
I saw Othello's visage in his mind,
And to his honors and his valiant parts
Did I my soul and fortunes consecrate.
So that, dear lords, if I be left behind,
A moth of peace, and he go to the war, 250
The rites° for why I love him are bereft me,
And I a heavy interim shall support
By his dear absence. Let me go with him.

OTHELLO: Let her have your voice.°
Vouch with me, heaven, I therefore beg it not 255
To please the palate of my appetite,
Nor to comply with heat°—the young affects°
In me defunct—and proper satisfaction;°
But to be free and bounteous to her mind;
And heaven defend° your good souls that you think 260
I will your serious and great business scant
When she is with me. No, when light-winged toys
Of feathered Cupid seel° with wanton° dullness
My speculative and officed instrument,°
That my disports corrupt and taint my business, 265
Let housewives make a skillet of my helm,
And all indign° and base adversities
Make head° against my estimation!°—

DUKE: Be it as you shall privately determine,
Either for her stay or going. Th' affair cries haste, 270
And speed must answer it.

FIRST SENATOR: You must away tonight.

OTHELLO: With all my heart.

DUKE: At nine i' th' morning here we'll meet again.
Othello, leave some officer behind,
And he shall our commission bring to you, 275
And such things else of quality and respect
As doth import you.

OTHELLO: So please your grace, my ancient;
A man he is of honesty and trust.

---

²⁴⁴⁻²⁴⁵**My . . . lord** *i.e., I have become one in nature and being with the man I married (therefore, I too would go to the wars like a soldier).* ²⁵¹**rites** *(may refer either to the marriage rites or to the rites, formalities, of war).* ²⁵⁴**voice** *consent.* ²⁵⁷**heat** *lust.* ²⁵⁷**affects** *passions.* ²⁵⁸**proper satisfaction** *i.e., consummation of the marriage.* ²⁶⁰**defend** *forbid.* ²⁶³**seel** *sew up.* ²⁶³**wanton** *lascivious.* ²⁶⁴**speculative . . . instrument** *i.e., sight (and, by extension, the mind).* ²⁶⁷**indign** *unworthy.* ²⁶⁸**Make head** *form an army, i.e., attack.* ²⁶⁸**estimation** *reputation.*

To his conveyance I assign my wife,
With what else needful your good grace shall think   280
  to be sent after me.
DUKE: Let it be so.
  Good night to every one. [*To* BRABANTIO] And, noble signior,
  If virtue no delighted° beauty lack,
  Your son-in-law is far more fair than black.
FIRST SENATOR: Adieu, brave Moor. Use Desdemona well.   285
BRABANTIO: Look to her, Moor, if thou hast eyes to see:
  She has deceived her father, and may thee.

        [*Exeunt* DUKE, SENATORS, OFFICERS, *& c.*]

OTHELLO: My life upon her faith! Honest Iago,
  My Desdemona must I leave to thee.
  I prithee let thy wife attend on her,   290
  And bring them after in the best advantage.°
  Come, Desdemona. I have but an hour
  Of love, of worldly matter, and direction
  To spend with thee. We must obey the time.

        Exit [MOOR *with* DESDEMONA].

RODERIGO: Iago?   295
IAGO: What say'st thou, noble heart?
RODERIGO: What will I do, think'st thou?
IAGO: Why, go to bed and sleep.
RODERIGO: I will incontinently° drown myself.
IAGO: If thou dost, I shall never love thee after. Why, thou silly gentleman?   300
RODERIGO: It is silliness to live when to live is torment; and then have we a
  prescription to die when death is our physician.
IAGO: O villainous! I have looked upon the world for four times seven years, and
  since I could distinguish betwixt a benefit and an injury, I never found man that
  knew how to love himself. Ere I would say I would drown myself for the love   305
  of a guinea hen, I would change my humanity with a baboon.
RODERIGO: What should I do? I confess it is my shame to be so fond, but it is not
  in my virtue° to amend it.
IAGO: Virtue? A fig! 'Tis in ourselves that we are thus, or thus. Our bodies are our   310
  gardens, to the which our wills are gardeners; so that if we will plant nettles or
  sow lettuce, set hyssop and weed up thyme, supply it with one gender of herbs
  or distract° it with many—either to have it sterile with idleness or manured
  with industry—why, the power and corrigible° authority of this lies in our
  wills. If the balance of our lives had not one scale of reason to poise another of   315
  sensuality, the blood and baseness of our natures would conduct us to most
  prepost'rous conclusions.° But we have reason to cool our raging motions, our

---

283*delighted* delightful.   291*advantage* opportunity.   299*incontinently* at once.   309*virtue*
strength (Roderigo is saying that his nature controls him).   313*distract* vary.   314*corrigible* corrective.
317*conclusions* ends.

carnal sting or unbitted° lusts, whereof I take this that you call love to be a sect or scion.°

RODERIGO: It cannot be.   320

IAGO: It is merely a lust of the blood and a permission of the will. Come, be a man! Drown thyself? Drown cats and blind puppies! I have professed me thy friend, and I confess me knit to thy deserving with cables of perdurable toughness. I could never better stead° thee than now. Put money in thy purse. Follow thou the wars; defeat thy favor° with an usurped° beard. I say, put 325 money in thy purse. It cannot be long that Desdemona should continue her love to the Moor. Put money in thy purse. Nor he his to her. It was a violent commencement in her and thou shalt see an answerable° sequestration—put but money in thy purse. These Moors are changeable in their wills—fill thy 330 purse with money. The food that to him now is as luscious as locusts° shall be to him shortly as bitter as coloquintida.° She must change for youth; when she is sated with his body, she will find the errors of her choice. Therefore, put money in thy purse. If thou wilt needs damn thyself, do it a more delicate way than drowning. Make all the money thou canst. If sanctimony° and a frail vow 335 betwixt an erring° barbarian and supersubtle Venetian be not too hard for my wits, and all the tribe of hell, thou shalt enjoy her. Therefore, make money. A pox of drowning thyself, it is clean out of the way. Seek thou rather to be hanged in compassing° thy joy than to be drowned and go without her.   340

RODERIGO: Wilt thou be fast to my hopes, if I depend on the issue?

IAGO: Thou art sure of me. Go, make money. I have told thee often, and I retell thee again and again, I hate the Moor. My cause is hearted;° thine hath no less reason. Let us be conjunctive° in our revenge against him. If thou canst cuckold him, thou dost thyself a pleasure, me a sport. There are many events in the 345 womb of time, which will be delivered. Traverse, go, provide thy money! We will have more of this tomorrow. Adieu.

RODERIGO: Where shall we meet i' th' morning?

IAGO: At my lodging.

RODERIGO: I'll be with thee betimes.   350

IAGO: Go to, farewell. Do you hear, Roderigo?

RODERIGO: I'll sell all my land.   *Exit.*

IAGO: Thus do I ever make my fool my purse;
   For I mine own gained knowledge° should profane
   If I would time expend with such snipe   355
   But for my sport and profit. I hate the Moor,
   And it is thought abroad that 'twixt my sheets
   H'as done my office. I know not if't be true,
   But I, for mere suspicion in that kind,
   Will do, as if for surety.° He holds me well;   360

---

³¹⁸*unbitted* *i.e., uncontrolled.*   ³¹⁹*sect or scion* *off-shoot.*   ³²⁴*stead* *serve.*   ³²⁵*defeat thy favor*
disguise your face.   ³²⁵*usurped* *assumed.*   ³²⁹*answerable* *similar.*   ³³¹*locusts* *(a sweet fruit).*
³³²*coloquintida* *a purgative derived from a bitter apple.*   ³³⁵*sanctimony* *sacred bond (of marriage).*
³³⁶*erring* *wandering.*   ³³⁹*compassing* *encompassing, achieving.*   ³⁴³*hearted* *deepseated in the heart.*
³⁴⁴*conjunctive* *joined.*   ³⁵⁴*gained knowledge* *i.e., practical, worldly wisdom.*   ³⁶⁰*surety* *certainty.*

The better shall my purpose work on him.
Cassio's a proper° man. Let me see now:
To get his place, and to plume up my will°
In double knavery. How? How? Let's see.
After some time, to abuse Othello's ears   365
That he is too familiar with his wife.
He hath a person and a smooth dispose°
To be suspected—framed° to make women false.
The Moor is of a free and open nature
That thinks men honest that but seem to be so;   370
And will as tenderly be led by th' nose
As asses are.
I have't! It is engendered! Hell and night
Must bring this monstrous birth to the world's light.   [*Exit.*]

ACT II

Scene I [*Cyprus.*]

Enter MONTANO *and two* GENTLEMEN [*one above*]°.

MONTANO: What from the cape can you discern at sea?
FIRST GENTLEMAN: Nothing at all, it is a high-wrought flood.
   I cannot 'twixt the heaven and the main
   Descry a sail.
MONTANO: Methinks the wind hath spoke aloud at land;   5
   A fuller blast ne'er shook our battlements.
   If it hath ruffianed so upon the sea,
   What ribs of oak, when mountains melt on them,
   Can hold the mortise? What shall we hear of this?
SECOND GENTLEMAN: A segregation° of the Turkish fleet.   10
   For do but stand upon the foaming shore,
   The chidden billow seems to pelt the clouds;
   The wind-shaked surge, with high and monstrous main,°
   Seems to cast water on the burning Bear
   And quench the guards of th' ever-fixèd pole.°   15
   I never did like molestation view
   On the enchafèd flood.

362*proper* handsome.   363*plume up my will* (*many explanations have been offered for this crucial line, which in Q1, reads "make up my will." The general sense is something like "to make more proud and gratify my ego"*). 367*dispose* manner.   368*framed* designed.   **II.i. s.d. above** (*the Folio arrangement of this scene requires that the First Gentleman stand above—on the upper stage—and act as a lookout reporting sights which cannot be seen by Montano standing below on the main stage*).   10*segregation* separation.   13*main* (*both "ocean" and "strength"*).   14–15*Seems . . . pole* (*the constellation Ursa Minor contains two stars which are the guards, or companions, of the pole, or North Star*).

MONTANO: If that the Turkish fleet
   Be not ensheltered and embayed, they are drowned;
   It is impossible to bear it out.

Enter a [third] GENTLEMAN.

THIRD GENTLEMAN: News, lads! Our wars are done.   20
   The desperate tempest hath so banged the Turks
   That their designment halts. A noble ship of Venice
   Hath seen a grievous wrack and sufferance°
   On most part of their fleet.
MONTANO: How? Is this true?
THIRD GENTLEMAN: The ship is here put in,   25
   A Veronesa; Michael Cassio,
   Lieutenant to the warlike Moor Othello,
   Is come on shore; the Moor himself at sea,
   And is in full commission here for Cyprus.
MONTANO: I am glad on't. 'Tis a worthy governor.   30
THIRD GENTLEMAN: But this same Cassio, though he speak of comfort
   Touching the Turkish loss, yet he looks sadly
   And prays the Moor be safe, for they were parted
   With foul and violent tempest.
MONTANO: Pray heavens he be;
   For I have served him, and the man commands   35
   Like a full soldier. Let's to the seaside, ho!
   As well to see the vessel that's come in
   As to throw out our eyes for brave Othello,
   Even till we make the main and th' aerial blue
   An indistinct regard.°
THIRD GENTLEMAN: Come, let's do so;   40
   For every minute is expectancy
   Of more arrivancie.°

Enter CASSIO.

CASSIO: Thanks, you the valiant of the warlike isle,
   That so approve° the Moor. O, let the heavens
   Give him defense against the elements,   45
   For I have lost him on a dangerous sea.
MONTANO: Is he well shipped?
CASSIO: His bark is stoutly timbered, and his pilot
   Of very expert and approved allowance;°
   Therefore my hopes, not surfeited to death,°   50
   Stand in bold cure.° (*Within:* A sail, a sail, a sail!)

---

²³*sufferance* damage.   ³⁹⁻⁴⁰*the main . . . regard* *i.e., the sea and sky become indistinguishable.*   ⁴²*ar-rivancie* *arrivals.*   ⁴⁴*approve* *("honor" or, perhaps, "are as warlike and valiant as your governor").*   ⁴⁹*approved allowance* *known and tested.*   ⁵⁰*not surfeited to death* *i.e., not so great as to be in danger.*   ⁵¹*Stand in bold cure* *i.e., are likely to be restored.*

CASSIO: What noise?

FIRST GENTLEMAN: The town is empty; on the brow o' th' sea
　　Stand ranks of people, and they cry, "A sail!"

CASSIO: My hopes do shape him for the governor.　　　　　　　　　　[*A shot.*] 55

SECOND GENTLEMAN: They do discharge their shot of courtesy:
　　Our friends at least.

CASSIO:　　　　　　　　　I pray you, sir, go forth
　　And give us truth who 'tis that is arrived.

SECOND GENTLEMAN: I shall.　　　　　　　　　　　　　　　　　[*Exit.*]

MONTANO: But, good lieutenant, is your general wived?　　　　　　60

CASSIO: Most fortunately. He hath achieved a maid
　　That paragons° description and wild fame;°
　　One that excels the quirks of blazoning pens,°
　　And in th' essential vesture of creation°
　　Does tire the ingener.°

　　　　　　　　　　Enter [*Second*] GENTLEMAN.

　　　　　　　　　How now? Who has put in?　　　　　　　　　65

SECOND GENTLEMAN: 'Tis one Iago, ancient to the general.

CASSIO: H'as had most favorable and happy speed:
　　Tempests themselves, high seas, and howling winds,
　　The guttered° rocks and congregated° sands,
　　Traitors ensteeped° to enclog the guiltless keel,　　　　　　　70
　　As having sense° of beauty, do omit
　　Their mortal° natures, letting go safely by
　　The divine Desdemona.

MONTANO:　　　　　　　　What is she?

CASSIO: She that I spake of, our great captain's captain,
　　Left in the conduct of the bold Iago,　　　　　　　　　　75
　　Whose footing° here anticipates our thoughts
　　A se'nnight's° speed. Great Jove, Othello guard,
　　And swell his sail with thine own pow'rful breath,
　　That he may bless this bay with his tall° ship,
　　Make love's quick pants in Desdemona's arms,　　　　　　80
　　Give renewed fire to our extincted spirits,
　　And bring all Cyprus comfort!

　　　　　　Enter DESDEMONA, IAGO, RODERIGO, *and* EMILIA.

　　O, behold! The riches of the ship is come on shore!
　　You men of Cyprus, let her have your knees.　　　　　　[*Kneeling.*]
　　Hail to thee, lady! and the grace of heaven,
　　Before, behind thee, and on every hand,　　　　　　　　85

---

⁶²*paragons* exceeds.　　⁶²*wild fame* extravagant report.　　⁶³*quirks of blazoning pens* ingenuities of praising pens.　　⁶⁴*essential vesture of creation* essential human nature as given by the Creator.　　⁶⁵*tire the ingener* a difficult line that probably means something like "outdo the human ability to imagine and picture."　　⁶⁹*guttered* jagged.　　⁶⁹*congregated* gathered.　　⁷⁰*ensteeped* submerged.　　⁷¹*sense* awareness.　　⁷²*mortal* deadly.　　⁷⁶*footing* landing.　　⁷⁷*se'n-night's* week's.　　⁷⁹*tall* brave.

Enwheel thee round.

DESDEMONA: I thank you, valiant Cassio.
What tidings can you tell of my lord?

CASSIO: He is not yet arrived, nor know I aught
But that he's well and will be shortly here.

DESDEMONA: O but I fear. How lost you company?   90

CASSIO: The great contention of sea and skies
Parted our fellowship. (*Within:* A sail, a sail!)   [*A shot.*]
But hark. A sail!

SECOND GENTLEMAN: They give this greeting to the citadel;
This likewise is a friend.

CASSIO: See for the news.   [*Exit* GENTLEMAN.]   95
Good ancient, you are welcome. [*To* EMILIA] Welcome, mistress.
Let it not gall your patience, good Iago,
That I extend° my manners. 'Tis my breeding°
That gives me this bold show of courtesy.   [*Kisses* EMILIA.]

IAGO: Sir, would she give you so much of her lips   100
As of her tongue she oft bestows on me,
You would have enough.

DESDEMONA: Alas, she has no speech.

IAGO: In faith, too much.
I find it still when I have leave to sleep.°
Marry, before your ladyship,° I grant,   105
She puts her tongue a little in her heart
And chides with thinking.

EMILIA: You have little cause to say so.

IAGO: Come on, come on! You are pictures° out of door,
Bells in your parlors, wildcats in your kitchens,
Saints in your injuries,° devils being offended,   110
Players in your housewifery,° and housewives in your beds.

DESDEMONA: O, fie upon thee, slanderer!

IAGO: Nay, it is true, or else I am a Turk:
You rise to play, and go to bed to work.

EMILIA: You shall not write my praise.

IAGO: No, let me not.   115

DESDEMONA: What wouldst write of me, if thou shouldst praise me?

IAGO: O gentle lady, do not put me to't.
For I am nothing if not critical.

DESDEMONA: Come on, assay. There's one gone to the harbor?

IAGO: Ay, madam.

---

⁹⁸**extend**   *stretch.*   ⁹⁸**breeding**   *careful training in manners (Cassio is considerably more the polished gentleman than Iago, and aware of it).*   ¹⁰⁴**still . . . sleep**   *i.e., even when she allows me to sleep she continues to scold.*
¹⁰⁵**before your ladyship**   *in your presence.*   ¹⁰⁸**pictures**   *models (of virtue).*   ¹¹⁰**in your injuries**   *when you injure others.*   ¹¹¹**housewifery**   *this word can mean "careful, economical household management," and Iago would then be accusing women of only pretending to be good housekeepers, while in bed they are either [1] economical of their favors, or more likely [2] serious and dedicated workers.*

DESDEMONA [*Aside*]: I am not merry; but I do beguile   120
  The thing I am by seeming otherwise.—
  Come, how wouldst thou praise me?
IAGO: I am about it; but indeed my invention
  Comes from my pate as birdlime° does from frieze°—
  It plucks out brains and all. But my Muse labors,   125
  And thus she is delivered:
  If she be fair° and wise: fairness and wit,
  The one's for use, the other useth it.
DESDEMONA: Well praised. How if she be black° and witty?
IAGO: If she be black, and thereto have a wit,   130
  She'll find a white that shall her blackness fit.
DESDEMONA: Worse and worse!
EMILIA: How if fair and foolish?
IAGO: She never yet was foolish that was fair,
  For even her folly helped her to an heir.   135
DESDEMONA: Those are old fond° paradoxes to make fools laugh i' th' alehouse.
  What miserable praise hast thou for her that's foul and foolish?
IAGO: There's none so foul, and foolish thereunto,
  But does foul pranks which fair and wise ones do.
DESDEMONA: O heavy ignorance. Thou praisest the worst best. But what praise
  couldst thou bestow on a deserving woman indeed—one that in the authority 140
  of her merit did justly put on the vouch of very malice itself?°
IAGO: She that was ever fair, and never proud;
  Had tongue at will, and yet was never loud;   145
  Never lacked gold, and yet went never gay;
  Fled from her wish, and yet said "Now I may";
  She that being angered, her revenge being nigh,
  Bade her wrong stay, and her displeasure fly;
  She that in wisdom never was so frail   150
  To change the cod's head for the salmon's tail;°
  She that could think, and nev'r disclose her mind;
  See suitors following, and not look behind:
  She was a wight° (if ever such wights were)—
DESDEMONA: To do what?   155
IAGO: To suckle fools and chronicle small beer.°
DESDEMONA: O most lame and impotent conclusion. Do not learn of him, Emilia,
  though he be thy husband. How say you, Cassio? Is he not a most profane and
  liberal° counselor?
CASSIO: He speaks home,° madam. You may relish him more in° the soldier than 160
  in the scholar. [*Takes* DESDEMONA's *hand.*]

124**birdlime** *a sticky substance put on branches to catch birds.* 124**frieze** *rough cloth.* 127**fair** *light-complexioned.* 129**black** *brunette.* 136**fond** *foolish.* 141–143**one . . . itself** *i.e., a woman so honest and deserving that even malice would be forced to approve of her.* 151**To . . . tail** *i.e., to exchange something valuable for something useless.* 154**wight** *person.* 156**chronicle small beer** *i.e., keep household accounts (the most trivial of occupations in Iago's opinion).* 159**liberal** *licentious.* 160**speaks home** *thrusts deeply with his speech.* 60**relish him more in** *enjoy him more as.*

IAGO [*Aside*]: He takes her by the palm. Ay, well said, whisper! With as little a web
as this will I ensnare as great a fly as Cassio. Ay, smile upon her, do! I will gyve°
thee in thine own courtship.—You say true; 'tis so, indeed!—If such tricks as
these strip you out of your lieutenantry, it had been better you had not kissed   165
your three fingers so oft—which now again you are most apt to play the sir° in.
Very good! Well kissed! An excellent curtsy!° 'Tis so, indeed. Yet again your
fingers to your lips? Would they were clyster pipes° for your sake! [*Trumpets
within.*] The Moor! I know his trumpet.°   170
CASSIO: 'Tis truly so.
DESDEMONA: Let's meet him and receive him.
CASSIO: Lo, where he comes.

Enter OTHELLO *and* ATTENDANTS.

OTHELLO: O my fair warrior!
DESDEMONA: My dear Othello.
OTHELLO: It gives me wonder great as my content   175
    To see you here before me. O my soul's joy!
    If after every tempest come such calms,
    May the winds blow till they have wakened death.
    And let the laboring bark climb hills of seas
    Olympus-high, and duck again as low   180
    As hell's from heaven. If it were now to die,
    'Twere now to be most happy; for I fear
    My soul hath her content so absolute
    That not another comfort like to this
    Succeeds in unknown fate.
DESDEMONA: The heavens forbid   185
    But that our loves and comforts should increase
    Even as our days do grow.
OTHELLO: Amen to that, sweet powers!
    I cannot speak enough of this content:
    It stops me here [*touches his heart*]; it is too much of joy.
    And this, and this, the greatest discords be   [*They kiss.*] 190
    That e'er our hearts shall make!
IAGO [*Aside*]:   O, you are well tuned now!
    But I'll set down the pegs° that make this music,
    As honest as I am.
OTHELLO: Come, let us to the castle.
    News, friends! Our wars are done; the Turks are drowned.
    How does my old acquaintance of this isle?   195
    Honey, you shall be well desired in Cyprus;
    I have found great love amongst them. O my sweet,
    I prattle out of fashion, and I dote

---

¹⁶⁴**gyve** *bind.*   ¹⁶⁷**the sir** *the fashionable gentleman.*   ¹⁶⁸**curtsy** *courtesy, i.e., bow.*   ¹⁶⁹**clyster
pipes** *enema tubes.*   ¹⁷⁰**his trumpet** *(great men had their own distinctive calls).*   ¹⁹²**set down the pegs**
loosen the strings (to produce discord).

In mine own comforts. I prithee, good Iago,
Go to the bay and disembark my coffers.   200
Bring thou the master to the citadel;
He is a good one and his worthiness
Does challenge° much respect. Come, Desdemona,
Once more well met at Cyprus.

Exit OTHELLO *and* DESDEMONA [*and all but* IAGO *and* RODERIGO].

IAGO [*To an Attendant*]: Do thou meet me presently at the harbor. [*To* RODERIGO] 205
    Come hither. If thou be'st valiant (as they say base men being in love have then
    a nobility in their natures more than is native to them), list me. The lieutenant
    tonight watches on the court of guard.° First, I must tell thee this: Desdemona
    is directly in love with him.
RODERIGO: With him? Why, 'tis not possible.   210
IAGO: Lay thy finger thus [*puts his finger to his lips*], and let thy soul be instructed.
    Mark me with what violence she first loved the Moor but for bragging and
    telling her fantastical lies. To love him still for prating? Let not thy discreet heart
    think it. Her eye must be fed. And what delight shall she have to look on the
    devil? When the blood is made dull with the act of sport, there should be a   215
    game° to inflame it and to give satiety a fresh appetite, loveliness in favor,°
    sympathy in years,° manners, and beauties; all which the Moor is defective in.
    Now for want of these required conveniences,° her delicate tenderness will find
    itself abused, begin to heave the gorge,° disrelish and abhor the Moor. Very
    nature will instruct her in it and compel her to some second choice. Now sir,   220
    this granted—as it is a most pregnant° and unforced position—who stands so
    eminent in the degree of this fortune as Cassio does? A knave very voluble; no
    further conscionable° than in putting on the mere form of civil and humane°
    seeming for the better compass of his salt° and most hidden loose° affection.
    Why, none! Why, none! A slipper° and subtle knave, a finder of occasion, that   225
    has an eye can stamp and counterfeit advantages, though true advantage never
    present itself. A devilish knave. Besides, the knave is handsome, young, and hath
    all those requisites in him that folly and green minds look after. A pestilent
    complete knave, and the woman hath found him already.   230
RODERIGO: I cannot believe that in her; she's full of most blessed condition.
IAGO: Blessed fig's-end! The wine she drinks is made of grapes. If she had been
    blessed, she would never have loved the Moor. Blessed pudding! Didst thou not
    see her paddle with the palm of his hand? Didst not mark that?   235
RODERIGO: Yes, that I did; but that was but courtesy.
IAGO: Lechery, by this hand! [*Extends his index finger.*] An index° and obscure
    prologue to the history of lust and foul thoughts. They met so near with their
    lips that their breaths embraced together. Villainous thoughts, Roderigo. When

---

²⁰³*challenge*   *require, exact.*   ²⁰⁸*court of guard*   *guardhouse.*   ²¹⁶*game*   *sport (with the added sense of*
"gamey," "rank").   ²¹⁷*favor*   *countenance, appearance.*   ²¹⁷*sympathy in years*   *sameness of age.*
²¹⁹*conveniences*   *advantages.*   ²²⁰*heave the gorge*   *vomit.*   ²²²*pregnant*   *likely.*   ²²³⁻²²⁴*no fur-*
ther conscionable   *having no more conscience.*   ²²⁴*humane*   *polite.*   ²²⁵*salt*   *lecherous.*   ²²⁵*loose*
immoral.   ²²⁶*slipper*   *slippery.*   ²³⁷*index*   *pointer.*

these mutualities so marshal the way, hard at hand comes the master and main 240
exercise, th' incorporate° conclusion: Pish! But, sir, be you ruled by me. I have
brought you from Venice. Watch you tonight; for the command, I'll lay't upon
you. Cassio knows you not. I'll not be far from you. Do you find some occasion
to anger Cassio, either by speaking too loud, or tainting° his discipline, or from 245
what other course you please which the time shall more favorably minister.

RODERIGO: Well.

IAGO: Sir, he's rash and very sudden in choler,° and haply may strike at you.
Provoke him that he may; for even out of that will I cause these of Cyprus to
mutiny, whose qualification shall come into no true taste° again but by the 250
displanting of Cassio. So shall you have a shorter journey to your desires by the
means I shall then have to prefer them; and the impediment most profitably
removed without the which there were no expectation of our prosperity.

RODERIGO: I will do this if you can bring it to any opportunity. 255

IAGO: I warrant thee. Meet me by and by at the citadel. I must fetch his
necessaries ashore. Farewell.

RODERIGO: Adieu. *Exit.*

IAGO: That Cassio loves her, I do well believe't;
That she loves him, 'tis apt and of great credit. 260
The Moor, howbeit that I endure him not,
Is of a constant, loving, noble nature,
And I dare think he'll prove to Desdemona
A most dear° husband. Now I do love her too;
Not out of absolute° lust, though peradventure° 265
I stand accountant for as great a sin,
But partly led to diet° my revenge,
For that I do suspect the lusty Moor
Hath leaped into my seat; the thought whereof
Doth, like a poisonous mineral, gnaw my inwards; 270
And nothing can or shall content my soul
Till I am evened with him, wife for wife.
Or failing so, yet that I put the Moor
At least into a jealousy so strong
That judgment cannot cure. Which thing to do, 275
If this poor trash of Venice, whom I trace°
For his quick hunting, stand the putting on,
I'll have our Michael Cassio on the hip,
Abuse him to the Moor in the right garb°
(For I fear Cassio with my nightcap too), 280
Make the Moor thank me, love me, and reward me
For making him egregiously an ass

---

²⁴¹*incorporate* *carnal.* ²⁴⁵*tainting* *discrediting.* ²⁴⁸*choler* *anger.* ²⁵⁰*qualification . . . taste* *i.e., appeasement will not be brought about (wine was "qualified" by adding water).* ²⁶⁴*dear* *expensive* ²⁶⁵*out of absolute* *absolutely out of.* ²⁶⁵*peradventure* *perchance.* ²⁶⁷*diet* *feed.* ²⁷⁶*trace* *(most editors emend to "trash," meaning to hang weights on a dog to slow his hunting: but "trace" clearly means something like "put on the trace" or "set on the track").* ²⁷⁹*right garb* *i.e., "proper fashion."*

And practicing upon° his peace and quiet,
Even to madness. 'Tis here, but yet confused:
Knavery's plain face is never seen till used.   *Exit.* 285

Scene II [*A street.*]

Enter OTHELLO'S HERALD, *with a proclamation.*

HERALD: It is Othello's pleasure, our noble and valiant general, that upon certain
tidings now arrived importing the mere perdition° of the Turkish fleet, every
man put himself into triumph. Some to dance, some to make bonfires, each
man to what sport and revels his addition° leads him. For, besides these
beneficial news, it is the celebration of his nuptial. So much was his pleasure   5
should be proclaimed. All offices° are open, and there is full liberty of feasting
from this present hour of five till the bell have told eleven. Bless the isle of
Cyprus and our noble general Othello!   *Exit.*

Scene III [*The citadel of Cyprus.*]

Enter OTHELLO, DESDEMONA, CASSIO, *and* ATTENDANTS.

OTHELLO: Good Michael, look you to the guard tonight.
   Let's teach ourselves that honorable stop,
   Not to outsport discretion.
CASSIO: Iago hath direction what to do;
   But notwithstanding, with my personal eye   5
   Will I look to't.
OTHELLO: Iago is most honest.
   Michael, good night. Tomorrow with your earliest
   Let me have speech with you. [*To* DESDEMONA] Come, my dear love,
   The purchase made, the fruits are to ensue.
   That profit's yet to come 'tween me and you.   10
   Good night.   *Exit* [OTHELLO *with* DESDEMONA *and* ATTENDANTS].

Enter IAGO.

CASSIO: Welcome, Iago. We must to the watch.
IAGO: Not this hour, lieutenant; 'tis not yet ten o' th' clock. Our general cast° us
   thus early for the love of his Desdemona; who let us not therefore blame. He
   hath not yet made wanton the night with her, and she is sport for Jove.   15
CASSIO: She's a most exquisite lady.
IAGO: And, I'll warrant her, full of game.
CASSIO: Indeed, she's a most fresh and delicate creature.
IAGO: What an eye she has! Methinks it sounds a parley to provocation.
CASSIO: An inviting eye; and yet methinks right modest.   20

___

²⁸³**practicing upon** *scheming to destroy.*   **II.ii.** ²**mere perdition** *absolute destruction.*   ⁴**addition**
rank.   ⁶**offices** *kitchens and storerooms of food.*   **II.iii.** ¹³**cast** *dismissed.*

IAGO: And when she speaks, is it not an alarum° to love?

CASSIO: She is indeed perfection.

IAGO: Well, happiness to their sheets! Come, lieutenant, I have a stoup° of wine, and here without are a brace of Cyprus gallants that would fain have a measure 25 to the health of black Othello.

CASSIO: Not tonight, good Iago. I have very poor and unhappy brains for drinking; I could well wish courtesy would invent some other custom of entertainment.

IAGO: O, they are our friends. But one cup! I'll drink for you. 30

CASSIO: I have drunk but one tonight, and that was craftily qualified° too; and behold what innovation it makes here. I am unfortunate in the infirmity and dare not task my weakness with any more.

IAGO: What, man! 'Tis a night of revels, the gallants desire it.

CASSIO: Where are they? 35

IAGO: Here, at the door. I pray you call them in.

CASSIO: I'll do't, but it dislikes me.   *Exit.*

IAGO: If I can fasten but one cup upon him
 With that which he hath drunk tonight already,
 He'll be as full of quarrel and offense 40
 As my young mistress' dog. Now, my sick fool Roderigo,
 Whom love hath turned almost the wrong side out,
 To Desdemona hath tonight caroused
 Potations pottle-deep;° and he's to watch.
 Three else° of Cyprus, noble swelling spirits, 45
 That hold their honors in a wary distance,°
 The very elements of this warlike isle,
 Have I tonight flustered with flowing cups,
 And they watch too. Now, 'mongst this flock of drunkards
 Am I to put our Cassio in some action 50
 That may offend the isle. But here they come.

Enter CASSIO, MONTANO, *and* GENTLEMEN.

 If consequence do but approve my dream,
 My boat sails freely, both with wind and stream.

CASSIO: 'Fore God, they have given me a rouse° already.

MONTANO: Good faith, a little one; not past a pint, as I am a soldier. 55

IAGO: Some wine, ho!
 [*Sings*] And let me the canakin clink, clink;
    And let me the canakin clink.
     A soldier's a man;
     O man's life's but a span. 60
    Why then, let a soldier drink.
 Some wine, boys!

---

[22]*alarum* *the call to action, "general quarters."* [24]*stoup* *two-quart tankard.* [31]*qualified* *diluted.*
[44]*pottle-deep* *to the bottom of the cup.* [45]*else* *others.* [46]*hold . . . distance* *are scrupulous in main-taining their honor.* [54]*rouse* *drink.*

CASSIO: 'Fore God, an excellent song!

IAGO: I learned it in England, where indeed they are most potent in potting. Your Dane, your German, and your swag-bellied° Hollander—Drink, ho!—are   65
nothing to your English.

CASSIO: Is your Englishman so exquisite° in his drinking?

IAGO: Why, he drinks you with facility your Dane dead drunk; he sweats not to overthrow your Almain; he gives your Hollander a vomit ere the next pottle
can be filled.   70

CASSIO: To the health of our general!

MONTANO: I am for it, lieutenant, and I'll do you justice.

IAGO: O sweet England!

   [*Sings*] King Stephen was and a worthy peer;
       His breeches cost him but a crown;   75
       He held them sixpence all too dear,
       With that he called the tailor lown.°
       He was a wight of high renown,
       And thou art but of low degree:
       'Tis pride that pulls the country down;   80
       And take thine auld cloak about thee.

  Some wine, ho!

CASSIO: 'Fore God, this is a more exquisite song than the other.

IAGO: Will you hear't again?

CASSIO: No, for I hold him to be unworthy of his place that does those things.   85
Well, God's above all; and there be souls must be saved, and there be souls must
not be saved.

IAGO: It's true, good lieutenant.

CASSIO: For mine own part—no offense to the general, nor any man of quality—I
hope to be saved.   90

IAGO: And so do I too, lieutenant.

CASSIO: Ay, but, by your leave, not before me. The lieutenant is to be saved before
the ancient. Let's have no more of this; let's to our affairs.—God forgive us our
sins!—Gentlemen, let's look to our business. Do not think, gentlemen, I am
drunk. This is my ancient; this is my right hand, and this is my left. I am not   95
drunk now. I can stand well enough, and I speak well enough.

GENTLEMEN: Excellent well!

CASSIO: Why, very well then. You must not think then that I am drunk.

                                         Exit.

MONTANO: To th' platform, masters. Come, let's set the watch.   100

IAGO: You see this fellow that is gone before.
  He's a soldier fit to stand by Caesar
  And give direction; and do but see his vice.
  'Tis to his virtue a just equinox,°
  The one as long as th' other. 'Tis pity of him.   105
  I fear the trust Othello puts him in,
  On some odd time of his infirmity,

65**swag-bellied** *pendulous-bellied.*   67**exquisite** *superb.*   77**lown** *lout.*   104**just equinox** *exact balance (of dark and light).*

Will shake this island.
MONTANO: But is he often thus?
IAGO: 'Tis evermore his prologue to his sleep:
  He'll watch the horologe a double set°   110
  If drink rock not his cradle.
MONTANO: It were well
  The general were put in mind of it.
  Perhaps he sees it not, or his good nature
  Prizes the virtue that appears in Cassio
  And looks not on his evils. Is not this true?   115

                        Enter RODERIGO.

IAGO [*Aside*]: How now, Roderigo?
  I pray you after the lieutenant, go!   [*Exit* RODERIGO.]
MONTANO: And 'tis great pity that the noble Moor
  Should hazard such a place as his own second
  With one of an ingraft° infirmity.   120
  It were an honest action to say so
  To the Moor.
IAGO: Not I, for this fair island!
  I do love Cassio well and would do much
  To cure him of this evil.   (Help! Help! *Within*.)
  But hark! What noise?   125

                Enter CASSIO, *pursuing* RODERIGO.

CASSIO: Zounds, you rogue! You rascal!
MONTANO: What's the matter, lieutenant?
CASSIO: A knave teach me my duty? I'll beat the knave into a twiggen°
  bottle.
RODERIGO: Beat me?   130
CASSIO: Dost thou prate, rogue?   [*Strikes him*.]
MONTANO: Nay, good lieutenant! I pray you, sir, hold your hand.

                        [*Stays him*.]

CASSIO: Let me go, sir, or I'll knock you o'er the mazzard.°
MONTANO: Come, come, you're drunk!
CASSIO: Drunk?   [*They fight*.] 135
IAGO [*Aside to* RODERIGO]: Away, I say! Go out and cry a mutiny!

                                            [*Exit* RODERIGO.]

  Nay, good lieutenant. God's will, gentlemen!
  Help, ho! Lieutenant. Sir. Montano.
  Help, masters! Here's a goodly watch indeed!   [*A bell rung*.]
  Who's that which rings the bell? Diablo, ho!   140

---

¹¹⁰**watch . . . set**   *stay awake twice around the clock.*   ¹²⁰**ingraft**   *ingrained.*   ¹²⁸**twiggen**   *wicker-cov-*
ered.   ¹³³**mazzard**   *head.*

The two will rise. God's will, lieutenant,
You'll be ashamed forever.

Enter OTHELLO *and* ATTENDANTS.

OTHELLO: What is the matter here?
MONTANO: Zounds, I bleed still. I am hurt to the death.
He dies.   [*He and* CASSIO *fight again.*]
OTHELLO: Hold for your lives!   145
IAGO: Hold, ho! Lieutenant. Sir. Montano. Gentlemen!
   Have you forgot all place of sense and duty?
   Hold! The general speaks to you. Hold, for shame!
OTHELLO: Why, how now, ho? From whence ariseth this?
   Are we turned Turks, and to ourselves do that   150
   Which heaven hath forbid the Ottomites?°
   For Christian shame put by this barbarous brawl!
   He that stirs next to carve for his own rage
   Holds his soul light;° he dies upon his motion.
   Silence that dreadful bell! It frights the isle   155
   From her propriety.° What is the matter, masters?
   Honest Iago, that looks dead with grieving,
   Speak. Who began this? On thy love, I charge thee.
IAGO: I do not know. Friends all, but now, even now,
   In quarter° and in terms like bride and groom   160
   Devesting them for bed; and then, but now—
   As if some planet had unwitted men—
   Swords out, and tilting one at other's breasts
   In opposition bloody. I cannot speak
   Any beginning to this peevish odds,°   165
   And would in action glorious I had lost
   Those legs that brought me to a part of it!
OTHELLO: How comes it, Michael, you are thus forgot?
CASSIO: I pray you pardon me; I cannot speak.
OTHELLO: Worthy Montano, you were wont to be civil;   170
   Thy gravity and stillness of your youth
   The world hath noted, and your name is great
   In mouths of wisest censure.° What's the matter
   That you unlace° your reputation thus
   And spend your rich opinion° for the name   175
   Of a night-brawler? Give me answer to it.
MONTANO: Worthy Othello, I am hurt to danger.
   Your officer, Iago, can inform you.
   While I spare speech, which something now offends° me,

151**heaven . . . Ottomites**   *i.e., by sending the storm which dispersed the Turks.*   154**Holds his soul light**   *val-ues his soul lightly.*   156**propriety**   *proper order.*   160**In quarter**   *on duty.*   165**odds**   *quarrel.*
173**censure**   *judgment.*   174**unlace**   *undo (the term refers specifically to the dressing of a wild boar killed in the hunt).*   175**opinion**   *reputation.*   179**offends**   *harms, hurts.*

Of all that I do know; nor know I aught   180
By me that's said or done amiss this night,
Unless self-charity be sometimes a vice,
And to defend ourselves it be a sin
When violence assails us.
OTHELLO: Now, by heaven,
  My blood begins my safer guides to rule,   185
  And passion, having my best judgment collied,°
  Assays to lead the way. If I once stir
  Or do but lift this arm, the best of you
  Shall sink in my rebuke. Give me to know
  How this foul rout began, who set it on;   190
  And he that is approved in this offense,
  Though he had twinned with me, both at a birth,
  Shall lose me. What? In a town of war
  Yet wild, the people's hearts brimful of fear,
  To manage° private and domestic quarrel?   195
  In night, and on the court and guard of safety?
  'Tis monstrous. Iago, who began't?
MONTANO: If partially affined, or leagued in office,°
  Thou dost deliver more or less than truth,
  Thou art no soldier.
IAGO: Touch me not so near.   200
  I had rather have this tongue cut from my mouth
  Than it should do offense to Michael Cassio.
  Yet I persuade myself to speak the truth
  Shall nothing wrong him. This it is, general.
  Montano and myself being in speech,   205
  There comes a fellow crying out for help,
  And Cassio following him with determined sword
  To execute upon him. Sir, this gentleman
  Steps in to Cassio and entreats his pause.
  Myself the crying fellow did pursue,   210
  Lest by his clamor—as it so fell out—
  The town might fall in fright. He, swift of foot,
  Outran my purpose; and I returned then rather
  For that I heard the clink and fall of swords,
  And Cassio high in oath; which till tonight   215
  I ne'er might say before. When I came back—
  For this was brief—I found them close together
  At blow and thrust, even as again they were
  When you yourself did part them.
  More of this matter cannot I report;   220
  But men are men; the best sometimes forget.

186**collied**   *darkened.*   195**manage**   *conduct.*   198**If . . . office**   *if you are partial because you are related*
("affined") or the brother officer (of Cassio).

Though Cassio did some little wrong to him,
As men in rage strike those that wish them best,
Yet surely Cassio I believe received
From him that fled some strange indignity,   225
Which patience could not pass.°
OTHELLO: I know, Iago,
Thy honesty and love doth mince° this matter,
Making it light to Cassio. Cassio, I love thee;
But never more be officer of mine.

Enter DESDEMONA, *attended.*

Look if my gentle love be not raised up.   230
I'll make thee an example.
DESDEMONA: What is the matter, dear?
OTHELLO: All's well, sweeting; come away to bed.
[*To* MONTANO] Sir, for your hurts, myself will be your surgeon.
Lead him off.   [MONTANO *led off.*]
Iago, look with care about the town   235
And silence those whom this vile brawl distracted.
Come, Desdemona: 'tis the soldiers' life
To have their balmy slumbers waked with strife.

Exit [*with all but* IAGO *and* CASSIO].

IAGO: What, are you hurt, lieutenant?
CASSIO: Ay, past all surgery.   240
IAGO: Marry, God forbid!
CASSIO: Reputation, reputation, reputation! O, I have lost my reputation! I have
    lost the immortal part of myself, and what remains is bestial. My reputation,
    Iago, my reputation.
IAGO: As I am an honest man, I had thought you had received some bodily   245
    wound. There is more sense° in that than in reputation. Reputation is an idle
    and most false imposition,° oft got without merit and lost without deserving.
    You have lost no reputation at all unless you repute yourself such a loser. What,
    man, there are more ways to recover the general again. You are but now cast in
    his mood°—a punishment more in policy° than in malice—even so as one   250
    would beat his offenseless dog to affright an imperious lion. Sue to him again,
    and he's yours.
CASSIO: I will rather sue to be despised than to deceive so good a commander with
    so slight, so drunken, and so indiscreet an officer. Drunk! And speak parrot!°
    And squabble! Swagger! Swear! and discourse fustian° with one's own shadow!   255
    O thou invisible spirit of wine, if thou hast no name to be known by, let us call
    thee devil!

---

²²⁶**pass**   *allow to pass.*   ²²⁷**mince**   *cut up (i.e., tell only part of).*   ²⁴⁶**sense**   *physical feeling.*   ²⁴⁷**im-
position**   *external thing.*   ²⁵⁰**cast in his mood**   *dismissed because of his anger.*   ²⁵⁰**in policy**   *politically
necessary.*   ²⁵⁴⁻⁵⁵**speak parrot**   *gabble without sense.*   ²⁵⁵**discourse fustian**   *speak nonsense ("fustian"
was a coarse cotton cloth used for stuffing).*

IAGO: What was he that you followed with your sword?
　What had he done to you?
CASSIO: I know not.　　　　　　　　　　　　　　　　　　　　260
IAGO: Is't possible?
CASSIO: I remember a mass of things, but nothing distinctly: a quarrel, but nothing
　wherefore. O God, that men should put an enemy in their mouths to steal away
　their brains! that we should with joy, pleasance, revel, and applause transform
　ourselves into beasts!　　　　　　　　　　　　　　　　　　　265
IAGO: Why, but you are now well enough. How came you thus recovered?
CASSIO: It hath pleased the devil drunkenness to give place to the devil wrath. One
　unperfectness shows me another, to make me frankly despise myself.
IAGO: Come, you are too severe a moraler. As the time, the place, and the
　condition of this country stands, I could heartily wish this had not befall'n; but　270
　since it is as it is, mend it for your own good.
CASSIO: I will ask him for my place again: he shall tell me I am a drunkard. Had I
　as many mouths as Hydra, such an answer would stop them all. To be now a
　sensible man, by and by a fool, and presently a beast! O strange! Every
　inordinate cup is unblest, and the ingredient is a devil.　　　　　　275
IAGO: Come, come, good wine is a good familiar creature if it be well used.
　Exclaim no more against it. And, good lieutenant, I think you think I love you.
CASSIO: I have well approved it, sir. I drunk?
IAGO: You or any man living may be drunk at a time, man. I tell you what you　280
　shall do. Our general's wife is now the general. I may say so in this respect, for
　all he hath devoted and given up himself to the contemplation, mark, and
　devotement of her parts° and graces. Confess yourself freely to her; importune
　her help to put you in your place again. She is of so free, so kind, so apt, so
　blessed a disposition she holds it a vice in her goodness not to do more than she　285
　is requested. This broken joint between you and her husband entreat her to
　splinter;° and my fortunes against any lay° worth naming, this crack of your
　love shall grow stronger than it was before.
CASSIO: You advise me well.
IAGO: I protest, in the sincerity of love and honest kindness.　　　　290
CASSIO: I think it freely; and betimes in the morning I will beseech the virtuous
　Desdemona to undertake for me. I am desperate of my fortunes if they check°
　me.
IAGO: You are in the right. Good night, lieutenant; I must to the watch.
CASSIO: Good night, honest Iago.　　　　　　　　　　　*Exit* CASSIO.　295
IAGO: And what's he then that says I play the villain,
　When this advice is free° I give, and honest,
　Probal to° thinking, and indeed the course
　To win the Moor again? For 'tis most easy
　Th' inclining° Desdemona to subdue　　　　　　　　　　300
　In any honest suit; she's framed as fruitful°

---

²⁸³***devotement of her parts*** *devotion to her qualities.*　²⁸⁷***splinter*** *splint.*　²⁸⁷***lay*** *wager.*
²⁹³***check*** *repulse.*　²⁹⁷***free*** *generous and open.*　²⁹⁸***Probal to*** *provable by.*　³⁰⁰***inclining*** *inclined*
(to be helpful).　³⁰¹***framed as fruitful*** *made as generous.*

As the free elements.° And then for her
To win the Moor—were't to renounce his baptism,
All seals and symbols of redeemèd sin—
His soul is so enfettered to her love   305
That she may make, unmake, do what she list,
Even as her appetite° shall play the god
With his weak function.° How am I then a villain
To counsel Cassio to this parallel course,
Directly to his good? Divinity of hell!   310
When devils will the blackest sins put on,°
They do suggest at first with heavenly shows,°
As I do now. For whiles this honest fool
Plies Desdemona to repair his fortune,
And she for him pleads strongly to the Moor,   315
I'll pour this pestilence into his ear:
That she repeals him° for her body's lust;
And by how much she strives to do him good,
She shall undo her credit with the Moor.
So will I turn her virtue into pitch,   320
And out of her own goodness make the net
That shall enmesh them all. How now, Roderigo?

                                                            Enter RODERIGO.

RODERIGO: I do not follow here in the chase, not like a hound that hunts, but one
    that fills up the cry.° My money is almost spent; I have been tonight
    exceedingly well cudgeled; and I think the issue will be, I shall have so much   325
    experience for my pains; and so, with no money at all, and a little more wit,
    return again to Venice.
IAGO: How poor are they that have not patience!
    What wound did ever heal but by degrees?
    Thou know'st we work by wit, and not by witchcraft;   330
    And wit depends on dilatory time.
    Does't not go well? Cassio hath beaten thee,
    And thou by that small hurt hath cashiered Cassio.
    Though other things grow fair against the sun,
    Yet fruits that blossom first will first be ripe.   335
    Content thyself awhile. By the mass, 'tis morning!
    Pleasure and action make the hours seem short.
    Retire thee, go where thou art billeted.
    Away, I say! Thou shalt know more hereafter.
    Nay, get thee gone!   *Exit* RODERIGO.
            Two things are to be done: 340

---

³⁰²*elements*   *i.e., basic nature.*   ³⁰⁷*appetite*   *liking.*   ³⁰⁸*function*   *thought.*   ³¹¹**put on**   *advance,*
further.   ³¹²*shows*   *appearances.*   ³¹⁷*repeals him*   *asks for (Cassio's reinstatement).*   ³²⁴**fills up the**
cry   *makes up one of the hunting pack, adding to the noise but not actually tracking.*

My wife must move° for Cassio to her mistress;
I'll set her on;
Myself awhile° to draw the Moor apart
And bring him jump° when he may Cassio find
Soliciting his wife. Ay, that's the way!   345
Dull not device by coldness and delay.   *Exit.*

ACT III

Scene I [A street.]

Enter CASSIO [and] MUSICIANS.

CASSIO: Masters, play here. I will content your pains.°
    Something that's brief; and bid "Good morrow, general." [*They play.*]

[*Enter CLOWN.*°]

CLOWN: Why, masters, have your instruments been in Naples° that they speak i' th'
nose thus?
MUSICIAN: How, sir, how?   5
CLOWN: Are these, I pray you, wind instruments?
MUSICIAN: Ay, marry, are they, sir.
CLOWN: O, thereby hangs a tale.
MUSICIAN: Whereby hangs a tale, sir?
CLOWN: Marry, sir, by many a wind instrument that I know. But, masters, here's   10
    money for you; and the general so likes your music that he desires you, for
    love's sake, to make no more noise with it.
MUSICIAN: Well, sir, we will not.
CLOWN: If you have any music that may not be heard, to't again. But, as they say,
    to hear music the general does not greatly care.   15
MUSICIAN: We have none such, sir.
CLOWN: Then put up your pipes in your bag, for I'll away. Go, vanish into air,
    away!   *Exit MUSICIANS.*
CASSIO: Dost thou hear me, mine honest friend?
CLOWN: No. I hear not your honest friend. I hear you.   20
CASSIO: Prithee keep up thy quillets.° There's a poor piece of gold for
    thee. If the gentlewoman that attends the general's wife be stirring, tell her
    there's one Cassio entreats her a little favor of speech. Wilt thou do this?
CLOWN: She is stirring, sir. If she will stir hither, I shall seem to notify unto her.° 25

Exit CLOWN.

---

³⁴¹**move** *petition.*   ³⁴³**awhile** *at the same time.*   ³⁴⁴**jump** *at the precise moment and place.*   **III.i.**
¹**content your pains** *reward your efforts.*   **s.d. Clown** *fool.*   ³**Naples** *this may refer either to the
Neapolitan nasal tone, or to syphilis—rife in Naples—which breaks down the nose.*   ²¹**quillets** *puns.*
²⁵⁻²⁶**seem . . . her** *(the Clown is mocking Cassio's overly elegant manner of speaking).*

Enter IAGO.

CASSIO: In happy time, Iago.
IAGO: You have not been abed then?
CASSIO: Why no, the day had broke before we parted.
  I have made bold, Iago, to send in to your wife;
  My suit to her is that she will to virtuous Desdemona   30
  Procure me some access.
IAGO: I'll send her to you presently,
  And I'll devise a mean to draw the Moor
  Out of the way, that your converse and business
  May be more free.
CASSIO: I humbly thank you for't.   *Exit* [IAGO]. 35
                            I never knew
  A Florentine° more kind and honest.

Enter EMILIA.

EMILIA: Good morrow, good lieutenant. I am sorry
  For your displeasure;° but all will sure be well.
  The general and his wife are talking of it,   40
  And she speaks for you stoutly. The Moor replies
  That he you hurt is of great fame in Cyprus
  And great affinity,° and that in wholesome wisdom
  He might not but refuse you. But he protests he loves you.
  And needs no other suitor but his likings   45
  To bring you in again.
CASSIO: Yet I beseech you,
  If you think fit, or that it may be done,
  Give me advantage of some brief discourse
  With Desdemona alone.
EMILIA: Pray you come in.
  I will bestow you where you shall have time   50
  To speak your bosom° freely.
CASSIO: I am much bound to you. [*Exeunt.*]

Scene II [*The citadel.*]

Enter OTHELLO, IAGO, *and* GENTLEMEN.

OTHELLO: These letters give, Iago, to the pilot
  And by him do my duties to the Senate.
  That done, I will be walking on the works;
  Repair° there to me.
IAGO: Well, my good lord, I'll do't.
OTHELLO: This fortification, gentlemen, shall we see't?   5

---

³⁷**Florentine**   *i.e., Iago is as kind as if he were from Cassio's home town, Florence.*   ³⁹**displeasure**   *discom-*
forting.   ⁴³**affinity**   *family.*   ⁵¹**bosom**   *inmost thoughts.*   **III.ii.**   ⁴**Repair**   *go.*

GENTLEMEN: We'll wait upon your lordship.   [*Exeunt.*]

Scene III [*The citadel.*]

Enter DESDEMONA, CASSIO, *and* EMILIA.

DESDEMONA: Be thou assured, good Cassio, I will do
   All my abilities in thy behalf.
EMILIA: Good madam, do. I warrant it grieves my husband
   As if the cause were his.
DESDEMONA: O, that's an honest fellow. Do not doubt, Cassio,   5
   But I will have my lord and you again
   As friendly as you were.
CASSIO: Bounteous madam,
   Whatever shall become of Michael Cassio,
   He's never anything but your true servant.
DESDEMONA: I know't; I thank you. You do love my lord.   10
   You have known him long, and be you well assured
   He shall in strangeness stand no farther off
   Than in a politic distance.°
CASSIO: Ay, but, lady,
   That policy may either last so long,
   Or feed upon such nice° and waterish diet,   15
   Or breed itself so out of circumstances,°
   That, I being absent, and my place supplied,°
   My general will forget my love and service.
DESDEMONA: Do not doubt° that; before Emilia here
   I give thee warrant of thy place. Assure thee,   20
   If I do vow a friendship, I'll perform it
   To the last article. My lord shall never rest;
   I'll watch him tame° and talk him out of patience;
   His bed shall seem a school, his board a shrift;°
   I'll intermingle everything he does   25
   With Cassio's suit. Therefore be merry, Cassio,
   For thy solicitor shall rather die
   Than give thy cause away.

Enter OTHELLO *and* IAGO [*at a distance*].

EMILIA: Madam, here comes my lord.
CASSIO: Madam, I'll take my leave.   30
DESDEMONA: Why, stay, and hear me speak.
CASSIO: Madam, not now. I am very ill at ease,

III.iii.   12–13*He . . . distance*   *i.e., he shall act no more distant to you than is necessary for political reasons.*
15*nice* *trivial.*   16*Or . . . circumstances*   *i.e., or grow so on the basis of accidental happenings and political*
needs.   17*supplied* *filled.*   19*doubt* *imagine.*   23*watch him tame* *(animals were tamed by being*
kept awake).   24*board a shrift* *table (seem) a confessional.*

Unfit for mine own purposes.
DESDEMONA: Well, do your discretion.   *Exit* CASSIO.
IAGO: Ha! I like not that.
OTHELLO: What dost thou say?   35
IAGO: Nothing, my lord; or if—I know not what.
OTHELLO: Was not that Cassio parted from my wife?
IAGO: Cassio, my lord? No, sure, I cannot think it
  That he would steal away so guilty-like,
  Seeing you coming.
OTHELLO: I do believe 'twas he.   40
DESDEMONA [*Coming to them*]: How now, my lord?
  I have been talking with a suitor here,
  A man that languishes in your displeasure.
OTHELLO: Who is't you mean?
DESDEMONA: Why, your lieutenant, Cassio. Good my lord,   45
  If I have any grace or power to move you,
  His present° reconciliation take.
  For if he be not one that truly loves you,
  That errs in ignorance, and not in cunning,
  I have no judgment in an honest face.   50
  I prithee call him back.
OTHELLO: Went he hence now?
DESDEMONA: I' sooth so humbled
  That he hath left part of his grief with me
  To suffer with him. Good love, call him back.
OTHELLO: Not now, sweet Desdemon; some other time.   55
DESDEMONA: But shall't be shortly?
OTHELLO: The sooner, sweet, for you.
DESDEMONA: Shall't be tonight at supper?
OTHELLO: No, not tonight.
DESDEMONA: Tomorrow dinner then?
OTHELLO: I shall not dine at home;
  I meet the captains at the citadel.
DESDEMONA: Why then, tomorrow night, on Tuesday morn,   60
  On Tuesday noon, or night, on Wednesday morn.
  I prithee name the time, but let it not
  Exceed three days. In faith, he's penitent;
  And yet his trespass, in our common reason
  (Save that, they say, the wars must make example   65
  Out of her best), is not almost a fault
  T' incur a private check.° When shall he come?
  Tell me, Othello. I wonder in my soul
  What you would ask me that I should deny
  Or stand so mamm'ring° on. What? Michael Cassio,   70

---

⁴⁷**present** *immediate.*   ⁶⁶⁻⁶⁷**is ... check** *is almost not serious enough for a private rebuke (let alone a public disgrace).*   ⁷⁰**mamm'ring** *hesitating.*

That came awooing with you, and so many a time,
When I have spoke of you dispraisingly,
Hath ta'en your part—to have so much to do
To bring him in? By'r Lady, I could do much—
OTHELLO: Prithee no more. Let him come when he will!   75
 I will deny thee nothing.
DESDEMONA: Why, this is not a boon;
 'Tis as I should entreat you wear your gloves,
 Or feed on nourishing dishes, or keep you warm,
 Or sue to you to do a peculiar profit°
 To your own person. Nay, when I have a suit   80
 Wherein I mean to touch your love indeed,
 It shall be full of poise° and difficult weight,
 And fearful to be granted.
OTHELLO: I will deny thee nothing!
 Whereon I do beseech thee grant me this,
 To leave me but a little to myself.   85
DESDEMONA: Shall I deny you? No. Farewell, my lord.
OTHELLO: Farewell, my Desdemona: I'll come to thee straight.°
DESDEMONA: Emilia, come. Be as your fancies teach you;
 Whate'er you be, I am obedient.   *Exit [with* EMILIA].
OTHELLO: Excellent wretch! Perdition catch my soul   90
 But I do love thee! And when I love thee not,
 Chaos is come again.
IAGO: My noble lord—
OTHELLO: What dost thou say, Iago?
IAGO: Did Michael Cassio, when you wooed my lady,
 Know of your love?   95
OTHELLO: He did, from first to last. Why dost thou ask?
IAGO: But for a satisfaction of my thought,
 No further harm.
OTHELLO: Why of thy thought, Iago?
IAGO: I did not think he had been acquainted with her.
OTHELLO: O, yes, and went between us° very oft.   100
IAGO: Indeed?
OTHELLO: Indeed? Ay, indeed! Discern'st thou aught in that?
 Is he not honest?
IAGO: Honest, my lord?
OTHELLO: Honest? Ay, honest.
IAGO: My lord, for aught I know.
OTHELLO: What dost thou think?
IAGO: Think, my lord?
OTHELLO: Think, my lord?   105
 By heaven, thou echoest me,

---

⁷⁹**peculiar profit** *particularly personal good.*   ⁸²**poise** *weight.*   ⁸⁷**straight** *at once.*   ¹⁰⁰**between us**
i.e., as messenger.

As if there were some monster in thy thought
Too hideous to be shown. Thou dost mean something.
I heard thee say even now, thou lik'st not that,
When Cassio left my wife. What didst not like?   110
And when I told thee he was of my counsel°
Of my whole course of wooing, thou cried'st "Indeed?"
And didst contract and purse thy brow together,
As if thou then hadst shut up in thy brain
Some horrible conceit.° If thou dost love me,   115
Show me thy thought.
IAGO: My lord, you know I love you.
OTHELLO: I think thou dost;
    And, for I know thou'rt full of love and honesty
    And weigh'st thy words before thou giv'st them breath,
    Therefore these stops° of thine fright me the more;   120
    For such things in a false disloyal knave
    Are tricks of custom;° but in a man that's just
    They're close dilations,° working from the heart
    That passion cannot rule.
IAGO: For Michael Cassio,
    I dare be sworn, I think that he is honest.   125
OTHELLO: I think so too.
IAGO: Men should be what they seem;
    Or those that be not, would they might seem none!
OTHELLO: Certain, men should be what they seem.
IAGO: Why then, I think Cassio's an honest man.
OTHELLO: Nay, yet there's more in this?   130
    I prithee speak to me as to thy thinkings,
    As thou dost ruminate, and give thy worst of thoughts
    The worst of words.
IAGO: Good my lord, pardon me:
    Though I am bound to every act of duty,
    I am not bound to that all slaves are free to.   135
    Utter my thoughts? Why, say they are vile and false,
    As where's that palace whereinto foul things
    Sometimes intrude not? Who has that breast so pure
    But some uncleanly apprehensions
    Keep leets and law days,° and in sessions sit   140
    With meditations lawful?
OTHELLO: Thou dost conspire against thy friend, Iago,
    If thou but think'st him wronged, and mak'st his ear
    A stranger to thy thoughts.
IAGO: I do beseech you—

---

¹¹¹**of my counsel**   *in my confidence.*   ¹¹⁵**conceit**   *thought.*   ¹²⁰**stops**   *interruptions.*   ¹²²**of custom**
customary.   ¹²³**close dilations**   *expressions of hidden thoughts.*   ¹⁴⁰**leets and law days**   *meetings of local*
courts.

Though I perchance am vicious in my guess 145
(As I confess it is my nature's plague
To spy into abuses, and of my jealousy
Shape faults that are not), that your wisdom
From one that so imperfectly conceits
Would take no notice, nor build yourself a trouble 150
Out of his scattering and unsure observance.
It were not for your quiet nor your good,
Nor for my manhood, honesty, and wisdom,
To let you know my thoughts.

OTHELLO: What dost thou mean?

IAGO: Good name in man and woman, dear my lord, 155
   Is the immediate jewel of their souls.
   Who steals my purse steals trash; 'tis something, nothing;
   'Twas mine, 'tis his, and has been slave to thousands;
   But he that filches from me my good name
   Robs me of that which not enriches him 160
   And makes me poor indeed.

OTHELLO: By heaven, I'll know thy thoughts!

IAGO: You cannot, if my heart were in your hand;
   Nor shall not whilst 'tis in my custody.

OTHELLO: Ha!

IAGO: O, beware, my lord, of jealousy! 165
   It is the green-eyed monster, which doth mock
   The meat it feeds on. That cuckold lives in bliss
   Who, certain of his fate, loves not his wronger;
   But O, what damnèd minutes tells° he o'er
   Who dotes, yet doubts—suspects, yet fondly° loves! 170

OTHELLO: O misery.

IAGO: Poor and content is rich, and rich enough;
   But riches fineless° is as poor as winter
   To him that ever fears he shall be poor.
   Good God the souls of all my tribe defend 175
   From jealousy!

OTHELLO: Why? Why is this?
   Think'st thou I'd make a life of jealousy,
   To follow still° the changes of the moon
   With fresh suspicions? No! To be once in doubt
   Is to be resolved. Exchange me for a goat 180
   When I shall turn the business of my soul
   To such exsufflicate and blown° surmises,
   Matching thy inference. 'Tis not to make me jealous
   To say my wife is fair, feeds well, loves company,
   Is free of speech, sings, plays, and dances; 185

---

[169]***tells*** counts.   [170]***fondly*** *foolishly.*   [173]***fineless*** *infinite.*   [178]***To follow still*** *to change always (as the phases of the moon).*   [182]***exsufflicate and blown*** *inflated and flyblown.*

Where virtue is, these are more virtuous.
Nor from mine own weak merits will I draw
The smallest fear or doubt of her revolt,
For she had eyes, and chose me. No, Iago;
I'll see before I doubt; when I doubt, prove;   190
And on the proof there is no more but this:
Away at once with love or jealousy!
IAGO: I am glad of this; for now I shall have reason
    To show the love and duty that I bear you
    With franker spirit. Therefore, as I am bound,   195
    Receive it from me. I speak not yet of proof.
    Look to your wife; observe her well with Cassio;
    Wear your eyes thus: not jealous nor secure.
    I would not have your free and noble nature
    Out of self-bounty° be abused. Look to't.   200
    I know our country disposition well:
    In Venice they do let heaven see the pranks
    They dare not show their husbands; their best conscience
    Is not to leave't undone, but kept unknown.°
OTHELLO: Dost thou say so?   205
IAGO: She did deceive her father, marrying you;
    And when she seemed to shake and fear your looks,
    She loved them most.
OTHELLO: And so she did.
IAGO: Why, go to then!
    She that so young could give out such a seeming
    To seel° her father's eyes up close as oak°—   210
    He thought 'twas witchcraft. But I am much to blame.
    I humbly do beseech you of your pardon
    For too much loving you.
OTHELLO: I am bound to thee forever.
IAGO: I see this hath a little dashed your spirits.
OTHELLO: Not a jot, not a jot.
IAGO: Trust me, I fear it has.   215
    I hope you will consider what is spoke
    Comes from my love. But I do see y' are moved.
    I am to pray you not to strain° my speech
    To grosser issues nor to larger reach°
    Than to suspicion.   220
OTHELLO: I will not.
IAGO: Should you do so, my lord,
    My speech should fall into such vile success
    Which my thoughts aimed not. Cassio's my worthy friend—
    My lord, I see y' are moved.

200**self-bounty**   innate kindness (which attributes his own motives to others).   203–4**their ... unknown**   i.e., their morality does not forbid adultery, but it does forbid being found out.   210**seel**   hoodwink.   210**oak**   (a close-grained wood).   218**strain**   enlarge the meaning.   219**reach**   meaning.

OTHELLO: No, not much moved.
   I do not think but Desdemona's honest.   225
IAGO: Long live she so. And long live you to think so.
OTHELLO: And yet, how nature erring from itself—
IAGO: Ay, there's the point, as (to be bold with you)
   Not to affect many proposèd matches
   Of her own clime, complexion, and degree,°   230
   Whereto we see in all things nature tends°—
   Foh! one may smell in such a will most rank,
   Foul disproportions, thoughts unnatural.
   But, pardon me, I do not in position°
   Distinctly° speak of her; though I may fear   235
   Her will, recoiling to her better judgment,
   May fall to match° you with her country forms,°
   And happily° repent.
OTHELLO: Farewell, farewell!
   If more thou dost perceive, let me know more.
   Set on thy wife to observe. Leave me, Iago.   240
IAGO: My lord, I take my leave.   [*Going.*]
OTHELLO: Why did I marry? This honest creature doubtless
   Sees and knows more, much more, than he unfolds.
IAGO [*Returns*]: My lord, I would I might entreat your honor
   To scan this thing no farther. Leave it to time.   245
   Although 'tis fit that Cassio have his place,
   For sure he fills it up with great ability,
   Yet, if you please to hold him off awhile,
   You shall by that perceive him and his means.
   Note if your lady strains his entertainment°   250
   With any strong or vehement importunity;
   Much will be seen in that. In the meantime
   Let me be thought too busy in my fears
   (As worthy cause I have to fear I am)
   And hold her free, I do beseech your honor.   255
OTHELLO: Fear not my government.°
IAGO: I once more take my leave.   *Exit.*
OTHELLO: This fellow's of exceeding honesty,
   And knows all qualities,° with a learnèd spirit
   Of human dealings. If I do prove her haggard,°
   Though that her jesses° were my dear heartstrings,   260
   I'd whistle her off and let her down the wind°
   To prey at fortune. Haply for° I am black

---

[230]**degree** *social station*   [231]**in . . . tends**   *i.e., all things in nature seek out their own kind.*   [234]**position** *general argument.*   [235]**Distinctly** *specifically*   [237]**fall to match** *happen to compare.*   [237]**country forms** *i.e., the familiar appearance of her countrymen.*   [238]**happily** *by chance.*   [250]**strains his entertainment** *urge strongly that he be reinstated.*   [256]**government** *self-control.*   [258]**qualities** *natures, types of people.* [259]**haggard** *a partly trained hawk which has gone wild again.*   [260]**jesses** *straps which held the hawk's legs to the trainer's wrist.*   [261]**I'd . . . wind** *I would release her (like an untamable hawk and let her fly free.* [262]**Haply for** *it may be because.*

And have not those soft parts° of conversation
That chamberers° have, or for I am declined
Into the vale of years—yet that's not much—   265
She's gone. I am abused, and my relief
Must be to loathe her. O curse of marriage,
That we can call these delicate creatures ours,
And not their appetites! I had rather be a toad
And live upon the vapor of a dungeon   270
Than keep a corner in the thing I love
For others' uses. Yet 'tis the plague to great ones;
Prerogatived are they less than the base.
'Tis destiny unshunnable, like death.
Even then this forkèd° plague is fated to us   275
When we do quicken.° Look where she comes.

           Enter DESDEMONA *and* EMILIA.

If she be false, heaven mocked itself!
I'll not believe't.
DESDEMONA: How now, my dear Othello?
   Your dinner, and the generous islanders
   By you invited, do attend° your presence.   280
OTHELLO: I am to blame.
DESDEMONA: Why do you speak so faintly?
   Are you not well?
OTHELLO: I have a pain upon my forehead, here.°
DESDEMONA: Why, that's with watching; 'twill away again,
   Let me but bind it hard, within this hour   285
   It will be well.
OTHELLO: Your napkin° is too little;

      [*He pushes the handkerchief away, and it falls.*]

   Let it° alone. Come, I'll go in with you.
DESDEMONA: I am very sorry that you are not well.   *Exit* [*with* OTHELLO].
EMILIA: I am glad I have found this napkin;
   This was her first remembrance from the Moor.   290
   My wayward husband hath a hundred times
   Wooed me to steal it; but she so loves the token
   (For he conjured her she should ever keep it)
   That she reserves it evermore about her
   To kiss and talk to. I'll have the work ta'en out°   295
   And give't Iago. What he will do with it,

---

²⁶³**soft parts** *gentle qualities and manners.*   ²⁶⁴**chamberers** *courtiers—or, perhaps, accomplished seducers.*
²⁷⁵**forkèd** *horned (the sign of the cuckold was horns).*   ²⁷⁶**do quicken** *are born.*   ²⁸³**here** *(he points to his imaginary horns).*   ²⁸⁶**napkin** *elaborately worked handkerchief.*   ²⁸⁷**it** *(it makes a considerable differ-ence in the interpretation of later events whether this "it" refers to Othello's forehead or to the handkerchief; nothing in the text makes the reference clear).*   ²⁹⁵**work ta'en out** *needlework copied.*

Heaven knows, not I; I nothing° but to please his fantasy.°

Enter IAGO.

IAGO: How now? What do you here alone?
EMILIA: Do not you chide; I have a thing for you.
IAGO: You have a thing for me? It is a common thing—   300
EMILIA: Ha?
IAGO: To have a foolish wife.
EMILIA: O, is that all? What will you give me now
  For that same handkerchief?
IAGO: What handkerchief?
EMILIA: What handkerchief!   305
  Why, that the Moor first gave to Desdemona,
  That which so often you did bid me steal.
IAGO: Hast stol'n it from her?
EMILIA: No, but she let it drop by negligence,
  And to th' advantage,° I, being here, took't up.   310
  Look, here 't is.
IAGO: A good wench. Give it me.
EMILIA: What will you do with't, that you have been so earnest
  To have me filch it?
IAGO: Why, what is that to you?   [*Takes it.*]
EMILIA: If it be not for some purpose of import,°
  Give't me again. Poor lady, she'll run mad   315
  When she shall lack° it.
IAGO: Be not acknown on't.°
  I have use for it. Go, leave me.   *Exit* EMILIA.
  I will in Cassio's lodging lose this napkin
  And let him find it. Trifles light as air
  Are to the jealous confirmations strong   320
  As proofs of Holy Writ. This may do something.
  The Moor already changes with my poison:
  Dangerous conceits are in their natures poisons,
  Which at the first are scarce found to distaste,°
  But with a little,° act upon the blood,   325
  Burn like the mines of sulfur. I did say so.

Enter OTHELLO.

Look where he comes! Not poppy nor mandragora,°
Nor all the drowsy syrups of the world,
Shall ever medicine thee to that sweet sleep
Which thou owedst° yesterday.

---

²⁹⁷***I nothing*** *I wish nothing.*   ²⁹⁷***fantasy*** *fancy, whim.* ³¹⁰***to th' advantage*** *being lucky.*   ³¹⁴***import*** *importance.*   ³¹⁶***lack*** *miss.* ³¹⁶***Be not acknown on't.*** *forget you ever saw it.*   ³²⁴***are scarce
found to distaste*** *scarcely can be tasted.* ³²⁵***with a little*** *in a short time.* ³²⁷***poppy nor mandragora***
soporifics. ³³⁰***owedst*** *possessed.*

OTHELLO: Ha! ha! False to me?   330
IAGO: Why, how now, general? No more of that.
OTHELLO: Avaunt! be gone! Thou hast set me on the rack.
    I swear 'tis better to be much abused
    Than but to know't a little.
IAGO: How now, my lord?
OTHELLO: What sense had I of her stol'n hours of lust?   335
    I saw't not, thought it not, it harmed not me;
    I slept the next night well, fed well, was free and merry;
    I found not Cassio's kisses on her lips.
    He that is robbed, not wanting° what is stol'n,
    Let him not know't, and he's not robbed at all.   340
IAGO: I am sorry to hear this.
OTHELLO: I had been happy if the general camp,
    Pioners° and all, had tasted her sweet body,
    So I had nothing known. O now, forever
    Farewell the tranquil mind! Farewell content!   345
    Farewell the plumèd troops, and the big wars
    That make ambition virtue! O, farewell!
    Farewell the neighing steed and the shrill trump,
    The spirit-stirring drum, th' ear-piercing fife,
    The royal banner, and all quality,   350
    Pride, pomp, and circumstance° of glorious war!
    And O you mortal engines° whose rude throats
    Th' immortal Jove's dread clamors° counterfeit,
    Farewell! Othello's occupation's gone!
IAGO: Is't possible, my lord?   355
OTHELLO: Villain, be sure thou prove my love a whore!
    Be sure of it; give me the ocular proof;
    Or, by the worth of mine eternal soul,
    Thou hadst been better have been born a dog
    Than answer my waked wrath!
IAGO: Is't come to this?   360
OTHELLO: Make me to see't; or at the least so prove it
    That the probation° bear no hinge nor loop
    To hang a doubt on—or woe upon thy life!
IAGO: My noble lord—
OTHELLO: If thou dost slander her and torture me,   365
    Never pray more; abandon all remorse;
    On horror's head horrors accumulate;
    Do deeds to make heaven weep, all earth amazed;
    For nothing canst thou to damnation add
    Greater than that.

339**wanting** *missing.*   343**Pioners** *the basest manual laborers in the army, who dug trenches and mines.*
351**circumstance** *pageantry.*   352**mortal engines** *lethal weapons, i.e., cannon.*   353**clamors** *i.e., thun-*
der.   362**probation** *proof.*

IAGO: O grace! O heaven forgive me!   370
   Are you a man? Have you a soul or sense?
   God b' wi' you! Take mine office. O wretched fool,
   That lov'st to make thine honesty a vice!
   O monstrous world! Take note, take note, O world,
   To be direct and honest is not safe.   375
   I thank you for this profit, and from hence
   I'll love no friend, sith° love breeds such offense.
OTHELLO: Nay, stay. Thou shouldst be honest.
IAGO: I should be wise; for honesty's a fool
   And loses that it works for.
OTHELLO: By the world,   380
   I think my wife be honest, and think she is not;
   I think that thou art just, and think thou are not.
   I'll have some proof. My name, that was as fresh
   As Dian's° visage, is now begrimed and black
   As mine own face. If there be cords, or knives,   385
   Poison, or fire, or suffocating streams,
   I'll not endure it. Would I were satisfied!
IAGO: I see you are eaten up with passion.
   I do repent me that I put it to you.
   You would be satisfied?
OTHELLO: Would? Nay, and I will.   390
IAGO: And may; but how? How satisfied, my lord?
   Would you, the supervisor,° grossly gape on?
   Behold her topped?
OTHELLO: Death and damnation! O!
IAGO: It were a tedious° difficulty, I think,
   To bring them to that prospect.° Damn them then,   395
   If ever mortal eyes do see them bolster°
   More than their own! What then? How then?
   What shall I say? Where's satisfaction?
   It is impossible you should see this,
   Were they as prime° as goats, as hot as monkeys,   400
   As salt as wolves in pride,° and fools as gross
   As ignorance made drunk. But yet, I say,
   If imputation and strong circumstances
   Which lead directly to the door of truth
   Will give you satisfaction, you might hav't.   405
OTHELLO: Give me a living reason she's disloyal.
IAGO: I do not like the office.°
   But sith I am entered in this cause so far,
   Pricked° to't by foolish honesty and love,

377**sith** *since.*   384**Dian's** *Diana's (goddess of the moon and of chastity).*   392**supervisor** *onlooker.*
394**tedious** *hard to arrange.*   395**prospect** *sight (where they can be seen).*   396**bolster** *go to bed with*
400–01**prime, salt** *lustful.*   401**pride** *heat.*   407**office** *duty.*   409**Pricked** *spurred.*

I will go on. I lay with Cassio lately,   410
And being troubled with a raging tooth,
I could not sleep.
There are a kind of men so loose of soul
That in their sleeps will mutter their affairs.
One of this kind is Cassio.   415
In sleep I heard him say, "Sweet Desdemona,
Let us be wary, let us hide our loves!"
And then, sir, would he gripe° and wring my hand,
Cry "O sweet creature!" Then kiss me hard,
As if he plucked up kisses by the roots   420
That grew upon my lips; laid his leg o'er my thigh,
And sigh, and kiss, and then cry, "Cursèd fate
That gave thee to the Moor!"

OTHELLO: O monstrous! monstrous!

IAGO: Nay, this was but his dream.

OTHELLO: But this denoted a foregone conclusion,°   425
'Tis a shrewd doubt,° though it be but a dream.

IAGO: And this may help to thicken other proofs
That do demonstrate° thinly.

OTHELLO: I'll tear her all to pieces!

IAGO: Nay, yet be wise. Yet we see nothing done;
She may be honest yet. Tell me but this: 430
Have you not sometimes seen a handkerchief
Spotted with strawberries in your wife's hand?

OTHELLO: I gave her such a one; 'twas my first gift.

IAGO: I know not that; but such a handkerchief—
I am sure it was your wife's—did I today   435
See Cassio wipe his beard with.

OTHELLO: If it be that—

IAGO: If it be that or any that was hers,
It speaks against her with the other proofs.

OTHELLO: O, that the slave had forty thousand lives!
One is too poor, too weak for my revenge.   440
Now do I see 'tis true. Look here, Iago:
All my fond love thus do I blow to heaven.
'Tis gone.
Arise, black vengeance, from the hollow hell!
Yield up, O love, thy crown and hearted° throne   445
To tyrannous hate! Swell, bosom, with thy fraught,°
For 'tis of aspics'° tongues.

IAGO: Yet be content.°

OTHELLO: O, blood, blood, blood!

---

418 **gripe** *seize.*   425 **foregone conclusion** *consummated fact.*   426 **shrewd doubt** *penetrating guess.*
428 **demonstrate** *show, appear.*   445 **hearted** *seated in the heart.*   446 **fraught** *burden.*   447 **aspics'**
asps'.   447 **content** *patient, quiet.*

IAGO: Patience, I say. Your mind may change.

OTHELLO: Never, Iago. Like to the Pontic Sea,° 450
  Whose icy current and compulsive course
  Nev'r keeps retiring ebb, but keeps due on
  To the Propontic and the Hellespont,
  Even so my bloody thoughts, with violent pace,
  Shall nev'r look back, nev'r ebb to humble love, 455
  Till that a capable and wide° revenge
  Swallow them up. [*He kneels.*] Now, by yond marble heaven,
  In the due reverence of a sacred vow
  I here engage my words.

IAGO: Do not rise yet.   [IAGO *kneels.*]
  Witness, you ever-burning lights above, 460
  You elements that clip° us round about,
  Witness that here Iago doth give up
  The execution° of his wit, hands, heart
  To wronged Othello's service! Let him command,
  And to obey shall be in me remorse,° 465
  What bloody business ever.°   [*They rise.*]

OTHELLO: I greet thy love,
  Not with vain thanks but with acceptance bounteous,°
  And will upon the instant put thee to 't°
  Within these three days let me hear thee say
  That Cassio's not alive. 470

IAGO: My friend is dead. 'Tis done at your request.
  But let her live.

OTHELLO: Damn her, lewd minx! O, damn her! Damn her!
  Come, go with me apart. I will withdraw
  To furnish me with some swift means of death
  For the fair devil. Now art thou my lieutenant. 475

IAGO: I am your own forever.   *Exeunt.*

Scene IV [*A street.*]

Enter DESDEMONA, EMILIA, *and* CLOWN.

DESDEMONA: Do you know, sirrah, where Lieutenant Cassio lies?°

CLOWN: I dare not say he lies anywhere.

DESDEMONA: Why, man?

CLOWN: He's a soldier, and for me to say a soldier lies, 'tis stabbing.

DESDEMONA: Go to. Where lodges he? 5

450**Pontic Sea**   *the Black Sea (famous for the strong and constant current with which it flows through the Bosporus into the Mediterranean, where the water level is lower).*   456**capable and wide**   *sufficient and far-reaching.*
461**clip**   *enfold.*   463**execution**   *workings, action.*   465**remorse**   *pity.*   466**ever**   *soever.*
467**bounteous**   *absolute.*   468**to't**   *i.e., to the work you have said you are prepared to do.*   **III.iv.**   1**lies**
lodges.

CLOWN: To tell you where he lodges is to tell you where I lie.

DESDEMONA: Can anything be made of this?

CLOWN: I know not where he lodges, and for me to devise a lodging, and say he
  lies here or he lies there, were to lie in mine own throat.°

DESDEMONA: Can you enquire him out, and be edified° by report?   10

CLOWN: I will catechize the world for him; that is, make questions, and by them
  answer.

DESDEMONA: Seek him, bid him come hither. Tell him I have moved° my lord on
  his behalf and hope all will be well.

CLOWN: To do this is within the compass° of man's wit, and therefore I will attempt   15
  the doing it.   *Exit* CLOWN.

DESDEMONA: Where should° I lose the handkerchief, Emilia?

EMILIA: I know not, madam.

DESDEMONA: Believe me, I had rather have lost my purse
  Full of crusadoes.° And but my noble Moor   20
  Is true of mind, and made of no such baseness
  As jealous creatures are, it were enough
  To put him to ill thinking.

EMILIA: Is he not jealous?

DESDEMONA: Who? He? I think the sun where he was born
  Drew all such humors° from him.

EMILIA: Look where he comes.   25

Enter OTHELLO.

DESDEMONA: I will not leave him now till Cassio
  Be called to him. How is't with you, my lord?

OTHELLO: Well, my good lady. [*Aside*] O, hardness to dissemble!°—
  How do you, Desdemona?

DESDEMONA: Well, my good lord.

OTHELLO: Give me your hand. This hand is moist,° my lady.   30

DESDEMONA: It hath felt no age nor known no sorrow.

OTHELLO: This argues° fruitfulness and liberal° heart.
  Hot, hot, and moist. This hand of yours requires
  A sequester° from liberty; fasting and prayer;
  Much castigation; exercise devout;   35
  For here's a young and sweating devil here
  That commonly rebels. 'Tis a good hand,
  A frank one.

DESDEMONA: You may, indeed, say so;

---

⁹**lie in mine own throat** *(to lie in the throat is to lie absolutely and completely).*   ¹⁰**edified**   *enlightened (Desdemona mocks the Clown's overly elaborate diction).*   ¹³**moved** *pleaded with.*   ¹⁵**compass** *reach.*
¹⁷**should** *might.*   ²⁰**crusadoes** *Portuguese gold coins.*   ²⁵**humors** *characteristics.*   ²⁸**hardness to
dissemble** *(Othello may refer here either to the difficulty he has in maintaining his appearance of composure, or to
what he believes to be Desdemona's hardened hypocrisy).*   ³⁰**moist** *(a moist, hot hand was taken as a sign of a
lustful nature).*   ³²**argues** *suggests.*   ³²**liberal** *free, open (but also with a suggestion of "licentious"; from
here on in this scene Othello's words bear a double meaning, seeming to be normal but accusing Desdemona of being unfaithful).*   ³⁴**sequester** *separation.*

For 'twas that hand that gave away my heart.

OTHELLO: A liberal hand! The hearts of old gave hands,   40
    But our new heraldry° is hands, not hearts.

DESDEMONA: I cannot speak of this. Come now, your promise!

OTHELLO: What promise, chuck?

DESDEMONA: I have sent to bid Cassio come speak with you.

OTHELLO: I have a salt and sorry rheum° offends me.   45
    Lend me thy handkerchief.

DESDEMONA: Here, my lord.

OTHELLO: That which I gave you.

DESDEMONA: I have it not about me.

OTHELLO: Not?

DESDEMONA: No, indeed, my lord.

OTHELLO: That's a fault.   50
    That handkerchief
    Did an Egyptian to my mother give.
    She was a charmer,° and could almost read
    The thoughts of people. She told her, while she kept it
    'Twould make her amiable° and subdue my father
    Entirely to her love; but if she lost it   55
    Or made a gift of it, my father's eye
    Should hold her loathèd, and his spirits should hunt
    After new fancies. She, dying, gave it me,
    And bid me, when my fate would have me wived,
    To give it her. I did so; and take heed on't;   60
    Make it a darling like your precious eye.
    To lose't or give't away were such perdition
    As nothing else could match.

DESDEMONA: Is't possible?

OTHELLO: 'Tis true. There's magic in the web° of it.
    A sibyl that had numbered in the world   65
    The sun to course two hundred compasses,
    In her prophetic fury° sewed the work;
    The worms were hallowed that did breed the silk,
    And it was dyed in mummy° which the skillful
    Conserved of maidens' hearts.

DESDEMONA: Indeed? Is't true?   70

OTHELLO: Most veritable. Therefore look to't well.

DESDEMONA: Then would to God that I had never seen't!

OTHELLO: Ha! Wherefore?

DESDEMONA: Why do you speak so startingly and rash?

OTHELLO: Is't lost? Is't gone? Speak, is it out o' th' way?   75

DESDEMONA: Heaven bless us!

---

⁴¹**heraldry** *heraldic symbolism.*   ⁴⁵**a salt and sorry rheum** *a heavy, running head cold.*   ⁵²**charmer**
magician.   ⁵⁴**amiable** *desirable.*   ⁶⁴**web** *weaving.*   ⁶⁷**prophetic fury** *seized by the spirit and able to*
prophesy.   ⁶⁹**mummy** *liquid drained from embalmed bodies.*

OTHELLO: Say you?
DESDEMONA: It is not lost. But what an if it were?
OTHELLO: How?
DESDEMONA: I say it is not lost.   80
OTHELLO: Fetch't, let me see't!
DESDEMONA: Why, so I can; but I will not now.
    This is a trick to put me from my suit:
    Pray you let Cassio be received again.
OTHELLO: Fetch me the handkerchief! My mind misgives.   85
DESDEMONA: Come, come!
    You'll never meet a more sufficient° man—
OTHELLO: The handkerchief!
DESDEMONA: A man that all his time
    Hath founded his good fortunes on your love,
    Shared dangers with you—   90
OTHELLO: The handkerchief!
DESDEMONA: I'faith, you are to blame.
OTHELLO: Away!   *Exit* OTHELLO.
EMILIA: Is not this man jealous?
DESDEMONA: I nev'r saw this before.   95
    Sure there's some wonder in this handkerchief;
    I am most unhappy in the loss of it.
EMILIA: 'Tis not a year or two shows us a man.
    They are all but stomachs, and we all but food;
    They eat us hungerly, and when they are full,   100
    They belch us.

                    Enter IAGO *and* CASSIO.

            Look you, Cassio and my husband.
IAGO: There is no other way; 'tis she must do't.
    And lo the happiness! Go and importune her.
DESDEMONA: How now, good Cassio? What's the news with you?
CASSIO: Madam, my former suit. I do beseech you   105
    That by your virtuous means I may again
    Exist, and be a member of his love
    Whom I with all the office° of my heart
    Entirely honor. I would not be delayed.
    If my offense be of such mortal kind   110
    That nor my service past, nor present sorrows,
    Nor purposed merit in futurity,
    Can ransom me into his love again,
    But to know so must be my benefit.°
    So shall I clothe me in a forced content,   115
    And shut myself up in some other course
    To fortune's alms.

---

⁸⁷*sufficient*   *complete, with all proper qualities.*   ¹⁰⁸*office*   *duty.*   ¹¹⁴*benefit*   *good.*

DESMONA: Alas, thrice-gentle Cassio,
My advocation° is not now in tune.
My lord is not my lord; nor should I know him
Were he in favor° as in humor altered. 120
So help me every spirit sanctified
As I have spoken for you all my best
And stood within the blank° of his displeasure
For my free speech. You must awhile be patient.
What I can do I will; and more I will 125
Than for myself I dare. Let that suffice you.
IAGO: Is my lord angry?
EMILIA: He went hence but now,
And certainly in strange unquietness.
IAGO: Can he be angry? I have seen the cannon
When it hath blown his ranks into the air 130
And, like the devil, from his very arm
Puffed his own brother. And is he angry?
Something of moment° then. I will go meet him.
There's matter in't indeed if he be angry.
DESMONA: I prithee do so.   *Exit* [IAGO.]
                              Something sure of state,° 135
Either from Venice or some unhatched practice°
Made demonstrable here in Cyprus to him,
Hath puddled° his clear spirit; and in such cases
Men's natures wrangle with inferior things,
Though great ones are their object. 'Tis even so. 140
For let our finger ache, and it endues°
Our other, healthful members even to a sense
Of pain. Nay, we must think men are not gods,
Nor of them look for such observancy
As fits the bridal. Beshrew me much, Emilia, 145
I was, unhandsome warrior as I am,
Arraigning his unkindness with my soul;
But now I find I had suborned the witness,
And he's indicted falsely.
EMILIA: Pray heaven it be
State matters, as you think, and no conception 150
Nor no jealous toy° concerning you.
DESMONA: Alas the day! I never gave him cause.
EMILIA: But jealous souls will not be answered so;
They are not ever jealous for the cause,
But jealous for they're jealous. It is a monster 155
Begot upon itself, born on itself.

---

[118]*advocation* advocacy.   [120]*favor* countenance.   [123]*blank* bull's-eye of a target.   [133]*moment* importance.   [135]*of state* state affairs.   [136]*unhatched practice* undisclosed plot.   [138]*puddled* muddied.
[141]*endues* leads.   [151]*toy* trifle.

DESDEMONA: Heaven keep the monster from Othello's mind!
EMILIA: Lady, amen.
DESDEMONA: I will go seek him. Cassio, walk here about.
   If I do find him fit,° I'll move your suit   160
   And seek to effect it to my uttermost.
CASSIO: I humbly thank your ladyship.   *Exit* [DESDEMONA *with* EMILIA].

Enter BIANCA.

BIANCA: Save you, friend Cassio!
CASSIO: What make you from home?
   How is't with you, my most fair Bianca?
   I' faith, sweet love, I was coming to your house.   165
BIANCA: And I was going to your lodging, Cassio.
   What, keep a week away? Seven days and nights?
   Eightscore eight hours? And lovers' absent hours
   More tedious than the dial eightscore times?
   O weary reck'ning.°
CASSIO: Pardon me, Bianca.   170
   I have this while with leaden thoughts been pressed,
   But I shall in a more continuate° time
   Strike off this score° of absence. Sweet Bianca,

[*Gives her* DESDEMONA'S *handkerchief.*]

   Take me this work out.
BIANCA: O Cassio, whence came this?
   This is some token from a newer friend.   175
   To the felt absence now I feel a cause.
   Is't come to this? Well, well.
CASSIO: Go to, woman!
   Throw your vile guesses in the devil's teeth,
   From whence you have them. You are jealous now
   That this is from some mistress, some remembrance.   180
   No, by my faith, Bianca.
BIANCA: Why, whose is it?
CASSIO: I know not neither; I found it in my chamber.
   I like the work well; ere it be demanded,°
   As like enough it will, I would have it copied.
   Take it and do't, and leave me for this time.   185
BIANCA: Leave you? Wherefore?
CASSIO: I do attend here on the general
   And think it no addition, nor my wish,
   To have him see me womaned.
BIANCA: Why, I pray you?

---

¹⁶⁰*fit* receptive.   ¹⁷⁰*reck'ning* addition.   ¹⁷²*continuate* uninterrupted.   ¹⁷³***Strike off this score***
i.e., pay this bill (the score being the account of drinks kept in a tavern).   ¹⁸³***demanded*** *asked for (by the person who lost it).*

CASSIO: Not that I love you not.
BIANCA: But that you do not love me!   190
    I pray you bring° me on the way a little,
    And say if I shall see you soon at night.
CASSIO: 'Tis but a little way that I can bring you,
    For I attend here; but I'll see you soon.
BIANCA: 'Tis very good. I must be circumstanced.°   *Exeunt omnes.* 195

ACT IV

Scene I [A street.]

Enter OTHELLO *and* IAGO.

IAGO: Will you think so?
OTHELLO: Think so, Iago?
IAGO: What,
    To kiss in private?
OTHELLO: An unauthorized° kiss?
IAGO: Or to be naked with her friend in bed
    An hour or more, not meaning any harm?
OTHELLO: Naked in bed, Iago, and not mean harm?   5
    It is hypocrisy against the devil.
    They that mean virtuously, and yet do so,
    The devil their virtue tempts, and they tempt heaven.
IAGO: If they do nothing,'tis a venial slip.
    But if I give my wife a handkerchief—   10
OTHELLO: What then?
IAGO: Why, then 'tis hers, my lord; and being hers,
    She may, I think, bestow't on any man.
OTHELLO: She is protectress of her honor too.
    May she give that?   15
IAGO: Her honor is an essence that's not seen;
    They have it very oft that have it not.
    But for the handkerchief—
OTHELLO: By heaven, I would most gladly have forgot it!
    Thou said'st—O, it comes o'er my memory   20
    As doth the raven° o'er the infected house,
    Boding to all—he had my handkerchief.
IAGO: Ay, what of that?
OTHELLO: That's not so good now.
IAGO: What if I had said I had seen him do you wrong?

191**bring** *accompany.* 195**be circumstanced** *accept things as they are.* **IV.i.** 2**unauthorized** *illicit.*
21**raven** *(a harbinger of death).*

Or heard him say—as knaves be such abroad°   25
Who having, by their own importunate suit,
Or voluntary dotage° of some mistress,
Convincèd or supplied° them, cannot choose
But they must blab—
OTHELLO: Hath he said anything?
IAGO: He hath, my lord; but be you well assured,   30
No more than he'll unswear.
OTHELLO: What hath he said?
IAGO: Why, that he did—I know not what he did.
OTHELLO: What? what?
IAGO: Lie—
OTHELLO: With her?
IAGO: With her, on her; what you will.   35
OTHELLO: Lie with her? Lie on her?—We say lie on her when they belie her.—
    Lie with her! Zounds, that's fulsome.°—Handkerchief—confessions—   40
    handkerchief!—To confess, and be hanged for his labor—first to be hanged,
    and then to confess! I tremble at it. Nature would not invest herself in such
    shadowing passion without some instruction.° It is not words that shakes me
    thus.—Pish! Noses, ears, and lips? Is't possible?—Confess?—Handkerchief?—
    O devil!   *Falls in a trance.*
IAGO: Work on.
    My med'cine works! Thus credulous fools are caught,
    And many worthy and chaste dames even thus,   45
    All guiltless, meet reproach.° What, ho! My lord!
    My lord, I say! Othello!

                                Enter CASSIO.

                            How now, Cassio?
CASSIO: What's the matter?
IAGO: My lord is fall'n into an epilepsy.
    This is his second fit; he had one yesterday.   50
CASSIO: Rub him about the temples.
IAGO: The lethargy° must have his quiet course.
    If not, he foams at mouth, and by and by
    Breaks out to savage madness. Look, he stirs.
    Do you withdraw yourself a little while.   55
    He will recover straight. When he is gone,
    I would on great occasion° speak with you.   [*Exit* CASSIO.]
    How is it, general? Have you not hurt your head?
OTHELLO: Dost thou mock° me?

---

²⁵*abroad*   i.e., in the world.   ²⁷*voluntary dotage*   weakness of the will.   ²⁸*Convincèd or supplied*   per-
suaded or gratified (the mistress).   ³⁷*fulsome*   foul, repulsive.   ^{39–40}*Nature . . . instruction*   i.e., my
mind would not become so darkened (with anger) unless there were something in this (accusation); (it should be remembered that Othello believes in the workings of magic and supernatural forces).   ⁴⁶*reproach*   shame.
⁵²*lethargy*   coma.   ⁵⁷*great occasion*   very important matter.   ⁵⁹*mock*   (Othello takes Iago's comment as
a reference to his horns—which it is).

IAGO: I mock you not, by heaven.
   Would you would bear your fortune like a man.   60
OTHELLO: A hornèd man's a monster and a beast.
IAGO: There's many a beast then in a populous city,
   And many a civil° monster.
OTHELLO: Did he confess it?
IAGO: Good, sir, be a man.
   Think every bearded fellow that's but yoked   65
   May draw° with you. There's millions now alive
   That nightly lie in those unproper° beds
   Which they dare swear peculiar.° Your case is better.
   O, 'tis the spite of hell, the fiend's arch-mock,
   To lip a wanton in a secure couch,   70
   And to suppose her chaste. No, let me know;
   And knowing what I am, I know what she shall be.
OTHELLO: O, thou art wise! 'Tis certain.
IAGO: Stand you awhile apart;
   Confine yourself but in a patient list.°
   Whilst you were here, o'erwhelmèd with your grief—   75
   A passion most unsuiting such a man—
   Cassio came hither. I shifted him away°
   And laid good 'scuses upon your ecstasy,°
   Bade him anon return, and here speak with me;
   The which he promised. Do but encave° yourself   80
   And mark the fleers,° the gibes, and notable° scorns
   That dwell in every region of his face.
   For I will make him tell the tale anew:
   Where, how, how oft, how long ago, and when
   He hath, and is again to cope your wife.   85
   I say, but mark his gesture. Marry patience,
   Or I shall say you're all in all in spleen,°
   And nothing of a man.
OTHELLO: Dost thou hear, Iago?
   I will be found most cunning in my patience;
   But—dost thou hear?—most bloody.
IAGO: That's not amiss;   90
   But yet keep time in all. Will you withdraw?

[OTHELLO *moves to one side, where his remarks are not audible to* CASSIO *and* IAGO.]

   Now will I question Cassio of Bianca,
   A huswife° that by selling her desires

---

⁶³*civil* city-dwelling.   ⁶⁶*draw* i.e., like the horned ox.   ⁶⁷*unproper* i.e., not exclusively the husband's.
⁶⁸*peculiar* their own alone.   ⁷⁴*a patient list* the bounds of patience.   ⁷⁷*shifted him away* got rid of
him by a strategem.   ⁷⁸*ecstasy* trance (the literal meaning, "outside oneself," bears on the meaning of the change
Othello is undergoing).   ⁸⁰*encave* hide.   ⁸¹*fleers* mocking looks or speeches.   ⁸¹*notable* obvious.
⁸⁷*spleen* passion, particularly anger.   ⁹³*huswife* housewife (but with the special meaning here of "prostitute").

Buys herself bread and cloth. It is a creature
That dotes on Cassio, as 'tis the strumpet's plague   95
To beguile many and be beguiled by one.
He, when he hears of her, cannot restrain
From the excess of laughter. Here he comes.

Enter CASSIO.

As he shall smile, Othello shall go mad:
And his unbookish° jealousy must conster°   100
Poor Cassio's smiles, gestures, and light behaviors
Quite in the wrong. How do you, lieutenant?
CASSIO: The worser that you give me the addition°
   Whose want even kills me.
IAGO: Ply Desdemona well, and you are sure on't.   105
   Now, if this suit lay in Bianca's power,
   How quickly should you speed!
CASSIO: Alas, poor caitiff!°
OTHELLO: Look how he laughs already!
IAGO: I never knew woman love man so.
CASSIO: Alas, poor rogue! I think, i' faith, she loves me. 110
OTHELLO: Now he denies it faintly, and laughs it out.
IAGO: Do you hear, Cassio?
OTHELLO: Now he importunes him
   To tell it o'er. Go to! Well said, well said!
IAGO: She gives it out that you shall marry her.
   Do you intend it?   115
CASSIO: Ha, ha, ha!
OTHELLO: Do ye triumph, Roman? Do you triumph?
CASSIO: I marry? What, a customer?° Prithee bear some charity to my wit; do not
   think it so unwholesome. Ha, ha, ha!
OTHELLO: So, so, so, so. They laugh that win.   120
IAGO: Why, the cry goes that you marry her.
CASSIO: Prithee, say true.
IAGO: I am a very villain else.
OTHELLO: Have you scored° me? Well.   125
CASSIO: This is the monkey's own giving out. She is persuaded I will marry her
   out of her own love and flattery, not out of my promise.
OTHELLO: Iago beckons me; now he begins the story.

[OTHELLO *moves close enough to hear.*]

CASSIO: She was here even now; she haunts me in every place. I was the other day
   talking on the sea bank with certain Venetians, and thither comes the bauble,° 130
   and falls me thus about my neck—

---

¹⁰⁰**unbookish**   *ignorant.*   ¹⁰⁰**conster**   *construe.*   ¹⁰³**addition**   *title.*   ¹⁰⁷**caitiff**   *wretch.*
¹¹⁸**customer**   *one who sells, a merchant (here, a prostitute).*   ¹²⁴**scored**   *marked, defaced.*   ¹³⁰**bauble**
plaything.

OTHELLO: Crying "O dear Cassio!" as it were. His gesture imports it.

CASSIO: So hangs, and lolls, and weeps upon me; so shakes and pulls me! Ha, ha, ha!

OTHELLO: Now he tells how she plucked him to my chamber. O, I see that nose 135
of yours, but not that dog I shall throw it to.

CASSIO: Well, I must leave her company.

IAGO: Before me!° Look where she comes.

Enter BIANCA.

CASSIO: 'Tis such another fitchew!° Marry a perfumed one? What do you mean
by this haunting of me? 140

BIANCA: Let the devil and his dam haunt you! What did you mean by that same
handkerchief you gave me even now? I was a fine fool to take it. I must take out
the work? A likely piece of work that you should find it in your chamber and
know not who left it there! This is some minx's token, and I must take out the
work? There! [*She throws down the handkerchief.*] Give it your hobbyhorse.° 145
Wheresoever you had it, I'll take out no work on't.

CASSIO: How now, my sweet Bianca? How now? how now?

OTHELLO: By heaven, that should be my handkerchief!

BIANCA: If you'll come to supper tonight, you may; if you will not, come when 150
you are next prepared for.° *Exit.*

IAGO: After her, after her!

CASSIO: Faith, I must; she'll rail in the streets else.

IAGO: Will you sup there?

CASSIO: Yes, I intend so. 155

IAGO: Well, I may chance to see you, for I would very fain speak with you.

CASSIO: Prithee come. Will you?

IAGO: Go to, say no more. [*Exit* CASSIO.]

OTHELLO [*Comes forward*]: How shall I murder him, Iago?

IAGO: Did you perceive how he laughed at his vice? 160

OTHELLO: O Iago!

IAGO: And did you see the handkerchief?

OTHELLO: Was that mine?

IAGO: Yours, by this hand! And to see how he prizes the foolish woman your wife!
She gave it him, and he hath giv'n it his whore. 165

OTHELLO: I would have him nine years a-killing!—A fine woman, a fair woman,
a sweet woman?

IAGO: Nay, you must forget that.

OTHELLO: Ay, let her rot, and perish, and be damned tonight; for she shall not live.
No, my heart is turned to stone; I strike it, and it hurts my hand. O, the world 170
hath not a sweeter creature! She might lie by an emperor's side and command
him tasks.

IAGO: Nay, that's not your way.°

---

[137]**Before me!** *(an exclamation of surprise).* [138]**fitchew** *polecat, i.e, strong-smelling creature.* [145]**hob-**
byhorse *prostitute.* [150]**next prepared for** *next expected—i.e., never.* [172]**way** *proper course.*

OTHELLO: Hang her! I do but say what she is. So delicate with her needle. An admirable musician. O, she will sing the savageness out of a bear! Of so high and
plenteous wit and invention°—   175

IAGO: She's the worse for all this.

OTHELLO: O, a thousand, a thousand times. And then, of so gentle a condition?°

IAGO: Ay, too gentle.

OTHELLO: Nay, that's certain. But yet the pity of it, Iago. O Iago, the pity of it,
Iago.   180

IAGO: If you are so fond over her iniquity, give her patent to offend; for if it touch°
not you, it comes near nobody.

OTHELLO: I will chop her into messes!° Cuckold me!

IAGO: O, 'tis foul in her.   185

OTHELLO: With mine officer!

IAGO: That's fouler.

OTHELLO: Get me some poison, Iago, this night. I'll not expostulate with her, lest
her body and beauty unprovide my mind° again. This night, Iago!

IAGO: Do it not with poison. Strangle her in her bed, even the bed she hath 190
contaminated.

OTHELLO: Good, good! The justice of it pleases. Very good!

IAGO: And for Cassio, let me be his undertaker.° You shall hear more by midnight.

OTHELLO: Excellent good!   [*A trumpet.*]

                     What trumpet is that same?   195

IAGO: I warrant something from Venice.

           Enter LODOVICO, DESDEMONA, *and* ATTENDANTS.

                  'Tis Lodovico.
This comes from the Duke. See, your wife's with him.

LODOVICO: God save you, worthy general.

OTHELLO: With° all my heart, sir.

LODOVICO: The Duke and the senators of Venice greet you.

                            [*Gives him a letter.*]

OTHELLO: I kiss the instrument of their pleasures.   200

                         [*Opens the letter and reads.*]

DESDEMONA: And what's the news, good cousin Lodovico?

IAGO: I am very glad to see you, signior.
Welcome to Cyprus.

LODOVICO: I thank you. How does Lieutenant Cassio?

IAGO: Lives, sir.

DESDEMONA: Cousin, there's fall'n between him and my lord   205
An unkind° breach; but you shall make all well.

OTHELLO: Are you sure of that?

DESDEMONA: My lord?

---

[175]*invention* *imagination.*   [177–78]*gentle a condition* *(1) well born (2) of a gentle nature.*   [183]*touch affects.*   [184]*messes bits.*   [189]*unprovide my mind undo my resolution.*   [193]*undertaker (not "burier"
but "one who undertakes to do something").*   [198]*With i.e., I greet you with.*   [206]*unkind unnatural.*

OTHELLO [*Reads*]: "This fail you not to do, as you will—"
LODOVICO: He did not call; he's busy in the paper.   210
   Is there division 'twixt my lord and Cassio?
DESDEMONA: A most unhappy one. I would do much
   T' atone° them, for the love I bear to Cassio.
OTHELLO: Fire and brimstone!
DESDEMONA: My lord?
OTHELLO: Are you wise?
DESDEMONA: What, is he angry?
LODOVICO: May be th' letter moved him;   215
   For, as I think, they do command him home,
   Deputing Cassio in his government.°
DESDEMONA: Trust me, I am glad on't.
OTHELLO: Indeed?
DESDEMONA: My lord?
OTHELLO: I am glad to see you mad.
DESDEMONA: Why, sweet Othello—
OTHELLO: Devil!   [*Strikes her.*] 220
DESDEMONA: I have not deserved this.
LODOVICO: My lord, this would not be believed in Venice,
   Though I should swear I saw't. 'Tis very much.
   Make her amends; she weeps.
OTHELLO: O devil, devil!
   If that the earth could teem° with woman's tears,   225
   Each drop she falls° would prove a crocodile.°
   Out of my sight!
DESDEMONA: I will not stay to offend you.   [*Going.*]
LODOVICO: Truly, an obedient lady.
   I do beseech your lordship call her back.
OTHELLO: Mistress!
DESDEMONA: My lord?
OTHELLO: What would you with her, sir?   230
LODOVICO: Who? I, my lord?
OTHELLO: Ay! You did wish that I would make her turn.
   Sir, she can turn, and turn, and yet go on
   And turn again; and she can weep, sir, weep;
   And she's obedient; as you say, obedient.   235
   Very obedient. Proceed you in your tears.
   Concerning this, sir—O well-painted passion!
   I am commanded home.—Get you away;
   I'll send for you anon.—Sir, I obey the mandate
   And will return to Venice.—Hence, avaunt!   [*Exit* DESDEMONA.] 240
   Cassio shall have my place. And, sir, tonight
   I do entreat that we may sup together.

---

²¹³*atone*   reconcile.   ²¹⁷*government*   office.   ²²⁵*teem*   conceive.   ²²⁶*falls*   drops.   ²²⁶*crocodile*
(*the crocodile was supposed to shed false tears to lure its victims*).

You are welcome, sir, to Cyprus.—Goats and monkeys!   *Exit.*
LODOVICO: Is this the noble Moor whom our full Senate
    Call all in all sufficient? Is this the nature   245
    Whom passion could not shake? whose solid virtue
    The shot of accident nor dart of chance
    Could neither graze nor pierce?
IAGO: He is much changed.
LODOVICO: Are his wits safe? Is he not light of brain?
IAGO: He's that he is; I may not breathe my censure.   250
    What he might be (if, what he might, he is not)
    I would to heaven he were!
LODOVICO: What, strike his wife?
IAGO: Faith, that was not so well; yet would I knew
    That stroke would prove the worst.
LODOVICO: Is it his use?°
    Or did the letters work upon his blood°   255
    And new-create his fault?
IAGO: Alas, alas!
    It is not honesty in me to speak
    What I have seen and known. You shall observe him,
    And his own courses° will denote him so
    That I may save my speech. Do but go after   260
    And mark how he continues.
LODOVICO: I am sorry that I am deceived in him.   *Exeunt.*

Scene II [*The citadel.*]

               Enter OTHELLO *and* EMILIA.

OTHELLO: You have seen nothing then?
EMILIA: Nor ever heard, nor ever did suspect.
OTHELLO: Yes, you have seen Cassio and she together.
EMILIA: But then I saw no harm, and then I heard
    Each syllable that breath made up° between them.   5
OTHELLO: What, did they never whisper?
EMILIA: Never, my lord.
OTHELLO: Nor send you out o' th' way?
EMILIA: Never.
OTHELLO: To fetch her fan, her gloves, her mask, nor nothing?
EMILIA: Never, my lord.   10
OTHELLO: That's strange.
EMILIA: I durst, my lord, to wager she is honest,
    Lay down my soul at stake.° If you think other,
    Remove your thought. It doth abuse your bosom.

---

²⁵⁴**use** *habit*   ²⁵⁵**blood** *passion.*   ²⁵⁹**courses** *actions.*   **IV.ii.**   ⁵**that breath made up** *spoken.*
¹³**at stake** *as the wager.*

If any wretch have put this in your head,   15
Let heaven requite it with the serpent's curse,°
For if she be not honest,° chaste, and true,
There's no man happy. The purest of their wives
Is foul as slander.
OTHELLO: Bid her come hither. Go.   *Exit* EMILIA.
 She says enough; yet she's a simple bawd°   20
 That cannot say as much. This is a subtle whore,
 A closet lock and key of villainous secrets,
 And yet she'll kneel and pray; I have seen her do't.

Enter DESDEMONA *and* EMILIA.

DESDEMONA: My lord, what is your will?
OTHELLO: Pray you, chuck, come hither.
DESDEMONA: What is your pleasure?
OTHELLO: Let me see your eyes.   25
 Look in my face.
DESDEMONA: What horrible fancy's this?
OTHELLO [*To* EMILIA]: Some of your function°, mistress:
 Leave procreants alone and shut the door;
 Cough or cry hem if anybody come.
 Your mystery°, your mystery! Nay, dispatch!   *Exit* EMILIA. 30
DESDEMONA: Upon my knee, what doth your speech import?
 I understand a fury in your words.°
OTHELLO: Why, what art thou?
DESDEMONA: Your wife, my lord; your true
 And loyal wife.
OTHELLO: Come, swear it, damn thyself;
 Lest, being like one of heaven, the devils themselves   35
 Should fear to seize thee. Therefore be doubledamned:
 Swear thou art honest.
DESDEMONA: Heaven doth truly know it.
OTHELLO: Heaven truly knows that thou art false as hell.
DESDEMONA: To whom, my lord? With whom? How am I false?
OTHELLO: Ah, Desdemon! Away! Away! Away!   40
DESDEMONA: Alas the heavy day! Why do you weep?
 Am I the motive° of these tears, my lord?
 If haply° you my father do suspect
 An instrument of this your calling back,
 Lay not your blame on me. If you have lost him,   45
 I have lost him too.
OTHELLO: Had it pleased heaven
 To try me with affliction, had they rained

---

¹⁶**serpent's curse** *(God's curse on the serpent after the fall of Eden).* ¹⁷**honest** *chaste.* ²⁰**bawd** *pro-*
curess. ²⁷**Some of your function** *do your proper work (as the operator of a brothel).* ³⁰**mystery** *trade.*
³²**words** *words (Q1 adds to this line, "But not the words").* ⁴²**motive** *cause.* ⁴³**haply** *by chance.*

All kinds of sores and shames on my bare head,
Steeped° me in poverty to the very lips,
Given to captivity me and my utmost hopes,   50
I should have found in some place of my soul
A drop of patience. But alas, to make me
The fixèd figure for the time of scorn°
To point his slow and moving finger at.
Yet could I bear that too, well, very well.   55
But there where I have garnered up my heart,
Where either I must live or bear no life,
The fountain from the which my current runs
Or else dries up—to be discarded thence,
Or keep it as a cistern for foul toads   60
To knot and gender° in—turn thy complexion there,
Patience, thou young and rose-lipped cherubin!
I here look grim as hell!°
DESDEMONA: I hope my noble lord esteems me honest.
OTHELLO: O, ay, as summer flies are in the shambles,°   65
    That quicken even with blowing.° O thou weed,
    Who art so lovely fair, and smell'st so sweet,
    That the sense aches at thee, would thou hadst never been born!
DESDEMONA: Alas, what ignorant° sin have I committed?
OTHELLO: Was this fair paper, this most goodly book,   70
    Made to write "whore" upon? What committed?
    Committed? O thou public commoner,°
    I should make very forges of my cheeks
    That would to cinders burn up modesty,
    Did I but speak thy deeds. What committed?   75
    Heaven stops the nose at it, and the moon winks;°
    The bawdy wind that kisses all it meets
    Is hushed within the hollow mine of earth
    And will not hear't. What committed?
DESDEMONA: By heaven, you do me wrong!   80
OTHELLO: Are not you a strumpet?
DESDEMONA: No, as I am a Christian!
    If to preserve this vessel for my lord
    From any other foul unlawful touch
    Be not to be a strumpet, I am none.
OTHELLO: What, not a whore?
DESDEMONA: No, as I shall be saved!   85
OTHELLO: Is't possible?

---

⁴⁹**Steeped** *submerged.*   ⁵³**The . . . scorn** *the very image of scorn in our time.*   ⁶¹**knot and gender**
twist in bunches and procreate.   ⁶¹⁻⁶³**turn . . . hell** *(the rough sense would seem to be "even Patience would*
grow pale, turn complexion, at Desdemona's perfidy, but that Othello looks grimly on).   ⁶⁵**shambles** *abattoirs.*
⁶⁶**quicken even with blowing** *become impregnated as soon as they lay their eggs.*   ⁶⁹**ignorant** *unknowing.*
⁷²**commonor** *prostitute.*   ⁷⁶**winks** *closes its eyes (the moon was the symbol of chastity).*

DESDEMONA: O, heaven forgive us!

OTHELLO: I cry you mercy° then.

   I took you for that cunning whore of Venice

   That married with Othello. [*Calling*] You, mistress,

Enter EMILIA.

   That have the office opposite to Saint Peter   90

   And keep the gate of hell! You, you, ay, you!

   We have done our course; there's money for your pains.

[Throws her some coins.]

   I pray you turn the key and keep our counsel.   *Exit.*

EMILIA: Alas, what does this gentleman conceive?

   How do you, madam? How do you, my good lady?   95

DESDEMONA: Faith, half asleep.

EMILIA: Good madam, what's the matter with my lord?

DESDEMONA: With who?

EMILIA: Why, with my lord, madam.

DESDEMONA: Who is thy lord?

EMILIA: He that is yours, sweet lady.   100

DESDEMONA: I have none. Do not talk to me, Emilia.

   I cannot weep, nor answers have I none

   But what should go by water.° Prithee tonight

   Lay on my bed my wedding sheets, remember;

   And call thy husband hither.

EMILIA: Here's a change indeed!   *Exit.* 105

DESDEMONA: 'Tis meet I should be used so, very meet.

   How have I been behaved, that he might stick

   The small'st opinion on my least misuse?°

Enter IAGO and EMILIA.

IAGO: What is your pleasure, madam? How is't with you?

DESDEMONA: I cannot tell. Those that do teach young babes   110

   Do it with gentle means and easy tasks.

   He might have chid me so; for, in good faith,

   I am a child to chiding.

IAGO: What is the matter, lady?

EMILIA: Alas, Iago, my lord hath so bewhored her,

   Thrown such despite° and heavy terms upon her   115

   That true hearts cannot bear it.

DESDEMONA: Am I that name, Iago?

IAGO: What name, fair lady?

DESDEMONA: Such as she said my lord did say I was.

EMILIA: He called her whore. A beggar in his drink

---

[87]**cry you mercy** *ask your pardon.*   [103]**water** *tears.*   [107–8]**stick ... misuse** *base any doubt on my smallest fault.*   [115]**despite** *abuse.*

Could not have laid such terms upon his callet.°   120
IAGO: Why did he so?
DESDEMONA: I do not know; I am sure I am none such.
IAGO: Do not weep, do not weep. Alas the day.
EMILIA: Hath she forsook so many noble matches,
 Her father and her country, and her friends,   125
 To be called whore? Would it not make one weep?
DESDEMONA: It is my wretched fortune.
IAGO: Beshrew° him for't!
 How comes this trick upon him?
DESDEMONA: Nay, heaven doth know.
EMILIA: I will be hanged if some eternal villain,
 Some busy and insinuating rogue,   130
 Some cogging,° cozening slave, to get some office,
 Have not devised this slander. I will be hanged else.
IAGO: Fie, there is no such man! It is impossible.
DESDEMONA: If any such there be, heaven pardon him.
EMILIA: A halter pardon him! And hell gnaw his bones!   135
 Why should he call her whore? Who keeps her company?
 What place? What time? What form? What likelihood?
 The Moor's abused by some most villainous knave,
 Some base notorious knave, some scurvy fellow.
 O heavens, that such companions° thou'dst unfold,°   140
 And put in every honest hand a whip
 To lash the rascals naked through the world
 Even from the east to th' west!
IAGO: Speak within door.°
EMILIA: O, fie upon them! Some such squire° he was
 That turned your wit the seamy side without   145
 And made you to suspect me with the Moor.
IAGO: You are a fool. Go to.
DESDEMONA: Alas, Iago,
 What shall I do to win my lord again?
 Good friend, go to him, for, by this light of heaven,
 I know not how I lost him. Here I kneel: 150
 If e'er my will did trespass 'gainst his love
 Either in discourse of thought° or actual deed,
 Or that mine eyes, mine ears, or any sense
 Delighted them in any other form;
 Or that I do not yet, and ever did,   155
 And ever will (though he do shake me off
 To beggarly divorcement) love him dearly,
 Comfort forswear me. Unkindness may do much,

---

¹²⁰*callet* *slut.* ¹²⁷*Beshrew* *curse.* ¹³¹*cogging* *cheating.* ¹⁴⁰*companions* *fellows, rogues.*
¹⁴⁰*unfold* *disclose.* ¹⁴³*within door* *more quietly and moderately.* ¹⁴⁴*squire* *(a term of contempt).*
¹⁵²*discourse of thought* *thinking.*

And his unkindness may defeat° my life,
But never taint my love. I cannot say "whore." 160
It does abhor me now I speak the word;
To do the act that might the addition earn
Not the world's mass of vanity could make me.
IAGO: I pray you be content. 'Tis but his humor.°
The business of the state does him offense. 165
DESDEMONA: If 'twere no other.
IAGO: It is but so, I warrant.   [*Trumpets within.*]
Hark how these instruments summon to supper.
The messengers of Venice stay the meat.°
Go in, and weep not. All things shall be well.

[*Exeunt* DESDEMONA *and* EMILIA. *Enter* RODERIGO.]

How now, Roderigo? 170
RODERIGO: I do not find that thou deal'st justly with me.
IAGO: What in the contrary?
RODERIGO: Every day thou daff'st° me with some device,° Iago, and rather, as it
seems to me now, keep'st from me all conveniency° than suppliest me with the
least advantage of hope. I will indeed no longer endure it; nor am I yet 175
persuaded to put up° in peace what already I have foolishly suffered.
IAGO: Will you hear me, Roderigo?
RODERIGO: I have heard too much, and your words and performances are no kin
together. 180
IAGO: You charge me most unjustly.
RODERIGO: With naught but truth. I have wasted myself out of my means. The
jewels you have had from me to deliver Desdemona would half have corrupted
a votarist.° You have told me she hath received them, and returned me
expectations and comforts of sudden respect° and acquaintance; but I find none. 185
IAGO: Well, go to; very well.
RODERIGO: Very well? Go to? I cannot go to, man; nor 'tis not very well. Nay, I
think it is scurvy, and begin to find myself fopped° in it.
IAGO: Very well.
RODERIGO: I tell you 'tis not very well. I will make myself known to Desdemona. 190
If she will return me my jewels, I will give over my suit and repent my unlawful
solicitation. If not, assure yourself I will seek satisfaction of you.
IAGO: You have said now?
RODERIGO: Ay, and said nothing but what I protest° intendment of doing. 195
IAGO: Why, now I see there's mettle° in thee, and even from this instant do build
on thee a better opinion than ever before. Give me thy hand, Roderigo. Thou
hast taken against me a most just exception,° but yet I protest I have dealt most
directly° in thy affair.

---

¹⁵⁹*defeat* *destroy.*   ¹⁶⁴*humor* *mood.*   ¹⁶⁸*stay the meat* *await the meal.*   ¹⁷³*daff'st* *put off.*
¹⁷³*device* *scheme.*   ¹⁷⁴*conveniency* *what is needful.*   ¹⁷⁶*put up* *accept.*   ¹⁸⁵*sudden respect* *im-*
mediate *consideration.*   ¹⁸⁹*fopped* *duped.*   ¹⁸⁴*votarist* *nun.*   ¹⁹⁶*protest* *aver.*   ¹⁹⁷*mettle*
spirit.   ¹⁹⁹*exception* *objection.*   ²⁰⁰*directly* *straight-forwardly.*

RODERIGO: It hath not appeared.

IAGO: I grant indeed it hath not appeared, and your suspicion is not without wit and judgment. But, Roderigo, if thou hast that in thee indeed which I have greater reason to believe now than ever—I mean purpose, courage, and valor—this night show it. If thou the next night following enjoy not Desdemona, take 205 me from this world with treachery and devise engines for° my life.

RODERIGO: Well, what is it? Is it within reason and compass?°

IAGO: Sir, there is especial commission come from Venice to depute Cassio in Othello's place. 210

RODERIGO: Is that true? Why, then Othello and Desdemona return again to Venice.

IAGO: O, no; he goes into Mauritania and taketh away with him the fair Desdemona, unless his abode be lingered here by some accident; wherein none can be so determinate° as the removing of Cassio. 215

RODERIGO: How do you mean, removing him?

IAGO: Why, by making him uncapable of Othello's place—knocking out his brains.

RODERIGO: And that you would have me to do?

IAGO: Ay, if you dare do yourself a profit and a right. He sups tonight with a 220 harlotry,° and thither will I go to him. He knows not yet of his honorable fortune. If you will watch his going thence, which I will fashion to fall out° between twelve and one, you may take him at your pleasure. I will be near to second° your attempt, and he shall fall between us. Come, stand not amazed at it, but go along with me. I will show you such a necessity in his death that 225 you shall think yourself bound to put it on him. It is now high supper time, and the night grows to waste. About it.

RODERIGO: I will hear further reason for this.

IAGO: And you shall be satisfied.   *Exeunt.*

Scene III [The citadel.]

Enter OTHELLO, LODOVICO, DESDEMONA, EMILIA, *and* ATTENDANTS.

LODOVICO: I do beseech you, sir, trouble yourself no further.

OTHELLO: O, pardon me; 'twill do me good to walk.

LODOVICO: Madam, good night. I humbly thank your ladyship.

DESDEMONA: Your honor is most welcome.

OTHELLO: Will you walk, sir? O, Desdemona. 5

DESDEMONA: My lord?

OTHELLO: Get you to bed on th' instant; I will be returned forthwith. Dismiss your attendant there. Look 't be done.

DESDEMONA: I will, my lord.   *Exit* [OTHELLO, *with* LODOVICO *and* ATTENDANTS].

EMILIA: How goes it now? He looks gentler than he did. 10

DESDEMONA: He says he will return incontinent,°
    And hath commanded me to go to bed.

206–207*engines for* *schemes against.*   208*compass* *possibility.*   215*determinate* *effective.*   221*har-*
lotry female.   222–23*fall out* *occur.*   224*second* *support.*   **IV.iii.** 11*incontinent* *at once.*

And bade me to dismiss you.
EMILIA: Dismiss me?
DESDEMONA: It was his bidding; therefore, good Emilia,
   Give me my nightly wearing, and adieu.   15
   We must not now displease him.
EMILIA: I would you had never seen him!
DESDEMONA: So would not I. My love doth so approve him
   That even his stubbornness, his checks,° his frowns—
   Prithee unpin me—have grace and favor.   20
EMILIA: I have laid these sheets you bade me on the bed.
DESDEMONA: All's one.° Good Father, how foolish are our minds!
   If I do die before, prithee shroud me
   In one of these same sheets.
EMILIA: Come, come! You talk.
DESDEMONA: My mother had a maid called Barbary.   25
   She was in love; and he she loved proved mad
   And did forsake her. She had a song of "Willow";
   An old thing 'twas, but it expressed her fortune,
   And she died singing it. That song tonight
   Will not go from my mind; I have much to do   30
   But to go hang my head all at one side
   And sing it like poor Barbary. Prithee dispatch.
EMILIA: Shall I go fetch your nightgown?
DESDEMONA: No, unpin me here.
   This Lodovico is a proper man.   35
EMILIA: A very handsome man.
DESDEMONA: He speaks well.
EMILIA: I know a lady in Venice would have walked barefoot to Palestine for a
   touch of his nether lip.
DESDEMONA [*Sings*]:
   "The poor soul sat singing by a sycamore tree,   40
     Sing all a green willow;
   Her hand on her bosom, her head on her knee,
     Sing willow, willow, willow.
   The fresh streams ran by her and murmured her moans;
     Sing willow, willow, willow;   45
   Her salt tears fell from her, and soft'ned the stones—
     Sing willow, willow, willow—"
   Lay by these.   [*Gives* EMILIA *her clothes.*]
     "Willow, Willow"—
   Prithee hie° thee; he'll come anon.°   50
     "Sing all a green willow must be my garland
     Let nobody blame him; his scorn I approve"—
   Nay, that's not next. Hark! Who is't that knocks?
EMILIA: It is the wind.

---

¹⁹**checks**   *rebukes.*   ²²**All's one**   *no matter.*   ⁵⁰**hie**   *hurry.*   ⁵⁰**anon**   *at once.*

DESDEMONA [*Sings*]:
   "I called my love false love; but what said he then?   55
   Sing willow, willow, willow:
   If I court moe° women, you'll couch with moe men."
   So, get thee gone; good night. Mine eyes do itch.
   Doth that bode weeping?
EMILIA: 'Tis neither here nor there.
DESDEMONA: I have heard it said so. O, these men, these men.   60
   Dost thou in conscience think, tell me, Emilia,
   That there be women do abuse their husbands
   In such gross kind?
EMILIA: There be some such, no question.
DESDEMONA: Wouldst thou do such a deed for all the world?
EMILIA: Why, would not you?
DESDEMONA: No, by this heavenly light!   65
EMILIA: Nor I neither by this heavenly light.
   I might do't as well i' th' dark.
DESDEMONA: Wouldst thou do such a deed for all the world?
EMILIA: The world's a huge thing; it is a great price for a small vice.
DESDEMONA: In troth, I think thou wouldst not.   70
EMILIA: In troth, I think I should; and undo't when I had done. Marry, I would not
   do such a thing for a joint-ring,° nor for measures of lawn,° nor for gowns,
   petticoats, nor caps, nor any petty exhibition,° but for all the whole world?
   Why, who would not make her husband a cuckold to make him a monarch? I
   should venture purgatory for't.
DESDEMONA: Beshrew me if I would do such a wrong for the whole world.   75
EMILIA: Why, the wrong is but a wrong i' th' world; and having the world for your
   labor, 'tis a wrong in your own world, and you might quickly make it right.
DESDEMONA: I do not think there is any such woman.
EMILIA: Yes, a dozen; and as many to th' vantage as would store° the world they   80
   played for.
   But I do think it is their husbands' faults
   If wives do fall. Say that they slack their duties
   And pour our treasures into foreign° laps;   85
   Or else break out in peevish jealousies,
   Throwing restraint upon us; or say they strike us,
   Or scant our former having in despite°—
   Why, we have galls; and though we have some grace,
   Yet have we some revenge. Let husbands know   90
   Their wives have sense like them. They see, and smell,
   And have their palates both for sweet and sour,
   As husbands have. What is it that they do
   When they change° us for others? Is it sport?

57**moe** *more.*   72**joint-ring** *(a ring with two interlocking halves).*   72**lawn** *fine linen.*   73**exhibition** *payment.*   81**to . . . store** *in addition as would fill.*   85**foreign** *alien, i.e., other than the wife.*
88**scant . . . despite** *reduce, in spite, our household allowance (?).*   94**change** *exchange.*

I think it is. And doth affection° breed it? 95
I think it doth. Is't frailty that thus errs?
It is so too. And have not we affections?
Desires for sport? and frailty? as men have?
Then let them use us well; else let them know,
The ills we do, their ills instruct us so.° 100
DESDEMONA: Good night, good night. Heaven me such uses° send,
Not to pick bad from bad, but by bad mend. *Exeunt.*

ACT V

Scene I [*A street.*]

Enter IAGO *and* RODERIGO.

IAGO: Here, stand behind this bulk;° straight will he come.
Wear thy good rapier bare, and put it home.
Quick, quick! Fear nothing; I'll be at thy elbow.
It makes us, or it mars us, think on that,
And fix most firm thy resolution. 5
RODERIGO: Be near at hand; I may miscarry in't.
IAGO: Here, at thy hand. Be bold, and take thy stand. [*Moves to one side.*]
RODERIGO: I have no great devotion to the deed,
And yet he hath given me satisfying reasons.
'Tis but a man gone. Forth my sword! He dies! 10
IAGO: I have rubbed this young quat° almost to the sense,°
And he grows angry. Now, whether he kill Cassio,
Or Cassio him, or each do kill the other,
Every way makes my gain. Live Roderigo,
He calls me to a restitution large 15
Of gold and jewels that I bobbed° from him
As gifts to Desdemona.
It must not be. If Cassio do remain,
He hath a daily beauty in his life
That makes me ugly; and besides, the Moor 20
May unfold me to him; there stand I in much peril.
No, he must die. But so, I hear him coming.

Enter CASSIO.

RODERIGO: I know his gait. 'Tis he. Villain, thou diest! [*Thrusts at* CASSIO.]
CASSIO: That thrust had been mine enemy indeed
But that my coat° is better than thou know'st. 25

95**affection** *strong feeling, desire.*   100**instruct us so** *teach us to do likewise.*   101**uses** *practices.*
V.i. 1**bulk** *projecting stall of a shop.*   11**quat** *pimple.*   11**to the sense** *raw.*   16**bobbed** *swindled.*
25**coat** *i.e., a mail shirt or bullet-proof vest.*

I will make proof of thine.   [*Fights with* RODERIGO.]
RODERIGO: O, I am slain!°
CASSIO: I am maimed forever. Help, ho! Murder! Murder!

Enter OTHELLO [*to one side*].

OTHELLO: The voice of Cassio. Iago keeps his word.
RODERIGO: O, villain that I am!
OTHELLO: It is even so.
CASSIO: O help, ho! Light! A surgeon!   30
OTHELLO: 'Tis he. O brave Iago, honest and just,
   That hast such noble sense of thy friend's wrong!
   Thou teachest me. Minion,° your dear lies dead,
   And your unblest° fate hies.° Strumpet, I come.
   Forth of my heart those charms, thine eyes, are blotted.   35
   Thy bed, lust-stained, shall with lust's blood be spotted.

Exit OTHELLO. *Enter* LODOVICO *and* GRATIANO.

CASSIO: What, ho? No watch? No passage?° Murder! Murder!
GRATIANO: 'Tis some mischance. The voice is very direful.
CASSIO: O, help!
LODOVICO: Hark!   40
RODERIGO: O wretched villain!
LODOVICO: Two or three groan. 'Tis heavy night.
   These may be counterfeits. Let's think't unsafe
   To come into the cry without more help.
RODERIGO: Nobody come? Then shall I bleed to death.   45
LODOVICO: Hark!

Enter IAGO [*with a light*].

GRATIANO: Here's one comes in his shirt, with light and weapons.
IAGO: Who's there? Whose noise is this that cries on murder?
LODOVICO: We do not know.
IAGO: Do not you hear a cry?
CASSIO: Here, here! For heaven's sake, help me!
IAGO: What's the matter?   50
GRATIANO: This is Othello's ancient, as I take it.
LODOVICO: The same indeed, a very valiant fellow.
IAGO: What are you here that cry so grievously?
CASSIO: Iago? O, I am spoiled, undone by villains.
   Give me some help.   55

---

²⁶**slain**   *most editors add here a stage direction that has Iago wounding Cassio in the leg from behind, but remaining unseen. However, nothing in the text requires this, and Cassio's wound can be given him in the fight with Roderigo, for presumably when Cassio attacks Roderigo the latter would not simply accept the thrust but would parry. Since Iago enters again at line 46, he must exit at some point after line 22.*   ³³**Minion**   *hussy, i.e., Desdemona.*   ³⁴**un-blest**   *unsanctified.*   ³⁴**hies**   *approaches swiftly.*   ³⁷**passage**   *passers-by.*

IAGO: O me, lieutenant! What villains have done this?

CASSIO: I think that one of them is hereabout
And cannot make away.

IAGO: O treacherous villains!
[*To* LODOVICO *and* GRATIANO] What are you there?
Come in, and give some help. 60

RODERIGO: O, help me here!

CASSIO: That's one of them.

IAGO: O murd'rous slave! O villain! [*Stabs* RODERIGO.]

RODERIGO: O damned Iago! O inhuman dog!

IAGO: Kill men i' th' dark?—Where be these bloody thieves?—
How silent is this town!—Ho! Murder! Murder!— 65
What may you be? Are you of good or evil?

LODOVICO: As you shall prove us, praise us.

IAGO: Signior Lodovico?

LODOVICO: He, sir.

IAGO: I cry you mercy. Here's Cassio hurt by villains. 70

GRATIANO: Cassio?

IAGO: How is't, brother?

CASSIO: My leg is cut in two.

IAGO: Marry, heaven forbid!
Light, gentlemen. I'll bind it with my shirt.

Enter BIANCA.

BIANCA: What is the matter, ho? Who is't that cried? 75

IAGO: Who is't that cried?

BIANCA: O my dear Cassio! My sweet Cassio!
O Cassio, Cassio, Cassio!

IAGO: O notable strumpet!—Cassio, may you suspect
Who they should be that have thus mangled you? 80

CASSIO: No.

GRATIANO: I am sorry to find you thus. I have been to seek you.

IAGO: Lend me a garter. So. O for a chair
To bear him easily hence.

BIANCA: Alas, he faints! O Cassio, Cassio, Cassio! 85

IAGO: Gentlemen all, I do suspect this trash
To be a party in this injury.—
Patience awhile, good Cassio.—Come, come.
Lend me a light. Know we this face or no?
Alas, my friend and my dear countryman 90
Roderigo? No.—Yes, sure.—Yes, 'tis Roderigo!

GRATIANO: What, of Venice?

IAGO: Even he, sir. Did you know him?

GRATIANO: Know him? Ay.

IAGO: Signior Gratiano? I cry your gentle pardon.
These bloody accidents must excuse my manners 95
That so neglected you.

GRATIANO: I am glad to see you.
IAGO: How do you, Cassio?—O, a chair, a chair!
GRATIANO: Roderigo?
IAGO: He, he, 'tis he! [*A chair brought in.*] O, that's well said;° the chair.
   Some good man bear him carefully from hence.   100
   I'll fetch the general's surgeon. [*To* BIANCA] For you, mistress,
   Save you your labor. [*To* CASSIO] He that lies slain here, Cassio,
   Was my dear friend. What malice was between you?
CASSIO: None in the world; nor do I know the man.
IAGO: What, look you pale?—O, bear him out o' th' air.   105

[CASSIO *is carried off.*]

   Stay you, good gentlemen.—Look you pale, mistress?
   Do you perceive the gastness° of her eye?
   Nay, if you stare, we shall hear more anon.
   Behold her well; I pray you look upon her.
   Do you see, gentlemen? Nay, guiltiness will speak,   110
   Though tongues were out of use.°

[*Enter* EMILIA.]

EMILIA: Alas, what is the matter? What is the matter, husband?
IAGO: Cassio hath here been set on in the dark
   By Roderigo and fellows that are scaped.
   He's almost slain, and Roderigo quite dead.   115
EMILIA: Alas, good gentleman! Alas, good Cassio!
IAGO: This is the fruits of whoring. Prithee, Emilia,
   Go know of Cassio where he supped tonight.
   [*To* BIANCA] What, do you shake at that?
BIANCA: He supped at my house; but I therefore shake not.   120
IAGO: O, did he so? I charge° you go with me.
EMILIA: Oh fie upon thee, strumpet!
BIANCA: I am no strumpet, but of life as honest
   As you that thus abuse me.
EMILIA: As I? Fie upon thee!
IAGO: Kind gentlemen, let's go see poor Cassio dressed.°   125
   [*To* BIANCA] Come, mistress, you must tell's another tale.
   Emilia, run you to the citadel
   And tell my lord and lady what hath happed   [*Exit* EMILIA.]
   Will you go on afore?   *Exeunt* [*all but* IAGO].
          This is the night
   That either makes me or fordoes me quite.°   [*Exit.*] 130

99**well said** *well done*   107**gastness** *terror.*   111**tongues out of use** *men no longer spoke.*
121**charge** *command.*   125**dressed** *bandaged.*   130**fordoes me quite** *completely ruins me.*

Scene II. [DESDEMONA'S *chamber.*]

    Enter OTHELLO [*with a light*]; *and* DESDEMONA *in her bed.*

OTHELLO: It is the cause, it is the cause, my soul.
    Let me not name it to you, you chaste stars.
    It is the cause. Yet I'll not shed her blood,
    Nor scar that whiter skin of hers than snow
    And smooth as monumental alabaster.   5
    Yet she must die, else she'll betray more men.
    Put out the light, and then put out the light.
    If I quench thee, thou flaming minister,°
    I can again thy former light restore,
    Should I repent me; but once put out thy light,   10
    Thou cunning'st° pattern of excelling nature,
    I know not where is that Promethean heat°
    That can thy light relume.° When I have plucked the rose,
    I cannot give it vital° growth again;
    It needs must wither. I'll smell thee on the tree.   [*He kisses her.*] 15
    O balmy breath, that dost almost persuade
    Justice to break her sword. One more, one more!
    Be thus when thou art dead, and I will kill thee,
    And love thee after. One more, and that's the last!
    So sweet was ne'er so fatal. I must weep,   20
    But they are cruel tears. This sorrow's heavenly;
    It strikes where it doth love. She wakes.
DESDEMONA: Who's there? Othello?
OTHELLO: Ay, Desdemona.
DESDEMONA: Will you come to bed, my lord?
OTHELLO: Have you prayed tonight, Desdemon?
DESDEMONA: Ay, my lord.   25
OTHELLO: If you bethink yourself of any crime
    Unreconciled as yet to heaven and grace,
    Solicit for it straight.
DESDEMONA: Alack, my lord, what may you mean by that?
OTHELLO: Well, do it, and be brief; I will walk by.°   30
    I would not kill thy unpreparèd spirit.
    No; heavens forfend! I would not kill thy soul.
DESDEMONA: Talk you of killing?
OTHELLO: Ay, I do.
DESDEMONA: Then heaven
    Have mercy on me!
OTHELLO: Amen, with all my heart.

V.ii.   [8]*minister*   *worker, servant.*   [11]*cunning'st*   *most intricate and skilfully wrought (by nature excelling it-self).*   [12]***Promethean heat***   *divine fire (Prometheus is the Titan who stole fire from heaven and gave it to man).* [13]*relume*   *relight.*   [14]*vital*   *living.*   [30]*by*   *nearby.*

DESDEMONA: If you say so, I hope you will not kill me.   35
OTHELLO: Humh.
DESDEMONA: And yet I fear you; for you're fatal then
   When your eyes roll so. Why I should fear I know not,
   Since guiltiness I know not; but yet I feel I fear.
OTHELLO: Think on thy sins.
DESDEMONA: They are loves I bear to you.   40
OTHELLO: Ay, and for that thou diest.
DESDEMONA: That death's unnatural that kills for loving.
   Alas, why gnaw you so your nether lip?
   Some bloody passion shakes your very frame.
   These are portents; but yet I hope, I hope,   45
   They do not point on me.
OTHELLO: Peace and be still.
DESDEMONA: I will so. What's the matter?
OTHELLO: That handkerchief which I so loved and gave thee,
   Thou gav'st to Cassio.
DESDEMONA: No, by my life and soul!
   Send for the man and ask him.
OTHELLO: Sweet soul, take heed,   50
   Take heed of perjury; thou art on thy deathbed.
DESDEMONA: Ay, but not yet to die.
OTHELLO: Presently.°
   Therefore confess thee freely of thy sin,
   For to deny each article° with oath
   Cannot remove nor choke the strong conception   55
   That I do groan withal. Thou art to die.
DESDEMONA: Then Lord have mercy on me.
OTHELLO: I say, amen.
DESDEMONA: And have you mercy too. I never did
   Offend you in my life; never loved Cassio
   But with such general warranty° of heaven   60
   As I might love. I never gave him token.
OTHELLO: By heaven, I saw my handkerchief in's hand!
   O perjured woman! thou dost stone° my heart,
   And mak'st me call what I intend to do
   A murder, which I thought a sacrifice.   65
   I saw the handkerchief.
DESDEMONA: He found it then.
   I never gave it him. Send for him hither.
   Let him confess a truth.
OTHELLO: He hath confessed.
DESDEMONA: What, my lord?
OTHELLO: That he hath used thee.
DESDEMONA: How? Unlawfully?

---

52 **Presently** *immediately.*   54 **article** *item (of the charge of adultery. Othello makes heavy use of legal terms in this scene).*   60 **warranty** *allowance.*   63 **stone** *turn to stone.*

OTHELLO: Ay.   70
DESDEMONA: He will not say so.
OTHELLO: No, his mouth is stopped.
   Honest Iago hath ta'en order for't.°
DESDEMONA: O, my fear interprets. What, is he dead?
OTHELLO: Had all his hairs been lives, my great revenge
   Had stomach° for them all.   75
DESDEMONA: Alas, he is betrayed, and I undone!
OTHELLO: Out, strumpet! Weep'st thou for him to my face?
DESDEMONA: O, banish me, my lord, but kill me not!
OTHELLO: Down, strumpet!
DESDEMONA: Kill me tomorrow; let me live tonight!   80
OTHELLO: Nay, if you strive—
DESDEMONA: But half an hour!
OTHELLO: Being done, there is no pause.
DESDEMONA: But while I say one prayer!
OTHELLO: It is too late.   *Smothers her.*

           EMILIA *at the door.*

EMILIA [*Calls within*]: My lord, my lord! What, ho, my lord, my lord!
OTHELLO: What noise is this? Not dead? Not yet quite dead?   85
   I that am cruel am yet merciful;
   I would not have thee linger in thy pain.
EMILIA [*Within*]: What, ho! My lord, my lord!
OTHELLO: So, so. Who's there?
EMILIA [*Within*]: O, good my lord, I would speak a word with you.
OTHELLO: Yes, 'tis Emilia.—By and by.—She's dead.—   90
   'Tis like she comes to speak of Cassio's death.
   The noise was high.° Ha! No more moving?
   Still as the grave.—Shall she come in? Were't good?—
   I think she stirs again. No.—What's best to do?
   If she come in, she'll sure speak to my wife.   95
   My wife! My wife! What wife? I have no wife.
   O, insupportable! O heavy hour!
   Methinks° it should be now a huge eclipse
   Of sun and moon, and that th' affrighted globe
   Should yawn° at alteration.
EMILIA [*Within*]:   I do beseech you   100
   That I may speak with you, O good my lord!
OTHELLO: I had forgot thee. O, come in, Emilia.
   Soft, by and by.—Let me the curtains draw.—

       [*Draws the bed hangings and then opens the door.*]

Where art thou?

---

⁷²**ta'en order for't**   *made sure of it.*   ⁷⁵**stomach**   *appetite.*   ⁹²**high**   *loud (Q1 reads "here").*
⁹⁸⁻¹⁰⁰**Methinks . . . alteration**   *(the Elizabethans believed that great changes in human affairs were reflected by*
disorders in nature).   ¹⁰⁰**yawn**   *gape open (as in an earthquake).*

Enter EMILIA.

What's the matter with thee now?

EMILIA: O my good lord, yonder's foul murders done!   105

OTHELLO: What? Now?

EMILIA: But now, my lord.

OTHELLO: It is the very error° of the moon.
   She comes more nearer earth than she was wont
   And makes men mad.   110

EMILIA: Cassio, my lord, hath killed a young Venetian
   Called Roderigo.

OTHELLO: Roderigo killed?
   And Cassio killed?

EMILIA: No, Cassio is not killed.

OTHELLO: Not Cassio killed? Then murder's out of tune,
   And sweet revenge grows harsh.   115

DESDEMONA: O, falsely, falsely murdered!

EMILIA: O Lord! What cry is that?

OTHELLO: That? What?

EMILIA: Out and alas! that was my lady's voice.
   Help! Help, ho! Help! O lady, speak again!
   Sweet Desdemona! O sweet mistress, speak!   120

DESDEMONA: A guiltless death I die.

EMILIA: O, who hath done this deed?

DESDEMONA: Nobody—I myself. Farewell.
   Commend me to my kind lord. O, farewell!   [*She dies.*]

OTHELLO: Why, how should she be murd'red?

EMILIA: Alas, who knows?   125

OTHELLO: You heard her say herself, it was not I.

EMILIA: She said so. I must needs report the truth.

OTHELLO: She's like a liar gone to burning hell!
   'Twas I that killed her.

EMILIA: O, the more angel she,
   And you the blacker devil!   130

OTHELLO: She turned to folly, and she was a whore.

EMILIA: Thou dost belie her, and thou art a devil.

OTHELLO: She was false as water.

EMILIA: Thou art rash as fire to say
   That she was false. O, she was heavenly true!

OTHELLO: Cassio did top her. Ask thy husband else.   135
   O, I were damned beneath all depth in hell
   But that I did proceed upon just grounds
   To this extremity. Thy husband knew it all.

EMILIA: My husband?

108**error**   *wandering out of regular course (disorders in the heavens were believed by some to cause disorders on earth,*
as well as vice versa).

OTHELLO: Thy husband.
EMILIA: That she was false to wedlock?
OTHELLO: Ay, with Cassio. Had she been true,   140
  If heaven would make me such another world
  Of one entire and perfect chrysolite,°
  I'd not have sold her for it.
EMILIA: My husband?
OTHELLO: Ay, 'twas he that told me on her first.
  An honest man he is, and hates the slime   145
  That sticks on filthy deeds.
EMILIA: My husband?
OTHELLO: What needs this iterance? Woman, I say thy husband.
EMILIA: O mistress, villainy hath made mocks with love!
  My husband say she was false?
OTHELLO: He, woman.
  I say, thy husband. Dost understand the word?   150
  My friend, thy husband; honest, honest Iago.
EMILIA: If he say so, may his pernicious soul
  Rot half a grain a day! He lies to th' heart.
  She was too fond of her most filthy bargain.
OTHELLO: Hah?   155
EMILIA: Do thy worst.
  This deed of thine is no more worthy heaven
  Than thou wast worthy her.
OTHELLO: Peace, you were best.°
EMILIA: Thou hast not half that pow'r to do me harm
  As I have to be hurt. O gull! O dolt!   160
  As ignorant as dirt! Thou hast done a deed—

[OTHELLO *moves to draw his sword.*]

  I care not for thy sword; I'll make thee known,
  Though I lost twenty lives. Help! Help! Ho! Help!
  The Moor hath killed my mistress! Murder! murder!

Enter MONTANO, GRATIANO, *and* IAGO [*and Others*].

MONTANO: What is the matter? How now, general?   165
EMILIA: O, are you come, Iago? You have done well,
  That men must lay their murders on your neck.
GRATIANO: What is the matter?
EMILIA: Disprove this villain, if thou be'st a man.
  He says thou told'st him that his wife was false.   170
  I know thou didst not; thou'rt not such a villain.
  Speak, for my heart is full.
IAGO: I told him what I thought, and told no more
  Than what he found himself was apt and true.

---

¹⁴²*chrysolite* topaz.   ¹⁵⁸*Peace, you were best* i.e., you had better be silent.

EMILIA: But did you ever tell him she was false?   175
IAGO: I did.
EMILIA: You told a lie, an odious damnèd lie!
   Upon my soul, a lie! A wicked lie!
   She false with Cassio? Did you say with Cassio?
IAGO: With Cassio, mistress. Go to, charm° your tongue.   180
EMILIA: I will not charm my tongue; I am bound to speak:
   My mistress here lies murdered in her bed.
ALL: O heavens forfend!
EMILIA: And your reports have set the murder on.
OTHELLO: Nay, stare not, masters. It is true indeed.   185
GRATIANO: 'Tis a strange truth.
MONTANO: O monstrous act!
EMILIA: Villainy, villainy, villainy!
   I think upon't—I think I smell't!—O villainy!
   I thought so then.—I'll kill myself for grief.—
   O villainy, villainy!   190
IAGO: What, are you mad? I charge you get you home.
EMILIA: Good gentlemen, let me have leave to speak.
   'Tis proper I obey him, but not now.
   Perchance, Iago, I will ne'er go home.
OTHELLO: O! O! O!   [*Falls on the bed.*]   195
EMILIA: Nay, lay thee down and roar,
   For thou hast killed the sweetest innocent
   That e'er did lift up eye.
OTHELLO: O, she was foul!   [*Rises.*]
   I scarce did know you, uncle. There lies your niece,
   Whose breath, indeed, these hands have newly stopped.
   I know this act shows horrible and grim.   200
GRATIANO: Poor Desdemona! I am glad thy father's dead.
   Thy match was mortal to him, and pure grief
   Shore his old thread in twain. Did he live now,
   This sight would make him do a desperate turn;
   Yea, curse his better angel from his side,   205
   And fall to reprobation.°
OTHELLO: 'Tis pitiful; but yet Iago knows
   That she with Cassio hath the act of shame
   A thousand times committed. Cassio confessed it;
   And she did gratify his amorous works   210
   With that recognizance and pledge of love,
   Which I first gave her. I saw it in his hand.
   It was a handkerchief, an antique token
   My father gave my mother.
EMILIA: O God! O heavenly God!   215
IAGO: Zounds, hold your peace!

180*charm*   control.   206*reprobation*   damnation.

EMILIA: 'Twill out, 'twill out! I peace?
    No, I will speak as liberal as the north.°
    Let heaven and men and devils, let them all,
    All, all, cry shame against me, yet I'll speak.
IAGO: Be wise, and get you home.
EMILIA: I will not.   220

        [IAGO *draws and threatens* EMILIA.]

GRATIANO: Fie! Your sword upon a woman?
EMILIA: O thou dull Moor, that handkerchief thou speak'st of
    I found by fortune, and did give my husband;
    For often with a solemn earnestness—
    More than indeed belonged to such a trifle—   225
    He begged of me to steal't.
IAGO: Villainous whore!
EMILIA: She give it Cassio? No, alas, I found it,
    And I did give't my husband.
IAGO: Filth, thou liest!
EMILIA: By heaven, I do not, I do not, gentlemen.
    O murd'rous coxcomb! What should such a fool   230
    Do with so good a wife?
OTHELLO: Are there no stones° in heaven
    But what serves for the thunder? Precious villain!

    [*The* MOOR *runs at* IAGO, *but is disarmed by* MONTANO. IAGO *kills his wife.*]

GRATIANO: The woman falls. Sure he hath killed his wife.
EMILIA: Ay, ay. O, lay me by my mistress' side.   [*Exit* IAGO.]
GRATIANO: He's gone, but his wife's killed.   235
MONTANO: 'Tis a notorious° villain. Take you this weapon,
    Which I have recovered from the Moor.
    Come, guard the door without. Let him not pass,
    But kill him rather. I'll after that same villain,
    For 'tis a damnèd slave.   *Exit* [*with all but* OTHELLO *and* EMILIA].
OTHELLO: I am not valiant neither;   240
    But every puny whipster° gets my sword.
    But why should honor outlive honesty?
    Let it go all.
EMILIA: What did thy song bode, lady?
    Hark, canst thou hear me? I will play the swan,
    And die in music. [*Sings*] "Willow, willow, willow."   245
    Moor, she was chaste. She loved thee, cruel Moor,
    So come my soul to bliss as I speak true.
    So speaking as I think, alas, I die.   [*She dies.*]
OTHELLO: I have another weapon in this chamber;

---

²¹⁷**liberal as the north** *freely (and bitingly) as the north wind blows.*   ²³¹**stones** *thunderbolts.*   ²³⁶**notorious** *out-and-out.*   ²⁴¹**puny whipster** *small top-whipping boy (?).*

It was a sword of Spain, the ice-brook's temper.   250
　　O, here it is.—Uncle, I must come forth.
GRATIANO [*Within*]: If thou attempt it, it will cost thee dear.
　　Thou hast no weapon, and perforce must suffer.
OTHELLO: Look in upon me then and speak with me,
　　Or, naked as I am, I will assault thee.   255

　　　　　　　　　[*Enter* GRATIANO.]

GRATIANO: What is the matter?
OTHELLO:　　　　　　　　　Behold, I have a weapon;
　　A better never did itself sustain
　　Upon a soldier's thigh. I have seen the day
　　That with this little arm and this good sword
　　I have made my way through more impediments   260
　　Than twenty times your stop. But O vain boast!
　　Who can control his fate? 'Tis not so now.
　　Be not afraid, though you do see me weaponed.
　　Here is my journey's end, here is my butt,°
　　And very seamark of my utmost sail.°   265
　　Do you go back dismayed? 'Tis a lost fear.
　　Man but a rush° against Othello's breast.
　　And he retires. Where should Othello go?
　　Now, how dost thou look now? O ill-starred wench!
　　Pale as thy smock! When we shall meet at compt,°   270
　　This look of thine will hurl my soul from heaven,
　　And fiends will snatch at it. Cold, cold, my girl?
　　Even like thy chastity.
　　O cursèd, cursèd slave! Whip me, ye devils,
　　From the possession of ° this heavenly sight!   275
　　Blow me about in winds! roast me in sulfur!
　　Wash me in steep-down gulfs of liquid fire!
　　O Desdemon! Dead Desdemon; dead. O! O!

　　　Enter LODOVICO, CASSIO, MONTANO, *and* IAGO [*as prisoner,*] *with* OFFICERS.

LODOVICO: Where is this rash and most unfortunate man?
OTHELLO: That's he that was Othello? Here I am.   280
LODOVICO: Where is that viper? Bring the villain forth.
OTHELLO: I look down towards his feet°—but that's a fable.
　　If that thou be'st a devil, I cannot kill thee.   [*Wounds* IAGO.]
LODOVICO: Wrench his sword from him.   [OTHELLO *is disarmed.*]
IAGO:　　　　　　　　　I bleed, sir, but not killed.
OTHELLO: I am not sorry neither. I'd have thee live;   285
　　For in my sense, 'tis happiness to die.

---

²⁶⁴**butt**　target, stopping place.　　²⁶⁵**seamark of my utmost sail**　maker of my furthest journey.　　²⁶⁷**Man
but a rush**　attack with only a reed.　　²⁷⁰**compt**　Judgment Day.　　²⁷⁵**the possession of**　being possessed
by.　　²⁸²**towards his feet**　i.e., for his cloven hoofs.

LODOVICO: O thou Othello that was once so good,
   Fall'n in the practice° of a cursèd slave,
   What shall be said to thee?
OTHELLO: Why, anything:
   An honorable murderer, if you will;   290
   For naught I did in hate, but all in honor.
LODOVICO: This wretch hath part confessed his villainy.
   Did you and he consent in Cassio's death?
OTHELLO: Ay.
CASSIO: Dear general, I never gave you cause.   295
OTHELLO: I do believe it, and I ask your pardon.
   Will you, I pray, demand that demi-devil
   Why he hath thus ensnared my soul and body?
IAGO: Demand me nothing. What you know, you know.
   From this time forth I never will speak word.   300
LODOVICO: What, not to pray?
GRATIANO: Torments will ope your lips.
OTHELLO: Well, thou dost best.
LODOVICO: Sir, you shall understand what hath befall'n,
   Which, as I think, you know not. Here is a letter
   Found in the pocket of the slain Roderigo;   305
   And here another. The one of them imports
   The death of Cassio to be undertook
   By Roderigo.
OTHELLO: O villain!
CASSIO: Most heathenish and most gross!
LODOVICO: Now here's another discontented paper   310
   Found in his pocket too; and this, it seems,
   Roderigo meant t' have sent this damnèd villain;
   But that, belike, Iago in the interim
   Came in and satisfied him.
OTHELLO: O thou pernicious caitiff!
   How came you, Cassio, by that handkerchief   315
   That was my wife's?
CASSIO: I found it in my chamber;
   And he himself confessed it but even now
   That there he dropped it for a special purpose
   Which wrought to his desire.
OTHELLO: O fool! Fool! Fool!
CASSIO: There is besides in Roderigo's letter,   320
   How he upbraids Iago that he made him
   Brave me upon the watch; whereon it came
   That I was cast; and even but now he spake,
   After long seeming dead—Iago hurt him,
   Iago set him on.   325

288*practice* *plotting.*

LODOVICO: You must forsake this room and go with us.
  Your power and your command is taken off,
  And Cassio rules in Cyprus. For this slave,
  If there be any cunning cruelty
  That can torment him much and hold him long,   330
  It shall be his. You shall close prisoner rest
  Till that the nature of your fault be known
  To the Venetian state. Come, bring away.
OTHELLO: Soft you, a word or two before you go.
  I have done the state some service and they know't.   335
  No more of that. I pray you, in your letters,
  When you shall these unlucky deeds relate,
  Speak of me as I am. Nothing extenuate,
  Nor set down aught in malice. Then must you speak
  Of one that loved not wisely, but too well;   340
  Of one not easily jealous, but, being wrought,
  Perplexed in the extreme; of one whose hand,
  Like the base Judean,° threw a pearl away
  Richer than all his tribe; of one whose subdued eyes,
  Albeit unusèd to the melting mood,   345
  Drops tears as fast as the Arabian trees
  Their med'cinable gum. Set you down this.
  And say besides that in Aleppo once,
  Where a malignant and a turbaned Turk
  Beat a Venetian and traduced the state,   350
  I took by th' throat the circumcisèd dog
  And smote him—thus.   [He stabs himself.]
LODOVICO: O bloody period!°
GRATIANO: All that is spoke is marred.
OTHELLO: I kissed thee ere I killed thee. No way but this,
  Killing myself, to die upon a kiss.   [He falls over DESDEMONA and dies.] 355
CASSIO: This did I fear, but thought he had no weapon;
  For he was great of heart.
LODOVICO [To IAGO]:   O Spartan dog,
  More fell° than anguish, hunger, or the sea!
  Look on the tragic loading of this bed.
  This is thy work. The object poisons sight;   360
  Let it be hid.   [Bed curtains drawn.]
            Gratiano, keep° the house,
  And seize upon the fortunes of the Moor,
  For they succeed on you. To you, lord governor,
  Remains the censure of this hellish villain,
  The time, the place, the torture. O, enforce it!   365
  Myself will straight aboard, and to the state
  This heavy act with heavy heart relate.   Exeunt.

---

³⁴³**Judean**   (most editors use the Q1 reading, "Indian," here, but F is clear: both readings point toward the infidel, the unbeliever).   ³⁵³**period**   end.   ³⁵⁸**fell**   cruel.   ³⁶¹**keep**   remain in.

QUESTIONS FOR REFLECTION

Experience

1. Describe your experience in reading *Othello*. To what extent can you identify with any one of the play's characters?

Interpretation

2. What makes Othello a tragic figure? Is his tragedy self-inflicted or is it beyond his control? What is his tragic flaw?
3. Compare Othello's speeches from the beginning, middle, and end of the play (Acts I, III, and V). Explain the significance of their differences in style and tone.
4. Iago is a resourceful and clever character who knows how to manipulate people. Explain how he manipulates Roderigo, Cassio, and Othello.
5. What reason does Iago give for seeking Othello's destruction? Does this seem an adequate or a credible motive?
6. How does Emilia's role help us to better understand Iago? In what ways is she a *foil* (a contrasting character) to Desdemona? What other characters serve to balance each other?
7. Of what significance is Bianca's role in the play? Brabantio's?
8. *Othello* has a dual setting—Venice and Cyprus. With what values and ideas is each place associated, and how are these related to the action and themes of the play?
9. What ideas about love are expressed by Othello and Desdemona? What images of the sexual bond emerge in the speech and actions of Roderigo, Iago, and Emilia?
10. How does Shakespeare use Desdemona's handkerchief dramatically and symbolically? In which scenes is it most important? With what is it associated?
11. Examine the scene in which Othello kills Desdemona (Act V, Scene II). Read his speech beginning, "It is the cause" (lines 1–22). Explain how Othello sees himself at this point, and describe his state of mind.
12. Examine the scene in which Othello secretly watches Cassio talking to Bianca (Act IV, Scene I). Explain how Iago controls Othello's perception, leading him to misinterpret what he sees. In what other scenes does Iago direct other characters to misinterpret one another's actions and speech?
13. Any staging of Othello requires careful attention to lighting. Single out two scenes in which lighting is especially important, and explain how you would stage them.
14. Look carefully at the beginning and ending of any two acts. Consider how Shakespeare guides the audience's responses at these points. Consider also the effectiveness of each beginning and ending in relation to the development of the plot.
15. Locate two scenes in which characters' speeches shift between prose and verse. Explain the significance of these shifts.

Evaluation

16. What judgment does Shakespeare's *Othello* make about jealousy? About the power of evil over goodness?
17. How effectively do you think Shakespeare dramatizes Iago's power over others?

Hamlet

Hamlet, the most famous play in English literature, continues to fascinate and challenge both readers and audiences. Interpretations of Hamlet's character and actions abound, because the play has produced so many intense and varied responses. No small indication of the tragedy's power is that actors long to play its title role.

A brief summary can suggest the movement of the plot but not the depth of Hamlet's character. After learning of his father's death, Prince Hamlet returns to the Danish court from his university studies to find Claudius, the dead king's brother, ruling Denmark and married to Hamlet's mother, Gertrude. Her remarriage within two months of his father's death has left Hamlet disillusioned, confused, and suspicious of Claudius. When his father's ghost appears before Hamlet to reveal that Claudius murdered the king, Hamlet is confronted with having to avenge his father's death.

Hamlet's efforts to carry out this obligation would have been a familiar kind of plot to Elizabethan audiences. *Revenge tragedy* was a well-established type of drama that traced its antecedents to Greek and Roman plays, particularly through the Roman playwright Seneca (c. 3 B.C.–A.D. 65), whose plays were translated and produced in English in the late sixteenth century. Shakespeare's audiences knew its conventions, particularly from Thomas Kyd's popular *Spanish Tragedy* (c. 1587). Basically, this type of play consists of a murder that has to be avenged by a relative of the victim. Typically, the victim's ghost appears to demand revenge, and invariably madness of some sort is worked into subsequent events, which ultimately result in the deaths of the murderer, the avenger, and a number of other characters. Crime, madness, ghostly anguish, poison, overheard conversations, conspiracies, and a final scene littered with corpses: *Hamlet* subscribes to the basic ingredients of the formula, but it also transcends the conventions of revenge tragedy because Hamlet contemplates not merely revenge but suicide and the meaning of life itself.

Hamlet must face not only a diseased social order but also conflicts within himself when his indecisiveness becomes as agonizing as the corruption surrounding him. However, Hamlet is also a forceful and attractive character. His intelligence is repeatedly revealed in his penetrating use of language; through images and metaphors he creates a perspective on his world that is at once satiric and profoundly painful. His astonishing and sometimes shocking wit is leveled at his mother, his beloved Ophelia, and Claudius as well as at himself. Nothing escapes his critical eye and divided imagination. Hamlet, no less than the people around him, is perplexed by his alienation from life.

Hamlet's limitations as well as his virtues make him one of Shakespeare's most complex characters. His keen self-awareness is both agonizing and liberating. Although he struggles throughout the play with painful issues ranging from family loyalties to matters of state, he retains his dignity as a tragic hero, whom generations of audiences have found compelling.

Hamlet, Prince of Denmark

CHARACTERS

CLAUDIUS, *King of Denmark*
HAMLET, *son to the late and nephew to the present king*
POLONIUS, *lord chamberlain*
HORATIO, *friend to Hamlet*
LAERTES, *son to Polonius*
VOLTIMAND
CORNELIUS
ROSENCRANTZ } *courtiers*
GUILDENSTERN
OSRIC
A GENTLEMAN
A PRIEST
MARCELLUS }
BERNARDO } *officers*
FRANCISCO, *a soldier*
REYNALDO, *servant to Polonius*
PLAYERS
TWO CLOWNS, *grave-diggers*
FORTINBRAS, *Prince of Norway*
A CAPTAIN
ENGLISH AMBASSADORS
GERTRUDE, *Queen of Denmark, and mother to Hamlet*
OPHELIA, *daughter to Polonius*
GHOST *of Hamlet's father*
(LORDS, LADIES, OFFICERS, SOLDIERS, SAILORS, MESSENGERS, AND OTHER ATTENDANTS)

Scene. Denmark.

ACT I

Scene I [*Elsinore. A platform° before the castle.*]

> *Enter* BERNARDO *and* FRANCISCO, *two sentinels.*

BERNARDO: Who's there?

I.i.   s.d. platform   *a level space on the battlements of the royal castle at Elsinore, a Danish seaport; now Helsingör.*

FRANCISCO: Nay, answer me:° stand, and unfold yourself.
BERNARDO: Long live the king°!
FRANCISCO: Bernardo?
BERNARDO: He.   5
FRANCISCO: You come most carefully upon your hour.
BERNARDO: 'Tis now struck twelve; get thee to bed, Francisco.
FRANCISCO: For this relief much thanks: 'tis bitter cold,
    And I am sick at heart.
BERNARDO: Have you had quiet guard?
FRANCISCO: Not a mouse stirring.   10
BERNARDO: Well, good night.
    If you do meet Horatio and Marcellus,
    The rivals° of my watch, bid them make haste.

                    Enter HORATIO *and* MARCELLUS.

FRANCISCO: I think I hear them. Stand, ho! Who is there?
HORATIO: Friends to this ground.
MARCELLUS: And liegemen to the Dane.   15
FRANCISCO: Give you° good night.
MARCELLUS: O, farewell, honest soldier:
    Who hath reliev'd you?
FRANCISCO: Bernardo hath my place.
    Give you good night.   *Exit* FRANCISCO.
MARCELLUS: Holla! Bernardo!
BERNARDO: Say,
    What, is Horatio there?
HORATIO: A piece of him.
BERNARDO: Welcome, Horatio: welcome, good Marcellus.   20
MARCELLUS: What, has this thing appear'd again to-night?
BERNARDO: I have seen nothing.
MARCELLUS: Horatio says 'tis but our fantasy,
    And will not let belief take hold of him.
    Touching this dreaded sight, twice seen of us: 25
    Therefore I have entreated him along
    With us to watch the minutes of this night;
    That if again this apparition come,
    He may approve° our eyes and speak to it.
HORATIO: Tush, tush, 'twill not appear.
BERNARDO: Sit down awhile;   30
    And let us once again assail your ears,
    That are so fortified against our story
    What we have two nights seen.
HORATIO: Well, sit we down,

---

²**me**   *this is emphatic, since Francisco is the sentry.*   ³**Long live the king!**   *either a password or greeting; Hora-*
tio and Marcellus use a different one in line 15.   ¹³**rivals**   *partners.*   ¹⁶**Give you**   *God give you.*
²⁹**approve**   *corroborate.*

And let us hear Bernardo speak of this.

BERNARDO: Last night of all,   35
　　When yond same star that's westward from the pole°
　　Had made his course t' illume that part of heaven
　　Where now it burns, Marcellus and myself,
　　The bell then beating one,—

Enter GHOST.

MARCELLUS: Peace, break thee off; look, where it comes again!   40
BERNARDO: In the same figure, like the king that's dead.
MARCELLUS: Thou art a scholar;° speak to it, Horatio.
BERNARDO: Looks 'a not like the king? mark it, Horatio.
HORATIO: Most like: it harrows° me with fear and wonder.
BERNARDO: It would be spoke to.°
MARCELLUS:　　　　　　　　　Speak to it, Horatio.   45
HORATIO: What art thou that usurp'st this time of night,
　　Together with that fair and warlike form
　　In which the majesty of buried Denmark°
　　Did sometimes march? by heaven I charge thee, speak!
MARCELLUS: It is offended.
BERNARDO:　　　　　　　　See it stalks away!   50
HORATIO: Stay! speak, speak! I charge thee, speak!   *Exit* GHOST.
MARCELLUS: 'Tis gone, and will not answer.
BERNARDO: How now, Horatio! you tremble and look pale:
　　Is not this something more than fantasy?
　　What think you on 't?   55
HORATIO: Before my God, I might not this believe
　　Without the sensible and true avouch
　　Of mine own eyes.
MARCELLUS:　　　　　Is it not like the king?
HORATIO: As thou art to thyself:
　　Such was the very armour he had on   60
　　When he the ambitious Norway combated;
　　So frown'd he once, when, in an angry parle,
　　He smote° the sledded Polacks° on the ice.
　　'Tis strange.
MARCELLUS: Thus twice before, and jump° at this dead hour,   65
　　With martial stalk hath he gone by our watch.
HORATIO: In what particular thought to work I know not;
　　But in the gross and scope° of my opinion,
　　This bodes some strange eruption to our state.
MARCELLUS: Good now,° sit down, and tell me, he that knows,   70

---

³⁶**pole**　*polestar.*　　⁴²**scholar**　*exorcisms were performed in Latin, which Horatio as an educated man would be able to speak.*　　⁴⁴**harrows**　*lacerates the feelings.*　　⁴⁵**It ... to**　*a ghost could not speak until spoken to.* ⁴⁸**buried Denmark**　*the buried king of Denmark.*　　⁶³**smote**　*defeated.*　　⁶³**sledded Polacks**　*Polanders using sledges.*　　⁶⁵**jump**　*exactly.*　　⁶⁸**gross and scope**　*general drift.* ⁷⁰**Good now**　*an expression denoting entreaty or expostulation.*

Why this same strict and most observant watch
So nightly toils° the subject° of the land,
And why such daily cast° of brazen cannon,
And foreign mart° for implements of war;
Why such impress° of shipwrights, whose sore task   75
Does not divide the Sunday from the week;
What might be toward, that this sweaty haste
Doth make the night joint-labourer with the day:
Who is't that can inform me?
HORATIO: That can I;
At least, the whisper goes so. Our last king,   80
Whose image even but now appear'd to us,
Was, as you know, by Fortinbras of Norway,
Thereto prick'd on° by a most emulate° pride,
Dar'd to the combat; in which our valiant Hamlet—
For so this side of our known world esteem'd him—   85
Did slay this Fortinbras; who, by a seal'd compact,
Well ratified by law and heraldry,°
Did forfeit, with his life, all those his lands
Which he stood seiz'd° of, to the conqueror:
Against the which, a moiety competent°   90
Was gaged by our king; which had return'd
To the inheritance of Fortinbras,
Had he been vanquisher; as, by the same comart,°
And carriage° of the article design'd,
His fell to Hamlet. Now, sir, young Fortinbras,   95
Of unimproved° mettle hot and full,°
Hath in the skirts of Norway here and there
Shark'd up° a list of lawless resolutes,°
For food and diet,° to some enterprise
That hath a stomach in't; which is no other—   100
As it doth well appear unto our state—
But to recover of us, by strong hand
And terms compulsatory, those foresaid lands
So by his father lost: and this, I take it,
Is the main motive of our preparations,   105
The source of this our watch and the chief head
Of this post-haste and romage° in the land.
BERNARDO: I think it be no other but e'en so:
Well may it sort° that this portentous figure

72**toils** *causes or makes to toil.*   72**subject** *people, subjects.*   73**cast** *casting, founding.*   74**mart** *buying and selling, traffic.*   75**impress** *impressment.*   83**prick'd on** *incited.*   83**emulate** *rivaling.*
87**law and heraldry** *heraldic law, governing combat.*   89**seiz'd** *possessed.*   90**moiety competent** *adequate or sufficient portion.*   93**comart** *joint bargain.*   94**carriage** *import, bearing.*   96**unimproved** *not turned to account.*   96**hot and full** *full of fight.*   98**Shark'd up** *got together in haphazard fashion.*
98**resolutes** *desperadoes.*   99**food and diet** *no pay but their keep.*   107**romage** *bustle, commotion.*
109**sort** *suit.*

Comes armed through our watch; so like the king 110
That was and is the question of these wars.
HORATIO: A mote° it is to trouble the mind's eye.
In the most high and palmy state° of Rome,
A little ere the mightiest Julius fell,
The graves stood tenantless and the sheeted dead 115
Did squeak and gibber in the Roman streets:
As stars with trains of fire° and dews of blood,
Disasters° in the sun; and the moist star°
Upon whose influence Neptune's empire° stands
Was sick almost to doomsday with eclipse: 120
And even the like precurse° of fear'd events,
As harbingers preceding still the fates
And prologue to the omen coming on,
Have heaven and earth together demonstrated
Unto our climatures and countrymen.— 125

Enter GHOST.

But soft, behold! lo, where it comes again!
I'll cross° it, though it blast me. Stay, illusion!
If thou hast any sound, or use of voice,
Speak to me! *It° spreads his arms.*
If there be any good thing to be done, 130
That may to thee do ease and grace to me,
Speak to me!
If ° thou art privy to thy country's fate,
Which, happily, foreknowing may avoid,
O, speak! 135
Or if thou hast uphoarded in thy life
Extorted treasure in the womb of earth,
For which, they say, you spirits oft walk in death, *The cock crows.*
Speak of it: stay, and speak! Stop it, Marcellus.
MARCELLUS: Shall I strike at it with my partisan?° 140
HORATIO: Do, if it will not stand.
BERNARDO: 'Tis here!
HORATIO: 'Tis here!
MARCELLUS:'Tis gone! *[Exit* GHOST.]
We do it wrong, being so majestical,
To offer it the show of violence;
For it is, as the air, invulnerable, 145

112*mote*   speck of dust.   113*palmy state*   triumphant sovereignty.   117*stars* . . . *fire*   i.e., comets.
118*Disasters*   unfavorable aspects.   118*moist star*   the moon, governing tides.   119*Neptune's empire*   the
sea.   121*precurse*   heralding.   127*cross*   meet, face, thus bringing down the evil influence on the person who
crosses it.   129*It*   the Ghost, or perhaps Horatio.   133–139*If* . . . in the following seven lines, Horatio recites
the traditional reasons why ghosts might walk.   140*partisan*   long-handled spear with a blade having lateral pro-
jections.

And our vain blows malicious mockery.
BERNARDO: It was about to speak, when the cock crew.°
HORATIO: And then it started like a guilty thing
    Upon a fearful summons. I have heard,
    The cock, that is the trumpet to the morn,   150
    Doth with his lofty and shrill-sounding throat
    Awake the god of day; and, at his warning,
    Whether in sea or fire, in earth or air,
    Th' extravagant and erring° spirit hies
    To his confine:° and of the truth herein   155
    This present object made probation.°
MARCELLUS: It faded on the crowing of the cock.
    Some say that ever 'gainst° that season comes
    Wherein our Saviour's birth is celebrated,
    The bird of dawning singeth all night long: 160
    And then, they say, no spirit dare stir abroad;
    The nights are wholesome; then no planets strike,°
    No fairy takes, nor witch hath power to charm,
    So hallow'd and so gracious° is that time.
HORATIO: So have I heard and do in part believe it.   165
    But, look, the morn, in russet mantle clad,
    Walks o'er the dew of yon high eastward hill:
    Break we our watch up; and by my advice,
    Let us impart what we have seen to-night
    Unto young Hamlet; for, upon my life,   170
    This spirit, dumb to us, will speak to him.
    Do you consent we shall acquaint him with it,
    As needful in our loves, fitting our duty?
MARCELLUS: Let's do 't, I pray; and I this morning know
    Where we shall find him most conveniently.   *Exeunt.* 175

Scene II [A room of state in the castle.]

Flourish. Enter CLAUDIUS, *King of Denmark,* GERTRUDE *the Queen,* COUNCILORS, POLO-
NIUS *and his Son* LAERTES, HAMLET, *cum aliis*° [*including* VOLTIMAND *and* CORNELIUS].

KING: Though yet of Hamlet our dear brother's death
    The memory be green, and that it us befitted
    To bear our hearts in grief and our whole kingdom
    To be contracted in one brow of woe,
    Yet so far hath discretion fought with nature   5
    That we with wisest sorrow think on him,

147**cock crew**   *according to traditional ghost lore, spirits returned to their confines at cockcrow.*   154**extravagant
and erring**   *wandering. Both words mean the same thing.*   155**confine**   *place of confinement.*   156**probation**   *proof, trial.*   158**'gainst**   *just before.*   162**planets strike**   *it was thought that planets were malignant
and might strike travelers by night.*   164**gracious**   *full of goodness.*   **I.ii.**   **s.d. cum aliis**   *with others.*

Together with remembrance of ourselves.
Therefore our sometime sister, now our queen,
Th' imperial jointress° to this warlike state,
Have we, as 'twere with a defeated joy,— 10
With an auspicious and a dropping eye,
With mirth in funeral and with dirge in marriage,
In equal scale weighing delight and dole,—
Taken to wife: nor have we herein barr'd
Your better wisdoms, which have freely gone 15
With this affair along. For all, our thanks.
Now follows, that° you know, young Fortinbras,
Holding a weak supposal° of our worth,
Or thinking by our late dear brother's death
Our state to be disjoint° and out of frame,° 20
Colleagued° with this dream of his advantage,°
He hath not fail'd to pester us with message,
Importing° the surrender of those lands
Lost by his father, with all bands of law,
To our most valiant brother. So much for him. 25
Now for ourself and for this time of meeting:
Thus much the business is: we have here writ
To Norway, uncle of young Fortinbras,—
Who, impotent and bed-rid, scarcely hears
Of this his nephew's purpose,—to suppress 30
His further gait° herein; in that the levies,
The lists and full proportions, are all made
Out of his subject:° and we here dispatch
You, good Cornelius, and you, Voltimand,
For bearers of this greeting to old Norway; 35
Giving to you no further personal power
To business with the king, more than the scope
Of these delated° articles allow.
Farewell, and let your haste commend your duty.
CORNELIUS: ⎫
VOLTIMAND: ⎬ In that and all things will we show our duty. 40
KING: We doubt it nothing: heartily farewell.

[*Exeunt* VOLTIMAND *and* CORNELIUS.]

And now, Laertes, what's the news with you?
You told us of some suit; what is't, Laertes?
You cannot speak of reason to the Dane,°

---

⁹*jointress* *woman possessed of a jointure, or, joint tenancy of an estate.* ¹⁷*that* *that which.* ¹⁸*weak sup-*
posal *low estimate.* ²⁰*disjoint* *distracted, out of joint.* ²⁰*frame* *order.* ²¹*Colleagued* *added to.*
²¹*dream . . . advantage* *visionary hope of success.* ²³*Importing* *purporting, pertaining to.* ³¹*gait*
proceeding. ³³*Out of his subject* *at the expense of Norway's subjects (collectively).* ³⁸*delated* *expressly*
stated. ⁴⁴*the Dane* *Danish king.*

And lose your voice:° what wouldst thou beg, Laertes,   45
That shall not be my offer, not thy asking?
The head is not more native° to the heart,
The hand more instrumental° to the mouth,
Than is the throne of Denmark to thy father.
What wouldst thou have, Laertes?
LAERTES: My dread lord,   50
Your leave and favour to return to France;
From whence though willingly I came to Denmark,
To show my duty in your coronation,
Yet now, I must confess, that duty done,
My thoughts and wishes bend again toward France   55
And bow them to your gracious leave and pardon.°
KING: Have you your father's leave? What says Polonius?
POLONIUS: He hath, my lord, wrung from me my slow leave
By laboursome petition, and at last
Upon his will I seal'd my hard consent: 60
I do beseech you, give him leave to go.
KING: Take thy fair hour, Laertes; time be thine,
And thy best graces spend it at thy will!
But now, my cousin° Hamlet, and my son,—
HAMLET [aside]: A little more than kin, and less than kind!°   65
KING: How is it that the clouds still hang on you?
HAMLET: Not so, my lord; I am too much in the sun.°
QUEEN: Good Hamlet, cast thy nighted colour off,
And let thine eye look like a friend on Denmark.
Do not for ever with thy vailed lids   70
Seek for thy noble father in the dust:
Thou know'st 'tis common; all that lives must die,
Passing through nature to eternity.
HAMLET: Ay, madam, it is common.°
QUEEN: If it be,
Why seems it so particular with thee?   75
HAMLET: Seems, madam! nay, it is; I know not "seems."
'Tis not alone my inky cloak, good mother,
Nor customary suits° of solemn black,
Nor windy suspiration° of forc'd breath,
No, nor the fruitful river in the eye,   80
Nor the dejected 'haviour of the visage,

---

[45]**lose your voice** *speak in vain.*   [47]**native** *closely connected, related.*   [48]**instrumental** *serviceable.*
[56]**leave and pardon** *permission to depart.*   [64]**cousin** *any kin not of the immediate family.*   [65]**A little
... kind** *i.e., my relation to you has become more than kinship warrants; it has also become unnatural.*   [67]**I am
... sun** *the senses seem to be: I am too much out of doors, I am too much in the sun of your grace (ironical), I am
too much of a son to you. Possibly an allusion to the proverb "Out of heaven's blessing into the warm sun"; i.e., Hamlet is out of house and home in being deprived of the kingship.*   [74]**Ay ... common** *i.e., it is common, but it
hurts nevertheless; possibly a reference to the commonplace quality of the queen's remark.*   [78]**customary suits** *suits
prescribed by custom for mourning.*   [79]**windy suspiration** *heavy sighing.*

Together with all forms, moods, shapes of grief,
That can denote me truly: these indeed seem,
For they are actions that a man might play:
But I have that within which passeth show;   85
These but the trappings and the suits of woe.
KING: 'Tis sweet and commendable in your nature, Hamlet,
    To give these mourning duties to your father:
    But, you must know, your father lost a father;
    That father lost, lost his, and the survivor bound   90
    In filial obligation for some term
    To do obsequious° sorrow: but to persever
    In obstinate condolement° is a course
    Of impious stubbornness; 'tis unmanly grief;
    It shows a will most incorrect° to heaven,   95
    A heart unfortified, a mind impatient,
    An understanding simple and unschool'd:
    For what we know must be and is as common
    As any the most vulgar thing° to sense,
    Why should we in our peevish opposition   100
    Take it to heart? Fie! 'tis a fault to heaven,
    A fault against the dead, a fault to nature,
    To reason most absurd; whose common theme
    Is death of fathers, and who still hath cried,
    From the first corse till he that died to-day,   105
    "This must be so." We pray you, throw to earth
    This unprevailing° woe, and think of us
    As of a father: for let the world take note,
    You are the most immediate° to our throne;
    And with no less nobility° of love   110
    Than that which dearest father bears his son,
    Do I impart° toward you. For your intent
    In going back to school in Wittenberg,°
    It is most retrograde° to our desire:
    And we beseech you, bend you° to remain   115
    Here, in the cheer and comfort of our eye,
    Our chiefest courtier, cousin, and our son.
QUEEN: Let not thy mother lose her prayers, Hamlet:
    I pray thee, stay with us; go not to Wittenberg.
HAMLET: I shall in all my best obey you, madam.   120
KING: Why, 'tis a loving and a fair reply:
    Be as ourself in Denmark. Madam, come;
    This gentle and unforc'd accord of Hamlet

---

[92]**obsequious** *dutiful.*   [93]**condolement** *sorrowing.*   [95]**incorrect** *Untrained, uncorrected.*   [99]**vulgar thing** *common experience.*   [107]**unprevailing** *unavailing.*   [109]**most immediate** *next in succession.*   [110]**nobility** *high degree.*   [112]**impart** *the object is apparently love (1.110).*   [113]**Wittenberg** *famous German university founded in 1502.*   [114]**retrograde** *contrary.*   [115]**bend you** *incline yourself; imperative.*

Sits smiling to my heart: in grace whereof,
No jocund health that Denmark drinks to-day,   125
But the great cannon to the clouds shall tell,
And the king's rouse° the heaven shall bruit again,°
Re-speaking earthly thunder. Come away.

Flourish. Exeunt all but HAMLET.

HAMLET: O, that this too too sullied flesh would melt,
   Thaw and resolve itself into a dew!   130
   Or that the Everlasting had not fix'd
   His canon 'gainst self-slaughter! O God! God!
   How weary, stale, flat and unprofitable,
   Seem to me all the uses of this world!
   Fie on't! ah fie! 'tis an unweeded garden,   135
   That grows to seed; things rank and gross in nature
   Possess it merely.° That it should come to this!
   But two months dead: nay, not so much, not two:
   So excellent a king; that was, to this,
   Hyperion° to a satyr; so loving to my mother   140
   That he might not beteem° the winds of heaven
   Visit her face too roughly. Heaven and earth!
   Must I remember? why, she would hang on him,
   As if increase of appetite had grown
   By what it fed on: and yet, within a month—   145
   Let me not think on't—Frailty, thy name is woman!—
   A little month, or ere those shoes were old
   With which she followed my poor father's body,
   Like Niobe,° all tears: —why she, even she—
   O God! a beast, that wants discourse of reason,°   150
   Would have mourn'd longer—married with my uncle,
   My father's brother, but no more like my father
   Than I to Hercules: within a month:
   Ere yet the salt of most unrighteous tears
   Had left the flushing in her galled° eyes,   155
   She married. O, most wicked speed, to post
   With such dexterity° to incestuous sheets!
   It is not nor it cannot come to good:
   But break, my heart; for I must hold my tongue.

Enter HORATIO, MARCELLUS, *and* BERNARDO.

HORATIO: Hail to your lordship!

127*rouse*   *draft of liquor.*   127*bruit again*   *echo.*   137*merely*   *completely, entirely.*   140*Hyperion*
God of the sun in the older regime of ancient gods.   141*beteem*   *allow.*   149*Niobe*   *Tantalus's daughter, who*
boasted that she had more sons and daughters than Leto; for this Apollo and Artemis slew her children. She was turned
into stone by Zeus on Mount Sipylus.   150*discourse of reason*   *process or faculty of reason.*   155*galled*
irritated.   157*dexterity*   *facility.*

HAMLET: I am glad to see you well: 160
   Horatio!—or I do forget myself.
HORATIO: The same, my lord, and your poor servant ever.
HAMLET: Sir, my good friend; I'll change that name with you:°
   And what make you from Wittenberg, Horatio?
   Marcellus?   165
MARCELLUS: My good lord—
HAMLET: I am very glad to see you. Good even, sir.
   But what, in faith, make you from Wittenberg?
HORATIO: A truant disposition, good my lord.
HAMLET: I would not hear your enemy say so,   170
   Nor shall you do my ear that violence,
   To make it truster of your own report
   Against yourself: I know you are no truant.
   But what is your affair in Elsinore?
   We'll teach you to drink deep ere you depart.   175
HORATIO: My lord, I came to see your father's funeral.
HAMLET: I prithee, do not mock me, fellow-student;
   I think it was to see my mother's wedding.
HORATIO: Indeed, my lord, it follow'd hard° upon.
HAMLET: Thrift, thrift, Horatio! the funeral bak'd meats°   180
   Did coldly furnish forth the marriage tables.
   Would I had met my dearest° foe in heaven
   Or ever I had seen that day, Horatio!
   My father!—methinks I see my father.
HORATIO: Where, my lord!
HAMLET: In my mind's eye, Horatio.   185
HORATIO: I saw him once; 'a° was a goodly king.
HAMLET: 'A was a man, take him for all in all,
   I shall not look upon his like again.
HORATIO: My lord, I think I saw him yesternight.
HAMLET: Saw? who?   190
HORATIO: My lord, the king your father.
HAMLET: The king my father!
HORATIO: Season your admiration° for a while
   With an attent ear, till I may deliver,
   Upon the witness of these gentlemen,
   This marvel to you.
HAMLET: For God's love, let me hear.   195
HORATIO: Two nights together had these gentlemen,
   Marcellus and Bernardo, on their watch,
   In the dead waste and middle of the night,

---

[163]**I'll ... you** *I'll be your servant, you shall be my friend; also explained as "I;ll exchange the name of friend with you."*   [179]**hard** *close.*   [180]**bak'd meats** *meat pies.*   [182]**dearest** *direst; the adjective dear in Shakespeare has two different origins: O.E. deore, "beloved," and O.E. deor, "fierce." Dearest is the superlative of the second*   [186]**'a** *he.*   [192]**Season your admiration** *restrain your astonishment.*

Been thus encount'red. A figure like your father,
Armed at point exactly, cap-a-pe,°   200
Appears before them, and with solemn march
Goes slow and stately by them: thrice he walk'd
By their oppress'd° and fear-surprised eyes,
Within his truncheon's° length; whilst they, distill'd°
Almost to jelly with the act° of fear,   205
Stand dumb and speak not to him. This to me
In dreadful secrecy impart they did;
And I with them the third night kept the watch:
Where, as they had deliver'd, both in time,
Form of the thing, each word made true and good,   210
The apparition comes: I knew your father;
These hands are not more like.
HAMLET: But where was this?
MARCELLUS: My lord, upon the platform where we watch'd.
HAMLET: Did you not speak to it?
HORATIO: My lord, I did;
But answer made it none: yet once methought   215
It lifted up it° head and did address
Itself to motion, like as it would speak;
But even then the morning cock crew loud,
And at the sound it shrunk in haste away,
And vanish'd from our sight.
HAMLET: 'Tis very strange.   220
HORATIO: As I do live, my honour'd lord, 'tis true;
And we did think it writ down in our duty
To let you know of it.
HAMLET: Indeed, indeed, sirs, but this troubles me.
Hold you the watch to-night?
MARCELLUS: }
BERNARDO: }   We do, my lord.   225
HAMLET: Arm'd, say you?
MARCELLUS: }
BERNARDO: }   Arm'd, my lord.
HAMLET: From top to toe?
MARCELLUS: }
BERNARDO: }   My lord, from head to foot.
HAMLET: Then saw you not his face?
HORATIO: O, yes, my lord; he wore his beaver° up.   230
HAMLET: What, look'd he frowningly?
HORATIO: A countenance more
In sorrow than in anger.
HAMLET: Pale or red?
HORATIO: Nay, very pale.

---

²⁰⁰**cap-a-pe** *from head to foot.*   ²⁰³**oppress'd** *distressed.*   ²⁰⁴**truncheon** *officer's staff.*   ²⁰⁴**dis-**
till'd *softened, weakened.*   ²⁰⁵**act** *action.*   ²¹⁶**it** *its.*   ²³⁰**beaver** *visor on the helmet.*

HAMLET: And fix'd his eyes upon you?
HORATIO: Most constantly.
HAMLET: I would I had been there.
HORATIO: It would have much amaz'd you.   235
HAMLET: Very like, very like. Stay'd it long?
HORATIO: While one with moderate haste might tell a hundred.
MARCELLUS: ⎫
BERNARDO: ⎬ Longer, longer.
HORATIO: Not when I saw't.
HAMLET: His beard was grizzled,—no?
HORATIO: It was, as I have seen it in his life,   240
    A sable° silver'd.
HAMLET: I will watch to-night;
    Perchance 'twill walk again.
HORATIO: I warr'nt it will.
HAMLET: If it assume my noble father's person,
    I'll speak to it, though hell itself should gape
    And bid me hold my peace. I pray you all,   245
    If you have hitherto conceal'd this sight,
    Let it be tenable in your silence still;
    And whatsoever else shall hap to-night,
    Give it an understanding, but no tongue:
    I will requite your loves. So, fare you well: 250
    Upon the platform, 'twixt eleven and twelve,
    I'll visit you.
ALL: Our duty to your honour.
HAMLET: Your loves, as mine to you: farewell.   *Exeunt [all but* HAMLET].
    My father's spirit in arms! all is not well;
    I doubt° some foul play: would the night were come!   255
    Till then sit still, my soul: foul deeds will rise,
    Though all the earth o'erwhelm them, to men's eyes.   *Exit.*

Scene III [A room in Polonius's house.]

Enter LAERTES *and* OPHELIA, *his Sister.*

LAERTES: My necessaries are embark'd: farewell:
    And, sister, as the winds give benefit
    And convoy is assistant,° do not sleep,
    But let me hear from you.
OPHELIA: Do you doubt that?
LAERTES: For Hamlet and the trifling of his favour,   5
    Hold it a fashion° and a toy in blood,°
    A violet in the youth of primy° nature,
    Forward,° not permanent, sweet, not lasting,

---

[241]**sable**   *black color.*   [255]**doubt**   *fear.*   **I.iii.**   [3]**convoy is assistant** *means of conveyance are available.*
[6]**fashion**   *custom, prevailing usage.*   [6]**toy in blood**   *passing amorous fancy.*   [7]**primy**   *in its prime.*
[8]**Forward**   *precocious.*

The perfume and suppliance of a minute;°
No more.

OPHELIA: No more but so?

LAERTES: Think it no more: 10
For nature, crescent,° does not grow alone
In thews° and bulk, but, as this temple° waxes,
The inward service of the mind and soul
Grows wide withal. Perhaps he loves you now,
And now no soil° nor cautel° doth besmirch   15
The virtue of his will: but you must fear,
His greatness weigh'd,° his will is not his own;
For he himself is subject to his birth:
He may not, as unvalued persons do,
Carve for himself; for on his choice depends   20
The safety and health of this whole state;
And therefore must his choice be circumscrib'd
Unto the voice and yielding° of that body
Whereof he is the head. Then if he says he loves you,
It fits your wisdom so far to believe it   25
As he in his particular act and place
May give his saying deed;° which is no further
Than the main voice of Denmark goes withal.
Then weigh what loss your honour may sustain,
If with too credent° ear you list his songs,   30
Or lose your heart, or your chaste treasure open
To his unmast'red° importunity.
Fear it, Ophelia, fear it, my dear sister,
And keep you in the rear of your affection,
Out of the shot and danger of desire.   35
The chariest° maid is prodigal enough,
If she unmask her beauty to the moon:
Virtue itself 'scapes not calumnious strokes:
The canker galls the infants of the spring,°
Too oft before their buttons° be disclos'd,°   40
And in the morn and liquid dew° of youth
Contagious blastments° are most imminent.
Be wary then; best safety lies in fear:
Youth to itself rebels, though none else near.

OPHELIA: I shall the effect of this good lesson keep,   45
As watchman to my heart. But, good my brother,

---

⁹**suppliance of a minute** *diversion to fill up a minute.*   ¹¹**crescent** *growing, waxing.*   ¹²**thews** *bodily*
strength.   ¹²**temple** *body.*   ¹⁵**soil** *blemish.*   ¹⁵**cautel** *crafty device.*   ¹⁷**greatness weigh'd** *high*
position considered.   ²³**voice and yielding** *assent, approval.*   ²⁷**deed** *effect.*   ³⁰**credent** *credulous.*
³²**unmast'red** *unrestrained.*   ³⁶**chariest** *most scrupulously modest.*   ³⁹**The canker . . . spring** *the*
cankerworm destroys the young plants of spring.   ⁴⁰**buttons** *buds.*   ⁴⁰**disclos'd** *opened.*   ⁴¹**liquid dew**
i.e., time when dew is fresh.   ⁴²**blastments** *blights.*

Do not, as some ungracious° pastors do,
Show me the steep and thorny way to heaven;
Whiles, like a puff'd° and reckless libertine,
Himself the primrose path of dalliance treads, 50
And recks° not his own rede.°

Enter POLONIUS.

LAERTES: O, fear me not.
I stay too long: but here my father comes.
A double° blessing is a double grace;
Occasion° smiles upon a second leave.
POLONIUS: Yet here, Laertes? aboard, aboard, for shame! 55
The wind sits in the shoulder of your sail,
And you are stay'd for. There; my blessing with thee!
And these few precepts° in thy memory
Look thou character.° Give thy thoughts no tongue,
Nor any unproportion'd° thought his act. 60
Be thou familiar, but by no means vulgar.°
Those friends thou hast, and their adoption tried,
Grapple them to thy soul with hoops of steel;
But do not dull thy palm with entertainment
Of each new-hatch'd, unfledg'd° comrade. Beware 65
Of entrance to a quarrel, but being in,
Bear't that th' opposed may beware of thee.
Give every man thy ear, but few thy voice;
Take each man's censure, but reserve thy judgement.
Costly thy habit as thy purse can buy, 70
But not express'd in fancy;° rich, not gaudy;
For the apparel oft proclaims the man,
And they in France of the best rank and station
Are of a most select and generous chief in that.°
Neither a borrower nor a lender be; 75
For loan oft loses both itself and friend,
And borrowing dulleth edge of husbandry.°
This above all: to thine own self be true,
And it must follow, as the night the day,
Thou canst not then be false to any man. 80
Farewell: my blessing season° this in thee!
LAERTES: Most humbly do I take my leave, my lord.
POLONIUS: The time invites you; go; your servants tend.

---

⁴⁷**ungracious** *graceless.* ⁴⁹**puff'd** *bloated.* ⁵¹**recks** *heeds.* ⁵¹**rede** *counsel.* ⁵³**double** *i.e.,
Laertes has already bade his father good-by.* ⁵⁴**Occasion** *opportunity.* ⁵⁸**precepts** *many parallels have
been found to the series of maxims which follows, one of the closer being that in Lyly's Euphues.* ⁵⁹**character** *in-
scribe.* ⁶⁰**unproportion'd** *inordinate.* ⁶¹**vulgar** *common.* ⁶⁵**unfledg'd** *immature.* ⁷¹**express'd in fancy** *fantastical in design.* ⁷⁴**Are . . . that** *chief is usually taken as a substantive meaning
"head," "eminence."* ⁷⁷**husbandry** *thrift.* ⁸¹**season** *mature.*

LAERTES: Farewell, Ophelia; and remember well
    What I have said to you.
OPHELIA: 'Tis in my memory lock'd,   85
    And you yourself shall keep the key of it.
LAERTES: Farewell.   *Exit* LAERTES.
POLONIUS: What is 't, Ophelia, he hath said to you?
OPHELIA: So please you, something touching the Lord Hamlet.
POLONIUS: Marry, well bethought: 90
    'Tis told me, he hath very oft of late
    Given private time to you; and you yourself
    Have of your audience been most free and bounteous:
    If it be so, as so't is put on° me,
    And that in way of caution, I must tell you,   95
    You do not understand yourself so clearly
    As it behooves my daughter and your honour.
    What is between you? give me up the truth.
OPHELIA: He hath, my lord, of late made many tenders°
    Of his affection to me.   100
POLONIUS: Affection! pooh! you speak like a green girl,
    Unsifted° in such perilous circumstance.
    Do you believe his tenders, as you call them?
OPHELIA: I do not know, my lord, what I should think.
POLONIUS: Marry, I will teach you: think yourself a baby;   105
    That you have ta'en these tenders° for true pay,
    Which are not sterling.° Tender° yourself more dearly;
    Or—not to crack the wind° of the poor phrase,
    Running it thus—you'll tender me a fool.°
OPHELIA: My lord, he hath importun'd me with love   110
    In honourable fashion.
POLONIUS: Ay, fashion° you may call it; go to, go to.
OPHELIA: And hath given countenance° to his speech, my lord,
    With almost all the holy vows of heaven.
POLONIUS: Ay, springes° to catch woodcocks.° I do know,   115
    When the blood burns, how prodigal the soul
    Lends the tongue vows: these blazes, daughter,
    Giving more light than heat, extinct in both,
    Even in their promise, as it is a-making,
    You must not take for fire. From this time   120
    Be somewhat scanter of your maiden presence;
    Set your entreatments° at a higher rate
    Than a command to parley.° For Lord Hamlet,

---

[94]**put on** *impressed on.*   [99, 103]**tenders** *offers.*   [102]**Unsifted** *untried.*   [106]**tenders** *promises to pay*   [107]**sterling** *legal currency.*   [107]**Tender** *hold.*   [108]**crack the wind** *i.e., run it until it is broken-winded.*   [109]**tender . . . fool** *show me a fool (for a daughter).*   [112]**fashion** *mere form, pretense.* [113]**countenance** *credit, support.*   [115]**springes** *snares.*   [115]**woodcocks** *birds easily caught, type of stupidity.*   [122]**entreatments** *conversations, interviews.*   [123]**command to parley** *mere invitation to talk.*

Believe so much in him,° that he is young,
And with a larger tether may he walk   125
Than may be given you: in few,° Ophelia,
Do not believe his vows; for they are brokers;°
Not of that dye° which their investments° show,
But mere implorators of ° unholy suits,
Breathing° like sanctified and pious bawds,   130
The better to beguile. This is for all:
I would not, in plain terms, from this time forth,
Have you so slander° any moment leisure,
As to give words or talk with the Lord Hamlet.
Look to 't, I charge you: come your ways.   135
OPHELIA: I shall obey, my lord.   *Exeunt.*

Scene IV [*The platform.*]

Enter HAMLET, HORATIO, *and* MARCELLUS.

HAMLET: The air bites shrewdly; it is very cold.
HORATIO: It is a nipping and an eager air.
HAMLET: What hour now?
HORATIO: I think it lacks of twelve.
MARCELLUS: No, it is struck.
HORATIO: Indeed? I heard it not: then it draws near the season   5
Wherein the spirit held his wont to walk.

A flourish of trumpets, and two pieces go off.

What does this mean, my lord?
HAMLET: The king doth wake° to-night and takes his rouse,°
Keeps wassail,° and the swagg'ring up-spring° reels;°
And, as he drains his draughts of Rhenish° down,
The kettle-drum and trumpet thus bray out   10
The triumph of his pledge.°
HORATIO: Is it a custom?
HAMLET: Ay, marry, is 't:
But to my mind, though I am native here
And to the manner born,° it is a custom   15
More honour'd in the breach than the observance.
This heavy-headed revel east and west
Makes us traduc'd and tax'd of other nations:

---

[124] **so ... him** *this much concerning him.*   [126] **in few** *briefly.*   [127] **brokers** *go-betweens, procurers.*
[128] **dye** *color or sort.*   [128] **investments** *clothes.*   [129] **implorators of** *solicitors of.*   [130] **Breathing**
speaking.   [133] **slander** *bring disgrace or reproach upon.*   **I.iv.** [8] **wake** *stay awake, hold revel.*   [8] **rouse**
carouse, drinking bout.   [9] **wassail** *carousal.*   [9] **up-spring** *last and wildest dance at German merry-makings.*
[9] **reels** *reels through.*   [10] **Rhenish** *rhine wine.*   [12] **triumph ... pledge** *his glorious achievement as a*
drinker.   [15] **to ... born** *destined by birth to be subject to the custom in question.*

They clepe° us drunkards, and with swinish phrase°
Soil our addition;° and indeed it takes   20
From our achievements, though perform'd at height,
The pith and marrow of our attribute.°
So, oft it chances in particular men,
That for some vicious mole of nature° in them,   25
As, in their birth—wherein they are not guilty,
Since nature cannot choose his origin—
By the o'ergrowth of some complexion,
Oft breaking down the pales° and forts of reason,
Or by some habit that too much o'er-leavens°
The form of plausive° manners, that these men,   30
Carrying, I say, the stamp of one defect,
Being nature's livery,° or fortune's star,°—
Their virtues else—be they as pure as grace,
As infinite as man may undergo—
Shall in the general censure take corruption   35
From that particular fault: the dram of eale°
Doth all the noble substance of a doubt
To his own scandal.°

Enter GHOST.

HORATIO: Look, my lord, it comes!
HAMLET: Angels and ministers of grace° defend us!
    Be thou a spirit of health or goblin damn'd,   40
    Bring with thee airs from heaven or blasts from hell,
    Be thy intents wicked or charitable,
    Thou com'st in such a questionable° shape
    That I will speak to thee: I'll call thee Hamlet,
    King, father, royal Dane: O, answer me!   45
    Let me not burst in ignorance; but tell
    Why thy canoniz'd° bones, hearsed° in death,
    Have burst their cerements;° why the sepulchre,
    Wherein we saw thee quietly interr'd,
    Hath op'd his ponderous and marble jaws,   50
    To cast thee up again. What may this mean,
    That thou, dead corse, again in complete steel
    Revisits thus the glimpses of the moon,°
    Making night hideous; and we fools of nature°

---

[19]*clepe* *call.*   [19]***with swinish phrase*** *by calling us swine.*   [20]***addition*** *reputation*   [22]***attribute*** *reputation*   [24]***mole of nature*** *natural blemish in one's constitution.*   [28]***pales*** *palings (as of a fortification).*   [29]***o'er-leavens*** *induces a change throughout (as yeast works in bread).*   [30]***plausive*** *pleasing.*   [32]***nature's livery*** *endowment from nature.*   [32]***fortune's star*** *the position in which one is placed by fortune, a reference to astrology. The two phrases are aspects of the same thing.*   [36]***dram of eale*** *has had various interpretations, the preferred one being probably, "a dram of evil."*   [36–38]***the dram . . . scandal*** *a famous crux.*   [39]***ministers of grace*** *messengers of God.*   [43]***questionable*** *inviting question or conversation.*   [47]***canoniz'd*** *buried according to the canons of the church.*   [47]***hearsed*** *coffined.*   [48]***cerements*** *grave-clothes.*   [53]***glimpses of the moon*** *the earth by night.*   [54]***fools of nature*** *mere men, limited to natural knowledge.*

So horridly to shake our disposition   55
With thoughts beyond the reaches of our souls?
Say, why is this? wherefore? what should we do?

[GHOST] *beckons* [HAMLET].

HORATIO: It beckons you to go away with it,
   As if it some impartment° did desire
   To you alone.
MARCELLUS: Look, with what courteous action   60
   It waves you to a more removed° ground:
   But do not go with it.
HORATIO: No, by no means.
HAMLET: It will not speak; then I will follow it.
HORATIO: Do not, my lord!
HAMLET: Why, what should be the fear?
   I do not set my life at a pin's fee;   65
   And for my soul, what can it do to that,
   Being a thing immortal as itself?
   It waves me forth again: I'll follow it.
HORATIO: What if it tempt you toward the flood, my lord,
   Or to the dreadful summit of the cliff   70
   That beetles o'er° his base into the sea,
   And there assume some other horrible form,
   Which might deprive your sovereignty of reason°
   And draw you into madness? think of it:
   The very place puts toys of desperation,°   75
   Without more motive, into every brain
   That looks so many fathoms to the sea
   And hears it roar beneath.
HAMLET: It waves me still.
   Go on; I'll follow thee.
MARCELLUS: You shall not go, my lord.
HAMLET: Hold off your hands!   80
HORATIO: Be rul'd; you shall not go.
HAMLET: My fate cries out,
   And makes each petty artere° in this body
   As hardy as the Nemean lion's° nerve.°
   Still am I call'd. Unhand me, gentlemen.
   By heaven, I'll make a ghost of him that lets° me!   85
   I say, away! Go on; I'll follow thee.   *Exeunt* GHOST *and* HAMLET.

---

[59]*impartment* *communication.*   [61]*removed* *remote.*   [71]*beetles o'er* *overhangs threateningly.*
[73]*deprive . . . reason* *take away the sovereignty of your reason. It was thought that evil spirits would sometimes as-*
sume the form of departed spirits in order to work madness in a human creature.   [75]*toys of desperation* *freakish*
notions of suicide.   [82]*artere* *artery.*   [83]*Nemean lion's* *Nemean lion was one of the monsters slain by Her-*
cules.   [83]*nerve* *sinew, tendon. The point is that the arteries which were carrying the spirits out into the body were*
functioning and were as stiff and hard as the sinews of the lion.   [85]*lets* *hinders.*

HORATIO: He waxes desperate with imagination.
MARCELLUS: Let's follow; 'tis not fit thus to obey him.
HORATIO: Have after. To what issue° will this come?
MARCELLUS: Something is rotten in the state of Denmark.   90
HORATIO: Heaven will direct it.°
MARCELLUS: Nay, let's follow him.   *Exeunt.*

Scene V [Another part of the platform.]

Enter GHOST *and* HAMLET.

HAMLET: Whither wilt thou lead me? speak; I'll go no further.
GHOST: Mark me.
HAMLET: I will.
GHOST: My hour is almost come,
    When I to sulphurous and tormenting flames
    Must render up myself.
HAMLET: Alas, poor ghost!
GHOST: Pity me not, but lend thy serious hearing   5
    To what I shall unfold.
HAMLET: Speak; I am bound to hear.
GHOST: So art thou to revenge, when thou shalt hear.
HAMLET: What?
GHOST: I am thy father's spirit,
    Doom'd for a certain term to walk the night,   10
    And for the day confin'd to fast° in fires,
    Till the foul crimes done in my days of nature
    Are burnt and purg'd away. But that I am forbid
    To tell the secrets of my prison-house,
    I could a tale unfold whose lightest word   15
    Would harrow up thy soul, freeze thy young blood,
    Make thy two eyes, like stars, start from their spheres,°
    Thy knotted° and combined° locks to part
    And each particular hair to stand an end,
    Like quills upon the fretful porpentine: °   20
    But this eternal blazon° must not be
    To ears of flesh and blood. List, list, O, list!
    If thou didst ever thy dear father love—
HAMLET: O God!
GHOST: Revenge his foul and most unnatural° murder.   25
HAMLET: Murder!

89*issue*   outcome.   91*it*   i.e., the outcome.   **I.v.**   11*fast*   probably, do without food. It has been sometimes taken in the sense of doing general penance.   17*spheres*   orbits.   18*knotted*   perhaps intricately arranged. 18*combined*   tied, bound.   20*porpentine*   porcupine.   21*eternal blazon*   promulgation or proclamation of eternity, revelation of the hereafter.   25*unnatural*   i.e., pertaining to fratricide.

GHOST: Murder most foul, as in the best it is;
   But this most foul, strange and unnatural.
HAMLET: Haste me to know't, that I, with wings as swift
   As meditation or the thoughts of love, 30
   May sweep to my revenge.
GHOST: I find thee apt;
   And duller shouldst thou be than the fat weed°
   That roots itself in ease on Lethe wharf,°
   Wouldst thou not stir in this. Now, Hamlet, hear:
   'Tis given out that, sleeping in my orchard, 35
   A serpent stung me; so the whole ear of Denmark
   Is by a forged process of my death
   Rankly abus'd: but know, thou noble youth,
   The serpent that did sting thy father's life
   Now wears his crown.
HAMLET: O my prophetic soul! 40
   My uncle!
GHOST: Ay, that incestuous, that adulterate° beast,
   With witchcraft of his wit, with traitorous gifts,—
   O wicked wit and gifts, that have the power
   So to seduce!—won to his shameful lust 45
   The will of my most seeming-virtuous queen:
   O Hamlet, what a falling-off was there!
   From me, whose love was of that dignity
   That it went hand in hand even with the vow
   I made to her in marriage, and to decline 50
   Upon a wretch whose natural gifts were poor
   To those of mine!
   But virtue, as it never will be moved,
   Though lewdness court it in a shape of heaven,
   So lust, though to a radiant angel link'd, 55
   Will sate itself in a celestial bed,
   And prey on garbage.
   But, soft! methinks I scent the morning air;
   Brief let me be. Sleeping within my orchard,
   My custom always of the afternoon, 60
   Upon my secure° hour thy uncle stole,
   With juice of cursed hebona° in a vial,
   And in the porches of my ears did pour
   The leperous° distilment; whose effect
   Holds such an enmity with blood of man 65
   That swift as quicksilver it courses through

---

³²**fat weed** *many suggestions have been offered as to the particular plant intended, including asphodel; probably a general figure for plants growing along rotting wharves and piles.* ³³**Lethe wharf** *bank of the river of forgetfulness in Hades.* ⁴²**adulterate** *adulterous.* ⁶¹**secure** *confident, unsuspicious.* ⁶²**hebona** *generally supposed to mean henbane, conjectured hemlock; ebenus, meaning "yew."* ⁶⁴**leperous** *causing leprosy.*

The natural gates and alleys of the body,
And with a sudden vigour it doth posset°
And curd, like eager° droppings into milk,
The thin and wholesome blood: so did it mine;   70
And a most instant tetter bark'd about,
Most lazar-like,° with vile and loathsome crust,
All my smooth body.
Thus was I, sleeping, by a brother's hand
Of life, of crown, of queen, at once dispatch'd:°   75
Cut off even in the blossoms of my sin,
Unhous'led,° disappointed,° unanel'd,°
No reck'ning made, but sent to my account
With all my imperfections on my head:
O, horrible! O, horrible! most horrible!°   80
If thou hast nature in thee, bear it not;
Let not the royal bed of Denmark be
A couch for luxury° and damned incest.
But, howsomever thou pursues this act,
Taint not thy mind,° nor let thy soul contrive   85
Against thy mother aught: leave her to heaven
And to those thorns that in her bosom lodge,
To prick and sting her. Fare thee well at once!
The glow-worm shows the matin° to be near,
And 'gins to pale his uneffectual fire:°   90
Adieu, adieu, adieu! remember me.   [*Exit.*]
HAMLET: O all you host of heaven! O earth! what else?
And shall I couple° hell? O, fie! Hold, hold, my heart;
And you, my sinews, grow not instant old,
But bear me stiffly up. Remember thee!   95
Ay, thou poor ghost, whiles memory holds a seat
In this distracted globe.° Remember thee!
Yea, from the table of my memory
I'll wipe away all trivial fond records,
All saws° of books, all forms, all pressures° past,   100
That youth and observation copied there;
And thy commandment all alone shall live
Within the book and volume of my brain,
Unmix'd with baser matter: yes, by heaven!
O most pernicious woman!   105
O villain, villain, smiling, damned villain!

---

⁶⁸**posset** *coagulate, curdle.*   ⁶⁹**eager** *sour, acid.*   ⁷²**lazar-like** *leperlike.*   ⁷⁵**dispatch'd** *suddenly bereft.*   ⁷⁷**Unhous'led** *without having received the sacrament.*   ⁷⁷**disappointed** *unready, without equipment for the last journey.*   ⁷⁷**unanel'd** *without having received extreme unction.*   ⁸⁰**O ... horrible** *many editors give this line to Hamlet; Garrick and Sir Henry Irving spoke it in that part.*   ⁸³**luxury** *lechery.*   ⁸⁵**Taint ... mind** *probably, deprave not thy character, do nothing except in the pursuit of a natural revenge.*   ⁸⁹**matin** *morning.*   ⁹⁰**uneffectual fire** *cold light.*   ⁹³**couple** *add.*   ⁹⁷**distracted globe** *confused head.*   ¹⁰⁰**saws** *wise sayings.*   ¹⁰⁰**pressures** *impressions stamped.*

My tables,°—meet it is I set it down,
That one may smile, and smile, and be a villain;
At least I am sure it may be so in Denmark: [*Writing.*]
So, uncle, there you are. Now to my word;°   110
It is "Adieu, adieu! remember me,"
I have sworn't.

Enter HORATIO *and* MARCELLUS.

HORATIO: My lord, my lord—
MARCELLUS: Lord Hamlet,—
HORATIO: Heavens secure him!
HAMLET: So be it!
MARCELLUS: Hillo, ho, ho,° my lord!   115
HAMLET: Hillo, ho, ho, boy! come, bird, come.
MARCELLUS: How is't, my noble lord?
HORATIO: What news, my lord?
HAMLET: O, wonderful!
HORATIO: Good my lord, tell it.
HAMLET: No; you will reveal it.
HORATIO: Not I, my lord, by heaven.
MARCELLUS: Nor I, my lord.   120
HAMLET: How say you, then; would heart of man once think it?
　But you'll be secret?
HORATIO: }
　　　　　　 　 Ay, by heaven, my lord.
MARCELLUS: }
HAMLET: There's ne'er a villain dwelling in all Denmark
　But he's an arrant° knave.
HORATIO: There needs no ghost, my lord, come from the grave   125
　To tell us this.
HAMLET: Why, right; you are in the right;
　And so, without more circumstance at all,
　I hold it fit that we shake hands and part:
　You, as your business and desire shall point you;
　For every man has business and desire,   130
　Such as it is; and for my own poor part,
　Look you, I'll go pray.
HORATIO: These are but wild and whirling words, my lord.
HAMLET: I am sorry they offend you, heartily;
　Yes, 'faith, heartily.
HORATIO: There's no offence, my lord.   135
HAMLET: Yes, by Saint Patrick,° but there is, Horatio,
　And much offence too. Touching this vision here,
　It is an honest° ghost, that let me tell you:

---

[107]*tables*　*probably a small portable writing-tablet carried at the belt.*　[110]*word*　*watchword.*　[115]**Hillo,**
ho, ho　*a falconer's call to a hawk in air.*　[124]*arrant*　*thoroughgoing.*　[136]*Saint Patrick*　*St. Patrick was*
keeper of Purgatory and patron saint of all blunders and confusion.　[138]*honest*　*i.e., a real ghost and not an evil*
spirit.

For your desire to know what is between us,
O'ermaster 't as you may. And now, good friends,   140
As you are friends, scholars and soldiers,
Give me one poor request.
HORATIO: What is 't, my lord? we will.
HAMLET: Never make known what you have seen to-night.
HORATIO: } My lord, we will not.
MARCELLUS: }
HAMLET: Nay, but swear 't.
HORATIO: In faith,   145
    My lord, not I.
MARCELLUS: Nor I, my lord, in faith.
HAMLET: Upon my sword.°
MARCELLUS: We have sworn, my lord, already.
HAMLET: Indeed, upon my sword, indeed.   GHOST *cries under the stage.*
GHOST: Swear.
HAMLET: Ah, ha, boy! say'st thou so? art thou there, truepenny?°   150
    Come on—you hear this fellow in the cellarage—
    Consent to swear.
HORATIO: Propose the oath, my lord.
HAMLET: Never to speak of this that you have seen,
    Swear by my sword.
GHOST [*beneath*]: Swear.   155
HAMLET: Hic et ubique?° then we'll shift our ground.
    Come hither, gentlemen,
    And lay your hands again upon my sword:
    Swear by my sword,
    Never to speak of this that you have heard.   160
GHOST [*beneath*]: Swear by his sword.
HAMLET: Well said, old mole! canst work i' th' earth so fast?
    A worthy pioner!° Once more remove, good friends.
HORATIO: O day and night, but this is wondrous strange!
HAMLET: And therefore as a stranger give it welcome.   165
    There are more things in heaven and earth, Horatio,
    Than are dreamt of in your philosophy.
    But come;
    Here, as before, never, so help you mercy,
    How strange or odd soe'er I bear myself,   170
    As I perchance hereafter shall think meet
    To put an antic° disposition on,
    That you, at such times seeing me, never shall,
    With arms encumb'red° thus, or this head-shake,

147*sword*   i.e., the hilt in the form of a cross.   150*truepenny*   good old boy, or the like.   156**Hic et ubique?**
here and everywhere?   163**pioner**   digger, miner.   172**antic**   fantastic.   174**encumb'red**   folded or en-
twined.

Or by pronouncing of some doubtful phrase,   175
As "Well, well, we know," or "We could, an if we would,"
Or "If we list to speak," or "There be, an if they might,"
Or such ambiguous giving out,° to note°
That you know aught of me: this not to do,
So grace and mercy at your most need help you,   180
Swear.
GHOST [*beneath*]: Swear.
HAMLET: Rest, rest, perturbed spirit! [*They swear.*] So, gentlemen,
With all my love I do commend me to you:
And what so poor a man as Hamlet is   185
May do, t' express his love and friending° to you,
God willing, shall not lack. Let us go in together;
And still your fingers on your lips, I pray.
The time is out of joint: O cursed spite,
That ever I was born to set it right!   190
Nay, come, let's go together.   *Exeunt.*

ACT II

Scene I [A room in Polonius's house.]

Enter old POLONIUS *with his man* [REYNALDO].

POLONIUS: Give him this money and these notes, Reynaldo.
REYNALDO: I will, my lord.
POLONIUS: You shall do marvellous wisely, good Reynaldo,
Before you visit him, to make inquire
Of his behaviour.
REYNALDO: My lord, I did intend it.   5
POLONIUS: Marry, well said; very well said. Look you, sir,
Inquire me first what Danskers° are in Paris;
And how, and who, what means, and where they keep,°
What company, at what expense; and finding
By this encompassment° and drift° of question   10
That they do know my son, come you more nearer
Than your particular demands will touch it:°
Take° you as 'twere, some distant knowledge of him;
As thus, "I know his father and his friends;
And in part him": do you mark this, Reynaldo?   15

---

¹⁷⁸**giving out** *profession of knowledge.*   ¹⁷⁸**to note** *to give a sign.*   ¹⁸⁶**friending** *friendliness.*   **II.i.**
⁷**Danskers** *Danke was a common variant for "Denmark"; hence "Dane."*   ⁸**keep** *dwell.*   ¹⁰**encompass-
ment** *roundabout talking.*   ¹⁰**drift** *gradual approach or course.*   ^{11–12}**come . . . it** *i.e., you will find
out more this way than by asking pointed questions.*   ¹³**Take** *assume, pretend.*

REYNALDO: Ay, very well, my lord.
POLONIUS: "And in part him; but" you may say "not well:
　　But, if 't be he I mean, he's very wild;
　　Addicted so and so": and there put on° him
　　What forgeries° you please; marry, none so rank   20
　　As may dishonour him; take heed of that;
　　But, sir, such wanton,° wild and usual slips
　　As are companions noted and most known
　　To youth and liberty.
REYNALDO:　　　　　　　As gaming, my lord.
POLONIUS: Ay, or drinking, fencing,° swearing, quarrelling,   25
　　Drabbing;° you may go so far.
REYNALDO: My lord, that would dishonour him.
POLONIUS: 'Faith, no; as you may season it in the charge.
　　You must not put another scandal on him,
　　That he is open to incontinency;°   30
　　That's not my meaning: but breathe his faults so quaintly°
　　That they may seem the taints of liberty,°
　　The flash and outbreak of a fiery mind,
　　A savageness in unreclaimed° blood,
　　Of general assault.°
REYNALDO:　　　　　　But, my good lord,—   35
POLONIUS: Wherefore should you do this?
REYNALDO:　　　　　　　　　　　　Ay, my lord,
　　I would know that.
POLONIUS:　　　　　　Marry, sir, here's my drift;
　　And, I believe, it is a fetch of wit:°
　　You laying these slight sullies on my son,
　　As 'twere a thing a little soil'd i' th' working,   40
　　Mark you,
　　Your party in converse, him you would sound,
　　Having ever° seen in the prenominate° crimes
　　The youth you breathe of guilty, be assur'd
　　He closes with you in this consequence;°   45
　　"Good sir," or so, or "friend," or "gentleman,"
　　According to the phrase or the addition
　　Of man and country.
REYNALDO:　　　　　　　Very good, my lord.
POLONIUS: And then, sir, does 'a this—'a does—what was I about to say?
　　By the mass, I was about to say something: where did I leave?   50

---

[19]**put on** *impute to.* [20]**forgeries** *invented tales.* [22]**wanton** *sportive, unrestrained.* [25]**fencing** *in-dicative of the ill repute of professional fencers and fencing schools in Elizabethan times.* [26]**Drabbing** *associated with immoral women.* [30]**incontinency** *habitual loose behavior.* [31]**quaintly** *delicately, ingeniously.* [32]**taints of liberty** *blemishes due to freedom.* [34]**unreclaimed** *untamed.* [36]**general assault** *tendency that assails all untrained youth.* [38]**fetch of wit** *clever trick.* [43]**ever** *at any time.* [43]**prenominate** *before-mentioned.* [45]**closes ... consequence** *agrees with you in this conclusion.*

REYNALDO: At "closes in the consequence," at "friend or so," and "gentleman."
POLONIUS: At "closes in the consequence," ay, marry;
   He closes thus: "I know the gentleman;
   I saw him yesterday, or t' other day,   55
   Or then, or then; with such, or such; and, as you say,
   There was 'a gaming; there o'ertook in's rouse;°
   There falling out at tennis": or perchance,
   "I saw him enter such a house of sale,"
   Videlicet,° a brothel, or so forth.   60
   See you now;
   Your bait of falsehood takes this carp of truth:
   And thus do we of wisdom and of reach,°
   With windlasses° and with assays of bias,°
   By indirections° find directions° out: 65
   So by my former lecture° and advice,
   Shall you my son. You have me, have you not?
REYNALDO: My lord, I have.
POLONIUS: God bye ye;° fare ye well.
REYNALDO: Good my lord!
POLONIUS: Observe his inclination in yourself.°   70
REYNALDO: I shall, my lord.
POLONIUS: And let him ply his music.°
REYNALDO: Well, my lord.
POLONIUS: Farewell!   *Exit* REYNALDO.

Enter OPHELIA.

      How now, Ophelia! what's the matter?
OPHELIA: O, my lord, my lord, I have been so affrighted!
POLONIUS: With what, i' th' name of God?   75
OPHELIA: My lord, as I was sewing in my closet,°
   Lord Hamlet, with his doublet° all unbrac'd;°
   No hat upon his head; his stockings foul'd,
   Ungart'red, and down-gyved° to his ankle;
   Pale as his shirt; his knees knocking each other;   80
   And with a look so piteous in purport
   As if he had been loosed out of hell
   To speak of horrors,—he comes before me.
POLONIUS: Mad for thy love?
OPHELIA: My lord, I do not know;
   But truly, I do fear it.

---

[57] **o'ertook in's rouse** *overcome by drink.*   [60] **Videlicet** *namely.*   [63] **reach** *capacity, ability.*   [64] **wind-lasses** *i.e., circuitous paths.*   [64] **assays of bias** *attempts that resemble the course of the bowl, which, being weighted on one side, has a curving motion.*   [65] **indirections** *devious courses.*   [65] **directions** *straight courses, i.e., the truth.*   [66] **lecture** *admonition.*   [68] **bye ye** *be with you.*   [70] **Observe . . . yourself** *in your own person, not by spies; or conform your own conduct to his inclination; or test him by studying yourself.*   [72] **ply his music** *probably to be taken literally.*   [76] **closet** *private chamber.*   [77] **doublet** *close-fitting coat.*   [77] **unbrac'd** *unfastened.*   [79] **down-gyved** *fallen to the ankles (like gyves or fetters).*

POLONIUS: What said he?   85
OPHELIA: He took me by the wrist and held me hard;
   Then goes he to the length of all his arm;
   And, with his other hand thus o'er his brow,
   He falls to such perusal of my face
   As 'a would draw it. Long stay'd he so;   90
   At last, a little shaking of mine arm
   And thrice his head thus waving up and down,
   He rais'd a sigh so piteous and profound
   As it did seem to shatter all his bulk°
   And end his being: that done, he lets me go: 95
   And, with his head over his shoulder turn'd,
   He seem'd to find his way without his eyes;
   For out o'doors he went without their helps,
   And, to the last, bended their light on me.
POLONIUS: Come, go with me: I will go seek the king.   100
   This is the very ecstasy of love,
   Whose violent property° fordoes° itself
   And leads the will to desperate undertakings
   As oft as any passion under heaven
   That does afflict our natures. I am sorry.   105
   What, have you given him any hard words of late?
OPHELIA: No, my good lord, but, as you did command,
   I did repel his letters and denied
   His access to me.
POLONIUS: That hath made him mad.
   I am sorry that with better heed and judgement   110
   I had not quoted° him: I fear'd he did but trifle,
   And meant to wrack thee; but, beshrew my jealousy!°
   By heaven, it is as proper to our age
   To cast beyond° ourselves in our opinions
   As it is common for the younger sort   115
   To lack discretion. Come, go we to the king:
   This must be known; which, being kept close, might move
   More grief to hide than hate to utter love.°
   Come.   *Exeunt.*

Scene II [*A room in the castle.*]

   Flourish. Enter KING *and* QUEEN, ROSENCRANTZ, *and* GUILDENSTERN [*with others*].

KING: Welcome, dear Rosencrantz and Guildenstern!

94**bulk** *body.*   102**property** *nature.*   102**fordoes** *destroys.*   111**quoted** *observed.*   112**beshrew**
my jealousy *curse my suspicions.*   114**cast beyond** *overshoot, miscalculate.*   117–118**might . . . love**
*i.e., I might cause more grief to others by hiding the knowledge of Hamlet's love to Ophelia than hatred to me and mine
by telling of it.*

Moreover that° we much did long to see you,
The need we have to use you did provoke
Our hasty sending. Something have you heard
Of Hamlet's transformation; so call it, 5
Sith° nor th' exterior nor the inward man
Resembles that it was. What it should be,
More than his father's death, that thus hath put him
So much from th' understanding of himself,
I cannot dream of: I entreat you both, 10
That, being of so young days° brought up with him,
And sith so neighbour'd to his youth and haviour,
That you vouchsafe your rest° here in our court
Some little time: so by your companies
To draw him on to pleasures, and to gather, 15
So much as from occasion you may glean,
Whether aught, to us unknown, afflicts him thus,
That, open'd, lies within our remedy.
QUEEN: Good gentlemen, he hath much talk'd of you;
And sure I am two men there are not living 20
To whom he more adheres. If it will please you
To show us so much gentry° and good will
As to expend your time with us awhile,
For the supply and profit° of our hope,
Your visitation shall receive such thanks 25
As fits a king's remembrance.
ROSENCRANTZ: Both your majesties
Might, by the sovereign power you have of us,
Put your dread pleasures more into command
Than to entreaty.
GUILDENSTERN: But we both obey,
And here give up ourselves, in the full bent° 30
To lay our service freely at your feet,
To be commanded.
KING: Thanks, Rosencrantz and gentle Guildenstern.
QUEEN: Thanks, Guildenstern and gentle Rosencrantz:
And I beseech you instantly to visit 35
My too much changed son. Go, some of you,
And bring these gentlemen where Hamlet is.
GUILDENSTERN: Heavens make our presence and our practices
Pleasant and helpful to him!
QUEEN: Ay, amen!

Exeunt ROSENCRANTZ *and* GUILDENSTERN [*with some* ATTENDANTS].

II.ii. [2]***Moreover that*** *besides the fact that.*   [6]***Sith*** *since.*   [11]***of . . . days*** *from such early youth.*
[13]***vouchsafe your rest*** *please to stay.*   [22]***gentry*** *courtesy.*   [24]***supply and profit*** *aid and successful out-*
come.   [30]***in . . . bent*** *to the utmost degree of our mental capacity.*

Enter POLONIUS.

POLONIUS: Th' ambassadors from Norway, my good lord,   40
 Are joyfully return'd.
KING: Thou still hast been the father of good news.
POLONIUS: Have I, my lord? I assure my good liege,
 I hold my duty, as I hold my soul,
 Both to my God and to my gracious king: 45
 And I do think, or else this brain of mine
 Hunts not the trail of policy so sure
 As it hath us'd to do, that I have found
 The very cause of Hamlet's lunacy.
KING: O, speak of that; that do I long to hear.   50
POLONIUS: Give first admittance to th' ambassadors;
 My news shall be the fruit to that great feast.
KING: Thyself do grace to them, and bring them in.   [*Exit* POLONIUS.]
 He tells me, my dear Gertrude, he hath found
 The head and source of all your son's distemper.   55
QUEEN: I doubt° it is no other but the main;°
 His father's death, and our o'erhasty marriage.
KING: Well, we shall sift him.

Enter AMBASSADORS [VOLTIMAND *and* CORNELIUS, *with* POLONIUS].

   Welcome, my good friends!
 Say, Voltimand, what from our brother Norway?
VOLTIMAND: Most fair return of greetings and desires.   60
 Upon our first, he sent out to suppress
 His nephew's levies; which to him appear'd
 To be a preparation 'gainst the Polack;
 But, better look'd into, he truly found
 It was against your highness: whereat griev'd,   65
 That so his sickness, age and impotence
 Was falsely borne in hand,° sends out arrests
 On Fortinbras; which he, in brief, obeys;
 Receives rebuke from Norway, and in fine°
 Makes vow before his uncle never more   70
 To give th' assay° of arms against your majesty.
 Whereon old Norway, overcome with joy,
 Gives him three score thousand crowns in annual fee,
 And his commission to employ those soldiers,
 So levied as before, against the Polack: 75
 With an entreaty, herein further shown, [*giving a paper.*]
 That it might please you to give quiet pass
 Through your dominions for this enterprise,

---

[56]**doubt** *fear.*   [56]**main** *chief point, principal concern.*   [67]**borne in hand** *deluded.*   [69]**in fine** *in the end.*   [71]**assay** *assault, trial (of arms).*

On such regards of safety and allowance°
As therein are set down.
KING: It likes° us well;   80
And at our more consider'd° time we'll read,
Answer, and think upon this business.
Meantime we thank you for your well-took labour:
Go to your rest; at night we'll feast together:
Most welcome home!   *Exeunt* AMBASSADORS.
POLONIUS: This business is well ended.   85
My liege, and madam, to expostulate
What majesty should be, what duty is,
Why day is day, night night, and time is time,
Were nothing but to waste night, day and time.
Therefore, since brevity is the soul of wit,°   90
And tediousness the limbs and outward flourishes,°
I will be brief: your noble son is mad:
Mad call I it; for, to define true madness
What is 't but to be nothing else but mad?
But let that go.
QUEEN: More matter, with less art.   95
POLONIUS: Madam, I swear I use no art at all.
That he is mad, 'tis true: 'tis true 'tis pity;
And pity 'tis 'tis true: a foolish figure;°
But farewell it, for I will use no art.
Mad let us grant him, then: and now remains   100
That we find out the cause of this effect,
Or rather say, the cause of this defect,
For this effect defective comes by cause:
Thus it remains, and the remainder thus.
Perpend.°   105
I have a daughter—have while she is mine—
Who, in her duty and obedience, mark,
Hath given me this: now gather, and surmise.   [*Reads the letter*]
"To the celestial and my soul's idol, the most beautified Ophelia,"—   110
That's an ill phrase, a vile phrase; "beautified" is a vile phrase: but you shall hear.
Thus: [*Reads.*]
"In her excellent white bosom, these, & c."
QUEEN: Came this from Hamlet to her?
POLONIUS: Good madam, stay awhile; I will be faithful.   [*Reads.*] 115
                    "Doubt thou the stars are fire;
                         Doubt that the sun doth move;
                    Doubt truth to be a liar;
                         But never doubt I love.

---

⁷⁹**safety and allowance**   *pledges of safety to the country and terms of permission for the troops to pass.*
⁸⁰**likes**   *pleases.*   ⁸¹**consider'd**   *suitable for deliberation.*   ⁹⁰**wit**   *sound sense or judgment.*
⁹¹**flourishes**   *ostentation, embellishments.*   ⁹⁸**figure**   *figure of speech.*   ¹⁰⁵**Perpend**   *consider.*

"O dear Ophelia, I am ill at these numbers;° I have not art to reckon° my   120
groans: but that I love thee best, O most best, believe it. Adieu.
"Thine evermore, most dear lady, whilst this machine° is to him,

                                      HAMLET."

This, in obedience, hath my daughter shown me,
And more above,° hath his solicitings,   125
As they fell out° by time, by means° and place,
All given to mine ear.
KING: But how hath she
  Receiv'd his love?
POLONIUS: What do you think of me?
KING: As of a man faithful and honourable.
POLONIUS: I would fain prove so. But what might you think,   130
  When I had seen this hot love on the wing—
  As I perceiv'd it, I must tell you that,
  Before my daughter told me—what might you,
  Or my dear majesty your queen here, think,
  If I had play'd the desk or table-book,°   135
  Or given my heart a winking,° mute and dumb,
  Or look'd upon this love with idle sight;
  What might you think? No, I went round to work,
  And my young mistress thus I did bespeak: °
  "Lord Hamlet is a prince, out of thy star;°   140
  This must not be": and then I prescripts gave her,
  That she should lock herself from his resort,
  Admit no messengers, receive no tokens.
  Which done, she took the fruits of my advice;
  And he, repelled—a short tale to make—   145
  Fell into a sadness, then into a fast,
  Thence to a watch,° thence into a weakness,
  Thence to a lightness,° and, by this declension,°
  Into the madness wherein now he raves,
  And all we mourn for.
KING: Do you think 'tis this?   150
QUEEN: It may be, very like.
POLONIUS: Hath there been such a time—I would fain know that—
  That I have positively said "'Tis so,"
  When it prov'd otherwise?
KING: Not that I know.
POLONIUS [*pointing to his head and shoulder*]: Take this from this, if this be
  otherwise:

120*ill ... numbers* unskilled at writing verses.   120*reckon* number metrically, scan.   122*machine* bodily frame.   125*more above* moreover.   126*fill out* occurred.   126*means* opportunities (of access).
135*play'd ... table-book* i.e., remained shut up, concealed this information.   136*given ... winking* given
my heart a signal to keep silent.   139*bespeak* address.   140*out ... star* above thee in position.
147*watch* state of sleeplessness.   148*lightness* lightheartedness.   148*declension* decline, deterioration.

If circumstances lead me, I will find
Where truth is hid, though it were hid indeed
Within the centre.°
KING: How may we try it further?
POLONIUS: You know, sometimes he walks four hours together
Here in the lobby.
QUEEN: So he does indeed. 160
POLONIUS: At such a time I'll loose my daughter to him:
Be you and I behind an arras° then;
Mark the encounter: if he love her not
And be not from his reason fall'n thereon,°
Let me be no assistant for a state, 165
But keep a farm and carters.
KING: We will try it.

Enter HAMLET [*reading on a book*].

QUEEN: But, look, where sadly the poor wretch comes reading.
POLONIUS: Away, I do beseech you both, away:

Exeunt KING *and* QUEEN [*with* ATTENDANTS].

I'll board° him presently. O, give me leave.
How does my good Lord Hamlet? 170
HAMLET: Well, God-a-mercy.
POLONIUS: Do you know me, my lord?
HAMLET: Excellent well; you are a fishmonger.°
POLONIUS: Not I, my lord.
HAMLET: Then I would you were so honest a man. 175
POLONIUS: Honest, my lord!
HAMLET: Ay, sir; to be honest, as this world goes, is to be one man picked out of
ten thousand.
POLONIUS: That's very true, my lord.
HAMLET: For if the sun breed maggots in a dead dog, being a good kissing 180
carrion,°—Have you a daughter?
POLONIUS: I have, my lord.
HAMLET: Let her not walk i' the sun:° conception° is a blessing: but as your
daughter may conceive—Friend, look to 't.
POLONIUS [*aside*]: How say you by° that? Still harping on my daughter: yet he 185
knew me not at first; 'a said I was a fishmonger: 'a is far gone, far gone: and
truly in my youth I suffered much extremity for love; very near this. I'll speak
to him again. What do you read, my lord?
HAMLET: Words, words, words.

---

¹⁵⁸***centre*** *middle point of the earth.*   ¹⁶²***arras*** *hanging, tapestry.*   ¹⁶⁴***thereon*** *on that account.*
¹⁶⁹***board*** *accost.*   ¹⁷³***fishmonger*** *an opprobrious expression meaning "bawd," "procurer."*
¹⁸⁰⁻¹⁸¹***good kissing carrion*** *i.e., a good piece of flesh for kissing (?).*   ¹⁸³***i' the sun*** *in the sunshine of*
princely favors.   ¹⁸³***conception*** *quibble on "understanding" and "pregnancy."*   ¹⁸⁵***by*** *concerning.*

POLONIUS: What is the matter,° my lord?   190

HAMLET: Between who?°

POLONIUS: I mean, the matter that you read, my lord.

HAMLET: Slanders, sir: for the satirical rogue says here that old men have grey
beards, that their faces are wrinkled, their eyes purging° thick amber and plum- 195
tree gum and that they have a plentiful lack of wit, together with most weak
hams: all which, sir, though I most powerfully and potently believe, yet I hold
it not honesty° to have it thus set down, for yourself, sir, should be old as I am,
if like a crab you could go backward.

POLONIUS [*aside*]: Though this be madness, yet there is method in 't.—Will you 200
walk out of the air, my lord?

HAMLET: Into my grave.

POLONIUS: Indeed, that's out of the air. [*Aside.*] How pregnant sometimes his
replies are! a happiness° that often madness hits on, which reason and sanity
could not so prosperously° be delivered of. I will leave him, and suddenly con- 205
trive the means of meeting between him and my daughter.—My honourable
lord, I will most humbly take my leave of you.

HAMLET: You cannot, sir, take from me any thing that I will more willingly part
withal: except my life, except my life, except my life.

Enter GUILDENSTERN *and* ROSENCRANTZ.

POLONIUS: Fare you well, my lord.   210

HAMLET: These tedious old fools!

POLONIUS: You go to seek the Lord Hamlet; there he is.

ROSENCRANTZ [*to* POLONIUS]: God save you, sir!   [*Exit* POLONIUS.]

GUILDENSTERN: My honoured lord!

ROSENCRANTZ: My most dear lord!   215

HAMLET: My excellent good friends! How dost thou, Guildenstern? Ah, Rosencrantz! Good lads, how do ye both?

ROSENCRANTZ: As the indifferent° children of the earth.

GUILDENSTERN: Happy, in that we are not over-happy;
On Fortune's cap we are not the very button.   220

HAMLET: Nor the soles of her shoe?

ROSENCRANTZ: Neither, my lord.

HAMLET: Then you live about her waist, or in the middle of her favours?

GUILDENSTERN: 'Faith, her privates° we.

HAMLET: In the secret parts of Fortune? O, most true; she is a strumpet. What's the 225
news?

ROSENCRANTZ: None, my lord, but that the world's grown honest.

HAMLET: Then is doomsday near: but your news is not true. Let me question more
in particular: what have you, my good friends, deserved at the hands of Fortune, that she sends you to prison hither?   230

190*matter*   *substance.*   191*Between who?*   *Hamlet deliberately takes matter as meaning "basis of dispute."*
194*purging*   *discharging.*   197*honesty*   *decency.*   203*happiness*   *felicity of expression.*   204*prosper-
ously*   *successfully.*   217*indifferent*   *ordinary.*   223*privates*   *i.e., ordinary men (sexual pun on private
parts).*

GUILDENSTERN: Prison, my lord!

HAMLET: Denmark's a prison.

ROSENCRANTZ: Then is the world one.

HAMLET: A goodly one; in which there are many confines,° wards and dungeons, Denmark being one o' the worst.   235

ROSENCRANTZ: We think not so, my lord.

HAMLET: Why, then, 'tis none to you; for there is nothing either good or bad, but thinking makes it so: to me it is a prison.

ROSENCRANTZ: Why then, your ambition makes it one; 'tis too narrow for your mind.   240

HAMLET: O God, I could be bounded in a nutshell and count myself a king of infinite space, were it not that I have bad dreams.

GUILDENSTERN: Which dreams indeed are ambition, for the very substance of the ambitious° is merely the shadow of a dream.

HAMLET: A dream itself is but a shadow.   245

ROSENCRANTZ: Truly, and I hold ambition of so airy and light a quality that it is but a shadow's shadow.

HAMLET: Then are our beggars bodies, and our monarchs and outstretched heroes the beggars' shadows. Shall we to the court? for, by my fay,° I cannot reason.°

ROSENCRANTZ: 250
GUILDENSTERN: } We'll wait upon° you.

HAMLET: No such matter: I will not sort° you with the rest of my servants, for, to speak to you like an honest man, I am most dreadfully attended.° But, in the beaten way of friendship,° what make you at Elsinore?

ROSENCRANTZ: To visit you, my lord: no other occasion.   255

HAMLET: Beggar that I am, I am ever poor in thanks; but I thank you: and sure, dear friends, my thanks are too dear a° halfpenny. Were you not sent for? Is it your own inclining? Is it a free visitation? Come, come, deal justly with me: come, come; nay, speak.

GUILDENSTERN: What should we say, my lord?   260

HAMLET: Why, any thing, but to the purpose. You were sent for; and there is a kind of confession in your looks which your modesties have not craft enough to colour: I know the good king and queen have sent for you.

ROSENCRANTZ: To what end, my lord?

HAMLET: That you must teach me. But let me conjure° you, by the rights of our   265
fellowship, by the consonancy of our youth,° by the obligation of our ever-preserved love, and by what more dear a better proposer° could charge you withal, be even and direct with me, whether you were sent for, or no?

ROSENCRANTZ [*aside to* GUILDENSTERN]: What say you?   270

HAMLET [*aside*]: Nay, then, I have an eye of you.—If you love me, hold not off.

GUILDENSTERN: My lord, we were sent for.

---

²³³**confines** *places of confinement.*   ²⁴³**very ... ambitious** *that seemingly most substantial thing which the ambitious pursue.*   ²⁴⁸**fay** *faith.*   ²⁴⁹**reason** *argue.*   ²⁵⁰**wait upon** *accompany.*   ²⁵¹**sort** *class.*   ²⁵²**dreadfully attended** *poorly provided with servants.*   ²⁵³**in the ... friendship** *as a matter of course among friends.*   ²⁵⁶**a** *i.e., at a.*   ²⁶⁴**conjure** *adjure, entreat.*   ²⁶⁵**consonancy of our youth** *the fact that we are of the same age.*   ²⁶⁶**better proposer** *one more skillful in finding proposals.*

HAMLET: I will tell you why; so shall my anticipation prevent your discovery,° and
your secrecy to the king and queen moult no feather. I have of late—but
wherefore I know not—lost all my mirth, forgone all custom of exercises; and   275
indeed it goes so heavily with my disposition that this goodly frame, the earth,
seems to me a sterile promontory, this most excellent canopy, the air, look you,
this brave o'erhanging firmament, this majestical roof fretted° with golden fire,
why, it appeareth nothing to me but a foul and pestilent congregation of
vapours. What a piece of work is a man! how noble in reason! how infinite in   280
faculties!° in form and moving how express° and admirable! in action how like
an angel! in apprehension° how like a god! the beauty of the world! the
paragon of animals! And yet, to me, what is this quintessence° of dust? man
delights not me: no, nor woman neither, though by your smiling you seem to
say so.   285
ROSENCRANTZ: My lord, there was no such stuff in my thoughts.
HAMLET: Why did you laugh then, when I said "man delights not me"?
ROSENCRANTZ: To think, my lord, if you delight not in man, what lenten°
entertainment the players shall receive from you: we coted° them on the way;
and hither are they coming, to offer you service.   290
HAMLET: He that plays the king shall be welcome; his majesty shall have tribute of
me; the adventurous knight shall use his foil and target;° the lover shall not sigh
gratis; the humorous man° shall end his part in peace; the clown shall make
those laugh whose lungs are tickle o' the sere;° and the lady shall say her mind
freely, or the blank verse shall halt for 't.° What players are they?   295
ROSENCRANTZ: Even those you were wont to take delight in, the tragedians of the
city.
HAMLET: How chances it they travel? their residence,° both in reputation and
profit, was better both ways.
ROSENCRANTZ: I think their inhibition° comes by the means of the late   300
innovation.°
HAMLET: Do they hold the same estimation they did when I was in the city? are
they so followed?
ROSENCRANTZ: No, indeed, are they not.
HAMLET: How° comes it? do they grow rusty?   305
ROSENCRANTZ: Nay, their endeavour keeps in the wonted pace: but there is, sir,
an aery° of children, little eyases,° that cry out on the top of question,° and are

---

273*prevent your discovery*   *forestall your disclosure.*   278*fretted*   *adorned.*   281*faculties*   *capacity.*
281*express*   *well-framed (?), exact (?).*   283*apprehension*   *understanding.*   283*quintessence*   *the*
fifth essence of ancient philosophy, supposed to be the substance of the heavenly bodies and to be latent in all
things.   289*lenten*   *meager.*   289*coted*   *overtook and passed beyond.*   289*foil and target*   *sword*
and shield.   298*humorous man*   *actor who takes the part of the humor characters.*   293*tickle o' the*
sere   *easy on the trigger.*   296*the lady . . . for 't*   *the lady (fond of talking) shall have opportunity to*
talk, blank verse or no blank verse.   298*residence*   *remaining in one place.*   300*inhibition*   *formal pro-*
hibition (from acting plays in the city or, possibly, at court).   300*innovation*   *the new fashion in satirical*
plays performed by boy actors in the "private" theaters.   305–323*How . . . load too*   *the passage is the fa-*
mous one dealing with the War of the Theatres (1599–1602); namely, the rivalry between the children's compa-
nies and the adult actors.   307*aery*   *nest.*   307*eyases*   *young hawks.*   307*cry . . . question* *speak in a*
high key dominating conversation; clamor forth the height of controversy; probably "excel" (cf. line 459); perhaps intended
to decry leaders of the dramatic profession.

most tyrannically° clapped for 't: these are now the fashion, and so berattle° the
common stages°—so they call them—that many wearing rapiers° are afraid of
goose-quills° and dare scarce come thither.   310

HAMLET: What, are they children? who maintains 'em? how are they escoted?°
Will they pursue the quality° no longer than they can sing?° will they not say
afterwards, if they should grow themselves to common° players—as it is most
like, if their means are no better—their writers do them wrong, to make them
exclaim against their own succession?°   315

ROSENCRANTZ: 'Faith, there has been much to do on both sides; and the nation
holds it no sin to tarre° them to controversy: there was, for a while, no money
bid for argument,° unless the poet and the players went to cuffs° in the
question.°

HAMLET: Is't possible?   320

GUILDENSTERN: O, there has been much throwing about of brains.

HAMLET: Do the boys carry it away?°

ROSENCRANTZ: Ay, that they do, my lord; Hercules and his load° too.

HAMLET: It is not very strange; for my uncle is king of Denmark, and those that
would make mows° at him while my father lived, give twenty, forty, fifty, a   325
hundred ducats° a-piece for his picture in little.° 'Sblood, there is something in
this more than natural, if philosophy could find it out.

A flourish [of trumpets within].

GUILDENSTERN: There are the players.   330

HAMLET: Gentlemen, you are welcome to Elsinore. Your hands, come then: the
appurtenance of welcome is fashion and ceremony: let me comply° with you
in this garb,° lest my extent° to the players, which, I tell you, must show fairly
outwards, should more appear like entertainment than yours. You are welcome:
but my uncle-father and aunt-mother are deceived.   335

GUILDENSTERN: In what, my dear lord?

HAMLET: I am but mad north-north-west:° when the wind is southerly I know a
hawk from a handsaw.°

Enter POLONIUS.

POLONIUS: Well be with you, gentlemen!   340

308*tyrannically* outrageously.   308*berattle* berate.   309*common stages* public theaters.   309*many*
wearing rapiers many men of fashion, who were afraid to patronize the common players for fear of being satirized by the
poets who wrote for the children.   310*goose-quills* i.e., pens of satirists.   311*escoted* maintained.   32*qual-*
ity acting profession.   312*no longer ... sing* i.e., until their voices change.   313*common* regular, adult.
315*succession* future careers.   319*tarre* set on (as dogs).   318*argument* probably, plot for a play.
320*went to cuffs* came to blows.   319*question* controversy.   322*carry it away* win the day.   323*Her-*
cules ... load regarded as an allusion to the sign of the Globe Theatre, which was Hercules bearing the world on his
shoulder.   325*mows* grimaces.   326*ducats* gold coins worth 9s. 4d.   326*in little* in miniature.
332*comply* observe the formalities of courtesy.   333*garb* manner.   333*extent* showing of kindness.   338*I*
am ... north-north-west I am only partly mad, i.e., in only one point of the compass.   339*handsaw* a proposed reading of hernshaw would mean "heron"; handsaw may be an early corruption of hernshaw. Another view regards
hawk as the variant of hack, a tool of the pickax type, and handsaw as a saw operated by hand.

HAMLET: Hark you, Guildenstern; and you too: at each ear a hearer: that great baby
    you see there is not yet out of his swaddling-clouts.°

ROSENCRANTZ: Happily he is the second time come to them; for they say an old
    man is twice a child.

HAMLET: I will prophesy he comes to tell me of the players; mark it.—You say   345
    right, sir: o' Monday morning;° 'twas then indeed.

POLONIUS: My lord, I have news to tell you.

HAMLET: My lord, I have news to tell you. When Roscius° was an actor in
    Rome,—

POLONIUS: The actors are come hither, my lord.   350

HAMLET: Buz, buz!°

POLONIUS: Upon my honour,—

HAMLET: Then came each actor on his ass,—

POLONIUS: The best actors in the world, either for tragedy, comedy, history,
    pastoral, pastoral-comical, historical-pastoral, tragical-historical, tragical-   355
    comical-historical-pastoral, scene individable,° or poem unlimited:° Seneca°
    cannot be too heavy, nor Plautus° too light. For the law of writ and the liberty,°
    these are the only men.

HAMLET: O Jephthah, judge of Israel,° what a treasure hadst thou!

POLONIUS: What a treasure had he, my lord?   360

HAMLET: Why,

        "One fair daughter, and no more,
        The which he loved passing well."

POLONIUS [aside]:Still on my daughter.

HAMLET: Am I not i' the right, old Jephthah?   365

POLONIUS: If you call me Jephthah, my lord, I have a daughter that I love passing°
    well.

HAMLET: Nay, that follows not.

POLONIUS: What follows, then, my lord?

HAMLET: Why,   370

        "As by lot, God wot,"
    and then, you know,

        "It came to pass, as most like° it was,"—
    the first row° of the pious chanson° will show you more; for look, where my
    abridgement comes.°   375

Enter the PLAYERS.

You are welcome, masters; welcome, all. I am glad to see thee well. Welcome,
    good friends. O, old friend! why, thy face is valanced° since I saw thee last:

---

³⁴²*swaddling-clouts* *clothes in which to wrap a newborn baby.*   ³⁴⁶*o' Monday morning* *said to mislead
Polonius.*   ³⁴⁸*Roscius* *a famous Roman actor.*   ³⁵¹*Buz, buz* *an interjection used at Oxford to denote
stale news.*   ³⁵⁶*scene individable* *a play observing the unity of place.*   ³⁵⁶*poem unlimited* *a play disre-
garding the unities of time and place.*   ³⁵⁷*Seneca* *writer of Latin tragedies, model of early Elizabethan writers of
tragedy.*   ³⁵⁷*Plautus* *writer of Latin comedy.*   ³⁵⁷*law . . . liberty* *pieces written according to rules and
without rules, i.e., "classical" and "romantic" dramas.*   ³⁵⁹*Jephthah . . . Israel* *Jephthah had to sacrifice his
daughter; see Judges 11.*   ³⁶⁷*passing* *surpassingly.*   ³⁷³*like* *probable.*   ³⁷⁴*row* *stanza.*
³⁷⁴*chanson* *ballad.*   ³⁷⁵*abridgement comes* *opportunity comes for cutting short the conversation.*
³⁷⁷*valanced* *fringed (with a beard).*

comest thou to beard me in Denmark? What, my young lady and mistress! By'r lady, your ladyship is nearer to heaven than when I saw you last, by the altitude of a chopine.° Pray God, your voice, like a piece of uncurrent° gold, be not 380 cracked within the ring.° Masters, you are all welcome. We'll e'en to 't like French falconers, fly at any thing we see: we'll have a speech straight: come, give us a taste of your quality; come, a passionate speech.

FIRST PLAYER: What speech, my good lord?

HAMLET: I heard thee speak me a speech once, but it was never acted; or, if it was, 385 not above once; for the play, I remember, pleased not the million; 'twas caviary to the general:° but it was—as I received it, and others, whose judgements in such matters cried in the top of° mine—an excellent play, well digested in the scenes, set down with as much modesty as cunning.° I remember, one said there were no sallets° in the lines to make the matter savoury, nor no matter in 390 the phrase that might indict° the author of affectation; but called it an honest method, as wholesome as sweet, and by very much more handsome than fine.° One speech in 't I chiefly loved: 'twas Æneas' tale to Dido;° and thereabout of it especially, where he speaks of Priam's slaughter: if it live in your memory, begin at this line: let me see, let me see— 395
"The rugged Pyrrhus,° like th' Hyrcanian beast,"°—
'tis not so:—it begins with Pyrrhus:—
"The rugged Pyrrhus, he whose sable arms,
Black as his purpose, did the night resemble
When he lay couched in the ominous horse,° 400
Hath now this dread and black complexion smear'd
With heraldry more dismal; head to foot
Now is he total gules;° horridly trick'd°
With blood of fathers, mothers, daughters, sons,
Bak'd and impasted° with the parching streets, 405
That lend a tyrannous and a damned light
To their lord's murder: roasted in wrath and fire,
And thus o'er-sized° with coagulate gore,
With eyes like carbuncles, the hellish Pyrrhus
Old grandsire Priam seeks." 410
So, proceed you.

POLONIUS: 'Fore God, my lord, well spoken, with good accent and good discretion.

---

[380]**chopine** *kind of shoe raised by the thickness of the heel; worn in Italy, particularly at Venice.* [380]**un-current** *not passable as lawful coinage.* [381]**cracked within the ring** *in the center of coins were rings enclosing the sovereign's head; if the coin was cracked within this ring, it was unfit for currency.* [387]**caviary to the general** *not relished by the multitude.* [388]**cried in the top of** *spoke with greater authority than.* [390]**cunning** *skill.* [390]**sallets** *salads: here, spicy improprieties.* [391]**indict** *convict.* [392]**as wholesome . . . fine** *its beauty was not that of elaborate ornament, but that of order and proportion.* [393]**Æneas' tale to Dido** *the lines recited by the player are imitated from Marlowe and Nashe's Dido Queen of Carthage (II.i. 214 ff.). They are written in such a way that the conventionality of the play within a play is raised above that of ordinary drama.* [396]**Pyrrhus** *a Greek hero in the Trojan War.* [396]**Hyrcanian beast** *the tiger; see Virgil, Aeneid, IV. 266.* [400]**ominous horse** *Trojan horse.* [403]**gules** *red, a heraldic term.* [403]**trick'd** *spotted, smeared.* [405]**impasted** *made into a paste.* [408]**o'er-sized** *covered as with size or glue.*

FIRST PLAYER: "Anon he finds him
　　Striking too short at Greeks; his antique sword,
　　Rebellious to his arm, lies where it falls,
　　Repugnant° to command: unequal match'd,
　　Pyrrhus at Priam drives; in rage strikes wide;　　　　　　　　420

　　But with the whiff and wind of his fell sword
　　Th' unnerved father falls. Then senseless Ilium,°
　　Seeming to feel this blow, with flaming top
　　Stoops to his base, and with a hideous crash
　　Takes prisoner Pyrrhus' ear: for, lo! his sword　　　　　　　425
　　Which was declining on the milky head
　　Of reverend Priam, seem'd i' th' air to stick:
　　So, as a painted tyrant,° Pyrrhus stood,
　　And like a neutral to his will and matter,°
　　Did nothing.　　　　　　　　　　　　　　　　　　　430
　　But, as we often see, against° some storm,
　　A silence in the heavens, the rack° stand still,
　　The bold winds speechless and the orb below
　　As hush as death, anon the dreadful thunder
　　Doth rend the region,° so, after Pyrrhus' pause,　　　　　　435
　　Aroused vengeance sets him new a-work;
　　And never did the Cyclops' hammers fall
　　On Mars's armour forg'd for proof eterne°
　　With less remorse than Pyrrhus' bleeding sword
　　Now falls on Priam.　　　　　　　　　　　　　　　440
　　Out, out, thou strumpet, Fortune! All you gods,
　　In general synod,° take away her power;
　　Break all the spokes and fellies° from her wheel,
　　And bowl the round nave° down the hill of heaven,
　　As low as to the fiends!"　　　　　　　　　　　　445
POLONIUS: This is too long.
HAMLET: It shall to the barber's, with your beard. Prithee, say on: he's for a jig° or
　　a tale of bawdry,° or he sleeps: say on: come to Hecuba.°
FIRST PLAYER: "But who, ah woe! had seen the mobled° queen—"
HAMLET: "The mobled queen?"　　　　　　　　　　　　450
POLONIUS: That's good; "mobled queen" is good.
FIRST PLAYER: "Run barefoot up and down, threat'ning the flames
　　With bisson rheum;° a clout° upon that head
　　Where late the diadem stood, and for a robe,
　　About her lank and all o'er-teemed° loins,　　　　　　　455
　　A blanket, in the alarm of fear caught up;

---

⁴¹⁹**Repugnant** *disobedient.*　　⁴²²**Then senseless Ilium** *insensate Troy.*　　⁴²⁸**painted tyrant** *tyrant in a picture.*　　⁴²⁹**matter** *task.*　　⁴³¹**against** *before.*　　⁴³²**rack** *mass of clouds.*　　⁴³⁵**region** *assembly.* ⁴³⁸**proof eterne** *external resistance to assault.*　　⁴⁴²**synod** *assembly.*　　⁴⁴³**fellies** *pieces of wood forming the rim of a wheel.*　　⁴⁴⁴**nave** *hub.*　　⁴⁴⁸**jig** *comic performance given at the end or in an interval of a play.* ⁴⁴⁸**bawdry** *indecency.*　　⁴⁴⁸**Hecuba** *wife of Priam, king of Troy.*　　⁴⁴⁹**mobled** *muffled.*　　⁴⁵³**bisson rheum** *blinding tears.*　　⁴⁵³**clout** *piece of cloth.*　　⁴⁵⁵**o'er-teemed** *worn out with bearing children.*

Who this had seen, with tongue in venom steep'd,
'Gainst Fortune's state would treason have pronounc'd:°
But if the gods themselves did see her then
When she saw Pyrrhus make malicious sport   460
In mincing with his sword her husband's limbs,
The instant burst of clamour that she made,
Unless things mortal move them not at all,
Would have made milch° the burning eyes of heaven,
And passion in the gods."   465

POLONIUS: Look, whe'r he has not turned° his colour and has tears in 's eyes.
Prithee, no more.

HAMLET: 'Tis well; I'll have thee speak out the rest soon. Good my lord, will you
see the players well bestowed? Do you hear, let them be well used; for they are
the abstract° and brief chronicles of the time: after your death you were better   470
have a bad epitaph than their ill report while you live.

POLONIUS: My lord, I will use them according to their desert.

HAMLET: God's bodykins,° man, much better: use every man after his desert, and
who shall 'scape whipping? Use them after your own honour and dignity: the
less they deserve, the more merit is in your bounty. Take them in.   475

POLONIUS: Come, sirs.

HAMLET: Follow him, friends: we'll hear a play tomorrow. [*Aside to* FIRST PLAYER.]
Dost thou hear me, old friend; can you play the Murder of Gonzago?

FIRST PLAYER: Ay, my lord.

HAMLET: We'll ha 't to-morrow night. You could, for a need, study a speech of   480
some dozen or sixteen lines,° which I would set down and insert in 't, could
you not?

FIRST PLAYER: Ay, my lord.

HAMLET: Very well. Follow that lord; and look you mock him not.—My good
friends, I'll leave you till night: you are welcome to Elsinore.   485

Exeunt POLONIUS *and* PLAYERS.

ROSENCRANTZ: Good my lord!   *Exeunt* [ROSENCRANTZ *and* GUILDENSTERN.]

HAMLET: Ay, so, God bye to you.—Now I am alone.
O, what a rogue and peasant° slave am I!   490
Is it not monstrous that this player here,
But in a fiction, in a dream of passion,
Could force his soul so to his own conceit
That from her working all his visage wann'd,°
Tears in his eyes, distraction in 's aspect,   495
A broken voice, and his whole function suiting
With forms to his conceit?° and all for nothing!
For Hecuba!

---

[458]**pronounc'd** *proclaimed.*   [464]**milch** *moist with tears.*   [466]**turned** *changed.*   [470]**abstract** *sum-*
mary account.   [473]**bodykins** *diminutive form of the oath "by God's body."*   [483]**dozen or sixteen lines**
critics have amused themselves by trying to locate Hamlet's lines. Lucianus's speech III.ii. 226–231 is the best guess.
[490]**peasant** *base.*   [494]**wann'd** *grew pale.*   [496-97]**his whole … conceit** *his whole being responded*
with forms to suit his thought.

What's Hecuba to him, or he to Hecuba,
That he should weep for her? What would he do,   500
Had he the motive and the cue for passion
That I have? He would drown the stage with tears
And cleave the general ear with horrid speech,
Make mad the guilty and appall the free,
Confound the ignorant, and amaze indeed   505
The very faculties of eyes and ears.
Yet I,
A dull and muddy-mettled° rascal, peak,°
Like John-a-dreams,° unpregnant of° my cause,
And can say nothing; no, not for a king.   510
Upon whose property° and most dear life
A damn'd defeat was made. Am I a coward?
Who calls me villain? breaks my pate across?
Plucks off my beard, and blows it in my face?
Tweaks me by the nose? gives me the lie i' th' throat,   515
As deep as to the lungs? who does me this?
Ha!
'Swounds, I should take it: for it cannot be
But I am pigeon-liver'd° and lack gall
To make oppression bitter, or ere this   520
I should have fatted all the region kites°
With this slave's offal: bloody, bawdy villain!
Remorseless, treacherous, lecherous, kindless° villain!
O, vengeance!
Why, what an ass am I! This is most brave,   525
That I, the son of a dear father murder'd,
Prompted to my revenge by heaven and hell,
Must, like a whore, unpack my heart with words,
And fall a-cursing, like a very drab,°
A stallion!°   530
Fie upon 't! foh! About,° my brains! Hum, I have heard
That guilty creatures sitting at a play
Have by the very cunning of the scene
Been struck so to the soul that presently
They have proclaim'd their malefactions;   535
For murder, though it have no tongue, will speak
With most miraculous organ. I'll have these players
Play something like the murder of my father

508*muddy-mettled* *dull-spirited.*   508*peak* *mope, pine.*   509*John-a-dreams* *an expression occurring elsewhere in Elizabethan literature to indicate a dreamer.*   509*unpregnant of* *not quickened by.*   511*property* *proprietorship (of crown and life).*   519*pigeon-liver'd* *the pigeon was supposed to secrete no gall; if Hamlet, so he says, had had gall, he would have felt the bitterness of oppression, and avenged it.*   521*region kites* *kites of the air.*   523*kindless* *unnatural.*   529*drab* *prostitute.*   530*stallion* *prostitute (male or female).*   531*About* *about it, or turn thou right about.*

Before mine uncle: I'll observe his looks:
I'll tent° him to the quick: if 'a do blench,°   540
I know my course. The spirit that I have seen
May be the devil:° and the devil hath power
T' assume a pleasing shape; yea, and perhaps
Out of my weakness and my melancholy,
As he is very potent with such spirits,°   545
Abuses me to damn me: I'll have grounds
More relative° than this:° the play's the thing
Wherein I'll catch the conscience of the king.   *Exit.*

ACT III

Scene I [A room in the castle.]

Enter KING, QUEEN, POLONIUS, OPHELIA, ROSENCRANTZ, GUILDENSTERN, LORDS.

KING: And can you, by no drift of conference,°
  Get from him why he puts on this confusion,
  Grating so harshly all his days of quiet
  With turbulent and dangerous lunacy?
ROSENCRANTZ: He does confess he feels himself distracted;   5
  But from what cause 'a will by no means speak.
GUILDENSTERN: Nor do we find him forward° to be sounded,
  But, with a crafty madness, keeps aloof,
  When we would bring him on to some confession
  Of his true state.
QUEEN: Did he receive you well?   10
ROSENCRANTZ: Most like a gentleman.
GUILDENSTERN: But with much forcing of his disposition.°
ROSENCRANTZ: Niggard of question;° but, of our demands,
  Most free in his reply.
QUEEN: Did you assay° him
  To any pastime?   15
ROSENCRANTZ: Madam, it so fell out, that certain players
  We o'er-raught° on the way: of these we told him;
  And there did seem in him a kind of joy
  To hear of it: they are here about the court,
  And, as I think, they have already order   20

---

⁵⁴⁰*tent*   probe.   ⁵⁴⁰*blench*   quail, flinch.   ⁵⁴²*May be the devil*   *Hamlet's suspicion is properly grounded in the belief of the time.*   ⁵⁴⁵*spirits*   humors.   ⁵⁴⁷*relative*   closely related, definite.   ⁵⁴⁷*this*   i.e., the ghost's story.   **III.i.**   ¹*drift of conference*   device of conversation.   ⁷*forward*   willing.   ¹²*forcing of his disposition*   i.e., against his will.   ¹³*Niggard of question*   sparing of conversation.   ¹⁴*assay*   try to win.   ¹⁷*o'er-raught*   overtook.

This night to play before him.

POLONIUS: 'Tis most true:
And he beseech'd me to entreat your majesties
To hear and see the matter.

KING: With all my heart; and it doth much content me
To hear him so inclin'd.   25
Good gentlemen, give him a further edge,°
And drive his purpose into these delights.

ROSENCRANTZ: We shall, my lord.   *Exeunt* ROSENCRANTZ *and* GUILDENSTERN.

KING: Sweet Gertrude, leave us too;
For we have closely° sent for Hamlet hither,
That he, as 'twere by accident, may here   30
Affront° Ophelia:
Her father and myself, lawful espials,°
Will so bestow ourselves that, seeing, unseen,
We may of their encounter frankly judge,
And gather by him, as he is behav'd,   35
If 't be th' affliction of his love or no
That thus he suffers for.

QUEEN: I shall obey you.
And for your part, Ophelia, I do wish
That your good beauties be the happy cause
Of Hamlet's wildness:° so shall I hope your virtues   40
Will bring him to his wonted way again,
To both your honours.

OPHELIA: Madam, I wish it may.   [*Exit* QUEEN.]

POLONIUS: Ophelia, walk you here. Gracious,° so please you,
We will bestow ourselves. [*To* OPHELIA.] Read on this book;
That show of such an exercise° may colour°   45
Your loneliness. We are oft to blame in this,—
'Tis too much prov'd—that with devotion's visage
And pious action we do sugar o'er
The devil himself.

KING: [*Aside*] O, 'tis too true!
How smart a lash that speech doth give my conscience!   50
The harlot's cheek, beautied with plast'ring art,
Is not more ugly to° the thing° that helps it
Than is my deed to my most painted word:
O heavy burthen!

POLONIUS: I hear him coming: let's withdraw, my lord.   55

                              [*Exeunt* KING *and* POLONIUS.]

                         Enter HAMLET.

---

²⁶*edge* incitement.   ²⁹*closely* secretly.   ³¹*Affront* confront.   ³²*lawful espials* legitimate spies.
⁴⁰*wildness* madness.   ⁴³*Gracious* your grace (addressed to the king).   ⁴⁵*exercise* act of devotion (the
book she reads is one of devotion).   ⁴⁵*colour* give a plausible appearance to.   ⁵²*to* compared to.
⁵²*thing* i.e., the cosmetic.

HAMLET: To be, or not to be: that is the question:
   Whether 'tis nobler in the mind to suffer
   The slings and arrows of outrageous fortune,
   Or to take arms against a sea° of troubles,
   And by opposing end them? To die: to sleep;   60
   No more; and by a sleep to say we end
   The heart-ache and the thousand natural shocks
   That flesh is heir to, 'tis a consummation
   Devoutly to be wish'd. To die, to sleep;
   To sleep: perchance to dream: ay, there's the rub;   65
   For in that sleep of death what dreams may come
   When we have shuffled° off this mortal coil,°
   Must give us pause: there's the respect°
   That makes calamity of so long life;°
   For who would bear the whips and scorns of time,°   70
   Th' oppressor's wrong, the proud man's contumely,
   The pangs of despis'd° love, the law's delay,
   The insolence of office° and the spurns°
   That patient merit of th' unworthy takes,
   When he himself might his quietus° make   75
   With a bare bodkin?° who would fardels° bear,
   To grunt and sweat under a weary life,
   But that the dread of something after death,
   The undiscover'd country from whose bourn°
   No traveller returns, puzzles the will   80
   And makes us rather bear those ills we have
   Than fly to others that we know not of?
   Thus conscience° does make cowards of us all;
   And thus the native hue° of resolution
   Is sicklied o'er° with the pale cast° of thought,   85
   And enterprises of great pitch° and moment°
   With this regard° their currents° turn awry,
   And lose the name of action—Soft you now!
   The fair Ophelia! Nymph, in thy orisons°
   Be all my sins rememb'red.
OPHELIA: Good my lord,   90
   How does your honour for this many a day?

---

[59]*sea*   the mixed metaphor of this speech has often been commented on; a later emendation siege has sometimes been spoken on the stage.   [67]*shuffled*   sloughed, cast.   [67]*coil*   usually means "turmoil"; here, possibly "body" (conceived of as wound about the soul like rope); clay, soil, veil, have been suggested as emendations.   [68]*respect* consideration.   [69]*of . . . life*   so long-lived.   [70]*time*   the world.   [72]*despis'd*   rejected.   [73]*office* office-holders.   [73]*spurns*   insults.   [75]*quietus*   acquittance; here, death.   [76]*bare bodkin*   mere dagger; bare is sometimes understood as "unsheathed."   [76]*fardels*   burdens.   [79]*bourn*   boundary.   [83]*conscience* probably, inhibition by the faculty of reason restraining the will from doing wrong.   [84]*native hue*   natural color; metaphor derived from the color of the face.   [85]*sicklied o'er*   given a sickly tinge.   [85]*cast*   shade of color. [86]*pitch*   height (as of falcon's flight).   [86]*moment*   importance.   [87]*regard*   respect, consideration. [87]*currents*   courses.   [89]*orisons*   prayers.

HAMLET: I humbly thank you; well, well, well.

OPHELIA: My lord, I have remembrances of yours,
　That I have longed long to re-deliver;
　I pray you, now receive them.

HAMLET: No, not I;　　　　　　　　　　　　　　　　　　　　　　95
　I never gave you aught.

OPHELIA: My honour'd lord, you know right well you did;
　And, with them, words of so sweet breath compos'd
　As made the things more rich: their perfume lost,
　Take these again; for to the noble mind　　　　　　　　　100
　Rich gifts wax poor when givers prove unkind.
　There, my lord.

HAMLET: Ha, ha! are you honest?°

OPHELIA: My lord?

HAMLET: Are you fair?　　　　　　　　　　　　　　　　　　　105

OPHELIA: What means your lordship?

HAMLET: That if you be honest and fair, your honesty° should admit no discourse
　to° your beauty.

OPHELIA: Could beauty, my lord, have better commerce° than with honesty?

HAMLET: Ay, truly; for the power of beauty will sooner transform honesty from   110
　what it is to a bawd than the force of honesty can translate beauty into his
　likeness: this was sometime a paradox, but now the time° gives it proof. I did
　love you once.

OPHELIA: Indeed, my lord, you made me believe so.

HAMLET: You should not have believed me; for virtue cannot so inoculate° our old   115
　stock but we shall relish of it:° I loved you not.

OPHELIA: I was the more deceived.

HAMLET: Get thee to a nunnery: why wouldst thou be a breeder of sinners? I am
　myself indifferent honest;° but yet I could accuse me of such things that it were
　better my mother had not borne me: I am very proud, revengeful, ambitious,   120
　with more offences at my beck° than I have thoughts to put them in,
　imagination to give them shape, or time to act them in. What should such
　fellows as I do crawling between earth and heaven? We are arrant knaves, all;
　believe none of us. Go thy ways to a nunnery. Where's your father?

OPHELIA: At home, my lord.　　　　　　　　　　　　　　　　125

HAMLET: Let the doors be shut upon him, that he may play the fool no where but
　in 's own house. Farewell.

OPHELIA: O, help him, you sweet heavens!

HAMLET: If thou dost marry, I'll give thee this plague for thy dowry: be thou as
　chaste as ice, as pure as snow, thou shalt not escape calumny. Get thee to a   130

103–8 **are you honest ... beauty** _honest meaning "truthful" and "chaste" and fair meaning "just, honorable" (line 105) and "beautiful" (line 107) are not mere quibbles; the speech has the irony of a double entendre._   107 **your honesty** _your chastity._   108 **discourse to** _familiar intercourse with._   109 **commerce** _intercourse._ 112 **the time** _the present age._   115 **inoculate** _graft (metaphorical)._   116 **but ... it** _i.e., that we do not still have about us a taste of the old stock, i.e., retain our sinfulness._   119 **indifferent honest** _moderately virtuous._ 121 **beck** _command._

nunnery, go: farewell. Or, if thou wilt needs marry, marry a fool; for wise men
know well enough what monsters° you make of them. To a nunnery, go, and
quickly too. Farewell.

OPHELIA: O heavenly powers, restore him! 135

HAMLET: I have heard of your° paintings too, well enough; God hath given you
one face, and you make yourselves another: you jig,° you amble, and you lisp;
you nick-name God's creatures, and make your wantonness your ignorance.°
Go to, I'll no more on 't; it hath made me mad. I say, we will have no more
marriage: those that are married already, all but one,° shall live; the rest shall 140
keep as they are. To a nunnery, go. *Exit.*

OPHELIA: O, what a noble mind is here o'er-thrown!
The courtier's, soldier's, scholar's, eye, tongue, sword;
Th' expectancy and rose° of the fair state,
The glass of fashion and the mould of form,° 145
Th' observ'd of all observers,° quite, quite down!
And I, of ladies most deject and wretched,
That suck'd the honey of his music vows,
Now see that noble and most sovereign reason,
Like sweet bells jangled, out of time and harsh; 150
That unmatch'd form and feature of blown° youth
Blasted with ecstasy:° O, woe is me,
T' have seen what I have seen, see what I see!

Enter KING *and* POLONIUS.

KING: Love! his affections do not that way tend;
Nor what he spake, though it lack'd form a little, 155
Was not like madness. There's something in his soul,
O'er which his melancholy sits on brood;
And I do doubt° the hatch and the disclose°
Will be some danger: which for to prevent,
I have in quick determination 160
Thus set it down: he shall with speed to England,
For the demand of our neglected tribute:
Haply the seas and countries different
With variable° objects shall expel
This something-settled° matter in his heart, 165
Whereon his brains still beating puts him thus
From fashion of himself.° What think you on 't?

POLONIUS: It shall do well: but yet do I believe
The origin and commencement of his grief

133**monsters**   *an allusion to the horns of a cuckold*   136**your**   *indefinite use.*   137**jig**   *move with jerky motion; probably allusion to the jig, or song and dance, of the current stage.*   138–139**make . . . ignorance**   *i.e., excuse your wantonness on the ground of your ignorance.*   140**one**   *i.e., the king.*   144**expectancy and rose**
source of hope.   145**The glass . . . form**   *the mirror of fashion and the pattern of courtly behavior.*   146**observ'd . . . observers**   *i.e., the center of attention in the court.*   151**blown**   *blooming.*   152**ecstasy**   *madness.*   158**doubt**   *fear.*   158**disclose**   *disclosure or revelation (by chipping of the shell).*   164**variable**
various.   165**something-settled**   *somewhat settled.*   167**From . . . himself**   *out of his natural manner.*

Sprung from neglected love. How now, Ophelia!   170
You need not tell us what Lord Hamlet said;
We heard it all. My lord, do as you please;
But, if you hold it fit, after the play
Let his queen mother all alone entreat him
To show his grief: let her be round° with him;   175
And I'll be plac'd, so please you, in the ear
Of all their conference. If she find him not,
To England send him, or confine him where
Your wisdom best shall think.
KING: It shall be so:
Madness in great ones must not unwatch'd go.   *Exeunt.*   180

Scene II [*A hall in the castle.*]

Enter HAMLET *and three of the* PLAYERS.

HAMLET: Speak the speech, I pray you, as I pronounced it to you, trippingly on the
tongue: but if you mouth it, as many of your° players do, I had as lief the town-
crier spoke my lines. Nor do not saw the air too much with your hand, thus,
but use all gently; for in the very torrent, tempest, and, as I may say, whirlwind
of your passion, you must acquire and beget a temperance that may give it   5
smoothness. O, it offends me to the soul to hear a robustious° periwig-pated°
fellow tear a passion to tatters, to very rags, to split the ears of the groundlings,°
who for the most part are capable of ° nothing but inexplicable° dumb-shows
and noise: I would have such a fellow whipped for o'er-doing Termagant;° it
out-herods Herod:° pray you, avoid it.   10
FIRST PLAYER: I warrant your honour.
HAMLET: Be not too tame neither, but let your own discretion be your tutor: suit
the action to the word, the word to the action; with this special observance, that
you o'er-step not the modesty of nature: for any thing so overdone is from the
purpose of playing, whose end, both at the first and now, was and is, to hold, as 15
't were, the mirror up to nature; to show virtue her own feature, scorn her own
image, and the very age and body of the time his form and pressure.° Now this
overdone, or come tardy off,° though it make the unskilful laugh, cannot but
make the judicious grieve; the censure of the which one° must in your
allowance o'erweigh a whole theatre of others. O, there be players that I have   20
seen play, and heard others praise, and that highly, not to speak it profanely, that,
neither having the accent of Christians nor the gait of Christian, pagan, nor

---

175*round* blunt.   **III.ii.** ²*your* indefinite use.   ⁶*robustious* violent, boisterous.   ⁶*periwig-pated*
⁷*groundlings* those who stood in the yard of the theater.   ⁸*capable of* susceptible of being influenced by.
⁸*inexplicable* of no significance worth explaining.   ⁹*Termagant* a god of the Saracens; a character in the St.
Nicholas play, where one of his worshipers, leaving him in charge of goods, returns to find them stolen; whereupon he
beats the god (or idol), which howls vociferously.   ¹⁰*Herod* Herod of Jewry; a character in The Slaughter of the
Innocents and other cycle plays. The part was played with great noise and fury.   ¹⁷*pressure* stamp, impressed character.   ¹⁸*come tardy off* inadequately done.   ¹⁹*the censure ... one* the judgment of even one of whom.

man, have so strutted and bellowed that I have thought some of nature's
journeymen° had made men and not made them well, they imitated humanity
so abominably.   25
FIRST PLAYER: I hope we have reformed that indifferently° with us, sir.
HAMLET: O, reform it altogether. And let those that play your clowns speak no
    more than is set down for them; for there be of ° them that will themselves
    laugh, to set on some quantity of barren° spectators to laugh too; though, in the
    mean time, some necessary question of the play be then to be considered: that's   30
    villanous, and shows a most pitiful ambition in the fool that uses it. Go, make
    you ready.

[*Exeunt* PLAYERS.]

Enter POLONIUS, GUILDENSTERN, *and* ROSENCRANTZ.

How now, my lord! will the king hear this piece of work?   35
POLONIUS: And the queen too, and that presently.
HAMLET: Bid the players make haste.   [*Exit* POLONIUS.]
    Will you two help to hasten them?
ROSENCRANTZ: ⎫   *Exeunt they two.*
GUILDENSTERN: ⎬ We will, my lord.
HAMLET: What ho! Horatio!

Enter HORATIO.

HORATIO: Here, sweet lord, at your service.   40
HAMLET: Horatio, thou art e'en as just° a man
    As e'er my conversation cop'd withal.
HORATIO: O, my dear lord,—
HAMLET: Nay, do not think I flatter;
    For what advancement may I hope from thee
    That no revenue hast but thy good spirits,   45
    To feed and clothe thee? Why should the poor be flatter'd?
    No, let the candied tongue lick absurd pomp,
    And crook the pregnant° hinges of the knee
    Where thrift° may follow fawning. Dost thou hear?
    Since my dear soul was mistress of her choice   50
    And could of men distinguish her election,
    S' hath seal'd thee for herself; for thou hast been
    As one, in suff'ring all, that suffers nothing,
    A man that fortune's buffets and rewards
    Hast ta'en with equal thanks: and blest are those   55
    Whose blood and judgement are so well commeddled,
    That they are not a pipe for fortune's finger
    To sound what stop° she please. Give me that man

---

²⁴*journeymen*   laborers not yet masters in their trade.   ²⁶*indifferently*   *fairly, tolerably.*   ²⁸*of*   i.e., some
among them.   ²⁹*barren*   i.e., of wit.   ⁴¹*just*   honest, honorable.   ⁴⁸*pregnant*   pliant.   ⁴⁹*thrift*
profit.   ⁵⁸*stop*   hole in a wind instrument for controlling the sound.

That is not passion's slave, and I will wear him
In my heart's core, ay, in my heart of heart,   60
As I do thee.—Something too much of this.—
There is a play to-night before the king;
One scene of it comes near the circumstance
Which I have told thee of my father's death:
I prithee, when thou seest that act afoot,   65
Even with the very comment of thy soul°
Observe my uncle: if his occulted° guilt
Do not itself unkennel in one speech,
It is a damned° ghost that we have seen,
And my imaginations are as foul   70
As Vulcan's stithy.° Give him heedful note;
For I mine eyes will rivet to his face,
And after we will both our judgements join
In censure of his seeming.°
HORATIO: Well, my lord:
     If 'a steal aught the whilst this play is playing,   75
     And 'scape detecting, I will pay the theft.

Enter trumpets and kettledrums, KING, QUEEN, POLONIUS, OPHELIA, [ROSENCRANTZ,
GUILDENSTERN, *and* OTHERS].

HAMLET: They are coming to the play; I must be idle:° Get you a place.
KING: How fares our cousin Hamlet?
HAMLET: Excellent, i' faith; of the chameleon's dish:° I eat the air, promise-
     crammed: you cannot feed capons so.   80
KING: I have nothing with° this answer, Hamlet; these words are not mine.°
HAMLET: No, nor mine now. [*To* POLONIUS.] My lord, you played once i' the
     university, you say?
POLONIUS: That did I, my lord; and was accounted a good actor.
HAMLET: What did you enact?   85
POLONIUS: I did enact Julius Cæsar: I was killed i' the Capitol; Brutus killed me.
HAMLET: It was a brute part of him to kill so capital a calf there. Be the players
     ready?
ROSENCRANTZ: Ay, my lord; they stay upon your patience.
QUEEN: Come hither, my dear Hamlet, sit by me.   90
HAMLET: No, good mother, here's metal more attractive.
POLONIUS [*to the king*]: O, ho! do you mark that?
HAMLET: Lady, shall I lie in your lap?   [*Lying down at* OPHELIA'*s feet.*]
OPHELIA: No, my lord.
HAMLET: I mean, my head upon your lap?   95

66very ... soul *inward and sagacious criticism.*   **67occulted** *hidden.*   **69damned** *in league with Sa-*
tan.   **71stithy** *smithy, place of stiths (anvils).*   **74censure ... seeming** *judgment of his appearance or be-*
havior.   **77idle** *crazy, or not attending to anything serious.*   **79chameleon's dish** *chameleons were supposed*
to feed on air. (Hamlet deliberately misinterprets the king's "fares" as "feeds.")   **81have ... with** *make nothing*
of.   **81are not mine** *do not respond to what I ask.*

OPHELIA: Ay, my lord.

HAMLET: Do you think I meant country° matters?

OPHELIA: I think nothing, my lord.

HAMLET: That's a fair thought to lie between maids' legs.   100

OPHELIA: What is, my lord?

HAMLET: Nothing.

OPHELIA: You are merry, my lord.

HAMLET: Who, I?

OPHELIA: Ay, my lord.   105

HAMLET: O God, your only° jig-maker.° What should a man do but be merry?
for, look you, how cheerfully my mother looks, and my father died within's
two hours.

OPHELIA: Nay, 'tis twice two months, my lord.

HAMLET: So long? Nay then, let the devil wear black, for I'll have a suit of sables.°   110
O heavens! die two months ago, and not forgotten yet? Then there's hope a
great man's memory may outlive his life half a year: but, by 'r lady, 'a must build
churches, then; or else shall 'a suffer not thinking on,° with the hobbyhorse,
whose epitaph is "For, O, for, O, the hobbyhorse is forgot."°   115

The trumpets sound. Dumb show follows.

Enter a KING *and a* QUEEN [*very lovingly*]; *the* QUEEN *embracing him, and he her.* [*She
kneels, and makes show of protestation unto him.*] *He takes her up, and declines his head upon her
neck: he lies him down upon a bank of flowers: she, seeing him asleep, leaves him. Anon comes in
another man, takes off his crown, kisses it, pours poison in the sleeper's ears, and leaves him. The*
QUEEN *returns; finds the* KING *dead, makes passionate action. The* POISONER, *with some three
or four come in again, seem to condole with her. The dead body is carried away. The* POISONER
woos the QUEEN *with gifts: she seems harsh awhile, but in the end accepts love.* [*Exeunt.*]

OPHELIA: What means this, my lord?

HAMLET: Marry, this is miching mallecho;° it means mischief.

OPHELIA: Belike this show imports the argument of the play.

Enter PROLOGUE.

HAMLET: We shall know by this fellow: the players cannot keep counsel; they'll
tell all.   120

OPHELIA: Will 'a tell us what this show meant?

HAMLET: Ay, or any show that you'll show him: be not you ashamed to show, he'll
not shame to tell you what it means.

OPHELIA: You are naught, you are naught:° I'll mark the play.

PROLOGUE: For us, and for our tragedy,   125
Here stooping° to your clemency,
We beg your hearing patiently.   [*Exit.*]

---

[98]*country*   *with a bawdy pun.*   [106]*your only*   *only your.*   [106]*jig-maker*   *composer of jigs (song and
dance).*   [110]*suit of sables*   *garments trimmed with the fur of the sable, with a quibble on sable meaning "black."*
[114]*suffer ... on*   *undergo oblivion.*   [115]*"For ... forgot"*   *verse of a song occurring also in Love's Labour's
Lost, III.i.30; the hobbyhorse was a character in the Morris Dance.*   [117]*miching mallecho*   *sneaking mischief.*
[124]*naught*   *indecent.*   [126]*stooping*   *bowing.*

HAMLET: Is this a prologue, or the posy° of a ring?
OPHELIA: 'Tis brief, my lord.
HAMLET: As woman's love.   130

Enter [two Players as] KING *and* QUEEN.

PLAYER KING: Full thirty times hath Phoebus' cart gone round
  Neptune's salt wash° and Tellus'° orbed ground,
  And thirty dozen moons with borrowed° sheen
  About the world have times twelve thirties been,
  Since love our hearts and Hymen° did our hands   135
  Unite commutual° in most sacred bands.
PLAYER QUEEN: So many journeys may the sun and moon
  Make us again count o'er ere love be done!
  But, woe is me, you are so sick of late,
  So far from cheer and from your former state,   140
  That I distrust° you. Yet, though I distrust,
  Discomfort you, my lord, it nothing must:
  For women's fear and love holds quantity;°
  In neither aught, or in extremity.
  Now, what my love is, proof hath made you know;   145
  And as my love is siz'd, my fear is so:
  Where love is great, the littlest doubts are fear;
  Where little fears grow great, great love grows there.
PLAYER KING: 'Faith, I must leave thee, love, and shortly too;
  My operant° powers their functions leave° to do: 150
  And thou shalt live in this fair world behind,
  Honour'd, belov'd; and haply one as kind
  For husband shalt thou—
PLAYER QUEEN: O, confound the rest!
  Such love must needs be treason in my breast:
  In second husband let me be accurst!   155
  None wed the second but who kill'd the first.
HAMLET (*aside*): Wormwood, wormwood.
PLAYER QUEEN: The instances that second marriage move
  Are base respects of thrift, but none of love:
  A second time I kill my husband dead,   160
  When second husband kisses me in bed.
PLAYER KING: I do believe you think what now you speak;
  But what we do determine oft we break.
  Purpose is but the slave to memory,
  Of violent birth, but poor validity: 165
  Which now, like fruit unripe, sticks on the tree;
  But fall, unshaken, when they mellow be.

---

[128] **posy** *motto.* [132] **salt wash** *the sea.* [132] **Tellus** *goddess of the earth* (orbed ground). [133] **bor-rowed** *i.e., reflected.* [135] **Hymen** *god of matrimony.* [136] **commutual** *mutually.* [141] **distrust** *an anxious about.* [143] **holds quantity** *keeps proportion between.* [150] **operant** *active.* [150] **leave** *cease.*

Most necessary 'tis that we forget
To pay ourselves what to ourselves is debt:
What to ourselves in passion we propose,   170
The passion ending, doth the purpose lose.
The violence of either grief or joy
Their own enactures° with themselves destroy:
Where joy most revels, grief doth most lament;
Grief joys, joy grieves, on slender accident.   175
This world is not for aye,° nor 'tis not strange
That even our loves should with our fortunes change;
For 'tis a question left us yet to prove,
Whether love lead fortune, or else fortune love.
The great man down, you mark his favourite flies;   180
The poor advanc'd makes friends of enemies.
And hitherto doth love on fortune tend;
For who° not needs shall never lack a friend,
And who in want a hollow friend doth try,
Directly seasons° him his enemy.   185
But, orderly to end where I begun,
Our wills and fates do so contrary run
That our devices still are overthrown;
Our thoughts are ours, their ends° none of our own:
So think thou wilt no second husband wed;   190
But die thy thoughts when thy first lord is dead.
PLAYER QUEEN: Nor earth to me give food, nor heaven light!
  Sport and repose lock from me day and night!
  To desperation turn my trust and hope!
  An anchor's° cheer° in prison be my scope!   195
  Each opposite° that blanks° the face of joy
  Meet what I would have well and it destroy!
  Both here and hence pursue me lasting strife,
  If, once a widow, ever I be wife!
HAMLET: If she should break it now!   200
PLAYER KING: 'Tis deeply sworn. Sweet, leave me here awhile;
  My spirits grow dull, and fain I would beguile
  The tedious day with sleep.   *[Sleeps.]*
PLAYER QUEEN: Sleep rock thy brain;
  And never come mischance between us twain!   *Exit.*
HAMLET: Madam, how like you this play?   205
QUEEN: The lady doth protest too much, methinks.
HAMLET: O, but she'll keep her word.
KING: Have you heard the argument? Is there no offence in 't?
HAMLET: No, no, they do but jest, poison in jest; no offence i' the world.

---

¹⁷³**enactures** *fulfillments.*   ¹⁷⁶**aye** *ever.*   ¹⁸³**who** *whoever.*   ¹⁸⁵**seasons** *matures,*   *ripens.*
¹⁸⁹**ends** *results.*   ¹⁹⁵**An anchor's** *an anchorite's.*   ¹⁹⁵**cheer** *fare; sometimes printed as* chair.
¹⁹⁶**opposite** *adverse thing.*   ¹⁹⁶**blanks** *causes to* blanch *or grow pale.*

KING: What do you call the play?   210

HAMLET: The Mouse-trap. Marry, how? Tropically.° This play is the image of a
murder done in Vienna: Gonzago° is the duke's name; his wife, Baptista: you
shall see anon; 't is a knavish piece of work: but what o' that? your majesty and
we that have free souls, it touches us not: let the galled jade° winch,° our
withers° are unwrung.°

Enter LUCIANUS.

This is one Lucianus, nephew to the king.

OPHELIA: You are as good as a chorus,° my lord.

HAMLET: I could interpret between you and your love, if I could see the puppets
dallying.°

OPHELIA: You are keen, my lord, you are keen.   220

HAMLET: It would cost you a groaning to take off my edge.

OPHELIA: Still better, and worse.°

HAMLET: So you mistake° your husbands. Begin, murderer; pox,° leave thy
damnable faces, and begin. Come: the croaking raven doth bellow for revenge.

LUCIANUS: Thoughts black, hands apt, drugs fit, and time agreeing;   225
Confederate° season, else no creature seeing;
Thou mixture rank, of midnight weeds collected,
With Hecate's° ban° thrice blasted, thrice infected,
Thy natural magic and dire property,   230
On wholesome life usurp immediately.

[Pours the poison into the sleeper's ears.]

HAMLET: 'A poisons him i' the garden for his estate. His name's Gonzago: the story
is extant, and written in very choice Italian: you shall see anon how the
murderer gets the love of Gonzago's wife.

OPHELIA: The king rises.   235

HAMLET: What, frighted with false fire!°

QUEEN: How fares my lord?

POLONIUS: Give o'er the play.

KING: Give me some light away!

POLONIUS: Lights, lights, lights!   *Exeunt all but* HAMLET *and* HORATIO.   240

HAMLET: Why, let the strucken deer go weep,
The hart ungalled play;

---

211 **Tropically** *figuratively,* trapically *suggests a pun on* trap *in* Mouse-trap *(1.211).*   212 **Gonzago** *in
1538 Luigi Gonzago murdered the Duke of Urbano by pouring poisoned lotion in his ears.*   214 **galled jade**
horse whose hide is rubbed by saddle or harness.   215 **winch** *wince.*   215 **withers** *the part between the horse's
shoulder blades.*   215 **unwrung** *not wrung or twisted.*   217 **chorus** *in many Elizabethan plays the action
was explained by an actor known as the "chorus"; at a puppet show the actor who explained the action was known as
an "interpreter," as indicated by the lines following.*   219–21 **dallying** *with sexual suggestion, continued in* keen
(sexually aroused), groaning *(i.e., in pregnancy), and* edge *(i.e., sexual desire or impetuosity).*   222 **Still . . .
worse** *more keen, less decorous.*   223 **mistake** *err in taking.*   223 **pox** *an imprecation.*   227 **Confed-
erate** *conspiring (to assist the murderer).*   229 **Hecate** *the goddess of witchcraft.*   229 **ban** *curse.*
236 **false fire** *fireworks, or a blank discharge.*   241–44 **Why . . . away** *probably from an old ballad, with allusion to the popular belief that a wounded deer retires to weep and die. Cf. As You Like It, II,i.66.*

For some must watch, while some must sleep:
   Thus runs the world away.°
Would not this,° sir, and a forest of feathers°—if the rest of my fortunes turn
Turk with° me—with two Provincial roses° on my razed° shoes, get me a
fellowship in a cry° of players,° sir?

HORATIO: Half a share.°

HAMLET: A whole one, I.
For thou dost know, O Damon dear,   250
   This realm dismantled° was
Of Jove himself; and now reigns here
   A very, very°—pajock.°

HORATIO: You might have rhymed.

HAMLET: O good Horatio, I'll take the ghost's word for a thousand pound.   255
Didst perceive?

HORATIO: Very well, my lord.

HAMLET: Upon the talk of the poisoning?

HORATIO: I did very well note him.

HAMLET: Ah, ha! Come, some music! come, the recorders!°   260
For if the king like not the comedy,
Why then, belike, he likes it not, perdy.°
Come, some music!

Enter ROSENCRANTZ *and* GUILDENSTERN.

GUILDENSTERN: Good my lord, vouchsafe me a word with you.

HAMLET: Sir, a whole history.   265

GUILDENSTERN: The king, sir,—

HAMLET: Ay, sir, what of him?

GUILDENSTERN: Is in his retirement marvellous distempered.

HAMLET: With drink, sir?

GUILDENSTERN: No, my lord, rather with choler.°   270

HAMLET: Your wisdom should show itself more richer to signify this to his doctor;
for, for me to put him to his purgation would perhaps plunge him into far
more choler.

GUILDENSTERN: Good my lord, put your discourse into some frame° and start not
so wildly from my affair.   275

HAMLET: I am tame, sir: pronounce.

GUILDENSTERN: The queen, your mother, in most great affliction of spirit, hath
sent me to you.

---

²⁴⁵*this* *i.e., the play.*   ²⁴⁵*feathers* *allusion to the plumes which Elizabethan actors were fond of wearing.*
²⁴⁶*turn Turk with* *go back on.*   ²⁴⁶*two Provincial roses* *rosettes of ribbon like the roses of Provins near Paris,
or else the roses of Provence.*   ²⁴⁶*razed* *cut, slashed (by way of ornament).*   ²⁴⁷*cry* *pack (as of hounds).*
²⁴⁷*fellowship . . . players* *partnership in a theatrical company.*   ²⁴⁸*Half a share* *allusion to the custom in
dramatic companies of dividing the ownership into a number of shares among the householders.*   ²⁵¹*dismantled*
stripped, divested.   ²⁵⁰⁻⁵³*For . . . very* *probably from an old ballad having to do with Damon and Pythias.*
²⁵³*pajock* *peacock (a bird with a bad reputation). Possibly the word was patchock, diminutive of patch, clown.*
²⁶⁰*recorders* *wind instruments of the flute kind.*   ²⁶²*perdy* *corruption of par dieu.*   ²⁷⁰*choler* *bilious disorder, with quibble on the sense "anger."*   ²⁷⁴*frame* *order.*

HAMLET: You are welcome.

GUILDENSTERN: Nay, good my lord, this courtesy is not of the right breed. If it 280
   shall please you to make me a wholesome° answer, I will do your mother's
   commandment; if not, your pardon and my return shall be the end of my
   business.

HAMLET: Sir, I cannot.

GUILDENSTERN: What, my lord?   285

HAMLET: Make you a wholesome answer; my wit's diseased: but, sir, such answer as
   I can make, you shall command; or, rather, as you say, my mother: therefore no
   more, but to the matter:° my mother, you say,—

ROSENCRANTZ: Then thus she says; your behaviour hath struck her into
   amazement and admiration.   290

HAMLET: O wonderful son, that can so 'stonish a mother! But is there no sequel at
   the heels of this mother's admiration? Impart.

ROSENCRANTZ: She desires to speak with you in her closet, ere you go to bed.

HAMLET: We shall obey, were she ten times our mother. Have you any further
   trade with us?   295

ROSENCRANTZ: My lord, you once did love me.

HAMLET: And do still, by these pickers and stealers.°

ROSENCRANTZ: Good my lord, what is your cause of distemper? you do, surely, bar
   the door upon your own liberty, if you deny your griefs to your friend.

HAMLET: Sir, I lack advancement.   300

ROSENCRANTZ: How can that be, when you have the voice° of the king himself
   for your succession in Denmark?

HAMLET: Ay, sir, but "While the grass grows,"°—the proverb is something musty.

Enter the PLAYERS *with recorders.*

O, the recorders! let me see one. To withdraw° with you:—why do you go 305
   about to recover the wind° of me, as if you would drive me into a toil?°

GUILDENSTERN: O, my lord, if my duty be too bold, my love is too unmannerly.°

HAMLET: I do not well understand that. Will you play upon this pipe?

GUILDENSTERN: My lord, I cannot.

HAMLET: I pray you.   310

GUILDENSTERN: Believe me, I cannot.

HAMLET: I beseech you.

GUILDENSTERN: I know no touch of it, my lord.

HAMLET: 'Tis as easy as lying: govern these ventages° with your fingers and thumb,
   give it breath with your mouth, and it will discourse most eloquent music. 315
   Look you, these are the stops.

GUILDENSTERN: But these cannot I command to any utterance of harmony; I have
   not the skill.

281*wholesome* *sensible.*   288*matter* *matter in hand.*   297*pickers and stealers* *hands, so called from the*
catechism "to keep my hands from picking and stealing."   301*voice* *support.*   303*While . . . grows"* *the*
rest of the proverb is "the silly horse starves." Hamlet may be destroyed while he is waiting for the succession to the king-
dom.   305*withdraw* *speak in private.*   306*recover the wind* *get to the windward side.*   306*toil*
snare.   307*if . . . unmannerly* *if I am using an unmannerly boldness, it is my love which occasions it.*
314*ventages* *stops of the recorders.*

HAMLET: Why, look you now, how unworthy a thing you make of me! You would play upon me; you would seem to know my stops; you would pluck out the heart of my mystery; you would sound me from my lowest note to the top of my compass:° and there is much music, excellent voice, in this little organ;° yet cannot you make it speak. 'Sblood, do you think I am easier to be played on than a pipe? Call me what instrument you will, though you can fret° me, you cannot play upon me.

Enter POLONIUS.

God bless you, sir!

POLONIUS: My lord, the queen would speak with you, and presently. 330

HAMLET: Do you see yonder cloud that 's almost in shape of a camel?

POLONIUS: By the mass, and 'tis like a camel, indeed.

HAMLET: Methinks it is like a weasel.

POLONIUS: It is backed like a weasel.

HAMLET: Or like a whale? 335

POLONIUS: Very like a whale.

HAMLET: Then I will come to my mother by and by. [*Aside.*] They fool me to the top of my bent.°—I will come by and by.°

POLONIUS: I will say so. [*Exit.*]

HAMLET: By and by is easily said. 340

Leave me, friends. [*Exeunt all but* HAMLET.]

'Tis now the very witching time° of night,

When churchyards yawn and hell itself breathes out

Contagion to this world: now could I drink hot blood,

And do such bitter business as the day 345

Would quake to look on. Soft! now to my mother.

O heart, lose not thy nature; let not ever

The soul of Nero° enter this firm bosom:

Let me be cruel, not unnatural:

I will speak daggers to her, but use none; 350

My tongue and soul in this be hypocrites;

How in my words somever she be shent,°

To give them seals° never, my soul, consent! *Exit.*

Scene III [*A room in the castle.*]

Enter KING, ROSENCRANTZ, *and* GUILDENSTERN.

KING: I like him not, nor stands it safe with us

To let his madness range. Therefore prepare you;

---

³²²**compass** *range of voice.*   ³²²**organ** *musical instrument, i.e., the pipe.*   ³²⁴**fret** *quibble on meaning "irritate" and the piece of wood, gut, or metal which regulates the fingering.*   ³³⁵**top of my bent** *limit of endurance, i.e., extent to which a bow may be bent.*   ³³⁵**by and by** *immediately.*   ³³⁹**witching time** *i.e., time when spells are cast.*   ³⁴⁵**Nero** *murderer of his mother, Agrippina.*   ³⁴⁹**shent** *rebuked.*   ³⁵⁰**give them seals** *confirm with deeds.*

I your commission will forthwith dispatch,°
And he to England shall along with you:
The terms° of our estate° may not endure   5
Hazard so near us as doth hourly grow
Out of his brows.°
GUILDENSTERN: We will ourselves provide:
Most holy and religious fear it is
To keep those many many bodies safe
That live and feed upon your majesty.   10
ROSENCRANTZ: The single and peculiar° life is bound,
With all the strength and armour of the mind,
To keep itself from noyance;° but much more
That spirit upon whose weal depend and rest
The lives of many. The cess° of majesty   15
Dies not alone; but, like a gulf,° doth draw
What's near it with it: it is a massy wheel,
Fix'd on the summit of the highest mount,
To whose huge spokes ten thousand lesser things
Are mortis'd and adjoin'd; which, when it falls,   20
Each small annexment, petty consequence,
Attends° the boist'rous ruin. Never alone
Did the king sigh, but with a general groan.
KING: Arm° you, I pray you, to this speedy voyage;
For we will fetters put about this fear,   25
Which now goes too free-footed.
ROSENCRANTZ: We will haste us.

Exeunt GENTLEMEN [ROSENCRANTZ *and* GUILDENSTERN].

Enter POLONIUS.

POLONIUS: My lord, he's going to his mother's closet:
Behind the arras° I'll convey° myself,
To hear the process;° I'll warrant she'll tax him home:°
And, as you said, and wisely was it said,   30
'Tis meet that some more audience than a mother,
Since nature makes them partial, should o'erhear
The speech, of vantage.° Fare you well, my liege:
I'll call upon you ere you go to bed,
And tell you what I know.
KING: Thanks, dear my lord.   *Exit* [POLONIUS].   35

III.iii.   ³*dispatch* prepare.   ⁵*terms* condition, circumstances.   ⁵*estate* state.   ⁷*brows* effronteries.
¹¹*single and peculiar* individual and private.   ¹³*noyance* harm.   ¹⁵*cess* decease.   ¹⁶*gulf*
whirlpool.   ²²*Attends* participates in.   ²⁴*Arm* prepare.   ²⁸*arras* screen of tapestry placed around
the walls of household apartments.   ²⁸*convey* implication of secrecy; convey was often used to mean "steal."
²⁹*process* proceedings.   ²⁹*tax him home* reprove him severely.   ³³*of vantage* from an advantageous
place.

O, my offence is rank, it smells to heaven;
It hath the primal eldest curse° upon't,
A brother's murder. Pray can I not,
Though inclination be as sharp as will:°
My stronger guilt defeats my strong intent;   40
And, like a man to double business bound,
I stand in pause where I shall first begin,
And both neglect. What if this cursed hand
Were thicker than itself with brother's blood,
Is there not rain enough in the sweet heavens   45
To wash it white as snow? Whereto serves mercy
But to confront° the visage of offence?
And what's in prayer but this two-fold force,
To be forestalled° ere we come to fall,
Or pardon'd being down? Then I'll look up;   50
My fault is past. But, O, what form of prayer
Can serve my turn? "Forgive me my foul murder"?
That cannot be: since I am still possess'd
Of those effects for which I did the murder,
My crown, mine own ambition° and my queen.   55
May one be pardon'd and retain th' offence?°
In the corrupted currents° of this world
Offence's gilded hand° may shove by justice,
And oft 'tis seen the wicked prize° itself
Buys out the law: but 'tis not so above;   60
There is no shuffling,° there the action lies°
In his true nature; and we ourselves compell'd,
Even to the teeth and forehead° of our faults,
To give in evidence. What then? what rests?°
Try what repentance can: what can it not?   65
Yet what can it when one can not repent?
O wretched state! O bosom black as death!
O limed° soul, that, struggling to be free,
Art more engag'd!° Help, angels! Make assay!°
Bow, stubborn knees; and, heart with strings of steel,   70
Be soft as sinews of the new-born babe!
All may be well.   [*He kneels.*]

Enter HAMLET.

HAMLET: Now might I do it pat,° now he is praying;
 And now I'll do't. And so 'a goes to heaven;

---

³⁷**primal eldest curse** *the curse of Cain, the first to kill his brother.* ³⁹**sharp as will** *i.e., his desire is as strong as his determination.* ⁴⁷**confront** *oppose directly.* ⁴⁹**forestalled** *prevented.* ⁵⁵**ambition** *i.e., realization of ambition.* ⁵⁶**offence** *benefit accruing from offense.* ⁵⁷**currents** *courses.* ⁵⁸**gilded hand** *hand offering gold as a bribe.* ⁵⁹**wicked prize** *prize won by wickedness.* ⁶¹**shuffling** *escape by trickery.* ⁶¹**lies** *is sustainable.* ⁶³**teeth and forehead** *very face.* ⁶⁴**rests** *remains.* ⁶⁸**limed** *caught as with birdlime.* ⁶⁹**engag'd** *embedded.* ⁶⁹**assay** *trial.* ⁷³**pat** *opportunely.*

And so am I reveng'd. That would be scann'd:°   75
A villain kills my father; and for that,
I, his sole son, do this same villain send
To heaven.
Why, this is hire and salary, not revenge.
'A took my father grossly, full of bread;°   80
With all his crimes broad blown,° as flush° as May;
And how his audit stands who knows save heaven?
But in our circumstance and course° of thought,
'Tis heavy with him: and am I then reveng'd,
To take him in the purging of his soul,   85
When he is fit and season'd for his passage?°
No!
Up, sword; and know thou a more horrid hent:°
When he is drunk asleep,° or in his rage,
Or in th' incestuous pleasure of his bed;   90
At game, a-swearing, or about some act
That has no relish of salvation in't;
Then trip him, that his heels may kick at heaven,
And that his soul may be as damn'd and black
As hell, whereto it goes. My mother stays: 95
This physic° but prolongs thy sickly days.   *Exit.*
KING [*Rising*]: My words fly up, my thoughts remain below:
   Words without thoughts never to heaven go.   *Exit.*

Scene IV [*The Queen's closet.*]

Enter [QUEEN] GERTRUDE *and* POLONIUS.

POLONIUS: 'A will come straight. Look you lay° home to him:
   Tell him his pranks have been too broad° to bear with,
   And that your grace hath screen'd and stood between
   Much heat° and him. I'll sconce° me even here.
   Pray you, be round° with him.   5
HAMLET (*within*): Mother, mother, mother!
QUEEN: I'll warrant you,
   Fear me not: withdraw, I hear him coming.
                                 [POLONIUS *hides behind the arras.*]

Enter HAMLET.

HAMLET: Now, mother, what's the matter?

75**would be scann'd** *needs to be looked into.*   80**full of bread** *enjoying his worldly pleasures (see Ezekiel 16:49).*   81**broad blown** *in full bloom.*   81**flush** *lusty.*   83**in . . . course** *as we see it in our mortal situation.*   86**fit . . . passage** *i.e., reconciled to heaven by forgiveness of his sins.*   88**hent** *seizing; or more probably, occasion of seizure.*   89**drunk asleep** *in a drunken sleep.*   96**physic** *purging (by prayer).*
III.iv. 1**lay** *thrust.*   2**broad** *unrestrained.*   4**Much heat** *i.e., the king's anger.*   4**sconce** *hide.*
5**round** *blunt.*

QUEEN: Hamlet, thou hast thy father much offended.

HAMLET: Mother, you have my father° much offended. 10

QUEEN: Come, come, you answer with an idle tongue.

HAMLET: Go, go, you question with a wicked tongue.

QUEEN: Why, how now, Hamlet!

HAMLET: What's the matter now?

QUEEN: Have you forgot me?

HAMLET: No, by the rood,° not so:

  You are the queen, your husband's brother's wife; 15

  And—would it were not so!—you are my mother.

QUEEN: Nay, then, I'll set those to you that can speak.

HAMLET: Come, come, and sit you down; you shall not budge;

  You go not till I set you up a glass

  Where you may see the inmost part of you. 20

QUEEN: What wilt thou do? thou wilt not murder me?

  Help, help, ho!

POLONIUS [*behind*]: What, ho! help, help; help!

HAMLET [*drawing*]: How now! a rat? Dead, for a ducat, dead!

                               [*Makes a pass through the arras.*]

POLONIUS [*behind*]: O, I am slain!   [*Falls and dies.*] 25

QUEEN: O me, what hast thou done?

HAMLET: Nay, I know not:

  Is it the king?

QUEEN: O, what a rash and bloody deed is this!

HAMLET: A bloody deed! almost as bad, good mother,

  As kill a king, and marry with his brother. 30

QUEEN: As kill a king!

HAMLET: Ay, lady, it was my word.

              [*Lifts up the arras and discovers* POLONIUS.]

  Thou wretched, rash, intruding fool, farewell!

  I took thee for thy better: take thy fortune;

  Thou find'st to be too busy is some danger.

  Leave wringing of your hands: peace! sit you down, 35

  And let me wring your heart; for so I shall,

  If it be made of penetrable stuff,

  If damned custom have not braz'd° it so

  That it be proof and bulwark against sense.

QUEEN: What have I done, that thou dar'st wag thy tongue 40

  In noise so rude against me?

HAMLET: Such an act

  That blurs the grace and blush of modesty,

  Calls virtue hypocrite, takes off the rose

  From the fair forehead of an innocent love

  And sets a blister° there, makes marriage-vows 45

---

⁹⁻¹⁰**thy father . . . my father** *i.e., Claudius, the elder Hamlet.*   ¹⁴**rood** *cross.*   ³⁸**braz'd** *brazened,*
hardened.   ⁴⁵**sets a blister** *brands as a harlot.*

As false as dicers' oaths: O, such a deed
As from the body of contraction° plucks
The very soul, and sweet religion° makes
A rhapsody° of words: heaven's face does glow
O'er this solidity and compound mass   50
With heated visage, as against the doom
Is thought-sick at the act.°
QUEEN: Ay me, what act,
That roars so loud, and thunders in the index?°
HAMLET: Look here, upon this picture, and on this.
The counterfeit presentment° of two brothers.   55
See, what a grace was seated on this brow;
Hyperion's° curls; the front° of Jove himself;
An eye Mars, to threaten and command;
A station° like the herald Mercury
New-lightned on a heaven-kissing hill;   60
A combination and form indeed,
Where every god did seem to set his seal,
To give the world assurance° of a man:
This was your husband. Look you now, what follows: 65
Here is your husband; like a mildew'd ear,°
Blasting his wholesome brother. Have you eyes?
Could you on this fair mountain leave to feed,
And batten° on this moor?° Ha! have you eyes?
You cannot call it love; for at your age
The hey-day° in the blood is tame, it's humble,   70
And waits upon the judgement: and what judgement
Would step from this to this? Sense, sure, you have,
Else could you not have motion,° but sure, that sense
Is apoplex'd° for madness would not err.
Nor sense to ecstasy was ne'er so thrall'd°   75
But it reserv'd some quality of choice,°
To serve in such a difference. What devil was't
Tha thus hath cozen'd° you ar hoodman-blind?°
Eyes without feeling, feeling without sight,
Ears without hands or eyes, smelling sans° all,   80

47contraction the marriage contract.   48religion religious vows.   49rhapsody senseless string.
49–52heaven's ... act heaven's face blushes to look down upon this world, compounded of the four elements,
with hot face as though the day of doom were near, and thought-sick at the deed (i.e., Gertrude's marriage).
53index prelude or preface.   55counterfeit presentment portrayed representation.   57Hyperion's
the sun god's.   57front brow.   59station manner of standing.   63assurance pledge, guarantee.
65mildew'd ear see Genesis 41:5–7 .68batten grow fat.   68moor barren upland.   70hey-day
state of excitement.   72–73Sense ... motion sense and motion are functions of the middle or sensible soul,
the possession of sense being the basis of motion.   74apoplex'd paralyzed; mental derangement was thus of
three sorts: apoplexy, ecstasy, and diabolic possession.   75thrall'd enslaved.   76quantity of choice frag-
ment of the power to choose.   78cozen'd tricked, cheated.   78hoodman-blind blindman's buff.
80sans without.

Or but a sickly part of one true sense
Could not so mope.°
O shame! where is thy blush? Rebellious hell,
If thou canst mutine° in a matron's bones,
To flaming youth let virtue be as wax, 85
And melt in her own fire: proclaim no shame
When the compulsive ardour gives the charge,°
Since frost itself as actively doth burn
And reason panders will°

QUEEN: O Hamlet, speak no more:
Thou turn'st mine eyes into my very soul; 90
And there I see such black and grained° spots
As will not leave their tint.

HAMLET: Nay, but to live
In the rank sweat of an enseamed° bed,
Stew'd in corruption, honeying and making love
Over the nasty sty,—

QUEEN: O, speak to me no more; 95
These words, like daggers, enter in mine ears;
No more, sweet Hamlet!

HAMLET: A murderer and a villain;
A slave that is not twentieth part the tithe
Of your precedent lord;° a vice of kings;°
A cutpurse of the empire and the rule, 100
That from a shelf the precious diadem stole,
And put it in his pocket!

QUEEN: No more!

Enter GHOST.

HAMLET: A king of shreds and patches,°—
Save me, and hover o'er me with your wings,
You heavenly guards! What would your gracious figure? 105

QUEEN: Alas, he's mad!

HAMLET: Do you not come your tardy son to chide,
That, laps'd in time and passion,° lets go by
Th' important° acting of your dread command?
O, say! 110

GHOST: Do not forget: this visitation
Is but to whet thy almost blunted purpose.

---

⁸²*mope*   *be in a depressed, spiritless state, act aimlessly.*   ⁸⁴*mutine*   *mutiny, rebel.*   ⁸⁷*gives the charge* *delivers the attack.*   ⁸⁹*reason pandars will*   *the normal and proper situation was one in which reason guided the will in the direction of good; here, reason is perverted and leads in the direction of evil.*   ⁹¹*grained*   *dyed in grain.*   ⁹³*enseamed*   *loaded with grease, greased.*   ⁹⁹*precedent lord*   *i.e., the elder Hamlet.*   ⁹⁹*vice of kings*   *buffoon of kings; a referenced to the Vice, or clown, of the morality plays and interludes.*   ¹⁰³*shreds and patches*   *i.e., motley, the traditional costume of the Vice.*   ¹⁰⁸*laps'd . . . passion*   *having suffered time to slip and passion to cool; also explained as "engrossed in casual events and lapsed into mere fruitless passion, so that he no longer entertains a rational purpose."*   ¹⁰⁹*important*   *urgent.*

But, look, amazement° on thy mother sits:
O, step between her and her fighting soul:
Conceit in weakest bodies strongest works: 115
Speak to her, Hamlet.
HAMLET: How is it with you, lady?
QUEEN: Alas, how is 't with you,
    That you do bend your eye on vacancy
    And with th' incorporal° air do hold discourse?
    Forth at your eyes your spirits wildly peep;   120
    And, as the sleeping soldiers in th' alarm,
    Your bedded° hair, like life in excrements,°
    Start up, and stand an° end. O gentle son,
    Upon the heat and flame of thy distemper
    Sprinkle cool patience. Whereon do you look?   125
HAMLET: On him, on him! Look you, how pale he glares!
    His form and cause conjoin'd,° preaching to stones,
    Would make them capable.—Do not look upon me;
    Lest with this piteous action you convert
    My stern effects:° then what I have to do   130
    Will want true colour;° tears perchance for blood.
QUEEN: To whom do you speak this?
HAMLET: Do you see nothing there?
QUEEN: Nothing at all; yet all that is I see.
HAMLET: Nor did you nothing hear?
QUEEN: No, nothing but ourselves.
HAMLET: Why, look you there! look, how it steals away!   135
    My father, in his habit as he liv'd!
    Look, where he goes, even now, out at the portal!   *Exit* GHOST.
QUEEN: This is the very coinage of your brain:
    This bodiless creation ecstasy
    Is very cunning in.
HAMLET: Ecstasy!   140
    My pulse, as yours, doth temperately keep time,
    And makes as healthful music: it is not madness
    That I have utt'red: bring me to the test,
    And I the matter will re-word,° which madness
    Would gambol° from. Mother, for love of grace,   145
    Lay not that flattering unction° to your soul,
    That not your trespass, but my madness speaks:
    It will but skin and film the ulcerous place,

---

¹¹³**amazement** *frenzy, distraction.*   ¹¹⁹**incorporal** *immaterial.*   ¹²²**bedded** *laid in smooth layers.*
¹²²**excrements** *the hair was considered an excrement or voided part of the body.*   ¹²³**an** *on.*   ¹²⁷**con-**
join'd *united.*   ¹²⁹⁻³⁰**convert ... effects** *divert me from my stern duty. For effects, possibly affects (affec-*
tions of the mind).   ¹³¹**want true colour** *lack good reason so that (with a play on the normal sense of*
colour) I shall shed tears instead of blood.   ¹⁴⁴**re-word** *repeat in words.*   ¹⁴⁵**gambol** *skip away.*
¹⁴⁶**unction** *ointment used medicinally or as a rite; suggestion that forgiveness for sin may not be so easily achieved.*

Whiles rank corruption, mining° all within,
Infects unseen. Confess yourself to heaven; 150
Repent what's past; avoid what is to come;°
And do not spread the compost° on the weeds,
To make them ranker. Forgive me this my virtue;°
For in the fatness° of these pursy° times
Virtue itself of vice must pardon beg, 155
Yea, curb° and woo for leave to do him good.
QUEEN: O Hamlet, thou hast cleft my heart in twain.
HAMLET: O, throw away the worser part of it,
And live the purer with the other half.
Good night: but go not to my uncle's bed; 160
Assume a virtue, if you have it not.
That monster, custom, who all sense doth eat,
Of habits devil, is angel yet in this,
That to the use of actions fair and good
He likewise gives a frock or livery, 165
That aptly is put on. Refrain to-night,
And that shall lend a kind of easiness
To the next abstinence: the next more easy;
For use almost can change the stamp of nature,
And either . . . the devil, or throw him out° 170
With wondrous potency. Once more, good night:
And when you are desirous to be bless'd,°
I'll blessing beg of you. For this same lord,   *[Pointing to* POLONIUS.]
I do repent: but heaven hath pleas'd it so,
To punish me with this and this with me, 175
That I must be their scourge and minister.
I will bestow him, and will answer well
The death I gave him. So, again, good night.
I must be cruel, only to be kind:
Thus bad begins and worse remains behind. 180
One word more, good lady.
QUEEN: What shall I do?
HAMLET: Not this, by no means, that I bid you do:
Let the bloat° king tempt you again to bed;
Pinch wanton on your cheek; call you his mouse;
And let him, for a pair of reechy° kisses, 185
Or paddling in your neck with his damn'd fingers,
Make you to ravel all this matter out,
That I essentially° am not in madness,
But mad in craft. 'Twere good you let him know;

---

¹⁴⁹**mining** *working under the surface.*   ¹⁵¹**what is to come** *i.e., the sins of the future.*   ¹⁵²**compost**
manure.   ¹⁵³**this my virtue** *my virtuous talk in reproving you.*   ¹⁵⁴**fatness** *grossness.*   ¹⁵⁴**pursy**
short-winded, corpulent.   ¹⁵⁶**curb** *bow, bend the knee.*   ¹⁷⁰*defective line usually emended by inserting mas-*
ter after either.   ¹⁷²**be bless'd** *become blessed, i.e., repentant.*   ¹⁸³**bloat** *bloated.*   ¹⁸⁵**reechy** *dirty,*
filthy   ¹⁸⁸**essentially** *in my essential nature.*

For who, that's but a queen, fair, sober, wise,   190
Would from a paddock,° from a bat, a gib,°
Such dear concernings° hide? who would do so?
No, in despite of sense and secrecy,
Unpeg the basket on the house's top,
Let the birds fly, and, like the famous ape,°   195
To try conclusions,° in the basket creep,
And break your own neck down.
QUEEN: Be thou assur'd, if words be made of breath,
  And breath of life, I have no life to breathe
  What thou hast said to me.   200
HAMLET: I must to England; you know that?
QUEEN: Alack,
  I had forgot: 'tis so concluded on.
HAMLET: There's letters seal'd: and my two schoolfellows,
  Whom I will trust as I will adders fang'd,
  They bear the mandate; they must sweep my way,°   205
  And marshal me to knavery. Let it work;
  For 'tis the sport to have the enginer°
  Hoist° with his own petar:° and 't shall go hard
  But I will delve one yard below their mines,
  And blow them at the moon: O, 'tis most sweet,   210
  When in one line two crafts° directly meet.
  This man shall set me packing:°
  I'll lug the guts into the neighbour room.
  Mother, good night. Indeed this counsellor
  Is now most still, most secret and most grave,   215
  Who was in life a foolish prating knave.
  Come, sir, to draw° toward an end with you.
  Good night, mother.

  Exeunt [severally; HAMLET dragging in POLONIUS.]

---

[191]**paddock**   toad.   [191]**gib**   tomcat.   [192]**dear concernings**   *important affairs.*   [195]**the famous ape**
*a letter from Sir John Suckling seems to supply other details of the story, otherwise not identified: "It is the story of the
jackanapes and the partridges; thou starest after a beauty till it be lost to thee, then let'st out another, and starest after
that till it is gone too."*   [196]**conclusions**   *experiments.*   [205]**sweep my way**   *clear my path.*   [207]**enginer**   *constructor of military works, or possibly, artilleryman.*   [208]**Hoist**   *blown up.*   [208]**petar**   *defined
as a small enginer of war used to blow in a door or make a breach, and as a case filled with explosive materials.*
[211]**two crafts**   *two acts of guile, with quibble on the sense of "two ships."*   [212]**set me packing**   *set me to making schemes, and set me to lugging (him), and, also, send me off in a hurry.*   [217]**draw**   *come, with quibble on literal sense.*

ACT IV

Scene I [A room in the castle.]

Enter KING *and* QUEEN, *with* ROSENCRANTZ *and* GUILDENSTERN.

KING: There's matter in these sighs, these profound heaves:
    You must translate: 'tis fit we understand them.
    Where is your son?
QUEEN: Bestow this place on us a little while.
                               [Exeunt ROSENCRANTZ *and* GUILDENSTERN.*]*
    Ah, mine own lord, what have I seen to-night!   5
KING: What, Gertrude? How does Hamlet?
QUEEN: Mad as the sea and wind, when both contend
    Which is the mightier: in his lawless fit,
    Behind the arras hearing something stir,
    Whips out his rapier, cries, "A rat, a rat!"   10
    And, in this brainish° apprehension,° kills
    The unseen good old man.
KING: O heavy deed!
    It had been so with us, had we been there:
    His liberty is full of threats to all;
    To you yourself, to us, to every one.   15
    Alas, how shall this bloody deed be answer'd?
    It will be laid to us, whose providence°
    Should have kept short,° restrain'd and out of haunt,°
    This mad young man: but so much was our love,
    We would not understand what was most fit;   20
    But, like the owner of a foul disease,
    To keep it from divulging,° let it feed
    Even on the pith of life. Where is he gone?
QUEEN: To draw apart the body he hath kill'd:
    O'er whom his very madness, like some ore   25
    Among a mineral° of metals base,
    Shows itself pure; 'a weeps for what is done.
KING: O Gertrude, come away!
    The sun no sooner shall the mountains touch,
    But we will ship him hence: and this vile deed   30
    We must, with all our majesty and skill,
    Both countenance and excuse. Ho, Guildenstern!

Enter ROSENCRANTZ *and* GUILDENSTERN.

Friends both, go join you with some further aid:

IV.i. ¹¹**brainish** *headstrong, passionate.*   ¹¹**apprehension** *conception, imagination.*   ¹⁷**providence** *foresight.*   ¹⁸**short** *i.e., on a short tether.*   ¹⁸**out of haunt** *secluded.*   ²²**divulging** *becoming evident.*   ²⁶**mineral** *mine.*

Hamlet in madness hath Polonius slain,
And from his mother's closet hath he dragg'd him: 35
Go seek him out; speak fair, and bring the body
Into the chapel. I pray you, haste in this.

> [*Exeunt* ROSENCRANTZ *and* GUILDENSTERN.]

Come, Gertrude, we'll call up our wisest friends;
And let them know, both what we mean to do,
And what's untimely done . . . °   40
Whose whisper o'er the world's diameter,°
As level° as the cannon to his blank,°
Transports his pois'ned shot, may miss our name,
And hit the woundless° air. O, come away!
My soul is full of discord and dismay.   *Exeunt.* 45

Scene II [*Another room in the castle.*]

Enter HAMLET.

HAMLET: Safely stowed.
ROSENCRANTZ:
GUILDENSTERN: } (*WITHIN*) Hamlet! Lord Hamlet!
HAMLET: But soft, what noise? Who calls on Hamlet? O, here they come.

Enter ROSENCRANTZ *and* GUILDENSTERN.

ROSENCRANTZ: What have you done, my lord, with the dead body?
HAMLET: Compounded it with dust, whereto 'tis kin.
ROSENCRANTZ: Tell us where 'tis, that we may take it thence   5
    And bear it to the chapel.
HAMLET: Do not believe it.
ROSENCRANTZ: Believe what?
HAMLET: That I can keep your counsel° and not mine own. Besides, to be de-
    manded of a sponge! What replication° should be made by the son of a king?   10
ROSENCRANTZ: Take you me for a sponge, my lord?
HAMLET: Ay, sir, that soaks up the king's countenance, his rewards, his authorities.°
    But such officers do the king best service in the end: he keeps them, like an ape
    an apple, in the corner of his jaw; first mouthed, to be last swallowed: when he
    needs what you have gleaned, it is but squeezing you, and, sponge, you shall be
    dry again.   15
ROSENCRANTZ: I understand you not, my lord.
HAMLET: I am glad of it: a knavish speech sleeps in a foolish ear.
ROSENCRANTZ: My lord, you must tell us where the body is, and go with us to the
    king.

40*defective line; some editors add:* so haply, slander; *others add:* for, haply, slander; *other conjectures.*   41**diame-
ter** *extent from side to side.*   42**level** *straight.*   42**blank** *white spot in the center of a target.*
44**woundless** *invulnerable.*   **IV.ii.** 9**keep your counsel** *Hamlet is aware of their treachery but says nothing
about it.*   10**replication** *reply.*   12**authorities** *authoritative backing.*

HAMLET: The body is with the king, but the king is not with the body.° The king 20
    is a thing—
GUILDENSTERN: A thing, my lord!
HAMLET: Of nothing: bring me to him. Hide fox, and all after.°   *Exeunt*

Scene III [*Another room in the castle.*]

Enter KING, *and two or three.*

KING: I have sent to seek him, and to find the body.
    How dangerous is it that this man goes loose!
    Yet must not we put the strong law on him:
    He's lov'd of the distracted° multitude,
    Who like not in their judgement, but their eyes;   5
    And where 'tis so, th' offender's scourge° is weigh'd,°
    But never the offence. To bear all smooth and even,
    This sudden sending him away must seem
    Deliberate pause:° diseases desperate grown
    By desperate appliance are reliev'd,   10
    Or not at all.

Enter ROSENCRANTZ, [GUILDENSTERN,] *and all the rest.*

    How now! what hath befall'n?
ROSENCRANTZ: Where the dead body is bestow'd, my lord,
    We cannot get from him.
KING: But where is he?
ROSENCRANTZ: Without, my lord; guarded, to know your pleasure.
KING: Bring him before us.   15
ROSENCRANTZ: Ho! bring in the lord.

They enter [*with* HAMLET].

KING: Now, Hamlet, where's Polonius?
HAMLET: At supper.
KING: At supper! where?
HAMLET: Not where he eats, but where 'a is eaten: a certain convocation of 20
    politic° worms° are e'en at him. Your worm is your only emperor for diet: we fat
    all creatures else to fat us, and we fat ourselves for maggots: your fat king and your
    lean beggar is but variable service,° two dishes, but to one table: that's the end.
KING: Alas, alas!   25
HAMLET: A man may fish with the worm that hath eat of a king, and eat of the fish
    that hath fed of that worm.

---

[20]**The body ... body** *there are many interpretations; possibly, "The body lies in death with the king, my father;
but my father walks disembodied"; or "Claudius has the bodily possession of kingship, but kingliness, or justice of
inheritance, is not with him."*   [24]**Hide ... after** *an old signal cry in the game of hide-and-seek.*   **IV.iii.**
[4]**distracted** *i.e., without power of forming logical judgments.*   [6]**scourge** *punishment.*   [6]**weigh'd** *taken
into consideration.*   [9]**Deliberate pause** *considered action.*   [20–21]**convocation ... worms** *allusion to the
Diet of Worms (1521).*   [21]**politic** *crafty.*   [23]**variable service** *a variety of dishes.*

KING: What dost thou mean by this?

HAMLET: Nothing but to show you how a king may go a progress° through the guts   30
    of a beggar.

KING: Where is Polonius?

HAMLET: In heaven; send thither to see: if your messenger find him not there, seek
    him i' the other place yourself. But if indeed you find him not within this
    month, you shall nose him as you go up the stairs into the lobby.

KING [to some ATTENDANTS]: Go seek him there.   35

HAMLET: 'A will stay till you come.   [Exeunt ATTENDANTS.]

KING: Hamlet, this deed, for thine especial safety,—
    Which we do tender,° as we dearly grieve
    For that which thou hast done,—must send thee hence
    With fiery quickness: therefore prepare thyself;   40
    The bark is ready, and the wind at help,
    Th' associates tend, and everything is bent
    For England.

HAMLET: For England!

KING: Ay, Hamlet.

HAMLET: Good.

KING: So is it, if thou knew'st our purposes.

HAMLET: I see a cherub° that sees them. But, come; for England! Farewell,   45
    dear mother.

KING: Thy loving father, Hamlet.

HAMLET: My mother: father and mother is man and wife; man and wife is one flesh;
    and so, my mother. Come, for England!   Exit.

KING: Follow him at foot;° tempt him with speed aboard;   50
    Delay it not; I'll have him hence to-night:
    Away! for every thing is seal'd and done
    That else leans on th' affair: pray you, make haste.

    [Exeunt all but the KING.]

    And, England, if my love thou hold'st at aught—
    As my great power thereof may give thee sense,   55
    Since yet thy cicatrice° looks raw and red
    After the Danish sword, and thy free awe°
    Pays homage to us—thou mayst not coldly set
    Our sovereign process; which imports at full,
    By letters congruing to that effect,   60
    The present death of Hamlet. Do it, England;
    For like the hectic° in my blood he rages,
    And thou must cure me: till I know 'tis done,
    Howe'er my haps,° my joys were ne'er begun.   Exit.

---

³⁰**progress** *royal journey of state.* ³⁸**tender** *regard, hold dear.* ⁴⁵**cherub** *cherubim are angels of knowl-*
edge. ⁵⁰**at foot** *close behind, at heel.* ⁵⁶**cicatrice** *scar.* ⁵⁷**free awe** *voluntary show of respect.*
⁶²**hectic** *fever.* ⁶⁴**haps** *fortunes.*

Scene IV [A plain in Denmark.]

Enter FORTINBRAS *with his Army over the stage.*

FORTINBRAS: Go, captain, from me greet the Danish king;
  Tell him that, by his license,° Fortinbras
  Craves the conveyance° of a promis'd march
  Over his kingdom. You know the rendezvous.
  If that his majesty would aught with us,   5
  We shall express our duty in his eye;°
  And let him know so.
CAPTAIN: I will do't, my lord.
FORTINBRAS: Go softly° on.   *[Exeunt all but* CAPTAIN.*]*

Enter HAMLET, ROSENCRANTZ, [GUILDENSTERN,] &c.

HAMLET: Good sir, whose powers are these?
CAPTAIN: They are of Norway, sir.   10
HAMLET: How purpos'd, sir, I pray you?
CAPTAIN: Against some part of Poland.
HAMLET: Who commands them, sir?
CAPTAIN: The nephew to old Norway, Fortinbras.
HAMLET: Goes it against the main° of Poland, sir,   15
  Or for some frontier?
CAPTAIN: Truly to speak, and with no addition,
  We go to gain a little patch of ground
  That hath in it no profit but the name.
  To pay five ducats, five, I would not farm it;°   20
  Nor will it yield to Norway or the Pole
  A ranker rate, should it be sold in fee.°
HAMLET: Why, then the Polack never will defend it.
CAPTAIN: Yes, it is already garrison'd.
HAMLET: Two thousand souls and twenty thousand ducats 25
  Will not debate the question of this straw;°
  This is th' imposthume° of much wealth and peace,
  That inward breaks, and shows no cause without
  Why the man dies. I humbly thank you, sir.
CAPTAIN: God be wi' you, sir.   *[Exit.]*
ROSENCRANTZ: Will 't please you go, my lord?   30
HAMLET: I'll be with you straight. Go a little before.
[Exeunt all except HAMLET.*]*
  How all occasions° do inform against° me,
  And spur my dull revenge! What is a man,

IV.iv. ²*license* *leave.*   ³*conveyance* *escort, convey.*   ⁶*in his eye* *in his presence.*   ⁸*softly* *slowly.*
¹⁵*main* *country itself.*   ²⁰*farm it* *take a lease of it.*   ²²*fee* *fee simple.*   ²⁶*debate . . . straw* *settle this*
trifling matter.   ²⁷*imposthume* *purulent abscess or swelling.*   ³²*occasions* *incidents, events.*   ³²*inform against*
generally defined as "show," "betray" (i.e., his tardiness); more probably inform means "take shape," as in Macbeth, II.i.48.

If his chief good and market of his time°
Be but to sleep and feed? a beast, no more.   35
Sure, he that made us with such large discourse,
Looking before and after, gave us not
That capability and god-like reason
To fust° in us unus'd. Now, whether it be
Bestial oblivion, or some craven scruple   40
Of thinking too precisely on th' event,
A thought which, quarter'd, hath but one part wisdom
And ever three parts coward, I do not know
Why yet I live to say "This thing 's to do";
Sith I have cause and will and strength and means   45
To do 't. Examples gross as earth exhort me:
Witness this army of such mass and charge
Led by a delicate and tender prince,
Whose spirit with divine ambition puff'd
Makes mouths at the invisible event,   50
Exposing what is mortal and unsure
To all that fortune, death and danger dare,
Even for an egg-shell. Rightly to be great
Is not to stir without great argument,
But greatly to find quarrel in a straw   55
When honour's at the stake. How stand I then,
That have a father kill'd, a mother stain'd,
Excitements of ° my reason and my blood,
And let all sleep? while, to my shame, I see
The imminent death of twenty thousand men,   60
That, for a fantasy and trick° of fame,
Go to their graves like beds, fight for a plot°
Whereon the numbers cannot try the cause,
Which is not tomb enough and continent
To hide the slain? O, from this time forth,   65
My thoughts be bloody, or be nothing worth!   *Exit.*

Scene V [*Elsinore. A room in the castle.*]

Enter HORATIO, [QUEEN] GERTRUDE, *and a* GENTLEMAN.

QUEEN: I will not speak with her.
GENTLEMAN: She is importunate, indeed distract:
   Her mood will needs be pitied.
QUEEN: What would she have?
GENTLEMAN: She speaks much of her father; says she hears
   There's tricks° i' th' world; and hems, and beats her heart;°   5

---

[34]**market of his time**   *the best use he makes of his time, or, that for which he sells his time.*   [39]**fust**   *grow moldy.*
[58]**Excitements of**   *incentives to.*   [61]**trick** *toy, trifle.*   [62]**plot**   *i.e., of ground.*   **IV.v.**[5]**tricks**   *deceptions.*
[5]**heart**   *i.e., breast.*

Spurns enviously at straws;° speaks things in doubt,
That carry but half sense: her speech is nothing,
Yet the unshaped° use of it doth move
The hearers to collection;° they yawn° at it,
And botch° the words up fit to their own thoughts;   10
Which, as her winks, and nods, and gestures yield° them,
Indeed would make one think there might be thought,
Though nothing sure, yet much unhappily.°
HORATIO: 'Twere good she were spoken with: for she may strew
Dangerous conjectures in ill-breeding minds.°   15
QUEEN: Let her come in.   [*Exit* GENTLEMAN.]
  [*Aside.*] To my sick soul, as sin's true nature is,
  Each toy seems prologue to some great amiss:°
  So full of artless jealousy is guilt,
  It spills itself in fearing to be spilt.°   20

                    Enter OPHELIA [*distracted*].

OPHELIA: Where is the beauteous majesty of Denmark?
QUEEN: How now, Ophelia!
OPHELIA (*she sings*): How should I your true love know
    From another one?
  By his cockle hat° and staff,   25
    And his sandal shoon.°
QUEEN: Alas, sweet lady, what imports this song?
OPHELIA: Say you? nay, pray you mark.
  (*Song*) He is dead and gone, lady,
    He is dead and gone;   30
  At his head a grass-green turf,
    At his heels a stone.
  O, ho!
QUEEN: Nay, but, Ophelia—
OPHELIA: Pray you, mark   35
  [*Sings.*] White his shroud as the mountain snow,—
                    Enter KING.
QUEEN: Alas, look here, my lord.
OPHELIA (*Song*): Larded° all with flowers;
  Which bewept to the grave did not go
    With true-love showers.   40
KING: How do you, pretty lady?

---

⁶**Spurns ... straws** *kicks spitefully at small objects in her path.* ⁸**unshaped** *unformed, artless.* ⁹**col-
lection** *inference, a guess at some sort of meaning.* ⁹**yawn** *wonder.* ¹⁰**botch** *patch.* ¹¹**yield**
deliver, bring forth (her words). ¹³**much unhappily** *expressive of much unhappiness.* ¹⁵**ill-breeding
minds** *minds bent on mischief.* ¹⁸**great amiss** *calamity, disaster.* ^{19–20}**So ... split** *guilt is so full
of suspicion that it unskillfully betrays itself in fearing to be betrayed.* ²⁵**cockle hat** *hat with cockleshell stuck
in it as a sign that the wearer has been a pilgrim to the shrine of St. James of Compostella; the pilgrim's garb was a
conventional disguise for lovers.* ²⁶**schoon** *shoes.* ³⁸**Larded** *decorated.*

OPHELIA: Well, God 'ild° you! They say the owl° was a baker's daughter. Lord, we
  know what we are, but know not what we may be. God be at your table!

KING: Conceit upon her father.

OPHELIA: Pray let's have no words of this; but when they ask you what it   45
  means, say you this:
  (*Song*) To-morrow is Saint Valentine's day,
    All in the morning betime,
  And I a maid at your window,
    To be your Valentine.°   50
  Then up he rose, and donn'd his clothes,
    And dupp'd° the chamber-door;
  Let in the maid, that out a maid
    Never departed more.

KING: Pretty Ophelia!   55

OPHELIA: Indeed, la, without an oath, I'll make an end on 't:
  [*Sings.*] By Gis° and by Saint Charity,
    Alack, and fie for shame!
  Young men will do 't, if they come to 't;
    By cock,° they are to blame.   60
  Quoth she, before you tumbled me,
    You promis'd me to wed.
  So would I ha' done, by yonder sun,
    An thou hadst not come to my bed.

KING: How long hath she been thus?   65

OPHELIA: I hope all will be well. We must be patient: but I cannot choose but weep,
  to think they would lay him i' the cold ground. My brother shall know of it: and
  so I thank you for your good counsel. Come, my coach! Good night, ladies; good
  night, sweet ladies; good night, good night.   [*Exit.*]

KING: Follow her close; give her good watch, I pray you.   [*Exit* HORATIO.]
  O, this is the poison of deep grief; it springs
  All from her father's death. O Gertrude, Gertrude,
  When sorrows come, they come not single spies,
  But in battalions. First, her father slain: 75
  Next your son gone; and he most violent author
  Of his own just remove: the people muddied,
  Thick and unwholesome in their thoughts and whispers,
  For good Polonius' death; and we have done but greenly,°
  In hugger-mugger° to inter him: poor Ophelia   80
  Divided from herself and her fair judgement,
  Without the which we are pictures, or mere beasts:
  Last, and as much containing as all these,
  Her brother is in secret come from France;

---

⁴²**God 'ild**   *god yield or reward.*   ⁴²**owl**   *reference to a monkish legend that a baker's daughter was turned into
an owl for refusing bread to the Savior.*   ⁵⁰**Valentine**   *this song alludes to the belief that the first girl seen by a
man on the morning of this day was his valentine or true love.*   ⁵²**dupp'd**   *opened.*   ⁵⁷**Gis**   *Jesus.*
⁶⁰**cock**   *perversion of "God" in oaths.*   ⁷⁹**greenly**   *foolishly.*   ⁸⁰**hugger-mugger**   *secret haste.*

Feeds on his wonder, keeps himself in clouds,°   85
And wants not buzzers° to infect his ear
With pestilent speeches of his father's death;
Wherein necessity, of matter beggar'd,°
Will nothing stick° our person to arraign
In ear and ear.° O my dear Gertrude, this,   90
Like to a murd'ring-piece,° in many places
Gives me superfluous death.   *A noise within.*

QUEEN: Alack, what noise is this?
KING: Where are my Switzers?° Let them guard the door.

                         Enter a MESSENGER.

What is the matter?
MESSENGER: Save yourself, my lord:
   The ocean, overpeering° of his list,°   95
   Eats not the flats with more impiteous haste
   Than young Laertes, in a riotous head,
   O'erbears your officers. The rabble call him lord;
   And, as the world were now but to begin,
   Antiquity forgot, custom not known,   100
   The ratifiers and props of every word,°
   They cry "Choose we: Laertes shall be king":
   Caps, hands, and tongues, applaud it to the clouds:
   "Laertes shall be king, Laertes king!"   *A noise within.*
QUEEN: How cheerfully on the false trail they cry!   105
   O, this is counter,° you false Danish dogs!
KING: The doors are broke.

                     Enter LAERTES *with others.*

LAERTES: Where is this king? Sirs, stand you all without.
DANES: No, let's come in.
LAERTES: I pray you, give me leave.
DANES: We will, we will.   [*They retire without the door.*]   110
LAERTES: I thank you: keep the door. O thou vile king,
   Give me my father!
QUEEN: Calmly, good Laertes.
LAERTES: That drop of blood that's calm proclaims me bastard,
   Cries cuckold to my father, brands the harlot
   Even here, between the chaste unsmirched brow   115
   Of my true mother.
KING: What is the cause, Laertes,

---

⁸⁵*in clouds* *invisible.*   ⁸⁶*buzzers* *gossipers.*   ⁸⁸*of matter beggar'd* *unprovided with facts.*   ⁸⁹*noth-*
ing stick *not hesitate.*   ⁹⁰*In ear and ear* *in everybody's ears.*   ⁹¹*murd'ring-piece* *small cannon or mor-*
tar; suggestion of numerous missiles fired.   ⁹⁴*Switzers* *Swiss guards, mercenaries.*   ⁹⁵*overpeering*
overflowing.   ⁹⁵*list* *shore.*   ¹⁰¹*word* *promise.*   ¹⁰⁶*counter* *a hunting term meaning to follow the*
trail in a direction opposite to that which the game has taken.

That thy rebellion looks so giant-like?
Let him go, Gertrude; do not fear our person:
There's such divinity doth hedge a king,
That treason can but peep to° what it would,°   120
Acts little of his will. Tell me, Laertes,
Why thou art thus incens'd. Let him go, Gertrude.
Speak, man.

LAERTES: Where is my father?

KING: Dead.

QUEEN: But not by him.

KING: Let him demand his fill.   125

LAERTES: How came he dead? I'll not be juggled with:
  To hell, allegiance! vows, to the blackest devil!
  Conscience and grace, to the profoundest pit!
  I dare damnation. To this point I stand,
  That both the worlds I give to negligence,°   130
  Let come what comes; only I'll be reveng'd
  Most thoroughly° for my father.

KING: Who shall stay you?

LAERTES: My will,° not all the world's:
  And for my means, I'll husband them so well,
  They shall go far with little.

KING: Good Laertes,   135
  If you desire to know the certainty
  Of your dear father, is 't writ in your revenge,
  That, swoopstake,° you will draw both friend and foe,
  Winner and loser?

LAERTES: None but his enemies.

KING: Will you know them then?   140

LAERTES: To his good friends thus wide I'll ope my arms;
  And like the kind life-rend'ring pelican,°
  Repast° them with my blood.

KING: Why, now you speak
  Like a good child and a true gentleman.
  That I am guiltless of your father's death,   145
  And am most sensibly in grief for it,
  It shall as level to your judgement 'pear
  As day does to your eye.

A noise within: "Let her come in."

LAERTES: How now! what noise is that?

---

¹²⁰**peep to**   *i.e., look at from afar off.*   ¹²⁰**would**   *wishes to do.*   ¹³⁰**give to negligence**   *he despises both the here and the hereafter.*   ¹³²**throughly**   *thoroughly.*   ¹³³**My will**   *he will not be stopped except by his own will.*   ¹³⁸**swoopstake**   *literally, drawing the whole stake at once, i.e., indiscriminately.*   ¹⁴²**pelican**   *reference to the belief that the pelican feeds its young with its own blood.*   ¹⁴³**Repast**   *feed.*

Enter OPHELIA.

O heat,° dry up my brains! tears seven times salt,   150
Burn out the sense and virtue of mine eye!
By heaven, thy madness shall be paid with weight,
Till our scale turn the beam. O rose of May!
Dear maid, kind sister, sweet Ophelia!
O heavens! is 't possible, a young maid's wits   155
Should be as mortal as an old man's life?
Nature is fine in love, and where 'tis fine,
It sends some precious instance of itself
After the thing it loves.
OPHELIA (*Song*): They bore him barefac'd on the bier;   160
Hey non nonny, nonny, hey nonny;
And in his grave rain'd many a tear:—
Fare you well, my dove!
LAERTES: Hadst thou thy wits, and didst persuade revenge,
It could not move thus.   165
OPHELIA [*sings*]: You must sing a-down a-down,
  An you call him a-down-a.
O, how the wheel° becomes it! It is the false steward,° that stole his
master's daughter.
LAERTES: This nothing's more than matter.   170
OPHELIA: There's rosemary,° that's for remembrance; pray you, love, remember:
and there is pansies,° that's for thoughts.
LAERTES: A document° in madness, thoughts and remembrance fitted.
OPHELIA: There's fennel° for you, and columbines:° there's rue° for you; and here's 175
some for me: we may call it herb of grace o' Sundays: O, you must wear your
rue with a difference. There's a daisy:° I would give you some violets,° but they
withered all when my father died: they say 'a made a good end,—
[*Sings.*] For bonny sweet Robin is all my joy.°
LAERTES: Thought° and affliction, passion, hell itself,   180
She turns to favour and to prettiness.
OPHELIA (*Song*): And will 'a not come again?°
  And will 'a not come again?
    No, no, he is dead:
      Go to thy death-bed: 185
He never will come again.

---

[150]**heat**   *probably the heat generated by the passion of grief.*   [168]**wheel**   *spinning wheel as accompaniment to the song refrain.*   [168–69]**false steward . . . daughter**   *the story is unknown.*   [171]**rosemary**   *used as a symbol of remembrance both at weddings and at funerals.*   [172]**pansies**   *emblems of love and courtship. Cf. French pensées.*   [173]**document**   *piece of instruction or lesson.*   [174]**fennel**   *emblem of flattery.*   [174]**columbines**   *emblem of unchastity (?) or ingratitude (?).*   [174]**rue**   *emblem of repentance. It was usually mingled with holy water and then known as herb of grace. Ophelia is probably playing on the two meanings of rue "repentant" and "even for Ruth (pity)"; the former signification is for the queen, the latter for herself.*   [176]**daisy**   *emblem of dissembling, faithlessness.*   [177]**violets**   *emblems of faithfulness.*   [179]**For . . . joy**   *probably a line from a Robin Hood ballad.*   [180]**Thought**   *melancholy thought.*   [182]**And . . . again**   *this song appeared in the songbooks as "The Merry Milkmaids' Dumps."*

His beard was as white as snow,
All flaxen was his poll:°
  He is gone, he is gone,
    And we cast away° moan: 190
God ha' mercy on his soul!
And of all Christian souls, I pray God. God be wi' you.   [*Exit.*]
LAERTES: Do you see this, O God?
KING: Laertes, I must commune with your grief,
  Or you deny me right.° Go but apart,   195
  Make choice of whom your wisest friends you will,
  And they shall hear and judge 'twixt you and me:
  If by direct or by collateral° hand
  They find us touch'd,° we will our kingdom give,
  Our crown, our life, and all that we call ours,   200
  To you in satisfaction; but if not,
  Be you content to lend your patience to us,
  And we shall jointly labour with your soul
  To give it due content.
LAERTES: Let this be so;
  His means of death, his obscure funeral—   205
  No trophy, sword, nor hatchment° o'er his bones,
  No noble rite nor formal ostentation—
  Cry to be heard, as 'twere from heaven to earth,
  That I must call 't in question.
KING: So you shall;
  And where th' offence is let the great axe fall.   210
  I pray you, go with me.   *Exeunt.*

Scene VI [*Another room in the castle.*]

Enter HORATIO *and others.*

HORATIO: What are they that would speak with me?
GENTLEMAN: Sea-faring men, sir: they say they have letters for you.
HORATIO: Let them come in.   [*Exit* GENTLEMAN.]
  I do not know from what part of the world
  I should be greeted, if not from lord Hamlet.   5

Enter SAILORS.

FIRST SAILOR: God bless you, sir.
HORATIO: Let him bless thee too.
FIRST SAILOR: 'A shall sir, an 't please him. There's a letter for you, sir; it comes
  from the ambassador that was bound for England; if your name be Horatio, as I
  am let to know it is.   10

---

¹⁸⁸***poll*** head.   ¹⁹⁰***cast away*** shipwrecked.   ¹⁹⁵***right*** my rights.   ¹⁹⁸***collateral*** indirect.
¹⁹⁹***touch'd*** implicated.   ²⁰⁶***hatchment*** tablet displaying the armorial bearings of a deceased person.

HORATIO [reads]:"Horatio, when thou shalt have overlooked this, give these fellows
    some means° to the king: they have letters for him. Ere we were two days old at
    sea, a pirate of very warlike appointment gave us chase. Finding ourselves too
    slow of sail, we put on a compelled valour, and in the grapple I boarded them:
    on the instant they got clear of our ship; so I alone became their prisoner. They   15
    have dealt with me like thieves of mercy:° but they knew what they did; I am to
    do a good turn for them. Let the king have the letters I have sent; and repair
    thou to me with as much speed as thou wouldst fly death. I have words to speak
    in thine ear will make thee dumb; yet are they much too light for the bore° of
    the matter. These good fellows will bring thee where I am. Rosencrantz and   20
    Guildenstern hold their course for England: of them I have much to tell thee.
    Farewell.

                     "He that thou knowest thine, HAMLET."
Come, I will give you way for these your letters;   25
And do 't the speedier, that you may direct me
To him from whom you brought them.   *Exeunt.*

Scene VII [*Another room in the castle.*]

                Enter KING *and* LAERTES.

KING: Now must your conscience° my acquittance seal,
    And you must put me in your heart for friend,
    Sith you have heard, and with a knowing ear,
    That he which hath your noble father slain
    Pursued my life.
LAERTES: It well appears: but tell me   5
    Why you proceeded not against these feats,
    So criminal and so capital° in nature,
    As by your safety, wisdom, all things else,
    You mainly° were stirr'd up.
KING: O, for two special reasons;
    Which may to you, perhaps, seem much unsinew'd,°   10
    But yet to me th' are strong. The queen his mother
    Lives almost by his looks; and for myself—
    My virtue or my plague, be it either which—
    She's so conjunctive° to my life and soul,
    That, as the star moves not but in his sphere,°   15
    I could not but by her. The other motive,
    Why to a public count° I might not go,

IV.vi. [12]*means* *means of access.*   [16–17]*thieves of mercy* *merciful thieves.*   [20]*bore* *caliber, importance.*
IV.vii. [1]*conscience* *knowledge that this is true.*   [7]*capital* *punishable by death.*   [9]*mainly* *greatly.*
[10]*Unsinew'd* *weak.*   [14]*conjunctive* *conformable (the next line suggesting planetary conjunction).*
[15]*sphere* *the hollow sphere in which, according to Ptolemaic astronomy, the planets were supposed to move.*
[17]*count* *account, reckoning.*

Is the great love the general gender° bear him;
Who, dipping all his faults in their affection,
Would, like the spring° that turneth wood to stone,   20
Convert his gyves° to graces; so that my arrows,
Too slightly timber'd° for so loud° a wind,
Would have reverted to my bow again,
And not where I had aim'd them.
LAERTES: And so have I a noble father lost;   25
A sister driven into desp'rate terms,°
Whose worth, if praises may go back° again,
Stood challenger on mount° of all the age°
For her perfections: but my revenge will come.
KING: Break not your sleeps for that: you must not think   30
That we are made of stuff so flat and dull
That we can let our beard be shook with danger
And think it pastime. You shortly shall hear more:
I lov'd your father, and we love ourself;
And that, I hope, will teach you to imagine—   35

Enter a MESSENGER *with letters.*

How now! what news?
MESSENGER: Letters, my lord, from Hamlet:
These to your majesty; this to the queen.°
KING: From Hamlet! who brought them?
MESSENGER: Sailors, my lord, they say; I saw them not:
They were given me by Claudio;° he receiv'd them   40
Of him that brought them.
KING: Laertes, you shall hear them.
Leave us.   [*Exit* MESSENGER.]
[*Reads.*] "High and mighty, You shall know I am set naked° on your king-
dom. To-morrow shall I beg leave to see your kingly eyes: when I shall,
first asking your pardon thereunto, recount the occasion of my sudden and   45
more strange return.   "HAMLET."
What should this mean? Are all the rest come back?
Or is it some abuse, and no such thing?
LAERTES: Know you the hand?
KING: 'Tis Hamlet's character. "Naked!"
And in a postscript here, he says "alone."   50
Can you devise° me?
LAERTES: I'm lost in it, my lord. But let him come;
It warms the very sickness in my heart,

---

¹⁸**general gender**   *common people.*   ²⁰**spring**   *i.e., one heavily charged with lime.*   ²¹**gyves**   *fetters; here,*
faults, or possibly, punishments inflicted (on him).   ²²**slightly timber'd**   *light.*   ²²**loud**   *strong.*
²⁶**terms**   *state, condition.*   ²⁷**go back**   *i.e., to Ophelia's former virtues.*   ²⁸**on mount**   *set up on high,*
mounted (on horseback).   ²⁸**of all the age**   *qualifies* challenger *and not* mount.   ³⁷**to the queen**   *one*
hears no more of the letter to the queen.   ⁴⁰**Claudio**   *this character does not appear in the play.*   ⁴³**naked**
unprovided (with retinue).   ⁵¹**devise**   *explain to.*

That I shall live and tell him to his teeth,
"Thus didst thou."
KING: If it be so, Laertes—   55
As how should it be so? how otherwise?°—
Will you be rul'd by me?
LAERTES: Ay, my lord;
So you will not o'errule me to a peace.
KING: To thine own peace. If he be now return'd,
As checking at° his voyage, and that he means   60
No more to undertake it, I will work him
To an exploit, now ripe in my device,
Under the which he shall not choose but fall:
And for his death no wind of blame shall breathe,
But even his mother shall uncharge the practice°   65
And call it accident.
LAERTES: My lord, I will be rul'd;
The rather, if you could devise it so
That I might be the organ.°
KING: It falls right.
You have been talk'd of since your travel much,
And that in Hamlet's hearing, for a quality   70
Wherein, they say, you shine: your sum of parts
Did not together pluck such envy from him
As did that one, and that, in my regard,
Of the unworthiest siege.°
LAERTES: What part is that, my lord?
KING: A very riband in the cap of youth,   75
Yet needful too; for youth no less becomes
The light and careless livery that it wears
Than settled age his sables° and his weeds,
Importing health and graveness. Two months since,
Here was a gentleman of Normandy:—   80
I have seen myself, and serv'd against, the French,
And they can well° on horseback: but this gallant
Had witchcraft in 't; he grew unto his seat;
And to such wondrous doing brought his horse,
As had he been incorps'd and demi-natur'd°   85
With the brave beast: so far he topp'd° my thought,
That I, in forgery° of shapes and tricks,
Come short of what he did.
LAERTES: A Norman was 't?

---

⁵⁶*As ... otherwise?* *how can this (Hamlet's return) be true? (yet) how otherwise than true (since we have the evidence of his letter)? Some editors read "How should it not be so," etc., making the words refer to Laertes's desire to meet with Hamlet.* ⁶⁰*checking at* *used in falconry of a hawk's leaving the quarry to fly at a chance bird, turn aside.* ⁶⁵*uncharge the practice* *acquit the stratagem of being a plot.* ⁶⁸*organ* *agent, instrument.* ⁷⁴*siege* *rank.* ⁷⁸*sables* *rich garments.* ⁸²*can well* *are skilled.* ⁸⁵*incorps'd and demi-natur'd* *of one body and nearly of one nature (like the centaur).* ⁸⁶*topp'd* *surpassed.* ⁸⁷*forgery* *invention.*

KING: A Norman.

LAERTES: Upon my life, Lamord.°

KING: The very same.   90

LAERTES: I know him well: he is the brooch indeed
    And gem of all the nation.

KING: He made confession° of you,
    And gave you such a masterly report
    For art and exercise° in your defence°   95
    And for your rapier most especial,
    That he cried out, 'twould be a sight indeed,
    If one could match you: the scrimers° of their nation,
    He swore, had neither motion, guard, nor eye,
    If you oppos'd them. Sir, this report of his   100
    Did Hamlet so envenom with his envy
    That he could nothing do but wish and beg
    Your sudden coming o'er, to play° with you.
    Now, out of this,—

LAERTES: What out of this, my lord?

KING: Laertes, was your father dear to you?   105
    Or are you like the painting of a sorrow,
    A face without a heart?

LAERTES: Why ask you this?

KING: Not that I think you did not love your father;
    But that I know love is begun by time;
    And that I see, in passages of proof,°   110
    Time qualifies the spark and fire of it.
    There lives within the very flame of love
    A kind of wick or snuff that will abate it;
    And nothing is at a like goodness still;
    For goodness, growing to a plurisy,°   115
    Dies in his own too much:° that we would do,
    We should do when we would; for this "would" changes
    And hath abatements° and delays as many
    As there are tongues, are hands, are accidents;°
    And then this "should" is like a spendthrift° sigh,   120
    That hurts by easing. But, to the quick o' th' ulcer:°—
    Hamlet comes back: what would you undertake,
    To show yourself your father's son in deed
    More than in words?

LAERTES: To cut his throat i' th' church.

---

⁹⁰**Lamord**   *this refers possibly to Pietro Monte, instructor to Louis XII's master of the horse.*   ⁹³**confession**
grudging admission of superiority.   ⁹⁵**art and exercise**   *skillful exercise.*   ⁹⁵**defence**   *science of defense in
sword practice.*   ⁹⁸**scrimers**   *fencers.*   ¹⁰³**play**   *fence.*   ¹¹⁰**passages of proof**   *proved instances.*
¹¹⁵**plurisy**   *excess, plethora.*   ¹¹⁶**in his own too much**   *of its own excess.*   ¹¹⁸**abatements**   *diminutions.*
¹¹⁹**accidents**   *occurrences, incidents.*   ¹²⁰**spendthrift**   *an allusion to the belief that each sigh cost the heart a drop
of blood.*   ¹²¹**quick o' th' ulcer**   *heart of the difficulty.*

KING: No place, indeed, should murder sanctuarize;° 125
Revenge should have no bounds. But, good Laertes,
Will you do this, keep close within your chamber.
Hamlet return'd shall know you are come home:
We'll put on those shall praise your excellence
And set a double varnish on the fame 130
The Frenchman gave you, bring you in fine together
And wager on your heads: he, being remiss,
Most generous and free from all contriving,
Will not peruse the foils; so that, with ease,
Or with a little shuffling, you may choose 135
A sword unbated,° and in a pass of practice°
Requite him for your father.
LAERTES: I will do 't:
And, for that purpose, I'll anoint my sword.
I bought an unction of a mountebank,°
So mortal that, but dip a knife in it, 140
Where it draws blood no cataplasm° so rare,
Collected from all simples° that have virtue
Under the moon,° can save the thing from death
That is but scratch'd withal: I'll touch my point
With this contagion, that, if I gall° him slightly, 145
It may be death.
KING: Let's further think of this;
Weigh what convenience both of time and means
May fit us to our shape:° if this should fail,
And that our drift look through our bad performance,°
'Twere better not assay'd: therefore this project 150
Should have a back or second, that might hold,
If this should blast in proof.° Soft! let me see:
We'll make a solemn wager on your cunnings:°
I ha 't:
When in your motion you are hot and dry— 155
As make your bouts more violent to that end—
And that he calls for drink, I'll have prepar'd him
A chalice° for the nonce, whereon but sipping,
If he by chance escape your venom'd stuck,°
Our purpose may hold there. But stay, what noise? 160

---

¹²⁵**sanctuarize**   *protect from punishment; allusion to the right of sanctuary with which certain religious places were invested.*   ¹³⁶**unbated**   *not blunted, having no button.*   ¹³⁶**pass of practice**   *treacherous thrust.*   ¹³⁹**mountebank**   *quack doctor.*   ¹⁴¹**cataplasm**   *plaster or poultice.*   ¹⁴²**simples**   *herbs.*   ¹⁴³**Under the moon**   *i.e., when collected by moonlight to add to their medicinal value.*   ¹⁴⁵**gall**   *graze, wound.*   ¹⁴⁸**shape**   *part we propose to act.*   ¹⁴⁹**drift . . . performance**   *intention be disclosed by our bungling.*   ¹⁵²**blast in proof**   *burst in the test (like a cannon).*   ¹⁵³**cunnings**   *skills.*   ¹⁵⁸**chalice**   *cup.*   ¹⁵⁹**stuck**   *thrust (from stoccado).*

Enter QUEEN.

QUEEN: One woe doth tread upon another's heel,
  So fast they follow: your sister's drown'd, Laertes.
LAERTES: Drown'd! O, where?
QUEEN: There is a willow° grows askant° the brook,　　　　165
  That shows his hoar° leaves in the glassy stream;
  There with fantastic garlands did she make
  Of crow-flowers,° nettles, daisies, and long purples°
  That liberal° shepherds give a grosser name,
  But our cold maids do dead men's fingers call them:
  There, on the pendent boughs her crownet° weeds　　170
  Clamb'ring to hang, an envious sliver° broke;
  When down her weedy° trophies and herself
  Fell in the weeping brook. Her clothes spread wide;
  And, mermaid-like, awhile they bore her up:
  Which time she chanted snatches of old lauds;°　　175
  As one incapable° of her own distress,
  Or like a creature native and indued°
  Upon that element: but long it could not be
  Till that her garments, heavy with their drink,
  Pull'd the poor wretch from her melodious lay　　180
  To muddy death.
LAERTES:　　　　　　Alas, then, she is drown'd?
QUEEN: Drown'd, drown'd.
LAERTES: Too much of water hast thou, poor Ophelia,
  And therefore I forbid my tears: but yet
  It is our trick;° nature her custom holds,　　185
  Let shame say what it will: when these are gone,
  The woman will be out.° Adieu, my lord:
  I have a speech of fire, that fain would blaze,
  But that this folly drowns it.　　　　　　*Exit.*
KING:　　　　　　　　Let's follow, Gertrude:　　190
  How much I had to do to calm his rage!
  Now fear I this will give it start again;
  Therefore let 's follow.　　　　　　*Exeunt.*

---

[164]*willow*　*for its significance of forsaken love.*　[164]*askant*　*aslant.*　[165]*hoar*　*white (i.e., on the under-side).*　[167]*crow-flowers*　*buttercups.*　[167]*long purples*　*early purple orchids.*　[168]*liberal*　*probably, free-spoken.*　[170]*crownet*　*coronet; made into a chaplet.*　[171]*sliver*　*branch.*　[172]*weedy*　*i.e., of plants.*　[175]*lauds*　*hymns.*　[176]*incapable*　*lacking capacity to apprehend.*　[177]*indued*　*endowed with qualities fitting her for living in water.*　[185]*trick*　*way.*　[186-187]*when . . . out*　*when my tears are all shed, the woman in me will be satisfied.*

ACT V

Scene I [A churchyard.]

Enter two CLOWNS° *[with spades, &c.].*

FIRST CLOWN: Is she to be buried in Christian burial when she wilfully seeks her own salvation?

SECOND CLOWN: I tell thee she is; therefore make her grave straight:° the crowner° hath sat on her, and finds it Christian burial.

FIRST CLOWN: How can that be, unless she drowned herself in her own defence? 5

SECOND CLOWN: Why, 'tis found so.

FIRST CLOWN: It must be "se offendendo";° it cannot be else. For here lies the point: if I drown myself wittingly,° it argues an act: and an act hath three branches;° it is, to act, to do, and to perform: argal,° she drowned herself 10 wittingly.

SECOND CLOWN: Nay, but hear you, goodman delver,°—

FIRST CLOWN: Give me leave. Here lies the water; good: here stands the man; good: if the man go to this water, and drown himself, it is, will he, nill he, he goes,—mark you that; but if the water come to him and drown him, he 15 drowns not himself: argal, he that is not guilty of his own death shortens not his own life.

SECOND CLOWN: But is this law?

FIRST CLOWN: Ay, marry, is 't; crowner's quest° law.

SECOND CLOWN: Will you ha' the truth on 't? If this had not been a gentle- 20 woman, she should have been buried out o' Christian burial.

FIRST CLOWN: Why, there thou say'st:° and the more pity that great folk should have countenance° in this world to drown or hang themselves, more than their even° Christian. Come, my spade. There is no ancient gentlemen but gardeners, ditchers, and grave-makers: they hold up° Adam's profession. 25

SECOND CLOWN: Was he a gentleman?

FIRST CLOWN: 'A was the first that ever bore arms.

SECOND CLOWN: Why, he had none.

FIRST CLOWN: What, art a heathen? How dost thou understand the Scripture? 30 The Scripture says "Adam digged": could he dig without arms? I'll put another question to thee: if thou answerest me not to the purpose, confess thyself °—

SECOND CLOWN: Go to.°

Vi.i.   clowns   *the word clown was used to denote peasants as well as humorous characters; here applied to the rus-tic type of clown.*   ³**straight**   *straightway, immediately; some interpret "from east to west in a direct line, parallel with the church."*   ⁴**crowner**   *coroner.*   ⁷**"se offendendo"**   *for se defendendo, term used in verdicts of jus-tifiable homicide.*   ⁸**wittingly**   *intentionally.*   ⁸⁻⁹**three branches**   *parody of legal phraseology.*   ¹⁰**argal**   *corruption of ergo, therefore*   ¹²**delver**   *digger.*   ¹⁹**quest**   *inquest.*   ²²**there thou say'st**   *that's right.*   ²³**countenance**   *privilege.*   ²⁴**even**   *fellow.*   ²⁵**hold up**   *maintain, continue.*   ³²⁻³³**confess thyself**   *"and be hanged" completes the proverb.*   ³⁴**Go to**   *perhaps, "begin," or some other form of concession.*

FIRST CLOWN: What is he that builds stronger than either the mason, the ship-   35
    wright, or the carpenter?
SECOND CLOWN: The gallows-maker; for that frame outlives a thousand tenants.
FIRST CLOWN: I like thy wit well, in good faith: the gallows does well; but how
    does it well? it does well to those that do ill: now thou dost ill to say the gal-
    lows is built stronger than the church: argal, the gallows may do well to thee.   40
    To 't again, come.
SECOND CLOWN: Who builds stronger than a mason, a shipwright, or a
    carpenter?
FIRST CLOWN: Ay, tell me that, and unyoke.°
SECOND CLOWN: Marry, now I can tell.   45
FIRST CLOWN: To 't.
SECOND CLOWN: Mass,° I cannot tell.

Enter HAMLET and HORATIO [at a distance].

FIRST CLOWN: Cudgel thy brains no more about it, for your dull ass will not
    mend his pace with beating; and, when you are asked this question next, say   50
    "a grave-maker": the houses he makes lasts till doomsday. Go, get thee in, and
    fetch me a stoup° of liquor.

[Exit SECOND CLOWN.] Song. [He digs.]

In youth, when I did love, did love,
    Methought it was very sweet,
To contract—O—the time, for—a—my behove,°
    O, methought, there—a—was nothing—a—meet.   55
HAMLET: Has this fellow no feeling of his business, that 'a sings at gravemaking?
HORATIO: Custom hath made it in him a property of easiness.°
HAMLET: 'Tis e'en so: the hand of little employment hath the daintier sense.
FIRST CLOWN: (Song.) But age, with his stealing steps,   60
    Hath claw'd me in his clutch,
And hath shipped me into the land
    As if I had never been such.   [Throws up a skull.]
HAMLET: That skull had a tongue in it, and could sing once: how the knave
    jowls° it to the ground, as if 'twere Cain's jaw-bone,° that did the first   65
    murder! This might be the pate of a politician,° which this ass now o'er-
    reaches;° one that would circumvent God, might it not?
HORATIO: It might, my lord.
HAMLET: Or of a courtier; which could say "Good morrow, sweet lord! How dost
    thou, sweet lord?" This might be my lord such-a-one, that praised my lord   70
    such-a-one's horse, when he meant to beg it; might it not?

45**unyoke** *after this great effort you may unharness the team of your wits.*   48**Mass** *by the Mass.*   52**stoup**
two-quart measure.   55**behove** *benefit.*   59**property of easiness** *a peculiarity that now is easy.*
66**jowls** *dashes.*   66**Cain's jaw-bone** *allusion to the old tradition that Cain slew Abel with the jawbone of*
an ass.   67**politician** *schemer, plotter.*   67-68**o'er-reaches** *quibble on the literal sense and the sense*
"circumvent."

HORATIO: Ay, my lord.

HAMLET: Why, e'en so: and now my Lady Worm's; chapless,° and knocked about
the mazzard° with a sexton's spade: here's fine revolution, an we had the trick   75
to see 't. Did these bones cost no more the breeding, but to play at loggats°
with 'em? mine ache to think on 't.

FIRST CLOWN: (*Song.*) A pick-axe, and a spade, a spade,
　　For and° a shrouding sheet:
　　O, a pit of clay for to be made   80
　　For such a guest is meet.   [*Throws up another skull.*]

HAMLET: There's another: why may not that be the skull of a lawyer? Where be
his quiddities° now, his quillities,° his cases, his tenures,° and his tricks? why
does he suffer this mad knave now to knock him about the sconce° with a
dirty shovel, and will not tell him of his action of battery? Hum! This fellow   85
might be in 's time a great buyer of land, with his statutes, his recognizances,°
his fines, his double vouchers,° his recoveries:° is this the fine° of his fines, and
the recovery of his recoveries, to have his fine pate full of fine dirt? will his
vouchers vouch him no more of his purchases, and double ones too, than the
length and breadth of a pair of indentures?° The very conveyances of his lands   90
will scarcely lie in this box; and must the inheritor° himself have no more, ha?

HORATIO: Not a jot more, my lord.

HAMLET: Is not parchment made of sheep-skins?

HORATIO: Ay, my lord, and of calf-skins° too.   95

HAMLET: They are sheep and calves which seek out assurance in that.° I will
speak to this fellow. Whose grave's this, sirrah?

FIRST CLOWN: Mine, sir.
　　[*Sings.*] O, a pit of clay for to be made   100
　　For such a guest is meet.

HAMLET: I think it be thine, indeed; for thou liest in 't.

FIRST CLOWN: You lie out on't, sir, and therefore 't is not yours: for my part, I do
not lie in 't, yet it is mine.

HAMLET: Thou dost lie in 't, to be in 't and say it is thine: 'tis for the dead, not for
the quick; therefore thou liest.   105

FIRST CLOWN: 'Tis a quick lie, sir; 'twill away again, from me to you.

HAMLET: What man dost thou dig it for?

FIRST CLOWN: For no man, sir.

HAMLET: What woman, then?

FIRST CLOWN: For none, neither.   110

HAMLET: Who is to be buried in 't?

FIRST CLOWN: One that was a woman, sir; but, rest her soul, she's dead.

---

[74]**chapless**　*having no lower jaw.*　[75]**mazzard**　*head.*　[76]**loggats**　*a game in which six sticks are thrown to lie as near as possible to a stake fixed in the ground, or block of wood on a floor.*　[79]**For and**　*and moreover.*　[83]**quiddities**　*subtleties, quibbles.*　[83]**quillities**　*verbal niceties, subtle distinctions.*　[83]**tenures**　*the holding of a piece of property or office or the conditions or period of such holding.*　[84]**sconce**　*head.*　[86]**statutes, recognizances**　*legal terms connected with the transfer of land.*　[87]**vouchers**　*persons called on to warrant a tenant's title.*　[87]**recoveries**　*process for transfer of entailed estate.*　[87]**fine**　*the four uses of this word are as follows: (1) end, (2) legal process, (3) elegant, (4) small.*　[90]**indentures**　*conveyances or contracts.*　[91]**inheritor**　*possessor, owner.*　[95]**calf-skins**　*parchments.*　[96]**assurance in that**　*safety in legal parchments.*

HAMLET: How absolute° the knave is! we must speak by the card,° or equivoca-
tion° will undo us. By the Lord, Horatio, these three years I have taken note
of it; the age is grown so picked° that the toe of the peasant comes so near the   115
heel of the courtier, he galls° his kibe.° How long hast thou been a grave-
maker?

FIRST CLOWN: Of all the day i' the year, I came to 't that day that our last king
Hamlet overcame Fortinbras.

HAMLET: How long is that since?   120

FIRST CLOWN: Cannot you tell that? every fool can tell that: it was the very day
that young Hamlet was born; he that is mad, and sent into England.

HAMLET: Ay, marry, why was he sent into England?

FIRST CLOWN: Why, because 'a was mad: 'a shall recover his wits there; or, if 'a do
not, 'tis no great matter there.   125

HAMLET: Why?

FIRST CLOWN: 'Twill not be seen in him there; there the men are as mad as he.

HAMLET: How came he mad?

FIRST CLOWN: Very strangely, they say.   130

HAMLET: How strangely?

FIRST CLOWN: Faith, e'en with losing his wits.

HAMLET: Upon what ground?

FIRST CLOWN: Why, here in Denmark: I have been sexton here, man and boy,
thirty years.°

HAMLET: How long will a man lie i' the earth ere he rot?   135

FIRST CLOWN: Faith, if 'a be not rotten before 'a die—as we have many pocky°
corses now-a-days, that will scarce hold the laying in—'a will last you some
eight year or nine year: a tanner will last you nine year.

HAMLET: Why he more than another?

FIRST CLOWN: Why, sir, his hide is so tanned with his trade, that 'a will keep out   140
water a great while; and your water is a sore decayer of your whoreson dead
body. Here's a skull now hath lain you i' th' earth three and twenty years.

HAMLET: Whose was it?

FIRST CLOWN: A whoreson mad fellow's it was: whose do you think it was?   145

HAMLET: Nay, I know not.

FIRST CLOWN: A pestilence on him for a mad rogue! 'a poured a flagon of
Rhenish on my head once. This same skull, sir, was Yorick's skull, the king's
jester.

HAMLET: This?   150

FIRST CLOWN: E'en that.

HAMLET: Let me see. [*Takes the skull.*] Alas, poor Yorick! I knew him, Horatio: a
fellow of infinite jest, of most excellent fancy: he hath borne me on his back
a thousand times; and now, how abhorred in my imagination it is! my gorge
rises at it. Here hung those lips that I have kissed I know not how oft. Where   155

---

¹¹³**absolute**   *positive, decided.*   ¹¹³**by the card**   *with precision, i.e., by the mariner's card on which the points of
the compass were marked.*   ¹¹³⁻¹⁴**equivocation**   *ambiguity in the use of terms.*   ¹¹⁵**picked**   *refined, fastid-
ious .*   ¹¹⁶**galls**   *chafes.*   ¹¹⁶**kibe**   *chilblain.*   ¹³⁴**thirty years**   *this statement with that in line 122
shows Hamlet's age to be thirty years.*   ¹³⁶**pocky**   *rotton, diseased.*

be your gibes now? your gambols? your songs? your flashes of merriment, that
were wont to set the table on a roar? Not one now, to mock your own grin-
ning? quite chap-fallen? Now get you to my lady's chamber, and tell her, let
her paint an inch thick, to this favour she must come; make her laugh at that.
Prithee, Horatio, tell me one thing.   160
HORATIO: What's that, my lord?
HAMLET: Dost thou think Alexander looked o' this fashion i' the earth?
HORATIO: E'en so.
HAMLET: And smelt so? pah!   [*Puts down the skull.*]
HORATIO: E'en so, my lord.   165
HAMLET: To what base uses we may return, Horatio! Why may not imagination
     trace the noble dust of Alexander, till'a find it stopping a bunghole?
HORATIO: 'Twere to consider too curiously,° to consider so.
HAMLET: No, faith, not a jot; but to follow him thither with modesty enough, and   170
     likelihood to lead it: as thus: Alexander died, Alexander was buried, Alexander
     returneth into dust; the dust is earth; of earth we make loam;° and why of that
     loam, whereto he was converted, might they not stop a beer-barrel?

       Imperious° Cæsar, dead and turn'd to clay,   175
       Might stop a hole to keep the wind away:
       O, that that earth, which kept the world in awe,
       Should patch a wall t'expel the winter's flaw!°
But soft! but soft awhile! here comes the king,

       Enter KING, QUEEN, LAERTES, *and the Corse of*
       [OPHELIA, *in procession, with* PRIEST, LORDS, *etc.*].

The queen, the courtiers: who is this they follow?   180
And with such maimed rites? This doth betoken
The corse they follow did with desp'rate hand
Fordo° it° own life: 'twas of some estate.
Couch° we awhile, and mark.   [*Retiring with* HORATIO.]
LAERTES: What ceremony else?
HAMLET: That is Laertes,   185
  A very noble youth: mark.
LAERTES: What ceremony else?
FIRST PRIEST: Her obsequies have been as far enlarg'd°
  As we have warranty: her death was doubtful;
  And, but that great command o'ersways the order,   190
  She should in ground unsanctified have lodg'd
  Till the last trumpet; for charitable prayers,
  Shards,° flints and pebbles should be thrown on her:
  Yet here she is allow'd her virgin crants,°

---

[168]**curiously** *minutely.* [172]**loam** *clay paste for brickmaking.* [175]**Imperious** *imperial.* [178]**flaw**
gust of wind. [183]**Fordo** *destroy.* [183]**it** *its.* [184]**Couch** *hide, lurk.* [188]**enlarg'd** *extended,*
referring to the fact that suicides are not given full burial rites. [193]**Shards** *broken bits of pottery.* [194]**crants**
garlands customarily hung upon the biers of unmarried women.

Her maiden strewments° and the bringing home   195
Of bell and burial.°
LAERTES: Must there no more be done?
FIRST PRIEST: No more be done:
  We should profane the service of the dead
  To sing a requiem and such rest to her
  As to peace-parted° souls.
LAERTES: Lay her i' th' earth: 200
  And from her fair and unpolluted flesh
  May violets spring! I tell thee, churlish priest,
  A minist'ring angel shall my sister be,
  When thou liest howling.°
HAMLET: What, the fair Ophelia!
QUEEN: Sweets to the sweet: farewell!   [Scattering flowers.] 205
  I hop'd thou shouldst have been my Hamlet's wife;
  I thought thy bride-bed to have deck'd, sweet maid,
  And not have strew'd thy grave.
LAERTES: O, treble woe
  Fall ten times treble on that cursed head,
  Whose wicked deed thy most ingenious sense°   210
  Depriv'd thee of! Hold off the earth awhile,
  Till I have caught her once more in mine arms: [Leaps into the grave.]
  Now pile your dust upon the quick and dead,
  Till of this flat a mountain you have made,
  T' o'ertop old Pelion,° or the skyish head   215
  Of blue Olympus.
HAMLET: [Advancing] What is he whose grief
  Bears such an emphasis? whose phrase of sorrow
  Conjures the wand'ring stars,° and makes them stand
  Like wonder-wounded hearers? This is I,
  Hamlet the Dane.   [Leaps into the grave.]
LAERTES: The devil take thy soul!   [Grappling with him.] 220
HAMLET: Thou pray'st not well.
  I prithee, take thy fingers from my throat;
  For, though I am not splenitive° and rash,
  Yet have I in me something dangerous,
  Which let thy wisdom fear: hold off thy hand.   225
KING: Pluck them asunder.
QUEEN: Hamlet, Hamlet!
ALL: Gentlemen,—
HORATIO: Good my lord, be quiet.

195*strewments*   *traditional strewing of flowers.*   195–96***bringing . . . burial***   *the laying to rest of the body, to the sound of the bell.*   200***peace-parted***   *allusion to the text "Lord, now lettest thy servant depart in peace."* 204***howling***   *i.e, in hell.*   210***ingenious sense***   *mind endowed with finest qualities.*   215***Pelion***   *Olympus, Pelion, and Ossa are mountains in the north of Thessaly.*   218***wand'ring stars***   *planets..*   223***splenitive*** *quick-tempered.*

[*The* ATTENDANTS *part them, and they come out of the grave.*]

HAMLET: Why, I will fight with him upon this theme
    Until my eyelids will no longer wag.°
QUEEN: O my son, what theme?   230
HAMLET: I lov'd Ophelia: forty thousand brothers
    Could not, with all their quantity° of love,
    Make up my sum. What wilt thou do for her?
KING: O, he is mad, Laertes.
QUEEN: For love of God, forbear° him.   235
HAMLET: 'Swounds,° show me what thou 'lt do:
    Woo 't° weep? woo 't fight? woo 't fast? woo 't tear thyself?
    Woo 't drink up eisel?° eat a crocodile?
    I'll do 't. Dost thou come here to whine?
    To outface me with leaping in her grave?   240
    Be buried quick with her, and so will I:
    And, if thou prate of mountains, let them throw
    Millions of acres on us, till our ground,
    Singeing his pate against the burning zone,°
    Make Ossa like a wart! Nay, an thou 'lt mouth,   245
    I'll rant as well as thou.
QUEEN: This is mere madness:
    And thus awhile the fit will work on him;
    Anon, as patient as the female dove.
    When that her golden couplets° are disclos'd,
    His silence will sit drooping.
HAMLET: Hear you, sir;   250
    What is the reason that you use me thus?
    I lov'd you ever: but it is no matter;
    Let Hercules himself do what he may,
    The cat will mew and dog will have his day.
KING: I pray thee, good Horatio, wait upon him.   *Exit* HAMLET *and* HORATIO. 255
    [*To* LAERTES.] Strengthen your patience in° our last night's speech;
    We'll put the matter to the present push.°
    Good Gertrude, set some watch over your son.
    This grave shall have a living° monument:
    An hour of quiet shortly shall we see;   260
    Till then, in patience our proceeding be.   *Exeunt.*

---

[229]*wag*   *move (not used ludicrously).*   [232]*quantity*   *some suggest that the word is used in a deprecatory sense (little bits, fragments).*   [235]*forbear*   *leave alone.*   [236]*'Swounds*   *oath, "God's wounds."*   [237]**Woo 't**   *wilt thou.*   [238]*eisel*   *vinegar. Some editors have taken this to be the name of a river, such as the Yssel, the Weissel, and the Nile.*   [244]**burning zone**   *sun's orbit.*   [249]**golden couplets**   *the pigeon lays two eggs; the young when hatched are covered with golden down.*   [256]*in*   *by recalling.*   [257]**present push**   *immediate test.*   [259]**living**   *lasting; also refers (for Laertes' benefit) to the plot against Hamlet.*

Scene II [*A hall in the castle.*]

Enter HAMLET *and* HORATIO.

HAMLET: So much for this, sir: now shall you see the other;
    You do remember all the circumstance?
HORATIO: Remember it, my lord!
HAMLET: Sir, in my heart there was a kind of fighting,
    That would not let me sleep: methought I lay   5
    Worse than the mutines° in the bilboes.° Rashly,°
    And prais'd be rashness for it, let us know,
    Our indiscretion sometime serves us well,
    When our deep plots do pall:° and that should learn us
    There's a divinity that shapes our ends,   10
    Rough-hew° them how we will,—
HORATIO: That is most certain.
HAMLET: Up from my cabin,
    My sea-gown° scarf'd about me, in the dark
    Grop'd I to find out them; had my desire,
    Finger'd° their packet, and in fine° withdrew   15
    To mine own room again; making so bold,
    My fears forgetting manners, to unseal
    Their grand commission; where I found, Horatio,—
    O royal knavery!—an exact command,
    Larded° with many several sorts of reasons   20
    Importing Denmark's health and England's too,
    With, ho! such bugs° and goblins in my life,°
    That, on the supervise,° no leisure bated,°
    No, not to stay the grinding of the axe,
    My head should be struck off.
HORATIO: Is 't possible?   25
HAMLET: Here's the commission: read it at more leisure.
    But wilt thou hear me how I did proceed?
HORATIO: I beseech you.
HAMLET: Being thus be-netted round with villanies,—
    Ere I could make a prologue to my brains,   30
    They had begun the play°—I sat me down,
    Devis'd a new commission, wrote it fair:
    I once did hold it, as our statists° do,
    A baseness to write fair° and labour'd much

V.ii. °*mutines* mutineers.   °*bilboes* shackels.   °*Rashly* goes with line 12.   °*pall* fail.
¹¹*Rough-hew* shape roughly; it may mean "bungle."   ¹³*sea-gown* "A sea-gown, or a corase, high-collered, and short-sleeved gowne, reaching down to the mid-leg, and used most by seamen and saylors" (Cotgrave, quoted by Singer).   ¹⁵*finger'd* pilfered, filched.   ¹⁵*in fine* finally.   ²⁰*Larded* enriched.   ²²*bugs* bug-bears.
²²*such . . . life* such imaginary dangers if I were allowed to live.   ²³*supervise* perusal.   ²³*leisure bated* delay allowed.   ²⁰⁻³¹*prologue . . . play* i.e., before I could begin to think, my mind had made its decision.
³³*statists* statesmen.   ³⁴*fair* in a clear hand.

How to forget that learning, but, sir, now   35
It did me yeoman's° service: wilt thou know
Th' effect of what I wrote?

HORATIO: Ay, good my lord.

HAMLET: An earnest conjuration from the king,
As England was his faithful tributary,
As love between them like the palm might flourish,   40
As peace should still her wheaten garland° wear
And stand a comma° 'tween their amities,
And many such-like 'As'es° of great charge,°
That, on the view and knowing of these contents,
Without debatement further, more or less,   45
He should the bearers put to sudden death,
Not shriving-time° allow'd.

HORATIO: How was this seal'd?

HAMLET: Why, even in that was heaven ordinant.°
I had my father's signet in my purse,
Which was the model of that Danish seal;   50
Folded the writ up in the form of th' other,
Subscrib'd it, gave 't th' impression, plac'd it safely,
The changeling never known. Now, the next day
Was our sea-fight; and what to this was sequent°
Thou know'st already.   55

HORATIO: So Guildenstern and Rosencrantz go to 't.

HAMLET: Why, man, they did make love to this employment;
They are not near my conscience; their defeat
Does by their own insinuation° grow:
'Tis dangerous when the baser nature comes   60
Between the pass° and fell incensed° points
Of mighty opposites.

HORATIO: Why, what a king is this!

HAMLET: Does it not, think thee, stand° me now upon—
He that hath kill'd my king and whor'd my mother,
Popp'd in between th' election° and my hopes,   65
Thrown out his angle° for my proper life,
And with such coz'nage°—is 't not perfect conscience,
To quit° him with this arm? and is 't not to be damn'd,
To let this canker° of our nature come
In further evil?   70

---

³⁶*yeoman's*   *i.e., faithful.*   ⁴¹*wheaten garland*   *symbol of peace.*   ⁴²*comma*   *smallest break or separation. Here amity begins and amity ends the period, and peace stands between like a dependent clause. The comma indicates continuity, link.*   ⁴³*'As'es*   *the "whereases" of a formal document, with play on the word ass.*   ⁴³*charge import, and burden.*   ⁴⁷*shriving-time*   *time for absolution.*   ⁴⁸*ordinant*   *directing.*   ⁵⁴*sequent*   *subsequent.*   ⁵⁹*insinuation*   *interference.*   ⁶¹*pass*   *thrust.*   ⁶¹*fell incensed*   *fiercely angered.*   ⁶³*stand become incumbent.*   ⁶⁵*election*   *the Danish throne was filled by election.*   ⁶⁶*angle*   *fishing line.*   ⁶⁷*coz'nage*   *trickery.*   ⁶⁸*quit*   *repay.*   ⁶⁹*canker*   *ulcer, or possibly the worm which destroys buds and leaves.*

HORATIO: It must be shortly known to him from England
   What is the issue of the business there.
HAMLET: It will be short: the interim is mine;
   And a man's life's no more than to say "One."
   But I am very sorry, good Horatio,   75
   That to Laertes I forgot myself;
   For, by the image of my cause, I see
   The portraiture of his: I'll court his favours:
   But, sure, the bravery° of his grief did put me
   Into a tow'ring passion.
HORATIO: Peace! who comes here?   80

Enter a COURTIER [OSRIC].

OSRIC: Your lordship is right welcome back to Denmark.
HAMLET: I humbly thank you, sir. [*To* HORATIO.] Dost know this water-fly?°
HORATIO: No, my good lord.
HAMLET: Thy state is the more gracious; for 'tis a vice to know him. He hath
   much land, and fertile: let a beast be lord of beasts,° and his crib shall stand at   85
   the king's mess:° 'tis a chough;° but, as I say, spacious in the possession of dirt.
OSRIC: Sweet lord, if your lordship were at leisure, I should impart a thing to you
   from his majesty.
HAMLET: I will receive it, sir, with all diligence of spirit. Put your bonnet to his   90
   right use; 'tis for the head.
OSRIC: I thank you lordship, it is very hot.
HAMLET: No, believe me, 'tis very cold; the wind is northerly.
OSRIC: It is indifferent° cold, my lord, indeed.
HAMLET: But yet methinks it is very sultry and hot for my complexion.   95
OSRIC: Exceedingly, my lord; it is very sultry,—as 'twere,—I cannot tell how.
   But, my lord, his majesty bade me signify to you that 'a has laid a great wager
   on your head: sir, this is the matter,—
HAMLET: I beseech you, remember°—

                                   [HAMLET *moves him to put on his hat.*]

OSRIC: Nay, good my lord; for mine ease,° in good faith. Sir, here is newly come   100
   to court Laertes; believe me, an absolute gentleman, full of most excellent differences, of very soft° society and great showing:° indeed, to speak feelingly°
   of him, he is the card° or calendar of gentry,° for you shall find in him the
   continent of what part a gentleman would see.
HAMLET: Sir, his definement° suffers no perdition° in you; though, I know, to   105
   divide him inventorially° would dozy° the arithmetic of memory, and yet but

---

⁷⁹**bravery** *bravado.*   ⁸²**water-fly** *vain or busily idle person.*   ⁸⁵**lord of beasts** *cf. Genesis 1:26, 28.*
⁸⁵⁻⁸⁶**his crib . . . mess** *he shall eat at the king's table, i.e., be one of the group of persons (usually four) constitut-*
ing a mess at a banquet.   ⁸⁶**chough** *probably, chattering jackdaw; also explained as chuff, provincial boor or churl.*
⁹⁴**indifferent** *somewhat.*   ⁹⁹**remember** *i.e., remember thy courtesy; conventional phrase for "Be covered."*
¹⁰⁰**mine ease** *conventional reply declining the invitation of "Remember thy courtesy."*   ¹⁰²**soft** *gentle.*
¹⁰²**showing** *distinguished appearance.*   ¹⁰³**feelingly** *with just perception.*   ¹⁰³**card** *chart, map.*
¹⁰³**gentry** *good breeding.*   ¹⁰⁵**definement** *definition.*   ¹⁰⁵**perdition** *loss, diminution.*   ¹⁰⁶**divide him**
inventorially *i.e., enumerate his graces.*   ¹⁰⁶**dozy** *dizzy.*

yaw° neither, in respect of his quick sail. But, in the verity of extolment, I take him to be a soul of great article;° and his infusion° of such dearth and rareness,° as, to make true diction of him, his semblable° is his mirror; and who else would trace° him, his umbrage,° nothing more. 110

OSRIC: Your lordship speaks most infallibly of him.

HAMLET: The concernancy,° sir? why do we wrap the gentleman in our more rawer breath?°

OSRIC: Sir? 115

HORATIO [*aside to* HAMLET]: Is 't not possible to understand in another tongue?° You will do 't, sir, really.

HAMLET: What imports the nomination° of this gentleman?

OSRIC: Of Laertes?

HORATIO [*aside to* HAMLET]: His purse is empty already; all 's golden words are 120 spent.

HAMLET: Of him, sir.

OSRIC: I know you are not ignorant—

HAMLET: I would you did, sir; yet, in faith, if you did, it would not much approve° me. Well, sir? 125

OSRIC: You are not ignorant of what excellence Laertes is—

HAMLET: I dare not confess that, lest I should compare with him in excellence; but, to know a man well, were to know himself.°

OSRIC: I mean, sir, for his weapon; but in the imputation° laid on him by them, in his meed° he's unfellowed. 130

HAMLET: What's his weapon?

OSRIC: Rapier and dagger.

HAMLET: That's two of his weapons: but, well.

OSRIC: The king, sir, hath wagered with him six Barbary horses: against the which he has impawned,° as I take it, six French rapiers and poniards, with their assigns, 135 as girdle, hangers,° and so: three of the carriages, in faith, are very dear to fancy,° very responsive° to the hilts, most delicate° carriages, and of very liberal conceit.°

HAMLET: What call you the carriages?

HORATIO [*aside to* HAMLET]: I knew you must be edified by the margent° ere 140 you had done.

OSRIC: The carriages, sir, are the hangers.

HAMLET: The phrase would be more german° to the matter, if we could carry cannon by our sides: I would it might be hangers till then. But, on: six Barbary horses against six French swords, their assigns, and three liberal-conceited 145

---

¹⁰⁷*yaw* to move unsteadily (of a ship). ¹⁰⁸*article* moment or importance. ¹⁰⁸*infusion* infused temperament, character imparted by nature. ¹⁰⁹*dearth and rareness* rarity. ¹⁰⁹*semblable* true likeness. ¹¹⁰*trace* follow. ¹¹⁰*umbrage* shadow. ¹¹³*concernancy* import. ¹¹⁴*breath* speech. ¹¹⁶⁻¹⁷*Is 't . . . tongue?* i.e., can one converse with Osric only in this outlandish jargon? ¹¹⁸*nomination* naming. ¹²⁵*approve* command. ¹²⁸*but . . . himself* but to know a man as excellent were to know Laertes. ¹²⁹*imputation* reputation. ¹³⁰*meed* merit. ¹³⁵*he has impawned* he has wagered. ¹³⁶*hangers* straps on the sword belt from which the sword hung. ¹³⁷*dear to fancy* fancifully made. ¹³⁷*responsive* probably, well balanced, corresponding closely. ¹³⁷*delicate* i.e., in workmanship. ¹³⁸*liberal conceit* elaborate design. ¹⁴⁰*margent* margin of a book, place for explanatory notes. ¹⁴³*german* germane, appropriate.

carriages; that's the French bet against the Danish. Why is this "impawned," as
you call it?

OSRIC: The king, sir, hath laid, that in a dozen passes between yourself and him,
he shall not exceed you three hits: he hath laid on twelve for nine; and it   150
would come to immediate trial, if your lordship would vouchsafe the answer.

HAMLET: How if I answer "no"?

OSRIC: I mean, my lord, the opposition of your person in trial.

HAMLET: Sir, I will walk here in the hall: if it please his majesty, it is the breathing
time° of day with me; let the foils be brought, the gentleman willing, and the   155
king hold his purpose, I will win for him as I can; if not, I will gain nothing
but my shame and the odd hits.

OSRIC: Shall I re-deliver you e'en so?

HAMLET: To this effect, sir; after what flourish your nature will.   160

OSRIC: I commend my duty to your lordship.

HAMLET: Yours, yours. [Exit OSRIC.] He does well to commend it himself; there
are no tongues else for 's turn.

HORATIO: This lapwing° runs away with the shell on his head.

HAMLET: 'A did comply, sir, with his dug,° before 'a sucked it. Thus has hey—and
many more of the same breed that I know the drossy° age dotes on—only got   165
the tune° of the time and out of an habit of encounter;° a kind of yesty° collection, which carries them through and through the most fann'd and win-
nowed° opinions; and do but blow them to their trial, the bubbles are out.°

Enter a LORD.

LORD: My lord, his majesty commended him to you by young Osric, who brings   170
back to him, that you attend him in the hall: he sends to know if your pleasure hold to play with Laertes, or that you will take longer time.

HAMLET: I am constant to my purposes; they follow the king's pleasure: if his fit-
ness speaks, mine is ready; now or whensoever, provided I be so able as now.   175

LORD: The king and queen and all are coming down.

HAMLET: In happy time.°

LORD: The queen desires you to use some gentle entertainment to Laertes before
you fall to play.

HAMLET: She well instructs me.   [Exit LORD.]   180

HORATIO: You will lose this wager, my lord.

HAMLET: I do not think so; since he went into France, I have been in continual
practice; I shall win at the odds. But thou wouldst not think how ill all 's here
about my heart: but it is no matter.

HORATIO: Nay, good my lord,—   185

HAMLET: It is but foolery; but it is such a kind of gain-giving,° as would perhaps
trouble a woman.

---

¹⁵⁵*breathing time*   *exercise period.*   ¹⁶³*lapwing*   *peewit; noted for its wiliness in drawing a visitor away from
its nest and its supposed habit of running about when newly hatched with its head in the shell; possibly an allusion to
Osric's hat.*   ¹⁶⁴*did comply . . . dug*   *paid compliments to his mother's breast.*   ¹⁶⁵*drossy*   *frivolous.*
¹⁶⁶*tune*   *temper, mood.*   ¹⁶⁶*habit of encounter*   *demeanor of social intercourse.*   ¹⁶⁷*yesty*   *frothy.*
¹⁶⁸*fann'd and winnowed*   *select and refined.*   ¹⁶⁸⁻⁶⁹*blow . . . out*   *i.e., put them to the test, and their
ignorance is exposed.*   ¹⁷⁷*in happy time*   *a phrase of courtesy.*   ¹⁸⁶*gain-giving*   *misgiving.*

HORATIO: If your mind dislike any thing, obey it: I will forestall their repair
hither, and say you are not fit.

HAMLET: Not a whit, we defy augury: there's a special providence in the fall of a   190
sparrow. If it be now, 'tis not to come; if it be not to come, it will be now; if it
be not now, yet it will come: the readiness is all:° since no man of aught he
leaves knows, what is 't to leave betimes? Let be.

A table prepared. [*Enter*] *Trumpets, Drums, and Officers with cushions;* KING, QUEEN, [OSRIC,]
and all the State; foils, daggers, [*and wine borne in;*] *and* LAERTES.

KING: Come, Hamlet, come, and take this hand from me.

[*The* KING *puts* LAERTES'S *hand into* HAMLET'S.]

HAMLET: Give me your pardon, sir: I have done you wrong;   195
But pardon 't as you are a gentleman.
This presence° knows,
And you must needs have heard, how I am punish'd
With a sore distraction. What I have done,
That might your nature, honour and exception°   200
Roughly awake, I here proclaim was madness.
Was 't Hamlet wrong'd Laertes? Never Hamlet:
If Hamlet from himself be ta'en away,
And when he's not himself does wrong Laertes,
Then Hamlet does it not, Hamlet denies it.   205
Who does it, then? His madness: if 't be so,
Hamlet is of the faction that is wrong'd;
His madness is poor Hamlet's enemy.
Sir, in this audience,
Let my disclaiming from a purpos'd evil   210
Free me so far in your most generous thoughts,
That I have shot mine arrow o'er the house,
And hurt my brother.

LAERTES: I am satisfied in nature,°
Whose motive, in this case, should stir me most
To my revenge: but in my terms of honour   215
I stand aloof; and will no reconcilement,
Till by some elder masters, of known honour,
I have a voice° and precedent of peace,
To keep my name ungor'd. But till that time,
I do receive your offer'd love like love,   220
And will not wrong it.

HAMLET: I embrace it freely;
And will this brother's wager frankly play.
Give us the foils. Come on.

---

¹⁹²***all***   all that matters.   ¹⁹⁷***presence***   royal assembly.   ²⁰⁰***exception***   disapproval.   ²¹³***nature***   i.e.,
he is personally satisfied, but his honor must be satisfied by the rules of the code of honor.   ²¹⁸***voice***   authoritative
pronouncement.

LAERTES: Come, one for me.
HAMLET: I'll be your foil,° Laertes: in mine ignorance
   Your skill shall, like a star i' th' darkest night,   225
   Stick fiery off ° indeed.
LAERTES: You mock me, sir.
HAMLET: No, by this hand.
KING: Give them the foils, young Osric. Cousin Hamlet,
   You know the wager?
HAMLET: Very well, my lord;
   Your grace has laid the odds o' th' weaker side.   230
KING: I do not fear it; I have seen you both:
   But since he is better'd, we have therefore odds.
LAERTES: This is too heavy, let me see another.
HAMLET: This likes me well. These foils have all a length?

                [*They prepare to play.*]

OSRIC: Ay, my good lord.   235
KING: Set me the stoups of wine upon that table.
   If Hamlet give the first or second hit,
   Or quit in answer of the third exchange,
   Let all the battlements their ordnance fire;
   The king shall drink to Hamlet's better breath;   240
   And in the cup an union° shall he throw,
   Richer than that which four successive kings
   In Denmark's crown have worn. Give me the cups;
   And let the kettle° to the trumpet speak,
   The trumpet to the cannoneer without,   245
   The cannons to the heavens, the heavens to earth,
   "Now the king drinks to Hamlet." Come begin: *Trumpets the while.*
   And you, the judges, bear a wary eye.
HAMLET: Come on, sir.
LAERTES: Come, my lord.   [*They play.*]
HAMLET: One.
LAERTES: No.
HAMLET: Judgement.
OSRIC: A hit, a very palpable hit.

      Drums, trumpets, and shot. Flourish. A piece goes off.

LAERTES: Well; again.   250
KING: Stay; give me drink. Hamlet, this pearl° is thine;
   Here's to thy health. Give him the cup.
HAMLET: I'll play this bout first; set it by awhile.
   Come. [*They play.*] Another hit; what say you?

---

²²⁴**foil**   *quibble on the two senses: "background which sets something off," and "blunted rapier for fencing."*
²²⁶**Stick fiery off**   *stand out brilliantly.*   ²⁴³**union**   *pearl.*   ²⁴⁴**kettle**   *kettledrum.*   ²⁵¹**pearl**   *i.e.,*
the poison.

LAERTES: A touch, a touch, I do confess 't. 255
KING: Our son shall win.
QUEEN: He's fat,° and scant of breath.
   Here, Hamlet, take my napkin, rub thy brows:
   The queen carouses° to thy fortune, Hamlet.
HAMLET: Good madam!
KING: Gertrude, do not drink.
QUEEN: I will, my lord; I pray you, pardon me.   [*Drinks.*] 260
KING [*aside*]: It is the poison'd cup: it is too late.
HAMLET: I dare not drink yet, madam; by and by.
QUEEN: Come, let me wipe thy face.
LAERTES: My lord, I'll hit him now.
KING: I do not think 't.
LAERTES [*aside*]:   And yet 'tis almost 'gainst my conscience. 265
HAMLET: Come, for the third, Laertes: you but dally;
   I pray you, pass with your best violence;
   I am afeard you make a wanton° of me.
LAERTES: Say you so? come on.   [*They play.*]
OSRIC: Nothing, neither way. 270
LAERTES: Have at you now!

[LAERTES *wounds* HAMLET; *then, in scuffling, they change rapiers,*° *and* HAMLET *wounds* LAERTES.]

KING: Part them; they are incens'd.
HAMLET: Nay, come again.   [*The* QUEEN *falls.*]
OSRIC: Look to the queen there, ho!
HORATIO: They bleed on both sides. How is it, my lord?
OSRIC: How is 't, Laertes?
LAERTES: Why, as a woodcock° to mine own springe,° Osric; 275
   I am justly kill'd with mine own treachery.
HAMLET: How does the queen?
KING: She swounds° to see them bleed.
QUEEN: No, no, the drink, the drink,—O my dear Hamlet,—
   The drink, the drink! I am poison'd.   [*Dies.*]
HAMLET: O villany! Ho! let the door be lock'd: 280
   Treachery! Seek it out.   [LAERTES *falls.*]
LAERTES: It is here, Hamlet: Hamlet, thou art slain;
   No med'cine in the world can do thee good;
   In thee there is not half an hour of life;
   The treacherous instrument is in thy hand, 285

---

²⁵⁶**fat** *not physically fit, out of training. Some earlier editors speculated that the term applied to the corpulence of Richard Burbage, who originally played the part, but the allusion now appears unlikely. "Fat" may also suggest "sweaty."* ²⁵⁸**carouses** *drinks a toast.* ²⁶⁸**wanton** *spoiled child.* ²⁷¹**in scuffling, they change rapiers** *according to a widespread stage tradition, Hamlet receives a scratch, realizes that Laertes's sword is unbated (not blunted), and accordingly forces an exchange.* ²⁷⁵**woodcock** *as type of stupidity or as decoy.* ²⁷⁵**springe** *trap, snare.* ²⁷⁷**swounds** *swoons.*

Unbated° and envenom'd: the foul practice
Hath turn'd itself on me; lo, here I lie,
Never to rise again: thy mother's poison'd:
I can no more: the king, the king's to blame.
HAMLET: The point envenom'd too!   290
   Then, venom, to thy work.   [Stabs the KING.]
ALL: Treason! treason!
KING: O, yet defend me, friends; I am but hurt.
HAMLET: Here, thou incestuous, murd'rous, damned Dane.
   Drink off this potion. Is thy union here?   295
   Follow my mother.   [KING dies.]
LAERTES: He is justly serv'd;
   It is a poison temper'd° by himself.
   Exchange forgiveness with me, noble Hamlet:
   Mine and my father's death come not upon thee,
   Nor thine on me!   [Dies.] 300
HAMLET: Heaven make thee free of it! I follow thee.
   I am dead, Horatio. Wretched queen, adieu!
   You that look pale and tremble at this chance,
   That are but mutes° or audience to this act,
   Had I but time—as this fell sergeant,° Death,   305
   Is strict in his arrest—O, I could tell you—
   But let it be. Horatio, I am dead;
   Thou livest; report me and my cause aright
   To the unsatisfied.
HORATIO: Never believe it:
   I am more an antique Roman° than a Dane: 310
   Here's yet some liquor left.
HAMLET: As th' art a man,
   Give me the cup: let go, by heaven, I'll ha 't.
   O God! Horatio, what a wounded name,
   Things standing thus unknown, shall live behind me!
   If thou didst ever hold me in thy heart,   315
   Absent thee from felicity awhile,
   And in this harsh world draw thy breath in pain,
   To tell my story.   A march afar off.
              What warlike noise is this?
OSRIC: Young Fortinbras, with conquest come from Poland,
   To the ambassadors of England gives   320
   This warlike volley.
HAMLET: O, I die, Horatio;
   The potent poison quite o'er-crows° my spirit:
   I cannot live to hear the news from England;
   But I do prophesy th' election lights

286**Unbated** *Not blunted with a button.*   297**temper'd** *mixed.*   304**mutes** *performers in a play who speak no words.*   305**sergeant** *sheriff's officer.*   310**Roman** *it was the Roman custom to follow masters in death.*   322**o'er-crows** *triumphs over.*

On Fortinbras: he has my dying voice;   325
So tell him, with th' occurrents,° more and less,
Which have solicited.° The rest is silence.   [*Dies.*]
HORATIO: Now cracks a noble heart. Good night, sweet prince;
And flights of angels sing thee to thy rest!
Why does the drum come hither?   [*March within.*] 330

    Enter FORTINBRAS, *with the* [English] AMBASSADORS [*and others*].

FORTINBRAS: Where is this sight?
HORATIO: What is it you would see?
If aught of woe or wonder, cease your search.
FORTINBRAS: This quarry° cries on havoc.° O proud Death,
What feast is toward in thine eternal cell,
That thou so many princes at a shot   335
So bloodily hast struck?
FIRST AMBASSADOR: The sight is dismal;
And our affairs from England come too late:
The ears are senseless that should give us hearing,
To tell him his commandment is fulfill'd,
That Rosencrantz and Guildenstern are dead: 340
Where should we have our thanks?
HORATIO: Not from his mouth,°
Had it th' ability of life to thank you:
He never gave commandment for their death.
But since, so jump° upon this bloody question,°
You from the Polack wars, and you from England,   345
Are here arriv'd, give order that these bodies
High on a stage° be placed to the view;
And let me speak to th' yet unknowing world
How these things came about: so shall you hear
Of carnal, bloody, and unnatural acts,   350
Of accidental judgements, casual slaughters,
Of deaths put on by cunning and forc'd cause,
And, in this upshot, purposes mistook
Fall'n on th' inventors' heads: all this can I
Truly deliver.
FORTINBRAS: Let us haste to hear it,   355
And call the noblest to the audience.
For me, with sorrow I embrace my fortune:
I have some rights of memory° in this kingdom,
Which now to claim my vantage doth invite me.
HORATIO: Of that I shall have also cause to speak,   360
And from his mouth whose voice will draw on more:°

---

³²⁶*occurrents*   *events, incidents.*   ³²⁷*solicited*   *moved, urged.*   ³³³*quarry*   *heap of dead.*   ³³³*cries on*
havoc   *proclaims a general slaughter.*   ³⁴¹*his mouth*   *i.e., the king's.*   ³⁴⁴*jump*   *precisely.*   ³⁴⁴*ques-*
tion   *dispute.*   ³⁴⁷ *stage*   *platform.*   ³⁵⁸*of memory*   *traditional, remembered.*   ³⁶¹*voice ... more*
vote will influence still others.

But let this same be presently perform'd,
Even while men's minds are wild; lest more mischance,
On° plots and errors, happen.
FORTINBRAS: Let four captains
Bear Hamlet, like a soldier, to the stage;   365
For he was likely, had he been put on,
To have prov'd most royal: and, for his passage,°
The soldiers' music and the rites of war
Speak loudly for him.
Take up the bodies: such a sight as this   370
Becomes the field,° but here shows much amiss.
Go, bid the soldiers shoot.

Exeunt [marching, bearing off the dead bodies; after which a peal of ordnance is shot off].

(1600)

QUESTIONS FOR REFLECTION

Experience

1. Describe your experience of reading *Hamlet*. If this is your second or later reading of the play, compare this reading experience with earlier ones.
2. If you have seen the play performed, compare your experience of seeing it with your experience of reading it.

Interpretation

3. What makes Hamlet a tragic figure? To what extent is he responsible for the tragic events of the play?
4. Compare Hamlet's speeches from the beginning and end of the play. Select one of his speeches from Act I or II and compare its tone, attitude, and feeling with a speech from the last act.
5. Explain the roles of Laertes and Fortinbras in the play.
6. What reasons are suggested for Hamlet's delay in exacting revenge for his father's death? Do you find these reasons plausible? Why or why not?
7. Identify the various settings in the play. Explain how each setting contributes to the play's dramatic mood and action. Compare, for example, the settings in Act I, scene i, and Act I, scene ii.
8. What images of women are found in the play? How are Ophelia and Gertrude characterized?
9. Discuss the character of Claudius. Can he be considered a tragic figure? Why or why not?

<hr>

364**On**   *on account of, or possibly, on top of, in addition to.*   367**passage**   *death.*   371**field**   *i.e., of battle.*

10. Characterize Horatio. What functions does Horatio serve in the play? Which of his personal qualities does Hamlet most admire? Why?
11. Rosencrantz and Guildenstern appear briefly and then disappear from the play. Explain their purpose for the plot of the play.
12. Explain how you would direct the actor playing Polonius. How, for example, would you advise the actor to deliver Polonius's counsel? How much self-knowledge and understanding do you think Polonius possesses?
13. Compare Hamlet and Othello as tragic heroes. What qualities of character distinguish them?
14. Compare Claudius and Iago as villains who precipitate tragedy in the lives of others.
15. What does the gravedigger scene in Act V, scene i, contribute to the play's tone and themes?
16. Any staging of *Hamlet* requires careful attention to lighting. Single out any two scenes in which lighting seems important and explain how you would stage these scenes.
17. Identify two scenes in which the characters' speeches shift between verse and prose. Explain the significance of these shifts.
18. One of the highlights of *Hamlet* is its language. Single out two places where you find the language especially rich, complex, and suggestive. You may choose soliloquies, dialogue exchanges, or both.

Evaluation

19. Whose values does the play most seriously question? Most rigorously criticize? Most generously support?
20. According to some critics, *Hamlet* is Shakespeare's greatest play. What are some of its most accomplished aspects?

CRITICS ON SHAKESPEARE

ADRIAN POOLE

Hamlet and Oedipus

FROM *TRAGEDY: SHAKESPEARE AND THE GREEK EXAMPLE*

For Freud, Hamlet was always closely associated with Oedipus. Again Freud finds a likeness solely in what the two fictional characters suffer from, the desires with which they are supposedly cursed. But Hamlet too has a side to him that Freud ignores. What Hamlet has in common with Oedipus and Freud is that he asks a lot of questions. Freud sees only half of each character, the half that could play the part of patient to his own analyst. And in extricating them from their own dramas and recasting them in his own, Freud seizes the role of analyst for himself, displacing the Oedipus and the Hamlet who make such courageous efforts to understand the story of their lives in the very act of its composition.

The most significant thing that Freud has to say about Sophocles' Oedipus is to do with the form and structure of the play rather than its hidden content: "The action of the play consists in nothing other than the process of revelation, with cunning delays and ever mounting excitement—a process that can be likened to the work of a psychoanalysis—that Oedipus himself is the murderer of Laius." "The work of a psychoanalysis": that is, the specific confrontation and intercourse between analyst and patient. This suggests that a psychoanalysis is constructed like a tragedy, or at least like this tragedy, and that what a psychoanalysis and a tragedy have in common is something to do with their work of discovery. In each case we are moved by the products of revelation only in so far as we are moved by the process of revelation.

When we consider the importance of Oedipus for Freud, we should therefore recall not only the image of a man who acts out our (supposedly) deepest fantasies, but also the action of the play through which Oedipus must discover the truth. If there is a "compulsion" in Sophocles' play, it is much less obviously the compulsion to act out infantile fantasies than the compulsion to know the truth. Sophocles' Oedipus and Shakespeare's Hamlet are the two characters in tragic drama most actively engaged in analysis and interpretation. Their importance for Freud is more to do with a passion for knowledge than with an occult or repressed guilt. Or rather, it is with their exploration of the mysterious relations between knowledge and guilt, a mystery which Freud radically simplifies by attributing guilt solely to the object of interpretation.

Oedipus and Hamlet are on their own within their worlds. Watching their efforts to interpret and understand from within the flow of their own lives, we recognize a universal predicament. Both Oedipus and Hamlet possess great powers of mind, but the questions to which they address themselves involve their whole being. The riddles they attempt to solve, the guilts discovered and incurred in the process of trying to solve them, these are written in flesh and blood, their own and others'.

JOHN ASHWORTH

Olivier, Freud, and Hamlet

FROM *THE ATLANTIC MONTHLY*

Following the fashion in movies and books, Sir Laurence Olivier has acted and directed a *Hamlet* with a simplified Freudian interpretation. The mad Ophelia makes caressing motions over a phallic ornament on the back of a chair, the camera focuses with heavy significance on the labial drapes over the Queen's bed, and why Hamlet doesn't kill the King in the first reel can be explained only in Hamlet's unconscious. In brief, the drama of Hamlet's life is replaced by the drama of what Hamlet might reveal from a couch.

At the beginning of the movie, a narrator intones through the fogs of Elsinore: "This is the tragedy of a man who couldn't make up his mind." Then Sir Laurence appears as the ineffective dreamer, the hysteric, the oversensitive "scholar." Hamlet's alleged procrastination, which for over a century was considered a literary enigma, is attributed—by Freudian trappings, by the neurasthenic quality of the acting, and by cutting significant parts of the play—to the Oedipus complex.

After writing that Shakespeare's play "does not give the cause or motive" of Hamlet's "hesitation," Freud himself explained it as follows: Hamlet can't take vengeance upon the man who takes his father's place with his mother, because Hamlet as a child has repressed the desire to do the same thing. So Hamlet's unconscious tells him that "he himself is no better than the murderer whom he is required to punish," and the "loathing" which should have driven him to revenge is replaced by "self-reproach" and "conscientious scruples." Thus Freud found an explanation for what most intellectuals of his generation, following Goethe and other nineteenth century critics, already believed in—Hamlet's "hesitation."

The main trouble with this "interpretation" is that Hamlet does not hesitate. He does in fact kill the King with remarkable dispatch, as a whole generation of Shakespearians since George Lyman Kittredge have pointed out. So Freud's description of Hamlet's character was based on a wrong premise. Because he couldn't perceive Hamlet's motives, he swallowed the nonsense that a workmanlike dramatist like Shakespeare had written a play without showing the motives of the central character. In consequence he was able to exchange for Hamlet's real motives the prevalent "interpretation" of his day that Hamlet was a procrastinator, and then to deal clinically with the alleged procrastination. . . .

Let's look at the play as Shakespeare intended it to be looked at—from the point of view of an Elizabethan audience. To them, Hamlet's "hesitation" is no occult problem because the play is half over before Hamlet can be sure that the King really did the murder. All that Hamlet has to go on is the word of a ghost, and he isn't sure of the Ghost's identity. For Hamlet, like nearly all Elizabethans, not only believes in ghosts, but also believes that demons can masquerade as ghosts. The apparition may be the ghost of his father or it may be a demon disguised as the ghost of his father, trying to trick him into killing an innocent man. This doubt about the Ghost was perfectly clear to an Elizabethan audience, if not to Freud; and because it is of first importance in understanding the plot, Shakespeare takes the trouble, as any competent dramatist might, to explain it three times: when Hamlet first speaks to the Ghost ("Be thou a spirit of health or goblin damn'd . . . ?"); in Horatio's warning not to follow the Ghost ("What is it tempt you toward the flood, my lord, . . . And there assume some other, horrible form . . . ?"); and in Hamlet's explanation that he will use the players to trick the King into revealing his guilt, if he is guilty.

When Freud ignores Hamlet's sensible precaution not to kill a man who might be innocent and assumes that Hamlet is hesitating to kill a man with whom he unconsciously identifies himself, he simply annihilates the Elizabethan audience for whom Shakespeare wrote, to whom Hamlet's scheme in the players' scene was obvious.

MAYNARD MACK

The Readiness Is All: Hamlet

FROM *Everybody's Shakespeare*

Hamlet's world is preeminently in the interrogative mood. It reverberates with questions, anguished, meditative, alarmed. There are questions that in this play, to an extent I think unparalleled in any other, mark the phases and even the nuances of the action, helping to establish its peculiar baffled tone. There are other questions whose interrogations, innocent at first glance, are subsequently seen to have reached beyond their contexts and to point toward some pervasive inscrutability in Hamlet's world as a whole. Such is that tense series of challenges with which the tragedy begins: Bernardo's of Francisco, "Who's there?" Francisco's of Horatio and Marcellus, "Who is there?" Horatio's of the ghost, "What art thou . . . ?"

And then there are the famous questions. In them the interrogations seem to point not only beyond the context but beyond the play, out of Hamlet's predicaments into everyone's: "What a piece of work is a man! . . . And yet to me what is this quintessence of dust?" (Act 2. Scene 2). "To be, or not to be—that is the question" (3.1.). "Get thee to a nunnery. Why wouldst thou be a breeder of sinners?" (3.1.). "I am very proud, revengeful, ambitious, with more offenses at my beck than I have thoughts to put them in, imagination to give them shape, or time to act them in. What should such fellows as I do crawling between earth and heaven?" (3.1.). "Dost thou think Alexander looked o' this fashion i' th' earth? . . . And smelt so?" (5.1.).

Further, Hamlet's world is a world of riddles. The hero's own language is often riddling, as the critics have pointed out. When he puns, his puns have receding depths in them, like the one which constitutes his first speech: "A little more than kin, and less than kind!" (1.2.). His utterances in madness, even if wild and whirling, are simultaneously, as Polonius discovers, pregnant: "Do you know me, my lord?" "Excellent well. You are a fishmonger" (2.2.). Even the madness itself is riddling: How much is real? How much is feigned? What does it mean?

Sane or mad, Hamlet's mind plays restlessly about his world, turning up one riddle upon another. The riddle of character, for example, and how it is that in a man whose virtues else are "pure as grace," some vicious mole of nature, some "dram of evil," can "all the noble substance [oft adulter]" (1.4.). Or the riddle of the player's art, and how a man can so project himself into a fiction, a dream of passion, that he can weep for Hecuba (2.2.). Or the riddle of action: how we may think too little—"What to ourselves in passion we propose," says the player-king. "The passion ending, doth the purpose lose" (3.2.); and again, how we may think too much: "Thus conscience does make cowards of us all, And thus the native hue of resolution Is sicklied o'er with the pale cast of thought" (3.1.).

There are also more immediate riddles. His mother—how could she "on this fair mountain leave to feed, And batten on this moor" (3.4.)? The ghost—which may be a devil, for "the devil hath power T' assume a pleasing shape" (2.2.). Ophelia—what does her behavior to him mean? Surprising her in her closet, he falls to such perusal of her face as he would draw it (2.1.). Even the king at his prayers is a riddle. Will a revenge that takes him in the purging of his soul be vengeance, or hire and salary (3.3.)? As for himself, Hamlet realizes, he is the greatest riddle of all—a mystery, he warns Rosencrantz and Guildenstern, from which he will not have the heart plucked out. He cannot tell why he has of late lost all his mirth, forgone all custom of exercises. Still less can he tell why he delays: "I do not know Why yet I live to say, 'This thing's to do,' Sith I have cause, and will, and strength, and means To do't" (4.4.).

Thus the mysteriousness of Hamlet's world is of a piece. It is not simply a matter of missing motivations, to be expunged if only we could find the perfect clue. It is built in. It is evidently an important part of what the play wishes to say to us. And it is certainly an element that the play thrusts upon us from the opening word. Everyone, I think, recalls the mysteriousness of that first scene. The cold middle of the night on the castle platform, the muffled sentries, the uneasy atmosphere of apprehension, the challenges leaping out of the dark, the questions that follow the challenges, feeling out the darkness, searching for identities, for relations, for assurance. "Bernardo?" "Have you had quiet guard?" "Who hath relieved you?" "What, is Horatio there?" "What, has this thing appeared again tonight?" "Looks 'a not like the king?" "How now, Horatio! . . . Is not this something more than fantasy? What think you on 't?" "Is it not like the King?" "Why this same strict and most observant watch . . . ?" "Shall I strike at it with my partisan?" "Do you consent we shall acquaint [young Hamlet] with it?"

We need not be surprised that critics and playgoers alike have been tempted to see in this an evocation not simply of Hamlet's world but of their own. Human beings in their aspect of bafflement, moving in darkness on a rampart between two worlds, unable to reject, or quite accept, the one that, when they face it, "to-shakes" their dispositions with thoughts beyond the reaches of their souls—comforting themselves with hints and guesses. We hear these hints and guesses whispering through the darkness as the several watchers speak. "At least, the whisper goes so" (1.1.), says one. "I think it be no other but e'en so," says another. "I have heard" that on the crowing of the cock "Th' extravagant and erring spirit hies To his confine," says a third. "Some say" at Christmas time "This bird of dawning" sings all night, "And then, they say, no spirit dare stir abroad." "So have I heard," says the first, "and do in part believe it." However we choose to take the scene, it is clear that it creates a world where uncertainties are of the essence.

CAROLYN HEILBRUN

The Character of Hamlet's Mother

FROM *HAMLET'S MOTHER AND OTHER WOMEN*

To understand Gertrude properly, it is only necessary to examine the lines Shakespeare has chosen for her to say. She is, except for her description of Ophelia's death, concise and pithy in speech, with a talent for seeing the essence of every situation presented before her eyes. If she is not profound, she is certainly never silly. We first hear her asking

Hamlet to stop wearing black, to stop walking about with his eyes downcast, and to realize that death is an inevitable part of life. She is, in short, asking him not to give way to the passion of grief, a passion of whose force and dangers the Elizabethans were aware, as Miss Campbell has shown. Claudius echoes her with a well-reasoned argument against grief which was, in its philosophy if not in its language, a piece of commonplace Elizabethan lore. After Claudius' speech, Gertrude asks Hamlet to remain in Denmark, where he is rightly loved. Her speeches have been short, however warm and loving, and conciseness of statement is not the mark of a dull and shallow woman.

We next hear her, as Queen and gracious hostess, welcoming Rosencrantz and Guildenstern to the court, hoping, with the King, that they may cheer Hamlet and discover what is depressing him. Claudius then tells Gertrude, when they are alone, that Polonius believes he knows what is upsetting Hamlet. The Queen answers:

> I doubt it is no other than the main,
> His father's death and our o'er-hasty marriage.
> (II.ii. 56–57)

This statement is concise, remarkably to the point, and not a little courageous. It is not the statement of a dull, slothful woman who can only echo her husband's words. Next, Polonius enters with his most unbrief apotheosis to brevity. The Queen interrupts him with five words: "More matter, with less art" (II. ii. 95). It would be difficult to find a phrase more applicable to Polonius. When this gentleman, in no way deterred from his loquacity, after purveying the startling news that he has a daughter, begins to read a letter, the Queen asks pointedly "Came this from Hamlet to her?" (II. ii. 114).

We see Gertrude next in Act III, asking Rosencrantz and Guildenstern, with her usual directness, if Hamlet received them well, and if they were able to tempt him to any pastime. But before leaving the room, she stops for a word of kindness to Ophelia. It is a humane gesture, for she is unwilling to leave Ophelia, the unhappy tool of the King and Polonius, without some kindly and intelligent appreciation of her help:

> And for your part, Ophelia, I do wish
> That your good beauties be the happy cause
> Of Hamlet's wildness. So shall I hope your virtues
> Will bring him to his wonted way again,
> To both your honors.   (III. i. 38–42)

[S]he dies. But before she dies she does not waste time on vituperation; she warns Hamlet that the drink is poisoned to prevent his drinking it. They are her last words. Those critics who have thought her stupid admire her death; they call it uncharacteristic.

In Act III, when Hamlet goes to his mother in her closet his nerves are pitched at the very height of tension; he is on the edge of hysteria. The possibility of murdering his mother has in fact entered his mind, and he has just met and refused an opportunity to kill Claudius. His mother, meanwhile, waiting for him, has told Polonius not to fear for her, but she knows when she sees Hamlet that he may be violently mad. Hamlet quips with her, insults her, tells her he wishes she were not his mother, and when she, still retaining dignity, attempts to end the interview, Hamlet seizes her and she cries for help. The important thing to note is that the Queen's cry "Thou wilt not murder me?" (III. iv. 21) is not foolish. She has seen from Hamlet's demeanor that he is capable of murder, as indeed in the next instant he proves himself to be.

We next learn from the Queen's startled "As kill a king?" (III. iv. 31) that she has no knowledge of the murder, though of course this is only confirmation here of what we already know. Then the Queen asks Hamlet why he is so hysterical:

> What have I done, that thou dar'st wag thy tongue
> In noise so rude against me?   (III. iv. 40–41)

Hamlet tells her: it is her lust, the need of sexual passion, which has driven her from the arms and memory of her husband to the incomparably cruder charms of his brother.

A. D. NUTTAL

Othello

FROM *A NEW MIMESIS*

Othello's tragedy indeed is strangely—and formally—introverted; it consists in the fact that he left the arena proper to tragedy, the battlefield, and entered a subtragic world for which he was not fitted. *Othello* is the story of a hero who went into a house.

Long ago A. C. Bradley observed that, if the heroes of *Hamlet* and *Othello* change places, each play ends very quickly. Hamlet would see through Iago in the first five minutes and be parodying him in the next. Othello, receiving clear instructions like "Kill that usurper" from a ghost, would simply have gone to work. Thus, as the classic problem of *Hamlet* is the hero's delay, so the classic problem of *Othello* is the hero's gullibility. The stronger our sense of Othello's incongruity in the domestic world, the less puzzling this becomes. Certainly, *Othello* is about a man who, having come from a strange and remote place, found his feet in the world of Venetian professional soldier-ship—and then exchanged that spacious world for a little, dim world of unimaginable horror. "War is no strife/To the dark house and the detested wife" comes not from Othello but from a comedy, but it will serve here. Its note of peculiarly masculine pain and hatred can still score the nerves. It is therefore not surprising that Shakespeare avails himself of the metaphor of the caged hawk. Desdemona says, "I'll watch him tame," at III. iii. 23. The real process of taming a hawk by keeping it awake and so breaking its spirit is described at length in T. H. White's *The Goshawk* [1953]. Othello turns the image round when he says of Desdemona,

> If I do prove her haggard,
> Though that her jesses were my dear heart-strings,
> I'd whistle her off and let her down the wind

To prey at fortune.   (III. iii. 259–62)

He speaks formally of Desdemona, but it is hard not to feel that in the last words it is his own dream of liberty which speaks.

Othello is also about insiders and outsiders. The exotic Moor finds when he leaves the public, martial sphere that he is not accepted, is not understood and cannot understand. The Venetian colour bar is sexual, not professional. Iago plays on this with his "old black ram . . . tupping your white ewe" (I. i. 85–86) and the same note is struck by Roderigo with his "gross clasps of a lascivious Moor" (I. i. 121). Othello's gullibility is not really so very strange. Coal-black among the glittering Venetians, he is visibly the outsider, and in his bewilderment he naturally looks for the man who is visibly the insider, the man who knows the ropes, the sort of man who is always around in the bar, the "good chap" or (as they said then) the "honest" man. And he finds him.

There are two schools of thought on the sort of actor who should play Iago. School A chooses a dark, waspish fellow. School B chooses a bluff, straw-haired, pink-faced sort of man, solid-looking with no nonsense about him. In production School B triumphs, for the role, cast in this way, becomes both credible and terrifying. Although Iago is everywhere spoken of as a "good chap," he has no friends, no loves, no positive desires. He, and not Othello, proves to be the true outsider of the play, for he is foreign to humanity itself. Othello comes from a remote clime, but Iago, in his simpler darkness, comes from the far side of chaos—hence the pathos of Shakespeare's best departure from his source. In Cinthio's *novella* the Ensign (that is, the Iago-figure) with a cunning affectation of reluctance, suggests that Desdemona is false and then seeing his chance, adds, "Your blackness already displeases her." In Shakespeare's play we have instead a note of bar-room masculine intimacy, in assumed complicity of sentiment. Iago says, in effect "Well, she went with black man, so what is one to think?" (III. iii. 228–33). Othello's need to be accepted and guided makes him an easy victim of this style. The hero is set for his sexual humiliation.

MAURICE CHARNEY

Shakespeare's Villains

FROM *HOW TO READ SHAKESPEARE*

The malevolence of Shakespeare's villains is difficult to account for either by their past history or by their present grievances. Shakespeare wants to avoid giving them a believable background that would justify or explain their evil. The villains are generally not motivated at all—at least not by detective-story standards—but are presented to us already securely entrenched in their moral condition. Their evil is a positive and active force, and its unquestioned energy makes the villains seem diabolic. We need to accept them as they appear without probing the origins of their conduct. This requires forbearance from the audience, whose love of scandalous explanation is deliberately frustrated.

What are we to make of the reasons Iago offers for his savage revenge on Othello? Is he acting from thwarted ambition, because Cassio has the promotion Iago thinks he himself deserves? Or are the reasons more subtle and more personal? As Iago tells us,

> I hate the Moor;
> And it is thought abroad that 'twixt my
>   sheets
> 'Has done my office. I know not if 't be true;
> Yet I, for mere suspicion in that kind,
> Will do as if for surety.   (1.3.356–60)

There is a cynical coldness in "I know not if 't be true," and Iago never troubles himself to find out. Personal honor means nothing to him, since in his view all women are whores and all human activity is base, coarse, gross, and disgusting. What is important is that Iago hates the Moor. That is enough, and reasons are alleged merely to satisfy public opinion.

In a much-quoted phrase, Coleridge spoke of this aspect of Iago's morality as the "motive-hunting of motiveless malignity." In other words, there are no motives and there is no cause that can account for Iago's evil. Othello never understands this, because even at the very end of the play he still wants to learn from that "demi-devil" "Why he hath thus ensnar'd my soul and body" (5.2.298). But Iago refuses any final comforts for Othello's tragic rationalism: "Demand me nothing. What you know, you know./ From this time forth I never will speak word" (299–300). Ultimately, there can be no answer to Othello's question. We have only a hint of explanation when Iago justifies the murder of Cassio: "He hath a daily beauty in his life/ That makes me ugly" (5.1.19–20). This judgment has the true satanic ring. Like Lucifer, Iago is irresistibly attracted to the beauty from which he has been excluded for all eternity, and this sense of damnation makes his revenge so monomaniacal.

Iago is Shakespeare's most brilliant villain, who dominates his play in a way no other villain can (except perhaps Macbeth, a villain-hero). He forces us to consider one of the most difficult paradoxes of tragedy: Why is the villain usually so much more intelligent, insightful, sensitive, and imaginative than his victim? The villain seems to be the surrogate for the diabolic-creative powers of the dramatist. Iago is wonderfully complex in his manipulation of the dramatic action; his plots and Shakespeare's seem to come together, so that one could speak of the stagecraft of villainy and its aesthetics. But in his moral nature Iago is wonderfully simple, if not actually simplified. The presence of both Iago and Desdemona in a single play assumes that good and evil exist as warring postulates. This is the morality play aspect of Shakespearean tragedy.

CHAPTER SEVEN

The Modern Realistic Theater: Ibsen

Realism can be defined as the representation of everyday life in literature. Concerned with the average, the commonplace, the ordinary, realism employs theatrical conventions to create the illusion of everyday life. With realistic drama came the depiction of subjects close to the lives of middle-class people: work, marriage, and family life. From this standpoint, Arthur Miller's *Death of a Salesman* and Henrik Ibsen's *A Doll House* are more realistic than Shakespeare's *Othello,* which in turn, is more realistic than Sophocles' *Oedipus Rex*. Though each of these plays possesses a true-to-life quality, each operates according to different theatrical conventions. Royal personages, gods, military heroes, and exalted language are absent from Miller's and Ibsen's plays, as modern dramatists turned to an approximation of the daily life of the lower and middle classes.

One means by which realistic drama creates the illusion of everyday life is through setting. Whereas settings consist primarily of painted backdrops in Molière's plays and are often established by dialogue in Shakespeare's plays, the settings of modern realistic plays are designed to look authentic. Moreover, setting in plays such as Ibsen's *A Doll House* often functions symbolically. In *Elements of Literature 3,* Robert Scholes has noted that the elaborately detailed setting of *A Doll House* symbolizes both "the impact of the Helmers' environment on their marriage" and the "very nature of their marriage"; it also embodies "the profound pressures placed on Helmer and Nora by the material and social conditions of their world."★

Other conventions designed to create and sustain the illusion that the audience was watching a slice of domestic life include the following: the use of a three-walled room with an open fourth wall into which the audience peers to view and overhear the action; dialogue that approximates the idiom of everyday discourse, polished to be sure, but designed especially to sound like speech rather than poetry; plots that, though highly contrived, seem to turn on a series of causally related actions; subjects not from mythology or history, but from the concerns of ordinary life.

INTRODUCTION TO HENRIK IBSEN

[1828–1906]

Besides accommodating himself to the conventions of realism in *A Doll House,* Ibsen also made the play a *cause célèbre* by raising questions in it about the rights of women, a subject that was beginning to receive attention in the late nineteenth century. *A Doll House,* written in 1879, performed in London (1889) and Paris (1894), attracted attention wherever it played. Nonetheless, Ibsen insisted that the play was less about the rights of women than about human rights generally, less about the particular social conditions responsible for the position of women in nineteenth-century Norway than about the need for individuals of both sexes to treat each other with mutual respect.

A Doll House

TRANSLATED BY ROLF FJELDE

CHARACTERS

TORVALD HELMER, *a lawyer*
NORA, *his wife*
DR. RANK
MRS. LINDE
NILS KROGSTAD, *a bank clerk*
THE HELMERS' THREE SMALL CHILDREN
ANNE-MARIE, *their nurse*
HELENE, *a maid*
A DELIVERY BOY

The action takes place in HELMER*'s residence.*

★Robert Scholes et al., *Elements of Literature 3* (New York: Oxford University Press, 1982), p. 966.

ACT I

A comfortable room, tastefully but not expensively furnished. A door to the right in the back wall leads to the entryway, another to the left leads to HELMER'*s study. Between these doors, a piano. Midway in the left-hand wall a door, and further back a window. Near the window a round table with an armchair and a small sofa. In the right-hand wall, toward the rear a door, and nearer the foreground a porcelain stove with two armchairs and a rocking chair beside it. Between the stove and the side door, a small table. Engravings on the walls. An* etagére *with china figures and other small art objects; a small bookcase with richly bound books; the floor carpeted; a fire burning in the stove. It is a winter day.*

A bell rings in the entryway; shortly after we hear the door being unlocked. NORA *comes into the room, humming happily to herself; she is wearing street clothes and carries an armload of packages, which she puts down on the table to the right. She has left the hall door open; and through it a* DELIVERY BOY *is seen, holding a Christmas tree and a basket which he gives to the* MAID *who let them in.*

NORA: Hide the tree well, Helene. The children mustn't get a glimpse of it till this evening, after it's trimmed. (*To the* DELIVERY BOY, *taking out her purse*) How much?

DELIVERY BOY: Fifty, ma'am.

NORA: There's a crown. No, keep the change. (*The* BOY *thanks her and leaves.* NORA *shuts the door. She laughs softly to herself while taking off her street things. Drawing a bag of macaroons from her pocket, she eats a couple, then steals over and listens at her husband's study door.*) Yes, he's home. (*Hums again as she moves to the table, right.*)

HELMER (*from the study*):   Is that my little lark twittering out there?

NORA (*busy opening some packages*):   Yes, it is.

HELMER: Is that my squirrel rummaging around?

NORA: Yes!

HELMER: When did my squirrel get in?

NORA: Just now. (*Putting the macaroon bag in her pocket and wiping her mouth*) Do come in, Torvald, and see what I've bought.

HELMER: Can't be disturbed. (*After a moment he opens the door and peers in, pen in hand.*) Bought, you say? All that there? Has the little spendthrift been out throwing money around again?

NORA: Oh, but Torvald, this year we really should let ourselves go a bit. It's the first Christmas we haven't had to economize.

HELMER: But you know we can't go squandering.

NORA: Oh yes, Torvald, we can squander a little now. Can't we? Just a tiny, wee bit. Now that you've got a big salary and are going to make piles and piles of money.

HELMER: Yes—starting New Year's. But then it's a full three months till the raise comes through.

NORA: Pooh! We can borrow that long.

HELMER: Nora! (*Goes over and playfully takes her by the ear*) Are your scatterbrains off again? What if today I borrowed a thousand crowns, and you squandered them over Christmas week, and then on New Year's Eve a roof tile fell on my head, and I lay there—

NORA (*putting her hand on his mouth*):   Oh! Don't say such things!

HELMER: Yes, but what if it happened—then what?

NORA: If anything so awful happened, then it just wouldn't matter if I had debts or not.

HELMER: Well, but the people I'd borrowed from?

NORA: Them? Who cares about them! They're strangers.

HELMER: Nora, Nora, how like a woman! No, but seriously, Nora, you know what I think about that. No debts! Never borrow! Something of freedom's lost—and something of beauty, too—from a home that's founded on borrowing and debt. We've made a brave stand up to now, the two of us; and we'll go right on like that the little while we have to.

NORA (*going toward the stove*):   Yes, whatever you say, Torvald.

HELMER (*following her*):   Now, now, the little lark's wings mustn't droop. Come on, don't be a sulky squirrel. (*Taking out his wallet*) Nora, guess what I have here.

NORA (*turning quickly*):   Money!

HELMER: There, see. (*Hands her some notes*) Good grief, I know how costs go up in a house at Christmastime.

NORA: Ten—twenty—thirty—forty. Oh, thank you. Torvald; I can manage no end on this.

HELMER: You really will have to.

NORA: Oh yes, I promise I will! But come here so I can show you everything I bought. And so cheap! Look, new clothes for Ivar here—and a sword. Here a horse and a trumpet for Bob. And a doll and a doll's bed here for Emmy; they're nothing much, but she'll tear them to bits in no time anyway. And here I have dress material and handkerchiefs for the maids. Old Anne-Marie really deserves something more.

HELMER: And what's in that package there?

NORA (*with a cry*):   Torvald, no! You can't see that till tonight!

HELMER: I see. But tell me now, you little prodigal, what have you thought of for yourself?

NORA: For myself? Oh, I don't want anything at all.

HELMER: Of course you do. Tell me just what—within reason—you'd most like to have.

NORA: I honestly don't know. Oh, listen, Torvald—

HELMER: Well?

NORA (*fumbling at his coat buttons, without looking at him*):   If you want to give me something, then maybe you could—you could—

HELMER: Come on, out with it.

NORA (*hurriedly*):   You could give me money, Torvald. No more than you think you can spare, then one of these days I'll buy something with it.

HELMER: But Nora—

NORA: Oh, please, Torvald darling, do that! I beg you, please. Then I could hang the bills in pretty gilt paper on the Christmas tree. Wouldn't that be fun?

HELMER: What are those little birds called that always fly through their fortunes?

NORA: Oh yes, spendthrifts; I know all that. But let's do as I say, Torvald; then I'll have time to decide what I really need most. That's very sensible, isn't it?

HELMER (*smiling*):   Yes, very—that is, if you actually hung onto the money I give you, and you actually used it to buy yourself something. But it goes for the house and for all sorts of foolish things, and then I only have to lay out some more.

NORA: Oh, but Torvald—

HELMER: Don't deny it, my dear little Nora. (*Putting his arm around her waist*) Spendthrifts are sweet, but they use up a frightful amount of money. It's incredible what it costs a man to feed such birds.

NORA: Oh, how can you say that! Really, I save everything I can.

HELMER (*laughing*):   Yes, that's the truth. Everything you can. But that's nothing at all.

NORA (*humming, with a smile of quiet satisfaction*):   Hm, if you only knew what expenses we larks and squirrels have, Torvald.

HELMER: You're an odd little one. Exactly the way your father was. You're never at a loss for scaring up money; but the moment you have it, it runs right out through your fingers; you never know what you've done with it. Well, one takes you as you are. It's deep in your blood. Yes, these things are hereditary, Nora.

NORA: Ah, I could wish I'd inherited many of Papa's qualities.

HELMER: And I couldn't wish you anything but just what you are, my sweet little lark. But wait; it seems to me you have a very—what should I call it?—a very suspicious look today—

NORA: I do?

HELMER: You certainly do. Look me straight in the eye.

NORA (*looking at him*):   Well?

HELMER (*shaking an admonitory finger*):   Surely my sweet tooth hasn't been running riot in town today, has she?

NORA: No. Why do you imagine that?

HELMER: My sweet tooth really didn't make a little detour through the confectioner's?

NORA: No, I assure you, Torvald—

HELMER: Hasn't nibbled some pastry?

NORA: No, not at all.

HELMER: Nor even munched a macaroon or two?

NORA: No, Torvald, I assure you, really—

HELMER: There, there now. Of course I'm only joking.

NORA (*going to the table, right*):   You know I could never think of going against you.

HELMER: No, I understand that; and you *have* given me your word. (*Going over to her.*) Well, you keep your little Christmas secrets to yourself, Nora darling. I expect they'll come to light this evening, when the tree is lit.

NORA: Did you remember to ask Dr. Rank?

HELMER: No. But there's no need for that; it's assumed he'll be dining with us. All the same, I'll ask him when he stops by here this morning. I've ordered some fine wine. Nora, you can't imagine how I'm looking forward to this evening.

NORA: So am I. And what fun for the children, Torvald!

HELMER: Ah, it's so gratifying to know that one's gotten a safe, secure job, and with a comfortable salary. It's a great satisfaction, isn't it?

NORA: Oh, it's wonderful!

HELMER: Remember last Christmas? Three whole weeks before, you shut yourself in every evening till long after midnight, making flowers for the Christmas tree, and all the other decorations to surprise us. Ugh, that was the dullest time I've ever lived through.

NORA: It wasn't at all dull for me.

HELMER (*smiling*):   But the outcome *was* pretty sorry, Nora.

NORA: Oh, don't tease me with that again. How could I help it that the cat came in and tore everything to shreds.

HELMER: No, poor thing, you certainly couldn't. You wanted so much to please us all, and that's what counts. But it's just as well that the hard times are past.

NORA: Yes, it's really wonderful.

HELMER: Now I don't have to sit here alone, boring myself, and you don't have to tire your precious eyes and your fair little delicate hands—

NORA (*clapping her hands*):   No, is it really true, Torvald, I don't have to? Oh, how wonderfully lovely to hear! (*Taking his arm.*) Now I'll tell you just how I've thought we should plan things. Right after Christmas—(*The doorbell rings.*) Oh, the bell. (*Straightening the room up a bit.*) Somebody would have to come. What a bore!

HELMER: I'm not at home to visitors, don't forget.

MAID (*from the hall doorway*):   Ma'am, a lady to see you—

NORA: All right, let her come in.

MAID (*to Helmer*):   And the doctor's just come too.

HELMER: Did he go right to my study?

MAID: Yes, he did.

HELMER *goes into his room. The* MAID *shows in* MRS. LINDE, *dressed in traveling clothes, and shuts the door after her.*

MRS. LINDE (*in a dispirited and somewhat hesitant voice*):   Hello, Nora.

NORA (*uncertain*):   Hello—

MRS. LINDE: You don't recognize me.

NORA: No, I don't know—but wait, I think—(*Exclaiming.*) What! Kristine! Is it really you?

MRS. LINDE: Yes, it's me.

NORA: Kristine! To think I didn't recognize you. But then, how could I? (*More quietly.*) How you've changed, Kristine!

MRS. LINDE: Yes, no doubt I have. In nine—ten long years.

NORA: Is it so long since we met! Yes, it's all of that. Oh, these last eight years have been a happy time, believe me. And so now you've come in to town, too. Made the long trip in the winter. That took courage.

MRS. LINDE: I just got here by ship this morning.

NORA: To enjoy yourself over Christmas, of course. Oh, how lovely! Yes, enjoy ourselves, we'll do that. But take your coat off. You're not still cold? (*Helping her.*) There now, let's get cozy here by the stove. No, the easy chair there! I'll take the rocker here. (*Seizing her hands.*) Yes, now you have your old look again; it was only in that first moment. You're a bit more pale, Kristine—and maybe a bit thinner.

MRS. LINDE: And much, much older, Nora.

NORA: Yes, perhaps, a bit older; a tiny, tiny bit; not much at all. (*Stopping short; suddenly serious*) Oh, but thoughtless me, to sit here, chattering away. Sweet, good Kristine, can you forgive me?

MRS. LINDE: What do you mean, Nora?

NORA (*softly*):   Poor Kristine, you've become a widow.

MRS. LINDE: Yes, three years ago.

NORA: Oh, I knew it, of course; I read it in the papers. Oh Kristine, you must believe me; I often thought of writing you then, but I kept postponing it, and something always interfered.

MRS. LINDE: Nora dear, I understand completely.

NORA: No, it was awful of me, Kristine. You poor thing, how much you must have gone through. And he left you nothing?

MRS. LINDE: No.

NORA: And no children?

MRS. LINDE: No.

NORA: Nothing at all, then?

MRS. LINDE: Not even a sense of loss to feed on.

NORA (*looking incredulously at her*):   But Kristine, how could that be?

MRS. LINDE (*smiling wearily and smoothing her hair*):   Oh, sometimes it happens, Nora.

NORA: So completely alone. How terribly hard that must be for you. I have three lovely children. You can't see them now; they're out with the maid. But now you must tell me everything—

MRS. LINDE: No, no, no, tell me about yourself.

NORA: No, you begin. Today I don't want to be selfish. I want to think only of you today. But there *is* something I must tell you. Did you hear of the wonderful luck we had recently?

MRS. LINDE: No, what's that?

NORA: My husband's been made manager in the bank, just think!

MRS. LINDE: Your husband? How marvelous!

NORA: Isn't it? Being a lawyer is such an uncertain living, you know, especially if one won't touch any cases that aren't clean and decent. And of course Torvald would never do that, and I'm with him completely there. Oh, we're simply delighted, believe me! He'll join the bank right after New Year's and start getting a huge salary and lots of commissions. From now on we can live quite differently—just as we want. Oh, Kristine, I feel so light and happy! Won't it be lovely to have stacks of money and not a care in the world?

MRS. LINDE: Well, anyway, it would be lovely to have enough for necessities.

NORA: No, not just for necessities, but stacks and stacks of money!

MRS. LINDE (*smiling*):   Nora, Nora, aren't you sensible yet? Back in school you were such a free spender.

NORA (*with a quiet laugh*):   Yes, that's what Torvald still says. (*Shaking her finger*) But "Nora, Nora" isn't as silly as you all think. Really, we've been in no position for me to go squandering. We've had to work, both of us.

MRS. LINDE: You too?

NORA: Yes, at odd jobs—needlework, crocheting, embroidery, and such—(*Casually*) and other things too. You remember that Torvald left the department when we were married? There was no chance of promotion in his office, and of course he needed to earn more money. But that first year he drove himself terribly. He took on all kinds of extra work that kept him going morning and night. It wore him down, and then he fell deathly ill. The doctors said it was essential for him to travel south.

MRS. LINDE: Yes, didn't you spend a whole year in Italy?

NORA: That's right. It wasn't easy to get away, you know. Ivar had just been born. But of course we had to go. Oh, that was a beautiful trip, and it saved Torvald's life. But it cost a frightful sum, Kristine.

MRS. LINDE: I can well imagine.

NORA: Four thousand, eight hundred crowns it cost. That's really a lot of money.

MRS. LINDE: But it's lucky you had it when you needed it.

NORA: Well, as it was, we got it from Papa.

MRS. LINDE: I see. It was just about the time your father died.

NORA: Yes, just about then. And, you know, I couldn't make the trip out to nurse him. I had to stay here, expecting Ivar any moment, and with my poor sick Torvald to care for. Dearest Papa, I never saw him again, Kristine. Oh, that was the worst time I've known in all my marriage.

MRS. LINDE: I know how you loved him. And then you went off to Italy?

NORA: Yes. We had the means now, and the doctors urged us. So we left a month after.

MRS. LINDE: And your husband came back completely cured?

NORA: Sound as a drum!

MRS. LINDE: But—the doctor?

NORA: Who?

MRS. LINDE: I thought the maid said he was a doctor, the man who came in with me.

NORA: Yes, that was Dr. Rank—but he's not making a sick call. He's our closest friend, and he stops by at least once a day. No, Torvald hasn't had a sick moment since, and the children are fit and strong, and I am, too. (*Jumping up and clapping her hands*) Oh, dear God, Kristine, what a lovely thing to live and be happy! But how disgusting of me—I'm talking of nothing but my own affairs. (*Sits on a stool close by* KRISTINE, *arms resting across her knees*) Oh, don't be angry with me! Tell me, is it really true that you weren't in love with your husband? Why did you marry him, then?

MRS. LINDE: My mother was still alive, but bedridden and helpless—and I had two younger brothers to look after. In all conscience, I didn't think I could turn him down.

NORA: No, you were right there. But was he rich at the time?

MRS. LINDE: He was very well off, I'd say. But the business was shaky, Nora. When he died, it all fell apart, and nothing was left.

NORA: And then—?

MRS. LINDE: Yes, so I had to scrape up a living with a little shop and a little teaching and whatever else I could find. The last three years have been like one endless workday without a rest for me. Now it's over, Nora. My poor mother doesn't need me, for she's passed on. Nor the boys, either; they're working now and can take care of themselves.

NORA: How free you must feel—

MRS. LINDE: No—only unspeakably empty. Nothing to live for now. (*Standing up anxiously*) That's why I couldn't take it any longer out in that desolate hole. Maybe here it'll be easier to find something to do and keep my mind occupied. If I could only be lucky enough to get a steady job, some office work—

NORA: Oh, but Kristine, that's so dreadfully tiring, and you already look so tired. It would be much better for you if you could go off to a bathing resort.

MRS. LINDE (*going toward the window*):   I have no father to give me travel money, Nora.

NORA (*rising*):   Oh, don't be angry with me.

MRS. LINDE (*going to her*):   Nora dear, don't you be angry with me. The worst of my kind of situation is all the bitterness that's stored away. No one to work for, and yet you're always having to snap up your opportunities. You have to live; and so you grow selfish. When you told me the happy change in your lot, do you know I was delighted less for your sakes than for mine?

NORA: How so? Oh, I see. You think maybe Torvald could do something for you.

MRS. LINDE: Yes, that's what I thought.

NORA: And he will, Kristine! Just leave it to me; I'll bring it up so delicately—find something attractive to humor him with. Oh, I'm so eager to help you.

MRS. LINDE: How very kind of you, Nora, to be so concerned over me—doubly kind, considering you really know so little of life's burdens yourself.

NORA: I—? I know so little—?

MRS. LINDE (smiling):   Well, my heavens—a little needlework and such—Nora, you're just a child.

NORA (tossing her head and pacing the floor):   You don't have to act so superior.

MRS. LINDE: Oh?

NORA: You're just like the others. You all think I'm incapable of anything serious—

MRS. LINDE: Come now—

NORA: That I've never had to face the raw world.

MRS. LINDE: Nora dear, you've just been telling me all your troubles.

NORA: Hm! Trivia! (Quietly) I haven't told you the big thing.

MRS. LINDE: Big thing? What do you mean?

NORA: You look down on me so, Kristine, but you shouldn't. You're proud that you worked so long and hard for your mother.

MRS. LINDE: I don't look down on a soul. But it is true; I'm proud—and happy, too—to think it was given to me to make my mother's last days almost free of care.

NORA: And you're also proud thinking of what you've done for your brothers.

MRS. LINDE: I feel I've a right to be.

NORA: I agree. But listen to this, Kristine—I've also got something to be proud and happy for.

MRS. LINDE: I don't doubt it. But whatever do you mean?

NORA: Not so loud. What if Torvald heard! He mustn't, not for anything in the world. Nobody must know, Kristine. No one but you.

MRS. LINDE: But what is it, then?

NORA: Come here. (Drawing her down beside her on the sofa) It's true—I've also got something to be proud and happy for. I'm the one who saved Torvald's life.

MRS. LINDE: Saved—? Saved how?

NORA: I told you about the trip to Italy. Torvald never would have lived if he hadn't gone south—

MRS. LINDE: Of course, your father gave you the means—

NORA (smiling):   That's what Torvald and all the rest think, but—

MRS. LINDE: But—?

NORA: Papa didn't give us a pin. I was the one who raised the money.

MRS. LINDE: You? The whole amount?

NORA: Four thousand, eight hundred crowns. What do you say to that?

MRS. LINDE: But Nora, how was it possible? Did you win the lottery?

NORA (disdainfully):   The lottery? Pooh! No art to that.

MRS. LINDE: But where did you get it from then?

NORA (humming, with a mysterious smile):   Hmm, tra-la-la-la.

MRS. LINDE: Because you couldn't have borrowed it.

NORA: No? Why not?

MRS. LINDE: A wife can't borrow without her husband's consent.

NORA (*tossing her head*): Oh, but a wife with a little business sense, a wife who knows how to manage—

MRS. LINDE: Nora, I simply don't understand—

NORA: You don't have to. Whoever said I *borrowed* the money? I could have gotten it other ways. (*Throwing herself back on the sofa*) I could have gotten it from some admirer or other. After all, a girl with my ravishing appeal—

MRS. LINDE: You lunatic.

NORA: I'll bet you're eaten up with curiosity, Kristine.

MRS. LINDE: Now listen here, Nora—you haven't done something indiscreet?

NORA (*sitting up again*): Is it indiscreet to save your husband's life?

MRS. LINDE: I think it's indiscreet that without his knowledge you—

NORA: But that's the point: he mustn't know! My Lord, can't you understand? He mustn't ever know the close call he had. It was to *me* the doctors came to say his life was in danger—that nothing could save him but a stay in the south. Didn't I try strategy then! I began talking about how lovely it would be for me to travel abroad like other young wives; I begged and I cried; I told him please to remember my condition, to be kind and indulge me; and then I dropped a hint that he could easily take out a loan. But at that, Kristine, he nearly exploded. He said I was frivolous, and it was his duty as man of the house not to indulge me in whims and fancies—as I think he called them. Aha, I thought, now you'll just have to be saved—and that's when I saw my chance.

MRS. LINDE: And your father never told Torvald the money wasn't from him?

NORA: No, never. Papa died right about then. I'd considered bringing him into my secret and begging him never to tell. But he was too sick at the time—and then, sadly, it didn't matter.

MRS. LINDE: And you've never confided in your husband since?

NORA: For heaven's sake, no! Are you serious? He's so strict on that subject. Besides—Torvald, with all his masculine pride—how painfully humiliating for him if he ever found out he was in debt to me. That would just ruin our relationship. Our beautiful happy home would never be the same.

MRS. LINDE: Won't you ever tell him?

NORA (*thoughtfully, half smiling*): Yes—maybe sometime, years from now, when I'm no longer so attractive. Don't laugh! I only mean when Torvald loves me less than now, when he stops enjoying my dancing and dressing up and reciting for him. Then it might be wise to have something in reserve—(*Breaking off*) How ridiculous! That'll never happen—Well, Kristine, what do you think of my big secret? I'm capable of something too, hm? You can imagine, of course, how this thing hangs over me. It really hasn't been easy meeting the payments on time. In the business world there's what they call quarterly interest and what they call amortization, and these are always so terribly hard to manage. I've had to skimp a little here and there, wherever I could, you know. I could hardly spare anything from my house allowance, because Torvald has to live well. I couldn't let the children go poorly dressed; whatever I got for them, I felt I had to use up completely—the darlings!

MRS. LINDE: Poor Nora, so it had to come out of your own budget, then?

NORA: Yes, of course. But I was the one most responsible, too. Every time Torvald gave me money for new clothes and such, I never used more than half; always bought the simplest, cheapest outfits. It was a godsend that everything looks so well on me that Torvald never noticed. But it did weigh me down at times, Kristine. It *is* such a joy to wear fine things. You understand.

MRS. LINDE: Oh, of course.

NORA: And then I found other ways of making money. Last winter I was lucky enough to get a lot of copying to do. I locked myself in and sat writing every evening till late in the night. Ah, I was tired so often, dead tired. But still it was wonderful fun, sitting and working like that, earning money. It was almost like being a man.

MRS. LINDE: But how much have you paid off this way so far?

NORA: That's hard to say, exactly. These accounts, you know, aren't easy to figure. I only know that I've paid out all I could scrape together. Time and again I haven't known where to turn. (*Smiling*) Then I'd sit here dreaming of a rich old gentleman who had fallen in love with me—

MRS. LINDE: What! Who is he?

NORA: Oh, really! And that he'd died, and when his will was opened, there in big letters it said, "All my fortune shall be paid over in cash, immediately, to that enchanting Mrs. Nora Helmer."

MRS. LINDE: But Nora dear—who *was* this gentleman?

NORA: Good grief, can't you understand? The old man never existed; that was only something I'd dream up time and again whenever I was at my wits' end for money. But it makes no difference now; the old fossil can go where he pleases for all I care; I don't need him or his will—because now I'm free. (*Jumping up*) Oh, how lovely to think of that, Kristine! Carefree! To know you're carefree, utterly carefree, to be able to romp and play with the children, and to keep up a beautiful, charming home— everything just the way Torvald likes it! And think, spring is coming, with big blue skies. Maybe we can travel a little then. Maybe I'll see the ocean again. Oh yes, it *is* so marvelous to live and be happy!

(*The front doorbell rings.*)

MRS. LINDE (*rising*):   There's the bell. It's probably best that I go.

NORA: No, stay. No one's expected. It must be for Torvald.

MAID (*from the hall doorway*):   Excuse me, ma'am—there's a gentleman here to see Mr. Helmer, but I didn't know—since the doctor's with him—

NORA: Who is the gentleman?

KROGSTAD (*from the doorway*):   It's me, Mrs. Helmer.

(MRS. LINDE *starts and turns away toward the window.*)

NORA (*stepping toward him, tense, her voice a whisper*):   You? What is it? Why do you want to speak to my husband?

KROGSTAD: Bank business—after a fashion. I have a small job in the investment bank, and I hear now your husband is going to be our chief—

NORA: In other words, it's—

KROGSTAD: Just dry business, Mrs. Helmer. Nothing but that.

NORA: Yes, then please be good enough to step into the study. (*She nods indifferently, as she sees him out by the hall door, then returns and begins stirring up the stove.*)

MRS. LINDE: Nora—who was that man?

NORA: That was a Mr. Krogstad—a lawyer.

MRS. LINDE: Then it really was him.

NORA: Do you know that person?

MRS. LINDE: I did once—many years ago. For a time he was a law clerk in our town.

NORA: Yes, he's been that.

MRS. LINDE: How he's changed.

NORA: I understand he had a very unhappy marriage.

MRS. LINDE: He's a widower now.

NORA: With a number of children. There now, it's burning. (*She closes the stove door and moves the rocker a bit to one side.*)

MRS. LINDE: They say he has a hand in all kinds of business.

NORA: Oh? That may be true; I wouldn't know. But let's not think about business. It's so dull.

(DR. RANK *enters from* HELMER'S *study.*)

RANK (*still in the doorway*):   No, no, really—I don't want to intrude, I'd just as soon talk a little while with your wife. (*Shuts the door, then notices* MRS. LINDE) Oh, beg pardon, I'm intruding here too.

NORA: No, not at all. (*Introducing him*) Dr. Rank, Mrs. Linde.

RANK: Well now, that's a name much heard in this house. I believe I passed the lady on the stairs as I came.

MRS. LINDE: Yes, I take the stairs very slowly. They're rather hard on me.

RANK: Uh-hm, some touch of internal weakness?

MRS. LINDE: More overexertion, I'd say.

RANK: Nothing else? Then you're probably here in town to rest up in a round of parties?

MRS. LINDE: I'm here to look for work.

RANK: Is that the best cure for overexertion?

MRS. LINDE: One has to live, Doctor.

RANK: Yes, there's a common prejudice to that effect.

NORA: Oh, come on, Dr. Rank—you really do want to live yourself.

RANK: Yes, I really do. Wretched as I am, I'll gladly prolong my torment indefinitely. All my patients feel like that. And it's quite the same, too, with the morally sick. Right at this moment there's one of those moral invalids in there with Helmer—

MRS. LINDE (*softly*):   Ah!

NORA: Who do you mean?

RANK: Oh, it's a lawyer, Krogstad, a type you wouldn't know. His character is rotten to the root—but even he began chattering all-importantly about how he had to *live.*

NORA: Oh? What did he want to talk to Torvald about?

RANK: I really don't know. I only heard something about the bank.

NORA: I didn't know that Krog—that this man Krogstad had anything to do with the bank.

RANK: Yes, he's gotten some kind of berth down there. (*To* MRS. LINDE) I don't know if you also have, in your neck of the woods, a type of person who scuttles about breathlessly, sniffing out hints of moral corruption, and then maneuvers his victim into some sort of key position where he can keep an eye on him. It's the healthy these days that are out in the cold.

MRS. LINDE: All the same, it's the sick who most need to be taken in.

RANK (*with a shrug*):   Yes, there we have it. That's the concept that's turning society into a sanatorium.

(NORA, *lost in her thoughts, breaks out into quiet laughter and claps her hands.*)

RANK: Why do you laugh at that? Do you have any real idea of what society is?

NORA: What do I care about dreary old society? I was laughing at something quite different—something terribly funny. Tell me, Doctor—is everyone who works in the bank dependent now on Torvald?

RANK: Is that what you find so terribly funny?

NORA (*smiling and humming*):   Never mind, never mind! (*Pacing the floor*) Yes, that's really immensely amusing: that we—that Torvald has so much power now over all those people. (*Taking the bag out of her pocket*) Dr. Rank, a little macaroon on that?

RANK: See here, macaroons! I thought they were contraband here.

NORA: Yes, but these are some that Kristine gave me.

MRS. LINDE: What? I—?

NORA: Now, now, don't be afraid. You couldn't possibly know that Torvald had forbidden them. You see, he's worried they'll ruin my teeth. But hmp! Just this once! Isn't that so, Dr. Rank? Help yourself! (*Puts a macaroon in his mouth*) And you too, Kristine. And I'll also have one, only a little one—or two, at the most. (*Walking about again*) Now I'm really tremendously happy. Now there's just one last thing in the world that I have an enormous desire to do.

RANK: Well! And what's that?

NORA: It's something I have such a consuming desire to say so Torvald could hear.

RANK: And why can't you say it?

NORA: I don't dare. It's quite shocking.

MRS. LINDE: Shocking?

RANK: Well, then it isn't advisable. But in front of us you certainly can. What do you have such a desire to say so Torvald could hear?

NORA: I have such a huge desire to say—to hell and be damned!

RANK: Are you crazy?

MRS. LINDE: My goodness, Nora!

RANK: Go on, say it. Here he is.

NORA (*hiding the macaroon bag*):   Shh, shh, shh!

(HELMER *comes in from his study, hat in hand, overcoat over his arm.*)

NORA (*going toward him*):   Well, Torvald dear, are you through with him?

HELMER: Yes, he just left.

NORA: Let me introduce you—this is Kristine, who's arrived here in town.

HELMER: Kristine—? I'm sorry, but I don't know—

NORA: Mrs. Linde, Torvald dear. Mrs. Kristine Linde.

HELMER: Of course. A childhood friend of my wife's, no doubt?

MRS. LINDE: Yes, we knew each other in those days.

NORA: And just think, she made the long trip down here in order to talk with you.

HELMER: What's this?

MRS. LINDE: Well, not exactly—

NORA: You see, Kristine is remarkably clever in office work, and so she's terribly eager to come under a capable man's supervision and add more to what she already knows—

HELMER: Very wise, Mrs. Linde.

NORA: And then when she heard that you'd become a bank manager—the story was wired out to the papers—then she came in as fast as she could and—Really, Torvald, for my sake you can do a little something for Kristine, can't you?

HELMER: Yes, it's not at all impossible. Mrs. Linde, I suppose you're a widow?

MRS. LINDE: Yes.

HELMER: Any experience in office work?

MRS. LINDE: Yes, a good deal.

HELMER: Well, it's quite likely that I can make an opening for you—

NORA (*clapping her hands*):   You see, you see!

HELMER: You've come at a lucky moment, Mrs. Linde.

MRS. LINDE: Oh, how can I thank you?

HELMER: Not necessary. (*Putting his overcoat on*) But today you'll have to excuse me—

RANK: Wait, I'll go with you. (*He fetches his coat from the hall and warms it at the stove.*)

NORA: Don't stay out long, dear.

HELMER: An hour; no more.

NORA: Are you going too, Kristine?

MRS. LINDE (*putting on her winter garments*):   Yes, I have to see about a room now.

HELMER: Then perhaps we can all walk together.

NORA (*helping her*):   What a shame we're so cramped here, but it's quite impossible for us to—

MRS. LINDE: Oh, don't even think of it! Good-bye, Nora dear, and thanks for everything.

NORA: Good-bye for now. Of course you'll be back again this evening. And you too, Dr. Rank. What? If you're well enough? Oh, you've got to be! Wrap up tight now.

(*In a ripple of small talk the company moves out into the hall; children's voices are heard outside on the steps.*)

NORA: There they are! There they are! (*She runs to open the door. The children come in with their nurse,* ANNE-MARIE.) Come in, come in! (*Bends down and kisses them*) Oh, you darlings—! Look at them, Kristine. Aren't they lovely!

RANK: No loitering in the draft here.

HELMER: Come, Mrs. Linde—this place is unbearable now for anyone but mothers.

(DR. RANK, HELMER, *and* MRS. LINDE *go down the stairs.* ANNE-MARIE *goes into the living room with the children.* NORA *follows, after closing the hall door.*)

NORA: How fresh and strong you look. Oh, such red cheeks you have! Like apples and roses. (*The children interrupt her throughout the following.*) And it was so much fun? That's wonderful. Really? You pulled both Emmy and Bob on the sled? Imagine, all together! Yes, you're a clever boy, Ivar. Oh, let me hold her a bit, Anne-Marie. My sweet little doll baby! (*Takes the smallest from the nurse and dances with her*) Yes, yes, Mama will dance with Bob as well. What? Did you throw snowballs? Oh, if I'd only been there! No, don't bother, Anne-Marie—I'll undress them myself. Oh yes, let me.

It's such fun. Go in and rest; you look half frozen. There's hot coffee waiting for you on the stove. (*The nurse goes into the room to the left. Nora takes the children's winter things off, throwing them about, while the children talk to her all at once.*) Is that so? A big dog chased you? But it didn't bite? No, dogs never bite little, lovely doll babies. Don't peek in the packages, Ivar! What is it? Yes, wouldn't you like to know. No, no, it's an ugly something. Well? Shall we play? What shall we play? Hide-and-seek? Yes, let's play hide-and-seek. Bob must hide first. I must? Yes, let me hide first. (*Laughing and shouting, she and the children play in and out of the living room and the adjoining room to the right. At last* NORA *hides under the table. The children come storming in, search, but cannot find her, then hear her muffled laughter, dash over to the table, lift the cloth and find her. Wild shouting. She creeps forward as if to scare them. More shouts. Meanwhile, a knock at the hall door; no one has noticed it. Now the door half opens, and* KROGSTAD *appears. He waits a moment; the game goes on.*)

KROGSTAD: Beg pardon, Mrs. Helmer—

NORA (*with a strangled cry, turning and scrambling to her knees*):   Oh! what do you want?

KROGSTAD: Excuse me. The outer door was ajar; it must be someone forgot to shut it—

NORA (*rising*):   My husband isn't home, Mr. Krogstad.

KROGSTAD: I know that.

NORA: Yes—then what do you want here?

KROGSTAD: A word with you.

NORA: With—? (*To the children, quietly*) Go in to Anne-Marie. What? No, the strange man won't hurt Mama. When he's gone, we'll play some more. (*She leads the children into the room to the left and shuts the door after them. Then, tense and nervous*) You want to speak to me?

KROGSTAD: Yes, I want to.

NORA: Today? But it's not yet the first of the month—

KROGSTAD: No, it's Christmas Eve. It's going to be up to you how merry a Christmas you have.

NORA: What is it you want? Today I absolutely can't—

KROGSTAD: We won't talk about that till later. This is something else. You do have a moment to spare, I suppose?

NORA: Oh yes, of course—I do, except—

KROGSTAD: Good. I was sitting over at Olsen's Restaurant when I saw your husband go down the street—

NORA: Yes?

KROGSTAD: With a lady.

NORA: Yes. So?

KROGSTAD: If you'll pardon my asking: wasn't that lady a Mrs. Linde?

NORA: Yes.

KROGSTAD: Just now come into town?

NORA: Yes, today.

KROGSTAD: She's a good friend of yours?

NORA: Yes, she is. But I don't see—

KROGSTAD: I also knew her once.

NORA: I'm aware of that.

KROGSTAD: Oh? You know all about it. I thought so, Well, then let me ask you short and sweet: is Mrs. Linde getting a job in the bank?

NORA: What makes you think you can cross-examine me, Mr. Krogstad—you, one of my husband's employees? But since you ask, you might as well know—yes, Mrs. Linde's going to be taken on at the bank. And I'm the one who spoke for her, Mr. Krogstad. Now you know.

KROGSTAD: So I guessed right.

NORA (*pacing up and down*):   Oh, one does have a tiny bit of influence, I should hope. Just because I am a woman, don't think it means that—When one has a subordinate position, Mr. Krogstad, one really ought to be careful about pushing somebody who—hm—

KROGSTAD: Who has influence?

NORA: That's right.

KROGSTAD (*in a different tone*):   Mrs. Helmer, would you be good enough to use your influence on my behalf?

NORA: What? What do you mean?

KROGSTAD: Would you please make sure that I keep my subordinate position in the bank?

NORA: What does that mean? Who's thinking of taking away your position?

KROGSTAD: Oh, don't play the innocent with me. I'm quite aware that your friend would hardly relish the chance of running into me again; and I'm also aware now whom I can thank for being turned out.

NORA: But I promise you—

KROGSTAD: Yes, yes, yes, to the point: there's still time, and I'm advising you to use your influence to prevent it.

NORA: But Mr. Krogstad, I have absolutely no influence.

KROGSTAD: You haven't? I thought you were just saying—

NORA: You shouldn't take me so literally. I! How can you believe that I have any such influence over my husband?

KROGSTAD: Oh, I've known your husband from our student days. I don't think the great bank manager's more steadfast than any other married man.

NORA: You speak insolently about my husband, and I'll show you the door.

KROGSTAD: The lady has spirit.

NORA: I'm not afraid of you any longer. After New Year's, I'll soon be done with the whole business.

KROGSTAD (*restraining himself*):   Now listen to me, Mrs. Helmer. If necessary, I'll fight for my little job in the bank as if it were life itself.

NORA: Yes, so it seems.

KROGSTAD: It's not just a matter of income; that's the least of it. It's something else—All right, out with it! Look, this is the thing. You know, just like all the others, of course, that once, a good many years ago, I did something rather rash.

NORA: I've heard rumors to that effect.

KROGSTAD: The case never got into court; but all the same, every door was closed in my face from then on. So I took up those various activities you know about. I had to grab hold somewhere; and I dare say I haven't been among the worst. But now I want to drop all that. My boys are growing up. For their sakes, I'll have to win back as much respect as possible here in town. That job in the bank was like the first rung in my ladder. And now your husband wants to kick me right back down in the mud again.

NORA: But for heaven's sake, Mr. Krogstad, it's simply not in my power to help you.

KROGSTAD: That's because you haven't the will to—but I have the means to make you.

NORA: You certainly won't tell my husband that I owe you money?

KROGSTAD: Hm—what if I told him that?

NORA: That would be shameful of you. (*Nearly in tears*) This secret—my joy and my pride—that he should learn it in such a crude and disgusting way—learn it from you. You'd expose me to the most horrible unpleasantness—

KROGSTAD: Only unpleasantness?

NORA (*vehemently*):   But go on and try. It'll turn out the worst for you, because then my husband will really see what a crook you are, and then you'll *never* be able to hold your job.

KROGSTAD: I asked if it was just domestic unpleasantness you were afraid of?

NORA: If my husband finds out, then of course he'll pay what I owe at once, and then we'd be through with you for good.

KROGSTAD (*a step closer*):   Listen, Mrs. Helmer—you've either got a very bad memory, or else no head at all for business. I'd better put you a little more in touch with the facts.

NORA: What do you mean?

KROGSTAD: When your husband was sick, you came to me for a loan of four thousand, eight hundred crowns.

NORA: Where else could I go?

KROGSTAD: I promised to get you that sum—

NORA: And you got it.

KROGSTAD: I promised to get you that sum, on certain conditions. You were so involved in your husband's illness, and so eager to finance your trip, that I guess you didn't think out all the details. It might just be a good idea to remind you. I promised you the money on the strength of a note I drew up.

NORA: Yes, and that I signed.

KROGSTAD: Right. But at the bottom I added some lines for your father to guarantee the loan. He was supposed to sign down there.

NORA: Supposed to? He did sign.

KROGSTAD: I left the date blank. In other words, your father would have dated his signature himself. Do you remember that?

NORA: Yes, I think—

KROGSTAD: Then I gave you the note for you to mail to your father. Isn't that so?

NORA: Yes.

KROGSTAD: And naturally you sent it at once—because only some five, six days later you brought me the note, properly signed. And with that, the money was yours.

NORA: Well, then; I've made my payments regularly, haven't I?

KROGSTAD: More or less. But—getting back to the point—those were hard times for you then, Mrs. Helmer.

NORA: Yes, they were.

KROGSTAD: Your father was very ill, I believe.

NORA: He was near the end.

KROGSTAD: He died soon after?

NORA: Yes.

KROGSTAD: Tell me, Mrs. Helmer, do you happen to recall the date of your father's death? The day of the month, I mean.

NORA: Papa died the twenty-ninth of September.

KROGSTAD: That's quite correct; I've already looked into that. And now we come to a curious thing—(*Taking out a paper*) which I simply cannot comprehend.

NORA: Curious thing? I don't know—

KROGSTAD: This is the curious thing: that your father co-signed the note for your loan three days after his death.

NORA: How—? I don't understand.

KROGSTAD: Your father died the twenty-ninth of September. But look. Here your father dated his signature October second. Isn't that curious, Mrs. Helmer? (NORA *is silent.*) Can you explain it to me? (NORA *remains silent.*) It's also remarkable that the words "October second" and the year aren't written in your father's hand, but rather in one that I think I know. Well, it's easy to understand. Your father forgot perhaps to date his signature, and then someone or other added it, a bit sloppily, before anyone knew of his death. There's nothing wrong in that. It all comes down to the signature. And there's no question about *that,* Mrs. Helmer. It really *was* your father who signed his own name here, wasn't it?

NORA (*after a short silence, throwing her head back and looking squarely at him*):   No, it wasn't. I signed Papa's name.

KROGSTAD: Wait, now—are you fully aware that this is a dangerous confession?

NORA: Why? You'll soon get your money.

KROGSTAD: Let me ask you a question—why didn't you send the paper to your father?

NORA: That was impossible. Papa was so sick. If I'd asked him for his signature, I also would have had to tell him what the money was for. But I couldn't tell him, sick as he was, that my husband's life was in danger. That was just impossible.

KROGSTAD: Then it would have been better if you'd given up the trip abroad.

NORA: I couldn't possibly. The trip was to save my husband's life. I couldn't give that up.

KROGSTAD: But didn't you ever consider that this was a fraud against me?

NORA: I couldn't let myself be bothered by that. You weren't any concern of mine. I couldn't stand you, with all those cold complications you made, even though you knew how badly off my husband was.

KROGSTAD: Mrs. Helmer, obviously you haven't the vaguest idea of what you've involved yourself in. But I can tell you this: it was nothing more and nothing worse than I once did—and it wrecked my whole reputation.

NORA: You? Do you expect me to believe that you ever acted bravely to save your wife's life?

KROGSTAD: Laws don't inquire into motives.

NORA: Then they must be very poor laws.

KROGSTAD: Poor or not—if I introduce this paper in court, you'll be judged according to law.

NORA: This I refuse to believe. A daughter hasn't a right to protect her dying father from anxiety and care? A wife hasn't a right to save her husband's life? I don't know much about laws, but I'm sure that somewhere in the books these things are allowed. And you don't know anything about it—you who practice the law? You must be an awful lawyer, Mr. Krogstad.

KROGSTAD: Could be. But business—the kind of business we two are mixed up in—don't you think I know about that? All right. Do what you want now. But I'm telling you *this:* if I get shoved down a second time, you're going to keep me company.
                                        (*He bows and goes out through the hall.*)

NORA (*pensive for a moment, then tossing her head*):   Oh, really! Trying to frighten me! I'm not so silly as all that. (*Begins gathering up the children's clothes, but soon stops*) But—? No, but that's impossible! I did it out of love.

THE CHILDREN (*in the doorway, left*):   Mama, that strange man's gone out the door.

NORA: Yes, yes, I know it. But don't tell anyone about the strange man. Do you hear. Not even Papa!

THE CHILDREN: No, Mama. But now will you play again?

NORA: No, not now.

THE CHILDREN: Oh, but Mama, you promised.

NORA: Yes, but I can't now. Go inside; I have too much to do. Go in, go in, my sweet darlings. (*She herds them gently back in the room and shuts the door after them. Settling on the sofa, she takes up a piece of embroidery and makes some stitches, but soon stops abruptly.*) No! (*Throws the work aside, rises, goes to the hall door and calls out*) Helene! Let me have the tree in here. (*Goes to the table, left, opens the table drawer, and stops again*) No, but that's utterly impossible!

MAID (*with the Christmas tree*):   Where should I put it, Ma'am?

NORA: There. The middle of the floor.

MAID: Should I bring anything else?

NORA: No, thanks. I have what I need.
                                        (*The MAID, who has set the tree down, goes out.*)

NORA (*absorbed in trimming the tree*):   Candles here—and flowers here. That terrible creature! Talk, talk, talk! There's nothing to it at all. The tree's going to be lovely. I'll do anything to please you, Torvald. I'll sing for you, dance for you—

(HELMER *comes in from the hall, with a sheaf of papers under his arm.*)

NORA: Oh! You're back so soon?

HELMER: Yes. Has anyone been here?

NORA: Here? No.

HELMER: That's odd. I saw Krogstad leaving the front door.

NORA: So? Oh yes, that's true. Krogstad was here a moment.

HELMER: Nora, I can see by your face that he's been here, begging you to put in a good word for him.

NORA: Yes.

HELMER: And it was supposed to seem like your own idea? You were to hide it from me that he'd been here. He asked you that, too, didn't he?

NORA: Yes, Torvald, but—

HELMER: Nora, Nora, and you could fall for that? Talk with that sort of person and promise him anything? And then in the bargain, tell me an untruth.

NORA: An untruth—?

HELMER: Didn't you say that no one had been here? (*Wagging his finger*) My little songbird must never do that again. A songbird needs a clean beak to warble with. No false notes. (*Putting his arm about her waist*) That's the way it should be, isn't it? Yes, I'm sure of it. (*Releasing her*) And so, enough of that. (*Sitting by the stove*) Ah, how snug and cozy it is here. (*Leafing among his papers*)

NORA (*busy with the tree, after a short pause*):   Torvald!

HELMER: Yes.

NORA: I'm so much looking forward to the Stenborg's costume party, day after tomorrow.

HELMER: And I can't wait to see what you'll surprise me with.

NORA: Oh, that stupid business.

HELMER: What?

NORA: I can't find anything that's right. Everything seems so ridiculous, so inane.

HELMER: So my little Nora's come to *that* recognition?

NORA (*going behind his chair, her arms resting on its back*):   Are you very busy, Torvald?

HELMER: Oh—

NORA: What papers are those?

HELMER: Bank matters.

NORA: Already?

HELMER: I've gotten full authority from the retiring management to make all necessary changes in personnel and procedure. I'll need Christmas week for that. I want to have everything in order by New Year's.

NORA: So that was the reason this poor Krogstad—

HELMER: Hm.

NORA (*still leaning on the chair and slowly stroking the nape of his neck*):   If you weren't so very busy, I would have asked you an enormous favor, Torvald.

HELMER: Let's hear. What is it?

NORA: You know, there isn't anyone who has your good taste—and I want so much to look well at the costume party. Torvald, couldn't you take over and decide what I should be and plan my costume?

HELMER: Ah, is my stubborn little creature calling for a lifeguard?

NORA: Yes, Torvald, I can't get anywhere without your help.

HELMER: All right—I'll think it over. We'll hit on something.

NORA: Oh, how sweet of you. (*Goes to the tree again. Pause.*) Aren't the red flowers pretty—? But tell me, was it really such a crime that this Krogstad committed?

HELMER: Forgery. Do you have any idea what that means?

NORA: Couldn't he have done it out of need?

HELMER: Yes, or thoughtlessness, like so many others. I'm not so heartless that I'd condemn a man categorically for just one mistake.

NORA: No, of course not, Torvald!

HELMER: Plenty of men have redeemed themselves by openly confessing their crimes and taking their punishments.

NORA: Punishment—?

HELMER: But now Krogstad didn't go that way. He got himself out by sharp practices, and that's the real cause of his moral breakdown.

NORA: Do you really think that would—?

HELMER: Just imagine how a man with that sort of guilt in him has to lie and cheat and deceive on all sides, has to wear a mask even with the nearest and dearest he has, even with his own wife and children. And with the children, Nora—that's where it's most horrible.

NORA: Why?

HELMER: Because that kind of atmosphere of lies infects the whole life of a home. Every breath the children take in is filled with the terms of something degenerate.

NORA (*coming closer behind him*):   Are you sure of that?

HELMER: Oh, I've seen it often enough as a lawyer. Almost everyone who goes bad early in life has a mother who's a chronic liar.

NORA: Why just—the mother?

HELMER: It's usually the mother's influence that's dominant, but the father's works in the same way, of course. Every lawyer is quite familiar with it. And still this Krogstad's been going home year in, year out, poisoning his own children with lies and pretense; that's why I call him morally lost. (*Reaching his hands out toward her*) So my sweet little Nora must promise me never to plead his cause. Your hand on it. Come, come, what's this? Give me your hand. There, now. All settled. I can tell you it'd be impossible for me to work alongside of him. I literally feel physically revolted when I'm anywhere near such a person.

NORA (*withdraws her hand and goes to the other side of the Christmas tree*):   How hot it is here! And I've got so much to do.

HELMER (*getting up and gathering his papers*):   Yes, and I have to think about getting some of these read through before dinner. I'll think about your costume, too. And something to hang on the tree in gilt paper, I may even see about that. (*Putting his hand on her head*) Oh you, my darling little songbird.

(*He goes into his study and closes the door after him.*)

NORA (*softly, after a silence*):   Oh, really! it isn't so. It's impossible. It must be impossible.

ANNE-MARIE (*in the doorway, left*):   The children are begging so hard to come in to Mama.

NORA: No, no, no, don't let them in to me! You stay with them, Anne-Marie.

ANNE-MARIE: Of course, Ma'am. (*Closes the door*)

NORA (*pale with terror*):   Hurt my children—! Poison my home? (*A moment's pause; then she tosses her head.*) That's not true. Never. Never in all the world.

ACT II

Same room. Beside the piano the Christmas tree now stands stripped of ornament, burned-down candle stubs on its ragged branches. NORA's *street clothes lie on the sofa.* NORA, *alone in the room, moves restlessly about; at last she stops at the sofa and picks up her coat.*

NORA (*dropping the coat again*):   Someone's coming! (*Goes toward the door, listens*) No—there's no one. Of course—nobody's coming today, Christmas Day—or tomorrow, either. But maybe—(*Opens the door and looks out*) No, nothing in the mailbox. Quite empty. (*Coming forward*) What nonsense! He won't do anything serious. Nothing terrible could happen. It's impossible. Why, I have three small children.

(ANNE-MARIE, *with a large carton, comes in from the room to the left.*)

ANNE-MARIE: Well, at last I found the box with the masquerade clothes.

NORA: Thanks. Put it on the table.

ANNE-MARIE (*does so*):   But they're all pretty much of a mess.

NORA: Ahh! I'd love to rip them in a million pieces!

ANNE-MARIE: Oh, mercy, they can be fixed right up. Just a little patience.

NORA: Yes, I'll go get Mrs. Linde to help me.

ANNE-MARIE: Out again now? In this nasty weather? Miss Nora will catch cold—get sick.

NORA: Oh, worse things could happen—How are the children?

ANNE-MARIE: The poor mites are playing with their Christmas presents, but—

NORA: Do they ask for me much?

ANNE-MARIE: They're so used to having Mama around, you know.

NORA: Yes, but Anne-Marie, I *can't* be together with them as much as I was.

ANNE-MARIE: Well, small children get used to anything.

NORA: You think so? Do you think they'd forget their mother if she was gone for good?

ANNE-MARIE: Oh, mercy—gone for good!

NORA: Wait, tell me, Anne-Marie—I've wondered so often—how could you ever have the heart to give your child over to strangers?

ANNE-MARIE: But I had to, you know, to become little Nora's nurse.

NORA: Yes, but how could you *do* it?

ANNE-MARIE: When I could get such a good place? A girl who's poor and who's gotten in trouble is glad enough for that. Because that slippery fish, he didn't do a thing for me, you know.

NORA: But your daughter's surely forgotten you.

ANNE-MARIE: Oh, she certainly has not. She's written to me, both when she was confirmed and when she was married.

NORA (*clasping her about the neck*):   You old Anne-Marie, you were a good mother for me when I was little.

ANNE-MARIE: Poor little Nora, with no other mother but me.

NORA: And if the babies didn't have one, then I know that you'd—What silly talk! (*Opening the carton*) Go in to them. Now I'll have to—Tomorrow you can see how lovely I'll look.

ANNE-MARIE: Oh, there won't be anyone at the party as lovely as Miss Nora.

(*She goes off into the room, left.*)

NORA (*begins unpacking the box, but soon throws it aside*):   Oh, if I dared to go out. If only nobody would come. If only nothing would happen here while I'm out. What craziness—nobody's coming. Just don't think. This muff—needs a brushing. Beautiful gloves, beautiful gloves. Let it go. Let it go! One, two, three, four, five, six—(*With a cry*) Oh, there they are! (*Poises to move toward the door, but remains irresolutely standing.* MRS. LINDE *enters from the hall, where she has removed her street clothes.*)

NORA: Oh, it's you, Kristine. There's no one else out there? How good that you've come.

MRS. LINDE: I hear you were up asking for me.

NORA: Yes, I just stopped by. There's something you really can help me with. Let's get settled on the sofa. Look, there's going to be a costume party tomorrow evening at the Stenborgs' right above us, and now Torvald wants me to go as a Neapolitan peasant girl and dance the tarantella that I learned in Capri.

MRS. LINDE: Really, you are giving a whole performance?

NORA: Torvald says yes, I should. See, here's the dress. Torvald had it made for me down there; but now it's all so tattered that I just don't know—

MRS. LINDE: Oh, we'll fix that up in no time. It's nothing more than the trimmings—they're a bit loose here and there. Needle and thread? Good, now we have what we need.

NORA: Oh, how sweet of you!

MRS. LINDE (*sewing*):   So you'll be in disguise tomorrow, Nora. You know what? I'll stop by then for a moment and have a look at you all dressed up. But listen, I've absolutely forgotten to thank you for that pleasant evening yesterday.

NORA (*getting up and walking about*):   I don't think it was as pleasant as usual yesterday. You should have come to town a bit sooner, Kristine—Yes, Torvald really knows how to give a home elegance and charm.

MRS. LINDE: And you do, too, if you ask me. You're not your father's daughter for nothing. But tell me, is Dr. Rank always so down in the mouth as yesterday?

NORA: No, that was quite an exception. But he goes around critically ill all the time—tuberculosis of the spine, poor man. You know, his father was a disgusting thing who kept mistresses and so on—and that's why the son's been sickly from birth.

MRS. LINDE (*lets her sewing fall to her lap*):   But my dearest Nora, how do you know about such things?

NORA (*walking more jauntily*):   Hmp! When you've had three children, then you've had a few visits from—women who know something of medicine, and they tell you this and that.

MRS. LINDE (*resumes sewing; a short pause*):   Does Dr. Rank come here every day?

NORA: Every blessed day. He's Torvald's best friend from childhood, and *my* good friend, too. Dr. Rank almost belongs to this house.

MRS. LINDE: But tell me—is he quite sincere? I mean, doesn't he rather enjoy flattering people?

NORA: Just the opposite. Why do you think that?

MRS. LINDE: When you introduced us yesterday, he was proclaiming that he'd often heard my name in this house; but later I noticed that your husband hadn't the slightest idea who I really was. So how could Dr. Rank—?

NORA: But it's all true, Kristine. You see, Torvald loves me beyond words, and, as he puts it, he'd like to keep me all to himself. For a long time he'd almost be jealous if I even mentioned any of my old friends back home. So of course I dropped that. But with Dr. Rank I talk a lot about such things, because he likes hearing about them.

MRS. LINDE: Now listen, Nora; in many ways you're still like a child. I'm a good deal older than you, with a little more experience. I'll tell you something; you ought to put an end to all this with Dr. Rank.

NORA: What should I put an end to?

MRS. LINDE: Both parts of it, I think. Yesterday you said something about a rich admirer who'd provide you with money—

NORA: Yes, one who doesn't exist—worse luck. So?

MRS. LINDE: Is Dr. Rank well off?

NORA: Yes, he is.

MRS. LINDE: With no dependents?

NORA: No, no one. But—

MRS. LINDE: And he's over here every day?

NORA: Yes, I told you that.

MRS. LINDE: How can a man of such refinement be so grasping?

NORA: I don't follow you at all.

MRS. LINDE: Now don't try to hide it, Nora. You think I can't guess who loaned you the forty-eight hundred crowns?

NORA: Are you out of your mind? How could you think of such a thing! A friend of ours, who comes here every single day. What an intolerable situation that would have been!

MRS. LINDE: Then it really wasn't him.

NORA: No, absolutely not. It never even crossed my mind for a moment—And he had nothing to lend in those days; his inheritance came later.

MRS. LINDE: Well, I think that was a stroke of luck for you, Nora dear.

NORA: No, it never would have occurred to me to ask Dr. Rank—Still, I'm quite sure that if I had asked him—

MRS. LINDE: Which you won't, of course.

NORA: No, of course not. I can't see that I'd ever need to. But I'm quite positive that if I talked to Dr. Rank—

MRS. LINDE: Behind your husband's back?

NORA: I've got to clear up this other thing; *that's* also behind his back. I've *got* to clear it all up.

MRS. LINDE: Yes, I was saying that yesterday, but—

NORA (*pacing up and down*): A man handles these problems so much better than a woman—

MRS. LINDE: One's husband does, yes.

NORA: Nonsense. (*Stopping*) When you pay everything you owe, then you get your note back, right?

MRS. LINDE: Yes, naturally.

NORA: And can rip it into a million pieces and burn it up—that filthy scrap of paper!

MRS. LINDE (*looking hard at her, laying her sewing aside, and rising slowly*): Nora, you're hiding something from me.

NORA: You can see it in my face?

MRS. LINDE: Something's happened to you since yesterday morning. Nora, what is it?

NORA (*hurrying toward her*): Kristine! (*Listening*) Shh! Torvald's home. Look, go in with the children a while. Torvald can't bear all this snipping and stitching. Let Anne-Marie help you.

MRS. LINDE (*gathering up some of the things*): All right, but I'm not leaving here until we've talked this out. (*She disappears into the room, left, as* TORVALD *enters from the hall.*)

NORA: Oh, how I've been waiting for you, Torvald dear.

HELMER: Was that the dressmaker?

NORA: No, that was Kristine. She's helping me fix up my costume. You know, it's going to be quite attractive.

HELMER: Yes, wasn't that a bright idea I had?

NORA: Brilliant! But then wasn't I good as well to give in to you?

HELMER: Good—because you give in to your husband's judgment? All right, you little goose, I know you didn't mean it like that. But I won't disturb you. You'll want to have a fitting, I suppose.

NORA: And you'll be working?

HELMER: Yes. (*Indicating a bundle of papers*) See. I've been down to the bank. (*Starts toward his study*)

NORA: Torvald.

HELMER (*stops*):   Yes.

NORA: If your little squirrel begged you, with all her heart and soul, for something—?

HELMER: What's that?

NORA: Then would you do it?

HELMER: First, naturally, I'd have to know what it was.

NORA: Your squirrel would scamper about and do tricks, if you'd only be sweet and give in.

HELMER: Out with it.

NORA: Your lark would be singing high and low in every room—

HELMER: Come on, she does that anyway.

NORA: I'd be a wood nymph and dance for you in the moonlight.

HELMER: Nora—don't tell me it's that same business from this morning?

NORA (*coming closer*):   Yes, Torvald, I beg you, please!

HELMER: And you actually have the nerve to drag that up again?

NORA: Yes, yes, you've got to give in to me; you have to let Krogstad keep his job in the bank.

HELMER: My dear Nora, I've slated his job for Mrs. Linde.

NORA: That's awfully kind of you. But you could just fire another clerk instead of Krogstad.

HELMER: This is the most incredible stubbornness! Because you go and give an impulsive promise to speak up for him, I'm expected to—

NORA: That's not the reason, Torvald. It's for your own sake. That man does writing for the worst papers; you said it yourself. He could do you any amount of harm. I'm scared to death of him—

HELMER: Ah, I understand. It's the old memories haunting you.

NORA: What do you mean by that?

HELMER: Of course, you're thinking about your father.

NORA: Yes, all right. Just remember how those nasty gossips wrote in the papers about Papa and slandered him so cruelly. I think they'd have had him dismissed if the department hadn't sent you up to investigate, and if you hadn't been so kind and open-minded toward him.

HELMER: My dear Nora, there's a notable difference between your father and me. Your father's official career was hardly above reproach. But mine is; and I hope it'll stay that way as long as I hold my position.

NORA: Oh, who can ever tell what vicious minds can invent? We could be so snug and happy now in our quiet, carefree home—you and I and the children, Torvald! That's why I'm pleading with you so—

HELMER: And just by pleading for him you make it impossible for me to keep him on. It's already known at the bank that I'm firing Krogstad. What if it's rumored around now that the new bank manager was vetoed by his wife—

NORA: Yes, what then—?

HELMER: Oh yes—as long as your little bundle of stubbornness gets her way—! I should go and make myself ridiculous in front of the whole office—whole office—

give people the idea I can be swayed by all kinds of outside pressure. Oh, you can bet I'd feel the effects of that soon enough! Besides—there's something that rules Krogstad right out at the bank as long as I'm the manager.

NORA: What's that?

HELMER: His moral failings I could maybe overlook if I had to—

NORA: Yes, Torvald, why not?

HELMER: And I hear he's quite efficient on the job. But he was a crony of mine back in my teens—one of those rash friendships that crop up again and again to embarrass you later in life. Well, I might as well say it straight out: we're on a first-name basis. And that tactless fool makes no effort at all to hide it in front of others. Quite the contrary—he thinks that entitles him to take a familiar air around me, and so every other second he comes booming out with his "Yes, Torvald!" and "Sure thing, Torvald!" I tell you, it's been excruciating for me. He's out to make my place in the bank unbearable.

NORA: Torvald, you can't be serious about all this.

HELMER: Oh no? Why not?

NORA: Because these are such petty considerations.

HELMER: What are you saying? Petty? You think I'm petty!

NORA: No, just the opposite, Torvald dear. That's exactly why—

HELMER: Never mind. You call my motives petty; then I might as well be just that. Petty! All right! We'll put a stop to this for good. (*Goes to the hall door and calls*) Helene!

NORA: What do you want?

HELMER (*searching among his papers*):   A decision. (*The* MAID *comes in.*) Look here; take this letter; go out with it at once. Get hold of a messenger and have him deliver it. Quick now. It's already addressed. Wait, here's some money.

MAID: Yes, sir. (*She leaves with the letter.*)

HELMER (*straightening his papers*):   There, now, little Miss Willful.

NORA (*breathlessly*):   Torvald, what was that letter?

HELMER: Krogstad's notice.

NORA: Call it back, Torvald! There's still time. Oh, Torvald, call it back! Do it for my sake—for your sake, for the children's sake! Do you hear, Torvald; do it! You don't know how this can harm us.

HELMER: Too late.

NORA: Yes, too late.

HELMER: Nora dear, I can forgive you this panic, even though basically you're insulting me. Yes, you are! Or isn't it an insult to think that I should be afraid of a courtroom hack's revenge? But I forgive you anyway, because this shows so beautifully how much you love me. (*Takes her in his arms*) This is the way it should be, my darling Nora. Whatever comes, you'll see: when it really counts, I have strength and courage enough as a man to take on the whole weight myself.

NORA (*terrified*):   What do you mean by that?

HELMER: The whole weight, I said.

NORA (*resolutely*):   No, never in all the world.

HELMER: Good. So we'll share it, Nora, as man and wife. That's as it should be. (*Fondling her*) Are you happy now? There, there, there—not these frightened dove's eyes. It's nothing at all but empty fantasies—Now you should run through your tarantella and practice your tambourine. I'll go to the inner office and shut both doors, so I won't hear a thing; you can make all the noise you like. (*Turning in the doorway*) And when Rank comes, just tell him where he can find me. (*He nods to her and goes with his papers into the study, closing the door.*)

NORA (*standing as though rooted, dazed with fright, in a whisper*):   He really could do it. He will do it. He'll do it in spite of everything. No, not that, never, never! Anything but that! Escape! A way out—(*The doorbell rings.*) Dr. Rank! Anything but that! Anything, whatever it is! (*Her hands pass over her face, smoothing it; she pulls herself together, goes over and opens the hall door.* DR. RANK *stands outside, hanging his fur coat up. During the following scene, it begins getting dark.*)

NORA: Hello, Dr. Rank. I recognized your ring. But you mustn't go in to Torvald yet; I believe he's working.

RANK: And you?

NORA: For you, I always have an hour to spare—you know that. (*He has entered, and she shuts the door after him.*)

RANK: Many thanks. I'll make use of these hours while I can.

NORA: What do you mean by that? While you can?

RANK: Does that disturb you?

NORA: Well, it's such an odd phrase. Is anything going to happen?

RANK: What's going to happen is what I've been expecting so long—but I honestly didn't think it would come so soon.

NORA (*gripping his arm*):   What is it you've found out? Dr. Rank, you have to tell me!

RANK (*sitting by the stove*):   It's all over with me. There's nothing to be done about it.

NORA (*breathing easier*):   Is it you—then—?

RANK: Who else? There's no point in lying to one's self. I'm the most miserable of all my patients, Mrs. Helmer. These past few days I've been auditing my internal accounts. Bankrupt! Within a month I'll probably be laid out and rotting in the churchyard.

NORA: Oh, what a horrible thing to say.

RANK: The thing itself is horrible. But the worst of it is all the other horror before it's over. There's only one final examination left; when I'm finished with that, I'll know about when my disintegration will begin. There's something I want to say. Helmer with his sensitivity has such a sharp distaste for anything ugly. I don't want him near my sickroom.

NORA: Oh, but Dr. Rank—

RANK: I won't have him in there. Under no condition. I'll lock my door to him— As soon as I'm completely sure of the worst, I'll send you my calling card marked with a black cross, and you'll know then the wreck has started to come apart.

NORA: No, today you're completely unreasonable. And I wanted you so much to be in a really good humor.

RANK: With death up my sleeve? And then to suffer this way for somebody else's sins. Is there any justice in that? And in every single family, in some way or another, this inevitable retribution of nature goes on—

NORA (*her hands pressed over her ears*):   Oh, stuff! Cheer up! Please—be gay!

RANK: Yes, I'd just as soon laugh at it all. My poor, innocent spine, serving time for my father's gay army days.

NORA (*by the table, left*):   He was so infatuated with asparagus tips and *pâté de foie gras,* wasn't that it?

RANK: Yes—and with truffles.

NORA: Truffles, yes. And then with oysters, I suppose?

RANK: Yes, tons of oysters, naturally.

NORA: And then the port and champagne to go with it. It's so sad that all these delectable things have to strike at our bones.

RANK: Especially when they strike at the unhappy bones that never shared in the fun.

NORA: Ah, that's the saddest of all.

RANK (*looks searchingly at her*):   Hm.

NORA (*after a moment*):   Why did you smile?

RANK: No, it was you who laughed.

NORA: No, it was you who smiled, Dr. Rank!

RANK (*getting up*):   You're even a bigger tease than I'd thought.

NORA: I'm full of wild ideas today.

RANK: That's obvious.

NORA (*putting both hands on his shoulders*):   Dear, dear Dr. Rank, you'll never die for Torvald and me.

RANK: Oh, that loss you'll easily get over. Those who go away are soon forgotten.

NORA (*looks fearfully at him*):   You believe that?

RANK: One makes new connections, and then—

NORA: Who makes new connections?

RANK: Both you and Torvald will when I'm gone. I'd say you're well under way already. What was that Mrs. Linde doing here last evening?

NORA: Oh, come—you can't be jealous of poor Kristine?

RANK: Oh yes, I am. She'll be my successor here in the house. When I'm down under, that woman will probably—

NORA: Shh! Not so loud. She's right in there.

RANK: Today as well. So you see.

NORA: Only to sew on my dress. Good gracious, how unreasonable you are. (*Sitting on the sofa*) Be nice now, Dr. Rank. Tomorrow you'll see how beautifully I'll dance, and you can imagine then that I'm dancing only for you—yes, and of course for Torvald, too—that's understood. (*Takes various items out of the carton*) Dr. Rank, sit over here and I'll show you something.

RANK (*sitting*):   What's that?

NORA: Look here. Look.

RANK: Silk stockings.

NORA: Flesh-colored. Aren't they lovely? Now it's so dark here, but tomorrow— No, no, no, just look at the feet. Oh well, you might as well look at the rest.

RANK: Hm—

NORA: Why do you look so critical? Don't you believe they'll fit?

RANK: I've never had any chance to form an opinion on that.

NORA (*glancing at him a moment*):   Shame on you. (*Hits him lightly on the ear with the stockings*) That's for you. (*Puts them away again*)

RANK: And what other splendors am I going to see now?

NORA: Not the least bit more, because you've been naughty. (*She hums a little and rummages among her things.*)

RANK (*after a short silence*):   When I sit here together with you like this, completely easy and open, then I don't know—I simply can't imagine—whatever would have become of me if I'd never come into this house.

NORA (*smiling*):   Yes, I really think you feel completely at ease with us.

RANK (*more quietly, staring straight ahead*):   And then to have to go away from it all—

NORA: Nonsense, you're not going away.

RANK (*his voice unchanged*):   —and not even be able to leave some poor show of gratitude behind, scarcely a fleeting regret—no more than a vacant place that anyone can fill.

NORA: And if I asked you now for—? No—

RANK: For what?

NORA: For a great proof of your friendship—

RANK: Yes, yes?

NORA: No, I mean—for an exceptionally big favor—

RANK: Would you really, for once, make me so happy?

NORA: Oh, you haven't the vaguest idea what it is.

RANK: All right, then tell me.

NORA: No, but I can't, Dr. Rank—it's all out of reason. It's advice and help, too—and a favor—

RANK: So much the better. I can't fathom what you're hinting at. Just speak out. Don't you trust me?

NORA: Of course. More than anyone else. You're my best and truest friend, I'm sure. That's why I want to talk to you. All right, then, Dr. Rank: there's something you can help me prevent. You know how deeply, how inexpressibly dearly Torvald loves me; he'd never hesitate a second to give up his life for me.

RANK (*leaning close to her*):   Nora—do you think he's the only one—

NORA (*with a slight start*):   Who—?

RANK: Who'd gladly give up his life for you.

NORA (*heavily*):   I see.

RANK: I swore to myself you should know this before I'm gone. I'll never find a better chance. Yes, Nora, now you know. And also you know now that you can trust me beyond anyone else.

NORA (*rising, natural and calm*):   Let me by.

RANK (*making room for her, but still sitting*):   Nora—

NORA (*in the hall doorway*):   Helene, bring the lamp in. (*Goes over to the stove*) Ah, dear Dr. Rank, that was really mean of you.

RANK (*getting up*):   That I've loved you just as deeply as somebody else? Was *that* mean?

NORA: No, but that you came out and told me. That was quite unnecessary—

RANK: What do you mean? Have you known—?

(*The* MAID *comes in with the lamp, sets it on the table, and goes out again.*)

RANK: Nora—Mrs. Helmer—I'm asking you: have you known about it?

NORA: Oh, how can I tell what I know or don't know? Really, I don't know what to say.—Why did you have to be so clumsy, Dr. Rank! Everything was so good.

RANK: Well, in any case, you now have the knowledge that my body and soul are at your command. So won't you speak out?

NORA (*Looking at him*):   After that?

RANK: Please, just let me know what it is.

NORA: You can't know anything now.

RANK: I have to. You mustn't punish me like this. Give me the chance to do whatever is humanly possible for you.

NORA: Now there's nothing you can do for me. Besides, actually, I don't need any help. You'll see—it's only my fantasies. That's what it is. Of course! (*Sits in the rocker, looks at him, and smiles*) What a nice one you are, Dr. Rank. Aren't you a little bit ashamed, now that the lamp is here?

RANK: No, not exactly. But perhaps I'd better go—for good?

NORA: No, you certainly can't do that. You must come here just as you always have. You know Torvald can't do without you.

RANK: Yes, but *you?*

NORA: You know how much I enjoy it when you're here.

RANK: That's precisely what threw me off. You're a mystery to me. So many times I've felt you'd almost rather be with me than with Helmer.

NORA: Yes—you see, there are some people that one loves most and other people that one would almost prefer being with.

RANK: Yes, there's something to that.

NORA: When I was back home, of course I loved Papa most. But I always thought it was so much fun when I could sneak down to the maids' quarters, because they never tried to improve me, and it was always so amusing, the way they talked to each other.

RANK: Aha, so it's *their* place that I've filled.

NORA (*jumping up and going to him*):   Oh, dear sweet Dr. Rank, that's not what I meant at all. But you can understand that with Torvald it's just the same as with Papa—

(*The* MAID *enters from the hall.*)

MAID: Ma'am—please! (*She whispers to* NORA *and hands her a calling card.*)

NORA (*glancing at the card*):   Ah! (*Slips it into her pocket*)

RANK: Anything wrong?

NORA: No, no, not at all. It's only some—it's my new dress—

RANK: Really? But—there's your dress.

NORA: Oh, that. But this is another one—I ordered it—Torvald mustn't know—

RANK: Ah, now we have the big secret.

NORA: That's right. Just go in with him—he's back in the inner study. Keep him there as long as—

RANK: Don't worry. He won't get away.   (*Goes into the study.*)

NORA (*to the* MAID):   And he's standing waiting in the kitchen.

MAID: Yes, he came up by the back stairs.

NORA: But didn't you tell him somebody was here?

MAID: Yes, but that didn't do any good.

NORA: He won't leave?

MAID: No, he won't go till he's talked with you, ma'am.

NORA: Let him come in, then—but quietly. Helene, don't breathe a word about this. It's a surprise for my husband.

MAID: Yes, yes, I understand—   (*Goes out.*)

NORA: This horror—it's going to happen. No, no, no, it can't happen, it mustn't. (*She goes and bolts* HELMER's *door. The* MAID *opens the hall door for* KROGSTAD *and shuts it behind him. He is dressed for travel in a fur coat, boots and a fur cap.*)

NORA (*going toward him*):   Talk softly. My husband's home.

KROGSTAD: Well, good for him.

NORA: What do you want?

KROGSTAD: Some information.

NORA: Hurry up, then. What is it?

KROGSTAD: You know, of course, that I got my notice.

NORA: I couldn't prevent it, Mr. Krogstad. I fought for you to the bitter end, but nothing worked.

KROGSTAD: Does your husband's love for you run so thin? He knows everything I can expose you too, and all the same he dares to—

NORA: How can you imagine he knows anything about this?

KROGSTAD: Ah, no—I can't imagine it either, now. It's not at all like my fine Torvald Helmer to have so much guts—

NORA: Mr. Krogstad, I demand respect for my husband!

KROGSTAD: Why, of course—all due respect. But since the lady's keeping it so carefully hidden, may I presume to ask if you're also a bit better informed than yesterday about what you've actually done?

NORA: More than you ever could teach me.

KROGSTAD: Yes, I *am* such an awful lawyer.

NORA: What is it you want from me?

KROGSTAD: Just a glimpse of how you are, Mrs. Helmer. I've been thinking about you all day long. A cashier, a night-court scribbler, a—well, a type like me also has a little of what they call a heart, you know.

NORA: Then show it. Think of my children.

KROGSTAD: Did you or your husband ever think of mine? But never mind. I simply wanted to tell you that you don't need to take this thing too seriously. For the present, I'm not proceeding with any action.

NORA: Oh no, really! Well—I knew that.

KROGSTAD: Everything can be settled in a friendly spirit. It doesn't have to get around town at all; it can stay just among us three.

NORA: My husband may never know anything of this.

KROGSTAD: How can you manage that? Perhaps you can pay me the balance?

NORA: No, not right now.

KROGSTAD: Or you know some way of raising the money in a day or two?

NORA: No way that I'm willing to use.

KROGSTAD: Well, it wouldn't have done you any good, anyway. If you stood in front of me with a fistful of bills, you still couldn't buy your signature back.

NORA: Then tell me what you're going to do with it.

KROGSTAD: I'll just hold onto it—keep it on file. There's no outsider who'll even get wind of it. So if you've been thinking of taking some desperate step—

NORA: I have.

KROGSTAD: Been thinking of running away from home—

NORA: I have!

KROGSTAD: Or even of something worse—

NORA: How could you guess that?

KROGSTAD: You can drop those thoughts.

NORA: How could you guess I was thinking of *that?*

KROGSTAD: Most of us think about *that* at first. I thought about it too, but I discovered I hadn't the courage—

NORA (*lifelessly*):   I don't either.

KROGSTAD (*relieved*):   That's true, you haven't the courage? You too?

NORA: I don't have it—I don't have it.

KROGSTAD: It would be terribly stupid, anyway. After that first storm at home blows out, why, then—I have here in my pocket a letter for your husband—

NORA: Telling everything?

KROGSTAD: As charitably as possible.

NORA (*quickly*):   He mustn't ever get that letter. Tear it up. I'll find some way to get money.

KROGSTAD: Beg pardon, Mrs. Helmer, but I think I just told you—

NORA: Oh, I don't mean the money I owe you. Let me know how much you want from my husband, and I'll manage it.

KROGSTAD: I don't want any money from your husband.

NORA: What do you want, then?

KROGSTAD: I'll tell you what. I want to recoup, Mrs. Helmer; I want to get on in the world—and there's where your husband can help me. For a year and a half I've kept myself clean of anything disreputable—all that time struggling with the worst conditions; but I was satisfied, working my way up step by step. Now I've been written right off, and I'm just not in the mood to come crawling back. I tell you, I want to move on. I want to get back in the bank—in a better position. Your husband can set up a job for me—

NORA: He'll never do that!

KROGSTAD: He'll do it. I know him. He won't dare breathe a word of protest. And once I'm in there together with him, you just wait and see! Inside of a year, I'll be the manager's right-hand man. It'll be Nils Krogstad, not Torvald Helmer, who runs the bank.

NORA: You'll never see the day!

KROGSTAD: Maybe you think you can—

NORA: I have the courage now—for *that*.

KROGSTAD: Oh, you don't scare me. A smart, spoiled lady like you—

NORA: You'll see; you'll see!

KROGSTAD: Under the ice, maybe? Down in the freezing, coal-black water? There, till you float up in the spring, ugly, unrecognizable, with your hair falling out—

NORA: You don't frighten me.

KROGSTAD: Nor do you frighten me. One doesn't do these things, Mrs. Helmer. Besides, what good would it be? I'd still have him safe in my pocket.

NORA: Afterwards? When I'm no longer—?

KROGSTAD: Are you forgetting that *I'll* be in control then over your final reputation? (NORA *stands speechless, staring at him.*) Good; now I've warned you. Don't do anything stupid. When Helmer's read my letter, I'll be waiting for his reply. And bear in mind that it's your husband himself who's forced me back to my old ways. I'll never forgive him for that. Good-bye, Mrs. Helmer.   (*He goes out through the hall.*)

NORA (*goes to the hall door, opens it a crack, and listens*):   He's gone. Didn't leave the letter. Oh no, no, that's impossible too! (*Opening the door more and more*) What's that?

He's standing outside—not going downstairs. He's thinking it over? Maybe he'll—? (*A letter falls in the mailbox; then* KROGSTAD's *footsteps are heard, dying away down a flight of stairs.* NORA *gives a muffled cry and runs over toward the sofa table. A short pause.*) In the mailbox. (*Slips warily over to the hall door*) It's lying there. Torvald, Torvald—now we're lost!

MRS. LINDE (*entering with the costume from the room, left*):   There now, I can't see anything else to mend. Perhaps you'd like to try—

NORA (*in a hoarse whisper*):   Kristine, come here.

MRS. LINDE (*tossing the dress on the sofa*):   What's wrong? You look upset.

NORA: Come here. See that letter? *There!* Look—through the glass in the mailbox.

MRS. LINDE: Yes, yes, I see it.

NORA: That letter's from Krogstad—

MRS. LINDE: Nora—it's Krogstad who loaned you the money!

NORA: Yes, and now Torvald will find out everything.

MRS. LINDE: Believe me, Nora, it's best for both of you.

NORA: There's more you don't know. I forged a name.

MRS. LINDE: But for heaven's sake—?

NORA: I only want to tell you that, Kristine, so that you can be my witness.

MRS. LINDE: Witness? Why should I—?

NORA: If I should go out of my mind—it could easily happen—

MRS. LINDE: Nora!

NORA: Or anything else occurred—so I couldn't be present here—

MRS. LINDE: Nora, Nora, you aren't yourself at all!

NORA: And someone should try to take on the whole weight, all of the guilt, you follow me—

MRS. LINDE: Yes, of course, but why do you think—?

NORA: Then you're the witness that it isn't true, Kristine. I'm very much myself; my mind right now is perfectly clear; and I'm telling you: nobody else has known about this; I alone did everything. Remember that.

MRS. LINDE: I will. But I don't understand all this.

NORA: Oh, how could you ever understand it? It's the miracle now that's going to take place.

MRS. LINDE: The miracle?

NORA: Yes, the miracle. But it's so awful, Kristine. It mustn't take place, not for anything in the world.

MRS. LINDE: I'm going right over and talk with Krogstad.

NORA: Don't go near him; he'll do you some terrible harm!

MRS. LINDE: There was a time once when he'd gladly have done anything for me.

NORA: He?

MRS. LINDE: Where does he live?

NORA: Oh, how do I know? Yes. (*Searches in her pocket*) Here's his card. But the letter, the letter—!

HELMER (*from the study, knocking on the door*):   Nora!

NORA (*with a cry of fear*):   Oh! What is it? What do you want?

HELMER: Now, now, don't be so frightened. We're not coming in. You locked the door—are you trying on the dress?

NORA: Yes, I'm trying it. I'll look just beautiful, Torvald.

MRS. LINDE (*who has read the card*):   He's living right around the corner.

NORA: Yes, but what's the use? We're lost. The letter's in the box.

MRS. LINDE: And your husband has the key?

NORA: Yes, always.

MRS. LINDE: Krogstad can ask for his letter back unread; he can find some excuse—

NORA: But it's just this time that Torvald usually—

MRS. LINDE: Stall him. Keep him in there. I'll be back as quick as I can. (*She hurries out through the hall entrance.*)

NORA (*goes to* HELMER'*s door, opens it, and peers in*):   Torvald!

HELMER (*from the inner study*):   Well—does one dare set foot in one's own living room at last? Come on, Rank, now we'll get a look—(*In the doorway*) But what's this?

NORA: What, Torvald dear?

HELMER: Rank had me expecting some grand masquerade.

RANK (*in the doorway*):   That was my impression, but I must have been wrong.

NORA: No one can admire me in my splendor—not until tomorrow.

HELMER: But Nora dear, you look so exhausted. Have you practiced too hard?

NORA: No, I haven't practiced at all yet.

HELMER: You know, it's necessary—

NORA: Oh, it's absolutely necessary, Torvald. But I can't get anywhere without your help. I've forgotten the whole thing completely.

HELMER: Ah, we'll soon take care of that.

NORA: Yes, take care of me, Torvald, please! Promise me that? Oh, I'm so nervous. That big party—You must give up everything this evening for me. No business—don't even touch your pen. Yes? Dear Torvald, promise?

HELMER: It's a promise. Tonight I'm totally at your service—you little helpless thing. Hm—but first there's one thing I want to—(*Goes toward the hall door*)

NORA: What are you looking for?

HELMER: Just to see if there's any mail.

NORA: No, no, don't do that, Torvald!

HELMER: Now what?

NORA: Torvald, please. There isn't any.

HELMER: Let me look, though. (*Starts out.* NORA, *at the piano, strikes the first notes of the tarantella.* HELMER, *at the door, stops.*) Aha!

NORA: I can't dance tomorrow if I don't practice with you.

HELMER (*going over to her*):   Nora dear, are you really so frightened?

NORA: Yes, so terribly frightened. Let me practice right now; there's still time before dinner. Oh, sit down and play for me, Torvald. Direct me. Teach me, the way you always have.

HELMER: Gladly, if it's what you want. (*Sits at the piano*)

NORA (*snatches the tambourine up from the box, then a long, varicolored shawl, which she throws around herself, whereupon she springs forward and cries out*):   Play for me now! Now I'll dance!

(HELMER *plays and* NORA *dances.* RANK *stands behind* HELMER *at the piano and looks on.*)

HELMER (*as he plays*):   Slower. Slow down.

NORA: Can't change it.

HELMER: Not so violent, Nora!

NORA: Has to be just like this.

HELMER (*stopping*):   No, no, that won't do at all.

NORA (*laughing and swinging her tambourine*):   Isn't that what I told you?

RANK: Let me play for her.

HELMER (*getting up*):   Yes, go on. I can teach her more easily then.

(RANK *sits at the piano and plays;* NORA *dances more and more wildly.* HELMER *has stationed himself by the stove and repeatedly gives her directions; she seems not to hear them; her hair loosens and falls over her shoulders; she does not notice, but goes on dancing.* MRS. LINDE *enters.*)

MRS. LINDE (*standing dumbfounded at the door*):   Ah—!

NORA (*still dancing*):   See what fun, Kristine!

HELMER: But Nora darling, you dance as if your life were at stake.

NORA: And it is.

HELMER: Rank, stop! This is pure madness. Stop it, I say!

(RANK *breaks off playing, and* NORA *halts abruptly.*)

HELMER (*going over to her*):   I never would have believed it. You've forgotten everything I taught you.

NORA (*throwing away the tambourine*):   You see for yourself.

HELMER: Well, there's certainly room for instruction here.

NORA: Yes, you see how important it is. You've got to teach me to the very last minute. Promise me that, Torvald?

HELMER: You can bet on it.

NORA: You mustn't, either today or tomorrow, think about anything else but me; you mustn't open any letters—or the mailbox—

HELMER: Ah, it's still the fear of that man—

NORA: Oh yes, yes, that too.

HELMER: Nora, it's written all over you—there's already a letter from him out there.

NORA: I don't know. I guess so. But you mustn't read such things now; there mustn't be anything ugly between us before it's all over.

RANK (*quietly to* HELMER):   You shouldn't deny her.

HELMER (*putting his arm around her*):   The child can have her way. But tomorrow night, after you've danced—

NORA: Then you'll be free.

MAID (*in the doorway, right*):   Ma'am, dinner is served.

NORA: We'll be wanting champagne, Helene.

MAID: Very good, ma'am.   (*Goes out*)

HELMER: So—a regular banquet, hm?

NORA: Yes, a banquet—champagne till daybreak! (*Calling out*) And some macaroons, Helene. Heaps of them—just this once.

HELMER (*taking her hands*):   Now, now, now—no hysterics. Be my own little lark again.

NORA: Oh, I will soon enough. But go on in—and you, Dr. Rank. Kristine, help me put up my hair.

RANK (*whispering, as they go*):   There's nothing wrong—really wrong, is there?

HELMER: Oh, of course not. It's nothing more than this childish anxiety I was telling you about.   (*They go out, right.*)

NORA: Well?

MRS. LINDE: Left town.

NORA: I could see by your face.

MRS. LINDE: He'll be home tomorrow evening. I wrote him a note.

NORA: You shouldn't have. Don't try to stop anything now. After all, it's a wonderful joy, this waiting here for the miracle.

MRS. LINDE: What is it you're waiting for?

NORA: Oh, you can't understand that. Go in to them, I'll be along in a moment.

(MRS. LINDE *goes into the dining room.* NORA *stands a short while as if composing herself; then she looks at her watch.*)

NORA: Five. Seven hours to midnight. Twenty-four hours to the midnight after, and then the tarantella's done. Seven and twenty-four? Thirty-one hours to live.

HELMER (*in the doorway, right*): What's become of the little lark?

NORA (*going toward him with open arms*): Here's your lark!

ACT III

Same scene. The table, with chairs around it, has been moved to the center of the room. A lamp on the table is lit. The hall door stands open. Dance music drifts down from the floor above. MRS. LINDE *sits at the table, absently paging through a book, trying to read, but apparently unable to focus her thoughts. Once or twice she pauses, tensely listening for a sound at the outer entrance.*

MRS. LINDE (*glancing at her watch*): Not yet—and there's hardly any time left. If only he's not—(*Listening again*) Ah, there he is. (*She goes out in the hall and cautiously opens the outer door. Quiet footsteps are heard on the stairs. She whispers.*) Come in. Nobody's here.

KROGSTAD (*in the doorway*): I found a note from you at home. What's back of all this?

MRS. LINDE: I just *had* to talk to you.

KROGSTAD: Oh? And it just *had* to be here in this house?

MRS. LINDE: At my place it was impossible; my room hasn't a private entrance. Come in; we're all alone. The maid's asleep, and the Helmers are at the dance upstairs.

KROGSTAD (*entering the room*): Well, well, the Helmers are dancing tonight? Really?

MRS. LINDE: Yes, why not?

KROGSTAD: How true—why not?

MRS. LINDE: All right, Krogstad, let's talk.

KROGSTAD: Do we two have anything more to talk about?

MRS. LINDE: We have a great deal to talk about.

KROGSTAD: I wouldn't have thought so.

MRS. LINDE: No, because you've never understood me, really.

KROGSTAD: Was there anything more to understand—except what's all too common in life? A calculating woman throws over a man the moment a better catch comes by.

MRS. LINDE: You think I'm so thoroughly calculating? You think I broke it off lightly?

KROGSTAD: Didn't you?

MRS. LINDE: Nils—is that what you really thought?

KROGSTAD: If you cared, then why did you write me the way you did?

MRS. LINDE: What else could I do? If I had to break off with you, then it was my job as well to root out everything you felt for me.

KROGSTAD (*wringing his hands*): So that was it. And this—all this, simply for money!

MRS. LINDE: Don't forget I had a helpless mother and two small brothers. We couldn't wait for you, Nils; you had such a long road ahead of you then.

KROGSTAD: That may be; but you still hadn't the right to abandon me for somebody else's sake.

MRS. LINDE: Yes—I don't know. So many, many times I've asked myself if I did have that right.

KROGSTAD (*more softly*): When I lost you, it was as if all the solid ground dissolved from under my feet. Look at me; I'm a half-drowned man now, hanging onto a wreck.

MRS. LINDE: Help may be near.

KROGSTAD: It was near—but then you came and blocked it off.

MRS. LINDE: Without my knowing it, Nils. Today for the first time I learned that it's you I'm replacing at the bank.

KROGSTAD: All right—I believe you. But now that you know, will you step aside?

MRS. LINDE: No, because that wouldn't benefit you in the slightest.

KROGSTAD: Not "benefit" me, hm! I'd step aside anyway.

MRS. LINDE: I've learned to be realistic. Life and hard, bitter necessity have taught me that.

KROGSTAD: And life's taught me never to trust fine phrases.

MRS. LINDE: Then life's taught you a very sound thing. But you do have to trust in actions, don't you?

KROGSTAD: What does that mean?

MRS. LINDE: You said you were hanging on like a half-drowned man to a wreck.

KROGSTAD: I've good reason to say that.

MRS. LINDE: I'm also like a half-drowned woman on a wreck. No one to suffer with; no one to care for.

KROGSTAD: You made your choice.

MRS. LINDE: There wasn't any choice then.

KROGSTAD: So—what of it?

MRS. LINDE: Nils, if only we two shipwrecked people could reach across to each other.

KROGSTAD: What are you saying?

MRS. LINDE: Two on one wreck are at least better off than each on his own.

KROGSTAD: Kristine!

MRS. LINDE: Why do you think I came into town?

KROGSTAD: Did you really have some thought of me?

MRS. LINDE: I have to work to go on living. All my born days, as long as I can remember, I've worked, and it's been my best and my only joy. But now I'm completely alone in the world; it frightens me to be so empty and lost. To work for yourself—there's no joy in that. Nils, give me something—someone to work for.

KROGSTAD: I don't believe all this. It's just some hysterical feminine urge to go out and make a noble sacrifice.

MRS. LINDE: Have you ever found me to be hysterical?

KROGSTAD: Can you honestly mean this? Tell me—do you know everything about my past?

MRS. LINDE: Yes.

KROGSTAD: And you know what they think I'm worth around here.

MRS. LINDE: From what you were saying before, it would seem that with me you could have been another person.

KROGSTAD: I'm positive of that.

MRS. LINDE: Couldn't it happen still?

KROGSTAD: Kristine—you're saying this in all seriousness? Yes, you are! I can see it in you. And do you really have the courage, then—?

MRS. LINDE: I need to have someone to care for; and your children need a mother. We both need each other. Nils, I have faith that you're good at heart—I'll risk everything together with you.

KROGSTAD (*gripping her hands*):   Kristine, thank you, thank you—Now I know I can win back a place in their eyes. Yes—but I forgot—

MRS. LINDE (*listening*):   Shh! The tarantella. Go now! Go on!

KROGSTAD: Why? What is it?

MRS. LINDE: Hear the dance up there? When that's over, they'll be coming down.

KROGSTAD: Oh, then I'll go. But—it's all pointless. Of course, you don't know the move I made against the Helmers.

MRS. LINDE: Yes, Nils, I know.

KROGSTAD: And all the same, you have the courage to—?

MRS. LINDE: I know how far despair can drive a man like you.

KROGSTAD: Oh, if I only could take it all back.

MRS. LINDE: You easily could—your letter's still lying in the mailbox.

KROGSTAD: Are you sure of that?

MRS. LINDE: Positive. But—

KROGSTAD (*looks at her searchingly*):   Is that the meaning of it, then? You'll have your friend at any price. Tell me straight out. Is that it?

MRS. LINDE: Nils—anyone who's sold herself for somebody else once isn't going to do it again.

KROGSTAD: I'll demand my letter back.

MRS. LINDE: No, no.

KROGSTAD: Yes, of course. I'll stay here till Helmer comes down; I'll tell him to give me my letter again—that it only involves my dismissal—that he shouldn't read it—

MRS. LINDE: No, Nils, don't call the letter back.

KROGSTAD: But wasn't that exactly why you wrote me to come here?

MRS. LINDE: Yes, in that first panic. But it's been a whole day and night since then, and in that time I've seen such incredible things in this house. Helmer's got to learn everything; this dreadful secret has to be aired; those two have to come to a full understanding; all these lies and evasions can't go on.

KROGSTAD: Well, then, if you want to chance it. But at least there's one thing I can do, and do right away—

MRS. LINDE (*listening*):   Go now, go quick! The dance is over. We're not safe another second.

KROGSTAD: I'll wait for you downstairs.

MRS. LINDE: Yes, please do; take me home.

KROGSTAD: I can't believe it; I've never been so happy. (*He leaves by way of the outer door; the door between the room and the hall stays open.*)

MRS. LINDE (*straightening up a bit and getting together her street clothes*):   How different now! How different! Someone to work for, to live for—a home to build. Well, it is worth the try! Oh, if they'd only come! (*Listening*) Ah, there they are. Bundle up. (*She picks up her hat and coat.* NORA*'s and* HELMER*'s voices can be heard outside; a key turns in the lock, and* HELMER *brings* NORA *into the hall almost by force. She is wearing the Italian costume with a large black shawl about her; he has on evening dress, with a black domino open over it.*)

NORA (*struggling in the doorway*):   No, no, no, not inside! I'm going up again. I don't want to leave so soon.

HELMER: But Nora dear—

NORA: Oh, I beg you, please, Torvald. From the bottom of my heart, *please*—only an hour more!

HELMER: Not a single minute, Nora darling. You know our agreement. Come on, in we go; you'll catch cold out here. (*In spite of her resistance, he gently draws her into the room.*)

MRS. LINDE: Good evening.

NORA: Kristine!

HELMER: Why, Mrs. Linde—are you here so late?

MRS. LINDE: Yes, I'm sorry, but I did want to see Nora in costume.

NORA: Have you been sitting here, waiting for me?

MRS. LINDE: Yes. I didn't come early enough; you were all upstairs; and then I thought I really couldn't leave without seeing you.

HELMER (*removing* NORA*'s shawl*):   Yes, take a good look. She's worth looking at, I can tell you that, Mrs. Linde. Isn't she lovely?

MRS. LINDE: Yes, I should say—

HELMER: A dream of loveliness, isn't she? That's what everyone thought at the party, too. But she's horribly stubborn—this sweet little thing. What's to be done with her? Can you imagine, I almost had to use force to pry her away.

NORA: Oh, Torvald, you're going to regret you didn't indulge me, even for just a half hour more.

HELMER: There, you see. She danced her tarantella and got a tumultuous hand—which was well earned, although the performance may have been a bit too naturalistic—I mean it rather overstepped the proprieties of art. But never mind—what's important is, she made a success, an overwhelming success. You think I could let her stay on after that and spoil the effect? Oh no; I took my lovely little Capri girl—my capricious little Capri girl, I should say—took her under my arm; one quick tour of the ballroom, a curtsy to every side, and then—as they say in novels—the beautiful vision disappeared. An exit should always be effective, Mrs. Linde, but that's what I can't get Nora to grasp. Phew, it's hot in here. (*Flings the domino on a chair and opens the door to his room*) Why's it dark in here? Oh yes, of course. Excuse me. (*He goes in and lights a couple of candles.*)

NORA (*in a sharp, breathless whisper*):   So?

MRS. LINDE (*quietly*):   I talked with him.

NORA: And—?

MRS. LINDE: Nora—you must tell your husband everything.

NORA (*dully*):   I knew it.

MRS. LINDE: You've got nothing to fear from Krogstad, but you have to speak out.

NORA: I won't tell.

MRS. LINDE: Then the letter will.

NORA: Thanks, Kristine. I know now what's to be done. Shh!

HELMER (*reentering*):   Well, then, Mrs. Linde—have you admired her?

MRS. LINDE: Yes, and now I'll say good night.

HELMER: Oh, come, so soon? Is this yours, this knitting?

MRS. LINDE: Yes, thanks. I nearly forgot it.

HELMER: Do you knit, then?

MRS. LINDE: Oh yes.

HELMER: You know what? You should embroider instead.

MRS. LINDE: Really? Why?

HELMER: Yes, because it's a lot prettier. See here, one holds the embroidery so, in the left hand, and then one guides the needle with the right—so—in an easy, sweeping curve—right?

MRS. LINDE: Yes, I guess that's—

HELMER: But, on the other hand, knitting—it can never be anything but ugly. Look, see here, the arms tucked in, the knitting needles going up and down—there's something Chinese about it. Ah, that was really a glorious champagne they served.

MRS. LINDE: Yes, good night, Nora, and don't be stubborn anymore.

HELMER: Well put, Mrs. Linde!

MRS. LINDE: Good night, Mr. Helmer.

HELMER (*accompanying her to the door*):   Good night, good night. I hope you get home all right. I'd be very happy to—but you don't have far to go. Good night, good night. (*She leaves. He shuts the door after her and returns.*) There, now, at last we got her out the door. She's a deadly bore, that creature.

NORA: Aren't you pretty tired, Torvald?

HELMER: No, not a bit.

NORA: You're not sleepy?

HELMER: Not at all. On the contrary, I'm feeling quite exhilarated. But you? Yes, you really look tired and sleepy.

NORA: Yes, I'm very tired. Soon now I'll sleep.

HELMER: See! You see! I was right all along that we shouldn't stay longer.

NORA: Whatever you do is always right.

HELMER (*kissing her brow*):   Now my little lark talks sense. Say, did you notice what a time Rank was having tonight?

NORA: Oh, was he? I didn't get to speak with him.

HELMER: I scarcely did either, but it's a long time since I've seen him in such high spirits. (*Gazes at her a moment, then comes nearer her*) Hm—it's marvelous, though, to be back home again—to be completely alone with you. Oh, you bewitchingly lovely young woman!

NORA: Torvald, don't look at me like that!

HELMER: Can't I look at my richest treasure? At all that beauty that's mine, mine alone—completely and utterly.

NORA (*moving around to the other side of the table*):   You mustn't talk to me that way tonight.

HELMER (*following her*):   The tarantella is still in your blood, I can see—and it makes you even more enticing. Listen. The guests are beginning to go. (*Dropping his voice*) Nora—it'll soon be quiet through this whole house.

NORA: Yes, I hope so.

HELMER: You do, don't you, my love? Do you realize—when I'm out at a party like this with you—do you know why I talk to you so little, and keep such a distance away; just send you a stolen look now and then—you know why I do it? It's because I'm imagining then that you're my secret darling, my secret young bride-to-be, and that no one suspects there's anything between us.

NORA: Yes, yes; oh, yes, I know you're always thinking of me.

HELMER: And then when we leave and I place the shawl over those fine young rounded shoulders—over that wonderful curving neck—then I pretend that you're my young bride, that we're just coming from the wedding, that for the first time I'm bringing you into my house—that for the first time I'm alone with you—completely alone with you, your trembling young beauty! All this evening I've longed for nothing but you. When I saw you turn and sway in the tarantella—my blood was pounding till I couldn't stand it—that's why I brought you down here so early—

NORA: Go away, Torvald! Leave me alone. I don't want all this.

HELMER: What do you mean? Nora, you're teasing me. You will, won't you? Aren't I your husband—?

(A knock at the outside door)

NORA *(startled)*:   What's that?

HELMER *(going toward the hall)*:   Who is it?

RANK *(outside)*:   It's me. May I come in a moment?

HELMER *(with quiet irritation)*:   Oh, what does he want now? *(Aloud)* Hold on. *(Goes and opens the door)* Oh, how nice that you didn't just pass us by!

RANK: I thought I heard your voice, and then I wanted so badly to have a look in. *(Lightly glancing about)* Ah, me, these old familiar haunts. You have it snug and cozy in here, you two.

HELMER: You seemed to be having it pretty cozy upstairs, too.

RANK: Absolutely. Why shouldn't I? Why not take in everything in life? As much as you can, anyway, and as long as you can. The wine was superb—

HELMER: The champagne especially.

RANK: You noticed that too? It's amazing how much I could guzzle down.

NORA: Torvald also drank a lot of champagne this evening.

RANK: Oh?

NORA: Yes, and that always makes him so entertaining.

RANK: Well, why shouldn't one have a pleasant evening after a well-spent day?

HELMER: Well spent? I'm afraid I can't claim that.

RANK *(slapping him on the back)*:   But I can, you see!

NORA: Dr. Rank, you must have done some scientific research today.

RANK: Quite so.

HELMER: Come now—little Nora talking about scientific research!

NORA: And can I congratulate you on the results?

RANK: Indeed you may.

NORA: Then they were good?

RANK: The best possible for both doctor and patient—certainty.

NORA *(quickly and searchingly)*:   Certainty?

RANK: Complete certainty. So don't I owe myself a gay evening afterwards?

NORA: Yes, you're right, Dr. Rank.

HELMER: I'm with you—just so long as you don't have to suffer for it in the morning.

RANK: Well, one never gets something for nothing in life.

NORA: Dr. Rank—are you very fond of masquerade parties?

RANK: Yes, if there's a good array of odd disguises—

NORA: Tell me, what should we two go as at the next masquerade?

HELMER: You little feather head—already thinking of the next!

RANK: We two? I'll tell you what: you must go as Charmed Life—

HELMER: Yes, but find a costume for *that!*

RANK: Your wife can appear just as she looks every day.

HELMER: That was nicely put. But don't you know what you're going to be?

RANK: Yes, Helmer, I've made up my mind.

HELMER: Well?

RANK: At the next masquerade I'm going to be invisible.

HELMER: That's a funny idea.

RANK: They say there's a hat—black, huge—have you never heard of the hat that makes you invisible? You put it on, and then no one on earth can see you.

HELMER (*suppressing a smile*):   Ah, of course.

RANK: But I'm quite forgetting what I came for. Helmer, give me a cigar, one of the dark Havanas.

HELMER: With the greatest pleasure. (*Holds out his case*)

RANK: Thanks. (*Takes one and cuts off the tip*)

NORA (*striking a match*):   Let me give you a light.

RANK: Thank you. (*She holds the match for him; he lights the cigar.*) And now good-bye.

HELMER: Good-bye, good-bye, old friend.

NORA: Sleep well, Doctor.

RANK: Thanks for that wish.

NORA: Wish me the same.

RANK: You? All right, if you like—Sleep well. And thanks for the light.

(*He nods to them both and leaves.*)

HELMER (*his voice subdued*):   He's been drinking heavily.

NORA (*absently*):   Could be. (HELMER *takes his keys from his pocket and goes out in the hall.*) Torvald—what are you after?

HELMER: Got to empty the mailbox; it's nearly full. There won't be room for the morning papers.

NORA: Are you working tonight?

HELMER: You know I'm not. Why—what's this? Someone's been at the lock.

NORA: At the lock—?

HELMER: Yes, I'm positive. What do you suppose—? I can't imagine one of the maids—? Here's a broken hairpin. Nora, it's yours—

NORA (*quickly*):   Then it must be the children—

HELMER: You'd better break them of that. Hm, hm—well, opened it after all. (*Takes the contents out and calls into the kitchen*) Helene! Helene, would you put out the lamp in the hall. (*He returns to the room, shutting the hall door, then displays the handful of mail.*) Look how it's piled up. (*Sorting through them*) Now what's this?

NORA (*at the window*):   The letter! Oh, Torvald, no!

HELMER: Two calling cards—from Rank.

NORA: From Dr. Rank?

HELMER (*examining them*):   "Dr. Rank, Consulting Physician." They were on top. He must have dropped them in as he left.

NORA: Is there anything on them?

HELMER: There's a black cross over the name. See? That's a gruesome notion. He could almost be announcing his own death.

NORA: That's just what he's doing.

HELMER: What! You've heard something? Something he's told you?

NORA: Yes. That when those cards came, he'd be taking his leave of us. He'll shut himself in now and die.

HELMER: Ah, my poor friend! Of course I knew he wouldn't be here much longer. But so soon—And then to hide himself away like a wounded animal.

NORA: If it has to happen, then it's best it happens in silence—don't you think so, Torvald?

HELMER (*pacing up and down*):   He's grown right into our lives. I simply can't imagine him gone. He with his suffering and loneliness—like a dark cloud setting off our sunlit happiness. Well, maybe it's best this way. For him, at least. (*Standing still*) And maybe for us too, Nora. Now we're thrown back on each other, completely. (*Embracing her*) Oh you, my darling wife, how can I hold you close enough? You know what, Nora—time and again I've wished you were in some terrible danger, just so I could stake my life and soul and everything, for your sake.

NORA (*tearing herself away, her voice firm and decisive*):   Now you must read your mail, Torvald.

HELMER: No, no, not tonight. I want to stay with you, dearest.

NORA: With a dying friend on your mind?

HELMER: You're right. We've both had a shock. There's ugliness between us— these thoughts of death and corruption. We'll have to get free of them first. Until then—we'll stay apart.

NORA (*clinging about his neck*):   Torvald—good night! Good night!

HELMER (*kissing her on the cheek*):   Good night, little songbird. Sleep well, Nora. I'll be reading my mail now.

(*He takes the letters into his room and shuts the door after him.*)

NORA (*with bewildered glances, groping about, seizing* HELMER*'s domino, throwing it around her, and speaking in short, hoarse, broken whispers*):   Never see him again. Never, never. (*Putting her shawl over her head*) Never see the children either—them, too. Never, never. Oh, the freezing black water! The depths—down—Oh, I wish it were over—He has it now; he's reading it—now. Oh no, no, not yet. Torvald, good-bye, you and the children— (*She starts for the hall; as she does,* HELMER *throws open his door and stands with an open letter in his hand.*)

HELMER: Nora!

NORA (*screams*):   Oh—!

HELMER: What is this? You know what's in this letter?

NORA: Yes, I know. Let me go! Let me out!

HELMER (*holding her back*):   Where are you going?

NORA (*struggling to break loose*):   You can't save me, Torvald!

HELMER (*slumping back*):   True! Then it's true what he writes? How horrible! No, no, it's impossible—it can't be true.

NORA: It *is* true. I've loved you more than all this world.

HELMER: Ah, none of your slippery tricks.

NORA (*taking one step toward him*):   Torvald—!

HELMER: What *is* this you've blundered into!

NORA: Just let me loose. You're not going to suffer for my sake. You're not going to take on my guilt.

HELMER: No more playacting. (*Locks the hall door*) You stay right here and give me a reckoning. You understand what you've done? Answer! You understand?

NORA (*looking squarely at him, her face hardening*):   Yes. I'm beginning to understand everything now.

HELMER (*striding about*):   Oh, what an awful awakening! In all these eight years— she who was my pride and joy—a hypocrite, a liar—worse, worse—a criminal! How infinitely disgusting it all is! The shame! (*NORA says nothing and goes on looking straight at him. He stops in front of her.*) I should have suspected something of the kind. I should have known. All your father's flimsy values—Be still! All your father's flimsy values have come out in you. No religion, no morals, no sense of duty—Oh, how I'm punished for letting him off! I did it for your sake, and you repay me like this.

NORA: Yes, like this.

HELMER: Now you've wrecked all my happiness—ruined my whole future. Oh, it's awful to think of. I'm in a cheap little grafter's hands; he can do anything he wants with me, ask for anything, play with me like a puppet—and I can't breathe a word. I'll be swept down miserably into the depths on account of a featherbrained woman.

NORA: When I'm gone from this world, you'll be free.

HELMER: Oh, quit posing. Your father had a mess of those speeches too. What good would that ever do me if you were gone from this world, as you say? Not the slightest. He can still make the whole thing known; and if he does, I could be falsely suspected as your accomplice. They might even think that I was behind it—that I put you up to it. And all that I can thank you for—you that I've coddled the whole of our marriage. Can you see now what you've done to me?

NORA (*icily calm*):   Yes.

HELMER: It's so incredible, I just can't grasp it. But we'll have to patch up whatever we can. Take off the shawl. I said, take it off! I've got to appease him somehow or other. The thing has to be hushed up at any cost. And as for you and me, it's got to seem like everything between us is just as it was—to the outside world, that is. You'll go right on living in this house, of course. But you can't be allowed to bring up the children; I don't dare trust you with them.—Oh, to have to say this to someone I've loved so much! Well, that's done with. From now on happiness doesn't matter; all that matters is saving the bits and pieces, the appearance—(*The doorbell rings.* HELMER *starts.*) What's that? And so late. Maybe the worst—? You think he'd—? Hide, Nora! Say you're sick. (*NORA remains standing motionless.* HELMER *goes and opens the door.*)

MAID (*half dressed, in the hall*):   A letter for Mrs. Helmer.

HELMER: I'll take it. (*Snatches the letter and shuts the door*) Yes, it's from him. You don't get it; I'm reading it myself.

NORA: Then read it.

HELMER (*by the lamp*):   I hardly dare. We may be ruined, you and I. But—I've got to know. (*Rips open the letter, skims through a few lines, glances at an enclosure, then cries out joyfully*) Nora! (*NORA looks inquiringly at him.*) Nora! Wait—better check it again—Yes, yes, it's true. I'm saved. Nora, I'm saved!

NORA: And I?

HELMER: You too, of course. We're both saved, both of us. Look. He's sent back your note. He says he's sorry and ashamed—that a happy development in his life—oh, who cares what he says! Nora, we're saved! No one can hurt you. Oh, Nora, Nora— but first, this ugliness all has to go. Let me see—(*Takes a look at the note*) No, I don't want to see it; I want the whole thing to fade like a dream. (*Tears the note and both letters to pieces, throws them into the stove and watches them burn*) There—now there's nothing left.—He wrote that since Christmas Eve you—oh, they must have been three terrible days for you, Nora.

NORA: I fought a hard fight.

HELMER: And suffered pain and saw no escape but—no, we're not going to dwell on anything unpleasant. We'll just be grateful and keep on repeating; it's over now, it's over! You hear me, Nora? You don't seem to realize—it's over. What's it mean—that frozen look? Oh, poor little Nora, I understand. You can't believe I've forgiven you. But I have, Nora; I swear I have. I know that what you did, you did out of love for me.

NORA: That's true.

HELMER: You loved me the way a wife ought to love her husband. It's simply the means that you couldn't judge. But you think I love you any the less for not knowing how to handle your affairs? No, no—just lean on me: I'll guide you and teach you. I wouldn't be a man if this feminine helplessness didn't make you twice as attractive to me. You mustn't mind those sharp words I said—that was all in the first confusion of thinking my world had collapsed. I've forgiven you, Nora; I swear I've forgiven you.

NORA: My thanks for your forgiveness.   (*She goes out through the door, right.*)

HELMER: No, wait—(*Peers in*) What are you doing in there?

NORA (*inside*):   Getting out of my costume.

HELMER (*by the open door*):   Yes, do that. Try to calm yourself and collect your thoughts again, my frightened little songbird. You can rest easy now; I've got wide wings to shelter you with. (*Walking about close by the door*) How snug and nice our home is, Nora. You're safe here; I'll keep you like a hunted dove I've rescued out of a hawk's claws. I'll bring peace to your poor, shuddering heart. Gradually it'll happen, Nora; you'll see. Tomorrow all this will look different to you; then everything will be as it was. I won't have to go on repeating I forgive you; you'll feel it for yourself. How can you imagine I'd ever conceivably want to disown you—or even blame you in any way? Ah, you don't know a man's heart, Nora. For a man there's something indescribably sweet and satisfying in knowing he's forgiven his wife—and forgiven her out of a full and open heart. It's as if she belongs to him in two ways now: in a sense he's given her fresh into the world again, and she's become his wife and his child as well. From now on that's what you'll be to me—you little, bewildered, helpless thing. Don't be afraid of anything, Nora; just open your heart to me, and I'll be conscience and will to you both—(NORA *enters in her regular clothes.*) What's this? Not in bed? You've changed your dress?

NORA: Yes, Torvald, I've changed my dress.

HELMER: But why now, so late?

NORA: Tonight I'm not sleeping.

HELMER: But Nora dear—

NORA (*looking at her watch*):   It's still not so very late. Sit down, Torvald; we have a lot to talk over. (*She sits at one side of the table.*)

HELMER: Nora—what is this? That hard expression—

NORA: Sit down. This'll take some time. I have a lot to say.

HELMER (*sitting at the table directly opposite her*):   You worry me, Nora. And I don't understand you.

NORA: No, that's exactly it. You don't understand me. And I've never understood you either—until tonight. No, don't interrupt. You can just listen to what I say. We're closing out accounts, Torvald.

HELMER: How do you mean that?

NORA (*after a short pause*):   Doesn't anything strike you about our sitting here like this?

HELMER: What's that?

NORA: We've been married now eight years. Doesn't it occur to you that this is the first time we two, you and I, man and wife, have ever talked seriously together?

HELMER: What do you mean—seriously?

NORA: In eight whole years—longer even—right from our first acquaintance, we've never exchanged a serious word on any serious thing.

HELMER: You mean I should constantly go and involve you in problems you couldn't possibly help me with?

NORA: I'm not talking of problems, I'm saying that we've never sat down seriously together and tried to get to the bottom of anything.

HELMER: But dearest, what good would that ever do you?

NORA: That's the point right there: you've never understood me. I've been wronged greatly, Torvald—first by Papa, and then by you.

HELMER: What! By us—the two people who've loved you more than anyone else?

NORA (*shaking her head*):   You never loved me. You've thought it fun to be in love with me, that's all.

HELMER: Nora, what a thing to say!

NORA: Yes, it's true now, Torvald. When I lived at home with Papa, he told me all his opinions, so I had the same ones too; or if they were different I hid them, since he wouldn't have cared for that. He used to call me his doll-child, and he played with me the way I played with my dolls. Then I came into your house—

HELMER: How can you speak of our marriage like that?

NORA (*unperturbed*):   I mean, then I went from Papa's hands into yours. You arranged everything to your own taste, and so I got the same taste as you—or I pretended to; I can't remember. I guess a little of both, first one, then the other. Now when I look back, it seems as if I'd lived here like a beggar—just from hand to mouth. I've lived by doing tricks for you, Torvald. But that's the way you wanted it. It's a great sin what you and Papa did to me. You're to blame that nothing's become of me.

HELMER: Nora, how unfair and ungrateful you are! Haven't you been happy here?

NORA: No, never. I thought so—but I never have.

HELMER: Not—not happy!

NORA: No, only lighthearted. And you've always been so kind to me. But our home's been nothing but a playpen. I've been your doll-wife here, just as at home I was Papa's doll-child. And in turn the children have been my dolls. I thought it was fun when you played with me, just as they thought it fun when I played with them. That's been our marriage, Torvald.

HELMER: There's some truth in what you're saying—under all the raving exaggeration. But it'll all be different after this. Playtime's over; now for the schooling.

NORA: Whose schooling—mine or the children's?

HELMER: Both yours and the children's, dearest.

NORA: Oh, Torvald, you're not the man to teach me to be a good wife to you.

HELMER: And you can say that?

NORA: And I—how am I equipped to bring up children?

HELMER: Nora!

NORA: Didn't you say a moment ago that that was no job to trust me with?

HELMER: In a flare of temper! Why fasten on that?

NORA: Yes, but you were so very right. I'm not up to the job. There's another job I have to do first. I have to try to educate myself. You can't help me with that. I've got to do it alone. And that's why I'm leaving you now.

HELMER (*jumping up*):   What's that?

NORA: I have to stand completely alone, if I'm ever going to discover myself and the world out there. So I can't go on living with you.

HELMER: Nora, Nora!

NORA: I want to leave right away. Kristine should put me up for the night—

HELMER: You're insane! You've no right! I forbid you!

NORA: From here on, there's no use forbidding me anything. I'll take with me whatever is mine. I don't want a thing from you, either now or later.

HELMER: What kind of madness is this!

NORA: Tomorrow I'm going home—I mean, home where I came from. It'll be easier up there to find something to do.

HELMER: Oh, you blind, incompetent child!

NORA: I must learn to be competent, Torvald.

HELMER: Abandon your home, your husband, your children! And you're not even thinking what people will say.

NORA: I can't be concerned about that. I only know how essential this is.

HELMER: Oh, it's outrageous. So you'll run out like this on your most sacred vows.

NORA: What do you think are my most sacred vows?

HELMER: And I have to tell you that! Aren't they your duties to your husband and children?

NORA: I have other duties equally sacred.

HELMER: That isn't true. What duties are they?

NORA: Duties to myself.

HELMER: Before all else, you're a wife and a mother.

NORA: I don't believe in that anymore. I believe that, before all else, I'm a human being, no less than you—or anyway, I ought to try to become one. I know the majority thinks you're right, Torvald, and plenty of books agree with you, too. But I can't go on believing what the majority says, or what's written in books. I have to think over these things myself and try to understand them.

HELMER: Why can't you understand your place in your own home? On a point like that, isn't there one everlasting guide you can turn to? Where's your religion?

NORA: Oh, Torvald, I'm really not sure what religion is.

HELMER: What—?

NORA: I only know what the minister said when I was confirmed. He told me religion was this thing and that. When I get clear and away by myself, I'll go into that problem too. I'll see if what the minister said was right, or, in any case, if it's right for me.

HELMER: A young woman your age shouldn't talk like that. If religion can't move you, I can try to rouse your conscience. You do have some moral feeling? Or, tell me—has that gone too?

NORA: It's not easy to answer that, Torvald. I simply don't know. I'm all confused about these things. I just know I see them so differently from you. I find out, for one thing, that the law's not at all what I'd thought—but I can't get it through my head that the law is fair. A woman hasn't a right to protect her dying father or save her husband's life! I can't believe that.

HELMER: You talk like a child. You don't know anything of the world you live in.

NORA: No, I don't. But now I'll begin to learn for myself. I'll try to discover who's right, the world or I.

HELMER: Nora, you're sick; you've got a fever. I almost think you're out of your head.

NORA: I've never felt more clearheaded and sure in my life.

HELMER: And—clearheaded and sure—you're leaving your husband and children?

NORA: Yes.

HELMER: Then there's only one possible reason.

NORA: What?

HELMER: You no longer love me.

NORA: No. That's exactly it.

HELMER: Nora! You can't be serious!

NORA: Oh, this is so hard, Torvald—you've been so kind to me always. But I can't help it. I don't love you anymore.

HELMER (*struggling for composure*):   Are you also clearheaded and sure about that?

NORA: Yes, completely. That's why I can't go on staying here.

HELMER: Can you tell me what I did to lose your love?

NORA: Yes, I can tell you. It was this evening when the miraculous thing didn't come—then I knew you weren't the man I'd imagined.

HELMER: Be more explicit; I don't follow you.

NORA: I've waited now so patiently eight long years—for, my Lord, I know miracles don't come every day. Then this crisis broke over me, and such a certainty filled me: *now* the miraculous event would occur. While Krogstad's letter was lying out there, I never for an instant dreamed that you could give in to his terms. I was so utterly sure you'd say to him: go on, tell your tale to the whole wide world. And when he'd done that—

HELMER: Yes, what then? When I'd delivered my own wife into shame and disgrace—!

NORA: When he'd done that, I was so utterly sure that you'd step forward, take the blame on yourself and say: I am the guilty one.

HELMER: Nora—!

NORA: You're thinking I'd never accept such a sacrifice from you? No, of course not. But what good would my protests be against you? That was the miracle I was waiting for, in terror and hope. And to stave that off, I would have taken my life.

HELMER: I'd gladly work for you day and night, Nora—and take on pain and deprivation. But there's no one who gives up honor for love.

NORA: Millions of women have done just that.

HELMER: Oh, you think and talk like a silly child.

NORA: Perhaps. But you neither think nor talk like the man I could join myself to. When your big fright was over—and it wasn't from any threat against me, only for what might damage you—when all the danger was past, for you it was just as if nothing had happened. I was exactly the same, your little lark, your doll, that you'd have to handle with double care now that I'd turned out so brittle and frail. (*Gets up*) Torvald—in that instant it dawned on me that for eight years I've been living here with a stranger, and that I'd even conceived three children—oh, I can't stand the thought of it! I could tear myself to bits.

HELMER (*heavily*): I see. There's a gulf that's opened between us—that's clear. Oh, but Nora, can't we bridge it somehow?

NORA: The way I am now, I'm no wife for you.

HELMER: I have the strength to make myself over.

NORA: Maybe—if your doll gets taken away.

HELMER: But to part! To part from you! No, Nora, no—I can't imagine it.

NORA (*going out, right*): All the more reason why it has to be. (*She reenters with her coat and a small overnight bag, which she puts on a chair by the table.*)

HELMER: Nora, Nora, not now! Wait till tomorrow.

NORA: I can't spend the night in a strange man's room.

HELMER: But couldn't we live here like brother and sister—

NORA: You know very well how long that would last. (*Throws her shawl about her*) Good-bye, Torvald. I won't look in on the children. I know they're in better hands than mine. The way I am now, I'm no use to them.

HELMER: But someday, Nora—someday—?

NORA: How can I tell? I haven't the least idea what'll become of me.

HELMER: But you're my wife, now and wherever you go.

NORA: Listen, Torvald—I've heard that when a wife deserts her husband's house just as I'm doing, then the law frees him from all responsibility. In any case, I'm freeing you from being responsible. Don't feel yourself bound, any more than I will. There has to be absolute freedom for us both. Here, take your ring back. Give me mine.

HELMER: That too?

NORA: That too.

HELMER: There it is.

NORA: Good. Well, now it's all over. I'm putting the keys here. The maids know all about keeping up the house—better than I do. Tomorrow, after I've left town, Kristine will stop by to pack up everything that's mine from home. I'd like those things shipped to me.

HELMER: Over! All over! Nora, won't you ever think about me?

NORA: I'm sure I'll think of you often, and about the children and the house here.

HELMER: May I write you?

NORA: No—never. You're not to do that.

HELMER: Oh, but let me send you—

NORA: Nothing. Nothing.

HELMER: Or help you if you need it.

NORA: No. I accept nothing from strangers.

HELMER: Nora—can I never be more than a stranger to you?

NORA (*picking up the overnight bag*): Ah, Torvald—it would take the greatest miracle of all—

HELMER: Tell me the greatest miracle!

NORA: You and I both would have to transform ourselves to the point that—oh, Torvald, I've stopped believing in miracles.

HELMER: But I'll believe. Tell me! Transform ourselves to the point that—?

NORA: That our living together could be a true marriage.

(She goes out down the hall.)

HELMER *(sinks down on a chair by the door, face buried in his hands)*: Nora! Nora! *(Looking about and rising)* Empty. She's gone. *(A sudden hope leaps in him)* The greatest miracle—?

(From below, the sound of a door slamming shut)

(1879)

QUESTIONS FOR REFLECTION

Experience

1. Describe your experience of reading (or viewing) *A Doll House*. How do you respond to Torvald Helmer's treatment of his wife, Nora? How do you respond to Nora's behavior? Why?
2. Describe Torvald Helmer. What aspects of his character are most evident in the early scenes? Does he give any evidence of having changed by the end of the play? Do you think he is capable of sharing the kind of marriage Nora describes at the end of the play?

Interpretation

3. Consider the function of the following characters: Nils Krogstad, Dr. Rank, and Kristine Linde.
4. Examine the play's plot. How does Ibsen control our responses and arouse our curiosity? Point out places where the tempo or pace of the play changes. What effects do these changes have?
5. Identify two or three visual details or objects that function as symbols, and explain their significance.
6. Choose one scene important for its revelation of character and explain how you would dramatize it.

Evaluation

7. Evaluate Nora's behavior. Does she make the right decision in leaving her family? Why or why not?
8. Ibsen has remarked that *A Doll House* is more about human rights than women's rights. What kind of rights do you think he had in mind?
9. *A Doll House* has been performed with an alternative ending in which Nora and Torvald are reconciled, and Nora remains with her family. Is this an artistically appropriate and theatrically effective ending? Why or why not?

CHAPTER EIGHT

A Collection of Modern and Contemporary Plays

All the world's a stage,
And all the men and women merely players:
They have their exits and their entrances,
And one man in his time plays many parts. . . .

WILLIAM SHAKESPEARE, *AS YOU LIKE IT,* II, VII

ISABELLA AUGUSTA PERSSE, LADY GREGORY

[1859–1932]

Born to a wealthy landowning family in Galway, in western Ireland, Isabella Augusta Persse, who married Sir William Gregory, a former governor of Ceylon, was a patroness of the Irish poet William Butler Yeats before she became a writer. Although she edited legendary Irish tales and translated Gaelic epics, she is best known as a writer of witty nationalistic plays like *The Rising of the Moon*. With Yeats, she founded the Irish Literary Theatre, an institution central to the rise of the Irish nationalist movement at the beginning of the twentieth century.

ISABELLA AUGUSTA PERSSE,
LADY GREGORY

The Rising of the Moon

Scene: *Side of a quay in a seaport town. Some posts and chains. A large barrel. Enter three policemen. Moonlight.*

SERGEANT, *who is older than the others, crosses the stage to right and looks down steps. The others put down a pastepot and unroll a bundle of placards.*

POLICEMAN B: I think this would be a good place to put up a notice. (*He points to a barrel.*)

POLICEMAN X: Better ask him. (*Calls to* SERGEANT) Will this be a good place for a placard? (*No answer.*)

POLICEMAN B: Will we put up a notice here on the barrel? (*No answer.*)

SERGEANT: There's a flight of steps here that leads down to the water. This is a place that should be minded well. If he got down here, his friends might have a boat to meet him; they might send it in here from outside.

POLICEMAN B: Would the barrel be a good place to put a notice up?

SERGEANT: It might; you can put it there.

(*They paste the notice up.*)

SERGEANT (*reading it*): Dark hair—dark eyes, smooth face, height over five feet five—there's not much to take hold of in that—It's a pity I had no chance of seeing him before he broke out of gaol. They say he's a wonder, that it's he makes all the plans for the whole organization. There isn't another man in Ireland would have broken gaol the way he did. He must have some friends among the gaolers.

POLICEMAN B: A hundred pounds is little enough for the Government to offer for him. You may be sure any man in the force that takes him will get promotion.

SERGEANT: I'll mind this place myself. I wouldn't wonder at all if he came this way. He might come slipping along there (*points to side of quay*), and his friends might be waiting for him there (*points down steps*), and once he got away it's little chance we'd have of finding him; it's maybe under a load of kelp he'd be in a fishing boat, and not one to help a married man that wants it to the reward.

POLICEMAN X: And if we get him itself, nothing but abuse on our heads for it from the people, and maybe from our own relations.

SERGEANT: Well, we have to do our duty in the force. Haven't we the whole country depending on us to keep law and order? It's those that are down would be up and those that are up would be down, if it wasn't for us. Well, hurry on, you have plenty of other places to placard yet, and come back here then to me. You can take the lantern. Don't be too long now. It's very lonesome here with nothing but the moon.

POLICEMAN B: It's a pity we can't stop with you. The Government should have brought more police into the town, with *him* in gaol, and at assize time too. Well, good luck to your watch. (*They go out.*)

SERGEANT (*walks up and down once or twice and looks at placard*): A hundred pounds and promotion sure. There must be a great deal of spending in a hundred pounds. It's a pity some honest man not to be the better of that.

(*A ragged man appears at left and tries to slip past.* SERGEANT *suddenly turns.*)

SERGEANT: Where are you going?

MAN: I'm a poor ballad-singer, your honor. I thought to sell some of these (*holds out bundle of ballads*) to the sailors. (*He goes on.*)

SERGEANT: Stop! Didn't I tell you to stop? You can't go on there.

MAN: Oh, very well. It's a hard thing to be poor. All the world's against the poor!

SERGEANT: Who are you?

MAN: You'd be as wise as myself if I told you, but I don't mind. I'm one Jimmy Walsh, a ballad-singer.

SERGEANT: Jimmy Walsh? I don't know that name.

MAN: Ah, sure, they know it well enough in Ennis. Were you ever in Ennis, Sergeant?

SERGEANT: What brought you here?

MAN: Sure, it's to the assizes I came, thinking I might make a few shillings here or there. It's in the one train with the judges I came.

SERGEANT: Well, if you came so far, you may as well go farther, for you'll walk out of this.

MAN: I will, I will; I'll just go on where I was going. (*Goes toward steps.*)

SERGEANT: Come back from those steps; no one has leave to pass down them tonight.

MAN: I'll just sit on the top of the steps till I see will some sailor buy a ballad off me that would give me my supper. They do be late going back to the ship. It's often I saw them in Cork carried down the quay in a hand-cart.

SERGEANT: Move on, I tell you. I won't have any one lingering about the quay tonight.

MAN: Well, I'll go. It's the poor have the hard life! Maybe yourself might like one, Sergeant. Here's a good sheet now. (*Turns one over*) "Content and a pipe"—that's not much. "The Peeler and the Goat"—you wouldn't like that. "Johnny Hart"—that's a lovely song.

SERGEANT: Move on.

MAN: Ah, wait till you hear it.

(*Sings.*)

> There was a rich farmer's daughter lived near the town of Ross;
> She courted a Highland soldier, his name was Johnny Hart;
> Says the mother to her daughter, "I'll go distracted mad
> If you marry that Highland soldier dressed up in Highland plaid."

SERGEANT: Stop that noise.

(MAN *wraps up his ballads and shuffles toward the steps.*)

SERGEANT: Where are you going?

MAN: Sure you told me to be going, and I am going.

SERGEANT: Don't be a fool. I didn't tell you to go that way; I told you to go back to the town.

MAN: Back to the town, is it?

SERGEANT (*taking him by the shoulder and shoving him before him*):   Here, I'll show you the way. Be off with you. What are you stopping for?

MAN (*who has been keeping his eye on the notice, points to it*):   I think I know what you're waiting for, Sergeant.

SERGEANT: What's that to you?

MAN: And I know well the man you're waiting for—I know him well—I'll be going. (*He shuffles on.*)

SERGEANT: You know him? Come back here. What sort is he?

MAN: Come back is it, Sergeant? Do you want to have me killed?

SERGEANT: Why do you say that?

MAN: Never mind. I'm going. I wouldn't be in your shoes if the reward was ten times as much. (*Goes on off stage to left*) Not if it was ten times as much.

SERGEANT (*rushing after him*):   Come back here, come back. (*Drags him back*) What sort is he? Where did you see him?

MAN: I saw him in my own place, in the County Clare. I tell you you wouldn't like to be looking at him. You'd be afraid to be in the one place with him. There isn't a weapon he doesn't know the use of, and as to strength, his muscles are as hard as that board. (*Slaps barrel.*)

SERGEANT: Is he as bad as that?

MAN: He is then.

SERGEANT: Do you tell me so?

MAN: There was a poor man in our place, a sergeant from Ballyvaughan.—It was with a lump of stone he did it.

SERGEANT: I never heard of that.

MAN: And you wouldn't, Sergeant. It's not everything that happens gets into the papers. And there was a policeman in plain clothes, too . . . It is in Limerick he was. . . . It was after the time of the attack on the police barrack at Kilmallock. . . . Moonlight . . . just like this . . . waterside. . . . Nothing was known for certain.

SERGEANT: Do you say so? It's a terrible county to belong to.

MAN: That's so, indeed! You might be standing there, looking out that way, thinking you saw him coming up this side of the quay (*points*) and he might be coming up this other side (*points*), and he'd be on you before you knew where you were.

SERGEANT: It's a whole troop of police they ought to put here to stop a man like that.

MAN: But if you'd like me to stop with you, I could be looking down this side. I could be sitting up here on this barrel.

SERGEANT: And you know him well, too?

MAN: I'd know him a mile off, Sergeant.

SERGEANT: But you wouldn't want to share the reward?

MAN: Is it a poor man like me, that has to be going the roads and singing in fairs, to have the name on him that he took a reward? But you don't want me. I'll be safer in the town.

SERGEANT: Well, you can stop.

MAN (*getting up on barrel*):   All right, Sergeant. I wonder, now, you're not tired out, Sergeant, walking up and down the way you are.

SERGEANT: If I'm tired I'm used to it.

MAN: You might have hard work before you tonight yet. Take it easy while you can. There's plenty of room up here on the barrel, and you see farther when you're higher up.

SERGEANT: Maybe so. (*Gets up beside him on barrel, facing right. They sit back to back, looking different ways*) You made me feel a bit queer with the way you talked.

MAN: Give me a match, Sergeant (*he gives it and* MAN *lights pipe*); take a draw yourself? It'll quiet you. Wait now till I give you a light, but you needn't turn round. Don't take your eye off the quay for the life of you.

SERGEANT: Never fear, I won't. (*Lights pipe. They both smoke*) Indeed it's a hard thing to be in the force, out at night and no thanks for it, for all the danger we're in. And it's little we get but abuse from the people, and no choice but to obey our orders, and never asked when a man is sent into danger, if you are a married man with a family.

MAN (*sings*):

> As through the hills I walked to view the hills and shamrock plain,
> I stood awhile where nature smiles to view the rocks and streams,
> On a matron fair I fixed my eyes beneath a fertile vale,
> As she sang her song it was on the wrong of poor old Granuaile.

SERGEANT: Stop that; that's no song to be singing in these times.

MAN: Ah, Sergeant, I was only singing to keep my heart up. It sinks when I think of him. To think of us two sitting here, and he creeping up the quay, maybe, to get to us.

SERGEANT: Are you keeping a good lookout?

MAN: I am; and for no reward too. Amn't I the foolish man? But when I saw a man in trouble, I never could help trying to get him out of it. What's that? Did something hit me? (*Rubs his heart.*)

SERGEANT (*patting him on the shoulder*):   You will get your reward in heaven.

MAN: I know that, I know that, Sergeant, but life is precious.

SERGEANT: Well, you can sing if it gives you more courage.

MAN (*sings*):

> Her head was bare, her hands and feet with iron bands were bound,
> Her pensive strain and plaintive wail mingles with the evening gale,
> And the song she sang with mournful air, I am old Granuaile.
> Her lips so sweet that monarchs kissed . . .

SERGEANT: That's not it. . . . "Her gown she wore was stained with gore." . . . That's it—you missed that.

MAN: You're right, Sergeant, so it is; I missed it. (*Repeats line*) But to think of a man like you knowing a song like that.

SERGEANT: There's many a thing a man might know and might not have any wish for.

MAN: Now, I daresay, Sergeant, in your youth, you used to be sitting up on a wall, the way you are sitting up on this barrel now, and the other lads beside you, and you singing "Granuaile"? . . .

SERGEANT: I did then.

MAN: And the "Shan Bhean Bhocht"? . . .

SERGEANT: I did then.

MAN: And the "Green on the Cape"?

SERGEANT: That was one of them.

MAN: And maybe the man you are watching for tonight used to be sitting on the wall, when he was young, and singing those same songs. . . . It's a queer world.

SERGEANT: Whisht! . . . I think I see something coming. . . . It's only a dog.

MAN: And isn't it a queer world? . . . Maybe it's one of the boys you used to be singing with that time you will be arresting today or tomorrow, and sending into the dock.

SERGEANT: That's true indeed.

MAN: And maybe one night, after you had been singing, if the other boys had told you some plan they had, some plan to free the country, you might have joined with them . . . and maybe it is you might be in trouble now.

SERGEANT: Well, who knows but I might? I had a great spirit in those days.

MAN: It's a queer world, Sergeant, and it's little any mother knows when she sees her child creeping on the floor what might happen to it before it has gone through its life, or who will be who in the end.

SERGEANT: That's a queer thought now, and a true thought. Wait now till I think it out. . . . If it wasn't for the sense I have, and for my wife and family, and for me joining the force the time I did, it might be myself now would be after breaking gaol and hiding in the dark, and it might be him that's hiding in the dark and that got out of gaol would be sitting up where I am on this barrel. . . . And it might be myself would be creeping up trying to make my escape from himself, and it might be himself would be keeping the law, and myself would be breaking it, and myself would be trying maybe to put a bullet in his head, or to take up a lump of a stone the way you said he did . . . no, that myself did. . . . Oh! (*Gasps. After a pause*) What's that? (*Grasps* MAN's *arm.*)

MAN (*jumps off barrel and listens, looking out over water*):   It's nothing, Sergeant.

SERGEANT: I thought it might be a boat. I had a notion there might be friends of his coming about the quays with a boat.

MAN: Sergeant, I am thinking it was with the people you were, and not with the law you were, when you were a young man.

SERGEANT: Well, if I was foolish then, that time's gone.

MAN: Maybe, Sergeant, it comes into your head sometimes, in spite of your belt and your tunic, that it might have been as well for you to have followed Granuaile.

SERGEANT: It's no business of yours what I think.

MAN: Maybe, Sergeant, you'll be on the side of the country yet.

SERGEANT (*gets off barrel*):   Don't talk to me like that. I have my duties and I know them. (*Looks round*) That was a boat; I hear the oars. (*Goes to the steps and looks down.*)

MAN (*sings*):

> *O, then, tell me, Shawn O'Farrell,*
> *Where the gathering is to be.*
> *In the old spot by the river*
> *Right well known to you and me!*

SERGEANT: Stop that! Stop that, I tell you!

MAN (*sings louder*):

> *One word more, for signal token,*
> *Whistle up the marching tune,*
> *with your pike upon your shoulder,*
> *At the Rising of the Moon.*

SERGEANT: If you don't stop that, I'll arrest you.

(*A whistle from below answers, repeating the air.*)

SERGEANT: That's a signal. (*Stands between him and steps*) You must not pass this way. . . . Step farther back. . . . Who are you? You are no ballad-singer.

MAN: You needn't ask who I am; that placard will tell you. (*Points to placard.*)

SERGEANT: You are the man I am looking for.

MAN (*takes off hat and wig.* SERGEANT *seizes them*):   I am. There's a hundred pounds on my head. There is a friend of mine below in a boat. He knows a safe place to bring me to.

SERGEANT (*looking still at hat and wig*):   It's a pity! It's a pity. You deceived me. You deceived me well.

MAN: I am a friend of Granuaile. There is a hundred pounds on my head.

SERGEANT: It's a pity, it's a pity!

MAN: Will you let me pass, or must I make you let me?

SERGEANT: I am in the force. I will not let you pass.

MAN: I thought to do it with my tongue. (*Puts hand in breast*) What is that?
       (*Voice of* POLICEMAN X *outside.*) Here, this is where we left him.

SERGEANT: It's my comrades coming.

MAN: You won't betray me . . . the friend of Granuaile. (*Slips behind barrel.*)
       (*Voice of* POLICEMAN B.) That was the last of the placards.

POLICEMAN X (*as they come in*):   If he makes his escape it won't be unknown he'll make it.

(SERGEANT *puts hat and wig behind his back.*)

POLICEMAN B: Did any one come this way?

SERGEANT (*after a pause*):   No one.

POLICEMAN B: No one at all?

SERGEANT: No one at all.

POLICEMAN B: We had no orders to go back to the station; we can stop along with you.

SERGEANT: I don't want you. There is nothing for you to do here.

POLICEMAN B: You bade us to come back here and keep watch with you.

SERGEANT: I'd sooner be alone. Would any man come this way and you making all that talk? It is better the place be quiet.

POLICEMAN B: Well, we'll leave you the lantern anyhow. (*Hands it to him.*)

SERGEANT: I don't want it. Bring it with you.

POLICEMAN B: You might want it. There are clouds coming up and you have the darkness of the night before you yet. I'll leave it over here on the barrel. (*Goes to barrel.*)

SERGEANT: Bring it with you I tell you. No more talk.

POLICEMAN B: Well, I thought it might be a comfort to you. I often think when I have it in my hand and can be flashing it about into every dark corner (*doing so*) that it's the same as being beside the fire at home, and the bits of bogwood blazing up now and again. (*Flashes it about, now on the barrel, now on* SERGEANT.)

SERGEANT (*furious*):   Be off the two of you, yourselves and your lantern!

(*They go out.* MAN *comes from behind barrel. He and* SERGEANT *stand looking at one another.*)

SERGEANT: What are you waiting for?

MAN: For my hat, of course, and my wig. You wouldn't wish me to get my death of cold?

(SERGEANT *gives them.*)

MAN (*going toward steps*):   Well, good night, comrade, and thank you. You did me a good turn tonight, and I'm obliged to you. Maybe I'll be able to do as much for you when the small rise up and the big fall down . . . when we all change places at the Rising (*waves his hand and disappears*) of the Moon.

SERGEANT (*turning his back to audience and reading placard*):   A hundred pounds reward! A hundred pounds! (*Turns toward audience*) I wonder, now, am I as great a fool as I think I am?

(*1907*)

QUESTIONS FOR REFLECTION

Experience

1. As you read *The Rising of the Moon,* at what point did you realize the Sergeant's divided loyalties? How do you respond to the Sergeant's predicament? To what extent do you sympathize with him? To what extent have you experienced an analogous division of loyalties? With what consequences?

Interpretation

2. What are the central issues of the play?
3. Which side do you think the playwright takes on the issues? Why?
4. What is ironic about the situations of the Sergeant and the hunted man?

Evaluation

5. Lady Gregory's play turns on a conflict of values, with the Sergeant caught between his sympathy for the hunted man and his desire to earn a substantial reward for turning him in. What do you think the Sergeant should do? Why?

JOHN MILLINGTON SYNGE

[1871–1909]

Like Lady Gregory and William Butler Yeats, John Millington Synge was an Irish dramatist intensely involved in the Irish literary renaissance. With Yeats and Lady Gregory, Synge served as codirector of the Abbey Theatre in Dublin. At Yeats's suggestion, Synge brought his knowledge and experience of the Irish peasantry, especially from his visits to the Aran Islands, into the language and dramatic situations of his plays. Yeats convinced Synge to abandon writing criticism and to write plays about simple people whose language reflected an intimate contact with earth, sea, and sky. In addition to *Riders to the Sea* (1904), which shows the extent to which he took Yeats's advice, Synge is best known for his masterful comedy, *The Playboy of the Western World* (1907). His journal of impressions (*The Aran Islands*) provides important information about the life of the island people and a helpful glimpse into the raw material Synge shaped into dramatic art.

JOHN MILLINGTON SYNGE

Riders to the Sea

CHARACTERS

MAURYA, *an old woman*
BARTLEY, *her son*
CATHLEEN, *her daughter*
NORA, *a younger daughter*
MEN AND WOMEN

Scene. *An island off the West of Ireland.*

Cottage kitchen, with nets, oilskins, spinning-wheel, some new boards standing by the wall, etc. CATHLEEN, *a girl of about twenty, finishes kneading cake, and puts it down in the pot-oven by the fire; then wipes her hands, and begins to spin at the wheel.* NORA, *a young girl, puts her head in at the door.*

NORA (*in a low voice*):   Where is she?
CATHLEEN: She's lying down, God help her, and maybe sleeping, if she's able.

> NORA *comes in softly, and takes a bundle from under her shawl.*

CATHLEEN (*spinning the wheel rapidly*):   What is it you have?

NORA: The young priest is after bringing them. It's a shirt and a plain stocking were got off a drowned man in Donegal.

CATHLEEN *stops her wheel with a sudden movement, and leans out to listen.*

NORA: We're to find out if it's Michael's they are, some time herself will be down looking by the sea.

CATHLEEN: How would they be Michael's, Nora? How would he go the length of that way to the far north?

NORA: The young priest says he's known the like of it. 'If it's Michael's they are,' says he, 'you can tell herself he's got a clean burial, by the grace of God; and if they're not his, let no one say a word about them, for she'll be getting her death,' says he, 'with crying and lamenting.'

The door which NORA *half closed is blown open by a gust of wind.*

CATHLEEN (*looking out anxiously*):   Did you ask him would he stop Bartley going this day with the horses to the Galway fair?

NORA: 'I won't stop him,' says he; 'but let you not be afraid. Herself does be saying prayers half through the night, and the Almighty God won't leave her destitute,' says he, 'with no son living.'

CATHLEEN: Is the sea bad by the white rocks, Nora?

NORA: Middling bad, God help us. There's a great roaring in the west, and it's worse it'll be getting when the tide's turned to the wind. (*She goes over to the table with the bundle.*) Shall I open it now?

CATHLEEN: Maybe she'd wake up on us, and come in before we'd done (*coming to the table*). It's a long time we'll be, and the two of us crying.

NORA (*goes to the inner door and listens*):   She's moving about on the bed. She'll be coming in a minute.

CATHLEEN: Give me the ladder, and I'll put them up in the turf-loft, the way she won't know of them at all, and maybe when the tide turns she'll be going down to see would he be floating from the east.

They put the ladder against the gable of the chimney; CATHLEEN *goes up a few steps and hides the bundle in the turf-loft.* MAURYA *comes from the inner room.*

MAURYA (*looking up at* CATHLEEN *and speaking querulously*):   Isn't it turf enough you have for this day and evening?

CATHLEEN: There's a cake baking at the fire for a short space (*throwing down the turf*), and Bartley will want it when the tide turns if he goes to Connemara.

NORA *picks up the turf and puts it round the pot-oven.*

MAURYA (*sitting down on a stool at the fire*):   He won't go this day with the wind rising from the south and west. He won't go this day, for the young priest will stop him surely.

NORA: He'll not stop him, mother; and I heard Eamon Simon and Stephen Pheety and Colum Shawn saying he would go.

MAURYA: Where is he itself?

NORA: He went down to see would there be another boat sailing in the week, and I'm thinking it won't be long till he's here now, for the tide's turning at the green head, and the hooker's tacking from the east.

CATHLEEN: I hear some one passing the big stones.

NORA (*looking out*):   He's coming now, and he in a hurry.

BARTLEY (*comes in and looks round the room. Speaking sadly and quietly*):   Where is the bit of new rope, Cathleen, was bought in Connemara?

CATHLEEN (*coming down*):   Give it to him, Nora; it's on a nail by the white boards. I hung it up this morning, for the pig with the black feet was eating it.

NORA (*giving him a rope*):   Is that it, Bartley?

MAURYA: You'd do right to leave that rope, Bartley, hanging by the boards (BARTLEY *takes the rope*). It will be wanting in this place, I'm telling you, if Michael is washed up tomorrow morning or the next morning, or any morning in the week; for it's a deep grave we'll make him, by the grace of God.

BARTLEY (*beginning to work with the rope*):   I've no halter the way I can ride down on the mare, and I must go now quickly. This is the one boat going for two weeks or beyond it, and the fair will be a good fair for horses, I heard them saying below.

MAURYA: It's a hard thing they'll be saying below if the body is washed up and there's no man in it to make the coffin, and I after giving a big price for the finest white boards you'd find in Connemara.

She looks round at the boards.

BARTLEY: How would it be washed up, and we after looking each day for nine days, and a strong wind blowing a while back from the west and south?

MAURYA: If it isn't found itself, that wind is raising the sea, and there was a star up against the moon, and it rising in the night. If it was a hundred horses, or a thousand horses, you had itself, what is the price of a thousand horses against a son where there is one son only?

BARTLEY (*working at the halter, to* CATHLEEN):   Let you go down each day, and see the sheep aren't jumping in on the rye, and if the jobber comes you can sell the pig with the black feet if there is a good price going.

MAURYA: How would the like of her get a good price for a pig?

BARTLEY (*to* CATHLEEN):   If the west wind holds with the last bit of the moon let you and Nora get up weed enough for another cock for the kelp. It's hard set we'll be from this day with no one in it but one man to work.

MAURYA: It's hard set we'll be surely the day you're drowned with the rest. What way will I live and the girls with me, and I an old woman looking for the grave?

BARTLEY *lays down the halter, takes off his old coat, and puts on a newer one of the same flannel.*

BARTLEY (*to* NORA):   Is she coming to the pier?

NORA (*looking out*):   She's passing the green head and letting fall her sails.

BARTLEY (*getting his purse and tobacco*):   I'll have half an hour to go down, and you'll see me coming again in two days, or in three days, or maybe in four days if the wind is bad.

MAURYA (*turning round to the fire, and putting her shawl over her head*):   Isn't it a hard and cruel man won't hear a word from an old woman, and she holding him from the sea?

CATHLEEN: It's the life of a young man to be going on the sea, and who would listen to an old woman with one thing and she saying it over?

BARTLEY (*taking the halter*):   I must go now quickly. I'll ride down on the red mare, and the grey pony 'ill run behind me. . . . The blessing of God on you.

He goes out.

MAURYA (*crying out as he is in the door*):   He's gone now, God spare us, and we'll not see him again. He's gone now, and when the black night is falling I'll have no son left me in the world.

CATHLEEN: Why wouldn't you give him your blessing and he looking round in the door? Isn't it sorrow enough is on every one in this house without you sending him out with an unlucky word behind him, and a hard word in his ear?

MAURYA *takes up the tongs and begins raking the fire aimlessly without looking round.*

NORA (*turning towards her*):   You're taking away the turf from the cake.

CATHLEEN (*crying out*):   The Son of God forgive us, Nora, we're after forgetting his bit of bread. (*She comes over to the fire.*)

NORA: And it's destroyed he'll be going till dark night, and he after eating nothing since the sun went up.

CATHLEEN (*turning the cake out of the oven*):   It's destroyed he'll be, surely. There's no sense left on any person in a house where an old woman will be talking for ever.

MAURYA *sways herself on her stool.*

CATHLEEN (*cutting off some of the bread and rolling it in a cloth; to* MAURYA):   Let you go down now to the spring well and give him this and he passing. You'll see him then and the dark word will be broken, and you can say 'God speed you,' the way he'll be easy in his mind.

MAURYA (*taking the bread*):   Will I be in it as soon as himself?

CATHLEEN: If you go now quickly.

MAURYA (*standing up unsteadily*):   It's hard set I am to walk.

CATHLEEN (*looking at her anxiously*):   Give her the stick, Nora, or maybe she'll slip on the big stones.

NORA: What stick?

CATHLEEN: The stick Michael brought from Connemara.

MAURYA (*taking a stick* NORA *gives her*).   In the big world the old people do be leaving things after them for their sons and children, but in this place it is the young men do be leaving things behind for them that do be old.

She goes out slowly. NORA *goes over to the ladder.*

CATHLEEN: Wait, Nora, maybe she'd turn back quickly. She's that sorry, God help her, you wouldn't know the thing she'd do.

NORA: Is she gone round by the bush?

CATHLEEN (*looking out*):   She's gone now. Throw it down quickly, for the Lord knows when she'll be out of it again.

NORA (*getting the bundle from the loft*):   The young priest said he'd be passing to-morrow, and we might go down and speak to him below if it's Michael's they are surely.

CATHLEEN (*taking the bundle*):   Did he say what way they were found?

NORA (*coming down*): 'There were two men,' says he, 'and they rowing round with poteen before the cocks crowed, and the oar of one of them caught the body, and they passing the black cliffs of the north.'

CATHLEEN (*trying to open the bundle*): Give me a knife, Nora; the string's perished with salt water, and there's a black knot on it you wouldn't loosen in a week.

NORA (*giving her a knife*): I've heard tell it was a long way to Donegal.

CATHLEEN (*cutting the string*): It is surely. There was a man in here a while ago—the man sold us that knife—and he said if you set off walking from the rocks beyond, it would be in seven days you'd be in Donegal.

NORA: And what time would a man take, and he floating?

CATHLEEN *opens the bundle and takes out a bit of a shirt and a stocking. They look at them eagerly.*

CATHLEEN (*in a low voice*): The Lord spare us, Nora! isn't it a queer hard thing to say if it's his they are surely?

NORA: I'll get his shirt off the hook the way we can put the one flannel on the other. (*She looks through some clothes hanging in the corner.*) It's not with them, Cathleen, and where will it be?

CATHLEEN: I'm thinking Bartley put it on him in the morning, for his own shirt was heavy with the salt in it. (*Pointing to the corner.*) There's a bit of a sleeve was of the same stuff. Give me that and it will do.

NORA *brings it to her and they compare the flannel.*

CATHLEEN: It's the same stuff, Nora; but if it is itself, aren't there great rolls of it in the shops of Galway, and isn't it many another man may have a shirt of it as well as Michael himself?

NORA (*who has taken up the stocking and counted the stitches, crying out*): It's Michael, Cathleen, it's Michael; God spare his soul, and what will herself say when she hears this story, and Bartley on the sea?

CATHLEEN (*taking the stocking*): It's a plain stocking.

NORA: It's the second one of the third pair I knitted, and I put up three-score stitches, and I dropped four of them.

CATHLEEN (*counts the stitches*): It's that number is in it (*crying out*). Ah, Nora, isn't it a bitter thing to think of him floating that way to the far north, and no one to keen him but the black hags that do be flying on the sea?

NORA (*swinging herself half round, and throwing out her arms on the clothes*): And isn't it a pitiful thing when there is nothing left of a man who was a great rower and fisher but a bit of an old shirt and a plain stocking?

CATHLEEN (*after an instant*): Tell me is herself coming, Nora? I hear a little sound on the path.

NORA (*looking out*): She is, Cathleen. She's coming up to the door.

CATHLEEN: Put these things away before she'll come in. Maybe it's easier she'll be after giving her blessing to Bartley, and we won't let on we've heard anything the time he's on the sea.

NORA (*helping* CATHLEEN *to close the bundle*): We'll put them here in the corner.

They put them into a hole in the chimney corner. CATHLEEN *goes back to the spinning-wheel.*

NORA: Will she see it was crying I was?

CATHLEEN: Keep your back to the door the way the light'll not be on you.

NORA *sits down at the chimney corner, with her back to the door.* MAURYA *comes in very slowly, without looking at the girls, and goes over to her stool at the other side of the fire. The cloth with the bread is still in her hand. The girls look at each other, and* NORA *points to the bundle of bread.*

CATHLEEN (*after spinning for a moment*): You didn't give him his bit of bread?

MAURYA *begins to keen softly, without turning round.*

CATHLEEN: Did you see him riding down?

MAURYA *goes on keening.*

CATHLEEN (*a little impatiently*): God forgive you; isn't it a better thing to raise your voice and tell what you seen, than to be making lamentation for a thing that's done? Did you see Bartley, I'm saying to you?
MAURYA (*with a weak voice*): My heart's broken from this day.
CATHLEEN (*as before*): Did you see Bartley?
MAURYA: I seen the fearfulest thing.
CATHLEEN (*leaves her wheel and looks out*): God forgive you; he's riding the mare now over the green head, and the grey pony behind him.
MAURYA (*Starts, so that her shawl falls back from her head and shows her white tossed hair. With a frightened voice*): The grey pony behind him. . . .
CATHLEEN (*coming to the fire*): What is it ails you at all?
MAURYA (*speaking very slowly*): I've seen the fearfulest thing any person has seen since the day Bride Dara seen the dead man with the child in his arms.
CATHLEEN *and* NORA: Uah.

They crouch down in front of the old woman at the fire.

NORA: Tell us what it is you seen.
MAURYA: I went down to the spring well, and I stood there saying a prayer to myself. Then Bartley came along, and he riding on the red mare with the grey pony behind him (*she puts up her hands, as if to hide something from her eyes*). The Son of God spare us, Nora!
CATHLEEN: What is it you seen?
MAURYA: I seen Michael himself.
CATHLEEN (*speaking softly*): You did not, mother. It wasn't Michael you seen, for his body is after being found in the far north, and he's got a clean burial, by the grace of God.
MAURYA (*a little defiantly*): I'm after seeing him this day, and he riding and galloping. Bartley came first on the red mare; and I tried to say 'God speed you,' but something choked the words in my throat. He went by quickly; and 'the blessing of God on you,' says he, and I could say nothing. I looked up then, and I crying, at the grey pony, and there was Michael upon it—with fine clothes on him, and new shoes on his feet.
CATHLEEN (*begins to keen*): It's destroyed we are from this day. It's destroyed, surely.
NORA: Didn't the young priest say the Almighty God won't leave her destitute with no son living?
MAURYA (*in a low voice, but clearly*): It's little the like of him knows of the sea. . . . Bartley will be lost now, and let you call in Eamon and make me a good coffin out of the white boards, for I won't live after them. I've had a husband, and a husband's father,

and six sons in this house—six fine men, though it was a hard birth I had with every one of them and they coming to the world—and some of them were found and some of them were not found, but they're gone now the lot of them. . . . There were Stephan and Shawn were lost in the great wind, and found after in the Bay of Gregory of the Golden Mouth, and carried up the two of them on one plank, and in by that door.

She pauses for a moment, the girls start as if they heard something through the door that is half open behind them.

    NORA (*in a whisper*):   Did you hear that, Cathleen? Did you hear a noise in the north-east?

    CATHLEEN (*in a whisper*):   There's someone after crying out by the seashore.

    MAURYA (*continues without hearing anything*):   There was Sheamus and his father, and his own father again, were lost in a dark night, and not a stick or sign was seen of them when the sun went up. There was Patch after was drowned out of a curagh that turned over. I was sitting here with Bartley, and he a baby lying on my two knees, and I seen two women, and three women, and four women coming in, and they crossing themselves and not saying a word. I looked out then, and there were men coming after them, and they holding a thing in the half of a red sail, and water dripping out of it—it was a dry day, Nora—and leaving a track to the door.

She pauses again with her hand stretched out towards the door. It opens softly and old women begin to come in, crossing themselves on the threshold, and kneeling down in front of the stage with red petticoats over their heads.

    MAURYA (*half in a dream, to* CATHLEEN):   Is it Patch, or Michael, or what is it at all?

    CATHLEEN: Michael is after being found in the far north, and when he is found there how could he be here in this place?

    MAURYA: There does be a power of young men floating round in the sea, and what way would they know if it was Michael they had, or another man like him, for when a man is nine days in the sea, and the wind blowing, it's hard set his own mother would be to say what man was in it.

    CATHLEEN: It's Michael, God spare him, for they're after sending us a bit of his clothes from the far north.

She reaches out and hands MAURYA *the clothes that belonged to Michael.* MAURYA *stands up slowly, and takes them in her hands.* NORA *looks out.*

    NORA: They're carrying a thing among them, and there's water dripping out of it and leaving a track by the big stones.

    CATHLEEN (*in a whisper to the women who have come in*):   Is it Bartley it is?

    ONE OF THE WOMEN: It is, surely, God rest his soul.

Two younger women come in and pull out the table. Then men carry in the body of BARTLEY, *laid on a plank, with a bit of a sail over it, and lay it on the table.*

    CATHLEEN (*to the women as they are doing so*):   What way was he drowned?

    ONE OF THE WOMEN: The grey pony knocked him over into the sea, and he was washed out where there is a great surf on the white rocks.

MAURYA *has gone over and knelt down at the head of the table. The women are keening softly and swaying themselves with a slow movement.* CATHLEEN *and* NORA *kneel at the other end of the table. The men kneel near the door.*

MAURYA (*raising her head and speaking as if she did not see the people around her*): They're all gone now, and there isn't anything more the sea can do to me. . . . I'll have no call now to be up crying and praying when the wind breaks from the south, and you can hear the surf is in the east, and the surf is in the west, making a great stir with the two noises, and they hitting one on the other. I'll have no call now to be going down and getting Holy Water in the dark nights after Samhain, and I won't care what way the sea is when the other women will be keening. (*To* NORA.) Give me the Holy Water, Nora; there's a small sup still on the dresser.

NORA *gives it to her.*

MAURYA (*drops Michael's clothes across* BARTLEY*'s feet, and sprinkles the Holy Water over him*): It isn't that I haven't prayed for you, Bartley, to the Almighty God. It isn't that I haven't said prayers in the dark night till you wouldn't know what I'd be saying; but it's a great rest I'll have now, and it's time, surely. It's a great rest I'll have now, and great sleeping in the long nights after Samhain, if it's only a bit of wet flour we do have to eat, and maybe a fish that would be stinking.

She kneels down again, crossing herself, and saying prayers under her breath.

CATHLEEN (*to an old man*): Maybe yourself and Eamon would make a coffin when the sun rises. We have fine white boards herself bought, God help her, thinking Michael would be found, and I have a new cake you can eat while you'll be working.
THE OLD MAN (*looking at the boards*): Are there nails with them?
CATHLEEN: There are not, Colum; we didn't think of the nails.
ANOTHER MAN: It's a great wonder she wouldn't think of the nails, and all the coffins she's seen made already.
CATHLEEN: It's getting old she is, and broken.

MAURYA *stands up again very slowly and spreads out the pieces of Michael's clothes beside the body, sprinkling them with the last of the Holy Water.*

NORA (*in a whisper to* CATHLEEN): She's quiet now and easy; but the day Michael was drowned you could hear her crying out from this to the spring well. It's fonder she was of Michael, and would anyone have thought that?
CATHLEEN (*slowly and clearly*): An old woman will be soon tired with anything she will do, and isn't it nine days herself is after crying and keening, and making great sorrow in the house?
MAURYA (*puts the empty cup mouth downwards on the table, and lays her hands together on* BARTLEY*'s feet*): They're all together this time, and the end is come. May the Almighty God have mercy on Bartley's soul, and on Michael's soul, and on the souls of Sheamus and Patch, and Stephen and Shawn (*bending her head*); and may He have mercy on my soul, Nora, and on the soul of every one is left living in the world.

She pauses, and the keen rises a little more loudly from the women, then sinks away.

MAURYA (*continuing*):   Michael has a clean burial in the far north, by the grace of Almighty God. Bartley will have a fine coffin out of the white boards, and a deep grave surely. What more can we want than that? No man at all can be living for ever, and we must be satisfied.

She kneels down again and the curtain falls slowly.

(*1904*)

QUESTIONS FOR REFLECTION

Experience

1. To what extent can you appreciate the characters' tragic situation? How has your experience prepared you to understand their predicament?

Interpretation

2. To what extent can *Riders to the Sea* be described as a tragedy?
3. Characterize the play's language, especially the speech style of the central characters. Of what importance is its religious dimension?
4. Distinguish between the rank and roles of Nora and Cathleen.
5. What is Maurya's role? Describe in general terms the kind of actress you imagine would be well suited to her role.
6. Identify the props used, and comment on their dramatic and symbolic significance.
7. Explain the significance of the title. How does Synge make the presence and the power of the sea felt?

Evaluation

8. Do you think this is a successful drama? Do you find it a tragic play? Why or why not?

SUSAN GLASPELL

[1882–1948]

Susan Glaspell, an American novelist and playwright, was one of the co-founders of the Provincetown Players, an influential theatrical company. With her husband, George Cram Cook, she collaborated on a number of plays, including her one-act satire on Freudian psychoanalysis, *Suppressed Desires*, published in 1916. In the same year Glaspell produced another fine one-act play, *Trifles*, which has continued to be her most frequently performed play.

SUSAN GLASPELL

Trifles

CHARACTERS

GEORGE HENDERSON, *County Attorney*
HENRY PETERS, *Sheriff*
LEWIS HALE, *A Neighboring Farmer*
MRS. PETERS
MRS. HALE

Scene. *The kitchen in the now abandoned farmhouse of* JOHN WRIGHT, *a gloomy kitchen, and left without having been put in order—unwashed pans under the sink, a loaf of bread outside the breadbox, a dish towel on the table—other signs of incompleted work. At the rear the outer door opens and the* SHERIFF *comes in followed by the* COUNTY ATTORNEY *and* HALE. *The* SHERIFF *and* HALE *are men in middle life, the* COUNTY ATTORNEY *is a young man; all are much bundled up and go at once to the stove. They are followed by two women—the* SHERIFF'*s wife first; she is a slight wiry woman, a thin nervous face.* MRS. HALE *is larger and would ordinarily be called more comfortable looking, but she is disturbed now and looks fearfully about as she enters. The women have come in slowly, and stand close together near the door.*

COUNTY ATTORNEY [*rubbing his hands*]:   This feels good. Come up to the fire, ladies.

MRS. PETERS [*after taking a step forward*]:   I'm not—cold.

SHERIFF [*unbuttoning his overcoat and stepping away from the stove as if to mark the beginning of official business*]:   Now, Mr. Hale, before we move things about, you explain to Mr. Henderson just what you saw when you came here yesterday morning.

COUNTY ATTORNEY: By the way, has anything been moved? Are things just as you left them yesterday?

SHERIFF [*looking about*]:   It's just the same. When it dropped below zero last night I thought I'd better send Frank out this morning to make a fire for us—no use getting pneumonia with a big case on, but I told him not to touch anything except the stove—and you know Frank.

COUNTY ATTORNEY: Somebody should have been left here yesterday.

SHERIFF: Oh—yesterday. When I had to send Frank to Morris Center for that man who went crazy—I want you to know I had my hands full yesterday, I knew you could get back from Omaha by today and as long as I went over everything here myself—

COUNTY ATTORNEY: Well, Mr. Hale, tell just what happened when you came here yesterday morning.

HALE: Harry and I had started to town with a load of potatoes. We came along the road from my place and as I got here I said, "I'm going to see if I can't get John Wright to go in with me on a party telephone." I spoke to Wright about it once before and he put me off, saying folks talked too much anyway, and all he asked was peace and quiet—I guess you know about how much he talked himself; but I thought maybe if I went to the house and talked about it before his wife, though I said to Harry that I didn't know as what his wife wanted made much difference to John—

COUNTY ATTORNEY: Let's talk about that later, Mr. Hale. I do want to talk about that, but tell now just what happened when you got to the house.

HALE: I didn't hear or see anything; I knocked at the door, and still it was all quiet inside. I knew they must be up, it was past eight o'clock. So I knocked again, and I thought I heard somebody say, "Come in." I wasn't sure, I'm not sure yet, but I opened the door—this door [*Indicating the door by which the two women are still standing*] and there in that rocker—[*Pointing to it*] sat Mrs. Wright.

[*They all look at the rocker.*]

COUNTY ATTORNEY: What—was she doing?

HALE: She was rockin' back and forth. She had her apron in her hand and was kind of—pleating it.

COUNTY ATTORNEY: And how did she—look?

HALE: Well, she looked queer.

COUNTY ATTORNEY: How do you mean—queer?

HALE: Well, as if she didn't know what she was going to do next. And kind of done up.

COUNTY ATTORNEY: How did she seem to feel about your coming?

HALE: Why, I don't think she minded—one way or other. She didn't pay much attention. I said, "How do, Mrs. Wright, it's cold, ain't it?" And she said, "Is it?"—and went on kind of pleating at her apron. Well, I was surprised; she didn't ask me to come up to the stove, or to set down, but just sat there, not even looking at me, so I said, "I want to see John." And then she—laughed. I guess you would call it a laugh. I thought of Harry and the team outside, so I said a little sharp: "Can't I see John?" "No," she says, kind o' dull like. "Ain't he home?" says I. "Yes," says she, "he's home." "Then why can't I see him?" I asked her, out of patience. "'Cause he's dead," says she. *"Dead?"* says I. She just nodded her head, not getting a bit excited, but rockin' back and forth. "Why—where is he?" says I, not knowing what to say. She just pointed upstairs—like that [*Himself pointing to the room above*]. I got up, with the idea of going up there. I walked from there to here—then I says, "Why, what did he die of?" "He died of a rope round his neck," says she, and just went on pleatin' at her apron. Well, I went out and called Harry. I thought I might—need help. We went upstairs and there he was lyin'—

COUNTY ATTORNEY: I think I'd rather have you go into that upstairs, where you can point it all out. Just go on now with the rest of the story.

HALE: Well, my first thought was to get that rope off. It looked . . . [*Stops, his face twitches.*] . . . but Harry, he went up to him, and he said, "No, he's dead all right, and we'd better not touch anything." So we went back down stairs. She was still sitting that same way. "Has anybody been notified?" I asked. "No," says she, unconcerned. "Who did this, Mrs. Wright?" said Harry. He said it businesslike—and she stopped pleatin' of her apron. "I don't know," she says. "You don't *know?*" says Harry. "No," says she. "Weren't you sleepin' in the bed with him?" says Harry. "Yes," says she, "but I was on the inside." "Somebody slipped a rope round his neck and strangled him and you didn't wake up?" says Harry. "I didn't wake up," she said after him. We must 'a looked as if we didn't see how that could be, for after a minute she said, "I sleep sound." Harry was going to ask her more questions but I said maybe we ought to let her tell her story first to the coroner, or the sheriff, so Harry went fast as he could to Rivers' place, where there's a telephone.

COUNTY ATTORNEY: And what did Mrs. Wright do when she knew that you had gone for the coroner?

HALE: She moved from that chair to this one over here [*Pointing to a small chair in the corner*] and just sat there with her hands held together and looking down. I got a feeling that I ought to make some conversation, so I said I had come in to see if John wanted to put in a telephone, and at that she started to laugh, and then she stopped and looked at me—scared. [*The* COUNTY ATTORNEY, *who has had his notebook out, makes a note.*] I dunno, maybe it wasn't scared. I wouldn't like to say it was. Soon Harry got back, and then Dr. Lloyd came, and you, Mr. Peters, and so I guess that's all I know that you don't.

COUNTY ATTORNEY [*looking around*]:   I guess we'll go upstairs first—and then out to the barn and around there. [*to the* SHERIFF] You're convinced that there was nothing important here—nothing that would point to any motive.

SHERIFF: Nothing here but kitchen things.

[*The* COUNTY ATTORNEY, *after again looking around the kitchen, opens the door of a cupboard closet. He gets up on a chair and looks on a shelf. Pulls his hand away, sticky.*]

COUNTY ATTORNEY: Here's a nice mess.

[*The women draw nearer.*]

MRS. PETERS [*to the other woman*]:   Oh, her fruit; it did freeze. [*To the* COUNTY ATTORNEY] She worried about that when it turned so cold. She said the fire'd go out and her jars would break.

SHERIFF: Well, can you beat the women! Held for murder and worryin' about her preserves.

COUNTY ATTORNEY: I guess before we're through she may have something more serious than preserves to worry about.

HALE: Well, women are used to worrying over trifles.

[*The two women move a little closer together.*]

COUNTY ATTORNEY [*with the gallantry of a young politician*]:   And yet, for all their worries, what would we do without the ladies? [*The women do not unbend. He goes to the sink, takes a dipperful of water from the pail and pouring it into a basin, washes his hands. Starts to wipe them on the roller towel, turns it for a cleaner place.*] Dirty towels! [*Kicks his foot against the pans under the sink.*] Not much of a housekeeper, would you say, ladies?

MRS. HALE [*stiffly*]:   There's a great deal of work to be done on a farm.

COUNTY ATTORNEY: To be sure. And yet [*With a little bow to her*] I know there are some Dickson county farmhouses which do not have such roller towels.

[*He gives it a pull to expose its full length again.*]

MRS. HALE: Those towels get dirty awful quick. Men's hands aren't always as clean as they might be.

COUNTY ATTORNEY: Ah, loyal to your sex, I see. But you and Mrs. Wright were neighbors. I suppose you were friends, too.

MRS. HALE [*shaking her head*]:   I've not seen much of her of late years. I've not been in this house—it's more than a year.

COUNTY ATTORNEY: And why was that? You didn't like her?

MRS. HALE: I liked her all well enough. Farmers' wives have their hands full, Mr. Henderson. And then—

COUNTY ATTORNEY: Yes—?

MRS. HALE [*looking about*]:   It never seemed a very cheerful place.

COUNTY ATTORNEY: No—it's not cheerful. I shouldn't say she had the homemaking instinct.

MRS. HALE: Well, I don't know as Wright had, either.

COUNTY ATTORNEY: You mean that they didn't get on very well?

MRS. HALE: No, I don't mean anything. But I don't think a place'd be any cheerfuller for John Wright's being in it.

COUNTY ATTORNEY: I'd like to talk more of that a little later. I want to get the lay of things upstairs now.

[*He goes to the left, where three steps lead to a stair door.*]

SHERIFF: I suppose anything Mrs. Peters does'll be all right. She was to take in some clothes for her, you know, and a few little things. We left in such a hurry yesterday.

COUNTY ATTORNEY: Yes, but I would like to see what you take, Mrs. Peters, and keep an eye out for anything that might be of use to us.

MRS. PETERS: Yes, Mr. Henderson.

[*The women listen to the men's steps on the stairs, then look about the kitchen.*]

MRS. HALE: I'd hate to have men coming into my kitchen, snooping around and criticising.

[*She arranges the pans under sink which the* COUNTY ATTORNEY *had shoved out of place.*]

MRS. PETERS: Of course it's no more than their duty.

MRS. HALE: Duty's all right, but I guess that deputy sheriff that came out to make the fire might have got a little of this on. [*Gives the roller towel a pull.*] Wish I'd thought of that sooner. Seems mean to talk about her for not having things slicked up when she had to come away in such a hurry.

MRS. PETERS [*Who has gone to a small table in the left rear corner of the room, and lifted one end of a towel that covers a pan*]:   She had bread set.

[*Stands still.*]

MRS. HALE [*eyes fixed on a loaf of bread beside the breadbox, which is on a low shelf at the other side of the room. Moves slowly toward it*]:   She was going to put this in there. [*Picks up loaf, then abruptly drops it. In a manner of returning to familiar things.*] It's a shame about her fruit. I wonder if it's all gone. [*Gets up on the chair and looks.*] I think there's some here that's all right, Mrs. Peters. Yes—here; [*Holding it toward the window.*] this is cherries, too. [*Looking again.*] I declare I believe that's the only one. [*Gets down, bottle in her hand. Goes to the sink and wipes it off on the outside.*] She'll feel awful bad after all her hard work in the hot weather. I remember the afternoon I put up my cherries last summer.

[*She puts the bottle on the big kitchen table, center of the room. With a sigh, is about to sit down in the rocking-chair. Before she is seated realizes what chair it is; with a slow look at it, steps back. The chair which she has touched rocks back and forth.*]

MRS. PETERS: Well, I must get those things from the front room closet. [*She goes to the door at the right, but after looking into the other room, steps back.*] You coming with me, Mrs. Hale? You could help me carry them.

[*They go in the other room; reappear,* MRS. PETERS *carrying a dress and skirt,* MRS. HALE *following with a pair of shoes.*]

MRS. PETERS: My, it's cold in there.

[*She puts the clothes on the big table, and hurries to the stove.*]

MRS. HALE [*examining her skirt*]:   Wright was close. I think maybe that's why she kept so much to herself. She didn't even belong to the Ladies Aid. I suppose she felt she couldn't do her part, and then you don't enjoy things when you feel shabby. She used to wear pretty clothes and be lively, when she was Minnie Foster, one of the town girls singing in the choir. But that—oh, that was thirty years ago. This all you was to take in?

MRS. PETERS: She said she wanted an apron. Funny thing to want, for there isn't much to get you dirty in jail, goodness knows. But I suppose just to make her feel more natural. She said they was in the top drawer in this cupboard. Yes, here. And then her little shawl that always hung behind the door. [*Opens stair door and looks.*] Yes, here it is.

[*Quickly shuts door leading upstairs.*]

MRS. HALE [*abruptly moving toward her*]:   Mrs. Peters?
MRS. PETERS: Yes, Mrs. Hale?
MRS. HALE: Do you think she did it?
MRS. PETERS [*in a frightened voice*]:   Oh, I don't know.
MRS. HALE: Well, I don't think she did. Asking for an apron and her little shawl. Worrying about her fruit.
MRS. PETERS [*starts to speak, glances up, where footsteps are heard in the room above. In a low voice*]:   Mr. Peters says it looks bad for her. Mr. Henderson is awful sarcastic in a speech and he'll make fun of her sayin' she didn't wake up.
MRS. HALE: Well, I guess John Wright didn't wake when they was slipping that rope under his neck.
MRS. PETERS: No, it's strange. It must have been done awful crafty and still. They say it was such a—funny way to kill a man, rigging it all up like that.
MRS. HALE: That's just what Mr. Hale said. There was a gun in the house. He says that's what he can't understand.
MRS. PETERS: Mr. Henderson said coming out that what was needed for the case was a motive; something to show anger, or—sudden feeling.
MRS. HALE [*who is standing by the table*]:   Well, I don't see any signs of anger around here. [*She puts her hand on the dish towel which lies on the table, stands looking down at table,*

one half of which is clean, the other half messy.] It's wiped to here. [*Makes a move as if to finish work, then turns and looks at loaf of bread outside the breadbox. Drops towel. In that voice of coming back to familiar things.*] Wonder how they are finding things upstairs. I hope she had it a little more red-up up there. You know, it seems kind of *sneaking.* Locking her up in town and then coming out here and trying to get her own house to turn against her!

MRS. PETERS: But Mrs. Hale, the law is the law.

MRS. HALE: I s'pose 'tis. [*Unbuttoning her coat.*] Better loosen up your things, Mrs. Peters. You won't feel them when you go out.

[MRS. PETERS *takes off her fur tippet, goes to hang it on hook at back of room, stands looking at the under part of the small corner table.*]

MRS. PETERS: She was piecing a quilt.

[*She brings the large sewing basket and they look at the bright pieces.*]

MRS. HALE: It's log cabin pattern. Pretty, isn't it? I wonder if she was goin' to quilt it or just knot it?

[*Footsteps have been heard coming down the stairs. The* SHERIFF *enters followed by* HALE *and the* COUNTY ATTORNEY.]

SHERIFF: They wonder if she was going to quilt it or just knot it!

[*The men laugh; the women look abashed.*]

COUNTY ATTORNEY [*rubbing his hands over the stove*]:   Frank's fire didn't do much up there, did it? Well, let's go out to the barn and get that cleared up.

[*The men go outside.*]

MRS. HALE [*resentfully*]:   I don't know as there's anything so strange, our takin' up our time with little things while we're waiting for them to get the evidence. [*She sits down at the big table smoothing out a block with decision.*] I don't see as it's anything to laugh about.

MRS. PETERS [*apologetically*]:   Of course they've got awful important things on their minds.

[*Pulls up a chair and joins* MRS. HALE *at the table.*]

MRS. HALE [*examining another block*]:   Mrs. Peters, look at this one. Here, this is the one she was working on, and look at the sewing! All the rest of it has been so nice and even. And look at this! It's all over the place! Why, it looks as if she didn't know what she was about!

[*After she has said this they look at each other, then start to glance back at the door. After an instant* MRS. HALE *has pulled at a knot and ripped the sewing.*]

MRS. PETERS: Oh, what are you doing, Mrs. Hale?

MRS. HALE [*mildly*]:   Just pulling out a stitch or two that's not sewed very good. [*Threading a needle.*] Bad sewing always made me fidgety.

MRS. PETERS [*nervously*]:   I don't think we ought to touch things.

MRS. HALE: I'll just finish up this end. [*Suddenly stopping and leaning forward.*] Mrs. Peters?

MRS. PETERS: Yes, Mrs. Hale?

MRS. HALE: What do you suppose she was so nervous about?

MRS. PETERS: Oh—I don't know. I don't know as she was nervous. I sometimes sew awful queer when I'm just tired. [MRS. HALE *starts to say something, looks at* MRS. PETERS, *then goes on sewing.*] Well, I must get these things wrapped up. They may be through sooner than we think. [*Putting apron and other things together.*] I wonder where I can find a piece of paper, and string.

MRS. HALE: In that cupboard, maybe.

MRS. PETERS [*looking in cupboard*]:   Why, here's a birdcage. [*Holds it up.*] Did she have a bird, Mrs. Hale?

MRS. HALE: Why, I don't know whether she did or not—I've not been here for so long. There was a man around last year selling canaries cheap, but I don't know as she took one; maybe she did. She used to sing real pretty herself.

MRS. PETERS [*glancing around*]:   Seems funny to think of a bird here. But she must have had one, or why would she have a cage? I wonder what happened to it.

MRS. HALE: I s'pose maybe the cat got it.

MRS. PETERS: No, she didn't have a cat. She's got that feeling some people have about cats—being afraid of them. My cat got in her room and she was real upset and asked me to take it out.

MRS. HALE: My sister Bessie was like that. Queer, ain't it?

MRS. PETERS [*examining the cage*]:   Why, look at this door. It's broke. One hinge is pulled apart.

MRS. HALE [*looking too*]:   Looks as if someone must have been rough with it.

MRS. PETERS: Why, yes.

[*She brings the cage forward and puts it on the table.*]

MRS. HALE: I wish if they're going to find any evidence they'd be about it. I don't like this place.

MRS. PETERS: But I'm awful glad you came with me, Mrs. Hale. It would be lonesome for me sitting here alone.

MRS. HALE: It would, wouldn't it? [*Dropping her sewing.*] But I tell you what I do wish, Mrs. Peters. I wish I had come over sometimes when *she* was here. I—[*Looking around the room.*]—wish I had.

MRS. PETERS: But of course you were awful busy, Mrs. Hale—your house and your children.

MRS. HALE: I could've come. I stayed away because it weren't cheerful—and that's why I ought to have come. I—I've never liked this place. Maybe because it's down in a hollow and you don't see the road. I dunno what it is but it's a lonesome place and always was. I wish I had come over to see Minnie Foster sometimes. I can see now—

[*Shakes her head.*]

MRS. PETERS: Well, you mustn't reproach yourself, Mrs. Hale. Somehow we just don't see how it is with other folks until—something comes up.

MRS. HALE: Not having children makes less work—but it makes a quiet house, and Wright out to work all day, and no company when he did come in. Did you know John Wright, Mrs. Peters?

MRS. PETERS: Not to know him; I've seen him in town. They say he was a good man.

MRS. HALE: Yes—good; he didn't drink, and kept his word as well as most, I guess, and paid his debts. But he was a hard man, Mrs. Peters. Just to pass the time of day with him—[*Shivers.*] Like a raw wind that gets to the bone. [*Pauses, her eye falling on the cage.*] I should think she would 'a wanted a bird. But what do you suppose went with it?

MRS. PETERS: I don't know, unless it got sick and died.

[*She reaches over and swings the broken door, swings it again. Both women watch it.*]

MRS. HALE: You weren't raised round here, were you? [MRS. PETERS *shakes her head.*] You didn't know—her?

MRS. PETERS: Not till they brought her yesterday.

MRS. HALE: She—come to think of it, she was kind of like a bird herself—real sweet and pretty, but kind of timid and—fluttery. How—she—did—change. [*Silence; then as if struck by a happy thought and relieved to get back to every day things.*] Tell you what, Mrs. Peters, why don't you take the quilt in with you? It might take up her mind.

MRS. PETERS: Why, I think that's a real nice idea, Mrs. Hale. There couldn't possibly be any objection to it, could there? Now, just what would I take? I wonder if her patches are in here—and her things.

[*They look in the sewing basket.*]

MRS. HALE: Here's some red. I expect this has got sewing things in it. [*Brings out a fancy box.*] What a pretty box. Looks like something somebody would give you. Maybe her scissors are in here. [*Opens box. Suddenly puts her hand to her nose.*] Why—[MRS. PETERS *bends nearer, then turns her face away.*] There's something wrapped up in this piece of silk.

MRS. PETERS: Why, this isn't her scissors.

MRS. HALE [*lifting the silk*]:   Oh, Mrs. Peters—it's—

[MRS. PETERS *bends closer.*]

MRS. PETERS: It's the bird.

MRS. HALE [*jumping up*]:   But, Mrs. Peters—look at it! Its neck! Look at its neck! It's all—other side *to.*

MRS. PETERS: Somebody—wrung—its—neck.

[*Their eyes meet. A look of growing comprehension, of horror. Steps are heard outside.* MRS. HALE *slips box under quilt pieces, and sinks into her chair. Enter* SHERIFF *and* COUNTY ATTORNEY. MRS. PETERS *rises.*]

COUNTY ATTORNEY [*as one turning from serious things to little pleasantries*]:   Well, ladies have you decided whether she was going to quilt it or knot it?

MRS. PETERS: We think she was going to—knot it.

COUNTY ATTORNEY: Well, that's interesting, I'm sure. [*Seeing the birdcage.*] Has the bird flown?

MRS. HALE [*putting more quilt pieces over the box*]:   We think the—cat got it.

COUNTY ATTORNEY [*Preoccupied*]:   Is there a cat?

[MRS. HALE *glances in a quick covert way at* MRS. PETERS.]

MRS. PETERS: Well, not *now*. They're superstitious, you know. They leave.

COUNTY ATTORNEY [*to* SHERIFF PETERS, *continuing an interrupted conversation*]:   No sign at all of anyone having come from the outside. Their own rope. Now let's go up again and go over it piece by piece. [*They start upstairs.*] It would have to have been someone who knew just the—

[MRS. PETERS *sits down. The two women sit there not looking at one another, but as if peering into something and at the same time holding back. When they talk now it is in the manner of feeling their way over strange ground, as if afraid of what they are saying, but as if they can not help saying it.*]

MRS. HALE: She liked the bird. She was going to bury it in that pretty box.

MRS. PETERS [*in a whisper*]:   When I was a girl—my kitten—there was a boy took a hatchet, and before my eyes—and before I could get there—[*Covers her face an instant.*] If they hadn't held me back I would have—[*Catches herself, looks upstairs where steps are heard, falters weakly.*]—hurt him.

MRS. HALE [*with a slow look around her*]:   I wonder how it would seem never to have had any children around. [*Pause.*] No, Wright wouldn't like the bird—a thing that sang. She used to sing. He killed that, too.

MRS. PETERS [*moving uneasily*]:   We don't know who killed the bird.

MRS. HALE: I knew John Wright.

MRS. PETERS: It was an awful thing was done in this house that night, Mrs. Hale. Killing a man while he slept, slipping a rope around his neck that choked the life out of him.

MRS. HALE: His neck. Choked the life out of him.

[*Her hand goes out and rests on the birdcage.*]

MRS. PETERS [*with rising voice*]:   We don't know who killed him. We don't *know*.

MRS. HALE [*her own feeling not interrupted*]:   If there'd been years and years of nothing, then a bird to sing to you, it would be awful—still, after the bird was still.

MRS. PETERS [*something within her speaking*]:   I know what stillness is. When we homesteaded in Dakota, and my first baby died—after he was two years old, and me with no other then—

MRS. HALE [*moving*]:   How soon do you suppose they'll be through, looking for the evidence?

MRS. PETERS: I know what stillness is. [*Pulling herself back.*] The law has got to punish crime, Mrs. Hale.

MRS. HALE [*not as if answering that*]:   I wish you'd seen Minnie Foster when she wore a white dress with blue ribbons and stood up there in the choir and sang. [*A look around the room.*] Oh, I *wish* I'd come over here once in a while! That was a crime! That was a crime! Who's going to punish that?

MRS. PETERS [*looking upstairs*]:   We mustn't—take on.

MRS. HALE: I might have known she needed help! I know how things can be—for women. I tell you, it's queer, Mrs. Peters. We live close together and we live far apart. We all go through the same things—it's all just a different kind of the same thing.

[*Brushes her eyes; noticing the bottle of fruit, reaches out for it.*] If I was you I wouldn't tell her her fruit was gone. Tell her it *ain't*. Tell her it's all right. Take this in to prove it to her. She—she may never know whether it was broke or not.

MRS. PETERS [*takes the bottle, looks about for something to wrap it in; takes petticoat from the clothes brought from the other room, very nervously begins winding this around the bottle. In a false voice*]:   My, it's a good thing the men couldn't hear us. Wouldn't they just laugh! Getting all stirred up over a little thing like a—dead canary. As if that could have anything to do with—with—wouldn't they *laugh!*

[*The men are heard coming down stairs.*]

MRS. HALE [*under her breath*]:   Maybe they would—maybe they wouldn't.

COUNTY ATTORNEY: No, Peters, it's all perfectly clear except a reason for doing it. But you know juries when it comes to women. If there was some definite thing. Something to show—something to make a story about—a thing that would connect up with this strange way of doing it—

[*The women's eyes meet for an instant. Enter* HALE *from outer door.*]

HALE: Well, I've got the team around. Pretty cold out there.

COUNTY ATTORNEY: I'm going to stay here a while by myself. [*To the* SHERIFF.] You can send Frank out for me, can't you? I want to go over everything. I'm not satisfied that we can't do better.

SHERIFF: Do you want to see what Mrs. Peters is going to take in?

[*The* COUNTY ATTORNEY *goes to the table, picks up the apron, laughs.*]

COUNTY ATTORNEY: Oh, I guess they're not very dangerous things the ladies have picked out. [*Moves a few things about, disturbing the quilt pieces which cover the box. Steps back.*] No, Mrs. Peters doesn't need supervising. For that matter, a sheriff's wife is married to the law. Ever think of it that way, Mrs. Peters?

MRS. PETERS: Not—just that way.

SHERIFF [*Chuckling*]:   Married to the law. [*Moves toward the other room.*] I just want you to come in here a minute, George. We ought to take a look at these windows.

COUNTY ATTORNEY [*scoffingly*]:   Oh, windows!

SHERIFF: We'll be right out, Mr. Hale.

[HALE *goes outside. The* SHERIFF *follows the* COUNTY ATTORNEY *into the other room. Then* MRS. HALE *rises, hands tight together, looking intensely at* MRS. PETERS, *whose eyes make a slow turn, finally meeting* MRS. HALE'*s. A moment* MRS. HALE *holds her, then her own eyes point the way to where the box is concealed. Suddenly* MRS. PETERS *throws back quilt pieces and tries to put the box in the bag she is wearing. It is too big. She opens box, starts to take bird out, cannot touch it, goes to pieces, stands there helpless. Sound of a knob turning in the other room.* MRS. HALE *snatches the box and puts it in the pocket of her big coat. Enter* COUNTY ATTORNEY *and* SHERIFF.]

COUNTY ATTORNEY [*facetiously*]:   Well, Henry, at least we found out that she was not going to quilt it. She was going to—what is it you call it, ladies?

MRS. HALE [*her hand against her pocket*]:   We call it—knot it, Mr. Henderson.

Curtain

(*1916*)

QUESTIONS FOR REFLECTION

Experience

1. At what point in reading *Trifles* did you realize that Mrs. Wright had murdered her husband?
2. What is your response to the women's behavior? To the behavior of the men? Why?

Interpretation

3. Explain the significance of the title. Do you prefer this title or the one Glaspell gave her rewriting of the play as a short story, "A Jury of Her Peers"? Why?
4. How does Glaspell characterize the men in the play? The sheriff? The attorney? The neighboring farmer? What attitudes toward women do the men display?
5. How does Glaspell enlist our sympathy for the women? How do Mrs. Hale and Mrs. Peters get along with the men?
6. Which of the stage props are most important for the play's dramatic action? For its theme? Why?
7. Explain the significance of the final line of dialogue.

Evaluation

8. What does Glaspell's play suggest about the relative merits of men's and women's perspectives? What implications might we derive about men's and women's ways of seeing things after reading or viewing this play? Why?

ARTHUR MILLER

[*b. 1915*]

Death of a Salesman is Arthur Miller's most famous and notable play. Produced and published in 1949, it had a long original Broadway run and has been frequently revived, most recently with noted film actor Brian Dennehy as the salesman Willy Loman. The play is in the tradition of social realism inaugurated by Ibsen and continued by Chekhov, Strindberg, and Shaw. The dialogue of the characters, their financial and emotional problems, and their behavior are all indicative of a typically realistic drama. Like Ibsen's *A Doll House,* Miller's *Salesman* raises questions about social values and attitudes—in this case, the pursuit of success and the American dream. Like Chekhov's tone in *The Cherry Orchard,* Miller's tone mixes sympathy and judgment, criticism and compassion. Miller provides extensive and detailed stage directions. Miller furnishes information about the lives his characters lead, giving us a better sense of their past.

These realistic touches blend, however, with other dramatic elements that are less realistic and that we will call *expressionistic.* Expressionistic playwrights attempt to dramatize a subjective picture of reality as seen by an individual consciousness. They attempt to show the inner life of a character, portraying external reality as he or she sees it. *Death of a Salesman* is expressionistic in that it dramatizes Willy Loman's subjective sense of things, rather than exhibiting a concern for a strict and exact representation of external detail. The play is particularly expressionistic in its memory scenes, in which Willy recalls events from the past in such a way that he reenacts rather than merely remembers them. In these scenes different times, places, and states of mind fluctuate and merge as Miller reveals Willy's thoughts, attitudes, and beliefs, his inflated hopes and deflated dreams. The expressionistic quality of the play is enhanced by lighting and music that signal flashbacks and contribute to its mood.

One issue readers, audiences, and critics have consistently raised about *Death of a Salesman* concerns its status as tragedy. The main question turns on whether Willy Loman is a tragic figure. Is he grand and noble enough to be a tragic hero? Is his failure tragic or merely pathetic? Over the years Miller has written about these and related questions in essays such as "On Social Drama" and "Tragedy and the Common Man." He has suggested that "the common man is as apt a subject for tragedy as kings"; and also that "the tragic feeling is evoked in us when we are in the presence of a character who is ready to lay down his life" to secure his dignity. How far these observations apply to Willy Loman is a matter for discussion.

ARTHUR MILLER

Death of a Salesman

CERTAIN PRIVATE CONVERSATIONS IN TWO ACTS AND A REQUIEM

CHARACTERS

WILLY LOMAN

LINDA

BIFF

HAPPY

BERNARD

THE WOMAN

CHARLEY

UNCLE BEN

HOWARD WAGNER

JENNY

STANLEY

MISS FORSYTHE

LETTA

The action takes place in WILLY LOMAN*'s house and yard and in various places he visits in the New York and Boston of today.*

Throughout the play, in the stage directions, left and right mean stage left and stage right.

ACT I

A melody is heard, played upon a flute. It is small and fine, telling of grass and trees and the horizon. The curtain rises.

Before us is the Salesman's house. We are aware of towering, angular shapes behind it, surrounding it on all sides. Only the blue light of the sky falls upon the house and forestage; the surrounding area shows an angry glow of orange. As more light appears, we see a solid vault of apartment houses around the small, fragile-seeming home. An air of the dream clings to the place, a dream rising out of reality. The kitchen at center seems actual enough, for there is a kitchen table with three chairs, and a refrigerator. But no other fixtures are seen. At the back of the kitchen there is a draped entrance, which leads to the livingroom. To the right of the kitchen, on a level raised two feet, is a bedroom furnished only with a brass bedstead and a straight chair. On a shelf over the bed a silver athletic trophy stands. A window opens onto the apartment house at the side.

Behind the kitchen, on a level raised six and a half feet, is the boys' bedroom, at present barely visible. Two beds are dimly seen, and at the back of the room a dormer window. (This bedroom is above the unseen livingroom.) At the left a stairway curves up to it from the kitchen.

The entire setting is wholly or, in some places, partially transparent. The roof-line of the house is one-dimensional; under and over it we see the apartment buildings. Before the house lies an apron, curving beyond the forestage into the orchestra. This forward area serves as the back yard as well as the locale of all WILLY*'s imaginings and of his city scenes. Whenever the action is in the present the actors observe the imaginary wall-lines, entering the house only through the door at the left. But in the scenes of the past these boundaries are broken, and characters enter or leave a room by stepping "through" a wall onto the forestage.*

From the right, WILLY LOMAN, *the Salesman, enters, carrying two large sample cases. The flute plays on. He hears but is not aware of it. He is past sixty years of age, dressed quietly. Even as he crosses the stage to the doorway of the house, his exhaustion is apparent. He unlocks the door, comes into the kitchen, and thankfully lets his burden down, feeling the soreness of his palms. A word-sigh escapes his lips—it might be "Oh, boy, oh, boy." He closes the door, then carries his cases out into the livingroom, through the draped kitchen doorway.*

LINDA, *his wife, has stirred in her bed at the right. She gets out and puts on a robe, listening. Most often jovial, she has developed an iron repression of her exceptions to* WILLY*'s behavior— she more than loves him, she admires him, as though his mercurial nature, his temper, his massive dreams and little cruelties, served her only as sharp reminders of the turbulent longings within him, longings which she shares but lacks the temperament to utter and follow to their end.*

LINDA (*hearing* WILLY *outside the bedroom, calls with some trepidation*):   Willy!

WILLY: It's all right. I came back.

LINDA: Why? What happened? (*Slight pause.*) Did something happen, Willy?

WILLY: No, nothing happened.

LINDA: You didn't smash the car, did you?

WILLY (*with casual irritation*):   I said nothing happened. Didn't you hear me?

LINDA: Don't you feel well?

WILLY: I am tired to the death. (*The flute has faded away. He sits on the bed beside her, a little numb.*) I couldn't make it. I just couldn't make it, Linda.

LINDA (*very carefully, delicately*):   Where were you all day? You look terrible.

WILLY: I got as far as a little above Yonkers. I stopped for a cup of coffee. Maybe it was the coffee.

LINDA: What?

WILLY (*after a pause*):   I suddenly couldn't drive any more. The car kept going onto the shoulder, y'know?

LINDA (*helpfully*):   Oh. Maybe it was the steering again. I don't think Angelo knows the Studebaker.

WILLY: No, it's me, it's me. Suddenly I realize I'm goin' sixty miles an hour and I don't remember the last five minutes. I'm—I can't seem to—keep my mind to it.

LINDA: Maybe it's your glasses. You never went for your new glasses.

WILLY: No, I see everything. I came back ten miles an hour. It took me nearly four hours from Yonkers.

LINDA (*resigned*):   Well, you'll just have to take a rest, Willy, you can't continue this way.

WILLY: I just got back from Florida.

LINDA: But you didn't rest your mind. Your mind is overactive, and the mind is what counts, dear.

WILLY: I'll start out in the morning. Maybe I'll feel better in the morning. (*She is taking off his shoes.*) These goddam arch supports are killing me.

LINDA: Take an aspirin. Should I get you an aspirin? It'll soothe you.

WILLY (*with wonder*):   I was driving along, you understand? And I was fine. I was even observing the scenery. You can imagine, me looking at scenery, on the road every week of my life. But it's so beautiful up there, Linda, the trees are so thick, and the sun is warm. I opened the windshield and just let the warm air bathe over me. And then all of a sudden I'm goin' off the road! I'm tellin' ya, I absolutely forgot I was driving. If I'd've gone the other way over the white line I might've killed somebody. So I went on again—and five minutes later I'm dreamin' again, and I nearly—(*He presses two fingers against his eyes.*) I have such thoughts, I have such strange thoughts.

LINDA: Willy, dear. Talk to them again. There's no reason why you can't work in New York.

WILLY: They don't need me in New York. I'm the New England man. I'm vital in New England.

LINDA: But you're sixty years old. They can't expect you to keep traveling every week.

WILLY: I'll have to send a wire to Portland. I'm supposed to see Brown and Morrison tomorrow morning at ten o'clock to show the line. Goddammit, I could sell them! (*He starts putting on his jacket.*)

LINDA (*taking the jacket from him*):   Why don't you go down to the place tomorrow and tell Howard you've simply got to work in New York? You're too accommodating, dear.

WILLY: If old man Wagner was alive I'd a been in charge of New York now! That man was a prince, he was a masterful man. But that boy of his, that Howard, he don't appreciate. When I went north the first time, the Wagner Company didn't know where New England was!

LINDA: Why don't you tell those things to Howard, dear?

WILLY (*encouraged*): I will, I definitely will. Is there any cheese?

LINDA: I'll make you a sandwich.

WILLY: No, go to sleep. I'll take some milk. I'll be up right away. The boys in?

LINDA: They're sleeping. Happy took Biff on a date tonight.

WILLY (*interested*): That so?

LINDA: It was so nice to see them shaving together, one behind the other, in the bathroom. And going out together. You notice? The whole house smells of shaving lotion.

WILLY: Figure it out. Work a lifetime to pay off a house. You finally own it, and there's nobody to live in it.

LINDA: Well, dear, life is a casting off. It's always that way.

WILLY: No, no, some people—some people accomplish something. Did Biff say anything after I went this morning?

LINDA: You shouldn't have criticized him, Willy, especially after he just got off the train. You mustn't lose your temper with him.

WILLY: When the hell did I lose my temper? I simply asked him if he was making any money. Is that a criticism?

LINDA: But, dear, how could he make any money?

WILLY (*worried and angered*): There's such an undercurrent in him. He became a moody man. Did he apologize when I left this morning?

LINDA: He was crestfallen, Willy. You know how he admires you. I think if he finds himself, then you'll both be happier and not fight any more.

WILLY: How can he find himself on a farm? Is that a life? A farmhand? In the beginning, when he was young, I thought, well, a young man, it's good for him to tramp around, take a lot of different jobs. But it's more than ten years now and he has yet to make thirty-five dollars a week!

LINDA: He's finding himself, Willy.

WILLY: Not finding yourself at the age of thirty-four is a disgrace!

LINDA: Shh!

WILLY: The trouble is he's lazy, goddammit!

LINDA: Willy, please!

WILLY: Biff is a lazy bum!

LINDA: They're sleeping. Get something to eat. Go on down.

WILLY: Why did he come home? I would like to know what brought him home.

LINDA: I don't know. I think he's still lost, Willy. I think he's very lost.

WILLY: Biff Loman is lost. In the greatest country in the world a young man with such—personal attractiveness, gets lost. And such a hard worker. There's one thing about Biff—he's not lazy.

LINDA: Never.

WILLY (*with pity and resolve*): I'll see him in the morning; I'll have a nice talk with him. I'll get him a job selling. He could be big in no time. My God! Remember how they used to follow him around in high school? When he smiled at one of them their faces lit up. When he walked down the street . . . (*He loses himself in reminiscences.*)

LINDA (*trying to bring him out of it*): Willy, dear, I got a new kind of American-type cheese today. It's whipped.

WILLY: Why do you get American when I like Swiss?

LINDA: I just thought you'd like a change—

WILLY: I don't want a change! I want Swiss cheese. Why am I always being contradicted?

LINDA (*with a covering laugh*):   I thought it would be a surprise.

WILLY: Why don't you open a window in here, for God's sake?

LINDA (*with infinite patience*):   They're all open, dear.

WILLY: The way they boxed us in here. Bricks and windows, windows and bricks.

LINDA: We should've bought the land next door.

WILLY: The street is lined with cars. There's not a breath of fresh air in the neighborhood. The grass don't grow any more, you can't raise a carrot in the back yard. They should've had a law against apartment houses. Remember those two beautiful elm trees out there? When I and Biff hung the swing between them?

LINDA: Yeah, like being a million miles from the city.

WILLY: They should've arrested the builder for cutting those down. They massacred the neighborhood. (*Lost.*) More and more I think of those days, Linda. This time of year it was lilac and wisteria. And then the peonies would come out, and the daffodils. What fragrance in this room!

LINDA: Well, after all, people had to move somewhere.

WILLY: No, there's more people now.

LINDA: I don't think there's more people. I think—

WILLY: There's more people! That's what's ruining this country! Population is getting out of control. The competition is maddening! Smell the stink from that apartment house! And another on the other side . . . How can they whip cheese?

On WILLY's *last line,* BIFF *and* HAPPY *raise themselves up in their beds, listening.*

LINDA: Go down, try it. And be quiet.

WILLY (*turning to* LINDA, *guiltily*):   You're not worried about me, are you, sweetheart?

BIFF: What's the matter?

HAPPY: Listen!

LINDA: You've got too much on the ball to worry about.

WILLY: You're my foundation and my support, Linda.

LINDA: Just try to relax, dear. You make mountains out of molehills.

WILLY: I won't fight with him any more. If he wants to go back to Texas, let him go.

LINDA: He'll find his way.

WILLY: Sure. Certain men just don't get started till later in life. Like Thomas Edison, I think. Or B. F. Goodrich. One of them was deaf. (*He starts for the bedroom doorway.*) I'll put my money on Biff.

LINDA: And Willy—if it's warm Sunday we'll drive in the country. And we'll open the windshield, and take lunch.

WILLY: No, the windshields don't open on the new cars.

LINDA: But you opened it today.

WILLY: Me? I didn't. (*He stops.*) Now isn't that peculiar! Isn't that a remarkable— (*He breaks off in amazement and fright as the flute is heard distantly.*)

LINDA: What, darling?

WILLY: That is the most remarkable thing.

LINDA: What, dear?

WILLY: I was thinking of the Chevvy. (*Slight pause.*) Nineteen twenty-eight . . . when I had that red Chevvy—(*Breaks off.*) That funny? I coulda sworn I was driving that Chevvy today.

LINDA: Well, that's nothing. Something must've reminded you.

WILLY: Remarkable. Ts. Remember those days? The way Biff used to simonize that car? The dealer refused to believe there was eighty thousand miles on it. (*He shakes his head.*) Heh! (*To* LINDA.) Close your eyes, I'll be right up. (*He walks out of the bedroom.*)

HAPPY (*to Biff*):   Jesus, maybe he smashed up the car again!

LINDA (*calling after* WILLY):   Be careful on the stairs, dear! The cheese is on the middle shelf! (*She turns, goes over to the bed, takes his jacket, and goes out of the bedroom.*)

Light has risen on the boys' room. Unseen, WILLY *is heard talking to himself, "Eighty thousand miles," and a little laugh.* BIFF *gets out of bed, comes downstage a bit, and stands attentively.* BIFF *is two years older than his brother* HAPPY, *well built, but in these days bears a worn air and seems less self-assured. He has succeeded less, and his dreams are stronger and less acceptable than* HAPPY's. HAPPY *is tall, powerfully made. Sexuality is like a visible color on him, or a scent that many women have discovered. He, like his brother, is lost, but in a different way, for he has never allowed himself to turn his face toward defeat and is thus more confused and hard-skinned, although seemingly more content.*

HAPPY (*getting out of bed*):   He's going to get his license taken away if he keeps that up. I'm getting nervous about him, y'know, Biff?

BIFF: His eyes are going.

HAPPY: No, I've driven with him. He sees all right. He just doesn't keep his mind on it. I drove into the city with him last week. He stops at a green light and then it turns red and he goes. (*He laughs.*)

BIFF: Maybe he's color-blind.

HAPPY: Pop? Why he's got the finest eye for color in the business. You know that.

BIFF (*sitting down on his bed*):   I'm going to sleep.

HAPPY: You're not still sour on Dad, are you, Biff?

BIFF: He's all right, I guess.

WILLY (*underneath them, in the livingroom*):   Yes, sir, eighty thousand miles—eighty-two thousand!

BIFF: You smoking?

HAPPY (*holding out a pack of cigarettes*):   Want one?

BIFF (*taking a cigarette*):   I can never sleep when I smell it.

WILLY: What a simonizing job, heh!

HAPPY (*with deep sentiment*):   Funny, Biff, y'know? Us sleeping in here again? The old beds. (*He pats his bed affectionately.*) All the talk that went across those two beds, huh? Our whole lives.

BIFF: Yeah. Lotta dreams and plans.

HAPPY (*with a deep and masculine laugh*):   About five hundred women would like to know what was said in this room.

They share a soft laugh.

BIFF: Remember that big Betsy something—what the hell was her name—over on Bushwick Avenue?

HAPPY (*combing his hair*):   With the collie dog!

BIFF: That's the one. I got you in there, remember?

HAPPY: Yeah, that was my first time—I think. Boy, there was a pig! (*They laugh, almost crudely.*) You taught me everything I know about women. Don't forget that.

BIFF: I bet you forgot how bashful you used to be. Especially with girls.

HAPPY: Oh, I still am, Biff.

BIFF: Oh, go on.

HAPPY: I just control it, that's all. I think I got less bashful and you got more so. What happened, Biff? Where's the old humor, the old confidence? (*He shakes* BIFF's *knee.* BIFF *gets up and moves restlessly about the room.*) What's the matter?

BIFF: Why does Dad mock me all the time?

HAPPY: He's not mocking you, he—

BIFF: Everything I say there's a twist of mockery on his face. I can't get near him.

HAPPY: He just wants you to make good, that's all. I wanted to talk to you about Dad for a long time, Biff. Something's—happening to him. He—talks to himself.

BIFF: I noticed that this morning. But he always mumbled.

HAPPY: But not so noticeable. It got so embarrassing I sent him to Florida. And you know something? Most of the time he's talking to you.

BIFF: What's he say about me?

HAPPY: I can't make it out.

BIFF: What's he say about me?

HAPPY: I think the fact that you're not settled, that you're still kind of up in the air . . .

BIFF: There's one or two other things depressing him, Happy.

HAPPY: What do you mean?

BIFF: Never mind. Just don't lay it all to me.

HAPPY: But I think if you just got started—I mean—is there any future for you out there?

BIFF: I tell ya, Hap, I don't know what the future is. I don't know—what I'm supposed to want.

HAPPY: What do you mean?

BIFF: Well, I spent six or seven years after high school trying to work myself up. Shipping clerk, salesman, business of one kind or another. And it's a measly manner of existence. To get on that subway on the hot mornings in summer. To devote your whole life to keeping stock, or making phone calls, or selling or buying. To suffer fifty weeks of the year for the sake of a two-week vacation, when all you really desire is to be outdoors, with your shirt off. And always to have to get ahead of the next fella. And still—that's how you build a future.

HAPPY: Well, you really enjoy it on a farm? Are you content out there?

BIFF (*with rising agitation*):   Hap, I've had twenty or thirty different kinds of jobs since I left home before the war, and it always turns out the same. I just realized it lately. In Nebraska when I herded cattle, and the Dakotas, and Arizona, and now in Texas. It's why I came home now, I guess, because I realized it. This farm I work on, it's spring there now, see? And they've got about fifteen new colts. There's nothing more inspiring or—beautiful than the sight of a mare and a new colt. And it's cool there now, see? Texas is cool now, and it's spring. And whenever spring comes to where I am, I suddenly get the feeling, my God, I'm not gettin' anywhere! What the hell am I doing, playing around with horses, twenty-eight dollars a week! I'm thirty-four years old, I oughta be makin' my future. That's when I come running home. And now, I get here, and I don't know what to do with myself. (*After a pause.*) I've always made a point of not wasting my life, and everytime I come back here I know that all I've done is to waste my life.

HAPPY: You're a poet, you know that, Biff? You're a—you're an idealist!

BIFF: No, I'm mixed up very bad. Maybe I oughta get married. Maybe I oughta get stuck into something. Maybe that's my trouble. I'm like a boy. I'm not married, I'm not in business, I just—I'm like a boy. Are you content, Hap? You're a success, aren't you? Are you content?

HAPPY: Hell, no!

BIFF: Why? You're making money, aren't you?

HAPPY (*moving about with energy, expressiveness*): All I can do now is wait for the merchandise manager to die. And suppose I get to be merchandise manager? He's a good friend of mine, and he just built a terrific estate on Long Island. And he lived there about two months and sold it, and now he's building another one. He can't enjoy it once it's finished. And I know that's just what I would do. I don't know what the hell I'm workin' for. Sometimes I sit in my apartment—all alone. And I think of the rent I'm paying. And it's crazy. But then, it's what I always wanted. My own apartment, a car, and plenty of women. And still, goddammit, I'm lonely.

BIFF (*with enthusiasm*): Listen, why don't you come out West with me?

HAPPY: You and I, heh?

BIFF: Sure, maybe we could buy a ranch. Raise cattle, use our muscles. Men built like we are should be working out in the open.

HAPPY (*avidly*): The Loman Brothers, heh?

BIFF (*with vast affection*): Sure, we'd be known all over the counties!

HAPPY (*enthralled*): That's what I dream about, Biff. Sometimes I want to just rip my clothes off in the middle of the store and outbox that goddam merchandise manager. I mean I can outbox, outrun, and outlift anybody in that store, and I have to take orders from those common, petty, sons-of-bitches till I can't stand it any more.

BIFF: I'm tellin' you, kid, if you were with me I'd be happy out there.

HAPPY (*enthused*): See, Biff, everybody around me is so false that I'm constantly lowering my ideals . . .

BIFF: Baby, together we'd stand up for one another, we'd have someone to trust.

HAPPY: If I were around you—

BIFF: Hap, the trouble is we weren't brought up to grub for money. I don't know how to do it.

HAPPY: Neither can I!

BIFF: Then let's go!

HAPPY: The only thing is—what can you make out there?

BIFF: But look at your friend. Builds an estate and then hasn't the peace of mind to live in it.

HAPPY: Yeah, but when he walks into the store the waves part in front of him. That's fifty-two thousand dollars a year coming through the revolving door, and I got more in my pinky finger than he's got in his head.

BIFF: Yeah, but you just said—

HAPPY: I gotta show some of those pompous, self-important executives over there that Hap Loman can make the grade. I want to walk into the store the way he walks in. Then I'll go with you, Biff. We'll be together yet, I swear. But take those two we had tonight. Now weren't they gorgeous creatures?

BIFF: Yeah, yeah, most gorgeous I've had in years.

HAPPY: I get that any time I want, Biff. Whenever I feel disgusted. The only trouble is, it gets like bowling or something. I just keep knockin' them over and it doesn't mean anything. You still run around a lot?

BIFF: Naa. I'd like to find a girl—steady, somebody with substance.

HAPPY: That's what I long for.

BIFF: Go on! You'd never come home.

HAPPY: I would! Somebody with character, with resistance! Like Mom, y'know? You're gonna call me a bastard when I tell you this. That girl Charlotte I was with tonight is engaged to be married in five weeks. (*He tries on his new hat.*)

BIFF: No kiddin'!

HAPPY: Sure, the guy's in line for the vice-presidency of the store. I don't know what gets into me, maybe I just have an overdeveloped sense of competition or something, but I went and ruined her, and furthermore I can't get rid of her. And he's the third executive I've done that to. Isn't that a crummy characteristic? And to top it all, I go to their weddings! (*Indignantly, but laughing.*) Like I'm not supposed to take bribes. Manufacturers offer me a hundred-dollar bill now and then to throw an order their way. You know how honest I am, but it's like this girl, see. I hate myself for it. Because I don't want the girl, and, still, I take it and—I love it!

BIFF: Let's go to sleep.

HAPPY: I guess we didn't settle anything, heh?

BIFF: I just got one idea that I think I'm going to try.

HAPPY: What's that?

BIFF: Remember Bill Oliver?

HAPPY: Sure, Oliver is very big now. You want to work for him again?

BIFF: No, but when I quit he said something to me. He put his arm on my shoulder, and he said, "Biff, if you ever need anything, come to me."

HAPPY: I remember that. That sounds good.

BIFF: I think I'll go to see him. If I could get ten thousand or even seven or eight thousand dollars I could buy a beautiful ranch.

HAPPY: I bet he'd back you. 'Cause he thought highly of you, Biff, I mean, they all do. You're well liked, Biff. That's why I say to come back here, and we both have the apartment. And I'm tellin' you, Biff, any babe you want . . .

BIFF: No, with a ranch I could do the work I like and still be something. I just wonder though. I wonder if Oliver still thinks I stole that carton of basketballs.

HAPPY: Oh, he probably forgot that long ago. It's almost ten years. You're too sensitive. Anyway, he didn't really fire you.

BIFF: Well, I think he was going to. I think that's why I quit. I was never sure whether he knew or not. I know he thought the world of me, though. I was the only one he'd let lock up the place.

WILLY (*below*):   You gonna wash the engine, Biff?

HAPPY: Shh!

BIFF *looks at* HAPPY, *who is gazing down, listening.* WILLY *is mumbling in the parlor.*

HAPPY: You hear that?

They listen. WILLY *laughs warmly.*

BIFF (*growing angry*):   Doesn't he know Mom can hear that?

WILLY: Don't get your sweater dirty, Biff!

A look of pain crosses BIFF's *face.*

HAPPY: Isn't that terrible? Don't leave again, will you? You'll find a job here. You gotta stick around. I don't know what to do about him, it's getting embarrassing.

WILLY: What a simonizing job!

BIFF: Mom's hearing that!

WILLY: No kiddin', Biff, you got a date? Wonderful!

HAPPY: Go on to sleep. But talk to him in the morning, will you?

BIFF (*reluctantly getting into bed*):   With her in the house. Brother!

HAPPY (*getting into bed*):   I wish you'd have a good talk with him.

The light on their room begins to fade.

BIFF (*to himself in bed*):   That selfish, stupid . . .

HAPPY: Sh . . . Sleep, Biff.

Their light is out. Well before they have finished speaking, WILLY's *form is dimly seen below in the darkened kitchen. He opens the refrigerator, searches in there, and takes out a bottle of milk. The apartment houses are fading out, and the entire house and surroundings become covered with leaves. Music insinuates itself as the leaves appear.*

WILLY: Just wanna be careful with those girls, Biff, that's all. Don't make any promises. No promises of any kind. Because a girl, y'know, they always believe what you tell 'em, and you're very young, Biff, you're too young to be talking seriously to girls.

Light rises on the kitchen. WILLY, *talking, shuts the refrigerator door and comes downstage to the kitchen table. He pours milk into a glass. He is totally immersed in himself, smiling faintly.*

WILLY: Too young entirely, Biff. You want to watch your schooling first. Then when you're all set, there'll be plenty of girls for a boy like you. (*He smiles broadly at a kitchen chair.*) That so? The girls pay for you? (*He laughs.*) Boy, you must really be makin' a hit.

WILLY *is gradually addressing—physically—a point offstage, speaking through the wall of the kitchen, and his voice has been rising in volume to that of a normal conversation.*

WILLY: I been wondering why you polish the car so careful. Ha! Don't leave the hubcaps, boys. Get the chamois to the hubcaps. Happy, use newspaper on the windows, it's the easiest thing. Show him how to do it, Biff! You see, Happy? Pad it up, use it like a pad. That's it, that's it, good work. You're doin' all right, Hap. (*He pauses, then nods in approbation for a few seconds, then looks upward.*) Biff, first thing we gotta do when we get time is clip that big branch over the house. Afraid it's gonna fall in a storm and hit the roof. Tell you what. We get a rope and sling her around, and then we climb up there with a couple of saws and take her down. Soon as you finish the car, boys, I wanna see ya. I got a surprise for you, boys.

BIFF (*offstage*):   Whatta ya got, Dad?

WILLY: No, you finish first. Never leave a job till you're finished—remember that. (*Looking toward the "big trees."*) Biff, up in Albany I saw a beautiful hammock. I think I'll buy it next trip, and we'll hang it right between those two elms. Wouldn't that be something? Just swingin' there under those branches. Boy, that would be . . .

YOUNG BIFF *and* YOUNG HAPPY *appear from the direction* WILLY *was addressing.* HAPPY *carries rags and a pail of water.* BIFF, *wearing a sweater with a block "S," carries a football.*

BIFF (*pointing in the direction of the car offstage*):   How's that, Pop, professional?

WILLY: Terrific. Terrific job, boys. Good work, Biff.

HAPPY: Where's the surprise, Pop?

WILLY: In the back seat of the car.

HAPPY: Boy! (*He runs off.*)

BIFF: What is it, Dad? Tell me, what'd you buy?

WILLY (*laughing, cuffs him*):   Never mind, something I want you to have.

BIFF (*turns and starts off*):   What is it, Hap?

HAPPY (*offstage*):   It's a punching bag!

BIFF: Oh, Pop!

WILLY: It's got Gene Tunney's signature on it!

HAPPY *runs onstage with a punching bag.*

BIFF: Gee, how'd you know we wanted a punching bag?

WILLY: Well, it's the finest thing for the timing.

HAPPY (*lies down on his back and pedals with his feet*):   I'm losing weight, you notice, Pop?

WILLY (*to* HAPPY):   Jumping rope is good too.

BIFF: Did you see the new football I got?

WILLY (*examining the ball*):   Where'd you get a new ball?

BIFF: The coach told me to practice my passing.

WILLY: That so? And he gave you the ball, heh?

BIFF: Well, I borrowed it from the locker room. (*He laughs confidentially.*)

WILLY (*laughing with him at the theft*):   I want you to return that.

HAPPY: I told you he wouldn't like it!

BIFF (*angrily*):   Well, I'm bringing it back!

WILLY (*stopping the incipient argument, to* HAPPY):   Sure, he's gotta practice with a regulation ball, doesn't he? (*To* BIFF.) Coach'll probably congratulate you on your initiative!

BIFF: Oh, he keeps congratulating my initiative all the time, Pop.

WILLY: That's because he likes you. If somebody else took that ball there'd be an uproar. So what's the report, boys, what's the report?

BIFF: Where'd you go this time, Dad? Gee we were lonesome for you.

WILLY (*pleased, puts an arm around each boy and they come down to the apron*):   Lonesome, heh?

BIFF: Missed you every minute.

WILLY: Don't say? Tell you a secret, boys. Don't breathe it to a soul. Someday I'll have my own business, and I'll never have to leave home any more.

HAPPY: Like Uncle Charley, heh?

WILLY: Bigger than Uncle Charley! Because Charley is not—liked. He's liked, but he's not—well liked.

BIFF: Where'd you go this time, Dad?

WILLY: Well, I got on the road, and I went north to Providence. Met the Mayor.

BIFF: The Mayor of Providence!

WILLY: He was sitting in the hotel lobby.

BIFF: What'd he say?

WILLY: He said, "Morning!" And I said, "You've got a fine city here, Mayor." And then he had coffee with me. And then I went to Waterbury. Waterbury is a fine city. Big clock city, the famous Waterbury clock. Sold a nice bill there. And then Boston—Boston is the cradle of the Revolution. A fine city. And a couple of other towns in Mass., and on to Portland and Bangor and straight home!

BIFF: Gee, I'd love to go with you sometime, Dad.

WILLY: Soon as summer comes.

HAPPY: Promise?

WILLY: You and Hap and I, and I'll show you all the towns. America is full of beautiful towns and fine, upstanding people. And they know me, boys, they know me up and down New England. The finest people. And when I bring you fellas up, there'll be open sesame for all of us, 'cause one thing, boys: I have friends. I can park my car in any street in New England, and the cops protect it like their own. This summer, heh?

BIFF *and* HAPPY (*together*): Yeah! You bet!

WILLY: We'll take our bathing suits.

HAPPY: We'll carry your bags, Pop!

WILLY: Oh, won't that be something! Me comin' into the Boston stores with you boys carryin' my bags. What a sensation!

BIFF *is prancing around, practicing passing the ball.*

WILLY: You nervous, Biff, about the game?

BIFF: Not if you're gonna be there.

WILLY: What do they say about you in school, now that they made you captain?

HAPPY: There's a crowd of girls behind him everytime the classes change.

BIFF (*taking* WILLY's *hand*): This Saturday, Pop, this Saturday—just for you, I'm going to break through for a touchdown.

HAPPY: You're supposed to pass.

BIFF: I'm takin' one play for Pop. You watch me, Pop, and when I take off my helmet, that means I'm breakin' out. Then you watch me crash through that line!

WILLY (*kisses* BIFF): Oh, wait'll I tell this in Boston!

BERNARD *enters in knickers. He is younger than* BIFF, *earnest and loyal, a worried boy.*

BERNARD: Biff, where are you? You're supposed to study with me today.

WILLY: Hey, looka Bernard. What're you lookin' so anemic about, Bernard?

BERNARD: He's gotta study, Uncle Willy. He's got Regents next week.

HAPPY (*tauntingly, spinning* BERNARD *around*): Let's box, Bernard!

BERNARD: Biff! (*He gets away from* HAPPY.) Listen, Biff, I heard Mr. Birnbaum say that if you don't start studyin' math he's gonna flunk you, and you won't graduate. I heard him!

WILLY: You better study with him, Biff. Go ahead now.

BERNARD: I heard him!

BIFF: Oh, Pop, you didn't see my sneakers! (*He holds up a foot for* WILLY *to look at.*)

WILLY: Hey, that's a beautiful job of printing!

BERNARD (*wiping his glasses*):   Just because he printed University of Virginia on his sneakers doesn't mean they've got to graduate him, Uncle Willy!

WILLY (*angrily*):   What're you talking about? With scholarships to three universities they're gonna flunk him?

BERNARD: But I heard Mr. Birnbaum say—

WILLY: Don't be a pest, Bernard! (*To his boys.*) What an anemic!

BERNARD: Okay, I'm waiting for you in my house, Biff.

BERNARD *goes off. The* LOMANS *laugh.*

WILLY: Bernard is not well liked, is he?

BIFF: He's liked, but he's not well liked.

HAPPY: That's right, Pop.

WILLY: That's just what I mean. Bernard can get the best marks in school, y'understand, but when he gets out in the business world, y'understand, you are going to be five times ahead of him. That's why I thank Almighty God you're both built like Adonises. Because the man who makes an appearance in the business world, the man who creates personal interest, is the man who gets ahead. Be liked and you will never want. You take me, for instance. I never have to wait in line to see a buyer. "Willy Loman is here!" That's all they have to know, and I go right through.

BIFF: Did you knock them dead, Pop?

WILLY: Knocked 'em cold in Providence, slaughtered 'em in Boston.

HAPPY (*on his back, pedaling again*):   I'm losing weight, you notice, Pop?

LINDA *enters, as of old, a ribbon in her hair, carrying a basket of washing.*

LINDA (*with youthful energy*):   Hello, dear!

WILLY: Sweetheart!

LINDA: How'd the Chevvy run?

WILLY: Chevrolet, Linda, is the greatest car ever built. (*To the boys.*) Since when do you let your mother carry wash up the stairs?

BIFF: Grab hold there, boy!

HAPPY: Where to, Mom?

LINDA: Hang them up on the line. And you better go down to your friends, Biff. The cellar is full of boys. They don't know what to do with themselves.

BIFF: Ah, when Pop comes home they can wait!

WILLY (*laughs appreciatively*):   You better go down and tell them what to do, Biff.

BIFF: I think I'll have them sweep out the furnace room.

WILLY: Good work, Biff.

BIFF (*goes through wall-line of kitchen to doorway at back and calls down*):   Fellas! Everybody sweep out the furnace room! I'll be right down!

VOICES: All right! Okay, Biff.

BIFF: George and Sam and Frank, come out back! We're hangin' up the wash! Come on, Hap, on the double! (*He and* HAPPY *carry out the basket.*)

LINDA: The way they obey him!

WILLY: Well, that's training, the training. I'm tellin' you, I was sellin' thousands and thousands, but I had to come home.

LINDA: Oh, the whole block'll be at that game. Did you sell anything?

WILLY: I did five hundred gross in Providence and seven hundred gross in Boston.

LINDA: No! Wait a minute, I've got a pencil. (*She pulls pencil and paper out of her apron pocket.*) That makes your commission . . . Two hundred—my God! Two hundred and twelve dollars!

WILLY: Well, I didn't figure it yet, but . . .

LINDA: How much did you do?

WILLY: Well, I—I did—about a hundred and eighty gross in Providence. Well, no—it came to—roughly two hundred gross on the whole trip.

LINDA(*without hesitation*):   Two hundred gross. That's . . . (*She figures.*)

WILLY: The trouble was that three of the stores were half closed for inventory in Boston. Otherwise I woulda broke records.

LINDA: Well, it makes seventy dollars and some pennies. That's very good.

WILLY: What do we owe?

LINDA: Well, on the first there's sixteen dollars on the refrigerator—

WILLY: Why sixteen?

LINDA: Well, the fan belt broke, so it was a dollar eighty.

WILLY: But it's brand new.

LINDA: Well, the man said that's the way it is. Till they work themselves in, y'know.

They move through the wall-line into the kitchen.

WILLY: I hope we didn't get stuck on that machine.

LINDA: They got the biggest ads of any of them!

WILLY: I know, it's a fine machine. What else?

LINDA: Well, there's nine-sixty for the washing machine. And for the vacuum cleaner there's three and a half due on the fifteenth. Then the roof, you got twenty-one dollars remaining.

WILLY: It don't leak, does it?

LINDA: No, they did a wonderful job. Then you owe Frank for the carburetor.

WILLY: I'm not going to pay that man! That goddam Chevrolet, they ought to prohibit the manufacture of that car!

LINDA: Well, you owe him three and a half. And odds and ends, comes to around a hundred and twenty dollars by the fifteenth.

WILLY: A hundred and twenty dollars! My God, if business don't pick up I don't know what I'm gonna do!

LINDA: Well, next week you'll do better.

WILLY: Oh, I'll knock them dead next week. I'll go to Hartford. I'm very well liked in Hartford. You know, the trouble is, Linda, people don't seem to take to me.

They move onto the forestage.

LINDA: Oh, don't be foolish.

WILLY: I know it when I walk in. They seem to laugh at me.

LINDA: Why? Why would they laugh at you? Don't talk that way, Willy.

WILLY *moves to the edge of the stage.* LINDA *goes into the kitchen and starts to darn stockings.*

WILLY: I don't know the reason for it, but they just pass me by. I'm not noticed.

LINDA: But you're doing wonderful, dear. You're making seventy to a hundred dollars a week.

WILLY: But I gotta be at it ten, twelve hours a day. Other men—I don't know—they do it easier. I don't know why—I can't stop myself—I talk too much. A man oughta come in with a few words. One thing about Charley. He's a man of few words, and they respect him.

LINDA: You don't talk too much, you're just lively.

WILLY (*smiling*):   Well, I figure, what the hell, life is short, a couple of jokes. (*To himself.*) I joke too much! (*The smile goes.*)

LINDA: Why? You're—

WILLY: I'm fat. I'm very—foolish to look at, Linda. I didn't tell you, but Christmas time I happened to be calling on F. H. Stewarts, and a salesman I know, as I was going in to see the buyer I heard him say something about—walrus. And I—I cracked him right across the face. I won't take that. I simply will not take that. But they do laugh at me. I know that.

LINDA: Darling . . .

WILLY: I gotta overcome it. I know I gotta overcome it. I'm not dressing to advantage, maybe.

LINDA: Willy, darling, you're the handsomest man in the world—

WILLY: Oh, no, Linda.

LINDA: To me you are. (*Slight pause.*) The handsomest.

From the darkness is heard the laughter of a woman. WILLY *doesn't turn to it, but it continues through* LINDA's *lines.*

LINDA: And the boys, Willy. Few men are idolized by their children the way you are.

Music is heard as behind a scrim, to the left of the house, THE WOMAN, *dimly seen, is dressing.*

WILLY (*with great feeling*):   You're the best there is, Linda, you're a pal, you know that? On the road—on the road I want to grab you sometimes and just kiss the life outa you.

The laughter is loud now, and he moves into a brightening area at the left, where THE WOMAN *has come from behind the scrim and is standing, putting on her hat, looking into a "mirror" and laughing.*

WILLY: 'Cause I get so lonely—especially when business is bad and there's nobody to talk to. I get the feeling that I'll never sell anything again, that I won't make a living for you, or a business, a business for the boys. (*He talks through* THE WOMAN's *subsiding laughter;* THE WOMAN *primps at the "mirror."*) There's so much I want to make for—

THE WOMAN: Me? You didn't make me, Willy. I picked you.

WILLY (*pleased*):   You picked me?

THE WOMAN (*who is quite proper-looking,* WILLY's *age*):   I did. I've been sitting at that desk watching all the salesmen go by, day in, day out. But you've got such a sense of humor, and we do have such a good time together, don't we?

WILLY: Sure, sure. (*He takes her in his arms.*) Why do you have to go now?

THE WOMAN: It's two o'clock . . .

WILLY: No, come on in! (*He pulls her.*)

THE WOMAN: . . . my sisters'll be scandalized. When'll you be back?

WILLY: Oh, two weeks about. Will you come up again?

THE WOMAN: Sure thing. You do make me laugh. It's good for me. (*She squeezes his arm, kisses him.*) And I think you're a wonderful man.

WILLY: You picked me, heh?

THE WOMAN: Sure. Because you're so sweet. And such a kidder.

WILLY: Well, I'll see you next time I'm in Boston.

THE WOMAN: I'll put you right through to the buyers.

WILLY (*slapping her bottom*):   Right. Well, bottoms up!

THE WOMAN (*slaps him gently and laughs*):   You just kill me, Willy. (*He suddenly grabs her and kisses her roughly.*) You kill me. And thanks for the stockings. I love a lot of stockings. Well, good night.

WILLY: Good night. And keep your pores open!

THE WOMAN: Oh, Willy!

THE WOMAN *bursts out laughing, and* LINDA'*s laughter blends in.* THE WOMAN *disappears into the dark. Now the area at the kitchen table brightens.* LINDA *is sitting where she was at the kitchen table, but now is mending a pair of silk stockings.*

LINDA: You are, Willy. The handsomest man. You've got no reason to feel that—

WILLY (*coming out of* THE WOMAN'*s dimming area and going over to* LINDA):   I'll make it all up to you, Linda, I'll—

LINDA: There's nothing to make up, dear. You're doing fine, better than—

WILLY (*noticing her mending*):   What's that?

LINDA: Just mending my stockings. They're so expensive—

WILLY (*angrily, taking them from her*):   I won't have you mending stockings in this house! Now throw them out!

LINDA *puts the stockings in her pocket.*

BERNARD (*entering on the run*):   Where is he? If he doesn't study!

WILLY (*moving to the forestage, with great agitation*):   You'll give him the answers!

BERNARD: I do, but I can't on a Regents! That's a state exam! They're liable to arrest me!

WILLY: Where is he? I'll whip him, I'll whip him!

LINDA: And he'd better give back that football, Willy, it's not nice.

WILLY: Biff! Where is he? Why is he taking everything?

LINDA: He's too tough with the girls, Willy. All the mothers are afraid of him!

WILLY: I'll whip him!

BERNARD: He's driving the car without a license!

THE WOMAN'*s laugh is heard.*

WILLY: Shut up!

LINDA: All the mothers—

WILLY: Shut up!

BERNARD (*backing quietly away and out*):   Mr. Birnbaum says he's stuck up.

WILLY: Get outa here!

BERNARD: If he doesn't buckle down he'll flunk math! (*He goes off.*)

LINDA: He's right, Willy, you've gotta—

WILLY (*exploding at her*):   There's nothing the matter with him! You want him to be a worm like Bernard? He's got spirit, personality . . .

As he speaks, LINDA, *almost in tears, exits into the livingroom.* WILLY *is alone in the kitchen, wilting and staring. The leaves are gone. It is night again, and the apartment houses look down from behind.*

WILLY: Loaded with it. Loaded! What is he stealing? He's giving it back, isn't he? Why is he stealing? What did I tell him? I never in my life told him anything but decent things.

HAPPY *in pajamas has come down the stairs;* WILLY *suddenly becomes aware of* HAPPY*'s presence.*

HAPPY: Let's go now, come on.

WILLY (*sitting down at the kitchen table*):   Huh! Why did she have to wax the floors herself? Everytime she waxes the floors she keels over. She knows that!

HAPPY: Shh! Take it easy. What brought you back tonight?

WILLY: I got an awful scare. Nearly hit a kid in Yonkers. God! Why didn't I go to Alaska with my brother Ben that time! Ben! That man was a genius, that man was success incarnate! What a mistake! He begged me to go.

HAPPY: Well, there's no use in—

WILLY: You guys! There was a man started with the clothes on his back and ended up with diamond mines!

HAPPY: Boy, someday I'd like to know how he did it.

WILLY: What's the mystery? The man knew what he wanted and went out and got it! Walked into a jungle, and comes out, the age of twenty-one, and he's rich! The world is an oyster, but you don't crack it open on a mattress!

HAPPY: Pop, I told you I'm gonna retire you for life.

WILLY: You'll retire me for life on seventy goddam dollars a week? And your women and your car and your apartment, and you'll retire me for life! Christ's sake, I couldn't get past Yonkers today! Where are you guys, where are you? The woods are burning! I can't drive a car!

CHARLEY *has appeared in the doorway. He is a large man, slow of speech, laconic, immovable. In all he says, despite what he says, there is pity, and, now, trepidation. He has a robe over his pajamas, slippers on his feet. He enters the kitchen.*

CHARLEY: Everything all right?

HAPPY: Yeah, Charley, everything's . . .

WILLY: What's the matter?

CHARLEY: I heard some noise. I thought something happened. Can't we do something about the walls? You sneeze in here, and in my house hats blow off.

HAPPY: Let's go to bed, Dad. Come on.

CHARLEY *signals to* HAPPY *to go.*

WILLY: You go ahead, I'm not tired at the moment.

HAPPY (*to* WILLY):   Take it easy, huh? (*He exits.*)

WILLY: What're you doin' up?

CHARLEY (*sitting down at the kitchen table opposite* WILLY):   Couldn't sleep good. I had a heartburn.

WILLY: Well, you don't know how to eat.

CHARLEY: I eat with my mouth.

WILLY: No, you're ignorant. You gotta know about vitamins and things like that.

CHARLEY: Come on, let's shoot. Tire you out a little.

WILLY (*hesitantly*):   All right. You got cards?

CHARLEY (*taking a deck from his pocket*):   Yeah, I got them. Someplace. What is it with those vitamins?

WILLY (*dealing*):   They build up your bones. Chemistry.

CHARLEY: Yeah, but there's no bones in a heartburn.

WILLY: What are you talkin' about? Do you know the first thing about it?

CHARLEY: Don't get insulted.

WILLY: Don't talk about something you don't know anything about.

They are playing. Pause.

CHARLEY: What're you doin' home?

WILLY: A little trouble with the car.

CHARLEY: Oh. (*Pause.*) I'd like to take a trip to California.

WILLY: Don't say.

CHARLEY: You want a job?

WILLY: I got a job, I told you that. (*After a slight pause.*) What the hell are you offering me a job for?

CHARLEY: Don't get insulted.

WILLY: Don't insult me.

CHARLEY: I don't see no sense in it. You don't have to go on this way.

WILLY: I got a good job. (*Slight pause.*) What do you keep comin' in here for?

CHARLEY: You want me to go?

WILLY (*after a pause, withering*):   I can't understand it. He's going back to Texas again. What the hell is that?

CHARLEY: Let him go.

WILLY: I got nothin' to give him, Charley, I'm clean, I'm clean.

CHARLEY: He won't starve. None a them starve. Forget about him.

WILLY: Then what have I got to remember?

CHARLEY: You take it too hard. To hell with it. When a deposit bottle is broken you don't get your nickel back.

WILLY: That's easy enough for you to say.

CHARLEY: That ain't easy for me to say.

WILLY: Did you see the ceiling I put up in the livingroom?

CHARLEY: Yeah, that's a piece of work. To put up a ceiling is a mystery to me. How do you do it?

WILLY: What's the difference?

CHARLEY: Well, talk about it.

WILLY: You gonna put up a ceiling?

CHARLEY: How could I put up a ceiling?

WILLY: Then what the hell are you bothering me for?

CHARLEY: You're insulted again.

WILLY: A man who can't handle tools is not a man. You're disgusting.

CHARLEY: Don't call me disgusting, Willy.

UNCLE BEN, *carrying a valise and an umbrella, enters the forestage from around the right corner of the house. He is a stolid man, in his sixties, with a mustache and an authoritative air. He is utterly certain of his destiny, and there is an aura of far places about him. He enters exactly as* WILLY *speaks.*

WILLY: I'm getting awfully tired, Ben.

BEN*'s music is heard.* BEN *looks around at everything.*

CHARLEY: Good, keep playing; you'll sleep better. Did you call me Ben?

BEN *looks at his watch.*

WILLY: That's funny. For a second there you reminded me of my brother Ben.

BEN: I have only a few minutes. (*He strolls, inspecting the place.* WILLY *and* CHARLEY *continue playing.*)

CHARLEY: You never heard from him again, heh? Since that time?

WILLY: Didn't Linda tell you? Couple of weeks ago we got a letter from his wife in Africa. He died.

CHARLEY: That so.

BEN (*chuckling*):   So this is Brooklyn, eh?

CHARLEY: Maybe you're in for some of his money.

WILLY: Naa, he had seven sons. There's just one opportunity I had with that man . . .

BEN: I must make a train, William. There are several properties I'm looking at in Alaska.

WILLY: Sure, sure! If I'd gone with him to Alaska that time, everything would've been totally different.

CHARLEY: Go on, you'd froze to death up there.

WILLY: What're you talking about?

BEN: Opportunity is tremendous in Alaska, William. Surprised you're not up there.

WILLY: Sure, tremendous.

CHARLEY: Heh?

WILLY: There was the only man I ever met who knew the answers.

CHARLEY: Who?

BEN: How are you all?

WILLY (*taking a pot, smiling*):   Fine, fine.

CHARLEY: Pretty sharp tonight.

BEN: Is Mother living with you?

WILLY: No, she died a long time ago.

CHARLEY: Who?

BEN: That's too bad. Fine specimen of a lady, Mother.

WILLY (*to* CHARLEY):   Heh?

BEN: I'd hoped to see the old girl.

CHARLEY: Who died?

BEN: Heard anything from Father, have you?

WILLY (*unnerved*):   What do you mean, who died?

CHARLEY (*taking a pot*):   What're you talkin' about?

BEN (*looking at his watch*):   William, it's half-past eight!

WILLY (*as though to dispel his confusion he angrily stops* CHARLEY's *hand*):   That's my build!

CHARLEY: I put the ace—

WILLY: If you don't know how to play the game I'm not gonna throw my money away on you!

CHARLEY (*rising*):   It was my ace, for God's sake!

WILLY: I'm through, I'm through!

BEN: When did Mother die?

WILLY: Long ago. Since the beginning you never knew how to play cards.

CHARLEY (*picks up the cards and goes to the door*):   All right! Next time I'll bring a deck with five aces.

WILLY: I don't play that kind of game!

CHARLEY (*turning to him*):   You should be ashamed of yourself!

WILLY: Yeah?

CHARLEY: Yeah! (*He goes out.*)

WILLY (*slamming the door after him*):   Ignoramus!

BEN (*as* WILLY *comes toward him through the wall-line of the kitchen*):   So you're William.

WILLY (*shaking* BEN's *hand*):   Ben! I've been waiting for you so long! What's the answer? How did you do it?

BEN: Oh, there's a story in that.

LINDA *enters the forestage, as of old, carrying the wash basket.*

LINDA: Is this Ben?

BEN (*gallantly*):   How do you do, my dear.

LINDA: Where've you been all these years? Willy's always wondered why you—

WILLY (*pulling* BEN *away from her impatiently*):   Where is Dad? Didn't you follow him? How did you get started?

BEN: Well, I don't know how much you remember.

WILLY: Well, I was just a baby, of course, only three or four years old—

BEN: Three years and eleven months.

WILLY: What a memory, Ben!

BEN: I have many enterprises, William, and I have never kept books.

WILLY: I remember I was sitting under the wagon in—was it Nebraska?

BEN: It was South Dakota, and I gave you a bunch of wild flowers.

WILLY: I remember you walking away down some open road.

BEN (*laughing*):   I was going to find Father in Alaska.

WILLY: Where is he?

BEN: At that age I had a very faulty view of geography, William. I discovered after a few days that I was heading due south, so instead of Alaska, I ended up in Africa.

LINDA: Africa!

WILLY: The Gold Coast!

BEN: Principally, diamond mines.

LINDA: Diamond mines!

BEN: Yes, my dear. But I've only a few minutes—

WILLY: No! Boys! Boys! (YOUNG BIFF *and* HAPPY *appear.*) Listen to this. This is your Uncle Ben, a great man! Tell my boys, Ben!

BEN: Why, boys, when I was seventeen I walked into the jungle, and when I was twenty-one I walked out. (*He laughs.*) And by God I was rich.

WILLY (*to the boys*):   You see what I been talking about? The greatest things can happen!

BEN (*glancing at his watch*):   I have an appointment in Ketchikan Tuesday week.

WILLY: No, Ben! Please tell about Dad. I want my boys to hear. I want them to know the kind of stock they spring from. All I remember is a man with a big beard, and I was in Mamma's lap, sitting around a fire, and some kind of high music.

BEN: His flute. He played the flute.

WILLY: Sure, the flute, that's right!

New music is heard, a high, rollicking tune.

BEN: Father was a very great and a very wild-hearted man. We would start in Boston, and he'd toss the whole family into the wagon, and then he'd drive the team right across the country; through Ohio, and Indiana, Michigan, Illinois, and all the Western states. And we'd stop in the towns and sell the flutes that he'd made on the way. Great inventor, Father. With one gadget he made more in a week than a man like you could make in a lifetime.

WILLY: That's just the way I'm bringing them up, Ben—rugged, well liked, all-around.

BEN: Yeah? (*To* BIFF.) Hit that, boy—hard as you can. (*He pounds his stomach.*)

BIFF: Oh, no, sir!

BEN (*taking boxing stance*):   Come on, get to me! (*He laughs.*)

WILLY: Go to it, Biff! Go ahead, show him!

BIFF: Okay! (*He cocks his fist and starts in.*)

LINDA (*to* WILLY):   Why must he fight, dear?

BEN (*sparring with* BIFF):   Good boy! Good boy!

WILLY: How's that, Ben, heh?

HAPPY: Give him the left, Biff!

LINDA: Why are you fighting?

BEN: Good boy! (*Suddenly comes in, trips* BIFF, *and stands over him, the point of his umbrella poised over* BIFF'S *eye.*)

LINDA: Look out, Biff!

BIFF: Gee!

BEN (*patting* BIFF'S *knee*):   Never fight fair with a stranger, boy. You'll never get out of the jungle that way. (*Taking* LINDA'*s hand and bowing.*) It was an honor and a pleasure to meet you, Linda.

LINDA (*withdrawing her hand coldly, frightened*):   Have a nice—trip.

BEN (*to* WILLY):   And good luck with your—what do you do?

WILLY: Selling.

BEN: Yes. Well . . . (*He raises his hand in farewell to all.*)

WILLY: No, Ben, I don't want you to think . . . (*He takes* BEN'S *arm to show him.*) It's Brooklyn, I know, but we hunt too.

BEN: Really, now.

WILLY: Oh, sure, there's snakes and rabbits and—that's why I moved out here. Why, Biff can fell any one of these trees in no time! Boys! Go right over to where they're building the apartment house and get some sand. We're gonna rebuild the entire front stoop right now! Watch this, Ben!

BIFF: Yes, sir! On the double, Hap!

HAPPY (*as he and* BIFF *run off*): I lost weight, Pop, you notice?

CHARLEY *enters in knickers, even before the boys are gone.*

CHARLEY: Listen, if they steal any more from that building the watchman'll put the cops on them!

LINDA (*to* WILLY): Don't let Biff . . .

BEN *laughs lustily.*

WILLY: You shoulda seen the lumber they brought home last week. At least a dozen six-by-tens worth all kinds a money.

CHARLEY: Listen, if that watchman—

WILLY: I gave them hell, understand. But I got a couple of fearless characters there.

CHARLEY: Willy, the jails are full of fearless characters.

BEN (*clapping* WILLY *on the back, with a laugh at* CHARLEY): And the stock exchange, friend!

WILLY (*joining in* BEN'S *laughter*): Where are the rest of your pants?

CHARLEY: My wife bought them.

WILLY: Now all you need is a golf club and you can go upstairs and go to sleep. (*To* BEN.) Great athlete! Between him and his son Bernard they can't hammer a nail!

BERNARD (*rushing in*): The watchman's chasing Biff!

WILLY (*angrily*): Shut up! He's not stealing anything!

LINDA (*alarmed, hurrying off left*): Where is he? Biff, dear! (*She exits.*)

WILLY (*moving toward the left, away from* BEN): There's nothing wrong. What's the matter with you?

BEN: Nervy boy. Good!

WILLY (*laughing*): Oh, nerves of iron, that Biff!

CHARLEY: Don't know what it is. My New England man comes back and he's bleedin', they murdered him up there.

WILLY: It's contacts, Charley, I got important contacts!

CHARLEY (*sarcastically*): Glad to hear it, Willy. Come in later, we'll shoot a little casino. I'll take some of your Portland money. (*He laughs at* WILLY *and exits.*)

WILLY (*turning to* BEN): Business is bad, it's murderous. But not for me, of course.

BEN: I'll stop by on my way back to Africa.

WILLY (*longingly*): Can't you stay a few days? You're just what I need, Ben, because I—I have a fine position here, but I—well, Dad left when I was such a baby and I never had a chance to talk to him and I still feel—kind of temporary about myself.

BEN: I'll be late for my train.

They are at opposite ends of the stage.

WILLY: Ben, my boys—can't we talk? They'd go into the jaws of hell for me, see, but I—

BEN: William, you're being first-rate with your boys. Outstanding, manly chaps!

WILLY (*hanging on to his words*):   Oh, Ben, that's good to hear! Because sometimes I'm afraid that I'm not teaching them the right kind of—Ben, how should I teach them?

BEN (*giving great weight to each word, and with a certain vicious audacity*):   William, when I walked into the jungle, I was seventeen. When I walked out I was twenty-one. And, by God, I was rich! (*He goes off into darkness around the right corner of the house.*)

WILLY: . . . was rich! That's just the spirit I want to imbue them with! To walk into a jungle! I was right! I was right! I was right!

BEN *is gone, but* WILLY *is still speaking to him as* LINDA, *in nightgown and robe, enters the kitchen, glances around for* WILLY, *then goes to the door of the house, looks out and sees him. Comes down to his left. He looks at her.*

LINDA: Willy, dear? Willy?

WILLY: I was right!

LINDA: Did you have some cheese? (*He can't answer.*) It's very late, darling. Come to bed, heh?

WILLY (*looking straight up*):   Gotta break your neck to see a star in this yard.

LINDA: You coming in?

WILLY: What ever happened to that diamond watch fob? Remember? When Ben came from Africa that time? Didn't he give me a watch fob with a diamond in it?

LINDA: You pawned it, dear. Twelve, thirteen years ago. For Biff's radio correspondence course.

WILLY: Gee, that was a beautiful thing. I'll take a walk.

LINDA: But you're in your slippers.

WILLY (*starting to go around the house at the left*):   I was right! I was! (*Half to* LINDA, *as he goes, shaking his head.*) What a man! There was a man worth talking to. I was right!

LINDA (*calling after* WILLY):   But in your slippers, Willy!

WILLY *is almost gone when* BIFF, *in his pajamas, comes down the stairs and enters the kitchen.*

BIFF: What is he doing out there?

LINDA: Sh!

BIFF: God Almighty, Mom, how long has he been doing this?

LINDA: Don't, he'll hear you.

BIFF: What the hell is the matter with him?

LINDA: It'll pass by morning.

BIFF: Shouldn't we do anything?

LINDA: Oh, my dear, you should do a lot of things, but there's nothing to do, so go to sleep.

HAPPY *comes down the stairs and sits on the steps.*

HAPPY: I never heard him so loud, Mom.

LINDA: Well, come around more often; you'll hear him. (*She sits down at the table and mends the lining of* WILLY'S *jacket.*)

BIFF: Why didn't you ever write me about this, Mom?

LINDA: How would I write to you? For over three months you had no address.

BIFF: I was on the move. But you know I thought of you all the time. You know that, don't you, pal?

LINDA: I know, dear, I know. But he likes to have a letter. Just to know that there's still a possibility for better things.

BIFF: He's not like this all the time, is he?

LINDA: It's when you come home he's always the worst.

BIFF: When I come home?

LINDA: When you write you're coming, he's all smiles, and talks about the future, and—he's just wonderful. And then the closer you seem to come, the more shaky he gets, and then, by the time you get here, he's arguing, and he seems angry at you. I think it's just that maybe he can't bring himself to—to open up to you. Why are you so hateful to each other? Why is that?

BIFF (*evasively*):   I'm not hateful, Mom.

LINDA: But you no sooner come in the door than you're fighting!

BIFF: I don't know why. I mean to change. I'm tryin', Mom, you understand?

LINDA: Are you home to stay now?

BIFF: I don't know. I want to look around, see what's doin'.

LINDA: Biff, you can't look around all your life, can you?

BIFF: I just can't take hold, Mom. I can't take hold of some kind of a life.

LINDA: Biff, a man is not a bird, to come and go with the springtime.

BIFF: Your hair . . . (*He touches her hair.*) Your hair got so gray.

LINDA: Oh, it's been gray since you were in high school. I just stopped dyeing it, that's all.

BIFF: Dye it again, will ya? I don't want my pal looking old. (*He smiles.*)

LINDA: You're such a boy! You think you can go away for a year and . . . You've got to get it into your head now that one day you'll knock on this door and there'll be strange people here—

BIFF: What are you talking about? You're not even sixty, Mom.

LINDA: But what about your father?

BIFF (*lamely*):   Well, I meant him too.

HAPPY: He admires Pop.

LINDA: Biff, dear, if you don't have any feeling for him, then you can't have any feeling for me.

BIFF: Sure I can, Mom.

LINDA: No. You can't just come to see me, because I love him. (*With a threat, but only a threat, of tears.*) He's the dearest man in the world to me, and I won't have anyone making him feel unwanted and low and blue. You've got to make up your mind now, darling, there's no leeway any more. Either he's your father and you pay him that respect, or else you're not to come here. I know he's not easy to get along with—nobody knows that better than me—but . . .

WILLY (*from the left, with a laugh*):   Hey, hey, Biffo!

BIFF (*starting to go out after* WILLY):   What the hell is the matter with him? (HAPPY *stops him.*)

LINDA: Don't—don't go near him!

BIFF: Stop making excuses for him! He always, always wiped the floor with you. Never had an ounce of respect for you.

HAPPY: He's always had respect for—

BIFF: What the hell do you know about it?

HAPPY (*surlily*):   Just don't call him crazy!

BIFF: He's got no character—Charley wouldn't do this. Not in his own house—spewing out that vomit from his mind.

HAPPY: Charley never had to cope with what he's got to.

BIFF: People are worse off than Willy Loman. Believe me, I've seen them!

LINDA: Then make Charley your father, Biff. You can't do that, can you? I don't say he's a great man. Willy Loman never made a lot of money. His name was never in the paper. He's not the finest character that ever lived. But he's a human being, and a terrible thing is happening to him. So attention must be paid. He's not to be allowed to fall into his grave like an old dog. Attention, attention must be finally paid to such a person. You called him crazy—

BIFF: I didn't mean—

LINDA: No, a lot of people think he's lost his—balance. But you don't have to be very smart to know what his trouble is. The man is exhausted.

HAPPY: Sure!

LINDA: A small man can be just as exhausted as a great man. He works for a company thirty-six years this March, opens up unheard-of territories to their trademark, and now in his old age they take his salary away.

HAPPY (indignantly):   I didn't know that, Mom.

LINDA: You never asked, my dear! Now that you get your spending money someplace else you don't trouble your mind with him.

HAPPY: But I gave you money last—

LINDA: Christmas time, fifty dollars! To fix the hot water it cost ninety-seven fifty! For five weeks he's been on straight commission, like a beginner, an unknown!

BIFF: Those ungrateful bastards!

LINDA: Are they any worse than his sons? When he brought them business, when he was young, they were glad to see him. But now his old friends, the old buyers that loved him so and always found some order to hand him in a pinch—they're all dead, retired. He used to be able to make six, seven calls a day in Boston. Now he takes his valises out of the car and puts them back and takes them out again and he's exhausted. Instead of walking he talks now. He drives seven hundred miles, and when he gets there no one knows him any more, no one welcomes him. And what goes through a man's mind, driving seven hundred miles home without having earned a cent? Why shouldn't he talk to himself? Why? When he has to go to Charley and borrow fifty dollars a week and pretend to me that it's his pay? How long can that go on? How long? You see what I'm sitting here and waiting for? And you tell me he has no character? The man who never worked a day but for your benefit? When does he get the medal for that? Is this his reward—to turn around at the age of sixty-three and find his sons, who he loved better than his life, one a philandering bum—

HAPPY: Mom!

LINDA: That's all you are, my baby! (To BIFF.) And you! What happened to the love you had for him? You were such pals! How you used to talk to him on the phone every night! How lonely he was till he could come home to you!

BIFF: All right, Mom. I'll live here in my room, and I'll get a job. I'll keep away from him, that's all.

LINDA: No, Biff. You can't stay here and fight all the time.

BIFF: He threw me out of this house, remember that.

LINDA: Why did he do that? I never knew why.

BIFF: Because I know he's a fake and he doesn't like anybody around who knows!

LINDA: Why a fake? In what way? What do you mean?

BIFF: Just don't lay it all at my feet. It's between me and him—that's all I have to say. I'll chip in from now on. He'll settle for half my pay check. He'll be all right. I'm going to bed. (*He starts for the stairs.*)

LINDA: He won't be all right.

BIFF (*turning on the stairs, furiously*):   I hate this city and I'll stay here. Now what do you want?

LINDA: He's dying, Biff.

> HAPPY *turns quickly to her, shocked.*

BIFF (*after a pause.*):   Why is he dying?

LINDA: He's been trying to kill himself.

BIFF (*with great horror*):   How?

LINDA: I live from day to day.

BIFF: What're you talking about?

LINDA: Remember I wrote you that he smashed up the car again? In February?

BIFF: Well?

LINDA: The insurance inspector came. He said that they have evidence. That all these accidents in the last year—weren't—weren't—accidents.

HAPPY: How can they tell that? That's a lie.

LINDA: It seems there's a woman . . . (*She takes a breath as—*)

BIFF (*sharply but contained*):   What woman?

LINDA (*simultaneously*):   . . . and this woman . . .

LINDA: What?

BIFF: Nothing. Go ahead.

LINDA: What did you say?

BIFF: Nothing. I just said what woman?

HAPPY: What about her?

LINDA: Well, it seems she was walking down the road and saw his car. She says that he wasn't driving fast at all, and that he didn't skid. She says he came to that little bridge, and then deliberately smashed into the railing, and it was only the shallowness of the water that saved him.

BIFF: Oh, no, he probably just fell asleep again.

LINDA: I don't think he fell asleep.

BIFF: Why not?

LINDA: Last month . . . (*With great difficulty.*) Oh, boys, it's so hard to say a thing like this! He's just a big stupid man to you, but I tell you there's more good in him than in many other people. (*She chokes, wipes her eyes.*) I was looking for a fuse. The lights blew out, and I went down the cellar. And behind the fuse box—it happened to fall out—was a length of rubber pipe—just short.

HAPPY: No kidding?

LINDA: There's a little attachment on the end of it. I knew right away. And sure enough, on the bottom of the water heater there's a new little nipple on the gas pipe.

HAPPY (*angrily*):   That—jerk.

BIFF: Did you have it taken off?

LINDA: I'm—I'm ashamed to. How can I mention it to him? Every day I go down and take away that little rubber pipe. But, when he comes home, I put it back where it was. How can I insult him that way? I don't know what to do. I live from day to day, boys. I tell you, I know every thought in his mind. It sounds so old-fashioned and silly, but I tell you he put his whole life into you and you've turned your backs on him. (*She is bent over in the chair, weeping, her face in her hands.*) Biff, I swear to God! Biff, his life is in your hands!

HAPPY (*to* BIFF):   How do you like that damned fool!

BIFF (*kissing her*):   All right, pal, all right. It's all settled now. I've been remiss. I know that, Mom. But now I'll stay, and I swear to you, I'll apply myself. (*Kneeling in front of her, in a fever of self-reproach.*) It's just—you see, Mom, I don't fit in business. Not that I won't try. I'll try, and I'll make good.

HAPPY: Sure you will. The trouble with you in business was you never tried to please people.

BIFF: I know, I—

HAPPY: Like when you worked for Harrison's. Bob Harrison said you were tops, and then you go and do some damn fool thing like whistling whole songs in the elevator like a comedian.

BIFF (*against* HAPPY):   So what? I like to whistle sometimes.

HAPPY: You don't raise a guy to a responsible job who whistles in the elevator!

LINDA: Well, don't argue about it now.

HAPPY: Like when you'd go off and swim in the middle of the day instead of taking the line around.

BIFF (*his resentment rising*):   Well, don't you run off? You take off sometimes, don't you? On a nice summer day?

HAPPY: Yeah, but I cover myself!

LINDA: Boys!

HAPPY: If I'm going to take a fade the boss can call any number where I'm supposed to be and they'll swear to him that I just left. I'll tell you something that I hate to say, Biff, but in the business world some of them think you're crazy.

BIFF (*angered*):   Screw the business world!

HAPPY: All right, screw it! Great, but cover yourself!

LINDA: Hap, Hap!

BIFF: I don't care what they think! They've laughed at Dad for years, and you know why? Because we don't belong in this nut-house of a city! We should be mixing cement on some open plain, or—or carpenters. A carpenter is allowed to whistle!

WILLY walks in from the entrance of the house, at left.

WILLY: Even your grandfather was better than a carpenter. (*Pause. They watch him.*) You never grew up. Bernard does not whistle in the elevator, I assure you.

BIFF (*as though to laugh* WILLY *out of it*):   Yeah, but you do, Pop.

WILLY: I never in my life whistled in an elevator! And who in the business world thinks I'm crazy?

BIFF: I didn't mean it like that, Pop. Now don't make a whole thing out of it, will ya?

WILLY: Go back to the West! Be a carpenter, a cowboy, enjoy yourself!

LINDA: Willy, he was just saying—

WILLY: I heard what he said!

HAPPY (*trying to quiet* WILLY):   Hey, Pop, come on now . . .

WILLY (*continuing over* HAPPY's *line*):   They laugh at me, heh? Go to Filene's, go to the Hub, go to Slattery's, Boston. Call out the name Willy Loman and see what happens! Big shot!

BIFF: All right, Pop.

WILLY: Big!

BIFF: All right!

WILLY: Why do you always insult me?

BIFF: I didn't say a word. (*To* LINDA.) Did I say a word?

LINDA: He didn't say anything, Willy.

WILLY (*going to the doorway of the livingroom*):   All right, good night, good night.

LINDA: Willy, dear, he just decided . . .

WILLY (*to* BIFF):   If you get tired hanging around tomorrow, paint the ceiling I put up in the livingroom.

BIFF: I'm leaving early tomorrow.

HAPPY: He's going to see Bill Oliver, Pop.

WILLY (*interestedly*):   Oliver? For what?

BIFF (*with reserve, but trying, trying*):   He always said he'd stake me. I'd like to go into business, so maybe I can take him up on it.

LINDA: Isn't that wonderful?

WILLY: Don't interrupt. What's wonderful about it? There's fifty men in the City of New York who'd stake him. (*To* BIFF.) Sporting goods?

BIFF: I guess so. I know something about it and—

WILLY: He knows something about it! You know sporting goods better than Spalding, for God's sake! How much is he giving you?

BIFF: I don't know, I didn't even see him yet, but—

WILLY: Then what're you talkin' about?

BIFF (*getting angry*):   Well, all I said was I'm gonna see him, that's all!

WILLY (*turning away*):   Ah, you're counting your chickens again.

BIFF (*starting left for the stairs*):   Oh, Jesus, I'm going to sleep!

WILLY (*calling after him*):   Don't curse in this house!

BIFF (*turning*):   Since when did you get so clean!

HAPPY (*trying to stop them*):   Wait a . . .

WILLY: Don't use that language to me! I won't have it!

HAPPY (*grabbing* BIFF, *shouts*):   Wait a minute! I got an idea. I got a feasible idea. Come here, Biff, let's talk this over now, let's talk some sense here. When I was down in Florida last time, I thought of a great idea to sell sporting goods. It just came back to me. You and I, Biff—we have a line, the Loman Line. We train a couple of weeks, and put on a couple of exhibitions, see?

WILLY: That's an idea!

HAPPY: Wait! We form two basketball teams, see? Two water-polo teams. We play each other. It's a million dollars' worth of publicity. Two brothers, see? The Loman Brothers. Displays in the Royal Palms—all the hotels. And banners over the ring and the basketball court: "Loman Brothers." Baby, we could sell sporting goods!

WILLY: That is a one-million-dollar idea.

LINDA: Marvelous!

BIFF: I'm in great shape as far as that's concerned.

HAPPY: And the beauty of it is, Biff, it wouldn't be like a business. We'd be out playin' ball again . . .

BIFF (*enthused*):   Yeah, that's . . .

WILLY: Million-dollar . . .

HAPPY: And you wouldn't get fed up with it, Biff. It'd be the family again. There'd be the old honor, and comradeship, and if you wanted to go off for a swim or somethin'—well, you'd do it! Without some smart cooky gettin' up ahead of you!

WILLY: Lick the world! You guys together could absolutely lick the civilized world.

BIFF: I'll see Oliver tomorrow. Hap, if we could work that out . . .

LINDA: Maybe things are beginning to—

WILLY (*wildly enthused, to* LINDA):   Stop interrupting! (*To* BIFF.) But don't wear sport jacket and slacks when you see Oliver.

BIFF: No, I'll—

WILLY: A business suit, and talk as little as possible, and don't crack any jokes.

BIFF: He did like me. Always liked me.

LINDA: He loved you!

WILLY (*to* LINDA):   Will you stop! (*To* BIFF.) Walk in very serious. You are not applying for a boy's job. Money is to pass. Be quiet, fine, and serious. Everybody likes a kidder, but nobody lends him money.

HAPPY: I'll try to get some myself, Biff. I'm sure I can.

WILLY: I can see great things for you, kids, I think your troubles are over. But remember, start big and you'll end big. Ask for fifteen. How much you gonna ask for?

BIFF: Gee, I don't know—

WILLY: And don't say "Gee." "Gee" is a boy's word. A man walking in for fifteen thousand dollars does not say "Gee!"

BIFF: Ten, I think, would be top though.

WILLY: Don't be so modest. You always started too low. Walk in with a big laugh. Don't look worried. Start off with a couple of your good stories to lighten things up. It's not what you say, it's how you say it—because personality always wins the day.

LINDA: Oliver always thought the highest of him—

WILLY: Will you let me talk?

BIFF: Don't yell at her, Pop, will ya?

WILLY (*angrily*):   I was talking, wasn't I?

BIFF: I don't like you yelling at her all the time, and I'm tellin' you, that's all.

WILLY: What're you, takin' over this house?

LINDA: Willy—

WILLY (*turning on her*):   Don't take his side all the time, goddammit!

BIFF (*furiously*):   Stop yelling at her!

WILLY (*suddenly pulling on his cheek, beaten down, guilt ridden*):   Give my best to Bill Oliver—he may remember me. (*He exits through the livingroom doorway.*)

LINDA (*her voice subdued*):   What'd you have to start that for? (BIFF *turns away.*) You see how sweet he was as soon as you talked hopefully? (*She goes over to* BIFF.) Come up and say good night to him. Don't let him go to bed that way.

HAPPY: Come on, Biff, let's buck him up.

LINDA: Please, dear. Just say good night. It takes so little to make him happy. Come. (*She goes through the livingroom doorway, calling upstairs from within the livingroom.*) Your pajamas are hanging in the bathroom. Willy!

HAPPY (*looking toward where* LINDA *went out*):   What a woman! They broke the mold when they made her. You know that, Biff?

BIFF: He's off salary. My God, working on commission!

HAPPY: Well, let's face it: he's no hot-shot selling man. Except that sometimes, you have to admit, he's a sweet personality.

BIFF (*deciding*):   Lend me ten bucks, will ya? I want to buy some new ties.

HAPPY: I'll take you to a place I know. Beautiful stuff. Wear one of my striped shirts tomorrow.

BIFF: She got gray. Mom got awful old. Gee, I'm gonna go in to Oliver tomorrow and knock him for a—

HAPPY: Come on up. Tell that to Dad. Let's give him a whirl. Come on.

BIFF (*steamed up*):   You know, with ten thousand bucks, boy!

HAPPY (*as they go into the livingroom*):   That's the talk, Biff, that's the first time I've heard the old confidence out of you! (*From within the livingroom, fading off.*) You're gonna live with me, kid, and any babe you want just say the word . . . (*The last lines are hardly heard. They are mounting the stairs to their parents' bedroom.*)

LINDA (*entering her bedroom and addressing* WILLY, *who is in the bathroom. She is straightening the bed for him*):   Can you do anything about the shower? It drips.

WILLY (*from the bathroom*):   All of a sudden everything falls to pieces! Goddam plumbing, oughta be sued, those people. I hardly finished putting it in and the thing . . . (*His words rumble off.*)

LINDA: I'm just wondering if Oliver will remember him. You think he might?

WILLY (*coming out of the bathroom in his pajamas*):   Remember him? What's the matter with you, you crazy? If he'd've stayed with Oliver he'd be on top by now! Wait'll Oliver gets a look at him. You don't know the average caliber any more. The average young man today—(*he is getting into bed*)—is got a caliber of zero. Greatest thing in the world for him was to bum around.

BIFF *and* HAPPY *enter the bedroom. Slight pause.*

WILLY (*stops short, looking at* BIFF):   Glad to hear it, boy.

HAPPY: He wanted to say good night to you, sport.

WILLY (*to* BIFF):   Yeah. Knock him dead, boy. What'd you want to tell me?

BIFF: Just take it easy, Pop. Good night. (*He turns to go.*)

WILLY (*unable to resist*):   And if anything falls off the desk while you're talking to him—like a package or something—don't you pick it up. They have office boys for that.

LINDA: I'll make a big breakfast—

WILLY: Will you let me finish? (*To* BIFF.) Tell him you were in the business in the West. Not farm work.

BIFF: All right, Dad.

LINDA: I think everything—

WILLY (*going right through her speech*):   And don't undersell yourself. No less than fifteen thousand dollars.

BIFF (*unable to bear him*):   Okay. Good night, Mom. (*He starts moving.*)

WILLY: Because you got a greatness in you, Biff, remember that. You got all kinds a greatness . . . (*He lies back, exhausted.* BIFF *walks out.*)

LINDA (*calling after* BIFF):   Sleep well, darling!

HAPPY: I'm gonna get married, Mom. I wanted to tell you.

LINDA: Go to sleep, dear.

HAPPY (*going*): I just wanted to tell you.

WILLY: Keep up the good work. (HAPPY *exits.*) God . . . remember that Ebbets Field game? The championship of the city?

LINDA: Just rest. Should I sing to you?

WILLY: Yeah. Sing to me. (LINDA *hums a soft lullaby.*) When that team came out— he was the tallest, remember?

LINDA: Oh, yes. And in gold.

BIFF *enters the darkened kitchen, takes a cigarette, and leaves the house. He comes downstage into a golden pool of light. He smokes, staring at the night.*

WILLY: Like a young god. Hercules—something like that. And the sun, the sun all around him. Remember how he waved to me? Right up from the field, with the representatives of three colleges standing by? And the buyers I brought, and the cheers when he came out—Loman, Loman, Loman! God Almighty, he'll be great yet. A star like that, magnificent, can never really fade away!

The light on WILLY *is fading. The gas heater begins to glow through the kitchen wall, near the stairs, a blue flame beneath red coils.*

LINDA (*timidly*): Willy, dear, what has he got against you?

WILLY: I'm so tired. Don't talk any more.

BIFF *slowly returns to the kitchen. He stops, stares toward the heater.*

LINDA: Will you ask Howard to let you work in New York?

WILLY: First thing in the morning. Everything'll be all right.

BIFF *reaches behind the heater and draws out a length of rubber tubing. He is horrified and turns his head toward* WILLY's *room, still dimly lit, from which the strains of* LINDA's *desperate but monotonous humming rise.*

WILLY (*staring through the window into the moonlight*): Gee, look at the moon moving between the buildings!

BIFF *wraps the tubing around his hand and quickly goes up the stairs. Curtain.*

ACT II

Music is heard, gay and bright. The curtain rises as the music fades away. WILLY, *in shirt sleeves, is sitting at the kitchen table, sipping coffee, his hat in his lap.* LINDA *is filling his cup when she can.*

WILLY: Wonderful coffee. Meal in itself.

LINDA: Can I make you some eggs?

WILLY: No. Take a breath.

LINDA: You look so rested, dear.

WILLY: I slept like a dead one. First time in months. Imagine, sleeping till ten on a Tuesday morning. Boys left nice and early, heh?

LINDA: They were out of here by eight o'clock.

WILLY: Good work!

LINDA: It was so thrilling to see them leaving together. I can't get over the shaving lotion in this house.

WILLY (*smiling*):   Mmm—

LINDA: Biff was very changed this morning. His whole attitude seemed to be hopeful. He couldn't wait to get downtown to see Oliver.

WILLY: He's heading for a change. There's no question, there simply are certain men that take longer to get—solidified. How did he dress?

LINDA: His blue suit. He's so handsome in that suit. He could be a—anything in that suit!

WILLY *gets up from the table.* LINDA *holds his jacket for him.*

WILLY: There's no question, no question at all. Gee, on the way home tonight I'd like to buy some seeds.

LINDA (*laughing*):   That'd be wonderful. But not enough sun gets back there. Nothing'll grow any more.

WILLY: You wait, kid, before it's all over we're gonna get a little place out in the country, and I'll raise some vegetables, a couple of chickens . . .

LINDA: You'll do it yet, dear.

WILLY *walks out of his jacket.* LINDA *follows him.*

WILLY: And they'll get married, and come for a weekend. I'd build a little guest house. 'Cause I got so many fine tools, all I'd need would be a little lumber and some peace of mind.

LINDA (*joyfully*):   I sewed the lining . . .

WILLY: I could build two guest houses, so they'd both come. Did he decide how much he's going to ask Oliver for?

LINDA (*getting him into the jacket*):   He didn't mention it, but I imagine ten or fifteen thousand. You going to talk to Howard today?

WILLY: Yeah. I'll put it to him straight and simple. He'll just have to take me off the road.

LINDA: And Willy, don't forget to ask for a little advance, because we've got the insurance premium. It's the grace period now.

WILLY: That's a hundred . . . ?

LINDA: A hundred and eight, sixty-eight. Because we're a little short again.

WILLY: Why are we short?

LINDA: Well, you had the motor job on the car . . .

WILLY: That goddam Studebaker!

LINDA: And you got one more payment on the refrigerator . . .

WILLY: But it just broke again!

LINDA: Well, it's old, dear.

WILLY: I told you we should've bought a well-advertised machine. Charley bought a General Electric and it's twenty years old and it's still good, that son-of-a-bitch.

LINDA: But, Willy—

WILLY: Whoever heard of a Hastings refrigerator? Once in my life I would like to own something outright before it's broken! I'm always in a race with the junkyard! I just finished paying for the car and it's on its last legs. The refrigerator consumes belts like a goddam maniac. They time those things. They time them so when you finally paid for them, they're used up.

LINDA (*buttoning up his jacket as he unbuttons it*):   All told, about two hundred dollars would carry us, dear. But that includes the last payment on the mortgage. After this payment, Willy, the house belongs to us.

WILLY: It's twenty-five years!

LINDA: Biff was nine years old when we bought it.

WILLY: Well, that's a great thing. To weather a twenty-five year mortgage is—

LINDA: It's an accomplishment.

WILLY: All the cement, the lumber, the reconstruction I put in this house! There ain't a crack to be found in it any more.

LINDA: Well, it served its purpose.

WILLY: What purpose? Some stranger'll come along, move in, and that's that. If only Biff would take this house, and raise a family . . . (*He starts to go.*) Good-by, I'm late.

LINDA (*suddenly remembering*):   Oh, I forgot! You're supposed to meet them for dinner.

WILLY: Me?

LINDA: At Frank's Chop House on Forty-eighth near Sixth Avenue.

WILLY: Is that so! How about you?

LINDA: No, just the three of you. They're gonna blow you to a big meal!

WILLY: Don't say! Who thought of that?

LINDA: Biff came to me this morning, Willy, and he said, "Tell Dad, we want to blow him to a big meal." Be there six o'clock. You and your two boys are going to have dinner.

WILLY: Gee whiz! That's really somethin'. I'm gonna knock Howard for a loop, kid. I'll get an advance, and I'll come home with a New York job. Goddammit, now I'm gonna do it!

LINDA: Oh, that's the spirit, Willy!

WILLY: I will never get behind a wheel the rest of my life!

LINDA: It's changing, Willy, I can feel it changing!

WILLY: Beyond a question. G'by, I'm late. (*He starts to go again.*)

LINDA (*calling after him as she runs to the kitchen table for a handkerchief*):   You got your glasses?

WILLY (*feels for them, then comes back in*):   Yeah, yeah, got my glasses.

LINDA (*giving him the handkerchief*):   And a handkerchief.

WILLY: Yeah, handkerchief.

LINDA: And your saccharine?

WILLY: Yeah, my saccharine.

LINDA: Be careful on the subway stairs.

She kisses him, and a silk stocking is seen hanging from her hand. WILLY *notices it.*

WILLY: Will you stop mending stockings? At least while I'm in the house. It gets me nervous. I can't tell you. Please.

LINDA *hides the stocking in her hand as she follows* WILLY *across the forestage in front of the house.*

LINDA: Remember, Frank's Chop House.

WILLY (*passing the apron*):   Maybe beets would grow out there.

LINDA (*laughing*):   But you tried so many times.

WILLY: Yeah. Well, don't work hard today. (*He disappears around the right corner of the house.*)

LINDA: Be careful!

As WILLY *vanishes,* LINDA *waves to him. Suddenly the phone rings. She runs across the stage and into the kitchen and lifts it.*

LINDA: Hello? Oh, Biff! I'm so glad you called, I just . . . Yes, sure, I just told him. Yes, he'll be there for dinner at six o'clock, I didn't forget. Listen, I was just dying to tell you. You know that little rubber pipe I told you about? That he connected to the gas heater? I finally decided to go down the cellar this morning and take it away and destroy it. But it's gone! Imagine? He took it away himself, it isn't there! (*She listens.*) When? Oh, then you took it. Oh—nothing, it's just that I'd hoped he'd taken it away himself. Oh, I'm not worried, darling, because this morning he left in such high spirits, it was like the old days! I'm not afraid any more. Did Mr. Oliver see you? . . . Well, you wait there then. And make a nice impression on him, darling. Just don't perspire too much before you see him. And have a nice time with Dad. He may have big news too! . . . That's right, a New York job. And be sweet to him tonight, dear. Be loving to him. Because he's only a little boat looking for a harbor. (*She is trembling with sorrow and joy.*) Oh, that's wonderful, Biff, you'll save his life. Thanks, darling. Just put your arm around him when he comes into the restaurant. Give him a smile. That's the boy . . . Good-by, dear. . . . You got your comb? . . . That's fine. Good-by, Biff dear.

In the middle of her speech, HOWARD WAGNER, *thirty-six, wheels in a small typewriter table on which is a wire-recording machine and proceeds to plug it in. This is on the left forestage. Light slowly fades on* LINDA *as it rises on* HOWARD. HOWARD *is intent on threading the machine and only glances over his shoulder as* WILLY *appears.*

WILLY: Pst! Pst!

HOWARD: Hello, Willy, come in.

WILLY: Like to have a little talk with you, Howard.

HOWARD: Sorry to keep you waiting. I'll be with you in a minute.

WILLY: What's that, Howard?

HOWARD: Didn't you ever see one of these? Wire recorder.

WILLY: Oh. Can we talk a minute?

HOWARD: Records things. Just got delivery yesterday. Been driving me crazy, the most terrific machine I ever saw in my life. I was up all night with it.

WILLY: What do you do with it?

HOWARD: I bought it for dictation, but you can do anything with it. Listen to this. I had it home last night. Listen to what I picked up. The first one is my daughter. Get this. (*He flicks the switch and "Roll out the Barrel" is heard being whistled.*) Listen to that kid whistle.

WILLY: That is lifelike, isn't it?

HOWARD: Seven years old. Get that tone.

WILLY: Ts, ts. Like to ask a little favor if you . . .

The whistling breaks off, and the voice of HOWARD'S DAUGHTER *is heard.*

HIS DAUGHTER: "Now you, Daddy."

HOWARD: She's crazy for me! (*Again the same song is whistled.*) That's me! Ha! (*He winks.*)

WILLY: You're very good!

The whistling breaks off again. The machine runs silent for a moment.

HOWARD: Sh! Get this now, this is my son.

HIS SON: "The capital of Alabama is Montgomery; the capital of Arizona is Phoenix; the capital of Arkansas is Little Rock; the capital of California is Sacramento . . ." (*And on, and on.*)

HOWARD (*holding up five fingers*):   Five years old, Willy!

WILLY: He'll make an announcer some day!

HIS SON (*continuing*):   "The capital . . ."

HOWARD: Get that—alphabetical order! (*The machine breaks off suddenly.*) Wait a minute. The maid kicked the plug out.

WILLY: It certainly is a—

HOWARD: Sh, for God's sake!

HIS SON: "It's nine o'clock, Bulova watch time. So I have to go to sleep."

WILLY: That really is—

HOWARD: Wait a minute! The next is my wife.

They wait.

HOWARD'S VOICE: "Go on, say something." (*Pause.*) "Well, you gonna talk?"

HIS WIFE: "I can't think of anything."

HOWARD'S VOICE: "Well, talk—it's turning."

HIS WIFE (*shyly, beaten*):   "Hello." (*Silence.*) "Oh, Howard, I can't talk into this . . ."

HOWARD (*snapping the machine off*):   That was my wife.

WILLY: That is a wonderful machine. Can we—

HOWARD: I tell you, Willy, I'm gonna take my camera, and my bandsaw, and all my hobbies, and out they go. This is the most fascinating relaxation I ever found.

WILLY: I think I'll get one myself.

HOWARD: Sure, they're only a hundred and a half. You can't do without it. Supposing you wanna hear Jack Benny, see? But you can't be at home at that hour. So you tell the maid to turn the radio on when Jack Benny comes on, and this automatically goes on with the radio . . .

WILLY: And when you come home you . . .

HOWARD: You can come home twelve o'clock, one o'clock, any time you like, and you get yourself a Coke and sit yourself down, throw the switch, and there's Jack Benny's program in the middle of the night!

WILLY: I'm definitely going to get one. Because lots of time I'm on the road, and I think to myself, what I must be missing on the radio!

HOWARD: Don't you have a radio in the car?

WILLY: Well, yeah, but who ever thinks of turning it on?

HOWARD: Say, aren't you supposed to be in Boston?

WILLY: That's what I want to talk to you about, Howard. You got a minute?

He draws a chair in from the wing.

HOWARD: What happened? What're you doing here?

WILLY: Well . . .

HOWARD: You didn't crack up again, did you?

WILLY: Oh, no. No . . .

HOWARD: Geez, you had me worried there for a minute. What's the trouble?

WILLY: Well, to tell you the truth, Howard, I've come to the decision that I'd rather not travel any more.

HOWARD: Not travel! Well, what'll you do?

WILLY: Remember, Christmas time, when you had the party here? You said you'd try to think of some spot for me here in town.

HOWARD: With us?

WILLY: Well, sure.

HOWARD: Oh, yeah, yeah. I remember. Well, I couldn't think of anything for you, Willy.

WILLY: I tell ya, Howard. The kids are all grown up, y'know. I don't need much any more. If I could take home—well, sixty-five dollars a week, I could swing it.

HOWARD: Yeah, but Willy, see I—

WILLY: I tell ya why, Howard. Speaking frankly and between the two of us, y'know—I'm just a little tired.

HOWARD: Oh, I could understand that, Willy. But you're a road man, Willy, and we do a road business. We've only got a half-dozen salesmen on the floor here.

WILLY: God knows, Howard, I never asked a favor of any man. But I was with the firm when your father used to carry you in here in his arms.

HOWARD: I know that, Willy, but—

WILLY: Your father came to me the day you were born and asked me what I thought of the name of Howard, may he rest in peace.

HOWARD: I appreciate that, Willy, but there just is no spot here for you. If I had a spot I'd slam you right in, but I just don't have a single, solitary spot.

He looks for his lighter. WILLY *has picked it up and gives it to him. Pause.*

WILLY (*with increasing anger*):   Howard, all I need to set my table is fifty dollars a week.

HOWARD: But where am I going to put you, kid?

WILLY: Look, it isn't a question of whether I can sell merchandise, is it?

HOWARD: No, but it's a business, kid, and everybody's gotta pull his own weight.

WILLY (*desperately*):   Just let me tell you a story, Howard—

HOWARD: 'Cause you gotta admit, business is business.

WILLY (*angrily*):   Business is definitely business, but just listen for a minute. You don't understand this. When I was a boy—eighteen, nineteen—I was already on the road. And there was a question in my mind as to whether selling had a future for me. Because in those days I had a yearning to go to Alaska. See, there were three gold strikes in one month in Alaska, and I felt like going out. Just for the ride, you might say.

HOWARD (*barely interested*):   Don't say.

WILLY: Oh, yeah, my father lived many years in Alaska. He was an adventurous man. We've got quite a little streak of self-reliance in our family. I thought I'd go out with my older brother and try to locate him, and maybe settle in the North with the old man. And I was almost decided to go, when I met a salesman in the Parker House. His name was Dave Singleman. And he was eighty-four years old, and he'd drummed merchandise in thirty-one states. And old Dave, he'd go up to his room, y'understand, put on his green velvet slippers—I'll never forget—and pick up his phone and call the buyers, and without ever leaving his room, at the age of eighty-four, he made his living. And when I saw that, I realized that selling was the greatest career a man could want. 'Cause what could be more satisfying than to be able to go, at the age of eighty-four, into twenty or thirty different cities, and pick up a phone, and be remembered and loved and helped by so many different people? Do you know? when he died—and by the way he died the death of a salesman, in his green velvet slippers in the smoker of the New York, New Haven and Hartford, going into Boston—when he died, hundreds of salesmen and buyers were at his funeral. Things were sad on a lotta trains for months after that. (*He stands up.* HOWARD *has not looked at him.*) In those days there was personality in it, Howard. There was respect, and comradeship, and gratitude in it. Today, it's all cut and dried, and there's no chance for bringing friendship to bear—or personality. You see what I mean? They don't know me any more.

HOWARD (*moving away, to the right*):   That's just the thing, Willy.

WILLY: If I had forty dollars a week—that's all I'd need. Forty dollars, Howard.

HOWARD: Kid, I can't take blood from a stone, I—

WILLY (*desperation is on him now*):   Howard, the year Al Smith was nominated, your father came to me and—

HOWARD (*starting to go off*):   I've got to see some people, kid.

WILLY (*stopping him*):   I'm talking about your father! There were promises made across this desk! You mustn't tell me you've got people to see—I put thirty-four years into this firm, Howard, and now I can't pay my insurance! You can't eat the orange and throw the peel away—a man is not a piece of fruit! (*After a pause.*) Now pay attention. Your father—in 1928 I had a big year. I averaged a hundred and seventy dollars a week in commissions.

HOWARD (*impatiently*):   Now, Willy, you never averaged—

WILLY (*banging his hand on the desk*):   I averaged a hundred and seventy dollars a week in the year of 1928! And your father came to me—or rather, I was in the office here—it was right over this desk—and he put his hand on my shoulder—

HOWARD (*getting up*):   You'll have to excuse me, Willy, I gotta see some people. Pull yourself together. (*Going out.*) I'll be back in a little while.

On HOWARD'*s exit, the light on his chair grows very bright and strange.*

WILLY: Pull myself together! What the hell did I say to him? My God, I was yelling at him! How could I! (WILLY *breaks off, staring at the light, which occupies the chair, animating it. He approaches this chair, standing across the desk from it.*) Frank, Frank, don't you remember what you told me that time? How you put your hand on my shoulder, and Frank . . . (*He leans on the desk and as he speaks the dead man's name he accidentally switches on the recorder, and instantly—*)

HOWARD'S SON: " . . . of New York is Albany. The capital of Ohio is Cincinnati, the capital of Rhode Island is . . ." (*The recitation continues.*)

WILLY (*leaping away with fright, shouting*):   Ha! Howard! Howard! Howard!

HOWARD (*rushing in*):   What happened?

WILLY (*pointing at the machine, which continues nasally, childishly, with the capital cities*): Shut it off! Shut it off!

HOWARD (*pulling the plug out*):   Look, Willy . . .

WILLY (*pressing his hands to his eyes*):   I gotta get myself some coffee. I'll get some coffee . . .

WILLY *starts to walk out.* HOWARD *stops him.*

HOWARD (*rolling up the cord*):   Willy, look . . .

WILLY: I'll go to Boston.

HOWARD: Willy, you can't go to Boston for us.

WILLY: Why can't I go?

HOWARD: I don't want you to represent us. I've been meaning to tell you for a long time now.

WILLY: Howard, are you firing me?

HOWARD: I think you need a good long rest, Willy.

WILLY: Howard—

HOWARD: And when you feel better, come back, and we'll see if we can work something out.

WILLY: But I gotta earn money, Howard. I'm in no position—

HOWARD: Where are your sons? Why don't your sons give you a hand?

WILLY: They're working on a very big deal.

HOWARD: This is no time for false pride, Willy. You go to your sons and tell them that you're tired. You've got two great boys, haven't you?

WILLY: Oh, no question, no question, but in the meantime . . .

HOWARD: Then that's that, heh?

WILLY: All right, I'll go to Boston tomorrow.

HOWARD: No, no.

WILLY: I can't throw myself on my sons. I'm not a cripple!

HOWARD: Look, kid, I'm busy this morning.

WILLY (*grasping* HOWARD'S *arm*):   Howard, you've got to let me go to Boston!

HOWARD (*hard, keeping himself under control*):   I've got a line of people to see this morning. Sit down, take five minutes, and pull yourself together, and then go home, will ya? I need the office, Willy. (*He starts to go, turns, remembering the recorder, starts to push off the table holding the recorder.*) Oh, yeah. Whenever you can this week, stop by and drop off the samples. You'll feel better, Willy, and then come back and we'll talk. Pull yourself together, kid, there's people outside.

HOWARD *exits, pushing the table off left.* WILLY *stares into space, exhausted. Now the music is heard—*BEN'S *music—first distantly, then closer, closer. As* WILLY *speaks,* BEN *enters from the right. He carries valise and umbrella.*

WILLY: Oh, Ben, how did you do it? What is the answer? Did you wind up the Alaska deal already?

BEN: Doesn't take much time if you know what you're doing. Just a short business trip. Boarding ship in an hour. Wanted to say good-by.

WILLY: Ben, I've got to talk to you.

BEN (*glancing at his watch*):   Haven't the time, William.

WILLY (*crossing the apron to* BEN):   Ben, nothing's working out. I don't know what to do.

BEN: Now, look here, William. I've bought timberland in Alaska and I need a man to look after things for me.

WILLY: God, timberland! Me and my boys in those grand outdoors!

BEN: You've a new continent at your doorstep, William. Get out of these cities, they're full of talk and time payments and courts of law. Screw on your fists and you can fight for a fortune up there.

WILLY: Yes, yes! Linda! Linda!

LINDA *enters as of old, with the wash.*

LINDA: Oh, you're back?

BEN: I haven't much time.

WILLY: No, wait! Linda, he's got a proposition for me in Alaska.

LINDA: But you've got—(*To* BEN.) He's got a beautiful job here.

WILLY: But in Alaska, kid, I could—

LINDA: You're doing well enough, Willy!

BEN (*to* LINDA):   Enough for what, my dear?

LINDA (*frightened of* BEN *and angry at him*):   Don't say those things to him! Enough to be happy right here, right now. (*To* WILLY, *while* BEN *laughs.*) Why must everybody conquer the world? You're well liked, and the boys love you, and someday—(*to* BEN)—why, old man Wagner told him just the other day that if he keeps it up he'll be a member of the firm, didn't he, Willy?

WILLY: Sure, sure. I am building something with this firm, Ben, and if a man is building something he must be on the right track, mustn't he?

BEN: What are you building? Lay your hand on it. Where is it?

WILLY (*hesitantly*):   That's true, Linda, there's nothing.

LINDA: Why? (*To* BEN.) There's a man eighty-four years old—

WILLY: That's right, Ben, that's right. When I look at that man I say, what is there to worry about?

BEN: Bah!

WILLY: It's true, Ben. All he has to do is go into any city, pick up the phone, and he's making his living and you know why?

BEN (*picking up his valise*):   I've got to go.

WILLY (*holding* BEN *back*):   Look at this boy!

BIFF, *in his high school sweater, enters carrying suitcase.* HAPPY *carries* BIFF's *shoulder guards, gold helmet, and football pants.*

WILLY: Without a penny to his name, three great universities are begging for him, and from there the sky's the limit, because it's not what you do, Ben. It's who you know and the smile on your face! It's contacts, Ben, contacts! The whole wealth of Alaska passes over the lunch table at the Commodore Hotel, and that's the wonder, the wonder of this country, that a man can end with diamonds here on the basis of being liked! (*He turns to* BIFF.) And that's why when you get out on that field today it's important. Because thousands of people will be rooting for you and loving you. (*To* BEN, *who has again begun to leave.*) And Ben! when he walks into a business office his name will sound out like a bell and all the doors will open to him! I've seen it, Ben, I've seen it a thousand times! You can't feel it with your hand like timber, but it's there!

BEN: Good-by, William.

WILLY: Ben, am I right? Don't you think I'm right? I value your advice.

BEN: There's a new continent at your doorstep, William. You could walk out rich. Rich. (*He is gone.*)

WILLY: We'll do it here, Ben! You hear me? We're gonna do it here!

Young BERNARD *rushes in. The gay music of the boys is heard.*

BERNARD: Oh, gee, I was afraid you left already!

WILLY: Why? What time is it?

BERNARD: It's half-past one!

WILLY: Well, come on, everybody! Ebbets Field next stop! Where's the pennants? (*He rushes through the wall-line of the kitchen and out into the livingroom.*)

LINDA (*to* BIFF):   Did you pack fresh underwear?

BIFF (*who has been limbering up*):   I want to go!

BERNARD: Biff, I'm carrying your helmet, ain't I?

HAPPY: No, I'm carrying the helmet.

BERNARD: Oh, Biff, you promised me.

HAPPY: I'm carrying the helmet.

BERNARD: How am I going to get in the locker room?

LINDA: Let him carry the shoulder guards. (*She puts her coat and hat on in the kitchen.*)

BERNARD: Can I, Biff? 'Cause I told everybody I'm going to be in the locker room.

HAPPY: In Ebbets Field it's the clubhouse.

BERNARD: I meant the clubhouse. Biff!

HAPPY: Biff!

BIFF (*grandly, after a slight pause*):   Let him carry the shoulder guards.

HAPPY (*as he gives* BERNARD *the shoulder guards*):   Stay close to us now.

WILLY *rushes in with the pennants.*

WILLY (*handing them out*):   Everybody wave when Biff comes out on the field. (HAPPY *and* BERNARD *run off.*) You set now, boy?

The music has died away.

BIFF: Ready to go, Pop. Every muscle is ready.

WILLY (*at the edge of the apron*):   You realize what this means?

BIFF: That's right, Pop.

WILLY (*feeling* BIFF'S *muscles*):   You're comin' home this afternoon captain of the All-Scholastic Championship Team of the City of New York.

BIFF: I got it, Pop. And remember, pal, when I take off my helmet, that touchdown is for you.

WILLY: Let's go! (*He is starting out, with his arm around* BIFF, *when* CHARLEY *enters, as of old, in knickers.*) I got no room for you, Charley.

CHARLEY: Room? For what?

WILLY: In the car.

CHARLEY: You goin' for a ride? I wanted to shoot some casino.

WILLY (*furiously*):   Casino! (*Incredulously*): Don't you realize what today is?

LINDA: Oh, he knows, Willy. He's just kidding you.

WILLY: That's nothing to kid about!

CHARLEY: No, Linda, what's goin' on?

LINDA: He's playing in Ebbets Field.

CHARLEY: Baseball in this weather?

WILLY: Don't talk to him. Come on, come on! (*He is pushing them out.*)

CHARLEY: Wait a minute, didn't you hear the news?

WILLY: What?

CHARLEY: Don't you listen to the radio? Ebbets Field just blew up.

WILLY: You go to hell! (CHARLEY *laughs. Pushing them out.*) Come on, come on! We're late.

CHARLEY (*as they go*):   Knock a homer, Biff, knock a homer!

WILLY (*the last to leave, turning to* CHARLEY):   I don't think that was funny, Charley. This is the greatest day of his life.

CHARLEY: Willy, when are you going to grow up?

WILLY: Yeah, heh? When this game is over, Charley, you'll be laughing out of the other side of your face. They'll be calling him another Red Grange. Twenty-five thousand a year.

CHARLEY (*kidding*):   Is that so?

WILLY: Yeah, that's so.

CHARLEY: Well, then, I'm sorry, Willy. But tell me something.

WILLY: What?

CHARLEY: Who is Red Grange?

WILLY: Put up your hands. Goddam you, put up your hands!

CHARLEY, *chuckling, shakes his head and walks away, around the left corner of the stage.* WILLY *follows him. The music rises to a mocking frenzy.*

WILLY: Who the hell do you think you are, better than everybody else? You don't know everything, you big, ignorant, stupid . . . Put up your hands!

Light rises, on the right side of the forestage, on a small table in the reception room of CHARLEY's *office. Traffic sounds are heard.* BERNARD, *now mature, sits whistling to himself. A pair of tennis rackets and an overnight bag are on the floor beside him.*

WILLY (*offstage*):   What are you walking away for? Don't walk away! If you're going to say something say it to my face! I know you laugh at me behind my back. You'll laugh out of the other side of your goddam face after this game. Touchdown! Touchdown! Eighty thousand people! Touchdown! Right between the goal posts.

BERNARD *is a quiet, earnest, but self-assured young man.* WILLY's *voice is coming from right upstage now.* BERNARD *lowers his feet off the table and listens.* JENNY, *his father's secretary, enters.*

JENNY (*distressed*):   Say, Bernard, will you go out in the hall?

BERNARD: What is that noise? Who is it?

JENNY: Mr. Loman. He just got off the elevator.

BERNARD (*getting up*):   Who's he arguing with?

JENNY: Nobody. There's nobody with him. I can't deal with him any more, and your father gets all upset everytime he comes. I've got a lot of typing to do, and your father's waiting to sign it. Will you see him?

WILLY (*entering*):   Touchdown! Touch—(*He sees* JENNY.) Jenny, Jenny, good to see you. How're ya? Workin'? Or still honest?

JENNY: Fine. How've you been feeling?

WILLY: Not much any more, Jenny. Ha, ha! (*He is surprised to see the rackets.*)

BERNARD: Hello, Uncle Willy.

WILLY (*almost shocked*):   Bernard! Well, look who's here! (*He comes quickly, guiltily, to* BERNARD *and warmly shakes his hand.*)

BERNARD: How are you? Good to see you.

WILLY: What are you doing here?

BERNARD: Oh, just stopped by to see Pop. Get off my feet till my train leaves. I'm going to Washington in a few minutes.

WILLY: Is he in?

BERNARD: Yes, he's in his office with the accountant. Sit down.

WILLY (*sitting down*):   What're you going to do in Washington?

BERNARD: Oh, just a case I've got there, Willy.

WILLY: That so? (*indicating the rackets.*) You going to play tennis there?

BERNARD: I'm staying with a friend who's got a court.

WILLY: Don't say. His own tennis court. Must be fine people, I bet.

BERNARD: They are, very nice. Dad tells me Biff's in town.

WILLY (*with a big smile*):   Yeah, Biff's in. Working on a very big deal, Bernard.

BERNARD: What's Biff doing?

WILLY: Well, he's been doing very big things in the West. But he decided to establish himself here. Very big. We're having dinner. Did I hear your wife had a boy?

BERNARD: That's right. Our second.

WILLY: Two boys! What do you know!

BERNARD: What kind of a deal has Biff got?

WILLY: Well, Bill Oliver—very big sporting-goods man—he wants Biff very badly. Called him in from the West. Long distance, carte blanche, special deliveries. Your friends have their own private tennis court?

BERNARD: You still with the old firm, Willy?

WILLY (*after a pause*):   I'm—I'm overjoyed to see how you made the grade, Bernard, overjoyed. It's an encouraging thing to see a young man really—really—Looks very good for Biff—very—(*He breaks off, then.*) Bernard—(*He is so full of emotion, he breaks off again.*)

BERNARD: What is it, Willy?

WILLY (*small and alone*):   What—what's the secret?

BERNARD: What secret?

WILLY: How—how did you? Why didn't he ever catch on?

BERNARD: I wouldn't know that, Willy.

WILLY (*confidentially, desperately*):   You were his friend, his boyhood friend. There's something I don't understand about it. His life ended after that Ebbets Field game. From the age of seventeen nothing good ever happened to him.

BERNARD: He never trained himself for anything.

WILLY: But he did, he did. After high school he took so many correspondence courses. Radio mechanics; television; God knows what, and never made the slightest mark.

BERNARD (*taking off his glasses*): Willy, do you want to talk candidly?

WILLY (*rising, faces* BERNARD): I regard you as a very brilliant man, Bernard. I value your advice.

BERNARD: Oh, the hell with the advice, Willy. I couldn't advise you. There's just one thing I've always wanted to ask you. When he was supposed to graduate, and the math teacher flunked him—

WILLY: Oh, that son-of-a-bitch ruined his life.

BERNARD: Yeah, but, Willy, all he had to do was go to summer school and make up that subject.

WILLY: That's right, that's right.

BERNARD: Did you tell him not to go to summer school?

WILLY: Me? I begged him to go. I ordered him to go!

BERNARD: Then why wouldn't he go?

WILLY: Why? Why! Bernard, that question has been trailing me like a ghost for the last fifteen years. He flunked the subject, and laid down and died like a hammer hit him!

BERNARD: Take it easy, kid.

WILLY: Let me talk to you—I got nobody to talk to. Bernard, Bernard, was it my fault? Y'see? It keeps going around in my mind, maybe I did something to him. I got nothing to give him.

BERNARD: Don't take it so hard.

WILLY: Why did he lay down? What is the story there? You were his friend!

BERNARD: Willy, I remember, it was June, and our grades came out. And he'd flunked math.

WILLY: That son-of-a-bitch!

BERNARD: No, it wasn't right then. Biff just got very angry, I remember, and he was ready to enroll in summer school.

WILLY (*surprised*): He was?

BERNARD: He wasn't beaten by it at all. But then, Willy, he disappeared from the block for almost a month. And I got the idea that he'd gone up to New England to see you. Did he have a talk with you then?

WILLY *stares in silence.*

BERNARD: Willy?

WILLY (*with a strong edge of resentment in his voice*): Yeah, he came to Boston. What about it?

BERNARD: Well, just that when he came back—I'll never forget this, it always mystifies me. Because I'd thought so well of Biff, even though he'd always taken advantage of me. I loved him, Willy, y'know? And he came back after that month and took his sneakers—remember those sneakers with "University of Virginia" printed on them? He was so proud of those, wore them every day. And he took them down in the cellar, and burned them up in the furnace. We had a fist fight. It lasted at least half an hour. Just the two of us, punching each other down the cellar, and crying right through it. I've often thought of how strange it was that I knew he'd given up his life. What happened in Boston, Willy?

WILLY *looks at him as at an intruder.*

BERNARD: I just bring it up because you asked me.

WILLY (*angrily*):   Nothing. What do you mean, "What happened?" What's that got to do with anything?

BERNARD: Well, don't get sore.

WILLY: What are you trying to do, blame it on me? If a boy lays down is that my fault?

BERNARD: Now, Willy, don't get—

WILLY: Well, don't—don't talk to me that way! What does that mean, "What happened?"

CHARLEY *enters. He is in his vest, and he carries a bottle of bourbon.*

CHARLEY: Hey, you're going to miss that train. (*He waves the bottle.*)

BERNARD: Yeah, I'm going. (*He takes the bottle.*) Thanks, Pop. (*He picks up his rackets and bag.*) Good-by, Willy, and don't worry about it. You know, "If at first you don't succeed . . ."

WILLY: Yes, I believe in that.

BERNARD: But sometimes, Willy, it's better for a man just to walk away.

WILLY: Walk away?

BERNARD: That's right.

WILLY: But if you can't walk away?

BERNARD (*after a slight pause*):   I guess that's when it's tough. (*Extending his hand.*) Good-by, Willy.

WILLY (*shaking* BERNARD'*s hand*):   Good-by, boy.

CHARLEY (*an arm on* BERNARD'*s shoulder*):   How do you like this kid? Gonna argue a case in front of the Supreme Court.

BERNARD (*protesting*):   Pop!

WILLY (*genuinely shocked, pained, and happy*):   No! The Supreme Court!

BERNARD: I gotta run. 'By, Dad!

CHARLEY: Knock 'em dead, Bernard!

BERNARD *goes off.*

WILLY (*as* CHARLEY *takes out his wallet*):   The Supreme Court! And he didn't even mention it!

CHARLEY (*counting out money on the desk*):   He don't have to—he's gonna do it.

WILLY: And you never told him what to do, did you? You never took any interest in him.

CHARLEY: My salvation is that I never took any interest in anything. There's some money—fifty dollars. I got an accountant inside.

WILLY: Charley, look . . . (*With difficulty.*) I got my insurance to pay. If you can manage it—I need a hundred and ten dollars.

CHARLEY *doesn't reply for a moment; merely stops moving.*

WILLY: I'd draw it from my bank but Linda would know, and I . . .

CHARLEY: Sit down, Willy.

WILLY (*moving toward the chair*):   I'm keeping an account of everything, remember. I'll pay every penny back. (*He sits.*)

CHARLEY: Now listen to me, Willy.

WILLY: I want you to know I appreciate . . .

CHARLEY (*sitting down on the table*):   Willy, what're you doin'? What the hell is goin' on in your head?

WILLY: Why? I'm simply . . .

CHARLEY: I offered you a job. You can make fifty dollars a week. And I won't send you on the road.

WILLY: I've got a job.

CHARLEY: Without pay? What kind of a job is a job without pay? (*He rises.*) Now, look, kid, enough is enough. I'm no genius but I know when I'm being insulted.

WILLY: Insulted!

CHARLEY: Why don't you want to work for me?

WILLY: What's the matter with you? I've got a job.

CHARLEY: Then what're you walkin' in here every week for?

WILLY (*getting up*):   Well, if you don't want me to walk in here—

CHARLEY: I am offering you a job.

WILLY: I don't want your goddam job!

CHARLEY: When the hell are you going to grow up?

WILLY (*furiously*):   You big ignoramus, if you say that to me again I'll rap you one! I don't care how big you are! (*He's ready to fight.*)

Pause.

CHARLEY (*kindly, going to him*):   How much do you need, Willy?

WILLY: Charley, I'm strapped. I'm strapped. I don't know what to do. I was just fired.

CHARLEY: Howard fired you?

WILLY: That snotnose. Imagine that? I named him. I named him Howard.

CHARLEY: Willy, when're you gonna realize that them things don't mean anything? You named him Howard, but you can't sell that. The only thing you got in this world is what you can sell. And the funny thing is that you're a salesman, and you don't know that.

WILLY: I've always tried to think otherwise, I guess. I always felt that if a man was impressive, and well liked, that nothing—

CHARLEY: Why must everybody like you? Who liked J. P. Morgan? Was he impressive? In a Turkish bath he'd look like a butcher. But with his pockets on he was very well liked. Now listen, Willy, I know you don't like me, and nobody can say I'm in love with you, but I'll give you a job because—just for the hell of it, put it that way. Now what do you say?

WILLY: I—I just can't work for you, Charley.

CHARLEY: What're you, jealous of me?

WILLY: I can't work for you, that's all, don't ask me why.

CHARLEY (*angered, takes out more bills*):   You been jealous of me all your life, you damned fool! Here, pay your insurance. (*He puts the money in* WILLY'S *hand.*)

WILLY: I'm keeping strict accounts.

CHARLEY: I've got some work to do. Take care of yourself. And pay your insurance.

WILLY (*moving to the right*):   Funny, y'know? After all the highways, and the trains, and the appointments, and the years, you end up worth more dead than alive.

CHARLEY: Willy, nobody's worth nothin' dead. (*After a slight pause.*) Did you hear what I said?

WILLY *stands still, dreaming.*

CHARLEY: Willy!

WILLY: Apologize to Bernard for me when you see him. I didn't mean to argue with him. He's a fine boy. They're all fine boys, and they'll end up big—all of them. Someday they'll all play tennis together. Wish me luck, Charley. He saw Bill Oliver today.

CHARLEY: Good luck.

WILLY (*on the verge of tears*): Charley, you're the only friend I got. Isn't that a remarkable thing? (*He goes out.*)

CHARLEY: Jesus!

CHARLEY *stares after him a moment and follows. All light blacks out. Suddenly raucous music is heard, and a red glow rises behind the screen at right.* STANLEY, *a young waiter, appears, carrying a table, followed by* HAPPY, *who is carrying two chairs.*

STANLEY (*putting the table down*): That's all right, Mr. Loman, I can handle it myself. (*He turns and takes the chairs from* HAPPY *and places them at the table.*)

HAPPY (*glancing around*): Oh, this is better.

STANLEY: Sure, in the front there you're in the middle of all kinds a noise. Whenever you got a party, Mr. Loman, you just tell me and I'll put you back here. Y'know, there's a lotta people they don't like it private, because when they go out they like to see a lotta action around them because they're sick and tired to stay in the house by theirself. But I know you, you ain't from Hackensack. You know what I mean?

HAPPY (*sitting down*): So how's it coming, Stanley?

STANLEY: Ah, it's a dog's life. I only wish during the war they'd a took me in the Army. I coulda been dead by now.

HAPPY: My brother's back, Stanley.

STANLEY: Oh, he come back, heh? From the Far West.

HAPPY: Yeah, big cattle man, my brother, so treat him right. And my father's coming too.

STANLEY: Oh, your father too!

HAPPY: You got a couple of nice lobsters?

STANLEY: Hundred per cent, big.

HAPPY: I want them with the claws.

STANLEY: Don't worry, I don't give you no mice. (HAPPY *laughs.*) How about some wine? It'll put a head on the meal.

HAPPY: No. You remember, Stanley, that recipe I brought you from overseas? With the champagne in it?

STANLEY: Oh, yeah, sure. I still got it tacked up yet in the kitchen. But that'll have to cost a buck apiece anyways.

HAPPY: That's all right.

STANLEY: What'd you, hit a number or somethin'?

HAPPY: No, it's a little celebration. My brother is—I think he pulled off a big deal today. I think we're going into business together.

STANLEY: Great! That's the best for you. Because a family business, you know what I mean?—that's the best.

HAPPY: That's what I think.

STANLEY: 'Cause what's the difference? Somebody steals? It's in the family. Know what I mean? (*Sotto voce.*) Like this bartender here. The boss is goin' crazy what kinda leak he's got in the cash register. You put it in but it don't come out.

HAPPY (*raising his head*):   Sh!

STANLEY: What?

HAPPY: You notice I wasn't lookin' right or left, was I!

STANLEY: No.

HAPPY: And my eyes are closed.

STANLEY: So what's the—?

HAPPY: Strudel's comin'.

STANLEY (*catching on, looks around*):   Ah, no, there's no—

He breaks off as a furred, lavishly dressed GIRL *enters and sits at the next table. Both follow her with their eyes.*

STANLEY: Geez, how'd ya know?

HAPPY: I got radar or something. (*Staring directly at her profile.*) Oooooooo . . . Stanley.

STANLEY: I think that's for you, Mr. Loman.

HAPPY: Look at that mouth. Oh, God. And the binoculars.

STANLEY: Geez, you got a life, Mr. Loman.

HAPPY: Wait on her.

STANLEY (*going to* THE GIRL'*s table*):   Would you like a menu, ma'am?

GIRL: I'm expecting someone, but I'd like a—

HAPPY: Why don't you bring her—excuse me, miss, do you mind? I sell champagne, and I'd like you to try my brand. Bring her a champagne, Stanley.

GIRL: That's awfully nice of you.

HAPPY: Don't mention it. It's all company money. (*He laughs.*)

GIRL: That's a charming product to be selling, isn't it?

HAPPY: Oh, gets to be like everything else. Selling is selling, y'know.

GIRL: I suppose.

HAPPY: You don't happen to sell, do you?

GIRL: No, I don't sell.

HAPPY: Would you object to a compliment from a stranger? You ought to be on a magazine cover.

GIRL (*looking at him a little archly*):   I have been.

STANLEY *comes in with a glass of champagne.*

HAPPY: What'd I say before, Stanley? You see? She's a cover girl.

STANLEY: Oh, I could see, I could see.

HAPPY (*to* THE GIRL):   What magazine?

GIRL: Oh, a lot of them. (*She takes the drink.*) Thank you.

HAPPY: You know what they say in France, don't you? "Champagne is the drink of the complexion"—Hya, Biff!

BIFF *has entered and sits with* HAPPY.

BIFF: Hello, kid. Sorry I'm late.

HAPPY: I just got here. Uh, Miss—?

GIRL: Forsythe.

HAPPY: Miss Forsythe, this is my brother.

BIFF: Is Dad here?

HAPPY: His name is Biff. You might've heard of him. Great football player.

GIRL: Really? What team?

HAPPY: Are you familiar with football?

GIRL: No, I'm afraid I'm not.

HAPPY: Biff is quarterback with the New York Giants.

GIRL: Well, that is nice, isn't it? (*She drinks.*)

HAPPY: Good health.

GIRL: I'm happy to meet you.

HAPPY: That's my name. Hap. It's really Harold, but at West Point they called me Happy.

GIRL (*now really impressed*):   Oh, I see. How do you do? (*She turns her profile.*)

BIFF: Isn't Dad coming?

HAPPY: You want her?

BIFF: Oh, I could never make that.

HAPPY: I remember the time that idea would never come into your head. Where's the old confidence, Biff?

BIFF: I just saw Oliver—

HAPPY: Wait a minute. I've got to see that old confidence again. Do you want her? She's on call.

BIFF: Oh, no. (*He turns to look at* THE GIRL.)

HAPPY: I'm telling you. Watch this. (*Turning to* THE GIRL.) Honey? (*She turns to him.*) Are you busy?

GIRL: Well, I am . . . but I could make a phone call.

HAPPY: Do that, will you, honey? And see if you can get a friend. We'll be here for a while. Biff is one of the greatest football players in the country.

GIRL (*standing up*):   Well, I'm certainly happy to meet you.

HAPPY: Come back soon.

GIRL: I'll try.

HAPPY: Don't try, honey, try hard.

THE GIRL *exits.* STANLEY *follows, shaking his head in bewildered admiration.*

HAPPY: Isn't that a shame now? A beautiful girl like that? That's why I can't get married. There's not a good woman in a thousand. New York is loaded with them, kid!

BIFF: Hap, look—

HAPPY: I told you she was on call!

BIFF (*strangely unnerved*):   Cut it out, will ya? I want to say something to you.

HAPPY: Did you see Oliver?

BIFF: I saw him all right. Now look, I want to tell Dad a couple of things and I want you to help me.

HAPPY: What? Is he going to back you?

BIFF: Are you crazy? You're out of your goddam head, you know that?

HAPPY: Why? What happened?

BIFF (*breathlessly*):   I did a terrible thing today, Hap. It's been the strangest day I ever went through. I'm all numb, I swear.

HAPPY: You mean he wouldn't see you?

BIFF: Well, I waited six hours for him, see? All day. Kept sending my name in. Even tried to date his secretary so she'd get me to him, but no soap.

HAPPY: Because you're not showin' the old confidence, Biff. He remembered you, didn't he?

BIFF (*stopping* HAPPY *with a gesture*):   Finally, about five o'clock, he comes out. Didn't remember who I was or anything. I felt like such an idiot, Hap.

HAPPY: Did you tell him my Florida idea?

BIFF: He walked away. I saw him for one minute. I got so mad I could've torn the walls down! How the hell did I ever get the idea I was a salesman there? I even believed myself that I'd been a salesman for him! And then he gave me one look and—I realized what a ridiculous lie my whole life has been! We've been talking in a dream for fifteen years. I was a shipping clerk.

HAPPY: What'd you do?

BIFF (*with great tension and wonder*):   Well, he left, see. And the secretary went out. I was all alone in the waiting-room. I don't know what came over me, Hap. The next thing I know I'm in his office—paneled walls, everything. I can't explain it. I—Hap, I took his fountain pen.

HAPPY: Geez, did he catch you?

BIFF: I ran out. I ran down all eleven flights. I ran and ran and ran.

HAPPY: That was an awful dumb—what'd you do that for?

BIFF (*agonized*):   I don't know, I just—wanted to take something, I don't know. You gotta help me, Hap. I'm gonna tell Pop.

HAPPY: You crazy? What for?

BIFF: Hap, he's got to understand that I'm not the man somebody lends that kind of money to. He thinks I've been spiting him all these years and it's eating him up.

HAPPY: That's just it. You tell him something nice.

BIFF: I can't.

HAPPY: Say you got a lunch date with Oliver tomorrow.

BIFF: So what do I do tomorrow?

HAPPY: You leave the house tomorrow and come back at night and say Oliver is thinking it over. And he thinks it over for a couple of weeks, and gradually it fades away and nobody's the worse.

BIFF: But it'll go on forever!

HAPPY: Dad is never so happy as when he's looking forward to something!

WILLY *enters.*

HAPPY: Hello, scout!

WILLY: Gee, I haven't been here in years!

STANLEY *has followed* WILLY *in and sets a chair for him.* STANLEY *starts off but* HAPPY *stops him.*

HAPPY: Stanley!

STANLEY *stands by, waiting for an order.*

BIFF (*going to* WILLY *with guilt, as to an invalid*):   Sit down, Pop. You want a drink?

WILLY: Sure, I don't mind.

BIFF: Let's get a load on.

WILLY: You look worried.

BIFF: N–no. (*To* STANLEY.) Scotch all around. Make it doubles.

STANLEY: Doubles, right. (*He goes.*)

WILLY: You had a couple already, didn't you?

BIFF: Just a couple, yeah.

WILLY: Well, what happened, boy? (*Nodding affirmatively, with a smile.*) Everything go all right?

BIFF (*takes a breath, then reaches out and grasps* WILLY*'s hand*): Pal . . . (*He is smiling bravely, and* WILLY *is smiling too.*) I had an experience today.

HAPPY: Terrific, Pop.

WILLY: That so? What happened?

BIFF (*high, slightly alcoholic, above the earth*): I'm going to tell you everything from first to last. It's been a strange day. (*Silence. He looks around, composes himself as best he can, but his breath keeps breaking the rhythm of his voice.*) I had to wait quite a while for him, and—

WILLY: Oliver?

BIFF: Yeah, Oliver. All day, as a matter of cold fact. And a lot of—instances—facts, Pop, facts about my life came back to me. Who was it, Pop? Who ever said I was a salesman with Oliver?

WILLY: Well, you were.

BIFF: No, Dad, I was a shipping clerk.

WILLY: But you were practically—

BIFF (*with determination*): Dad, I don't know who said it first, but I was never a salesman for Bill Oliver.

WILLY: What're you talking about?

BIFF: Let's hold on to the facts tonight, Pop. We're not going to get anywhere bullin' around. I was a shipping clerk.

WILLY (*angrily*): All right, now listen to me—

BIFF: Why don't you let me finish?

WILLY: I'm not interested in stories about the past or any crap of that kind because the woods are burning, boys, you understand? There's a big blaze going on all around. I was fired today.

BIFF (*shocked*): How could you be?

WILLY: I was fired, and I'm looking for a little good news to tell your mother, because the woman has waited and the woman has suffered. The gist of it is that I haven't got a story left in my head, Biff. So don't give me a lecture about facts and aspects. I am not interested. Now what've you got to say to me?

STANLEY *enters with three drinks. They wait until he leaves.*

WILLY: Did you see Oliver?

BIFF: Jesus, Dad!

WILLY: You mean you didn't go up there?

HAPPY: Sure he went up there.

BIFF: I did. I—saw him. How could they fire you?

WILLY (*on the edge of his chair*): What kind of a welcome did he give you?

BIFF: He won't even let you work on commission?

WILLY: I'm out! (*Driving.*) So tell me, he gave you a warm welcome?

HAPPY: Sure, Pop, sure!

BIFF (*driven*):   Well, it was kind of—

WILLY: I was wondering if he'd remember you. (*To* HAPPY.) Imagine, man doesn't see him for ten, twelve years and gives him that kind of a welcome!

HAPPY: Damn right!

BIFF (*trying to return to the offensive*):   Pop, look—

WILLY: You know why he remembered you, don't you? Because you impressed him in those days.

BIFF: Let's talk quietly and get this down to the facts, huh?

WILLY (*as though* BIFF *had been interrupting*):   Well, what happened? It's great news, Biff. Did he take you into his office or'd you talk in the waiting room?

BIFF: Well, he came in, see, and—

WILLY: (*with a big smile*):   What'd he say? Betcha he threw his arm around you.

BIFF: Well, he kinda—

WILLY: He's a fine man. (*To* HAPPY.) Very hard man to see, y'know.

HAPPY (*agreeing*):   Oh, I know.

WILLY (*to* BIFF):   Is that where you had the drinks?

BIFF: Yeah, he gave me a couple of—no, no!

HAPPY (*cutting in*):   He told him my Florida idea.

WILLY: Don't interrupt. (*To* BIFF.) How'd he react to the Florida idea?

BIFF: Dad, will you give me a minute to explain?

WILLY: I've been waiting for you to explain since I sat down here! What happened? He took you into his office and what?

BIFF: Well—I talked. And—and he listened, see.

WILLY: Famous for the way he listens, y'know. What was his answer?

BIFF: His answer was—(*He breaks off, suddenly angry.*) Dad, you're not letting me tell you what I want to tell you!

WILLY (*accusing, angered*):   You didn't see him, did you?

BIFF: I did see him!

WILLY: What'd you insult him or something? You insulted him, didn't you?

BIFF: Listen, will you let me out of it, will you just let me out of it!

HAPPY: What the hell!

WILLY: Tell me what happened!

BIFF (*to* HAPPY):   I can't talk to him!

A single trumpet note jars the ear. The light of green leaves stains the house, which holds the air of night and a dream. YOUNG BERNARD *enters and knocks on the door of the house.*

YOUNG BERNARD (*frantically*):   Mrs. Loman, Mrs. Loman!

HAPPY: Tell him what happened!

BIFF (*to* HAPPY):   Shut up and leave me alone!

WILLY: No, no! You had to go and flunk math!

BIFF: What math? What're you talking about?

YOUNG BERNARD: Mrs. Loman, Mrs. Loman!

LINDA *appears in the house, as of old.*

WILLY (*wildly*):   Math, math, math!

BIFF: Take it easy, Pop!

YOUNG BERNARD: Mrs. Loman!

WILLY (*furiously*):   If you hadn't flunked you'd've been set by now!

BIFF: Now, look, I'm gonna tell you what happened, and you're going to listen to me.

YOUNG BERNARD: Mrs. Loman!

BIFF: I waited six hours—

HAPPY: What the hell are you saying?

BIFF: I kept sending in my name but he wouldn't see me. So finally he . . . (*He continues unheard as light fades low on the restaurant.*)

YOUNG BERNARD: Biff flunked math!

LINDA: No!

YOUNG BERNARD: Birnbaum flunked him! They won't graduate him!

LINDA: But they have to. He's gotta go to the university. Where is he? Biff! Biff!

YOUNG BERNARD: No, he left. He went to Grand Central.

LINDA: Grand—You mean he went to Boston!

YOUNG BERNARD: Is Uncle Willy in Boston?

LINDA: Oh, maybe Willy can talk to the teacher. Oh, the poor, poor boy!

Light on house area snaps out.

BIFF (*at the table, now audible, holding up a gold fountain pen*):   . . . so I'm washed up with Oliver, you understand? Are you listening to me?

WILLY (*at a loss*):   Yeah, sure. If you hadn't flunked—

BIFF: Flunked what? What're you talking about?

WILLY: Don't blame everything on me! I didn't flunk math—you did! What pen?

HAPPY: That was awful dumb, Biff, a pen like that is worth—

WILLY (*seeing the pen for the first time*):   You took Oliver's pen?

BIFF (*weakening*):   Dad, I just explained it to you.

WILLY: You stole Bill Oliver's fountain pen!

BIFF: I didn't exactly steal it! That's just what I've been explaining to you!

HAPPY: He had it in his hand and just then Oliver walked in, so he got nervous and stuck it in his pocket!

WILLY: My God, Biff!

BIFF: I never intended to do it, Dad!

OPERATOR'S VOICE: Standish Arms, good evening!

WILLY (*shouting*):   I'm not in my room!

BIFF (*frightened*):   Dad, what's the matter? (*He and* HAPPY *stand up.*)

OPERATOR: Ringing Mr. Loman for you!

WILLY: I'm not there, stop it!

BIFF (*horrified, gets down on one knee before* WILLY):   Dad, I'll make good, I'll make good. (WILLY *tries to get to his feet.* BIFF *holds him down.*) Sit down now.

WILLY: No, you're no good, you're no good for anything.

BIFF: I am, Dad, I'll find something else, you understand? Now don't worry about anything. (*He holds up* WILLY'S *face.*) Talk to me, Dad.

OPERATOR: Mr. Loman does not answer. Shall I page him?

WILLY (*attempting to stand, as though to rush and silence the* OPERATOR):   No, no, no!

HAPPY: He'll strike something, Pop.

WILLY: No, no . . .

BIFF (*desperately, standing over* WILLY):   Pop, listen! Listen to me! I'm telling you something good. Oliver talked to his partner about the Florida idea. You listening? He—he talked to his partner, and he came to me . . . I'm going to be all right, you hear? Dad, listen to me, he said it was just a question of the amount!

WILLY: Then you . . . got it?

HAPPY: He's gonna be terrific, Pop!

WILLY (*trying to stand*):   Then you got it, haven't you? You got it! You got it!

BIFF (*agonized, holds* WILLY *down*):   No, no. Look, Pop. I'm supposed to have lunch with them tomorrow. I'm just telling you this so you'll know that I can still make an impression, Pop. And I'll make good somewhere, but I can't go tomorrow, see?

WILLY: Why not? You simply—

BIFF: But the pen, Pop!

WILLY: You give it to him and tell him it was an oversight!

HAPPY: Sure, have lunch tomorrow!

BIFF: I can't say that—

WILLY: You were doing a crossword puzzle and accidentally used his pen!

BIFF: Listen, kid, I took those balls years ago, now I walk in with his fountain pen? That clinches it, don't you see? I can't face him like that! I'll try elsewhere.

PAGE'S VOICE: Paging Mr. Loman!

WILLY: Don't you want to be anything?

BIFF: Pop, how can I go back?

WILLY: You don't want to be anything, is that what's behind it?

BIFF (*now angry at* WILLY *for not crediting his sympathy*):   Don't take it that way! You think it was easy walking into that office after what I'd done to him? A team of horses couldn't have dragged me back to Bill Oliver!

WILLY: Then why'd you go?

BIFF: Why did I go? Why did I go? Look at you! Look at what's become of you!

Off left, THE WOMAN *laughs.*

WILLY: Biff, you're going to go to that lunch tomorrow, or—

BIFF: I can't go. I've got no appointment!

HAPPY: Biff, for . . . !

WILLY: Are you spiting me?

BIFF: Don't take it that way! Goddammit!

WILLY (*strikes* BIFF *and falters away from the table*):   You rotten little louse! Are you spiting me?

THE WOMAN: Someone's at the door, Willy!

BIFF: I'm no good, can't you see what I am?

HAPPY (*separating them*):   Hey, you're in a restaurant! Now cut it out, both of you! (THE GIRLS *enter.*) Hello, girls, sit down.

THE WOMAN *laughs, off left.*

MISS FORSYTHE: I guess we might as well. This is Letta.

THE WOMAN: Willy, are you going to wake up?

BIFF (*ignoring* WILLY):   How're ya, miss, sit down. What do you drink?

MISS FORSYTHE: Letta might not be able to stay long.

LETTA: I gotta get up very early tomorrow. I got jury duty. I'm so excited! Were you fellows ever on a jury?

BIFF: No, but I been in front of them! (THE GIRLS *laugh*.) This is my father.

LETTA: Isn't he cute? Sit down with us, Pop.

HAPPY: Sit him down, Biff!

BIFF (*going to him*):   Come on, slugger, drink us under the table. To hell with it! Come on, sit down, pal.

On BIFF's *last insistence,* WILLY *is about to sit.*

THE WOMAN (*now urgently*):   Willy, are you going to answer the door!

THE WOMAN's *call pulls* WILLY *back. He starts right, befuddled.*

BIFF: Hey, where are you going?

WILLY: Open the door.

BIFF: The door?

WILLY: The washroom . . . the door . . . where's the door?

BIFF (*leading* WILLY *to the left*):   Just go straight down.

WILLY *moves left.*

THE WOMAN: Willy, Willy, are you going to get up, get up, get up, get up?

WILLY *exits left.*

LETTA: I think it's sweet you bring your daddy along.

MISS FORSYTHE: Oh, he isn't really your father!

BIFF (*at left, turning to her resentfully*):   Miss Forsythe, you've just seen a prince walk by. A fine, troubled prince. A hard-working, unappreciated prince. A pal, you understand? A good companion. Always for his boys.

LETTA: That's so sweet.

HAPPY: Well, girls, what's the program? We're wasting time. Come on, Biff. Gather round. Where would you like to go?

BIFF: Why don't you do something for him?

HAPPY: Me!

BIFF: Don't you give a damn for him, Hap?

HAPPY: What're you talking about? I'm the one who—

BIFF: I sense it, you don't give a good goddam about him. (*He takes the rolled-up hose from his pocket and puts it on the table in front of* HAPPY.) Look what I found in the cellar, for Christ's sake. How can you bear to let it go on?

HAPPY: Me? Who goes away? Who runs off and—

BIFF: Yeah, but he doesn't mean anything to you. You could help him—I can't! Don't you understand what I'm talking about? He's going to kill himself, don't you know that?

HAPPY: Don't I know it! Me!

BIFF: Hap, help him! Jesus . . . help him . . . Help me, help me, I can't bear to look at his face! (*Ready to weep, he hurries out, up right.*)

HAPPY (*starting after him*):   Where are you going?

MISS FORSYTHE: What's he so mad about?

HAPPY: Come on, girls, we'll catch up with him.

MISS FORSYTHE (*as* HAPPY *pushes her out*):   Say, I don't like that temper of his!

HAPPY: He's just a little overstrung, he'll be all right!

WILLY (*off left, as* THE WOMAN *laughs*):   Don't answer! Don't answer!

LETTA: Don't you want to tell your father—

HAPPY: No, that's not my father. He's just a guy. Come on, we'll catch Biff, and, honey, we're going to paint this town! Stanley, where's the check! Hey, Stanley!

They exit. STANLEY *looks toward left.*

STANLEY (*calling to* HAPPY *indignantly*):   Mr. Loman! Mr. Loman!

STANLEY *picks up a chair and follows them off. Knocking is heard off left.* THE WOMAN *enters, laughing.* WILLY *follows her. She is in a black slip; he is buttoning his shirt. Raw, sensuous music accompanies their speech.*

WILLY: Will you stop laughing? Will you stop?

THE WOMAN: Aren't you going to answer the door? He'll wake the whole hotel.

WILLY: I'm not expecting anybody.

THE WOMAN: Whyn't you have another drink, honey, and stop being so damn self-centered?

WILLY: I'm so lonely.

THE WOMAN: You know you ruined me, Willy? From now on, whenever you come to the office, I'll see that you go right through to the buyers. No waiting at my desk any more, Willy. You ruined me.

WILLY: That's nice of you to say that.

THE WOMAN: Gee, you are self-centered! Why so sad? You are the saddest self-centeredest soul I ever did see-saw. (*She laughs. He kisses her.*) Come on inside, drummer boy. It's silly to be dressing in the middle of the night. (*As knocking is heard.*) Aren't you going to answer the door?

WILLY: They're knocking on the wrong door.

THE WOMAN: But I felt the knocking. And he heard us talking in here. Maybe the hotel's on fire!

WILLY (*his terror rising*):   It's a mistake.

THE WOMAN: Then tell him to go away!

WILLY: There's nobody there.

THE WOMAN: It's getting on my nerves, Willy. There's somebody standing out there and it's getting on my nerves!

WILLY (*pushing her away from him*):   All right, stay in the bathroom here, and don't come out. I think there's a law in Massachusetts about it, so don't come out. It may be that new room clerk. He looked very mean. So don't come out. It's a mistake, there's no fire.

The knocking is heard again. He takes a few steps away from her, and she vanishes into the wing. The light follows him, and now he is facing YOUNG BIFF, *who carries a suitcase.* BIFF *steps toward him. The music is gone.*

BIFF: Why didn't you answer?

WILLY: Biff! What are you doing in Boston?

BIFF: Why didn't you answer? I've been knocking for five minutes, I called you on the phone—

WILLY: I just heard you. I was in the bathroom and had the door shut. Did anything happen home?

BIFF: Dad—I let you down.

WILLY: What do you mean?

BIFF: Dad . . .

WILLY: Biffo, what's this about? (*Putting his arm around* BIFF.) Come on, let's go downstairs and get you a malted.

BIFF: Dad, I flunked math.

WILLY: Not for the term?

BIFF: The term. I haven't got enough credits to graduate.

WILLY: You mean to say Bernard wouldn't give you the answers?

BIFF: He did, he tried, but I only got a sixty-one.

WILLY: And they wouldn't give you four points?

BIFF: Birnbaum refused absolutely. I begged him, Pop, but he won't give me those points. You gotta talk to him before they close the school. Because if he saw the kind of man you are, and you just talked to him in your way, I'm sure he'd come through for me. The class came right before practice, see, and I didn't go enough. Would you talk to him? He'd like you, Pop. You know the way you could talk.

WILLY: You're on. We'll drive right back.

BIFF: Oh, Dad, good work! I'm sure he'll change it for you!

WILLY: Go downstairs and tell the clerk I'm checkin' out. Go right down.

BIFF: Yes, Sir! See, the reason he hates me, Pop—one day he was late for class so I got up at the blackboard and imitated him. I crossed my eyes and talked with a lithp.

WILLY (*laughing*):   You did? The kids like it?

BIFF: They nearly died laughing!

WILLY: Yeah? What'd you do?

BIFF: The thquare root of thixthy twee is . . . (WILLY *bursts out laughing;* BIFF *joins him.*) And in the middle of it he walked in!

WILLY *laughs and* THE WOMAN *joins in offstage.*

WILLY (*without hesitating*):   Hurry downstairs and—

BIFF: Somebody in there?

WILLY: No, that was next door.

THE WOMAN *laughs offstage.*

BIFF: Somebody got in your bathroom!

WILLY: No, it's the next room, there's a party—

THE WOMAN (*enters, laughing. She lisps this*):   Can I come in? There's something in the bathtub, Willy, and it's moving!

WILLY *looks at* BIFF, *who is staring open-mouthed and horrified at* THE WOMAN.

WILLY: Ah—you better go back to your room. They must be finished painting by now. They're painting her room so I let her take a shower here. Go back, go back . . . (*He pushes her.*)

THE WOMAN (*resisting*):   But I've got to get dressed, Willy, I can't—

WILLY: Get out of here! Go back, go back . . . (*Suddenly striving for the ordinary.*) This is Miss Francis, Biff, she's a buyer. They're painting her room. Go back, Miss Francis, go back . . .

THE WOMAN: But my clothes, I can't go out naked in the hall!

WILLY (*pushing her offstage*):   Get outa here! Go back, go back!

BIFF *slowly sits down on his suitcase as the argument continues offstage.*

THE WOMAN: Where's my stockings? You promised me stockings, Willy!

WILLY: I have no stockings here!

THE WOMAN: You had two boxes of size nine sheers for me, and I want them!

WILLY: Here, for God's sake, will you get outa here!

THE WOMAN (*enters holding a box of stockings*):   I just hope there's nobody in the hall. That's all I hope. (*To* BIFF.) Are you football or baseball?

BIFF: Football.

THE WOMAN (*angry, humiliated*):   That's me too. G'night. (*She snatches her clothes from* WILLY, *and walks out.*)

WILLY (*after a pause*):   Well, better get going. I want to get to the school first thing in the morning. Get my suits out of the closet. I'll get my valise. (BIFF *doesn't move.*) What's the matter? (BIFF *remains motionless, tears falling.*) She's a buyer. Buys for J. H. Simmons. She lives down the hall—they're painting. You don't imagine—(*He breaks off. After a pause.*) Now listen, pal, she's just a buyer. She sees merchandise in her room and they have to keep it looking just so . . . (*Pause. Assuming command.*) All right, get my suits. (BIFF *doesn't move.*) Now stop crying and do as I say. I gave you an order. Biff, I gave you an order! Is that what you do when I give you an order? How dare you cry! (*Putting his arm around* BIFF.) Now look, Biff, when you grow up you'll understand about these things. You mustn't—you mustn't overemphasize a thing like this. I'll see Birnbaum first thing in the morning.

BIFF: Never mind.

WILLY (*getting down beside* BIFF):   Never mind! He's going to give you those points. I'll see to it.

BIFF: He wouldn't listen to you.

WILLY: He certainly will listen to me. You need those points for the U. of Virginia.

BIFF: I'm not going there.

WILLY: Heh? If I can't get him to change that mark you'll make it up in summer school. You've got all summer to—

BIFF (*his weeping breaking from him*):   Dad . . .

WILLY (*infected by it*):   Oh, my boy . . .

BIFF: Dad . . .

WILLY: She's nothing to me, Biff. I was lonely, I was terribly lonely.

BIFF: You—you gave her Mama's stockings! (*His tears break through and he rises to go.*)

WILLY (*grabbing for* BIFF):   I gave you an order!

BIFF: Don't touch me, you—liar!

WILLY: Apologize for that!

BIFF: You fake! You phony little fake! You fake! (*Overcome, he turns quickly and weeping fully goes out with his suitcase.* WILLY *is left on the floor on his knees.*)

WILLY: I gave you an order! Biff, come back here or I'll beat you! Come back here! I'll whip you!

STANLEY *comes quickly in from the right and stands in front of* WILLY.

WILLY (*shouts at* STANLEY):   I gave you an order . . .

STANLEY: Hey, let's pick it up, pick it up, Mr. Loman. (*He helps* WILLY *to his feet.*) Your boys left with the chippies. They said they'll see you home.

A second waiter watches some distance away.

WILLY: But we were supposed to have dinner together.

Music is heard, WILLY'*s theme.*

STANLEY: Can you make it?

WILLY: I'll—sure, I can make it. (*Suddenly concerned about his clothes.*) Do I—I look all right?

STANLEY: Sure, you look all right. (*He flicks a speck off* WILLY'S *lapel.*)

WILLY: Here—here's a dollar.

STANLEY: Oh, your son paid me. It's all right.

WILLY (*putting it in* STANLEY'S *hand*):   No, take it. You're a good boy.

STANLEY: Oh, no, you don't have to . . .

WILLY: Here—here's some more, I don't need it any more. (*After a slight pause.*) Tell me—is there a seed store in the neighborhood?

STANLEY: Seeds? You mean like to plant?

As WILLY *turns,* STANLEY *slips the money back into his jacket pocket.*

WILLY: Yes. Carrots, peas . . .

STANLEY: Well, there's hardware stores on Sixth Avenue, but it may be too late now.

WILLY (*anxiously*):   Oh, I'd better hurry. I've got to get some seeds. (*He starts off to the right.*) I've got to get some seeds, right away. Nothing's planted. I don't have a thing in the ground.

WILLY *hurries out as the light goes down.* STANLEY *moves over to the right after him, watches him off. The other waiter has been staring at* WILLY.

STANLEY (*to the waiter*):   Well, whatta you looking at?

The waiter picks up the chairs and moves off right. STANLEY *takes the table and follows him. The light fades on this area. There is a long pause, the sound of the flute coming over. The light gradually rises on the kitchen, which is empty.* HAPPY *appears at the door of the house, followed by* BIFF. HAPPY *is carrying a large bunch of long-stemmed roses. He enters the kitchen, looks around for* LINDA. *Not seeing her, he turns to* BIFF, *who is just outside the house door, and makes a gesture with his hands, indicating "Not here, I guess." He looks into the livingroom and freezes. Inside,* LINDA, *unseen, is seated,* WILLY'*s coat on her lap. She rises ominously and quietly and moves toward* HAPPY, *who backs up into the kitchen, afraid.*

HAPPY: Hey, what're you doing up? (LINDA *says nothing but moves toward him implacably.*) Where's Pop? (*He keeps backing to the right, and now* LINDA *is in full view in the doorway to the livingroom.*) Is he sleeping?

LINDA: Where were you?

HAPPY (*trying to laugh it off*):   We met two girls, Mom, very fine types. Here, we brought you some flowers. (*Offering them to her.*) Put them in your room, Ma.

She knocks them to the floor at BIFF'*s feet. He has now come inside and closed the door behind him. She stares at* BIFF, *silent.*

HAPPY: Now what'd you do that for? Mom, I want you to have some flowers—

LINDA (*cutting* HAPPY *off, violently to* BIFF):   Don't you care whether he lives or dies?

HAPPY (*going to the stairs*):   Come upstairs, Biff.

BIFF (*with a flare of disgust, to* HAPPY):   Go away from me! (*To* LINDA.) What do you mean, lives or dies? Nobody's dying around here, pal.

LINDA: Get out of my sight! Get out of here!

BIFF: I wanna see the boss.

LINDA: You're not going near him!

BIFF: Where is he? (*He moves into the livingroom and* LINDA *follows.*)

LINDA (*shouting after* BIFF):   You invite him for dinner. He looks forward to it all day—(BIFF *appears in his parents' bedroom, looks around, and exits*)—and then you desert him there. There's no stranger you'd do that to!

HAPPY: Why? He had a swell time with us. Listen, when I—(LINDA *comes back into the kitchen*)—desert him I hope I don't outlive the day!

LINDA: Get out of here!

HAPPY: Now look, Mom . . .

LINDA: Did you have to go to women tonight? You and your lousy rotten whores!

BIFF *re-enters the kitchen.*

HAPPY: Mom, all we did was follow Biff around trying to cheer him up! (*To* BIFF.) Boy, what a night you gave me!

LINDA: Get out of here, both of you, and don't come back! I don't want you tormenting him any more. Go on now, get your things together! (*To* BIFF.) You can sleep in his apartment. (*She starts to pick up the flowers and stops herself.*) Pick up this stuff, I'm not your maid any more. Pick it up, you bum, you!

HAPPY *turns his back to her in refusal.* BIFF *slowly moves over and gets down on his knees, picking up the flowers.*

LINDA: You're a pair of animals! Not one, not another living soul would have had the cruelty to walk out on that man in a restaurant!

BIFF (*not looking at her*):   Is that what he said?

LINDA: He didn't have to say anything. He was so humiliated he nearly limped when he came in.

HAPPY: But, Mom, he had a great time with us—

BIFF (*cutting him off violently*):   Shut up!

Without another word, HAPPY *goes upstairs.*

LINDA: You! You didn't even go in to see if he was all right!

BIFF (*still on the floor in front of* LINDA, *the flowers in his hand; with self-loathing*):   No. Didn't. Didn't do a damned thing. How do you like that, heh? Left him babbling in a toilet.

LINDA: You louse. You . . .

BIFF: Now you hit it on the nose! (*He gets up, throws the flowers in the wastebasket.*) The scum of the earth, and you're looking at him!

LINDA: Get out of here!

BIFF: I gotta talk to the boss, Mom. Where is he?

LINDA: You're not going near him. Get out of this house!

BIFF (*with absolute assurance, determination*):   No. We're gonna have an abrupt conversation, him and me.

LINDA: You're not talking to him!

Hammering is heard from outside the house, off right. BIFF *turns toward the noise.*

LINDA (*suddenly pleading*):   Will you please leave him alone?
BIFF: What's he doing out there?
LINDA: He's planting the garden!
BIFF (*quietly*):   Now? Oh, my God!

BIFF *moves outside,* LINDA *following. The light dies down on them and comes up on the center of the apron as* WILLY *walks into it. He is carrying a flashlight, a hoe and a handful of seed packets. He raps the top of the hoe sharply to fix it firmly, and then moves to the left, measuring off the distance with his foot. He holds the flashlight to look at the seed packets, reading off the instructions. He is in the blue of night.*

WILLY: Carrots . . . quarter-inch apart. Rows . . . one-foot rows. (*He measures it off.*) One foot. (*He puts down a package and measures off.*) Beets. (*He puts down another package and measures again.*) Lettuce. (*He reads the package, puts it down.*) One foot—(*He breaks off as* BEN *appears at the right and moves slowly down to him.*) What a proposition, ts, ts. Terrific, terrific. 'Cause she's suffered, Ben, the woman has suffered. You understand me? A man can't go out the way he came in, Ben, a man has got to add up to something. You can't, you can't—(BEN *moves toward him as though to interrupt.*) You gotta consider, now. Don't answer so quick. Remember, it's a guaranteed twenty-thousand-dollar proposition. Now look, Ben, I want you to go through the ins and outs of this thing with me. I've got nobody to talk to, Ben, and the woman has suffered, you hear me?
BEN (*standing still, considering*):   What's the proposition?
WILLY: It's twenty thousand dollars on the barrelhead. Guaranteed, gilt-edged, you understand?
BEN: You don't want to make a fool of yourself. They might not honor the policy.
WILLY: How can they dare refuse? Didn't I work like a coolie to meet every premium on the nose? And now they don't pay off? Impossible!
BEN: It's called a cowardly thing, William.
WILLY: Why? Does it take more guts to stand here the rest of my life ringing up a zero?
BEN (*yielding*):   That's a point, William. (*He moves, thinking, turns.*) And twenty thousand—that is something one can feel with the hand, it is there.
WILLY (*now assured, with rising power*):   Oh, Ben, that's the whole beauty of it! I see it like a diamond, shining in the dark, hard and rough, that I can pick up and touch in my hand. Not like—like an appointment! This would not be another damned-fool appointment, Ben, and it changes all the aspects. Because he thinks I'm nothing, see, and so he spites me. But the funeral—(*Straightening up.*) Ben, that funeral will be massive! They'll come from Maine, Massachusetts, Vermont, New Hampshire! All the old-timers with the strange license plates—that boy will be thunder-struck, Ben, because he never realized—I am known! Rhode Island, New York, New Jersey—I am known, Ben, and he'll see it with his eyes once and for all. He'll see what I am, Ben! He's in for a shock, that boy!
BEN (*coming down to the edge of the garden*):   He'll call you a coward.
WILLY (*suddenly fearful*):   No, that would be terrible.
BEN: Yes. And a damned fool.

WILLY: No, no, he mustn't, I won't have that! (*He is broken and desperate.*)

BEN: He'll hate you, William.

The gay music of the boys is heard.

WILLY: Oh, Ben, how do we get back to all the great times? Used to be so full of light, and comradeship, the sleigh-riding in winter, and the ruddiness on his cheeks. And always some kind of good news coming up, always something nice coming up ahead. And never even let me carry the valises in the house, and simonizing, simonizing that little red car! Why, why can't I give him something and not have him hate me?

BEN: Let me think about it. (*He glances at his watch.*) I still have a little time. Remarkable proposition, but you've got to be sure you're not making a fool of yourself.

BEN *drifts off upstage and goes out of sight.* BIFF *comes down from the left.*

WILLY (*suddenly conscious of* BIFF, *turns and looks up at him, then begins picking up the packages of seeds in confusion*):   Where the hell is that seed? (*Indignantly.*) You can't see nothing out here! They boxed in the whole goddam neighborhood!

BIFF: There are people all around here. Don't you realize that?

WILLY: I'm busy. Don't bother me.

BIFF (*taking the hoe from* WILLY):   I'm saying good-by to you, Pop. (WILLY *looks at him, silent, unable to move.*) I'm not coming back any more.

WILLY: You're not going to see Oliver tomorrow?

BIFF: I've got no appointment, Dad.

WILLY: He put his arm around you, and you've got no appointment?

BIFF: Pop, get this now, will you? Everytime I've left it's been a fight that sent me out of here. Today I realized something about myself and I tried to explain it to you and I—I think I'm just not smart enough to make any sense out of it for you. To hell with whose fault it is or anything like that. (*He takes* WILLY'*s arm.*) Let's just wrap it up, heh? Come on in, we'll tell Mom. (*He gently tries to pull* WILLY *to the left.*)

WILLY (*frozen, immobile, with guilt in his voice*):   No, I don't want to see her.

BIFF: Come on! (*He pulls again, and* WILLY *tries to pull away.*)

WILLY (*highly nervous*):   No, no, I don't want to see her.

BIFF (*tries to look into* WILLY'S *face, as if to find the answer there*):   Why don't you want to see her?

WILLY (*more harshly now*):   Don't bother me, will you?

BIFF: What do you mean, you don't want to see her? You don't want them calling you yellow, do you? This isn't your fault; it's me, I'm a bum. Now come inside! (WILLY *strains to get away.*) Did you hear what I said to you?

WILLY *pulls away and quickly goes by himself into the house.* BIFF *follows.*

LINDA (*to* WILLY):   Did you plant, dear?

BIFF (*at the door, to* LINDA):   All right, we had it out. I'm going and I'm not writing any more.

LINDA (*going to* WILLY *in the kitchen*):   I think that's the best way, dear. 'Cause there's no use drawing it out, you'll just never get along.

WILLY *doesn't respond.*

BIFF: People ask where I am and what I'm doing, you don't know, and you don't care. That way it'll be off your mind and you can start brightening up again. All right? That clears it, doesn't it? (WILLY *is silent, and* BIFF *goes to him.*) You gonna wish me luck, scout? (*He extends his hand.*) What do you say?

LINDA: Shake his hand, Willy.

WILLY (*turning to her, seething with hurt*):   There's no necessity to mention the pen at all, y'know.

BIFF (*gently*):   I've got no appointment, Dad.

WILLY (*erupting fiercely*):   He put his arm around . . . ?

BIFF: Dad, you're never going to see what I am, so what's the use of arguing? If I strike oil I'll send you a check. Meantime forget I'm alive.

WILLY (*to* LINDA):   Spite, see?

BIFF: Shake hands, Dad.

WILLY: Not my hand.

BIFF: I was hoping not to go this way.

WILLY: Well, this is the way you're going. Good-by.

BIFF *looks at him a moment, then turns sharply and goes to the stairs.*

WILLY (*stops him with*):   May you rot in hell if you leave this house!

BIFF (*turning*):   Exactly what is it that you want from me?

WILLY: I want you to know, on the train, in the mountains, in the valleys, wherever you go, that you cut down your life for spite!

BIFF: No, no.

WILLY: Spite, spite, is the word of your undoing! And when you're down and out, remember what did it. When you're rotting somewhere beside the railroad tracks, remember, and don't you dare blame it on me!

BIFF: I'm not blaming it on you!

WILLY: I won't take the rap for this, you hear?

HAPPY *comes down the stairs and stands on the bottom step, watching.*

BIFF: That's just what I'm telling you!

WILLY (*sinking into a chair at the table, with full accusation*):   You're trying to put a knife in me—don't think I don't know what you're doing!

BIFF: All right, phony! Then let's lay it on the line. (*He whips the rubber tube out of his pocket and puts it on the table.*)

HAPPY: You crazy—

LINDA: Biff! (*She moves to grab the hose, but* BIFF *holds it down with his hand.*)

BIFF: Leave it there! Don't move it!

WILLY (*not looking at it*):   What is that?

BIFF: You know goddam well what that is.

WILLY (*caged, wanting to escape*):   I never saw that.

BIFF: You saw it. The mice didn't bring it into the cellar! What is this supposed to do, make a hero out of you? This supposed to make me sorry for you?

WILLY: Never heard of it.

BIFF: There'll be no pity for you, you hear it? No pity!

WILLY (*to* LINDA): You hear the spite!

BIFF: No, you're going to hear the truth—what you are and what I am!

LINDA: Stop it!

WILLY: Spite!

HAPPY (*coming down toward* BIFF): You cut it now!

BIFF (*to* HAPPY): The man don't know who we are! The man is gonna know! (*To* WILLY.) We never told the truth for ten minutes in this house!

HAPPY: We always told the truth!

BIFF (*turning on him*): You big blow, are you the assistant buyer? You're one of the two assistants to the assistant, aren't you?

HAPPY: Well, I'm practically—

BIFF: You're practically full of it! We all are! And I'm through with it. (*To* WILLY.) Now hear this, Willy, this is me.

WILLY: I know you!

BIFF: You know why I had no address for three months? I stole a suit in Kansas City and I was in jail. (*To* LINDA, *who is sobbing*.) Stop crying. I'm through with it.

LINDA *turns away from them, her hands covering her face.*

WILLY: I suppose that's my fault!

BIFF: I stole myself out of every good job since high school!

WILLY: And whose fault is that?

BIFF: And I never got anywhere because you blew me so full of hot air I could never stand taking orders from anybody! That's whose fault it is!

WILLY: I hear that!

LINDA: Don't, Biff!

BIFF: It's goddam time you heard that! I had to be boss big shot in two weeks, and I'm through with it!

WILLY: Then hang yourself! For spite, hang yourself!

BIFF: No! Nobody's hanging himself, Willy! I ran down eleven flights with a pen in my hand today. And suddenly I stopped, you hear me? And in the middle of that office building, do you hear this? I stopped in the middle of that building and I saw—the sky. I saw the things that I love in this world. The work and the food and time to sit and smoke. And I looked at the pen and said to myself, what the hell am I grabbing this for? Why am I trying to become what I don't want to be? What am I doing in an office, making a contemptuous, begging fool of myself, when all I want is out there, waiting for me the minute I say I know who I am! Why can't I say that, Willy? (*He tries to make* WILLY *face him, but* WILLY *pulls away and moves to the left.*)

WILLY (*with hatred, threateningly*): The door of your life is wide open!

BIFF: Pop! I'm a dime a dozen, and so are you!

WILLY (*turning on him now in an uncontrolled outburst*): I am not a dime a dozen! I am Willy Loman, and you are Biff Loman!

BIFF *starts for* WILLY, *but is blocked by* HAPPY. *In his fury,* BIFF *seems on the verge of attacking his father.*

BIFF: I am not a leader of men, Willy, and neither are you. You were never anything but a hard-working drummer who landed in the ash can like all the rest of them!

I'm one dollar an hour, Willy! I tried seven states and couldn't raise it. A buck an hour! Do you gather my meaning? I'm not bringing home any prizes any more, and you're going to stop waiting for me to bring them home!

WILLY (*directly to* BIFF):   You vengeful, spiteful mutt!

> BIFF *breaks from* HAPPY. WILLY, *in fright, starts up the stairs.* BIFF *grabs him.*

BIFF (*at the peak of his fury*):   Pop, I'm nothing! I'm nothing, Pop. Can't you understand that? There's no spite in it any more. I'm just what I am, that's all.

> BIFF'*s fury has spent itself, and he breaks down, sobbing, holding on to* WILLY, *who dumbly fumbles for* BIFF'*s face.*

WILLY (*astonished*):   What're you doing? What're you doing? (*To* LINDA.) Why is he crying?

BIFF (*crying, broken*):   Will you let me go, for Christ's sake? Will you take that phony dream and burn it before something happens? (*Struggling to contain himself, he pulls away and moves to the stairs.*) I'll go in the morning. Put him—put him to bed. (*Exhausted,* BIFF *moves up the stairs to his room.*)

WILLY (*after a long pause, astonished, elevated*):   Isn't that remarkable? Biff—he likes me!

LINDA: He loves you, Willy!

HAPPY (*deeply moved*):   Always did, Pop.

WILLY: Oh, Biff! (*Staring wildly.*) He cried! Cried to me. (*He is choking with his love, and now cries out his promise.*) That boy—that boy is going to be magnificent!

> BEN *appears in the light just outside the kitchen.*

BEN: Yes, outstanding, with twenty thousand behind him.

LINDA (*sensing the racing of his mind, fearfully, carefully*):   Now come to bed, Willy. It's all settled now.

WILLY (*finding it difficult not to rush out of the house*):   Yes, we'll sleep. Come on. Go to sleep, Hap.

BEN: And it does take a great kind of man to crack the jungle.

> *In accents of dread,* BEN'*s idyllic music starts up.*

HAPPY (*his arm around* LINDA):   I'm getting married, Pop, don't forget it. I'm changing everything. I'm gonna run that department before the year is up. You'll see, Mom. (*He kisses her.*)

BEN: The jungle is dark but full of diamonds, Willy.

> WILLY *turns, moves, listening to* BEN.

LINDA: Be good. You're both good boys, just act that way, that's all.

HAPPY: 'Night, Pop. (*He goes upstairs.*)

LINDA (*to* WILLY):   Come, dear.

BEN (*with greater force*):   One must go in to fetch a diamond out.

WILLY (*to* LINDA, *as he moves slowly along the edge of the kitchen, toward the door*):   I just want to get settled down, Linda. Let me sit alone for a little.

LINDA (*almost uttering her fear*):   I want you upstairs.

WILLY (*taking her in his arms*):   In a few minutes, Linda. I couldn't sleep right now. Go on, you look awful tired. (*He kisses her.*)

BEN: Not like an appointment at all. A diamond is rough and hard to the touch.

WILLY: Go on now. I'll be right up.

LINDA: I think this is the only way, Willy.

WILLY: Sure, it's the best thing.

BEN: Best thing!

WILLY: The only way. Everything is gonna be—go on, kid, get to bed. You look so tired.

LINDA: Come right up.

WILLY: Two minutes.

LINDA *goes into the livingroom, then reappears in her bedroom.* WILLY *moves just outside the kitchen door.*

WILLY: Loves me. (*Wonderingly.*) Always loved me. Isn't that a remarkable thing? Ben, he'll worship me for it!

BEN (*with promise*):   It's dark there, but full of diamonds.

WILLY: Can you imagine that magnificence with twenty thousand dollars in his pocket?

LINDA (*calling from her room*):   Willy! Come up!

WILLY (*calling from the kitchen*):   Yes! Yes. Coming! It's very smart, you realize that, don't you, sweetheart? Even Ben sees it. I gotta go, baby. 'By! By! (*Going over to* BEN, *almost dancing.*) Imagine? When the mail comes he'll be ahead of Bernard again!

BEN: A perfect proposition all around.

WILLY: Did you see how he cried to me? Oh, if I could kiss him, Ben!

BEN: Time, William, time!

WILLY: Oh, Ben, I always knew one way or another we were gonna make it, Biff and I!

BEN (*looking at his watch*):   The boat. We'll be late. (*He moves slowly off into the darkness.*)

WILLY (*elegiacally, turning to the house*):   Now when you kick off, boy, I want a seventy-yard boot, and get right down the field under the ball, and when you hit, hit low and hit hard, because it's important, boy. (*He swings around and faces the audience.*) There's all kinds of important people in the stands, and the first thing you know . . . (*Suddenly realizing he is alone.*) Ben! Ben, where do I . . . ? (*He makes a sudden movement of search.*) Ben, how do I . . . ?

LINDA (*calling*):   Willy, you coming up?

WILLY (*uttering a gasp of fear, whirling about as if to quiet her*):   Sh! (*He turns around as if to find his way; sounds, faces, voices, seem to be swarming in upon him and he flicks at them, crying.*) Sh! Sh! (*Suddenly music, faint and high, stops him. It rises in intensity, almost to an unbearable scream. He goes up and down on his toes, and rushes off around the house.*) Shhh!

LINDA: Willy?

There is no answer. LINDA *waits.* BIFF *gets up off his bed. He is still in his clothes.* HAPPY *sits up.* BIFF *stands listening.*

LINDA (*with real fear*):   Willy, answer me! Willy!

There is the sound of a car starting and moving away at full speed.

LINDA: No!

BIFF (*rushing down the stairs*):   Pop!

As the car speeds off, the music crashes down in a frenzy of sound, which becomes the soft pulsation of a single cello string. BIFF *slowly returns to his bedroom. He and* HAPPY *gravely don their jackets.* LINDA *slowly walks out of her room. The music has developed into a dead march. The leaves of day are appearing over everything.* CHARLEY *and* BERNARD, *somberly dressed, appear and knock on the kitchen door.* BIFF *and* HAPPY *slowly descend the stairs to the kitchen as* CHARLEY *and* BERNARD *enter. All stop a moment when* LINDA, *in clothes of mourning, bearing a little bunch of roses, comes through the draped doorway into the kitchen. She goes to* CHARLEY *and takes his arm. Now all move toward the audience, through the wall-line of the kitchen. At the limit of the apron,* LINDA *lays down the flowers, kneels, and sits back on her heels. All stare down at the grave.*

REQUIEM

CHARLEY: It's getting dark, Linda.

LINDA *doesn't react. She stares at the grave.*

BIFF: How about it, Mom? Better get some rest, heh? They'll be closing the gate soon.

LINDA *makes no move. Pause.*

HAPPY (*deeply angered*):   He had no right to do that! There was no necessity for it. We would've helped him.

CHARLEY (*grunting*):   Hmmm.

BIFF: Come along, Mom.

LINDA: Why didn't anybody come?

CHARLEY: It was a very nice funeral.

LINDA: But where are all the people he knew? Maybe they blame him.

CHARLEY: Naa. It's a rough world, Linda. They wouldn't blame him.

LINDA: I can't understand it. At this time especially. First time in thirty-five years we were just about free and clear. He only needed a little salary. He was even finished with the dentist.

CHARLEY: No man only needs a little salary.

LINDA: I can't understand it.

BIFF: There were a lot of nice days. When he'd come home from a trip; or on Sundays, making the stoop; finishing the cellar; putting on the new porch; when he built the extra bathroom; and put up the garage. You know something, Charley, there's more of him in that front stoop than in all the sales he ever made.

CHARLEY: Yeah. He was a happy man with a batch of cement.

LINDA: He was so wonderful with his hands.

BIFF: He had the wrong dreams. All, all, wrong.

HAPPY (*almost ready to fight* BIFF):   Don't say that!

BIFF: He never knew who he was.

CHARLEY (*stopping* HAPPY's *movement and reply. To* BIFF.)   Nobody dast blame this man. You don't understand: Willy was a salesman. And for a salesman, there is no rock bottom to the life. He don't put a bolt to a nut, he don't tell you the law or give you medicine. He's a man out there in the blue, riding on a smile and a shoeshine. And when they start not smiling back—that's an earthquake. And then you get yourself a couple of spots on your hat, and you're finished. Nobody dast blame this man. A salesman is got to dream, boy. It comes with the territory.

BIFF: Charley, the man didn't know who he was.

HAPPY (*infuriated*):   Don't say that!

BIFF: Why don't you come with me, Happy?

HAPPY: I'm not licked that easily. I'm staying right in this city, and I'm gonna beat this racket! (*He looks at* BIFF, *his chin set.*) The Loman Brothers!

BIFF: I know who I am, kid.

HAPPY: All right, boy. I'm gonna show you and everybody else that Willy Loman did not die in vain. He had a good dream. It's the only dream you can have— to come out number-one man. He fought it out here, and this is where I'm gonna win it for him.

BIFF (*with a hopeless glance at* HAPPY, *bends toward his mother*):   Let's go, Mom.

LINDA: I'll be with you in a minute. Go on, Charley. (*He hesitates.*) I want to, just for a minute. I never had a chance to say good-by.

CHARLEY *moves away, followed by* HAPPY. BIFF *remains a slight distance up and left of* LINDA. *She sits there, summoning herself. The flute begins, not far away, playing behind her speech.*

LINDA: Forgive me, dear. I can't cry. I don't know what it is, but I can't cry. I don't understand it. Why did you ever do that? Help me, Willy, I can't cry. It seems to me that you're just on another trip. I keep expecting you. Willy, dear, I can't cry. Why did you do it? I search and search and I search, and I can't understand it, Willy. I made the last payment on the house today. Today, dear. And there'll be nobody home. (*A sob rises in her throat.*) We're free and clear. (*Sobbing more fully, released.*) We're free. (BIFF *comes slowly toward her.*) We're free . . . We're free . . .

BIFF *lifts her to her feet and moves out up right with her in his arms.* LINDA *sobs quietly.* BERNARD *and* CHARLEY *come together and follow them, followed by* HAPPY. *Only the music of the flute is left on the darkening stage as over the house the hard towers of the apartment buildings rise into sharp focus, and—*

Curtain

(*1949*)

QUESTIONS FOR REFLECTION

Experience

1. Identify the places in the play, if any, where you were confused. What may have accounted for your confusion?
2. To what extent do you identify with the dreams of the play's characters? Why?

Interpretation

3. Comment on the significance of the title. What kinds of deaths might be referred to? Explain.
4. What significance do you attach to the names of the characters?
5. Describe Biff's relationship with his father and with his brother, Happy.
6. How does Miller characterize Willy? Which of his characteristics are highlighted? What kind of man is he? To what extent and by what means is he considered a failure? Does anyone consider him a success? Why or why not?
7. What roles do women have in this play? Comment on Willy's relationships with them. Consider Biff's relationship with women as well.
8. Identify two minor characters and explain their significance for the play's action and theme(s).
9. Describe Miller's staging of the play. Consider his use of lighting and music, and the way he dramatizes dreams and memories.

Evaluation

10. What is typically "American" about Miller's play? What cultural attitudes and values displayed by the characters provide it with an American tone?
11. Published in 1947, *Death of a Salesman* has been among the most popular plays of the American theater. What accounts for the play's perennial appeal?
12. Read Miller's essay "Tragedy and the Common Man" and comment on the degree to which his remarks illuminate his intentions and define his achievement in the play.

LORRAINE HANSBERRY

[1930–1965]

Lorraine Hansberry was born and raised in Chicago. She studied painting at the Chicago Art Institute and the University of Wisconsin before turning to writing following a move to New York. *A Raisin in the Sun* (1959), her first Broadway play, was quickly made into a movie, starring Sidney Poitier and Claudia McNeil. Although the play reflects Hansberry's deep concern with civil rights, it transcends its racial and urban focus. Like Arthur Miller's *Death of a Salesman, A Raisin in the Sun* dramatizes the powerful attractions of the American dream of success. Like Miller's play also, Hansberry's is largely concerned with family life.

LORRAINE HANSBERRY

A Raisin in the Sun

What happens to a dream deferred?
Does it dry up
Like a raisin in the sun?
Or fester like a sore—
And then run?
Does it stink like rotten meat?
Or crust and sugar over—
Like a syrupy sweet?

Maybe it just sags
Like a heavy load.

Or does it explode?

LANGSTON HUGHES

CHARACTERS

(*In order of appearance*)
RUTH YOUNGER
TRAVIS YOUNGER
WALTER LEE YOUNGER (BROTHER)
BENEATHA YOUNGER
LENA YOUNGER (MAMA)
JOSEPH ASAGAI
GEORGE MURCHISON
KARL LINDNER
BOBO
MOVING MEN

The action of the play is set in Chicago's Southside, sometime between World War II and the present.

Act I
Scene One: Friday morning.
Scene Two: The following morning.
Act II
Scene One: Later, the same day.
Scene Two: Friday night, a few weeks later.
Scene Three: Moving day, one week later.
Act III
An hour later.

ACT I

Scene I

The YOUNGER *living room would be a comfortable and well-ordered room if it were not for a number of indestructible contradictions to this state of being. Its furnishings are typical and undistinguished and their primary feature now is that they have clearly had to accommodate the living of too many people for too many years—and they are tired. Still, we can see that at some time, a time probably no longer remembered by the family (except perhaps for* MAMA*), the furnishings of this room were actually selected with care and love and even hope—and brought to this apartment and arranged with taste and pride.*

That was a long time ago. Now the once loved pattern of the couch upholstery has to fight to show itself from under acres of crocheted doilies and couch covers which have themselves finally come to be more important than the upholstery. And here a table or a chair has been moved to disguise the worn places in the carpet; but the carpet has fought back by showing its weariness, with depressing uniformity, elsewhere on its surface.

Weariness has, in fact, won in this room. Everything has been polished, washed, sat on, used, scrubbed too often. All pretenses but living itself have long since vanished from the very atmosphere of this room.

Moreover, a section of this room, for it is not really a room unto itself, though the landlord's lease would make it seem so, slopes backward to provide a small kitchen area, where the family prepares the meals that are eaten in the living room proper, which must also serve as dining room. The single window that has been provided for these "two" rooms is located in this kitchen area. The sole natural light the family may enjoy in the course of a day is only that which fights its way through this little window.

At left, a door leads to a bedroom which is shared by MAMA *and her daughter,* BENEATHA. *At right, opposite, is a second room (which in the beginning of the life of this apartment was probably a breakfast room) which serves as a bedroom for* WALTER *and his wife,* RUTH.

Time: Sometime between World War II and the present.

Place: Chicago's Southside.

At Rise: It is morning dark in the living room. TRAVIS *is asleep on the make-down bed at center. An alarm clock sounds from within the bedroom at right, and presently* RUTH *enters from that room and closes the door behind her. She crosses sleepily toward the window. As she passes her sleeping son she reaches down and shakes him a little. At the window she raises the shade and a dusky Southside morning light comes in feebly. She fills a pot with water and puts it on to boil. She calls to the boy, between yawns, in a slightly muffled voice.*

RUTH *is about thirty. We can see that she was a pretty girl, even exceptionally so, but now it is apparent that life has been little that she expected, and disappointment has already begun to hang in her face. In a few years, before thirty-five even, she will be known among her people as a "settled woman."*

She crosses to her son and gives him a good, final, rousing shake.

RUTH: Come on now, boy, it's seven thirty! (*Her son sits up at last, in a stupor of sleepiness*) I say hurry up, Travis! You ain't the only person in the world got to use a bathroom! (*The child, a sturdy, handsome little boy of ten or eleven, drags himself out of the bed and almost blindly takes his towels and "today's clothes" from drawers and a closet and goes out to the bathroom, which is in an outside hall and which is shared by another family or families on the same floor.* RUTH *crosses to the bedroom door at right and opens it and calls in to her husband)* Walter Lee! . . . It's after seven thirty! Lemme see you do some waking up in there now! (*She waits*) You better get up from there, man! It's after seven thirty I tell you. (*She waits again*) All right, you just go ahead and lay there and next thing you know Travis be finished and Mr. Johnson'll be in there and you'll be fussing and cussing round here like a madman! And be late too! (*She waits, at the end of patience*) Walter Lee—it's time for you to GET UP!

(*She waits another second and then starts to go into the bedroom, but is apparently satisfied that her husband has begun to get up. She stops, pulls the door to, and returns to the kitchen area. She wipes her face with a moist cloth and runs her fingers through her sleep-disheveled hair in a vain effort and ties an apron around her housecoat. The bedroom door at right opens and her husband stands in the doorway in his pajamas, which are rumpled and mismated. He is a lean, intense young man in his middle thirties, inclined to quick nervous movements and erratic speech habits—and always in his voice there is a quality of indictment.*)

WALTER: Is he out yet?

RUTH: What you mean *out?* He ain't hardly got in there good yet.

WALTER (*wandering in, still more oriented to sleep than to a new day*):   Well, what was you doing all that yelling for if I can't even get in there yet? (*Stopping and thinking*) Check coming today?

RUTH: They *said* Saturday and this is just Friday and I hopes to God you ain't going to get up here first thing this morning and start talking to me 'bout no money— 'cause I 'bout don't want to hear it.

WALTER: Something the matter with you this morning?

RUTH: No—I'm just sleepy as the devil. What kind of eggs you want?

WALTER: Not scrambled. (RUTH *starts to scramble eggs*) Paper come? (RUTH *points impatiently to the rolled up Tribune on the table, and he gets it and spreads it out and vaguely reads the front page*) Set off another bomb yesterday.

RUTH (*maximum indifference*):   Did they?

WALTER (*looking up*):   What's the matter with you?

RUTH: Ain't nothing the matter with me. And don't keep asking me that this morning.

WALTER: Ain't nobody bothering you. (*Reading the news of the day absently again*) Say Colonel McCormick is sick.

RUTH (*affecting tea-party interest*):   Is he now? Poor thing.

WALTER (*sighing and looking at his watch*):   Oh, me. (*He waits*) Now what is that boy doing in that bathroom all this time? He just going to have to start getting up earlier. I can't be being late to work on account of him fooling around in there.

RUTH (*turning on him*):   Oh, no he ain't going to be getting up no earlier no such thing! It ain't his fault that he can't get to bed no earlier nights 'cause he got a bunch of crazy good-for-nothing clowns sitting up running their mouths in what is supposed to be his bedroom after ten o'clock at night . . .

WALTER: That's what you mad about, ain't it? The things I want to talk about with my friends just couldn't be important in your mind, could they?

(*He rises and finds a cigarette in her handbag on the table and crosses to the little window and looks out, smoking and deeply enjoying this first one*)

RUTH (*almost matter of factly, a complaint too automatic to deserve emphasis*):   Why you always got to smoke before you eat in the morning?

WALTER (*at the window*):   Just look at 'em down there . . . Running and racing to work . . . (*He turns and faces his wife and watches her a moment at the stove, and then, suddenly*) You look young this morning, baby.

RUTH (*indifferently*):   Yeah?

WALTER: Just for a second—stirring them eggs. Just for a second it was—you looked real young again. (*He reaches for her; she crosses away. Then, drily*) It's gone now—you look like yourself again!

RUTH: Man, if you don't shut up and leave me alone.

WALTER (*looking out to the street again*):   First thing a man ought to learn in life is not to make love to no colored woman first thing in the morning. You all some eeeevil people at eight o'clock in the morning.

(TRAVIS *appears in the hall doorway, almost fully dressed and quite wide awake now, his towels and pajamas across his shoulders. He opens the door and signals for his father to make the bathroom in a hurry*)

TRAVIS (*watching the bathroom*):   Daddy, come on!

(WALTER *gets his bathroom utensils and flies out to the bathroom*)

RUTH: Sit down and have your breakfast, Travis.

TRAVIS: Mama, this is Friday. (*Gleefully*) Check coming tomorrow, huh?

RUTH: You get your mind off money and eat your breakfast.

TRAVIS (*eating*):   This is the morning we supposed to bring the fifty cents to school.

RUTH: Well, I ain't got no fifty cents this morning.

TRAVIS: Teacher say we have to.

RUTH: I don't care what teacher say. I ain't got it. Eat your breakfast, Travis.

TRAVIS: I *am* eating.

RUTH: Hush up now and just eat!

(*The boy gives her an exasperated look for her lack of understanding, and eats grudgingly*)

TRAVIS: You think Grandmama would have it?

RUTH: No! And I want you to stop asking your grandmother for money, you hear me?

TRAVIS (*outraged*):   Gaaaleee! I don't ask her, she just gimme it sometimes!

RUTH: Travis Willard Younger—I got too much on me this morning to be—

TRAVIS: Maybe Daddy—

RUTH: *Travis!*

(*The boy hushes abruptly. They are both quiet and tense for several seconds*)

TRAVIS (*presently*):   Could I maybe go carry some groceries in front of the super-market for a little while after school then?

RUTH: Just hush, I said. (TRAVIS *jabs his spoon into his cereal bowl viciously, and rests his head in anger upon his fists*) If you through eating, you can get over there and make up your bed.

(*The boy obeys stiffly and crosses the room, almost mechanically, to the bed and more or less folds the bedding into a heap, then angrily gets his books and cap*)

TRAVIS (*sulking and standing apart from her unnaturally*):   I'm gone.

RUTH (*looking up from the stove to inspect him automatically*):   Come here. (*He crosses to her and she studies his head*) If you don't take this comb and fix this here head, you better! (TRAVIS *puts down his books with a great sigh of oppression, and crosses to the mirror. His mother mutters under her breath about his "slubbornness"*) 'Bout to march out of here with that head looking just like chickens slept in it! I just don't know where you get your slubborn ways . . . And get your jacket, too. Looks chilly out this morning.

TRAVIS (*with conspicuously brushed hair and jacket*):   I'm gone.

RUTH: Get carfare and milk money—(*Waving one finger*)—and not a single penny for no caps, you hear me?

TRAVIS (*with sullen politeness*):   Yes'm.

(*He turns in outrage to leave. His mother watches after him as in his frustration he approaches the door almost comically. When she speaks to him, her voice has become a very gentle tease*)

RUTH (*mocking; as she thinks he would say it*):   Oh, Mama makes me so mad sometimes, I don't know what to do! (*She waits and continues to his back as he stands stock-still in front of the door*) I wouldn't kiss that woman good-bye for nothing in this world this morning! (*The boy finally turns around and rolls his eyes at her, knowing the mood has changed and he is vindicated; he does not, however, move toward her yet*) Not for nothing in this world! (*She finally laughs aloud at him and holds out her arms to him and we see that it is a way between them, very old and practiced. He crosses to her and allows her to embrace him warmly but keeps his face fixed with masculine rigidity. She holds him back from her presently and looks at him and runs her fingers over the features of his face. With utter gentleness—*) Now—whose little old angry man are you?

TRAVIS (*the masculinity and gruffness start to fade at last*):   Aw gaalee—Mama . . .

RUTH (*Mimicking*):   Aw—gaaaaalleeeee, Mama! (*She pushes him, with rough playfulness and finality, toward the door*) Get on out of here or you going to be late.

TRAVIS (*in the face of love, new aggressiveness*):   Mama, could I *please* go carry groceries?

RUTH: Honey, it's starting to get so cold evenings.

WALTER (*coming in from the bathroom and drawing a make-believe gun from a make-believe holster and shooting at his son*):   What is it he wants to do?

RUTH: Go carry groceries after school at the supermarket.

WALTER: Well, let him go . . .

TRAVIS (*quickly, to the ally*):   I *have* to—she won't gimme the fifty cents . . .

WALTER (*to his wife only*):   Why not?

RUTH (*simply, and with flavor*):   'Cause we don't have it.

WALTER (*to RUTH only*):   What you tell the boy things like that for? (*Reaching down into his pants with a rather important gesture*) Here, son—

(*He hands the boy the coin, but his eyes are directed to his wife's.* TRAVIS *takes the money happily*)

TRAVIS: Thanks, Daddy.

(*He starts out.* RUTH *watches both of them with murder in her eyes.* WALTER *stands and stares back at her with defiance, and suddenly reaches into his pocket again on an afterthought*)

WALTER (*without even looking at his son, still staring hard at his wife*): In fact, here's another fifty cents . . . Buy yourself some fruit today—or take a taxicab to school or something!

TRAVIS: Whoopee—

(*He leaps up and clasps his father around the middle with his legs, and they face each other in mutual appreciation; slowly* WALTER LEE *peeks around the boy to catch the violent rays from his wife's eyes and draws his head back as if shot*)

WALTER: You better get down now—and get to school, man.

TRAVIS (*at the door*): O.K. Good-bye.

(*He exits*)

WALTER (*after him, pointing with pride*): That's *my* boy. (*She looks at him in disgust and turns back to her work*) You know what I was thinking 'bout in the bathroom this morning?

RUTH: No.

WALTER: How come you always try to be so pleasant!

RUTH: What is there to be pleasant 'bout!

WALTER: You want to know what I was thinking 'bout in the bathroom or not!

RUTH: I know what you thinking 'bout.

WALTER (*ignoring her*): 'Bout what me and Willy Harris was talking about last night.

RUTH (*immediately—a refrain*): Willy Harris is a good-for-nothing loudmouth.

WALTER: Anybody who talks to me has got to be a good-for-nothing loudmouth, ain't he? And what you know about who is just a good-for-nothing loudmouth? Charlie Atkins was just a "good-for-nothing loudmouth" too, wasn't he! When he wanted me to go in the dry-cleaning business with him. And now—he's grossing a hundred thousand a year. A hundred thousand dollars a year! You still call *him* a loudmouth!

RUTH (*bitterly*): Oh, Walter Lee . . .

(*She folds her head on her arms over the table*)

WALTER (*rising and coming to her and standing over her*): You tired, ain't you? Tired of everything. Me, the boy, the way we live—this beat-up hole—everything. Ain't you? (*She doesn't look up, doesn't answer*) So tired—moaning and groaning all the time, but you wouldn't do nothing to help, would you? You couldn't be on my side that long for nothing, could you?

RUTH: Walter, please leave me alone.

WALTER: A man needs for a woman to back him up . . .

RUTH: Walter—

WALTER: Mama would listen to you. You know she listen to you more than she do me and Bennie. She think more of you. All you have to do is just sit down with her when you drinking your coffee one morning and talking 'bout things like you do and—(*He sits down beside her and demonstrates graphically what he thinks her methods and tone should be*)—you just sip your coffee, see, and say easy like that you been thinking 'bout that deal Walter Lee is so interested in, 'bout the store and all, and sip some more coffee, like what you saying ain't really that important to you—And the next thing you know, she be listening good and asking you questions and when I come home—I can tell her the details. This ain't no fly-by-night proposition, baby. I mean we figured it out, me and Willy and Bobo.

RUTH (*with a frown*):   Bobo?

WALTER: Yeah. You see, this little liquor store we got in mind cost seventy-five thousand and we figured the initial investment on the place be 'bout thirty thousand, see. That be ten thousand each. Course, there's a couple of hundred you got to pay so's you don't spend your life just waiting for them clowns to let your license get approved—

RUTH: You mean graft?

WALTER (*frowning impatiently*):   Don't call it that. See there, that just goes to show you what women understand about the world. Baby, don't *nothing* happen for you in this world 'less you pay *somebody* off!

RUTH: Walter, leave me alone! (*She raises her head and stares at him vigorously—then says, more quietly*) *Eat* your eggs, they gonna be cold.

WALTER (*straightening up from her and looking off*):   That's it. There you are. Man say to his woman: I got me a dream. His woman say: Eat your eggs. (*Sadly, but gaining in power*) Man say: I got to take hold of this here world, baby! And a woman will say: Eat your eggs and go to work. (*Passionately now*) Man say: I got to change my life, I'm choking to death, baby! And his woman say—(*In utter anguish as he brings his fists down on his thighs*)—Your eggs is getting cold!

RUTH (*softly*):   Walter, that ain't none of our money.

WALTER (*not listening at all or even looking at her*):   This morning, I was lookin' in the mirror and thinking about it . . . I'm thirty-five years old; I been married eleven years and I got a boy who sleeps in the living room—(*Very, very quietly*)—and all I got to give him is stories about how rich white people live . . .

RUTH: Eat your eggs, Walter.

WALTER (*slams the table and jumps up*):   —DAMN MY EGGS—DAMN ALL THE EGGS THAT EVER WAS!

RUTH: Then go to work.

WALTER (*looking up at her*):   See—I'm trying to talk to you 'bout myself—(*Shaking his head with the repetition*)—and all you can say is eat them eggs and go to work.

RUTH (*wearily*):   Honey, you never say nothing new. I listen to you every day, every night and every morning, and you never say nothing new. (*Shrugging*) So you would rather *be* Mr. Arnold than be his chauffeur. So—I would *rather* be living in Buckingham Palace.

WALTER: That is just what is wrong with the colored woman in this world . . . Don't understand about building their men up and making 'em feel like they somebody. Like they can do something.

RUTH (*drily, but to hurt*):   There *are* colored men who do things.

WALTER: No thanks to the colored woman.

RUTH: Well, being a colored woman, I guess I can't help myself none.

(*She rises and gets the ironing board and sets it up and attacks a huge pile of rough-dried clothes, sprinkling them in preparation for the ironing and then rolling them into tight fat balls*)

WALTER (*mumbling*):   We one group of men tied to a race of women with small minds!

(*His sister BENEATHA enters. She is about twenty, as slim and intense as her brother. She is not as pretty as her sister-in-law, but her lean, almost intellectual face has a handsomeness of its own.*

She wears a bright-red flannel nightie, and her thick hair stands wildly about her head. Her speech is a mixture of many things; it is different from the rest of the family's insofar as education has permeated her sense of English—and perhaps the Midwest rather than the South has finally—at last—won out in her inflection; but not altogether, because over all of it is a soft slurring and transformed use of vowels which is the decided influence of the Southside. She passes through the room without looking at either RUTH *or* WALTER *and goes to the outside door and looks, a little blindly, out to the bathroom. She sees that it has been lost to the Johnsons. She closes the door with a sleepy vengeance and crosses to the table and sits down a little defeated)*

BENEATHA: I am going to start timing those people.

WALTER: You should get up earlier.

BENEATHA *(her face in her hands. She is still fighting the urge to go back to bed)*:   Really— would you suggest dawn? Where's the paper?

WALTER *(pushing the paper across the table to her as he studies her almost clinically, as though he has never seen her before)*:   You a horrible-looking chick at this hour.

BENEATHA *(drily)*:   Good morning, everybody.

WALTER *(senselessly)*:   How is school coming?

BENEATHA *(in the same spirit)*:   Lovely. Lovely. And you know, biology is the greatest. *(Looking up at him)* I dissected something that looked just like you yesterday.

WALTER: I just wondered if you've made up your mind and everything.

BENEATHA *(gaining in sharpness and impatience)*:   And what did I answer yesterday morning—and the day before that?

RUTH *(from the ironing board, like someone disinterested and old)*:   Don't be so nasty, Bennie.

BENEATHA *(still to her brother)*:   And the day before that and the day before that!

WALTER *(defensively)*:   I'm interested in you. Something wrong with that? Ain't many girls who decide—

WALTER *and* BENEATHA *(in unison)*:   —"to be a doctor."

(Silence)

WALTER: Have we figured out yet just exactly how much medical school is going to cost?

RUTH: Walter Lee, why don't you leave that girl alone and get out of here to work?

BENEATHA *(exits to the bathroom and bangs on the door)*:   Come on out of there, please!

(She comes back into the room)

WALTER *(looking at his sister intently)*:   You know the check is coming tomorrow.

BENEATHA *(turning on him with a sharpness all her own)*:   That money belongs to Mama, Walter, and it's for her to decide how she wants to use it. I don't care if she wants to buy a house or a rocket ship or just nail it up somewhere and look at it. It's hers. Not ours—*hers*.

WALTER *(bitterly)*:   Now ain't that fine! You just got your mother's interest at heart, ain't you, girl? You such a nice girl—but if Mama got that money she can always take a few thousand and help you through school too—can't she?

BENEATHA: I have never asked anyone around here to do anything for me!

WALTER: No! And the line between asking and just accepting when the time comes is big and wide—ain't it!

BENEATHA (*with fury*):   What do you want from me, Brother—that I quit school or just drop dead, which!

WALTER: I don't want nothing but for you to stop acting holy 'round here. Me and Ruth done made some sacrifices for you—why can't you do something for the family?

RUTH: Walter, don't be dragging me in it.

WALTER: You are in it—Don't you get up and go work in somebody's kitchen for the last three years to help put clothes on her back?

RUTH: Oh, Walter—that's not fair . . .

WALTER: It ain't that nobody expects you to get on your knees and say thank you, Brother; thank you, Ruth; thank you, Mama—and thank you, Travis, for wearing the same pair of shoes for two semesters—

BENEATHA (*dropping to her knees*):   Well—I *do*—all right?—thank everybody! And forgive me for ever wanting to be anything at all! (*Pursuing him on her knees across the floor*) FORGIVE ME, FORGIVE ME, FORGIVE ME!

RUTH: Please stop it! Your mama'll hear you.

WALTER: Who the hell told you you had to be a doctor? If you so crazy 'bout messing 'round with sick people—then go be a nurse like other women—or just get married and be quiet . . .

BENEATHA: Well—you finally got it said . . . It took you three years but you finally got it said. Walter, give up; leave me alone—it's Mama's money.

WALTER: *He was my father, too!*

BENEATHA: So what? He was mine, too—and Travis' grandfather—but the insurance money belongs to Mama. Picking on me is not going to make her give it to you to invest in any liquor stores—(*Underbreath, dropping into a chair*)—and I for one say, God bless Mama for that!

WALTER (*to* RUTH):   See—did you hear? Did you hear!

RUTH: Honey, please go to work.

WALTER: Nobody in this house is ever going to understand me.

BENEATHA: Because you're a nut.

WALTER: Who's a nut?

BENEATHA: You—you are a nut. Thee is mad, boy.

WALTER (*looking at his wife and his sister from the door, very sadly*):   The world's most backward race of people, and that's a fact.

BENEATHA (*turning slowly in her chair*):   And then there are all those prophets who would lead us out of the wilderness—(WALTER *slams out of the house*)—into the swamps!

RUTH: Bennie, why you always gotta be pickin' on your brother? Can't you be a little sweeter sometimes? (*Door opens.* WALTER *walks in. He fumbles with his cap, starts to speak, clears throat, looks everywhere but at* RUTH. *Finally:*)

WALTER (*to* RUTH):   I need some money for carfare.

RUTH (*looks at him, then warms; teasing, but tenderly*):   Fifty cents? (*She goes to her bag and gets money*) Here—take a taxi!

(WALTER *exits.* MAMA *enters. She is a woman in her early sixties, full-bodied and strong. She is one of those women of a certain grace and beauty who wear it so unobtrusively that it takes a while to notice. Her dark-brown face is surrounded by the total whiteness of her hair, and, being a woman who has adjusted to many things in life and overcome many more, her face is full of strength. She has, we can see, wit and faith of a kind that keep her eyes lit and full of interest and expectancy. She is, in a word, a beautiful woman. Her bearing is perhaps most like the noble bearing of the women of the Hereros of Southwest Africa—rather as if she imagines that as she walks she still bears a basket or a vessel upon her head. Her speech, on the other hand, is as careless as her carriage is precise—she is inclined to slur everything—but her voice is perhaps not so much quiet as simply soft)*

MAMA: Who that 'round here slamming doors at this hour?

(She crosses through the room, goes to the window, opens it, and brings in a feeble little plant growing doggedly in a small pot on the window sill. She feels the dirt and puts it back out)

RUTH: That was Walter Lee. He and Bennie was at it again.

MAMA: My children and they tempers. Lord, if this little old plant don't get more sun than it's been getting it ain't never going to see spring again. *(She turns from the window)* What's the matter with you this morning, Ruth? You looks right peaked. You aiming to iron all them things? Leave some for me. I'll get to 'em this afternoon. Bennie honey, it's too drafty for you to be sitting 'round half dressed. Where's your robe?

BENEATHA: In the cleaners.

MAMA: Well, go get mine and put it on.

BENEATHA: I'm not cold, Mama, honest.

MAMA: I know—but you so thin . . .

BENEATHA *(irritably)*:   Mama, I'm not cold.

MAMA *(seeing the make-down bed as* TRAVIS *has left it)*:   Lord have mercy, look at that poor bed. Bless his heart—he tries, don't he?

(She moves to the bed TRAVIS *has sloppily made up)*

RUTH: No—he don't half try at all 'cause he knows you going to come along behind him and fix everything. That's just how come he don't know how to do nothing right now—you done spoiled that boy so.

MAMA *(folding bedding)*:   Well—he's a little boy. Ain't supposed to know 'bout housekeeping. My baby, that's what he is. What you fix for his breakfast this morning?

RUTH *(angrily)*:   I feed my son, Lena!

MAMA: I ain't meddling—*(Underbreath; busy-bodyish)* I just noticed all last week he had cold cereal, and when it starts getting this chilly in the fall a child ought to have some hot grits or something when he goes out in the cold—

RUTH *(furious)*:   I gave him hot oats—is that all right!

MAMA: I ain't meddling. *(Pause)* Put a lot of nice butter on it? *(*RUTH *shoots her an angry look and does not reply)* He likes lots of butter.

RUTH *(exasperated)*:   Lena—

MAMA *(to* BENEATHA. MAMA *is inclined to wander conversationally sometimes)*:   What was you and your brother fussing 'bout this morning?

BENEATHA: It's not important, Mama.

(She gets up and goes to look out at the bathroom, which is apparently free, and she picks up her towels and rushes out)

MAMA: What was they fighting about?

RUTH: Now you know as well as I do.

MAMA (*shaking her head*):   Brother still worrying hisself sick about that money?

RUTH: You know he is.

MAMA: You had breakfast?

RUTH: Some coffee.

MAMA: Girl, you better start eating and looking after yourself better. You almost thin as Travis.

RUTH: Lena—

MAMA: Uh-hunh?

RUTH: What are you going to do with it?

MAMA: Now don't you start, child. It's too early in the morning to be talking about money. It ain't Christian.

RUTH: It's just that he got his heart set on that store—

MAMA: You mean that liquor store that Willy Harris want him to invest in?

RUTH: Yes—

MAMA: We ain't no business people, Ruth. We just plain working folks.

RUTH: Ain't nobody business people till they go into business. Walter Lee say colored people ain't never going to start getting ahead till they start gambling on some different kinds of things in the world—investments and things.

MAMA: What done got into you, girl? Walter Lee done finally sold you on investing.

RUTH: No. Mama, something is happening between Walter and me. I don't know what it is—but he needs something—something I can't give him any more. He needs this chance, Lena.

MAMA (*frowning deeply*):   But liquor, honey—

RUTH: Well—like Walter say—I spec people going to always be drinking themselves some liquor.

RUTH: Well—whether they drinks it or not ain't none of my business. But whether I go into business selling it to 'em *is,* and I don't want that on my ledger this late in life. (*Stopping suddenly and studying her daughter-in-law*) Ruth Younger, what's the matter with you today? You look like you could fall over right there.

RUTH: I'm tired.

MAMA: Then you better stay home from work today.

RUTH: I can't stay home. She'd be calling up the agency and screaming at them, "My girl didn't come in today—send me somebody! My girl didn't come in!" Oh, she just have a fit . . .

MAMA: Well, let her have it. I'll just call her up and say you got the flu—

RUTH (*laughing*):   Why the flu?

MAMA: 'Cause it sounds respectable to 'em. Something white people get, too. They know 'bout the flu. Otherwise they think you been cut up or something when you tell 'em you sick.

RUTH: I got to go in. We need the money.

MAMA: Somebody would of thought my children done all but starved to death the way they talk about money here late. Child, we got a great big old check coming tomorrow.

RUTH (*sincerely, but also self-righteously*):   Now that's your money. It ain't got nothing to do with me. We all feel like that—Walter and Bennie and me—even Travis.

MAMA (*thoughtfully, and suddenly very far away*):   Ten thousand dollars—

RUTH: Sure is wonderful.

MAMA: Ten thousand dollars.

RUTH: You know what you should do, Miss Lena? You should take yourself a trip somewhere. To Europe or South America or someplace—

MAMA (*throwing up her hands at the thought*):   Oh, child!

RUTH: I'm serious. Just pack up and leave! Go on away and enjoy yourself some. Forget about the family and have yourself a ball for once in your life—

MAMA (*drily*):   You should like I'm just about ready to die. Who'd go with me? What I look like wandering 'round Europe by myself?

RUTH: Shoot—these here rich white women do it all the time. They don't think nothing of packing up they suitcases and piling on one of them big steamships and— swoosh!—they gone, child.

MAMA: Something always told me I wasn't no rich white woman.

RUTH: Well—what are you going to do with it then?

MAMA: I ain't rightly decided. (*Thinking. She speaks now with emphasis*) Some of it got to be put away for Beneatha and her schoolin'—and ain't nothing going to touch that part of it. Nothing. (*She waits several seconds, trying to make up her mind about something, and looks at* RUTH *a little tentatively before going on*) Been thinking that we maybe could meet the notes on a little old two-story somewhere, with a yard where Travis could play in the summertime, if we use part of the insurance for a down payment and everybody kind of pitch in. I could maybe take on a little day work again, few days a week—

RUTH (*studying her mother-in-law furtively and concentrating on her ironing, anxious to encourage without seeming to*):   Well, Lord knows, we've put enough rent into this here rat trap to pay for four houses by now . . .

MAMA (*looking up at the words "rat trap" and then looking around and leaning back and sighing—in a suddenly reflective mood—*):   "Rat trap"—yes, that's all it is. (*Smiling*) I remember just as well the day me and Big Walter moved in here. Hadn't been married but two weeks and wasn't planning on living here no more than a year. (*She shakes her head at the dissolved dream*) We was going to set away, little by little, don't you know, and buy a little place out in Morgan Park. We had even picked out the house. (*Chuckling a little*) Looks right dumpy today. But Lord, child, you should know all the dreams I had 'bout buying that house and fixing it up and making me a little garden in the back— (*She waits and stops smiling*) And didn't none of it happen.

(*Dropping her hands in a futile gesture*)

RUTH (*keeps her head down, ironing*):   Yes, life can be a barrel of disappointments, sometimes.

MAMA: Honey, Big Walter would come in here some nights back then and slump down on that couch there and just look at the rug, and look at me and look at the rug and then back at me—and I'd know he was down then . . . really down. (*After a second very long and thoughtful pause; she is seeing back to times that only she can see*) And then, Lord, when I lost that baby—little Claude—I almost thought I was going to lose Big Walter too. Oh, that man grieved hisself! He was one man to love his children.

RUTH: Ain't nothin' can tear at you like losin' your baby.

MAMA: I guess that's how come that man finally worked hisself to death like he done. Like he was fighting his own war with this here world that took his baby from him.

RUTH: He sure was a fine man, all right. I always liked Mr. Younger.

MAMA: Crazy 'bout his children! God knows there was plenty wrong with Walter Younger—hard-headed, mean, kind of wild with women—plenty wrong with him. But he sure loved his children. Always wanted them to have something—be something. That's where Brother gets all these notions, I reckon. Big Walter used to say, he'd get right wet in the eyes sometimes, lean his head back with the water standing in his eyes and say, "Seem like God didn't see fit to give the black man nothing but dreams— but He did give us children to make them dreams seem worth while." (*She smiles*) He could talk like that, don't you know.

RUTH: Yes, he sure could. He was a good man, Mr. Younger.

MAMA: Yes, a fine man—just couldn't never catch up with his dreams, that's all.

(BENEATHA *comes in, brushing her hair and looking up to the ceiling, where the sound of a vacuum cleaner has started up*)

BENEATHA: What could be so dirty on that woman's rugs that she has to vacuum them every single day?

RUTH: I wish certain young women 'round here who I could name would take inspiration about certain rugs in a certain apartment I could also mention.

BENEATHA (*shrugging*):   How much cleaning can a house need, for Christ's sakes.

MAMA (*not liking the Lord's name used thus*):   Bennie!

RUTH: Just listen to her—just listen!

BENEATHA: Oh, God!

MAMA: If you use the Lord's name just one more time—

BENEATHA (*a bit of a whine*):   Oh, Mama—

RUTH: Fresh—just fresh as salt, this girl!

BENEATHA (*drily*):   Well—if the salt loses its savor—

MAMA: Now that will do. I just ain't going to have you 'round here reciting the scriptures in vain—you hear me?

BENEATHA: How did I manage to get on everybody's wrong side by just walking into a room?

RUTH: If you weren't so fresh—

BENEATHA: Ruth, I'm twenty years old.

MAMA: What time you be home from school today?

BENEATHA: Kind of late. (*With enthusiasm*) Madeline is going to start my guitar lessons today.

(MAMA *and* RUTH *look up with the same expression*)

MAMA: Your *what* kind of lessons?

BENEATHA: Guitar.

RUTH: Oh, Father!

MAMA: How come you done taken it in your mind to learn to play the guitar?

BENEATHA: I just want to, that's all.

MAMA (*smiling*):   Lord, child, don't you know what to do with yourself? How long it going to be before you get tired of this now—like you got tired of that little play-acting group you joined last year? (*Looking at* RUTH) And what was it the year before that?

RUTH: The horseback-riding club for which she bought that fifty-five-dollar riding habit that's been hanging in the closet ever since!

MAMA (*to* BENEATHA):   Why you got to flit so from one thing to another, baby?

BENEATHA (*sharply*): I just want to learn to play the guitar. Is there anything wrong with that?

MAMA: Ain't nobody trying to stop you. I just wonders sometimes why you has to flit so from one thing to another all the time. You ain't never done nothing with all that camera equipment you brought home—

BENEATHA: I don't flit! I—I experiment with different forms of expression—

RUTH: Like riding a horse?

BENEATHA: —People have to express themselves one way or another.

MAMA: What is it you want to express?

BENEATHA (*angrily*): Me! (MAMA *and* RUTH *look at each other and burst into raucous laughter*) Don't worry—I don't expect you to understand.

MAMA (*to change the subject*): Who you going out with tomorrow night?

BENEATHA (*with displeasure*): George Murchison again.

MAMA (*pleased*): Oh—you getting a little sweet on him?

RUTH: You ask me, this child ain't sweet on nobody but herself—(*Underbreath*) Express herself!

(*They laugh*)

BENEATHA: Oh—I like George all right, Mama. I mean I like him enough to go out with him and stuff, but—

RUTH (*for devilment*): What does *and stuff* mean?

BENEATHA: Mind your own business.

MAMA: Stop picking at her now, Ruth. (*She chuckles—then a suspicious sudden look at her daughter as she turns in her chair for emphasis*) What DOES it mean?

BENEATHA (*wearily*): Oh, I just mean I couldn't ever really be serious about George. He's—he's so shallow.

RUTH: Shallow—what do you mean he's shallow? He's *Rich*!

MAMA: Hush, Ruth.

BENEATHA: I know he's rich. He knows he's rich, too.

RUTH: Well—what other qualities a man got to have to satisfy you, little girl?

BENEATHA: You wouldn't even begin to understand. Anybody who married Walter could not possibly understand.

MAMA (*outraged*): What kind of way is that to talk about your brother?

BENEATHA: Brother is a flip—let's face it.

MAMA (*to* RUTH, *helplessly*): What's a flip?

RUTH (*glad to add kindling*): She's saying he's crazy.

BENEATHA: Not crazy. Brother isn't really crazy yet—he—he's an elaborate neurotic.

MAMA: Hush your mouth!

BENEATHA: As for George. Well. George looks good—he's got a beautiful car and he takes me to nice places and, as my sister-in-law says, he is probably the richest boy I will ever get to know and I even like him sometimes—but if the Youngers are sitting around waiting to see if their little Bennie is going to tie up the family with the Murchisons, they are wasting their time.

RUTH: You mean you wouldn't marry George Murchison if he asked you someday? That pretty, rich thing? Honey, I knew you was odd—

BENEATHA: No I would not marry him if all I felt for him was what I feel now. Besides, George's family wouldn't really like it.

MAMA: Why not?

BENEATHA: Oh, Mama—The Murchisons are honest-to-God-real-*live*-rich colored people, and the only people in the world who are more snobbish than rich white people are rich colored people. I thought everybody knew that. I've met Mrs. Murchison. She's a scene!

MAMA: You must not dislike people 'cause they well off, honey.

BENEATHA: Why not? It makes just as much sense as disliking people 'cause they are poor, and lots of people do that.

RUTH (*a wisdom-of-the-ages manner. To* MAMA):   Well, she'll get over some of this—

BENEATHA: Get over it? What are you talking about, Ruth? Listen, I'm going to be a doctor. I'm not worried about who I'm going to marry yet—if I ever get married.

MAMA *and* RUTH: *If!*

MAMA: Now, Bennie—

BENEATHA: Oh, I probably will . . . but first I'm going to be a doctor, and George, for one, still thinks that's pretty funny. I couldn't be bothered with that. I am going to be a doctor and everybody around here better understand that!

MAMA (*kindly*):   'Course you going to be a doctor, honey, God willing.

BENEATHA (*drily*):   God hasn't got a thing to do with it.

MAMA: Beneatha—that just wasn't necessary.

BENEATHA: Well—neither is God. I get sick of hearing about God.

MAMA: Beneatha!

BENEATHA: I mean it! I'm just tired of hearing about God all the time. What has He got to do with anything? Does he pay tuition?

MAMA: You 'bout to get your fresh little jaw slapped!

RUTH: That's just what she needs, all right!

BENEATHA: Why? Why can't I say what I want to around here, like everybody else?

MAMA: It don't sound nice for a young girl to say things like that—you wasn't brought up that way. Me and your father went to trouble to get you and Brother to church every Sunday.

BENEATHA: Mama, you don't understand. It's all a matter of ideas, and God is just one idea I don't accept. It's not important. I am not going out and be immoral or commit crimes because I don't believe in God. I don't even think about it. It's just that I get tired of Him getting credit for all the things the human race achieves through its own stubborn effort. There simply is no blasted God—there is only man and it is *he* who makes miracles!

(MAMA *absorbs this speech, studies her daughter and rises slowly and crosses to* BENEATHA *and slaps her powerfully across the face. After, there is only silence and the daughter drops her eyes from her mother's face, and* MAMA *is very tall before her*)

MAMA: Now—you say after me, in my mother's house there is still God. (*There is a long pause and* BENEATHA *stares at the floor wordlessly.* MAMA *repeats the phrase with precision and cool emotion*) In my mother's house there is still God.

BENEATHA: In my mother's house there is still God.

(*A long pause*)

MAMA (*walking away from* BENEATHA, *too disturbed for triumphant posture. Stopping and turning back to her daughter*):   There are some ideas we ain't going to have in this house. Not long as I am at the head of this family.

BENEATHA: Yes, ma'am.

(MAMA *walks out of the room*)

RUTH (*almost gently, with profound understanding*): You think you a woman, Bennie—but you still a little girl. What you did was childish—so you got treated like a child.

BENEATHA: I see. (*Quietly*) I also see that everybody thinks it's all right for Mama to be a tyrant. But all the tyranny in the world will never put a God in the heavens!

(*She picks up her books and goes out. Pause*)

RUTH (*goes to* MAMA'*s door*): She said she was sorry.

MAMA (*coming out, going to her plant*): They frightens me, Ruth. My children.

RUTH: You got good children, Lena. They just a little off sometimes—but they're good.

MAMA: No—there's something come down between me and them that don't let us understand each other and I don't know what it is. One done almost lost his mind thinking 'bout money all the time and the other done commence to talk about things I can't seem to understand in no form or fashion. What is it that's changing, Ruth.

RUTH (*soothingly, older than her years*): Now . . . you taking it all too seriously. You just got strong-willed children and it takes a strong woman like you to keep 'em in hand.

MAMA (*looking at her plant and sprinkling a little water on it*): They spirited all right, my children. Got to admit they got spirit—Bennie and Walter. Like this little old plant that ain't never had enough sunshine or nothing—and look at it . . .

(*She has her back to* RUTH, *who has had to stop ironing and lean against something and put the back of her hand to her forehead*)

RUTH (*trying to keep* MAMA *from noticing*): You . . . sure . . . loves that little old thing, don't you? . . .

MAMA: Well, I always wanted me a garden like I used to see sometimes at the back of the houses down home. This plant is close as I ever got to having one. (*She looks out of the window as she replaces the plant*) Lord, ain't nothing as dreary as the view from this window on a dreary day, is there? Why ain't you singing this morning, Ruth? Sing that "No Ways Tired." That song always lifts me up so—(*She turns at last to see that* RUTH *has slipped quietly to the floor, in a state of semiconsciousness*) Ruth! Ruth honey—what's the matter with you . . . Ruth!

Curtain

Scene II

It is the following morning; a Saturday morning, and house cleaning is in progress at the YOUNGERS. *Furniture has been shoved hither and yon and* MAMA *is giving the kitchen-area walls a washing down.* BENEATHA, *in dungarees, with a handkerchief tied around her face, is spraying insecticide into the cracks in the walls. As they work, the radio is on and a Southside disk-jockey program is inappropriately filling the house with a rather exotic saxophone blues.* TRAVIS, *the sole idle one, is leaning on his arms, looking out of the window.*

TRAVIS: Grandmama, that stuff Bennie is using smells awful. Can I go downstairs, please?

MAMA: Did you get all them chores done already? I ain't seen you doing much.

TRAVIS: Yes'm—finished early. Where did Mama go this morning?

MAMA (*looking at* BENEATHA):   She had to go on a little errand.

(*The phone rings.* BENEATHA *runs to answer it and reaches it before* WALTER, *who has entered from bedroom*)

TRAVIS: Where?

MAMA: To tend to her business.

BENEATHA: Haylo . . . (*Disappointed*) Yes, he is. (*She tosses the phone to* WALTER, *who barely catches it*) It's Willie Harris again.

WALTER (*as privately as possible under* MAMA'S *gaze*):   Hello, Willie. Did you get the papers from the lawyer? . . . No, not yet. I told you the mailman doesn't get here till ten-thirty . . . No, I'll come there . . . Yeah! Right away. (*He hangs up and goes for his coat*)

BENEATHA: Brother, where did Ruth go?

WALTER (*as he exits*):   How should I know!

TRAVIS: Aw come on, Grandma. Can I go outside?

MAMA: Oh, I guess so. You stay right in front of the house, though, and keep a good lookout for the postman.

TRAVIS: Yes'm. (*He darts into bedroom for stickball and bat, reenters, and sees* BENEATHA *on her knees spraying under sofa with behind upraised. He edges closer to the target, takes aim, and lets her have it. She screams*) Leave them poor little cockroaches alone, they ain't bothering you none! (*He runs as she swings the spray-gun at him viciously and playfully*) Grandma! Grandma!

MAMA: Look out there, girl, before you be spilling some of that stuff on that child!

TRAVIS (*safely behind the bastion of* MAMA):   That's right—look out, now! (*He exits*)

BENEATHA (*drily*):   I can't imagine that it would hurt him—it has never hurt the roaches.

MAMA: Well, little boys' hides ain't as tough as Southside roaches. You better get over there behind the bureau. I seen one marching out of there like Napoleon yesterday.

BENEATHA: There's really only one way to get rid of them, Mama—

MAMA: How?

BENEATHA: Set fire to this building! Mama, where did Ruth go?

MAMA (*looking at her with meaning*):   To the doctor, I think.

BENEATHA: The doctor? What's the matter? (*They exchange glances*) You don't think—

MAMA (*with her sense of drama*):   Now I ain't saying what I think. But I ain't never been wrong 'bout a woman neither.

(*The phone rings*)

BENEATHA (*at the phone*):   Hay-lo . . . (*Pause, and a moment of recognition*) Well—when did you get back! . . . And how was it? . . . Of course I've missed you—in my way . . . This morning? No . . . house cleaning and all that and Mama hates it if I let people come over when the house is like this . . . You *have*? Well, that's different . . . What is it—Oh, what the hell, come on over . . . Right, see you then. *Arrividerci.*

(*She hangs up*)

MAMA (*who has listened vigorously, as is her habit*):   Who is that you inviting over here with this house looking like this? You ain't got the pride you was born with!

BENEATHA: Asagai doesn't care how houses look, Mama—he's an intellectual.

MAMA: *Who?*

BENEATHA: Asagai—Joseph Asagai. He's an African boy I met on campus. He's been studying in Canada all summer.

MAMA: What's his name?

BENEATHA: Asagai, Joseph. Ah-sah-guy . . . He's from Nigeria.

MAMA: Oh, that's the little country that was founded by slaves way back . . .

BENEATHA: No, Mama—that's Liberia.

MAMA: I don't think I never met no African before.

BENEATHA: Well, do me a favor and don't ask him a whole lot of ignorant questions about Africans. I mean, do they wear clothes and all that—

MAMA: Well, now, I guess if you think we so ignorant 'round here maybe you shouldn't bring your friends here—

BENEATHA: It's just that people ask such crazy things. All anyone seems to know about when it comes to Africa is Tarzan—

MAMA (*indignantly*): Why should I know anything about Africa?

BENEATHA: Why do you give money at church for the missionary work?

MAMA: Well, that's to help save people.

BENEATHA: You mean save them from *heathenism*—

MAMA (*innocently*): Yes.

BENEATHA: I'm afraid they need more salvation from the British and the French.

(RUTH *comes in forlornly and pulls off her coat with dejection. They both turn to look at her*)

RUTH (*dispiritedly*): Well, I guess from all the happy faces—everybody knows.

BENEATHA: You pregnant?

MAMA: Lord have mercy, I sure hope it's a little old girl. Travis ought to have a sister.

(BENEATHA *and* RUTH *give her a hopeless look for this grandmotherly enthusiasm*)

BENEATHA: How far along are you?

RUTH: Two months.

BENEATHA: Did you mean to? I mean did you plan it or was it an accident?

MAMA: What do you know about planning or not planning?

BENEATHA: Oh, Mama.

RUTH (*wearily*): She's twenty years old, Lena.

BENEATHA: Did you plan it, Ruth?

RUTH: Mind your own business.

BENEATHA: It is my business—where is he going to live, on the *roof*? (*There is silence following the remark as the three women react to the sense of it*) Gee—I didn't mean that, Ruth, honest. Gee, I don't feel like that at all. I—I think it is wonderful.

RUTH (*dully*): Wonderful.

BENEATHA: Yes—really.

MAMA (*looking at* RUTH, *worried*): Doctor say everything going to be all right?

RUTH (*far away*): Yes—she says everything is going to be fine . . .

MAMA (*immediately suspicious*): "She"—What doctor you went to?

(RUTH *folds over, near hysteria*)

MAMA (*worriedly hovering over* RUTH): Ruth honey—what's the matter with you—you sick?

(RUTH *has her fists clenched on her thighs and is fighting hard to suppress a scream that seems to be rising in her*)

BENEATHA: What's the matter with her, Mama?

MAMA (*working her fingers in* RUTH'*s shoulders to relax her*):   She be all right. Women gets right depressed sometimes when they get her way. (*Speaking softly, expertly, rapidly*) Now you just relax. That's right . . . just lean back, don't think 'bout nothing at all . . . nothing at all—

RUTH: I'm all right . . .

(*The glassy-eyed look melts and then she collapses into a fit of heavy sobbing. The bell rings*)

BENEATHA: Oh, my God—that must be Asagai.

MAMA (*to* RUTH):   Come on now, honey. You need to lie down and rest awhile . . . then have some nice hot food.

(*They exit,* RUTH'*s weight on her mother-in-law.* BENEATHA, *herself profoundly disturbed, opens the door to admit a rather dramatic-looking young man with a large package*)

ASAGAI: Hello, Alaiyo—

BENEATHA (*holding the door open and regarding him with pleasure*):   Hello . . . (*Long pause*) Well—come in. And please excuse everything. My mother was very upset about my letting anyone come here with the place like this.

ASAGAI (*coming into the room*):   You look disturbed too . . . Is something wrong?

BENEATHA (*still at the door, absently*):   Yes . . . we've all got acute ghetto-itus. (*She smiles and comes toward him, finding a cigarette and sitting*) So—sit down! No! Wait! (*She whips the spraygun off sofa where she had left it and puts the cushions back. At last perches on arm of sofa. He sits*) So, how was Canada?

ASAGAI (*a sophisticate*):   Canadian.

BENEATHA (*looking at him*):   Asagai, I'm very glad you are back.

ASAGAI (*looking back at her in turn*):   Are you really?

BENEATHA: Yes—very.

ASAGAI: Why?—you were quite glad when I went away. What happened?

BENEATHA: You went away.

ASAGAI: Ahhhhhhhh.

BENEATHA: Before—you wanted to be so serious before there was time.

ASAGAI: How much time must there be before one knows what one feels?

BENEATHA (*stalling this particular conversation. Her hands pressed together, in a deliberately childish gesture*):   What did you bring me?

ASAGAI (*handing her the package*):   Open it and see.

BENEATHA (*eagerly opening the package and drawing out some records and the colorful robes of a Nigerian woman*):   Oh, Asagai! . . . You got them for me! . . . How beautiful . . . and the records too! (*She lifts out the robes and runs to the mirror with them and holds the drapery up in front of herself*)

ASAGAI (*coming to her at the mirror*):   I shall have to teach you how to drape it properly. (*He flings the material about her for the moment and stands back to look at her*) Ah—*Oh-pay-gay-day, oh-gbah-mu-shay.* (*A Yoruba exclamation for admiration*) You wear it well . . . very well . . . mutilated hair and all.

BENEATHA (*turning suddenly*): My hair—what's wrong with my hair?

ASAGAI (*shrugging*): Were you born with it like that?

BENEATHA (*reaching up to touch it*): No . . . of course not.

(*She looks back to the mirror, disturbed*)

ASAGAI (*smiling*): How then?

BENEATHA: You know perfectly well how . . . as crinkly as yours . . . that's how.

ASAGAI: And it is ugly to you that way?

BENEATHA (*quickly*): Oh, no—not ugly . . . (*More slowly, apologetically*) But it's so hard to manage when it's, well—raw.

ASAGAI: And so to accommodate that—you mutilate it every week?

BENEATHA: It's not mutilation!

ASAGAI (*laughing aloud at her seriousness*): Oh . . . please! I am only teasing you because you are so very serious about these things. (*He stands back from her and folds his arms across his chest as he watches her pulling at her hair and frowning in the mirror*) Do you remember the first time you met me at school? . . . (*He laughs*) You came up to me and you said—and I thought you were the most serious little thing I had ever seen—you said: (*He imitates her*) "Mr. Asagai—I want very much to talk with you. About Africa. You see, Mr. Asagai, I am looking for my *identity!*"

(*He laughs*)

BENEATHA (*turning to him, not laughing*): Yes—

(*Her face is quizzical, profoundly disturbed*)

ASAGAI (*still teasing and reaching out and taking her face in his hands and turning her profile to him*): Well . . . it is true that this is not so much a profile of a Hollywood queen as perhaps a queen of the Nile—(*A mock dismissal of the importance of the question*) But what does it matter? Assimilationism is so popular in your country.

BENEATHA (*wheeling, passionately, sharply*): I am not an assimilationist!

ASAGAI (*the protest hangs in the room for a moment and* ASAGAI *studies her, his laughter fading*): Such a serious one. (*There is a pause*) So—you like the robes? You must take excellent care of them—they are from my sister's personal wardrobe.

BENEATHA (*with incredulity*): You—you sent all the way home—for me?

ASAGAI (*with charm*): For you—I would do much more . . . Well, that is what I came for. I must go.

BENEATHA: Will you call me Monday?

ASAGAI: Yes . . . We have a great deal to talk about. I mean about identity and time and all that.

BENEATHA: Time?

ASAGAI: Yes. About how much time one needs to know what one feels.

BENEATHA: You see! You never understood that there is more than one kind of feeling which can exist between a man and a woman—or, at least, there should be.

ASAGAI (*shaking his head negatively but gently*): No. Between a man and a woman there need be only one kind of feeling. I have that for you . . . Now even . . . right this moment . . .

BENEATHA: I know—and by itself—it won't do. I can find that anywhere.

ASAGAI: For a woman it should be enough.

BENEATHA: I know—because that's what it says in all the novels that men write. But it isn't. Go ahead and laugh—but I'm not interested in being someone's little episode in America or—(*With feminine vengeance*)—one of them! (ASAGAI *has burst into laughter again*) That's funny as hell, huh!

ASAGAI: It's just that every American girl I have known has said that to me. White—black—in this you are all the same. And the same speech, too!

BENEATHA (*angrily*):   Yuk, yuk, yuk!

ASAGAI: It's how you can be sure that the world's most liberated women are not liberated at all. You all talk about it too much!

(MAMA *enters and is immediately all social charm because of the presence of a guest*)

BENEATHA: Oh—Mama—this is Mr. Asagai.

MAMA: How do you do?

ASAGAI (*total politeness to an elder*):   How do you do, Mrs. Younger. Please forgive me for coming at such an outrageous hour on a Saturday.

MAMA: Well, you are quite welcome. I just hope you understand that our house don't always look like this. (*Chatterish*) You must come again. I would love to hear all about—(*Not sure of the name*)—your country. I think it's so sad the way our American Negroes don't know nothing about Africa 'cept Tarzan and all that. And all that money they pour into these churches when they ought to be helping you people over there drive out them French and Englishmen done taken away your land.

(*The mother flashes a slightly superior look at her daughter upon completion of the recitation*)

ASAGAI (*taken aback by this sudden and acutely unrelated expression of sympathy*):   Yes . . . yes . . .

MAMA (*smiling at him suddenly and relaxing and looking him over*):   How many miles is it from here to where you come from?

ASAGAI: Many thousands.

MAMA (*looking at him as she would* WALTER):   I bet you don't half look after yourself, being away from your mama either. I spec you better come 'round here from time to time to get yourself some decent home-cooked meals . . .

ASAGAI (*moved*):   Thank you. Thank you very much. (*They are all quiet, then—*) Well . . . I must go. I will call you Monday, Alaiyo.

MAMA: What's that he call you?

ASAGAI: Oh—"Alaiyo." I hope you don't mind. It is what you would call a nickname, I think. It is a Yoruba word. I am a Yoruba.

MAMA (*looking at* BENEATHA):   I—I thought he was from—(*Uncertain*)

ASAGAI (*understanding*):   Nigeria is my country. Yoruba is my tribal origin—

BENEATHA: You didn't tell us what Alaiyo means . . . for all I know, you might be calling me Little Idiot or something . . .

ASAGAI: Well . . . let me see . . . I do not know how just to explain it . . . The sense of a thing can be so different when it changes languages.

BENEATHA: You're evading.

ASAGAI: No—really it is difficult . . . (*Thinking*) It means . . . it means One for Whom Bread—Food—Is Not Enough. (*He looks at her*) Is that all right?

BENEATHA (*understanding, softly*):   Thank you.

MAMA (*looking from one to the other and not understanding any of it*): Well . . . that's nice . . . You must come see us again—Mr.——

ASAGAI: Ah-sah-guy . . .

MAMA: Yes . . . Do come again.

ASAGAI: Good-bye.

(*He exits*)

MAMA (*after him*): Lord, that's a pretty thing just went out here! (*Insinuatingly, to her daughter*) Yes, I guess I see why we done commence to get so interested in Africa 'round here. Missionaries my aunt Jenny!

(*She exits*)

BENEATHA: Oh, Mama! . . .

(*She picks up the Nigerian dress and holds it up to her in front of the mirror again. She sets the headdress on haphazardly and then notices her hair again and clutches at it and then replaces the headdress and frowns at herself. Then she starts to wriggle in front of the mirror as she thinks a Nigerian woman might.* TRAVIS *enters and stands regarding her*)

TRAVIS: What's the matter, girl, you cracking up?

BENEATHA: Shut up.

(*She pulls the headdress off and looks at herself in the mirror and clutches at her hair again and squinches her eyes as if trying to imagine something. Then, suddenly, she gets her raincoat and kerchief and hurriedly prepares for going out*)

MAMA (*coming back into the room*): She's resting now. Travis, baby, run next door and ask Miss Johnson to please let me have a little kitchen cleanser. This here can is empty as Jacob's kettle.

TRAVIS: I just came in.

MAMA: Do as you told. (*He exits and she looks at her daughter*) Where you going?

BENEATHA (*halting at the door*): To become a queen of the Nile!

(*She exits in a breathless blaze of glory.* RUTH *appears in the bedroom doorway*)

MAMA: Who told you to get up?

RUTH: Ain't nothing wrong with me to be lying in no bed for. Where did Bennie go?

MAMA (*drumming her fingers*): Far as I could make out—to Egypt. (RUTH *just looks at her*) What time is it getting to?

RUTH: Ten twenty. And the mailman going to ring that bell this morning just like he done every morning for the last umpteen years.

(TRAVIS *comes in with the cleanser can*)

TRAVIS: She say to tell you that she don't have much.

MAMA (*angrily*): Lord, some people I could name sure is tight-fisted! (*Directing her grandson*) Mark two cans of cleanser down on the list there. If she that hard up for kitchen cleanser, I sure don't want to forget to get her none!

RUTH: Lena—maybe the woman is just short on cleanser—

MAMA (*not listening*): —Much baking powder as she done borrowed from me all these years, she could of done gone into the baking business!

(*The bell sounds suddenly and sharply and all three are stunned—serious and silent—mid-speech. In spite of all the other conversations and distractions of the morning, this is what they have been waiting for, even* TRAVIS, *who looks helplessly from his mother to his grandmother.* RUTH *is the first to come to life again*)

RUTH (*to* TRAVIS):   *Get down them steps, boy!*

(TRAVIS *snaps to life and flies out to get the mail*)

MAMA (*her eyes wide, her hand to her breast*):   You mean it done really come?

RUTH (*excited*):   Oh, Miss Lena!

MAMA (*collecting herself*):   Well . . . I don't know what we all so excited about 'round here for. We known it was coming for months.

RUTH: That's a whole lot different from having it come and being able to hold it in your hands . . . a piece of paper worth ten thousand dollars . . . (TRAVIS *bursts back into the room. He holds the envelope high above his head, like a little dancer, his face is radiant and he is breathless. He moves to his grandmother with sudden slow ceremony and puts the envelope into her hands. She accepts it, and then merely holds it and looks at it*) Come on! Open it . . . Lord have mercy, I wish Walter Lee was here!

TRAVIS: Open it, Grandmama!

MAMA (*staring at it*):   Now you all be quiet. It's just a check.

RUTH: Open it . . .

MAMA (*still staring at it*):   Now don't act silly . . . We ain't never been no people to act silly 'bout no money—

RUTH (*swiftly*):   We ain't never had none before—OPEN IT!

(MAMA *finally makes a good strong tear and pulls out the thin blue slice of paper and inspects it closely. The boy and his mother study it raptly over* MAMA's *shoulders*)

MAMA: *Travis!* (*She is counting off with doubt*) Is that the right number of zeros?

TRAVIS: Yes'm . . . ten thousand dollars. Gaalee, Grandmama, you rich.

MAMA (*she holds the check away from her, still looking at it. Slowly her face sobers into a mask of unhappiness*):   Ten thousand dollars. (*She hands it to* RUTH) Put it away somewhere, Ruth. (*She does not look at* RUTH; *her eyes seem to be seeing something somewhere very far off*) Ten thousand dollars they give you. Ten thousand dollars.

TRAVIS (*to his mother, sincerely*):   What's the matter with Grandmama—don't she want to be rich?

RUTH (*distractedly*):   You go on out and play now, baby. (TRAVIS *exits.* MAMA *starts wiping dishes absently, humming intently to herself.* RUTH *turns to her, with kind exasperation*) You've gone and got yourself upset.

MAMA (*not looking at her*):   I spec if it wasn't for you all . . . I would just put that money away or give it to the church or something.

RUTH: Now what kind of talk is that. Mr. Younger would just be plain mad if he could hear you talking foolish like that.

MAMA (*stopping and staring off*):   Yes . . . he sure would. (*Sighing*) We got enough to do with that money, all right. (*She halts then, and turns and looks at her daughter-in-law hard;* RUTH *avoids her eyes and* MAMA *wipes her hands with finality and starts to speak firmly to* RUTH) Where did you go today, girl?

RUTH: To the doctor.

MAMA (*impatiently*):   Now, Ruth . . . you know better than that. Old Doctor Jones is strange enough in his way but there ain't nothing 'bout him make somebody slip and call him "she"—like you done this morning.

RUTH: Well, that's what happened—my tongue slipped.

MAMA: You went to see that woman, didn't you?

RUTH (*defensively, giving herself away*):   What woman you talking about?

MAMA (*angrily*):   That woman who—

(WALTER *enters in great excitement*)

WALTER: Did it come?

MAMA (*quietly*):   Can't you give people a Christian greeting before you start asking about money?

WALTER (*to* RUTH):   Did it come? (RUTH *unfolds the check and lays it quietly before him, watching him intently with thoughts of her own.* WALTER *sits down and grasps it close and counts off the zeros*) Ten thousand dollars—(*He turns suddenly, frantically to his mother and draws some papers out of his breast pocket*) Mama—look. Old Willy Harris put everything on paper—

MAMA: Son—I think you ought to talk to your wife . . . I'll go on out and leave you alone if you want—

WALTER: I can talk to her later—Mama, look—

MAMA: Son—

WALTER: WILL SOMEBODY PLEASE LISTEN TO ME TODAY!

MAMA (*quietly*):   I don't 'low no yellin' in this house, Walter Lee, and you know it—(WALTER *stares at them in frustration and starts to speak several times*) And there ain't going to be no investing in no liquor stores.

WALTER: But, Mama, you ain't even looked at it.

MAMA: I don't aim to have to speak on that again.

(*A long pause*)

WALTER: You ain't looked at it and you don't aim to have to speak on that again? You ain't even looked at it and *you* have decided—(*Crumpling his papers*) Well, *you* tell that to my boy tonight when you put him to sleep on the living-room couch . . . (*Turning to* MAMA *and speaking directly to her*) Yeah—and tell it to my wife, Mama, to-morrow when she has to go out of here to look after somebody else's kids. And tell it to *me*, Mama, every time we need a new pair of curtains and I have to watch *you* go out and work in somebody's kitchen. Yeah, you tell me then!

(WALTER *starts out*)

RUTH: Where you going?

WALTER: I'm going out!

RUTH: Where?

WALTER: Just out of this house somewhere—

RUTH (*getting her coat*):   I'll come too.

WALTER: I don't want you to come!

RUTH: I got something to talk to you about, Walter.

WALTER: That's too bad.

MAMA (*still quietly*):   Walter Lee—(*She waits and he finally turns and looks at her*) Sit down.

WALTER: I'm a grown man, Mama.

MAMA: Ain't nobody said you wasn't grown. But you still in my house and my presence. And as long as you are—you'll talk to your wife civil. Now sit down.

RUTH (*suddenly*):   Oh, let him go on out and drink himself to death! He makes me sick to my stomach! (*She flings her coat against him and exits to bedroom*)

WALTER (*violently flinging the coat after her*):   And you turn mine too, baby! (*The door slams behind her*) That was my biggest mistake—

MAMA (*still quietly*):   Walter, what is the matter with you?

WALTER: Matter with me? Ain't nothing the matter with *me!*

MAMA: Yes there is. Something eating you up like a crazy man. Something more than me not giving you this money. The past few years I been watching it happen to you. You get all nervous acting and kind of wild in the eyes—(WALTER *jumps up impatiently at her words*) I said sit there now, I'm talking to you!

WALTER: Mama—I don't need no nagging at me today.

MAMA: Seem like you getting to a place where you always tied up in some kind of knot about something. But if anybody ask you 'bout it you just yell at 'em and bust out the house and go out and drink somewheres. Walter Lee, people can't live with that. Ruth's a good, patient girl in her way—but you getting to be too much. Boy, don't make the mistake of driving that girl away from you.

WALTER: Why—what she do for me?

MAMA: She loves you.

WALTER: Mama—I'm going out. I want to go off somewhere and be by myself for a while.

MAMA: I'm sorry 'bout your liquor store, son. It just wasn't the thing for us to do. That's what I want to tell you about—

WALTER: I got to go out, Mama—

(*He rises*)

MAMA: It's dangerous, son.

WALTER: What's dangerous?

MAMA: When a man goes outside his home to look for peace.

WALTER (*beseechingly*):   Then why can't there never be no peace in this house then?

MAMA: You done found it in some other house?

WALTER: No—there ain't no woman! Why do women always think there's a woman somewhere when a man gets restless. (*Picks up the check*) Do you know what this money means to me? Do you know what this money can do for us? (*Puts it back*) Mama—Mama—I want so many things . . .

MAMA: Yes, son—

WALTER: I want so many things that they are driving me kind of crazy . . . Mama—look at me.

MAMA: I'm looking at you. You a good-looking boy. You got a job, a nice wife, a fine boy and—

WALTER: A job. (*Looks at her*) Mama, a job? I open and close car doors all day long. I drive a man around in his limousine and I say, "Yes, sir; no, sir; very good, sir; shall I take the Drive, sir?" Mama, that ain't no kind of job . . . that ain't nothing at all. (*Very quietly*) Mama, I don't know if I can make you understand.

MAMA: Understand what, baby?

WALTER (*quietly*):   Sometimes it's like I can see the future stretched out in front of me—just plain as day. The future, Mama. Hanging over there at the edge of my days. Just waiting for me—a big, looming blank space—full of *nothing*. Just waiting for *me*. But it don't have to be. (*Pause. Kneeling beside her chair*) Mama—sometimes when I'm downtown and I pass them cool, quiet-looking restaurants where them white boys are sitting back and talking 'bout things . . . sitting there turning deals worth millions of dollars . . . sometimes I see guys don't look much older than me—

MAMA: Son—how come you talk so much 'bout money?

WALTER (*with immense passion*):   Because it is life, Mama!

MAMA (*quietly*):   Oh—(*Very quietly*) So now it's life. Money is life. Once upon a time freedom used to be life—now it's money. I guess the world really do change . . .

WALTER: No—it was always money, Mama. We just didn't know about it.

MAMA: No . . . something has changed. (*She looks at him*) You something new, boy. In my time we was worried about not being lynched and getting to the North if we could and how to stay alive and still have a pinch of dignity too . . . Now here come you and Beneatha—talking 'bout things we ain't never even thought about hardly, me and your daddy. You ain't satisfied or proud of nothing we done. I mean that you had a home; that we kept you out of trouble till you was grown; that you don't have to ride to work on the back of nobody's streetcar—You my children—but how different we done become.

WALTER (*a long beat. He pats her hand and gets up*):   You just don't understand, Mama, you just don't understand.

MAMA: Son—do you know your wife is expecting another baby? (WALTER *stands, stunned, and absorbs what his mother has said*) That's what she wanted to talk to you about. (WALTER *sinks down into a chair*) This ain't for me to be telling—but you ought to know. (*She waits*) I think Ruth is thinking 'bout getting rid of that child.

WALTER (*slowly understanding*):   —No—no—Ruth wouldn't do that.

MAMA: When the world gets ugly enough—a woman will do anything for her family. *The part that's already living.*

WALTER: You don't know Ruth, Mama, if you think she would do that.

(RUTH *opens the bedroom door and stands there a little limp*)

RUTH (*beaten*):   Yes I would too, Walter. (*Pause*) I gave her a five-dollar down payment.

(*There is total silence as the man stares at his wife and the mother stares at her son*)

MAMA (*presently*):   Well—(*Tightly*) Well—son, I'm waiting to hear you say something . . . (*She waits*) I'm waiting to hear how you be your father's son. Be the man he was . . . (*Pause. The silence shouts*) Your wife say she going to destroy your child. And I'm waiting to hear you talk like him and say we a people who give children life, not who destroys them—(*She rises*) I'm waiting to see you stand up and look like your daddy and say we done give up one baby to poverty and that we ain't going to give up nary another one . . . I'm waiting.

WALTER: Ruth—(*He can say nothing*)

MAMA: If you a son of mine, tell her! (WALTER *picks up his keys and his coat and walks out. She continues, bitterly*) You . . . you are a disgrace to your father's memory. Somebody get me my hat!

Curtain

ACT II

Scene I

Time: Later the same day.

At rise: RUTH *is ironing again. She has the radio going. Presently* BENEATHA's *bedroom door opens and* RUTH's *mouth falls and she puts down the iron in fascination.*

RUTH: What have we got on tonight!

BENEATHA (*emerging grandly from the doorway so that we can see her thoroughly robed in the costume Asagai brought*):   You are looking at what a well-dressed Nigerian woman wears—(*She parades for* RUTH, *her hair completely hidden by the headdress; she is coquettishly fanning herself with an ornate oriental fan, mistakenly more like Butterfly than any Nigerian that ever was*) Isn't it beautiful? (*She promenades to the radio and, with an arrogant flourish, turns off the good loud blues that is playing*) Enough of this assimilationist junk! (RUTH *follows her with her eyes as she goes to the phonograph and puts on a record and turns and waits ceremoniously for the music to come up. Then, with a shout—*) OCOMOGOSIAY!

(RUTH *jumps. The music comes up, a lovely Nigerian melody.* BENEATHA *listens, enraptured, her eyes far away—"back to the past." She begins to dance.* RUTH *is dumbfounded*)

RUTH: What kind of dance is that?
BENEATHA: A folk dance.
RUTH (*Pearl Bailey*):   What kind of folks do that, honey?
BENEATHA: It's from Nigeria. It's a dance of welcome.
RUTH: Who you welcoming?
BENEATHA: The men back to the village.
RUTH: Where they been?
BENEATHA: How should I know—out hunting or something. Anyway, they are coming back now . . .
RUTH: Well, that's good.
BENEATHA (*with the record*):
Alundi, alundi
Alundi alunya
Jop pu à jeepua
Ang gu sooooooooo
Ai yai yae . . .
Ayehaye—alundi . . .

(WALTER *comes in during this performance; he has obviously been drinking. He leans against the door heavily and watches his sister, at first with distaste. Then his eyes look off—"back to the past"—as he lifts both his fists to the roof, screaming*)

WALTER: YEAH . . . AND ETHIOPIA STRETCH FORTH HER HANDS AGAIN! . . .

RUTH (*drily, looking at him*):   Yes—and Africa sure is claiming her own tonight. (*She gives them both up and starts ironing again*)

WALTER (*all in a drunken, dramatic shout*):   Shut up! . . . I'm digging them drums . . . them drums move me! . . . (*He makes his weaving way to his wife's face and leans in close to her*) In my *heart of hearts*—(*He thumps his chest*)—I am much warrior!

RUTH (*without even looking up*):   In your heart of hearts you are much drunkard.

WALTER (*coming away from her and starting to wander around the room, shouting*):   Me and Jomo . . . (*Intently, in his sister's face. She has stopped dancing to watch him in this unknown mood*) That's my man, Kenyatta. (*Shouting and thumping his chest*) FLAMING SPEAR! HOT DAMN! (*He is suddenly in possession of an imaginary spear and actively spearing enemies all over the room*) OCOMOGOSIAY . . .

BENEATHA (*to encourage* WALTER, *thoroughly caught up with this side of him*):   OCO-MOGOSIAY, FLAMING SPEAR!

WALTER: THE LION IS WAKING . . . OWIMOWEH!

(*He pulls his shirt open and leaps up on the table and gestures with his spear*)

BENEATHA: OWIMOWEH!

WALTER (*on the table, very far gone, his eyes pure glass sheets. He sees what we cannot, that he is a leader of his people, a great chief, a descendant of Chaka, and that the hour to march has come*):   Listen, my black brothers—

BENEATHA: OCOMOGOSIAY!

WALTER: —Do you hear the waters rushing against the shores of the coastlands—

BENEATHA: OCOMOGOSIAY!

WALTER: —Do you hear the screeching of the cocks in yonder hills beyond where the chiefs meet in council for the coming of the mighty war—

BENEATHA: OCOMOGOSIAY!

(*And now the lighting shifts subtly to suggest the world of* WALTER*'s imagination, and the mood shifts from pure comedy. It is the inner* WALTER *speaking: the Southside chauffeur has assumed an unexpected majesty*)

WALTER: —Do you hear the beating of the wings of the birds flying low over the mountains and the low places of our land—

BENEATHA: OCOMOGOSIAY!

WALTER: —Do you hear the singing of the women, singing the war songs of our fathers to the babies in the great houses? Singing the sweet war songs! (*The doorbell rings*) OH, DO YOU HEAR, MY *BLACK* BROTHERS!

BENEATHA (*completely gone*):   We hear you, Flaming Spear—

(RUTH *shuts off the phonograph and opens the door.* GEORGE MURCHISON *enters*)

WALTER: Telling us to prepare for the GREATNESS OF THE TIME! (*Lights back to normal. He turns and sees* GEORGE) Black Brother!

(*He extends his hand for the fraternal clasp*)

GEORGE: Black Brother, hell!

RUTH (*having had enough, and embarrassed for the family*):   Beneatha, you got company—what's the matter with you? Walter Lee Younger, get down off that table and stop acting like a fool . . .

(WALTER *comes down off the table suddenly and makes a quick exit to the bathroom*)

RUTH: He's had a little to drink . . . I don't know what her excuse is.

GEORGE (*to* BENEATHA):   Look honey, we're going *to* the theatre—we're not going to be *in* it . . . so go change, huh?

(BENEATHA *looks at him and slowly, ceremoniously, lifts her hands and pulls off the headdress. Her hair is close-cropped and unstraightened.* GEORGE *freezes mid-sentence and* RUTH'*s eyes all but fall out of her head*)

GEORGE: What in the name of—

RUTH (*touching* BENEATHA'*s hair*):   Girl, you done lost your natural mind!? Look at your head!

GEORGE: What have you done to your head—I mean your hair!

BENEATHA: Nothing—except cut it off.

RUTH: Now that's the truth—it's what ain't been done to it! You expect this boy to go out with you with your head all nappy like that?

BENEATHA (*looking at* GEORGE):   That's up to George. If he's ashamed of his heritage—

GEORGE: Oh, don't be so proud of yourself, Bennie—just because you look eccentric.

BENEATHA: How can something that's natural be eccentric?

GEORGE: That's what being eccentric means—being natural. Get dressed.

BENEATHA: I don't like that, George.

RUTH: Why must you and your brother make an argument out of everything people say?

BENEATHA: Because I hate assimilationist Negroes!

RUTH: Will somebody please tell me what assimila-who-ever means!

GEORGE: Oh, it's just a college girl's way of calling people Uncle Toms—but that isn't what it means at all.

RUTH: Well, what does it mean?

BENEATHA (*cutting* GEORGE *off and staring at him as she replies to* RUTH):   It means someone who is willing to give up his own culture and submerge himself completely in the dominant, and in this case *oppressive* culture!

GEORGE: Oh, dear, dear, dear! Here we go! A lecture on the African past! On our Great West African Heritage! In one second we will hear all about the great Ashanti empires; the great Songhay civilizations; and the great sculpture of Bénin—and then some poetry in the Bantu—and the whole monologue will end with the word *heritage!* (*Nastily*) Let's face it, baby, your heritage is nothing but a bunch of raggedy-assed spirituals and some grass huts!

BENEATHA: GRASS HUTS! (RUTH *crosses to her and forcibly pushes her toward the bedroom*) See there . . . you are standing there in your splendid ignorance talking about people who were the first to smelt iron on the face of the earth! (RUTH *is pushing her through the door*) The Ashanti were performing surgical operations when the English— (RUTH *pulls the door to, with* BENEATHA *on the other side, and smiles graciously at* GEORGE. BENEATHA *opens the door and shouts the end of the sentence defiantly at* GEORGE)—were still tatooing themselves with blue dragons! (*She goes back inside*)

RUTH: Have a seat, George (*They both sit.* RUTH *folds her hands rather primly on her lap, determined to demonstrate the civilization of the family*) Warm, ain't it? I mean for September. (*Pause*) Just like they always say about Chicago weather: If it's too hot or cold for you, just wait a minute and it'll change. (*She smiles happily at this cliché of clichés*) Everybody say it's got to do with them bombs and things they keep setting off. (*Pause*) Would you like a nice cold beer?

GEORGE: No, thank you. I don't care for beer. (*He looks at his watch*) I hope she hurries up.

RUTH: What time is the show?

GEORGE: It's an eight-thirty curtain. That's just Chicago, though. In New York standard curtain time is eight forty.

(*He is rather proud of this knowledge*)

RUTH (*properly appreciating it*): You get to New York a lot?

GEORGE (*offhand*): Few times a year.

RUTH: Oh—that's nice. I've never been to New York.

(WALTER *enters. We feel he has relieved himself, but the edge of unreality is still with him*)

WALTER: New York ain't got nothing Chicago ain't. Just a bunch of hustling people all squeezed up together—being "Eastern."

(*He turns his face into a screw of displeasure*)

GEORGE: Oh—you've been?

WALTER: *Plenty* of times.

RUTH (*shocked at the lie*): Walter Lee Younger!

WALTER (*staring her down*): Plenty! (*Pause*) What we got to drink in this house? Why don't you offer this man some refreshment. (*To* GEORGE) They don't know how to entertain people in this house, man.

GEORGE: Thank you—I don't really care for anything.

WALTER (*feeling his head; sobriety coming*): Where's Mama?

RUTH: She ain't come back yet.

WALTER (*looking* MURCHISON *over from head to toe, scrutinizing his carefully casual tweed sports jacket over cashmere V-neck sweater over soft eyelet shirt and tie, and soft slacks, finished off with white buckskin shoes*): Why all you college boys wear them faggoty-looking white shoes?

RUTH: Walter Lee!

(GEORGE MURCHISON *ignores the remark*)

WALTER (*to* RUTH): Well, they look crazy as hell—white shoes, cold as it is.

RUTH (*crushed*): You have to excuse him—

WALTER: No he don't! Excuse me for what? What you always excusing me for! I'll excuse myself when I needs to be excused! (*A pause*) They look as funny as them black knee socks Beneatha wears out of here all the time.

RUTH: It's the college *style*, Walter.

WALTER: Style, hell. She looks like she got burnt legs or something!

RUTH: Oh, Walter—

WALTER (*an irritable mimic*): Oh, Walter! Oh, Walter! (*To* MURCHISON) How's your old man making out? I understand you all going to buy that big hotel on the Drive? (*He finds a beer in the refrigerator, wanders over to* MURCHISON, *sipping and wiping his lips with the back of his hand, and straddling a chair backwards to talk to the other man*) Shrewd move. Your old man is all right, man. (*Tapping his head and half winking for emphasis*) I mean he knows how to operate. I mean he thinks *big,* you know what I mean, I mean for a *home,* you know? But I think he's kind of running out of ideas now. I'd like to talk to him. Listen, man, I got some plans that could turn this city upside down. I mean think like he does. *Big.* Invest big, gamble big, hell, lose *big* if you have to, you know what I mean. It's hard to find a man on this whole Southside who understands my kind of thinking—you dig? (*He scrutinizes* MURCHISON *again, drinks his beer, squints his eyes and leans in close, confidential, man to man*) Me and you ought to sit down and talk sometimes, man. Man, I got me some ideas . . .

MURCHISON (*with boredom*):   Yeah—sometimes we'll have to do that, Walter.

WALTER (*understanding the indifference, and offended*):   Yeah—well, when you get the time, man. I know you a busy little boy.

RUTH: Walter, please—

WALTER (*bitterly, hurt*):   I know ain't nothing in this world as busy as you colored college boys with your fraternity pins and white shoes . . .

RUTH (*covering her face with humiliation*):   Oh, Walter Lee—

WALTER: I see you all all the time—with the books tucked under your arms—going to your (*British A—a mimic*) "clahsses." And for what! What the hell you learning over there? Filling up your heads—(*Counting off on his fingers*)—with the sociology and the psychology—but they teaching you how to be a man? How to take over and run the world? They teaching you how to run a rubber plantation or a steel mill? Naw—just to talk proper and read books and wear them faggoty-looking white shoes . . .

GEORGE (*looking at him with distaste, a little above it all*):   You're all wacked up with bitterness, man.

WALTER (*intently, almost quietly, between the teeth, glaring at the boy*):   And you—ain't you bitter, man? Ain't you just about had it yet? Don't you see no stars gleaming that you can't reach out and grab? You happy?—You contented son-of-a-bitch—you happy? You got it made? Bitter? Man, I'm a volcano. Bitter? Here I am a giant—surrounded by ants! Ants who can't even understand what it is the giant is talking about.

RUTH (*passionately and suddenly*):   Oh, Walter—ain't you with nobody!

WALTER (*violently*):   No! 'Cause ain't nobody with me! Not even my own mother!

RUTH: Walter, that's a terrible thing to say!

(BENEATHA *enters, dressed for the evening in a cocktail dress and earrings, hair natural*)

GEORGE: Well—hey—(*Crosses to* BENEATHA; *thoughtful, with emphasis, since this is a reversal*) You look great!

WALTER (*seeing his sister's hair for the first time*):   What's the matter with your head?

BENEATHA (*tired of the jokes now*):   I cut it off, Brother.

WALTER (*coming close to inspect it and walking around her*):   Well, I'll be damned. So that's what they mean by the African bush . . .

BENEATHA: Ha ha. Let's go, George.

GEORGE (*looking at her*):   You know something? I like it. It's sharp. I mean it really is. (*Helps her into her wrap*)

RUTH: Yes—I think so, too. (*She goes to the mirror and starts to clutch at her hair*)

WALTER: Oh no! You leave yours alone, baby. You might turn out to have a pin-shaped head or something!

BENEATHA: See you all later.

RUTH: Have a nice time.

GEORGE: Thanks. Good night. (*Half out the door, he reopens it. To* WALTER) Good night, Prometheus!

(BEANEATHA *and* GEORGE *exit*)

WALTER (*to* RUTH): Who is Prometheus?

RUTH: I don't know. Don't worry about it.

WALTER (*in fury, pointing after* GEORGE): See there—they get to a point where they can't insult you man to man—they got to go talk about something ain't nobody never heard of!

RUTH: How do you know it was an insult? (*To humor him*) Maybe Prometheus is a nice fellow.

WALTER: Prometheus! I bet there ain't even no such thing! I bet that simpleminded clown—

RUTH: Walter—

(*She stops what she is doing and looks at him*)

WALTER (*yelling*): Don't start!

RUTH: Start what?

WALTER: Your nagging! Where was I? Who was I with? How much money did I spend?

RUTH (*plaintively*): Walter Lee—why don't we just try to talk about it . . .

WALTER (*not listening*): I been out talking with people who understand me. People who care about the things I got on my mind.

RUTH (*wearily*): I guess that means people like Willy Harris.

WALTER: Yes, people like Willy Harris.

RUTH (*with a sudden flash of impatience*): Why don't you all just hurry up and go into the banking business and stop talking about it!

WALTER: Why? You want to know why? 'Cause we all tied up in a race of people that don't know how to do nothing but moan, pray and have babies!

(*The line is too bitter even for him and he looks at her and sits down*)

RUTH: Oh, Walter . . . (*Softly*) Honey, why can't you stop fighting me?

WALTER (*without thinking*): Who's fighting you? Who even cares about you?

(*This line begins the retardation of his mood*)

RUTH: Well—(*She waits a long time, and then with resignation starts to put away her things*) I guess I might as well go on to bed . . . (*More or less to herself*) I don't know where we lost it . . . but we have . . . (*Then, to him*) I—I'm sorry about this new baby, Walter. I guess maybe I better go on and do what I started . . . I guess I just didn't realize how bad things was with us . . . I guess I just didn't really realize—(*She starts out to the bedroom and stops*) You want some hot milk?

WALTER: Hot milk?

RUTH: Yes—hot milk.

WALTER: Why hot milk?

RUTH: 'Cause after all that liquor you come home with you ought to have something hot in your stomach.

WALTER: I don't want no milk.

RUTH: You want some coffee then?

WALTER: No, I don't want no coffee. I don't want nothing hot to drink. (*Almost plaintively*) Why you always trying to give me something to eat?

RUTH (*standing and looking at him helplessly*):   What *else* can I give you, Walter Lee Younger?

(*She stands and looks at him and presently turns to go out again. He lifts his head and watches her going away from him in a new mood which began to emerge when he asked her "Who cares about you?"*)

WALTER: It's been rough, ain't it, baby? (*She hears and stops but does not turn around and he continues to her back*) I guess between two people there ain't never as much understood as folks generally thinks there is. I mean like between me and you—(*She turns to face him*) How we gets to the place where we scared to talk softness to each other. (*He waits, thinking hard himself*) Why you think it got to be like that? (*He is thoughtful, almost as a child would be*) Ruth, what is it gets into people ought to be close?

RUTH: I don't know, honey. I think about it a lot.

WALTER: On account of you and me, you mean? The way things are with us. The way something done come down between us.

RUTH: There ain't so much between us, Walter . . . Not when you come to me and try to talk to me. Try to be with me . . . a little even.

WALTER (*total honesty*):   Sometimes . . . sometimes . . . I don't even know how to try.

RUTH: Walter—

WALTER: Yes?

RUTH (*coming to him, gently and with misgiving, but coming to him*):   Honey . . . life don't have to be like this. I mean sometimes people can do things so that things are better . . . You remember how we used to talk when Travis was born . . . about the way we were going to live . . . the kind of house . . . (*She is stroking his head*) Well, it's all starting to slip away from us . . .

(*He turns her to him and they look at each other and kiss, tenderly and hungrily. The door opens and* MAMA *enters—*WALTER *breaks away and jumps up. A beat*)

WALTER: Mama, where have you been?

MAMA: My—them steps is longer than they used to be. Whew! (*She sits down and ignores him*) How you feeling this evening, Ruth?

(RUTH *shrugs, disturbed at having been interrupted and watching her husband knowingly*)

WALTER: Mama, where have you been all day?

MAMA (*still ignoring him and leaning on the table and changing to more comfortable shoes*): Where's Travis?

RUTH: I let him go out earlier and he ain't come back yet. Boy, is he going to get it!

WALTER: Mama!

MAMA (*as if she has heard him for the first time*):   Yes, son?

WALTER: Where did you go this afternoon?

MAMA: I went downtown to tend to some business that I had to tend to.

WALTER: What kind of business?

MAMA: You know better than to question me like a child, Brother.

WALTER (*rising and bending over the table*):   Where were you, Mama? (*Bringing his fists down and shouting*) Mama, you didn't go do something with that insurance money, something crazy?

(*The front door opens slowly, interrupting him, and* TRAVIS *peeks his head in, less than hopefully*)

TRAVIS (*to his mother*):   Mama, I—

RUTH: "Mama I" nothing! You're going to get it, boy! Get on in that bedroom and get yourself ready!

TRAVIS: But I—

MAMA: Why don't you all never let the child explain hisself.

RUTH: Keep out of it now, Lena.

(MAMA *clamps her lips together, and* RUTH *advances toward her son menacingly*)

RUTH: A thousand times I have told you not to go off like that—

MAMA (*holding out her arms to her grandson*):   Well—at least let me tell him something. I want him to be the first one to hear . . . Come here, Travis. (*The boy obeys, gladly*) Travis—(*She takes him by the shoulder and looks into his face*)—you know that money we got in the mail this morning?

TRAVIS: Yes'm—

MAMA: Well—what you think your grandmama gone and done with that money?

TRAVIS: I don't know, Grandmama.

MAMA (*putting her finger on his nose for emphasis*):   She went out and she bought you a house! (*The explosion comes from* WALTER *at the end of the revelation and he jumps up and turns away from all of them in a fury.* MAMA *continues, to* TRAVIS) You glad about the house? It's going to be yours when you get to be a man.

TRAVIS: Yeah—I always wanted to live in a house.

MAMA: All right, gimme some sugar then—(TRAVIS *puts his arms around her neck as she watches her son over the boy's shoulder. Then, to* TRAVIS, *after the embrace*) Now when you say your prayers tonight, you thank God and your grandfather—'cause it was him who give you the house—in his way.

RUTH (*taking the boy from* MAMA *and pushing him toward the bedroom*):   Now you get out of here and get ready for your beating.

TRAVIS: Aw, Mama—

RUTH: Get on in there—(*Closing the door behind him and turning radiantly to her mother-in-law*) So you went and did it!

MAMA (*quietly, looking at her son with pain*):   Yes, I did.

RUTH (*raising both arms classically*):   PRAISE GOD! (*Looks at* WALTER *a moment, who says nothing. She crosses rapidly to her husband*) Please, honey—let me be glad . . . you be glad too. (*She has laid her hands on his shoulders, but he shakes himself free of her roughly, without turning to face her*) Oh, Walter . . . a home . . . a home. (*She comes back to* MAMA) Well—where is it? How big is it? How much it going to cost?

MAMA: Well—

RUTH: When we moving?

MAMA (*smiling at her*):   First of the month.

RUTH (*throwing back her head with jubilance*):   *Praise God!*

MAMA (*tentatively, still looking at her son's back turned against her and* RUTH):   It's—it's a nice house too . . . (*She cannot help speaking directly to him. An imploring quality in her voice, her manner, makes her almost like a girl now*) Three bedrooms—nice big one for you and Ruth. . . . Me and Beneatha still have to share our room, but Travis have one of his own—and (*With difficulty*) I figure if the—new baby—is a boy, we could get one of them double-decker outfits . . . And there's a yard with a little patch of dirt where I could maybe get to grow me a few flowers . . . And a nice big basement . . .

RUTH: Walter honey, be glad—

MAMA (*still to his back, fingering things on the table*):   'Course I don't want to make it sound fancier than it is . . . It's just a plain little old house—but it's made good and solid—and it will be *ours*. Walter Lee—it makes a difference in a man when he can walk on floors that belong to *him* . . .

RUTH: Where is it?

MAMA (*frightened at this telling*):   Well—well—it's out there in Clybourne Park—

(RUTH's *radiance fades abruptly, and* WALTER *finally turns slowly to face his mother with incredulity and hostility*)

RUTH: Where?

MAMA (*matter-of-factly*):   Four o six Clybourne Street, Clybourne Park.

RUTH: Clybourne Park? Mama, there ain't no colored people living in Clybourne Park.

MAMA (*almost idiotically*):   Well, I guess there's going to be some now.

WALTER (*bitterly*):   So that's the peace and comfort you went out and bought for us today!

MAMA (*raising her eyes to meet his finally*):   Son—I just tried to find the nicest place for the least amount of money for my family.

RUTH (*trying to recover from the shock*):   Well—well—'course I ain't one never been 'fraid of no crackers, mind you—but—well, wasn't there no other houses nowhere?

MAMA: Them houses they put up for colored in them areas way out all seem to cost twice as much as other houses. I did the best I could.

RUTH (*struck senseless with the news, in its various degrees of goodness and trouble, she sits a moment, her fists propping her chin in thought, and then she starts to rise, bringing her fists down with vigor, the radiance spreading from cheek to cheek again*):   Well—well!—All I can say is—if this is my time in life—MY TIME—to say good-bye—(*And she builds with momentum as she starts to circle the room with an exuberant, almost tearfully happy release*)—to these Goddamned cracking walls!—(*She pounds the walls*)—and these marching roaches!—(*She wipes at an imaginary army of marching roaches*)—and this cramped little closet which ain't now or never was no kitchen! . . . then I say it loud and good, HALLELUJAH! AND GOOD-BYE MISERY . . . I DON'T NEVER WANT TO SEE YOUR UGLY FACE AGAIN! (*She laughs joyously, having practically destroyed the apartment, and flings her arms up and lets them come down happily, slowly, reflectively, over her abdomen, aware for the first time perhaps that the life therein pulses with happiness and not despair*) Lena?

MAMA (*moved, watching her happiness*):   Yes, honey?

RUTH (*looking off*):   Is there—is there a whole lot of sunlight?

MAMA (*understanding*): Yes, child, there's a whole lot of sunlight.

(*Long pause*)

RUTH (*collecting herself and going to the door of the room* TRAVIS *is in*): Well—I guess I better see 'bout Travis. (*To* MAMA) Lord, I sure don't feel like whipping nobody today!

(*She exits*)

MAMA (*the mother and son are left alone now and the mother waits a long time, considering deeply, before she speaks*): Son—you—you understand what I done, don't you? (WALTER *is silent and sullen*) I—I just seen my family falling apart today . . . just falling to pieces in front of my eyes . . . We couldn't of gone on like we was today. We was going backwards 'stead of forwards—talking 'bout killing babies and wishing each other was dead . . . When it gets like that in life—you just got to do something different, push on out and do something bigger . . . (*She waits*) I wish you say something, son . . . I wish you'd say how deep inside you you think I done the right thing—

WALTER (*crossing slowly to his bedroom door and finally turning there and speaking measuredly*): What you need me to say you done right for? *You* the head of this family. You run our lives like you want to. It was your money and you did what you wanted with it. So what you need for me to say it was all right for? (*Bitterly, to hurt her as deeply as he knows is possible*) So you butchered up a dream of mine—you—who always talking 'bout your children's dreams . . .

MAMA: Walter Lee—

(*He just closes the door behind him.* MAMA *sits alone, thinking heavily*)

Curtain

Scene II

Time: Friday night. A few weeks later.

At rise: Packing crates mark the intention of the family to move. BENEATHA *and* GEORGE *come in, presumably from an evening out again.*

GEORGE: O.K. . . . O.K., whatever you say . . . (*They both sit on the couch. He tries to kiss her. She moves away*) Look, we've had a nice evening; let's not spoil it, huh? . . .

(*He again turns her head and tries to nuzzle in and she turns away from him, not with distaste but with momentary lack of interest; in a mood to pursue what they were talking about*)

BENEATHA: I'm *trying* to talk to you.
GEORGE: We always talk.
BENEATHA: Yes—and I love to talk.
GEORGE (*exasperated; rising*): I know it and I don't mind it sometimes . . . I want you to cut it out, see—The moody stuff, I mean. I don't like it. You're a nice-looking girl . . . all over. That's all you need, honey, forget the atmosphere. Guys aren't going to go for the atmosphere—they're going to go for what they see. Be glad for that. Drop the Garbo routine. It doesn't go with you. As for myself, I want a nice—(*Groping*)—simple (*Thoughtfully*)—sophisticated girl . . . not a poet—O.K.?

(He starts to kiss her, she rebuffs him again and he jumps up)

BENEATHA: Why are you angry, George?

GEORGE: Because this is stupid! I don't go out with you to discuss the nature of "quiet desperation" or to hear all about your thoughts—because the world will go on thinking what it thinks regardless—

BENEATHA: Then why read books? Why go to school?

GEORGE *(with artificial patience, counting on his fingers):*   It's simple. You read books—to learn facts—to get grades—to pass the course—to get a degree. That's all—it has nothing to do with thoughts.

(A long pause)

BENEATHA: I see. *(He starts to sit)* Good night, George.

(GEORGE looks at her a little oddly, and starts to exit. He meets MAMA coming in)

GEORGE: Oh—hello, Mrs. Younger.

MAMA: Hello, George, how you feeling?

GEORGE: Fine—fine, how are you?

MAMA: Oh, a little tired. You know them steps can get you after a day's work. You all have a nice time tonight?

GEORGE: Yes—a fine time. A fine time.

MAMA: Well, good night.

GEORGE: Good night. *(He exits.* MAMA *closes the door behind her)* Hello, honey. What you sitting like that for?

BENEATHA: I'm just sitting.

MAMA: Didn't you have a nice time?

BENEATHA: No.

MAMA: No? What's the matter?

BENEATHA: Mama, George is a fool—honest. *(She rises)*

MAMA *(hustling around unloading the packages she has entered with. She stops):*   Is he, baby?

BENEATHA: Yes.

(BENEATHA makes up TRAVIS' bed as she talks)

MAMA: You sure?

BENEATHA: Yes.

MAMA: Well—I guess you better not waste your time with no fools.

(BENEATHA looks up at her mother, watching her put groceries in the refrigerator. Finally she gathers up her things and starts into the bedroom. At the door she stops and looks back at her mother)

BENEATHA: Mama—

MAMA: Yes, baby—

BENEATHA: Thank you.

MAMA: For what?

BENEATHA: For understanding me this time.

(She exits quickly and the mother stands, smiling a little, looking at the place where BENEATHA just stood. RUTH enters)

RUTH: Now don't you fool with any of this stuff, Lena—

MAMA: Oh, I just thought I'd sort a few things out. Is Brother here?

RUTH: Yes.

MAMA (*with concern*): Is he—

RUTH (*reading her eyes*): Yes.

(MAMA *is silent and someone knocks on the door.* MAMA *and* RUTH *exchange weary and knowing glances and* RUTH *opens it to admit the neighbor,* MRS. JOHNSON,* *who is a rather squeaky wide-eyed lady of no particular age, with a newspaper under her arm*)

*This character and the scene of her visit were cut from the original production and early editions of the play.

MAMA (*changing her expression to acute delight and a ringing cheerful greeting*): Oh— hello there, Johnson.

JOHNSON (*This is a woman who decided long ago to be enthusiastic about EVERYTHING in life and she is inclined to wave her wrist vigorously at the height of her exclamatory comments*): Hello there, yourself! H'you this evening, Ruth?

RUTH (*not much of a deceptive type*): Fine, Mis' Johnson, h'you?

JOHNSON: Fine. (*Reaching out quickly, playfully, and patting* RUTH's *stomach*) Ain't you starting to poke out none yet! (*She mugs with delight at the over-familiar remark and her eyes dart around looking at the crates and packing preparation;* MAMA's *face is a cold sheet of endurance*) Oh, ain't we getting ready round here, though! Yessir! Lookathere! I'm telling you the Youngers is really getting ready to "move on up a little higher!"—Bless God!

MAMA (*a little drily, doubting the total sincerity of the Blesser*): Bless God.

JOHNSON: He's good, ain't He?

MAMA: Oh yes, He's good.

JOHNSON: I mean sometimes He works in mysterious ways . . . but He works, don't He!

MAMA (*the same*): Yes, he does.

JOHNSON: I'm just soooooo happy for y'all. And this here child—(*About* RUTH) looks like she could just pop open with happiness, don't she. Where's all the rest of the family?

MAMA: Bennie's gone to bed—

JOHNSON: Ain't no . . . (*The implication is pregnancy*) sickness done hit you—I hope . . . ?

MAMA: No—she just tired. She was out this evening.

JOHNSON (*all is a coo, an emphatic coo*): Aw—ain't that lovely. She still going out with the little Murchison boy?

MAMA (*drily*): Ummmm huh.

JOHNSON: That's lovely. You sure got lovely children, Younger. Me and Isaiah talks all the time 'bout what fine children you was blessed with. We sure do.

MAMA: Ruth, give Mis' Johnson a piece of sweet potato pie and some milk.

JOHNSON: Oh honey, I can't stay hardly a minute—I just dropped in to see if there was anything I could do. (*Accepting the food easily*) I guess y'all seen the news what's all over the colored paper this week . . .

MAMA: No—didn't get mine yet this week.

JOHNSON (*lifting her head and blinking with the spirit of catastrophe*): You mean you ain't read 'bout them colored people that was bombed out their place out there?

(RUTH *straightens with concern and takes the paper and reads it.* JOHNSON *notices her and feeds commentary*)

JOHNSON: Ain't it something how bad these here white folks is getting here in Chicago! Lord, getting so you think you right down in Mississippi! (*With a tremendous and rather insincere sense of melodrama*) 'Course I thinks it's wonderful how our folks keeps on pushing out. You hear some of these Negroes round here talking 'bout how they don't go where they ain't wanted and all that—but not me, honey! (*This is a lie*) Wilhemenia Othella Johnson goes anywhere, any time she feels like it! (*With head movement for emphasis*) Yes I do! Why if we left it up to these here crackers, the poor niggers wouldn't have nothing—(*She clasps her hand over her mouth*) Oh, I always forgets you don't 'low that word in your house.

MAMA (*quietly, looking at her*):   No—I don't 'low it.

JOHNSON (*vigorously again*):   Me neither! I was just telling Isaiah yesterday when he come using it in front of me—I said, "Isaiah, it's just like Mis' Younger says all the time—"

MAMA: Don't you want some more pie?

JOHNSON: No—no thank you; this was lovely. I got to get on over home and have my midnight coffee. I hear some people say it don't let them sleep but I finds I can't close my eyes right lessen I done had that laaaast cup of coffee . . . (*She waits. A beat. Undaunted*) My Goodnight coffee, I calls it!

MAMA (*with much eye-rolling and communication between herself and* RUTH):   Ruth, why don't you give Mis' Johnson some coffee.

(RUTH *gives* MAMA *an unpleasant look for her kindness*)

JOHNSON (*accepting the coffee*):   Where's Brother tonight?

MAMA: He's lying down.

JOHNSON: MMmmmmm, he sure gets his beauty rest, don't he? Good-looking man. Sure is a good-looking man! (*Reaching out to pat* RUTH'S *stomach again*) I guess that's how come we keep on having babies around here. (*She winks at* MAMA) One thing 'bout Brother, he always know how to have a *good* time. And soooooo ambitious! I bet it was his idea y'all moving out to Clybourne Park. Lord—I bet this time next month y'all's names will have been in the papers plenty—(*Holding up her hands to mark off each word of the headline she can see in front of her*) "NEGROES INVADE CLYBOURNE PARK—BOMBED!"

MAMA (*she and* RUTH *look at the woman in amazement*):   We ain't exactly moving out there to get bombed.

JOHNSON: Oh, honey—you know I'm praying to God every day that don't nothing like that happen! But you have to think of life like it is—and these here Chicago peckerwoods is some baaaad peckerwoods.

MAMA (*wearily*):   We done thought about all that Mis' Johnson.

(BENEATHA *comes out of the bedroom in her robe and passes through to the bathroom.* MRS. JOHNSON *turns*)

JOHNSON: Hello there, Bennie!

BENEATHA (*crisply*):   Hello, Mrs. Johnson.

JOHNSON: How is school?

BENEATHA (*crisply*):   Fine, thank you. (*She goes out.*)

JOHNSON (*insulted*):   Getting so she don't have much to say to nobody.

MAMA: The child was on her way to the bathroom.

JOHNSON: I know—but sometimes she act like ain't got time to pass the time of day with nobody ain't been to college. Oh—I ain't criticizing her none. It's just—you know how some of our young people gets when they get a little education. (MAMA *and* RUTH *say nothing, just look at her*) Yes—well. Well, I guess I better get on home. (*Unmoving*) 'Course I can understand how she must be proud and everything—being the only one in the family to make something of herself. I know just being a chauffeur ain't never satisfied Brother none. He shouldn't feel like that, though. Ain't nothing wrong with being a chauffeur.

MAMA: There's plenty wrong with it.

JOHNSON: What?

MAMA: Plenty. My husband always said being any kind of a servant wasn't a fit thing for a man to have to be. He always said a man's hands was made to make things, or to turn the earth with—not to drive nobody's car for 'em—or—(*She looks at her own hands*) carry they slop jars. And my boy is just like him—he wasn't meant to wait on nobody.

JOHNSON (*rising, somewhat offended*):   Mmmmmmmmmm. The Youngers is too much for me! (*She looks around*) You sure one proud-acting bunch of colored folks. Well—I always thinks like Booker T. Washington said that time—"Education has spoiled many a good plow hand"—

MAMA: Is that what old Booker T. said?

JOHNSON: He sure did.

MAMA: Well, it sounds just like him. The fool.

JOHNSON (*indignantly*):   Well—he was one of our great men.

MAMA: Who said so?

JOHNSON (*nonplussed*):   You know, me and you ain't never agreed about some things, Lena Younger. I guess I better be going—

RUTH (*quickly*):   Good night.

JOHNSON: Good night. Oh—(*Thrusting it at her*) You can keep the paper! (*With a trill*) 'Night.

MAMA: Good night, Mis' Johnson.

(MRS. JOHNSON *exits*)

RUTH: If ignorance was gold . . .

MAMA: Shush. Don't talk about folks behind their backs.

RUTH: You do.

MAMA: I'm old and corrupted. (BENEATHA *enters*) You was rude to Mis' Johnson, Beneatha, and I don't like it at all.

BENEATHA (*at her door*):   Mama, if there are two things we, as a people, have got to overcome, one is the Klu Klux Klan—and the other is Mrs. Johnson. (*She exits*)

MAMA: Smart aleck.

(*The phone rings*)

RUTH: I'll get it.

MAMA: Lord, ain't this a popular place tonight.

RUTH (*at the phone*):   Hello—Just a minute. (*Goes to door*) Walter, it's Mrs. Arnold. (*Waits. Goes back to the phone. Tense*) Hello. Yes, this is his wife speaking . . . He's lying down now. Yes . . . well, he'll be in tomorrow. He's been very sick. Yes—I know we should have called, but we were so sure he'd be able to come in today. Yes—yes, I'm very sorry. Yes . . . Thank you very much. (*She hangs up.* WALTER *is standing in the doorway of the bedroom behind her*) That was Mrs. Arnold.

WALTER (*indifferently*):   Was it?

RUTH: She said if you don't come in tomorrow that they are getting a new man . . .

WALTER: Ain't that sad—ain't that crying sad.

RUTH: She said Mr. Arnold has had to take a cab for three days . . . Walter, you ain't been to work for three days! (*This is a revelation to her*) Where you been, Walter Lee Younger? (WALTER *looks at her and starts to laugh*) You're going to lose your job.

WALTER: That's right . . . (*He turns on the radio*)

RUTH: Oh, Walter, and with your mother working like a dog every day—

(*A steamy, deep blues pours into the room*)

WALTER: That's sad too—Everything is sad.

MAMA: What you been doing for these three days, son?

WALTER: Mama—you don't know all the things a man what got leisure can find to do in this city . . . What's this—Friday night? Well—Wednesday I borrowed Willy Harris' car and I went for a drive . . . just me and myself and I drove and drove . . . Way out . . . way past South Chicago, and I parked the car and I sat and looked at the steel mills all day long. I just sat in the car and looked at them big black chimneys for hours. Then I drove back and I went to the Green Hat. (*Pause*) And Thursday—Thursday I borrowed the car again and I got in it and I pointed it the other way and I drove the other way—for hours—way, way up to Wisconsin, and I looked at the farms. I just drove and looked at the farms. Then I drove back and I went to the Green Hat. (*Pause*) And today—today I didn't get the car. Today I just walked. All over the Southside. And I looked at the Negroes and they looked at me and finally I just sat down on the curb at Thirty-ninth and South Parkway and I just sat there and watched the Negroes go by. And then I went to the Green Hat. You all sad? You all depressed? And you know where I am going right now—

(RUTH *goes out quietly*)

MAMA: Oh, Big Walter, is this the harvest of our days?

WALTER: You know what I like about the Green Hat? I like this little cat they got there who blows a sax . . . He blows. He talks to me. He ain't but 'bout five feet tall and he's got a conked head and his eyes is always closed and he's all music—

MAMA (*rising and getting some papers out of her handbag*):   Walter—

WALTER: And there's this other guy who plays the piano . . . and they got a sound. I mean they can work on some music . . . They got the best little combo in the world in the Green Hat . . . You can just sit there and drink and listen to them three men play and you realize that don't nothing matter worth a damn, but just being there—

MAMA: I've helped do it to you, haven't I, son? Walter I been wrong.

WALTER: Naw—you ain't never been wrong about nothing, Mama.

MAMA: Listen to me, now. I say I been wrong, son. That I been doing to you what the rest of the world been doing to you. (*She turns off the radio*) Walter—(*She stops and he looks up slowly at her and she meets his eyes pleadingly*) What you ain't never understood is that I ain't got nothing, don't own nothing, ain't never really wanted nothing that wasn't for you. There ain't nothing as precious to me . . . There ain't nothing worth holding on to, money, dreams, nothing else—if it means—if it means it's going to destroy my boy. (*She takes an envelope out of her handbag and puts it in front of him and he watches her without speaking or moving*) I paid the man thirty-five hundred dollars down on the house. That leaves sixty-five hundred dollars. Monday morning I want you to take this money and take three thousand dollars and put it in a savings account for Beneatha's medical schooling. The rest you put in a checking account—with your name on it. And from now on any penny that come out of it or that go in it is for you to look after. For you to decide. (*She drops her hands a little helplessly*) It ain't much, but it's all I got in the world and I'm putting it in your hands. I'm telling you to be the head of this family from now on like you supposed to be.

WALTER (*stares at the money*): You trust me like that, Mama?

MAMA: I ain't never stop trusting you. Like I ain't never stop loving you.

(*She goes out, and* WALTER *sits looking at the money on the table. Finally, in a decisive gesture, he gets up, and, in mingled joy and desperation, picks up the money. At the same moment,* TRAVIS *enters for bed*)

TRAVIS: What's the matter, Daddy? You drunk?

WALTER (*sweetly, more sweetly than we have ever known him*): No, Daddy ain't drunk. Daddy ain't going to never be drunk again. . . .

TRAVIS: Well, good night, Daddy.

(*The* FATHER *has come from behind the couch and leans over, embracing his son*)

WALTER: Son, I feel like talking to you tonight.

TRAVIS: About what?

WALTER: Oh, about a lot of things. About you and what kind of man you going to be when you grow up. . . . Son—son, what do you want to be when you grow up?

TRAVIS: A bus driver.

WALTER (*laughing a little*): A what? Man, that ain't nothing to want to be!

TRAVIS: Why not?

WALTER: 'Cause, man—it ain't big enough—you know what I mean.

TRAVIS: I don't know then. I can't make up my mind. Sometimes Mama asks me that too. And sometimes when I tell her I just want to be like you—she says she don't want me to be like that and sometimes she says she does. . . .

WALTER (*gathering him up in his arms*): You know what, Travis? In seven years you going to be seventeen years old. And things is going to be very different with us in seven years, Travis. . . . One day when you are seventeen I'll come home—home from my office downtown somewhere—

TRAVIS: You don't work in no office, Daddy.

WALTER: No—but after tonight. After what your daddy gonna do tonight, there's going to be offices—a whole lot of offices. . . .

TRAVIS: What you gonna do tonight, Daddy?

WALTER: You wouldn't understand yet, son, but your daddy's gonna make a transaction . . . a business transaction that's going to change our lives. . . . That's how come one day when you 'bout seventeen years old I'll come home and I'll be pretty tired, you know what I mean, after a day of conferences and secretaries getting things wrong the way they do . . . 'cause an executive's life is hell, man—(*The more he talks the farther away he gets*) And I'll pull the car up on the driveway . . . just a plain black Chrysler, I think, with white walls—no—black tires. More elegant. Rich people don't have to be flashy . . . though I'll have to get something a little sportier for Ruth—maybe a Cadillac convertible to do her shopping in. . . . And I'll come up the steps to the house and the gardener will be clipping away at the hedges and he'll say, "Good evening, Mr. Younger." And I'll say, "Hello, Jefferson, how are you this evening?" And I'll go inside and Ruth will come downstairs and meet me at the door and we'll kiss each other and she'll take my arm and we'll go up to your room to see you sitting on the floor with the catalogues of all the great schools in America around you. . . . All the great schools in the world! And—and I'll say, all right son—it's your seventeenth birthday, what is it you've decided? . . . Just tell me where you want to go to school and you'll *go*. Just tell me, what it is you want to be—and you'll *be* it. . . . Whatever you want to be—Yessir! (*He holds his arms open for* TRAVIS) You just name it, son . . . (TRAVIS *leaps into them*) and I hand you the world!

(WALTER's *voice has risen in pitch and hysterical promise and on the last line he lifts* TRAVIS *high*)

(Blackout)

Scene III

Time: Saturday, moving day, one week later.
Before the curtain rises, RUTH's *voice, a strident, dramatic church alto, cuts through the silence.*
It is, in the darkness, a triumphant surge, a penetrating statement of expectation: "Oh, Lord, *I don't feel no ways tired! Children, oh, glory hallelujah!"*
As the curtain rises we see that RUTH *is alone in the living room, finishing up the family's packing. It is moving day. She is nailing crates and tying cartons.* BENEATHA *enters, carrying a guitar case, and watches her exuberant sister-in-law.*

RUTH: Hey!
BENEATHA (*putting away the case*): Hi.
RUTH (*pointing at a package*): Honey—look in that package there and see what I found on sale this morning at the South Center. (RUTH *gets up and moves to the package and draws out some curtains*) Lookahere—hand-turned hems!
BENEATHA: How do you know the window size out there?
RUTH (*who hadn't thought of that*): Oh—Well, they bound to fit something in the whole house. Anyhow, they was too good a bargain to pass up. (RUTH *slaps her head, suddenly remembering something*) Oh, Bennie—I meant to put a special note on that carton over there. That's your mama's good china and she wants 'em to be very careful with it.
BENEATHA: I'll do it.

(BENEATHA *finds a piece of paper and starts to draw large letters on it*)

RUTH: You know what I'm going to do soon as I get in that new house?
BENEATHA: What?
RUTH: Honey—I'm going to run me a tub of water up to here . . . (*With her fingers practically up to her nostrils*) And I'm going to get in it—and I am going to sit . . . and sit . . . and sit in that hot water and the first person who knocks to tell *me* to hurry up and come out—
BENEATHA: Gets shot at sunrise.
RUTH (*laughing happily*): You said it, sister! (*Noticing how large* BENEATHA *is absent-mindedly making the note*) Honey, they ain't going to read that from no airplane.

BENEATHA (*laughing herself*):   I guess I always think things have more emphasis if they are big, somehow.

RUTH (*looking up at her and smiling*):   You and your brother seem to have that as a philosophy of life. Lord, that man—done changed so 'round here. You know—you know what we did last night? Me and Walter Lee?

BENEATHA: What?

RUTH (*smiling to herself*):   We went to the movies. (*Looking at* BENEATHA *to see if she understands*) We went to the movies. You know the last time me and Walter went to the movies together?

BENEATHA: No.

RUTH: Me neither. That's how long it been. (*Smiling again*) But we went last night. The picture wasn't much good, but that didn't seem to matter. We went—and we held hands.

BENEATHA: Oh, Lord!

RUTH: We held hands—and you know what?

BENEATHA: What?

RUTH: When we come out of the show it was late and dark and all the stores and things was closed up . . . and it was kind of chilly and there wasn't many people on the streets . . . and we was still holding hands, me and Walter.

BENEATHA: You're killing me.

(WALTER *enters with a large package. His happiness is deep in him; he cannot keep still with his new-found exuberance. He is singing and wiggling and snapping his fingers. He puts his package in a corner and puts a phonograph record, which he has brought in with him, on the record player. As the music, soulful and sensuous, comes up he dances over to* RUTH *and tries to get her to dance with him. She gives in at last to his raunchiness and in a fit of giggling allows herself to be drawn into his mood. They dip and she melts into his arms in a classic, body-melding "slow drag"*)

BENEATHA (*regarding them a long time as they dance, then drawing in her breath for a deeply exaggerated comment which she does not particularly mean*):   Talk about—olddddddddddd-fashionedddddddd—Negroes!

WALTER (*stopping momentarily*):   What kind of Negroes? (*He says this in fun. He is not angry with her today, nor with anyone. He starts to dance with his wife again*)

BENEATHA: Old-fashioned.

WALTER (*as he dances with* RUTH):   You know, when these *New Negroes* have their convention—(*Pointing at his sister*)—that is going to be the chairman of the Committee on Unending Agitation. (*He goes on dancing, then stops*) Race, race, race! . . . Girl, I do believe you are the first person in the history of the entire human race to successfully brainwash yourself. (BENEATHA *breaks up and he goes on dancing. He stops again, enjoying his tease*) Damn, even the N double A C P takes a holiday sometimes! (BENEATHA *and* RUTH *laugh. He dances with* RUTH *some more and starts to laugh and stops and pantomimes someone over an operating table*) I can just see that chick someday looking down at some poor cat on an operating table and before she starts to slice him, she says . . . (*Pulling his sleeves back maliciously*) "By the way, what are your views on civil rights down there? . . . "

(*He laughs at her again and starts to dance happily. The bell sounds*)

BENEATHA: Sticks and stones may break my bones but . . . words will never hurt me!

(BENEATHA *goes to the door and opens it as* WALTER *and* RUTH *go on with the clowning.* BENEATHA *is somewhat surprised to see a quiet-looking middle-aged white man in a business suit holding his hat and a briefcase in his hand and consulting a small piece of paper*)

MAN: Uh—how do you do, miss. I am looking for a Mrs.—(*He looks at the slip of paper*) Mrs. Lena Younger? (*He stops short, struck dumb at the sight of the oblivious* WALTER *and* RUTH)

BENEATHA (*smoothing her hair with slight embarrassment*):   Oh—yes, that's my mother. Excuse me (*She closes the door and turns to quiet the other two*) Ruth! Brother! (*Enunciating precisely but soundlessly:* "There's a white man at the door!" *They stop dancing,* RUTH *cuts off the phonograph,* BENEATHA *opens the door. The man casts a curious quick glance at all of them*) Uh—come in please.

MAN (*coming in*):   Thank you.

BENEATHA: My mother isn't here just now. Is it business?

MAN: Yes . . . well, of a sort.

WALTER (*freely, the Man of the House*):   Have a seat. I'm Mrs. Younger's son. I look after most of her business matters.

(RUTH *and* BENEATHA *exchange amused glances*)

MAN (*regarding* WALTER, *and sitting*):   Well—My name is Karl Lindner . . .

WALTER (*stretching out his hand*):   Walter Younger. This is my wife—(RUTH *nods politely*)—and my sister.

LINDNER: How do you do.

WALTER (*amiably, as he sits himself easily on a chair, leaning forward on his knees with interest and looking expectantly into the newcomer's face*):   What can we do for you, Mr. Lindner!

LINDNER (*some minor shuffling of the hat and briefcase on his knees*):   Well—I am a representative of the Clybourne Park Improvement Association—

WALTER (*pointing*):   Why don't you sit your things on the floor?

LINDNER: Oh—yes. Thank you. (*He slides the briefcase and hat under the chair*) And as I was saying—I am from the Clybourne Park Improvement Association and we have had it brought to our attention at the last meeting that you people—or at least your mother—has bought a piece of residential property at—(*He digs for the slip of paper again*)—four o six Clybourne Street . . .

WALTER: That's right. Care for something to drink? Ruth, get Mr. Lindner a beer.

LINDNER (*upset for some reason*):   Oh—no, really. I mean thank you very much, but no thank you.

RUTH (*innocently*):   Some coffee?

LINDNER: Thank you, nothing at all.

(BENEATHA *is watching the man carefully*)

LINDNER: Well, I don't know how much you folks know about our organization. (*He is a gentle man; thoughtful and somewhat labored in his manner*) It is one of these community organizations set up to look after—oh, you know, things like block upkeep and special projects and we also have what we call our New Neighbors Orientation Committee . . .

BENEATHA (*drily*):   Yes—and what do they do?

LINDNER (*turning a little to her and then returning the main force to* WALTER): Well—it's what you might call a sort of welcoming committee, I guess. I mean they, we—I'm the chairman of the committee—go around and see the new people who move into the neighborhood and sort of give them the lowdown on the way we do things in Clybourne Park.

BENEATHA (*with appreciation of the two meanings, which escape* RUTH *and* WALTER): Un-huh.

LINDNER: And we also have the category of what the association calls—(*He looks elsewhere*)—uh—special community problems . . .

BENEATHA: Yes—and what are some of those?

WALTER: Girl, let the man talk.

LINDNER (*with understated relief*): Thank you. I would sort of like to explain this thing in my own way. I mean I want to explain to you in a certain way.

WALTER: Go ahead.

LINDNER: Yes. Well. I'm going to try to get right to the point. I'm sure we'll all appreciate that in the long run.

BENEATHA: Yes.

WALTER: Be still now!

LINDNER: Well—

RUTH (*still innocently*): Would you like another chair—you don't look comfortable.

LINDNER (*more frustrated than annoyed*): No, thank you very much. Please. Well—to get right to the point I—(*A great breath, and he is off at last*) I am sure you people must be aware of some of the incidents which have happened in various parts of the city when colored people have moved into certain areas—(BENEATHA *exhales heavily and starts tossing a piece of fruit up and down in the air*) Well—because we have what I think is going to be a unique type of organization in American community life—not only do we deplore that kind of thing—but we are trying to do something about it. (BENEATHA *stops tossing and turns with a new and quizzical interest to the man*) We feel—(*gaining confidence in his mission because of the interest in the faces of the people he is talking to*)—we feel that most of the trouble in this world, when you come right down to it—(*He hits his knee for emphasis*)—most of the trouble exists because people just don't sit down and talk to each other.

RUTH (*nodding as she might in church, pleased with the remark*): You can say that again, mister.

LINDNER (*more encouraged by such affirmation*): That we don't try hard enough in this world to understand the other fellow's problem. The other guy's point of view.

RUTH: Now that's right.

(BENEATHA *and* WALTER *merely watch and listen with genuine interest*)

LINDNER: Yes—that's the way we feel out in Clybourne Park. And that's why I was elected to come here this afternoon and talk to you people. Friendly like, you know, the way people should talk to each other and see if we couldn't find some way to work this thing out. As I say, the whole business is a matter of *caring* about the other fellow. Anybody can see that you are a nice family of folks, hard working and honest I'm sure. (BENEATHA *frowns slightly, quizzically, her head tilted regarding him*) Today everybody knows what it means to be on the outside of *something*. And of course, there is always somebody who is out to take advantage of people who don't always understand.

WALTER: What do you mean?

LINDNER: Well—you see our community is made up of people who've worked hard as the dickens for years to build up that little community. They're not rich and fancy people; just hard-working, honest people who don't really have much but those little homes and a dream of the kind of community they want to raise their children in. Now, I don't say we are perfect and there is a lot wrong in some of the things they want. But you've got to admit that a man, right or wrong, has the right to want to have the neighborhood he lives in a certain kind of way. And at the moment the overwhelming majority of our people out there feel that people get along better, take more of a common interest in the life of the community, when they share a common background. I want you to believe me when I tell you that race prejudice simply doesn't enter into it. It is a matter of the people of Clybourne Park believing, rightly or wrongly, as I say, that for the happiness of all concerned that our Negro families are happier when they live in their *own* communities.

BENEATHA (*with a grand and bitter gesture*):   This, friends, is the Welcoming Committee!

WALTER (*dumbfounded, looking at* LINDNER):   Is this what you came marching all the way over here to tell us?

LINDNER: Well, now we've been having a fine conversation. I hope you'll hear me all the way through.

WALTER (*tightly*):   Go ahead, man.

LINDNER: You see—in the face of all the things I have said, we are prepared to make your family a very generous offer . . .

BENEATHA: Thirty pieces and not a coin less!

WALTER: Yeah?

LINDNER (*putting on his glasses and drawing a form out of the briefcase*):   Our association is prepared, through the collective effort of our people, to buy the house from you at a financial gain to your family.

RUTH: Lord have mercy, ain't this the living gall!

WALTER: All right, you through?

LINDNER: Well, I want to give you the exact terms of the financial arrangement—

WALTER: We don't want to hear no exact terms of no arrangements. I want to know if you got any more to tell us 'bout getting together?

LINDNER (*taking off his glasses*):   Well—I don't suppose that you feel . . .

WALTER: Never mind how I feel—you got any more to say 'bout how people ought to sit down and talk to each other? . . . Get out of my house, man.

(*He turns his back and walks to the door*)

LINDNER (*Looking around at the hostile faces and reaching and assembling his hat and briefcase*):   Well—I don't understand why you people are reacting this way. What do you think you are going to gain by moving into a neighborhood where you just aren't wanted and where some elements—well—people can get awful worked up when they feel that their whole way of life and everything they've ever worked for is threatened.

WALTER: Get out.

LINDNER (*at the door, holding a small card*):   Well—I'm sorry it went like this.

WALTER: Get out.

LINDNER (*almost sadly regarding* WALTER):   You just can't force people to change their hearts, son.

(*He turns and put his card on a table and exits.* WALTER *pushes the door to with stinging hatred, and stands looking at it.* RUTH *just sits and* BENEATHA *just stands. They say nothing.* MAMA *and* TRAVIS *enter*)

MAMA: Well—this all the packing got done since I left out of here this morning. I testify before God that my children got all the energy of the *dead!* What time the moving men due?

BENEATHA: Four o'clock. You had a caller, Mama.

(*She is smiling, teasingly*)

MAMA: Sure enough—who?

BENEATHA (*her arms folded saucily*):   The Welcoming Committee.

(WALTER *and* RUTH *giggle*)

MAMA (*innocently*):   Who?

BENEATHA: The Welcoming Committee. They said they're sure going to be glad to see you when you get there.

WALTER (*devilishly*):   Yeah, they said they can't hardly wait to see your face.

(*Laughter*)

MAMA (*sensing their facetiousness*):   What's the matter with you all?

WALTER: Ain't nothing the matter with us. We just telling you 'bout the gentleman who came to see you this afternoon. From the Clybourne Park Improvement Association.

MAMA: What he want?

RUTH (*in the same mood as* BENEATHA *and* WALTER):   To welcome you, honey.

WALTER: He said they can't hardly wait. He said the one thing they don't have, that they just *dying* to have out there is a fine family of fine colored people! (*To* RUTH *and* BENEATHA) Ain't that right!

RUTH (*mockingly*):   Yeah! He left his card—

BENEATHA (*handing card to* MAMA):   In case.

(MAMA *reads and throws it on the floor—understanding and looking off as she draws her chair up to the table on which she has put her plant and some sticks and some cord*)

MAMA: Father, give us strength. (*Knowingly—and without fun*) Did he threaten us?

BENEATHA: Oh—Mama—they don't do it like that any more. He talked Brotherhood. He said everybody ought to learn how to sit down and hate each other with good Christian fellowship.

(*She and* WALTER *shake hands to ridicule the remark*)

MAMA (*sadly*):   Lord, protect us . . .

RUTH: You should hear the money those folks raised to buy the house from us. All we paid and then some.

BENEATHA: What they think we going to do—eat 'em?

RUTH: No, honey, marry 'em.

MAMA (*shaking her head*):　Lord, Lord, Lord . . .

RUTH:　Well—that's the way the crackers crumble. (*A beat*) Joke.

BENEATHA (*laughingly noticing what her mother is doing*):　Mama, what are you doing?

MAMA:　Fixing my plant so it won't get hurt none on the way . . .

BENEATHA:　Mama, you going to take *that* to the new house?

MAMA:　Un-huh—

BENEATHA:　That raggedy-looking old thing?

MAMA (*stopping and looking at her*):　It expresses ME!

RUTH (*with delight, to* BENEATHA):　So there, Miss Thing!

(WALTER *comes to* MAMA *suddenly and bends down behind her and squeezes her in his arms with all his strength. She is overwhelmed by the suddenness of it and, though delighted, her manner is like that of* RUTH *and* TRAVIS)

MAMA:　Look out now, boy! You make me mess up my thing here!

WALTER (*his face lit, he slips down on his knees beside her, his arms still about her*):　Mama . . . you know what it means to climb up in the chariot?

MAMA (*gruffly, very happy*):　Get on away from me now . . .

RUTH (*near the gift-wrapped package, trying to catch* WALTER'S *eye*):　Psst—

WALTER:　What the old song say, Mama . . .

RUTH:　Walter—Now?

(*She is pointing at the package*)

WALTER (*speaking the lines, sweetly, playfully, in his mother's face*):

I got wings . . . you got wings . . .

All God's Children got wings . . .

MAMA:　Boy—get out of my face and do some work . . .

WALTER:

When I get to heaven gonna put on my wings,

Gonna fly all over God's heaven . . .

BENEATHA (*teasingly, from across the room*):　Everybody talking 'bout heaven ain't going there!

WALTER (*to* RUTH, *who is carrying the box across to them*):　I don't know, you think we ought to give her that . . . Seems to me she ain't been very appreciative around here.

MAMA (*eying the box, which is obviously a gift*):　What is that?

WALTER (*taking it from* RUTH *and putting it on the table in front of* MAMA):　Well—what you all think? Should we give it to her?

RUTH:　Oh—she was pretty good today.

MAMA:　I'll good you—

(*She turns her eyes to the box again*)

BENEATHA:　Open it, Mama.

(*She stands up, looks at it, turns and looks at all of them, and then presses her hands together and does not open the package*)

WALTER (*sweetly*):　Open it, Mama. It's for you. (MAMA *looks in his eyes. It is the first present in her life without its being Christmas. Slowly she opens her package and lifts out, one by one, a brand-new sparkling set of gardening tools.* WALTER *continues, prodding*) Ruth made up the note—read it . . .

MAMA (*picking up the card and adjusting her glasses*): "To our own Mrs. Miniver—Love from Brother, Ruth and Beneatha." Ain't that lovely . . .

TRAVIS (*tugging at his father's sleeve*): Daddy, can I give her mine now?

WALTER: All right, son. (TRAVIS *flies to get his gift*)

MAMA: Now I don't have to use my knives and forks no more . . .

WALTER: Travis didn't want to go in with the rest of us, Mama. He got his own. (*Somewhat amused*) We don't know what it is . . .

TRAVIS (*racing back in the room with a large hatbox and putting it in front of his grandmother*): Here!

MAMA: Lord have mercy, baby. You done gone and bought your grandmother a hat?

TRAVIS (*very proud*): Open it!

(*She does and lifts out an elaborate, but very elaborate, wide gardening hat, and all the adults break up at the sight of it*)

RUTH: Travis, honey, what is that?

TRAVIS (*who thinks it is beautiful and appropriate*): It's a gardening hat! Like the ladies always have on in the magazines when they work in their gardens.

BENEATHA (*giggling fiercely*): Travis—we were trying to make Mama Mrs. Miniver—not Scarlett O'Hara!

MAMA (*indignantly*): What's the matter with you all! This here is a beautiful hat! (*Absurdly*) I always wanted me one just like it!

(*She pops it on her head to prove it to her grandson, and the hat is ludicrous and considerably oversized*)

RUTH: Hot dog! Go, Mama!

WALTER (*doubled over with laughter*): I'm sorry, Mama—but you look like you ready to go out and chop you some cotton sure enough!

(*They all laugh except* MAMA, *out of deference to* TRAVIS' *feelings*)

MAMA (*gathering the boy up to her*): Bless your heart—this is the prettiest hat I ever owned—(WALTER, RUTH and BENEATHA *chime in—noisily, festively and insincerely congratulating* TRAVIS *on his gift*) What are we all standing around here for? We ain't finished packin' yet. Bennie, you ain't packed one book.

(*The bell rings*)

BENEATHA: That couldn't be the movers . . . it's not hardly two good yet—

(BENEATHA *goes into her room.* MAMA *starts for door*)

WALTER (*turning, stiffening*): Wait—wait—I'll get it.

(*He stands and looks at the door*)

MAMA: You expecting company, son?

WALTER (*just looking at the door*): Yeah—yeah . . .

(MAMA *looks at* RUTH, *and they exchange innocent and unfrightened glances*)

MAMA (*not understanding*): Well, let them in, son.

BENEATHA (*from her room*): We need some more string.

MAMA: Travis—you run to the hardware and get me some string cord.

(MAMA *goes out and* WALTER *turns and looks at* RUTH. TRAVIS *goes to a dish for money*)

RUTH: Why don't you answer the door, man?

WALTER (*suddenly bounding across the floor to embrace her*):   'Cause sometimes it hard to let the future begin!

(*Stooping down in her face*)

I got wings! You got wings!
All God's children got wings!

(*He crosses to the door and throws it open. Standing there is a very slight little man in a not too prosperous business suit and with haunted frightened eyes and a hat pulled down tightly, brim up, around his forehead.* TRAVIS *passes between the men and exits.* WALTER *leans deep in the man's face, still in his jubilance*)

When I get to heaven gonna put on my wings,
Gonna fly all over God's heaven . . .

(*The little man just stares at him*)

Heaven—

(*Suddenly he stops and looks past the little man into the empty hallway*) Where's Willy, man?

BOBO: He ain't with me.

WALTER (*not disturbed*):   Oh—come on in. You know my wife.

BOBO (*dumbly, taking off his hat*):   Yes—h'you, Miss Ruth.

RUTH (*quietly, a mood apart from her husband already, seeing* BOBO):   Hello, Bobo.

WALTER: You right on time today . . . Right on time. That's the way! (*He slaps* BOBO *on his back*) Sit down . . . lemme hear.

(RUTH *stands stiffly and quietly in back of them, as though somehow she senses death, her eyes fixed on her husband*)

BOBO (*his frightened eyes on the floor, his hat in his hands*):   Could I please get a drink of water, before I tell you about it, Walter Lee?

(WALTER *does not take his eyes off the man.* RUTH *goes blindly to the tap and gets a glass of water and brings it to* BOBO)

WALTER: There ain't nothing wrong, is there?

BOBO: Lemme tell you—

WALTER: Man—didn't nothing go wrong?

BOBO: Lemme tell you—Walter Lee. (*Looking at* RUTH *and talking to her more than to* WALTER) You know how it was. I got to tell you how it was. I mean first I got to tell you how it was all the way . . . I mean about the money I put in, Walter Lee . . .

WALTER (*with taut agitation now*):   What about the money you put in?

BOBO: Well—it wasn't much as we told you—me and Willy—(*He stops*) I'm sorry, Walter. I got a bad feeling about it. I got a real bad feeling about it . . .

WALTER: Man, what you telling me about all this for? . . . Tell me what happened in Springfield . . .

BOBO: Springfield.

RUTH (*like a dead woman*):   What was supposed to happen in Springfield?

BOBO (*to her*):   This deal that me and Walter went into with Willy—Me and Willy was going to go down to Springfield and spread some money 'round so's we wouldn't have to wait so long for the liquor license . . . That's what we were going to do. Everybody said that was the way you had to do, you understand, Miss Ruth?

WALTER: Man—what happened down there?

BOBO (*a pitiful man, near tears*):   I'm trying to tell you, Walter.

WALTER (*screaming at him suddenly*):   THEN TELL ME, GODDAMMIT . . . WHAT'S THE MATTER WITH YOU?

BOBO: Man . . . I didn't go to no Springfield, yesterday.

WALTER (*halted, life hanging in the moment*):   Why not?

BOBO (*the long way, the hard way to tell*):   'Cause I didn't have no reasons to . . .

WALTER: Man, what are you talking about!

BOBO: I'm talking about the fact that when I got to the train station yesterday morning—eight o'clock like we planned . . . Man—*Willy didn't never show up.*

WALTER: Why . . . where was he . . . where is he?

BOBO: That's what I'm trying to tell you . . . I don't know . . . I waited six hours . . . I called his house . . . and I waited . . . six hours . . . I waited in that train station six hours . . . (*Breaking into tears*) That was all the extra money I had in the world . . . (*Looking up at* WALTER *with the tears running down his face*) Man, *Willy is gone.*

WALTER: Gone, what you mean Willy is gone? Gone where? You mean he went by himself. You mean he went off to Springfield by himself—to take care of getting the license—(*Turns and looks anxiously at* RUTH) You mean maybe he didn't want too many people in on the business down there? (*Looks to* RUTH *again, as before*) You know Willy got his own ways. (*Looks back to* BOBO) Maybe you was late yesterday and he just went on down there without you. Maybe—maybe—he's been callin' you at home tryin' to tell you what happened or something. Maybe—maybe—he just got sick. He's somewhere—he's got to be somewhere. We just got to find him—me and you got to find him. (*Grabs* BOBO *senselessly by the collar and starts to shake him*) We got to!

BOBO (*in sudden angry, frightened agony*):   What's the matter with you, Walter! *When a cat take off with your money he don't leave you no road maps!*

WALTER (*turning madly, as though he is looking for* WILLY *in the very room*):   Willy! . . . Willy . . . don't do it . . . Please don't do it . . . Man, not with that money . . . Man, please, not with that money . . . Oh, God . . . Don't let it be true . . . (*He is wandering around, crying out for* WILLY *and looking for him or perhaps for help from God*) Man . . . I trusted you . . . Man, I put my life in your hands . . . (*He starts to crumple down on the floor as* RUTH *just covers her face in horror.* MAMA *opens the door and comes into the room, with* BENEATHA *behind her*) Man . . . (*He starts to pound the floor with his fists, sobbing wildly*) THAT MONEY IS MADE OUT OF MY FATHER'S FLESH——

BOBO (*standing over him helplessly*):   I'm sorry, Walter . . . (*Only* WALTER'*s sobs reply.* BOBO *puts on his hat*) I had my life staked on this deal, too . . .

(*He exits*)

MAMA (*to* WALTER):   Son—(*She goes to him, bends down to him, talks to his bent head*) Son . . . Is it gone? Son, I gave you sixty-five hundred dollars. Is it gone? All of it? Beneatha's money too?

WALTER (*lifting his head slowly*):   Mama . . . I never . . . went to the bank at all . . .

MAMA (*not wanting to believe him*):   You mean . . . your sister's school money . . . you used that too . . . Walter? . . .

WALTER: Yessss! All of it . . . It's all gone . . .

(*There is total silence.* RUTH *stands with her face covered with her hands;* BENEATHA *leans forlornly against a wall, fingering a piece of red ribbon from the mother's gift.* MAMA *stops and looks at her son without recognition and then, quite without thinking about it, starts to beat him senselessly in the face.* BENEATHA *goes to them and stops it*)

BENEATHA: Mama!

(MAMA *stops and looks at both of her children and rises slowly and wanders vaguely, aimlessly away from them*)

MAMA: I seen . . . him . . . night after night . . . come in . . . and look at that rug . . . and then look at me . . . the red showing in his eyes . . . the veins moving in his head . . . I seen him grow thin and old before he was forty . . . working and working and working like somebody's old horse . . . killing himself . . . and you—you give it all away in a day—(*She raises her arms to strike him again*)

BENEATHA: Mama—

MAMA: Oh, God . . . (*She looks up to Him*) Look down here—and show me the strength.

BENEATHA: Mama—

MAMA (*folding over*):   Strength . . .

BENEATHA (*plaintively*):   Mama . . .

MAMA: Strength!

Curtain

ACT III

An hour later.

    At curtain, there is a sullen light of gloom in the living room, gray light not unlike that which began the first scene of Act One. At left we can see WALTER *within his room, alone with himself. He is stretched out on the bed, his shirt out and open, his arms under his head. He does not smoke, he does not cry out, he merely lies there, looking up at the ceiling, much as if he were alone in the world.*

    In the living room BENEATHA *sits at the table, still surrounded by the now almost ominous packing crates. She sits looking off. We feel that this is a mood struck perhaps an hour before, and it lingers now, full of the empty sound of profound disappointment. We see on a line from her brother's bedroom the sameness of their attitudes. Presently the bell rings and* BENEATHA *rises without ambition or interest in answering. It is* ASAGAI, *smiling broadly, striding into the room with energy and happy expectation and conversation.*

ASAGAI: I came over . . . I had some free time. I thought I might help with the packing. Ah, I like the look of packing crates! A household in preparation for a journey! It depresses some people . . . but for me . . . it is another feeling. Something full of the flow of life, do you understand? Movement, progress . . . It makes me think of Africa.

BENEATHA: Africa!

ASAGAI: What kind of a mood is this? Have I told you how deeply you move me?

BENEATHA: He gave away the money, Asagai . . .

ASAGAI: Who gave away what money?

BENEATHA: The insurance money. My brother gave it away.

ASAGAI: Gave it away?

BENEATHA: He made an investment! With a man even Travis wouldn't have trusted with his most worn-out marbles.

ASAGAI: And it's gone?

BENEATHA: Gone!

ASAGAI: I'm very sorry . . . And you, now?

BENEATHA: Me? . . . Me? . . . Me, I'm nothing . . . Me. When I was very small . . . we used to take our sleds out in the wintertime and the only hills we had were the ice-covered stone steps of some houses down the street. And we used to fill them in with snow and make them smooth and slide down them all day . . . and it was very danger-ous, you know . . . far too steep . . . and sure enough one day a kid named Rufus came down too fast and hit the sidewalk and we saw his face just split open right there in front of us . . . And I remember standing there looking at his bloody open face thinking that was the end of Rufus. But the ambulance came and they took him to the hospital and they fixed the broken bones and they sewed it all up . . . and the next time I saw Rufus he just had a little line down the middle of his face . . . I never got over that . . .

ASAGAI: What?

BENEATHA: That that was what one person could do for another, fix him up—sew up the problem, make him all right again. That was the most marvelous thing in the world . . . I wanted to do that. I always thought it was the one concrete thing in the world that a human being could do. Fix up the sick, you know—and make them whole again. This was truly being God . . .

ASAGAI: You wanted to be God?

BENEATHA: No—I wanted to cure. It used to be so important to me. I wanted to cure. It used to matter. I used to care. I mean about people and how their bodies hurt . . .

ASAGAI: And you've stopped caring?

BENEATHA: Yes—I think so.

ASAGAI: Why?

BENEATHA (*bitterly*):   Because it doesn't seem deep enough, close enough to what ails mankind! It was a child's way of seeing things—or an idealist's.

ASAGAI: Children see things very well sometimes—and idealists even better.

BENEATHA: I know that's what you think. Because you are still where I left off. You with all your talk and dreams about Africa! You still think you can patch up the world. Cure the Great Sore of Colonialism—(*Loftily, mocking it*) with the Penicillin of Independence—!

ASAGAI: Yes!

BENEATHA: Independence *and then what?* What about all the crooks and thieves and just plain idiots who will come into power and steal and plunder the same as be-fore—only now they will be black and do it in the name of the new Independence—WHAT ABOUT THEM?!

ASAGAI: That will be the problem for another time. First we must get there.

BENEATHA: And where does it end?

ASAGAI: End? Who even spoke of an end? To life? To living?

BENEATHA: An end to misery! To stupidity! Don't you see there isn't any real progress, Asagai, there is only one large circle that we march in, around and around, each of us with our own little picture in front of us—our own little mirage that we think is the future.

ASAGAI: That is the mistake.

BENEATHA: What?

ASAGAI: What you just said—about the circle. It isn't a circle—it is simply a long line—as in geometry, you know, one that reaches into infinity. And because we cannot see the end—we also cannot see how it changes. And it is very odd but those who see the changes—who dream, who will not give up—are called idealists . . . and those who see only the circle—we call *them* the "realists"!

BENEATHA: Asagai, while I was sleeping in that bed in there, people went out and took the future right out of my hands! And nobody asked me, nobody consulted me— they just went out and changed my life!

ASAGAI: Was it your money?

BENEATHA: What?

ASAGAI: Was it your money he gave away?

BENEATHA: It belonged to all of us.

ASAGAI: But did you earn it? Would you have had it at all if your father had not died?

BENEATHA: No.

ASAGAI: Then isn't there something wrong in a house—in a world—where all dreams, good or bad, must depend on the death of a man? I never thought to see *you* like this, Alaiyo. You! Your brother made a mistake and you are grateful to him so that now you can give up the ailing human race on account of it! You talk about what good is struggle, what good is anything! Where are we all going and why are we bothering!

BENEATHA: AND YOU CANNOT ANSWER IT!

ASAGAI (*shouting over her*):   I LIVE THE ANSWER! (*Pause*) In my village at home it is the exceptional man who can even read a newspaper . . . or who ever sees a book at all. I will go home and much of what I will have to say will seem strange to the people of my village. But I will teach and work and things will happen, slowly and swiftly. At times it will seem that nothing changes at all . . . and then again the sudden dramatic events which make history leap into the future. And then quiet again. Retrogression even. Guns, murder, revolution. And I even will have moments when I wonder if the quiet was not better than all that death and hatred. But I will look about my village at the illiteracy and disease and ignorance and I will not wonder long. And perhaps . . . perhaps I will be a great man . . . I mean perhaps I will hold on to the substance of truth and find my way always with the right course . . . and perhaps for it I will be butchered in my bed some night by the servants of empire . . .

BENEATHA: *The martyr!*

ASAGAI (*he smiles*):   . . . or perhaps I shall live to be a very old man, respected and esteemed in my new nation . . . And perhaps I shall hold office and this is what I'm trying to tell you, Alaiyo: Perhaps the things I believe now for my country will be wrong and outmoded, and I will not understand and do terrible things to have things my way or merely to keep my power. Don't you see that there will be young men and women—not British soldiers then, but my own black countrymen—to step out of the shadows some evening and slit my then useless throat? Don't you see they have always been there . . . that they always will be. And that such a thing as my own death will be an advance? They who might kill me even . . . actually replenish all that I was.

BENEATHA: Oh, Asagai, I know all that.

ASAGAI: Good! Then stop moaning and groaning and tell me what you plan to do.

BENEATHA: Do?

ASAGAI: I have a bit of a suggestion.

BENEATHA: What?

ASAGAI (*rather quietly for him*):   That when it is all over—that you come home with me—

BENEATHA (*staring at him and crossing away with exasperation*):   Oh—Asagai—at this moment you decide to be romantic!

ASAGAI (*quickly understanding the misunderstanding*):   My dear, young creature of the New World—I do not mean across the city—I mean across the ocean: home—to Africa.

BENEATHA (*slowly understanding and turning to him with murmured amazement*):   To Africa?

ASAGAI: Yes! . . . (*Smiling and lifting his arms playfully*) Three hundred years later the African Prince rose up out of the seas and swept the maiden back across the middle passage over which her ancestors had come—

BENEATHA (*unable to play*):   To—to Nigeria?

ASAGAI: Nigeria. Home. (*Coming to her with genuine romantic flippancy*) I will show you our mountains and our stars; and give you cool drinks from gourds and teach you the old songs and the ways of our people—and, in time, we will pretend that—(*Very Softly*)—you have only been away for a day. Say that you'll come—(*He swings her around and takes her full in his arms in a kiss which proceeds to passion*)

BENEATHA (*pulling away suddenly*):   You're getting me all mixed up—

ASAGAI: Why?

BENEATHA: Too many things—too many things have happened today. I must sit down and think. I don't know what I feel about anything right this minute.

(*She promptly sits down and props her chin on her fist*)

ASAGAI (*charmed*):   All right, I shall leave you. No—don't get up. (*Touching her, gently, sweetly*) Just sit awhile and think . . . Never be afraid to sit awhile and think. (*He goes to door and looks at her*) How often I have looked at you and said, "Ah—so this is what the New World hath finally wrought . . ."

(*He exits.* BENEATHA *sits on alone. Presently* WALTER *enters from his room and starts to rummage through things, feverishly looking for something. She looks up and turns in her seat*)

BENEATHA (*hissingly*):   Yes—just look at what the New World hath wrought! . . . Just look! (*She gestures with bitter disgust*) There he is! *Monsieur le petit bourgeois noir*—himself! There he is—Symbol of a Rising Class! Entrepreneur! Titan of the system! (WALTER *ignores her completely and continues frantically and destructively looking for something and hurling things to floor and tearing things out of their place in his search.* BENEATHA *ignores the eccentricity of his actions and goes on with the monologue of insult*) Did you dream of yachts on Lake Michigan, Brother? Did you see yourself on that Great Day sitting down at the Conference Table, surrounded by all the mighty bald-headed men in America? All halted, waiting, breathless, waiting for your pronouncements on industry? Waiting for you—Chairman of the Board! (WALTER *finds what he is looking for—a small piece of white paper—and pushes it in his pocket and puts on his coat and rushes out without ever having looked at her. She shouts after him*) I look at you and I see the final triumph of stupidity in the world!

(*The door slams and she returns to just sitting again.* RUTH *comes quickly out of* MAMA*'s room*)

RUTH: Who was that?

BENEATHA: Your husband.

RUTH: Where did he go?

BENEATHA: Who knows—maybe he has an appointment at U.S. Steel.

RUTH (*anxiously, with frightened eyes*):   You didn't say nothing bad to him, did you?

BENEATHA: Bad? Say anything bad to him? No—I told him he was a sweet boy and full of dreams and everything is strictly peachy keen, as the ofay kids say!

(MAMA *enters from her bedroom. She is lost, vague, trying to catch hold, to make some sense of her former command of the world, but it still eludes her. A sense of waste overwhelms her gait; a measure of apology rides on her shoulders. She goes to her plant, which has remained on the table, looks at it, picks it up and takes it to the window sill and sets it outside, and she stands and looks at it a long moment. Then she closes the window, straightens her body with effort and turns around to her children*)

MAMA: Well—ain't it a mess in here, though? (*A false cheerfulness, a beginning of something*) I guess we all better stop moping around and get some work done. All this unpacking and everything we got to do. (RUTH *raises her head slowly in response to the sense of the line; and* BENEATHA *in similar manner turns very slowly to look at her mother*) One of you all better call the moving people and tell 'em not to come.

RUTH: Tell 'em not to come?

MAMA: Of course, baby. Ain't no need in 'em coming all the way here and having to go back. They charges for that too. (*She sits down, fingers to her brow, thinking*) Lord, ever since I was a little girl, I always remembers people saying, "Lena—Lena Eggleston, you aims too high all the time. You needs to slow down and see life a little more like it is. Just slow down some." That's what they always used to say down home—"Lord, that Lena Eggleston is a high-minded thing. She'll get her due one day!"

RUTH: No, Lena . . .

MAMA: Me and Big Walter just didn't never learn right.

RUTH: Lena, no! We gotta go. Bennie—tell her . . . (*She rises and crosses to* BENEATHA *with her arms outstretched.* BENEATHA *doesn't respond*) Tell her we can still move . . . the notes ain't but a hundred and twenty-five a month. We got four grown people in this house—we can work . . .

MAMA (*to herself*):   Just aimed too high all the time—

RUTH (*turning and going to* MAMA *fast—the words pouring out with urgency and desperation*):   Lena—I'll work . . . I'll work twenty hours a day in all the kitchens in Chicago . . . I'll strap my baby on my back if I have to and scrub all the floors in America and wash all the sheets in America if I have to—but we got to MOVE! We got to get OUT OF HERE!!

(MAMA *reaches out absently and pats* RUTH's *hand*)

MAMA: No—I sees things differently now. Been thinking 'bout some of the things we could do to fix this place up some. I seen a second-hand bureau over on Maxwell Street just the other day that could fit right there. (*She points to where the new furniture might go.* RUTH *wanders away from her*) Would need some new handles on it and then a little varnish and it look like something brand-new. And—we can put up them new curtains in the kitchen . . . Why this place be looking fine. Cheer us all up so that we forget trouble ever come . . . (*To* RUTH) And you could get some nice screens to put up in your room round the baby's bassinet . . . (*She looks at both of them, pleadingly*) Sometimes you just got to know when to give up some things . . . and hold on to what you got. . . .

(WALTER *enters from the outside, looking spent and leaning against the door, his coat hanging from him*)

MAMA: Where you been, son?
WALTER (*breathing hard*):   Made a call.
MAMA: To who, son?
WALTER: To The Man. (*He heads for his room*)
MAMA: What man, baby?
WALTER (*stops in the door*):   The Man, Mama. Don't you know who The Man is?
RUTH: Walter Lee?
WALTER: *The Man.* Like the guys in the streets say—The Man. Captain Boss—Mistuh Charley . . . Old Cap'n Please Mr. Bossman . . .
BENEATHA (*suddenly*):   Lindner!
WALTER: That's right! That's good. I told him to come right over.
BENEATHA (*fiercely, understanding*):   For what? What do you want to see him for!
WALTER (*looking at his sister*):   We going to do business with him.
MAMA: What you talking 'bout, son?
WALTER: Talking 'bout life, Mama. You all always telling me to see life like it is. Well—I laid in there on my back today . . . and I figured it out. Life just like it is. Who gets and who don't get. (*He sits down with his coat on and laughs*) Mama, you know it's all divided up. Life is. Sure enough. Between the takers and the "tooken." (*He laughs*) I've figured it out finally. (*He looks around at them*) Yeah. Some of us always getting "tooken." (*He laughs*) People like Willy Harris, they don't never get "tooken." And you know why the rest of us do? 'Cause we all mixed up. Mixed up bad. We get to looking 'round for the right and the wrong; and we worry about it and cry about it and stay up nights trying to figure out 'bout the wrong and the right of things all the time . . . And all the time, man, them takers is out there operating, just taking and taking. Willy Harris? Shoot—Willy Harris don't even count. He don't even count in the big scheme of things. But I'll say one thing for old Willy Harris . . . he's taught me something. He's taught me to keep my eye on what counts in this world. Yeah—(*Shouting out a little*) Thanks, Willy!
RUTH: What did you call that man for, Walter Lee?
WALTER: Called him to tell him to come on over to the show. Gonna put on a show for the man. Just what he wants to see. You see, Mama, the man came here today and he told us that them people out there where you want us to move—well they so

upset they willing to pay us *not* to move! (*He laughs again*) And—and oh, Mama—you would of been proud of the way me and Ruth and Bennie acted. We told him to get out . . . Lord have mercy! We told the man to get out! Oh, we was some proud folks this afternoon, yeah. (*He lights a cigarette*) We were still full of that old-time stuff . . .

RUTH (*coming toward him slowly*):   You talking 'bout taking them people's money to keep us from moving in that house?

WALTER: I ain't just talking 'bout it, baby—I'm telling you that's what's going to happen!

BENEATHA: Oh, God! Where is the bottom! Where is the real honest-to-God bottom so he can't go any farther!

WALTER: See—that's the old stuff. You and that boy that was here today. You all want everybody to carry a flag and a spear and sing some marching songs, huh? You wanna spend your life looking into things and trying to find the right and the wrong part, huh? Yeah. You know what's going to happen to that boy someday—he'll find himself sitting in a dungeon, locked in forever—and the takers will have the key! Forget it, baby! There ain't no causes—there ain't nothing but taking in this world, and he who takes most is smartest—and it don't make a damn bit of difference *how.*

MAMA: You making something inside me cry, son. Some awful pain inside me.

WALTER: Don't cry, Mama. Understand. That white man is going to walk in that door able to write checks for more money than we ever had. It's important to him and I'm going to help him . . . I'm going to put on the show, Mama.

MAMA: Son—I come from five generations of people who was slaves and sharecroppers—but ain't nobody in my family never let nobody pay 'em no money that was a way of telling us we wasn't fit to walk the earth. We ain't never been that poor. (*Raising her eyes and looking at him*) We ain't never been that—dead inside.

BENEATHA: Well—we are dead now. All the talk about dreams and sunlight that goes on in this house. It's all dead now.

WALTER: What's the matter with you all! I didn't make this world! It was give to me this way! Hell, yes, I want me some yachts someday! Yes, I want to hang some real pearls 'round my wife's neck. Ain't she supposed to wear no pearls? Somebody tell me—tell me, who decides which women is suppose to wear pearls in this world. I tell you I am a *man*—and I think my wife should wear some pearls in this world!

(*This last line hangs a good while and* WALTER *begins to move about the room. The word "Man" has penetrated his consciousness; he mumbles it to himself repeatedly between strange agitated pauses as he moves about*)

MAMA: Baby, how you going to feel on the inside?

WALTER: Fine! . . . Going to feel fine . . . a man . . .

MAMA: You won't have nothing left then, Walter Lee.

WALTER (*coming to her*):   I'm going to feel fine, Mama. I'm going to look that son-of-a-bitch in the eyes and say—(*He falters*)—and say, "All right, Mr. Lindner—(*He falters even more*)—that's *your* neighborhood out there! You got the right to keep it like you want! You got the right to have it like you want! Just write the check and—the house is yours." And—and I am going to say—(*His voice almost breaks*) "And you—you people just put the money in my hand and you won't have to live next to this bunch of stinking niggers! . . . " (*He straightens up and moves away from his mother, walking around the room*) And maybe—maybe I'll just get down on my black knees . . . (*He does so;*

RUTH *and* BENNIE *and* MAMA *watch him in frozen horror*) "Captain, Mistuh, Bossman— (*Groveling and grinning and wringing his hands in profoundly anguished imitation of the slow-witted movie stereotype*) A-hee-hee-hee! Oh, yassuh boss! Yasssssuh! Great white—(*Voice breaking, he forces himself to go on*)—Father, just gi' ussen de money, fo' God's sake, and we's—we's ain't gwine come out deh and dirty up yo' white folks neighborhood . . ." (*He breaks down completely*) And I'll feel fine! Fine! FINE! (*He gets up and goes into the bedroom*)

BENEATHA: That is not a man. That is nothing but a toothless rat.

MAMA: Yes—death done come in this here house. (*She is nodding, slowly, reflectively*) Done come walking in my house on the lips of my children. You what supposed to be my beginning again. You—what supposed to be my harvest. (*To* BENEATHA) You—you mourning your brother?

BENEATHA: He's no brother of mine.

MAMA: What you say?

BENEATHA: I said that that individual in that room is no brother of mine.

MAMA: That's what I thought you said. You feeling like you better than he is today? (BENEATHA *does not answer*) Yes? What you tell him a minute ago? That he wasn't a man? Yes? You give him up for me? You done wrote his epitaph too—like the rest of the world? Well, who give you the privilege?

BENEATHA: Be on my side for once! You saw what he just did, Mama! You saw him—down on his knees. Wasn't it you who taught me to despise any man who would do that? Do what he's going to do?

MAMA: Yes—I taught you that. Me and your daddy. But I thought I taught you something else too . . . I thought I taught you to love him.

BENEATHA: Love him? There is nothing left to love.

MAMA: There is *always* something left to love. And if you ain't learned that, you ain't learned nothing. (*Looking at her*) Have you cried for that boy today? I don't mean for yourself and for the family 'cause we lost the money. I mean for him: what he been through and what it done to him. Child, when do you think is the time to love somebody the most? When they done good and made things easy for everybody? Well then, you ain't through learning—because that ain't the time at all. It's when he's at his lowest and can't believe in hisself 'cause the world done whipped him so! When you starts measuring somebody, measure him right, child, measure him right. Make sure you done taken into account what hills and valleys he come through before he got to wherever he is.

(TRAVIS *bursts into the room at the end of the speech, leaving the door open*)

TRAVIS: Grandmama—the moving men are downstairs! The truck just pulled up.

MAMA (*turning and looking at him*): Are they, baby? They downstairs?

(*She sighs and sits.* LINDNER *appears in the doorway. He peers in and knocks lightly, to gain attention, and comes in. All turn to look at him*)

LINDNER (*hat and briefcase in hand*): Uh—hello . . .

(RUTH *crosses mechanically to the bedroom door and opens it and lets it swing open freely and slowly as the lights come up on* WALTER *within, still in his coat, sitting at the far corner of the room. He looks up and out through the room to* LINDNER)

RUTH: He's here.

(*A long minute passes and* WALTER *slowly gets up*)

LINDNER (*coming to the table with efficiency, putting his briefcase on the table and starting to unfold papers and unscrew fountain pens*):   Well, I certainly was glad to hear from you people. (WALTER *has begun the trek out of the room, slowly and awkwardly, rather like a small boy, passing the back of his sleeve across his mouth from time to time*) Life can really be so much simpler than people let it be most of the time. Well—with whom do I negotiate? You, Mrs. Younger, or your son here? (MAMA *sits with her hands folded on her lap and her eyes closed as* WALTER *advances.* TRAVIS *goes closer to* LINDNER *and looks at the papers curiously*) Just some official papers, sonny.

RUTH: Travis, you go downstairs—

MAMA (*opening her eyes and looking into* WALTER'*s*):   No. Travis, you stay right here. And you make him understand what you doing, Walter Lee. You teach him good. Like Willy Harris taught you. You show where our five generations done come to. (WALTER *looks from her to the boy, who grins at him innocently*) Go ahead, son—(*She folds her hands and closes her eyes*) Go ahead.

WALTER (*at last crosses to* LINDNER, *who is reviewing the contract*):   Well, Mr. Lindner. (BENEATHA *turns away*) We called you—(*There is a profound, simple groping quality in his speech*)—because, well, me and my family (*He looks around and shifts from one foot to the other*) Well—we are very plain people . . .

LINDNER: Yes—

WALTER: I mean—I have worked as a chauffeur most of my life—and my wife here, she does domestic work in people's kitchens. So does my mother. I mean—we are plain people . . .

LINDNER: Yes, Mr. Younger—

WALTER (*really like a small boy, looking down at his shoes and then up at the man*): And—uh—well, my father, well, he was a laborer most of his life. . . .

LINDNER (*absolutely confused*):   Uh, yes—yes, I understand. (*He turns back to the contract*)

WALTER (*a beat; staring at him*):   And my father—(*With sudden intensity*) My father almost *beat a man to death* once because this man called him a bad name or something, you know what I mean?

LINDNER (*looking up, frozen*):   No, no, I'm afraid I don't—

WALTER (*a beat. The tension hangs; then* WALTER *steps back from it*):   Yeah. Well—what I mean is that we come from people who had a lot of *pride.* I mean—we are very proud people. And that's my sister over there and she's going to be a doctor—and we are very proud—

LINDNER: Well—I am sure that is very nice, but—

WALTER: What I am telling you is that we called you over here to tell you that we are very proud and that this—(*Signaling to* TRAVIS) Travis, come here. (TRAVIS *crosses and* WALTER *draws him before him facing the man*) This is my son, and he makes the sixth generation our family in this country. And we have all thought about your offer—

LINDNER: Well, good . . . good—

WALTER: And we have decided to move into our house because my father—my father—he earned it for us brick by brick. (MAMA *has her eyes closed and is rocking back and forth as though she were in church, with her head nodding the Amen yes*) We don't want to make no trouble for nobody or fight no causes, and we will try to be good neighbors. And that's *all* we got to say about that. (*He looks the man absolutely in the eyes*) We don't want your money. (*He turns and walks away*)

LINDNER (*looking around at all of them*):   I take it then—that you have decided to occupy . . .

BENEATHA: That's what the man said.

LINDNER (*to* MAMA *in her reverie*):   Then I would like to appeal to you, Mrs. Younger. You are older and wiser and understand things better, I am sure . . .

MAMA: I am afraid you don't understand. My son said we was going to move and there ain't nothing left for me to say. (*Briskly*) You know how these young folks is nowadays, mister. Can't do a thing with 'em! (*As he opens his mouth, she rises*) Good-bye.

LINDNER (*folding up his materials*):   Well—if you are that final about it . . . there is nothing left for me to say. (*He finishes, almost ignored by the family, who are concentrating on* WALTER LEE. *At the door* LINDNER *halts and looks around*) I sure hope you people know what you're getting into.

(*He shakes his head and exits*)

RUTH (*looking around and coming to life*):   Well, for God's sake—if the moving men are here—LET'S GET THE HELL OUT OF HERE!

MAMA (*into action*):   Ain't it the truth! Look at all this here mess. Ruth, put Travis' good jacket on him . . . Walter Lee, fix your tie and tuck your shirt in, you look like somebody's hoodlum! Lord have mercy, where is my plant? (*She flies to get it amid the general bustling of the family, who are deliberately trying to ignore the nobility of the past moment*) You all start on down . . . Travis child, don't go empty-handed . . . Ruth, where did I put that box with my skillets in it? I want to be in charge of it myself . . . I'm going to make us the biggest dinner we ever ate tonight . . . Beneatha, what's the matter with them stockings? Pull them things up, girl . . .

(*The family starts to file out as two moving men appear and begin to carry out the heavier pieces of furniture, bumping into the family as they move about*)

BENEATHA: Mama, Asagai asked me to marry him today and go to Africa—

MAMA (*in the middle of her getting-ready activity*):   He did? You ain't old enough to marry nobody—(*Seeing the moving men lifting one of her chairs precariously*) Darling, that ain't no bale of cotton, please handle it so we can sit in it again! I had that chair twenty-five years . . .

(*The movers sigh with exasperation and go on with their work*)

BENEATHA (*girlishly and unreasonably trying to pursue the conversation*):   To go to Africa, Mama—be a doctor in Africa . . .

MAMA (*distracted*):   Yes, baby—

WALTER: *Africa!* What he want you to go to Africa for?

BENEATHA: To practice there . . .

WALTER: Girl, if you don't get all them silly ideas out your head! You better marry yourself a man with some loot . . .

BENEATHA (*angrily, precisely as in the first scene of the play*):   What have you got to do with who I marry!

WALTER: Plenty. Now I think George Murchison—

BENEATHA: *George Murchison!* I wouldn't marry him if he was Adam and I was Eve!

(WALTER *and* BENEATHA *go out yelling at each other vigorously and the anger is loud and real till their voices diminish.* RUTH *stands at the door and turns to* MAMA *and smiles knowingly*)

MAMA (*fixing her hat at last*):   Yeah—they something all right, my children . . .
RUTH: Yeah—they're something. Let's go, Lena.
MAMA (*stalling, starting to look around at the house*):   Yes—I'm coming. Ruth—
RUTH: Yes?
MAMA (*quietly, woman to woman*):   He finally come into his manhood today, didn't he? Kind of like a rainbow after the rain . . .
RUTH (*biting her lip lest her own pride explode in front of* MAMA):   Yes, Lena.

(WALTER*'s voice calls for them raucously*)

WALTER (*off stage*):   Y'all come on! These people charges by the hour, you know!
MAMA (*waving* RUTH *out vaguely*):   All right, honey—go on down. I be down directly.

(RUTH *hesitates, then exits.* MAMA *stands, at last alone in the living room, her plant on the table before her as the lights start to come down. She looks around at all the walls and ceilings and suddenly, despite herself, while the children call below, a great heaving thing rises in her and she puts her fist to her mouth to stifle it, takes a final desperate look, pulls her coat about her, pats her hat and goes out. The lights dim down. The door opens and she comes back in, grabs her plant, and goes out for the last time*)

Curtain

(*1959*)

QUESTIONS FOR REFLECTION

Experience

1. Did you find this play engaging or interesting? Why or why not? What makes it specifically an urban play? A "minority" play?
2. To what extent can you relate to the experiences of the play's characters?

Interpretation

3. Describe the relationship of Mama (Lena) with her daughter, Beneatha, and with her son, Walter. What expectations does she have for the future of each? Why?
4. Give two explanations for the primary conflicts of the play. What precipitates the various arguments and battles the characters wage with one another?
5. Explain the roles of Joseph Asagai and George Murchison. Does either character have thematic significance? Explain.
6. Identify and discuss a major theme of the play. Support your ideas with references to specific events and speeches.
7. Identify two important stage props and comment on their role in the play. Discuss whether either or both may be symbolic, and why.

8. Select a scene you find compelling and describe how to stage it.
9. Are you satisfied with the play's ending? Why or why not? How do you envision the future of the family, particularly of Ruth and Walter and of Beneatha?

Evaluation

10. Some readers consider this play a modern American classic. What do you think may have led them to such an assessment?
11. How is Hansberry's play a comment on the Langston Hughes poem that she uses as her epigraph?

TERRENCE MCNALLY

[*b. 1939*]

Terrence McNally has long been a fixture on and off Broadway. His plays have won wide acclaim for their wit, wisdom, and humanity. Among his numerous plays are *A Perfect Ganesh; Lips Together, Teeth Apart; Whisky; The Ritz;* and *Things That Go Bump in the Night.* McNally has also written screenplays, scripts for television, and the book for the musical adaptation of Manuel Puig's *The Kiss of the Spiderwoman.*

 Andre's Mother was written as a script for television. It won the 1990 Emmy Award for Best Writing in a Miniseries or Special.

TERRENCE MCNALLY

Andre's Mother

CHARACTERS

CAL
ARTHUR
PENNY
ANDRE'S MOTHER

Four people enter. They are nicely dressed and carry white helium-filled balloons on a string. They are CAL, *a young man;* ARTHUR, *his father;* PENNY, *his sister; and* ANDRE'S MOTHER.

 CAL: You know what's really terrible? I can't think of anything terrific to say. Goodbye. I love you. I'll miss you. And I'm supposed to be so great with words!

PENNY: What's that over there?

ARTHUR: Ask your brother.

CAL: It's a theatre. An outdoor theatre. They do plays there in the summer. Shakespeare's plays. (*To* ANDRE'S MOTHER.) God, how much he wanted to play Hamlet. It was his greatest dream. I think he would have sold his soul to play it. He would have gone to Timbuktu to have another go at that part. The summer he did it in Boston, he was so happy!

PENNY: Cal, I don't think she . . . ! It's not the time. Later.

ARTHUR: Your son was a . . . the Jews have a word for it . . .

PENNY (*Quietly appalled.*): Oh my God!

ARTHUR: Mensch, I believe it is and I think I'm using it right. It means warm, solid, the real thing. Correct me if I'm wrong.

PENNY: Fine, dad, fine. Just quit while you're ahead.

ARTHUR: I won't say he was like a son to me. Even my son isn't always like a son to me. I mean . . . ! In my clumsy way, I'm trying to say how much I liked Andre. And how much he helped me to know my own boy. Cal was always two hands full but Andre and I could talk about anything under the sun. My wife was very fond of him, too.

PENNY: Cal, I don't understand about the balloons.

CAL: They represent the soul. When you let go, it means you're letting his soul ascend to Heaven. That you're willing to let go. Breaking the last earthly ties.

PENNY: Does the Pope know about this?

ARTHUR: Penny!

PENNY: Andre loved my sense of humor. Listen, you can hear him laughing. (*She lets go of her white balloon.*) So long, you glorious, wonderful, I-know-what-Cal-means-about-words . . . *man!* God forgive me for wishing you were straight every time I laid eyes on you. But if any man was going to have you, I'm glad it was my brother! Look how fast it went up. I bet that means something. Something terrific.

ARTHUR: (ARTHUR *lets his balloon go.*) Goodbye. God speed.

PENNY: Cal?

CAL: I'm not ready yet.

PENNY: Okay. We'll be over there. Come on, pop, you can buy your little girl a Good Humor.

ARTHUR: They still make Good Humor?

PENNY: Only now they're called Dove Bars and they cost 12 dollars.

(PENNY *takes* ARTHUR *off.* CAL *and* ANDRE'S MOTHER *stand with their balloons.*)

CAL: I wish I knew what you were thinking. I think it would help me. You know almost nothing about me and I only know what Andre told me about you. I'd always had it in my mind that one day we would be friends, you and me. But if you didn't know about Andre and me . . . If this hadn't happened, I wonder if he would have ever told you. When he was so sick, if I asked him once I asked him a thousand times, tell her. She's your mother. She won't mind. But he was so afraid of hurting you and of your disapproval. I don't know which was worse. (*No response. He sighs.*) God, how many of us live in this city because we don't want to hurt our mothers and live in mortal terror of their disapproval. We lose ourselves here. Our lives aren't furtive, just our feelings toward people like you are! A city of fugitives from our parent's scorn or heartbreak. Sometimes he'd seem a little down and I'd say, "What's the matter, babe?" and this funny sweet, sad smile would cross his face and he'd say, "Just a little homesick, Cal, just a little bit." I always accused him of being a country boy just playing at being a hot shot, sophisticated New Yorker. (*He sighs.*) It's bullshit. It's all bullshit. (*Still no response.*) Do you remember the comic strip Little Lulu? Her mother had no name, she was so remote, so formidable to all the children. She was just Lulu's mother. "Hello, Lulu's Mother," Lulu's friends would say. She was almost anonymous in her remoteness. You remind me of her. Andre's Mother. Let me answer the questions you can't ask and then I'll leave you alone and you won't ever have to see me again. Andre died of AIDS. I don't know how he got it. I tested negative. He died bravely. You would have been proud of him. The only thing that frightened him was you. I'll have everything that was his sent to you. I'll pay for it. There isn't much. You should have come up the summer he played Hamlet. He was magnificent. Yes, I'm bitter. I'm bitter I've lost him. I'm bitter what's happening. I'm bitter even now, after all this, I can't reach you. I'm beginning to feel your disapproval and it's making me ill. (*He looks at his balloon.*) Sorry, old friend. I blew it. (*He lets go of the balloon.*) Good night, sweet prince, and flights of angels sing thee to thy rest! (*Beat.*) Goodbye, Andre's Mother. (*He goes.* ANDRE'S MOTHER *stands alone holding her white balloon. Her lip trembles. She looks on the verge of breaking down. She is about to let go of the balloon when she pulls it down to her. She looks at it a while before she gently kisses it. She lets go of the balloon. She follows it with her eyes as it rises and rises. The lights are beginning to fade.* ANDRE'S MOTHER*'s eyes are still on the balloon. Blackout.*)

(*1988*)

QUESTIONS FOR REFLECTION

Experience

1. To what extent do you sympathize with Andre's Mother?

Interpretation

2. Why is the play entitled "Andre's Mother"? What effect does the playwright achieve by making the mother's part silent?
3. What is the significance of Cal's allusion to Lulu's mother?
4. What is the effect of Cal's references to *Hamlet?* What is conveyed through Cal's quoting from Shakespeare's play?
5. What is the significance of the helium balloons and of what the characters do with them?
6. What is the significance of the final stage direction?
7. What is the overall theme of *Andre's Mother?*

Evaluation

8. What does the play suggest about the values of Andre, his mother, and lover?

AUGUST WILSON

[*b. 1945*]

August Wilson was born and raised in Pittsburgh, Pennsylvania. He quit school at sixteen and worked at various odd jobs until moving to Minneapolis–St. Paul, where he founded the Black Horizons Theatre Company. Having dropped out of school, Wilson educated himself at the public library, discovering there the work of Ralph Ellison, Richard Wright, and Langston Hughes, three modern African-American writers whose work inspired him. Wilson is the author of *Ma Rainey's Black Bottom, Fences, Joe Turner's Come and Gone, The Piano Lesson,* and *Two Trains Running,* all notable for their depiction of the urban lives of African-Americans. The recipient of many awards, including two Pulitzer Prizes, a New York Drama Critics Circle Award, and Tony Award, Wilson continues to provide a window on the lives of Americans struggling for success, equality, and survival.

AUGUST WILSON

Fences

CHARACTERS

TROY MAXSON
JIM BONO, TROY*'s friend*
ROSE, TROY*'s wife*
LYONS, TROY*'s oldest son by previous marriage*
GABRIEL, TROY*'s brother*
CORY, TROY *and* ROSE*'s son*
RAYNELL, TROY*'s daughter*

Setting. *The setting is the yard which fronts the only entrance to the Maxson household, an ancient two-story brick house set back off a small alley in a big-city neighborhood. The entrance to the house is gained by two or three steps leading to a wooden porch badly in need of paint.*

　　A relatively recent addition to the house and running its full width, the porch lacks congruence. It is a sturdy porch with a flat roof. One or two chairs of dubious value sit at one end where the kitchen window opens onto the porch. An old-fashioned icebox stands silent guard at the opposite end.

The yard is a small dirt yard, partially fenced, except for the last scene, with a wooden saw-horse, a pile of lumber, and other fence-building equipment set off to the side. Opposite is a tree from which hangs a ball made of rags. A baseball bat leans against the tree. Two oil drums serve as garbage receptacles and sit near the house at right to complete the setting.

The Play. Near the turn of the century, the destitute of Europe sprang on the city with tenacious claws and an honest and solid dream. The city devoured them. They swelled its belly until it burst into a thousand furnaces and sewing machines, a thousand butcher shops and bakers' ovens, a thousand churches and hospitals and funeral parlors and money-lenders. The city grew. It nourished itself and offered each man a partnership limited only by his talent, his guile, and his willingness and capacity for hard work. For the immigrants of Europe, a dream dared and won true.

The descendants of African slaves were offered no such welcome or participation. They came from places called the Carolinas and the Virginias, Georgia, Alabama, Mississippi, and Tennessee. They came strong, eager, searching. The city rejected them and they fled and settled along the riverbanks and under bridges in shallow, ramshackle houses made of sticks and tarpaper. They collected rags and wood. They sold the use of their muscles and their bodies. They cleaned houses and washed clothes, they shined shoes, and in quiet desperation and vengeful pride, they stole, and lived in pursuit of their own dream. That they could breathe free, finally, and stand to meet life with the force of dignity and whatever eloquence the heart could call upon.

By 1957, the hard-won victories of the European immigrants had solidified the industrial might of America. War had been confronted and won with new energies that used loyalty and patriotism as its fuel. Life was rich, full, and flourishing. The Milwaukee Braves won the World Series, and the hot winds of change that would make the sixties a turbulent, racing, dangerous, and provocative decade had not yet begun to blow full.

ACT I

Scene 1

It is 1957. TROY *and* BONO *enter the yard, engaged in conversation.* TROY *is fifty-three years old, a large man with thick, heavy hands; it is this largeness that he strives to fill out and make an accommodation with. Together with his blackness, his largeness informs his sensibilities and the choices he has made in his life.*

Of the two men, BONO *is obviously the follower. His commitment to their friendship of thirty-odd years is rooted in his admiration of* TROY's *honesty, capacity for hard work, and his strength, which* BONO *seeks to emulate.*

It is Friday night, payday, and the one night of the week the two men engage in a ritual of talk and drink. TROY *is usually the most talkative and at times he can be crude and almost vulgar, though he is capable of rising to profound heights of expression. The men carry lunch buckets and wear or carry burlap aprons and are dressed in clothes suitable to their jobs as garbage collectors.*

BONO: Troy, you ought to stop that lying!

TROY: I ain't lying! The nigger had a watermelon this big.

He indicates with his hands.

Talking about . . . "What watermelon, Mr. Rand?" I liked to fell out!
"What watermelon, Mr. Rand?" . . . And it sitting there big as life.

BONO: What did Mr. Rand say?

TROY: Ain't said nothing. Figure if the nigger too dumb to know he carrying a
watermelon, he wasn't gonna get much sense out of him. Trying to hide that great big
old watermelon under his coat. Afraid to let the white man see him carrying it home.

BONO: I'm like you . . . I ain't got no time for them kind of people.

TROY: Now what he looks like getting mad cause he see the man from the union
talking to Mr. Rand?

BONO: He come to me talking about . . . "Maxson gonna get us fired." I told him
to get away from me with that. He walked away from me calling you a troublemaker.
What Mr. Rand say?

TROY: Ain't said nothing. He told me to go down the Commissioner's office next
Friday. They called me down there to see them.

BONO: Well, as long as you got your complaint filed, they can't fire you. That's
what one of them white fellows tell me.

TROY: I ain't worried about them firing me. They gonna fire me cause I asked a
question? That's all I did. I went to Mr. Rand and asked him, "Why? Why you got the
white men driving and the colored lifting?" Told him, "what's the matter, don't I
count? You think only white fellows got sense enough to drive a truck. That ain't no
paper job! Hell, anybody can drive a truck. How come you got all whites driving and
the colored lifting?" He told me "take it to the union." Well, hell, that's what I done!
Now they wanna come up with this pack of lies.

BONO: I told Brownie if the man come and ask him any questions . . . just tell the
truth! It ain't nothing but something they done trumped up on you cause you filed a
complaint on them.

TROY: Brownie don't understand nothing. All I want them to do is change the job
description. Give everybody a chance to drive the truck. Brownie can't see that. He
ain't got that much sense.

BONO: How you figure he be making out with that gal be up at Taylors' all the
time . . . that Alberta gal?

TROY: Same as you and me. Getting just as much as we is. Which is to say nothing.

BONO: It is, huh? I figure you doing a little better than me . . . and I ain't saying
what I'm doing.

TROY: Aw, nigger, look here . . . I know you. If you had got anywhere near that
gal, twenty minutes later you be looking to tell somebody. And the first one you gonna
tell . . . that you gonna want to brag to . . . is gonna be me.

BONO: I ain't saying that. I see where you be eyeing her.

TROY: I eye all the women. I don't miss nothing. Don't never let nobody tell you
Troy Maxson don't eye the women.

BONO: You been doing more than eyeing her. You done bought her a drink or two.

TROY: Hell yeah, I bought her a drink! What that mean? I bought you one, too.
What that mean cause I buy her a drink? I'm just being polite.

BONO: It's all right to buy her one drink. That's what you call being polite. But
when you wanna be buying two or three . . . that's what you call eyeing her.

TROY: Look here, as long as you known me . . . you ever known me to chase after women?

BONO: Hell yeah! Long as I done known you. You forgetting I knew you when.

TROY: Naw, I'm talking about since I been married to Rose?

BONO: Oh, not since you been married to Rose. Now, that's the truth, there. I can say that.

TROY: All right then! Case closed.

BONO: I see you be walking up around Alberta's house. You supposed to be at Taylor's and you be walking up around there.

TROY: What are you watching where I'm walking for? I ain't watching after you.

BONO: I see you walking around there more than once.

TROY: Hell, you liable to see me walking anywhere! That don't mean nothing cause you see me walking around there.

BONO: Where she come from anyway? She just kinda showed up one day.

TROY: Tallahassee. You can look at her and tell she one of them Florida gals. They got some big healthy women down there. Grow them right up out the ground. Got a little bit of Indian in her. Most of them niggers down in Florida got some Indian in them.

BONO: I don't know about that Indian part. But she damn sure big and healthy. Woman wear some big stockings. Got them great big old legs and hips as wide as the Mississippi River.

TROY: Legs don't mean nothing. You don't do nothing but push them out of the way. But them hips cushion the ride!

BONO: Troy, you ain't got no sense.

TROY: It's the truth! Like you riding on Goodyears!

ROSE *enters from the house. She is ten years younger than* TROY, *her devotion to him stems from her recognition of the possibilities of her life without him: a succession of abusive men and their babies, a life of partying and running the streets, the Church, or aloneness with its attendant pain and frustration. She recognizes* TROY's *spirit as a fine and illuminating one and she either ignores or forgives his faults, only some of which she recognizes. Though she doesn't drink, her presence is an integral part of the Friday night rituals. She alternates between the porch and the kitchen, where supper preparations are under way.*

ROSE: What you all out here getting into?

TROY: What you worried about what we getting into for? This is men talk, woman.

ROSE: What I care what you all talking about? Bono, you gonna stay for supper?

BONO: No, I thank you, Rose. But Lucille say she cooking up a pot of pigfeet.

TROY: Pigfeet! Hell, I'm going home with you! Might even stay the night if you got some pigfeet. You got something in there to top them pigfeet, Rose?

ROSE: I'm cooking up some chicken. I got some chicken and collard greens.

TROY: Well, go on back in the house and let me and Bono finish what we was talking about. This is men talk. I got some talk for you later. You know what kind of talk I mean. You go on and powder it up.

ROSE: Troy Maxson, don't you start that now!

TROY [*puts his arm around her*]: Aw, woman . . . come here. Look here, Bono . . . when I met this woman . . . I got out that place, say, "Hitch up my pony, saddle up my mare . . . there's a woman out there for me somewhere. I looked here. Looked there.

Saw Rose and latched on to her." I latched on to her and told her—I'm gonna tell you the truth—I told her, "Baby, I don't wanna marry, I just wanna be your man." Rose told me . . . tell him what you told me, Rose.

ROSE: I told him if he wasn't the marrying kind, then move out the way so the marrying kind could find me.

TROY: That's what she told me. "Nigger, you in my way. You blocking the view! Move out the way so I can find me a husband." I thought it over two or three days. Come back—

ROSE: Ain't no two or three days nothing. You was back the same night.

TROY: Come back, told her . . . "Okay, baby . . . but I'm gonna buy me a banty rooster and put him out there in the backyard . . . and when he see a stranger come, he'll flap his wings and crow . . . " Look here, Bono, I could watch the front door by myself . . . it was that back door I was worried about.

ROSE: Troy, you ought not talk like that. Troy ain't doing nothing but telling a lie.

TROY: Only thing is . . . when we first got married . . . forget the rooster . . . we ain't had no yard!

BONO: I hear you tell it. Me and Lucille was staying down there on Logan Street. Had two rooms with the outhouse in the back. I ain't mind the outhouse none. But when that goddamn wind blow through there in the winter . . . that's what I'm talking about! To this day I wonder why in the hell I ever stayed down there for six long years. But see, I didn't know I could do no better. I thought only white folks had inside toilets and things.

ROSE: There's a lot of people don't know they can do no better than they doing now. That's just something you got to learn. A lot of folks still shop at Bella's.

TROY: Ain't nothing wrong with shopping at Bella's. She got fresh food.

ROSE: I ain't said nothing about if she got fresh food. I'm talking about what she charge. She charge ten cents more than the A&P.

TROY: The A&P ain't never done nothing for me. I spends my money where I'm treated right. I go down to Bella, say, "I need a loaf of bread, I'll pay you Friday." She give it to me. What sense that make when I got money to go and spend it somewhere else and ignore the person who done right by me? That ain't in the Bible.

ROSE: We ain't talking about what's in the Bible. What sense it made to shop there when she overcharge?

TROY: You shop where you want to. I'll do my shopping where the people been good to me.

ROSE: Well, I don't think it's right for her to overcharge. That's all I was saying.

BONO: Look here . . . I got to get on. Lucille going be raising all kind of hell.

TROY: Where you going, nigger? We ain't finished this pint. Come here, finish this pint.

BONO: Well, hell, I am . . . if you ever turn the bottle loose.

TROY [hands him the bottle]:   The only thing I say about the A&P is I'm glad Cory got that job down there. Help him take care of his school clothes and things. Gabe done moved out and things getting tight around here. He got that job. . . . He can start to look out for himself.

ROSE: Cory done went and got recruited by a college football team.

TROY: I told that boy about that football stuff. The white man ain't gonna let him get nowhere with that football. I told him when he first come to me with it. Now you come telling me he done went and got more tied up in it. He ought to go and get recruited in how to fix cars or something where he can make a living.

ROSE: He ain't talking about making no living playing football. It's just something the boys in school do. They gonna send a recruiter by to talk to you. He'll tell you he ain't talking about making no living playing football. It's a honor to be recruited.

TROY: It ain't gonna get him nowhere. Bono'll tell you that.

BONO: If he be like you in the sports . . . he's gonna be all right. Ain't but two men ever played baseball as good as you. That's Babe Ruth and Josh Gibson.* Them's the only two men ever hit more home runs than you.

TROY: What it ever get me? Ain't got a pot to piss in or a window to throw it out of.

ROSE: Times have changed since you was playing baseball, Troy. That was before the war. Times have changed a lot since then.

TROY: How in hell they done changed?

ROSE: They got lots of colored boys playing ball now. Baseball and football.

BONO: You right about that, Rose. Times have changed, Troy. You just come along too early.

TROY: There ought not never have been no time called too early! Now you take that fellow . . . what's that fellow they had playing right field for the Yankees back then? You know who I'm talking about, Bono. Used to play right field for the Yankees.

ROSE: Selkirk?

TROY: Selkirk! That's it! Man batting .269, understand? .269. What kind of sense that make? I was hitting .432 with thirty-seven home runs! Man batting .269 and playing right field for the Yankees! I saw Josh Gibson's daughter yesterday. She walking around with raggedy shoes on her feet. Now I bet you Selkirk's daughter ain't walking around with raggedy shoes on her feet! I bet you that!

ROSE: They got a lot of colored baseball players now. Jackie Robinson was the first. Folks had to wait for Jackie Robinson.

TROY: I done seen a hundred niggers play baseball better than Jackie Robinson. Hell, I know some teams Jackie Robinson couldn't even make! What you talking about Jackie Robinson. Jackie Robinson wasn't nobody. I'm talking about if you could play ball then they ought to have let you play. Don't care what color you were. Come telling me I come along too early. If you could play . . . then they ought to have let you play.

TROY *takes a long drink from the bottle.*

ROSE: You gonna drink yourself to death. You don't need to be drinking like that.

TROY: Death ain't nothing. I done seen him. Done wrassled with him. You can't tell me nothing about death. Death ain't nothing but a fastball on the outside corner. And you know what I'll do to that! Lookee here, Bono . . . am I lying? You get one of them fastballs, about waist high, over the outside corner of the plate where you can get the meat of the bat on it . . . and good god! You can kiss it goodbye. Now, am I lying?

BONO: Naw, you telling the truth there. I seen you do it.

TROY: If I'm lying . . . that 450 feet worth of lying!

Josh Gibson   *(1911–1947) powerful, black baseball player known in the 1930s as the Babe Ruth of the Negro leagues.*

Pause.

That's all death is to me. A fastball on the outside corner.

ROSE: I don't know why you want to get on talking about death.

TROY: Ain't nothing wrong with talking about death. That's part of life. Everybody gonna die. You gonna die, I'm gonna die. Bono's gonna die. Hell, we all gonna die.

ROSE: But you ain't got to talk about it. I don't like to talk about it.

TROY: You the one brought it up. Me and Bono was talking about baseball . . . you tell me I'm gonna drink myself to death. Ain't that right, Bono? You know I don't drink this but one night out of the week. That's Friday night. I'm gonna drink just enough to where I can handle it. Then I cuts it loose. I leave it alone. So don't you worry about me drinking myself to death. 'Cause I ain't worried about Death. I done seen him. I done wrestled with him.

Look here, Bono . . . I looked up one day and Death was marching straight at me. Like Soldiers on Parade! The Army of Death was marching straight at me. The middle of July, 1941. It got real cold just like it be winter. It seem like Death himself reached out and touched me on the shoulder. He touch me just like I touch you. I got cold as ice and Death standing there grinning at me.

ROSE: Troy, why don't you hush that talk.

TROY: I say . . . What you want, Mr. Death? You be wanting me? You done brought your army to be getting me? I looked him dead in the eye. I wasn't fearing nothing. I was ready to tangle. Just like I'm ready to tangle now. The Bible say be ever vigilant. That's why I don't get but so drunk. I got to keep watch.

ROSE: Troy was right down there in Mercy Hospital. You remember he had pneumonia? Laying there with a fever talking plumb out of his head.

TROY: Death standing there staring at me . . . carrying that sickle in his hand. Finally he say, "You want bound over for another year?" See, just like that . . . "You want bound over for another year?" I told him, "Bound over hell! Let's settle this now!"

It seem like he kinda fell back when I said that, and all the cold went out of me. I reached down and grabbed that sickle and threw it just as far as I could throw it . . . and me and him commenced to wrestling.

We wrestled for three days and three nights. I can't say where I found the strength from. Every time it seemed like he was gonna get the best of me, I'd reach way down deep inside myself and find the strength to do him one better.

ROSE: Every time Troy tell that story he find different ways to tell it. Different things to make up about it.

TROY: I ain't making up nothing. I'm telling you the facts of what happened. I wrestled with Death for three days and three nights and I'm standing here to tell you about it.

Pause.

All right. At the end of the third night we done weakened each other to where we can't hardly move. Death stood up, throwed on his robe . . . had him a white robe with a hood on it. He throwed on that robe and went off to look for his sickle. Say, "I'll be back." Just like that. "I'll be back." I told him, say, "Yeah, but . . . you gonna have to find me!" I wasn't no fool. I wasn't going looking for him. Death ain't nothing to play with. And I know he's gonna get me. I know I got to join his army . . . his camp followers.

But as long as I keep my strength and see him coming . . . as long as I keep up my vigilance . . . he's gonna have to fight to get me. I ain't going easy.

BONO: Well, look here, since you got to keep up your vigilance . . . let me have the bottle.

TROY: Aw hell, I shouldn't have told you that part. I should have left out that part.

ROSE: Troy be talking that stuff and half the time don't even know what he be talking about.

TROY: Bono know me better than that.

BONO: That's right. I know you. I know you got some Uncle Remus* in your blood. You got more stories than the devil got sinners.

TROY: Aw hell, I done seen him too! Done talked with the devil.

ROSE: Troy, don't nobody wanna be hearing all that stuff.

LYONS *enters the yard from the street. Thirty-four years old,* TROY*'s son by a previous marriage, he sports a neatly trimmed goatee, sport coat, white shirt, tieless and buttoned at the collar. Though he fancies himself a musician, he is more caught up in the rituals and "idea" of being a musician than in the actual practice of the music. He has come to borrow money from* TROY, *and while he knows he will be successful, he is uncertain as to what extent his lifestyle will be held up to scrutiny and ridicule.*

LYONS: Hey, Pop.

TROY: What you come "Hey, Popping" me for?

LYONS: How you doing, Rose?

He kisses her.

Mr. Bono. How you doing?

BONO: Hey, Lyons . . . how you been?

TROY: He must have been doing all right. I ain't seen him around here last week.

ROSE: Troy, leave your boy alone. He come by to see you and you wanna start all that nonsense.

TROY: I ain't bothering Lyons.

Offers him the bottle.

Here . . . get you a drink. We got an understanding. I know why he come by to see me and he know I know.

LYONS: Come on, Pop . . . I just stopped by to say hi . . . see how you was doing.

TROY: You ain't stopped by yesterday.

ROSE: You gonna stay for supper, Lyons? I got some chicken cooking in the oven.

LYONS: No, Rose . . . thanks. I was just in the neighborhood and thought I'd stop by for a minute.

TROY: You was in the neighborhood all right, nigger. You telling the truth there. You was in the neighborhood cause it's my payday.

LYONS: Well, hell, since you mentioned it . . . let me have ten dollars.

TROY: I'll be damned! I'll die and go to hell and play blackjack with the devil before I give you ten dollars.

BONO: That's what I wanna know about . . . that devil you done seen.

Uncle Remus   *Black storyteller who recounts traditional black tales in the book by Joel Chandler Harris.*

LYONS: What . . . Pop done seen the devil? You too much, Pops.

TROY: Yeah, I done seen him. Talked to him too!

ROSE: You ain't seen no devil. I done told you that man ain't had nothing to do with the devil. Anything you can't understand, you want to call it the devil.

TROY: Look here, Bono . . . I went down to see Hertzberger about some furniture. Got three rooms for two-ninety-eight. That what it say on the radio. "Three rooms . . . two-ninety-eight." Even made up a little song about it. Go down there . . . man tell me I can't get no credit. I'm working every day and can't get no credit. What to do? I got an empty house with some raggedy furniture in it. Cory ain't got no bed. He's sleeping on a pile of rags on the floor. Working every day and can't get no credit. Come back here—Rose'll tell you—madder than hell. Sit down . . . try to figure what I'm gonna do. Come a knock on the door. Ain't been living here but three days. Who know I'm here? Open the door . . . devil standing there bigger than life. White fellow . . . got on good clothes and everything. Standing there with a clipboard in his hand. I ain't had to say nothing. First words come out of his mouth was . . . "I understand you need some furniture and can't get no credit." I liked to fell over. He say, "I'll give you all the credit you want, but you got to pay the interest on it." I told him, "Give me three rooms worth and charge whatever you want." Next day a truck pulled up here and two men unloaded them three rooms. Man that drove the truck give me a book. Say send ten dollars, first of every month to the address in the book and everything will be all right. Say if I miss a payment the devil was coming back and it'll be hell to pay. That was fifteen years ago. To this day . . . the first of the month I send my ten dollars, Rose'll tell you.

ROSE: Troy lying.

TROY: I ain't never seen that man since. Now you tell me who else that could have been but the devil? I ain't sold my soul or nothing like that, you understand. Naw, I wouldn't have truck with the devil about nothing like that. I got my furniture and pays my ten dollars the first of the month just like clockwork.

BONO: How long you say you been paying this ten dollars a month?

TROY: Fifteen years!

BONO: Hell, ain't you finished paying for it yet? How much the man done charged you.

TROY: Ah hell, I done paid for it. I done paid for it ten times over! The fact is I'm scared to stop paying it.

ROSE: Troy lying. We got that furniture from Mr. Glickman. He ain't paying no ten dollars a month to nobody.

TROY: Aw hell, woman. Bono know I ain't that big a fool.

LYONS: I was just getting ready to say . . . I know where there's a bridge for sale.

TROY: Look here, I'll tell you this . . . it don't matter to me if he was the devil. It don't matter if the devil give credit. Somebody has got to give it.

ROSE: It ought to matter. You going around talking about having truck with the devil . . . God's the one you gonna have to answer to. He's the one gonna be at the Judgment.

LYONS: Yeah, well, look here, Pop . . . let me have that ten dollars. I'll give it back to you. Bonnie got a job working at the hospital.

TROY: What I tell you, Bono? The only time I see this nigger is when he wants something. That's the only time I see him.

LYONS: Come on, Pop, Mr. Bono don't want to hear all that. Let me have the ten dollars. I told you Bonnie working.

TROY: What that mean to me? "Bonnie working." I don't care if she working. Go ask her for the ten dollars if she working. Talking about "Bonnie working." Why ain't you working?

LYONS: Aw, Pop, you know I can't find no decent job. Where am I gonna get a job at? You know I can't get no job.

TROY: I told you I know some people down there. I can get you on the rubbish if you want to work. I told you that the last time you came by here asking me for something.

LYONS: Naw, Pop . . . thanks. That ain't for me. I don't wanna be carrying nobody's rubbish. I don't wanna be punching nobody's time clock.

TROY: What's the matter, you too good to carry people's rubbish? Where you think that ten dollars you talking about come from? I'm just supposed to haul people's rubbish and give my money to you cause you too lazy to work. You too lazy to work and wanna know why you ain't got what I got.

ROSE: What hospital Bonnie working at? Mercy?

LYONS: She's down at Passavant working in the laundry.

TROY: I ain't got nothing as it is. I give you that ten dollars and I got to eat beans the rest of the week. Naw . . . you ain't getting no ten dollars here.

LYONS: You ain't got to be eating no beans. I don't know why you wanna say that.

TROY: I ain't got no extra money. Gabe done moved over to Miss Pearl's paying her the rent and things done got tight around here. I can't afford to be giving you every payday.

LYONS: I ain't asked you to give me nothing. I asked you to loan me ten dollars. I know you got ten dollars.

TROY: Yeah, I got it. You know why I got it? Cause I don't throw my money away out there in the streets. You living the fast life . . . wanna be a musician . . . running around in them clubs and things . . . then, you learn to take care of yourself. You ain't gonna find me going and asking nobody for nothing. I done spent too many years without.

LYONS: You and me is two different people, Pop.

TROY: I done learned my mistake and learned to do what's right by it. You still trying to get something for nothing. Life don't owe you nothing. You owe it to yourself. Ask Bono. He'll tell you I'm right.

LYONS: You got your way of dealing with the world . . . I got mine. The only thing that matters to me is the music.

TROY: Yeah, I can see that! It don't matter how you gonna eat . . . where your next dollar is coming from. You telling the truth there.

LYONS: I know I got to eat. But I got to live too. I need something that gonna help me to get out of the bed in the morning. Make me feel like I belong in the world. I don't bother nobody. I just stay with my music cause that's the only way I can find to live in the world. Otherwise there ain't no telling what I might do. Now I don't come criticizing you and how you live. I just come by to ask you for ten dollars. I don't wanna hear all that about how I live.

TROY: Boy, your mamma did a hell of a job raising you.

LYONS: You can't change me, Pop. I'm thirty-four years old. If you wanted to change me, you should have been there when I was growing up. I come by to see you . . . ask for ten dollars and you want to talk about how I was raised. You don't know nothing about how I was raised.

ROSE: Let the boy have ten dollars, Troy.

TROY [to LYONS]:   What the hell you looking at me for? I ain't got no ten dollars. You know what I do with my money.

To ROSE.

Give him ten dollars if you want him to have it.

ROSE: I will. Just as soon as you turn it loose.

TROY [handing ROSE the money]:   There it is. Seventy-six dollars and forty-two cents. You see this, Bono? Now, I ain't gonna get but six of that back.

ROSE: You ought to stop telling that lie. Here, Lyons. [She hands him the money.]

LYONS: Thanks, Rose. Look . . . I got to run . . . I'll see you later.

TROY: Wait a minute. You gonna say, "thanks, Rose" and ain't gonna look to see where she got that ten dollars from? See how they do me, Bono?

LYONS: I know she got it from you, Pop. Thanks. I'll give it back to you.

TROY: There he go telling another lie. Time I see that ten dollars . . . he'll be owing me thirty more.

LYONS: See you, Mr. Bono.

BONO: Take care, Lyons!

LYONS: Thanks, Pop. I'll see you again.

LYONS exits the yard.

TROY: I don't know why he don't go and get him a decent job and take care of that woman he got.

BONO: He'll be all right, Troy. The boy is still young.

TROY: The *boy* is thirty-four years old.

ROSE: Let's not get off into all that.

BONO: Look here . . . I got to be going. I got to be getting on. Lucille gonna be waiting.

TROY [puts his arm around ROSE]:   See this woman, Bono? I love this woman. I love this woman so much it hurts. I love her so much . . . I done run out of ways of loving her. So I got to go back to basics. Don't you come by my house Monday morning talking about time to go to work . . . 'cause I'm still gonna be stroking!

ROSE: Troy! Stop it now!

BONO: I ain't paying him no mind, Rose. That ain't nothing but gin-talk. Go on, Troy. I'll see you Monday.

TROY: Don't you come by my house, nigger! I done told you what I'm gonna be doing.

The lights go down to black.

Scene 2

The lights come up on ROSE hanging up clothes. She hums and sings softly to herself. It is the following morning.

ROSE [Sings]:   Jesus, be a fence all around me every day
Jesus, I want you to protect me as I travel on my way.

Jesus, be a fence all around me every day.

TROY *enters from the house.*

Jesus, I want you to protect me
As I travel on my way.

[*To* TROY] 'Morning. You ready for breakfast? I can fix it soon as I finish hanging up these clothes?

TROY: I got the coffee on. That'll be all right. I'll just drink some of that this morning.

ROSE: That 651 hit yesterday. That's the second time this month. Miss Pearl hit for a dollar . . . seem like those that need the least always get lucky. Poor folks can't get nothing.

TROY: Them numbers don't know anybody. I don't know why you fool with them. You and Lyons both.

ROSE: It's something to do.

TROY: You ain't doing nothing but throwing your money away.

ROSE: Troy, you know I don't play foolishly. I just play a nickel here and a nickel there.

TROY: That's two nickels you done thrown away.

ROSE: Now I hit sometimes . . . that makes up for it. It always comes in handy when I do hit. I don't hear you complaining then.

TROY: I ain't complaining now. I just say it's foolish. Trying to guess out of six hundred ways which way the number gonna come. If I had all the money niggers, these Negroes, throw away on numbers for one week—just one week—I'd be a rich man.

ROSE: Well, you wishing and calling it foolish ain't gonna stop folks from playing numbers. That's one thing for sure. Besides . . . some good things come from playing numbers. Look where Pope done bought him that restaurant off of numbers.

TROY: I can't stand niggers like that. Man ain't had two dimes to rub together. He walking around with his shoes all run over bumming money for cigarettes. All right. Got lucky there and hit the numbers . . .

ROSE: Troy, I know all about it.

TROY: Had good sense, I'll say that for him. He ain't throwed his money away. I seen niggers hit the numbers and go through two thousand dollars in four days. Man bought him that restaurant down there . . . fixed it up real nice . . . and then didn't want nobody to come in it! A Negro go in there and can't get no kind of service. I seen a white fellow come in there and order a bowl of stew. Pope picked all the meat out the pot for him. Man ain't had nothing but a bowl of meat! Negro come behind him and ain't got nothing but the potatoes and carrots. Talking about what numbers do for people, you picked a wrong example. Ain't done nothing but make a worser fool out of him than he was before.

ROSE: Troy, you ought to stop worrying about what happened at work yesterday.

TROY: I ain't worried. Just told me to be down there at the Commissioner's office on Friday. Everybody think they gonna fire me. I ain't worried about them firing me. You ain't got to worry about that.

Pause.

Where's Cory? Cory in the house? [*Calls*] Cory?

ROSE: He gone out.

TROY: Out, huh? He gone out 'cause he know I want him to help me with this fence. I know how he is. That boy scared of work.

GABRIEL enters. He comes halfway down the alley and, hearing TROY's voice, stops.

TROY [*continues*]:   He ain't done a lick of work in his life.

ROSE: He had to go to football practice. Coach wanted them to get in a little extra practice before the season start.

TROY: I got his practice . . . running out of here before he gets his chores done.

ROSE: Troy, what is wrong with you this morning? Don't nothing set right with you. Go on back in there and go to bed . . . get up on the other side.

TROY: Why something got to be wrong with me? I ain't said nothing wrong with me.

ROSE: You got something to say about everything. First it's the numbers . . . then it's the way the man runs his restaurant . . . then you done got on Cory. What's it gonna be next? Take a look up there and see if the weather suits you . . . or is it gonna be how you gonna put up the fence with the clothes hanging in the yard.

TROY: You hit the nail on the head then.

ROSE: I know you like I know the back of my hand. Go on in there and get you some coffee . . . see if that straighten you up. 'Cause you ain't right this morning.

TROY starts into the house and sees GABRIEL. GABRIEL starts singing. TROY's brother, he is seven years younger than TROY. Injured in World War II, he has a metal plate in his head. He carries an old trumpet tied around his waist and believes with every fiber of his being that he is the Archangel Gabriel. He carries a chipped basket with an assortment of discarded fruits and vegetables he has picked up in the strip district and which he attempts to sell.

GABRIEL [*Singing*]:   Yes, ma'am, I got plums
              You ask me how I sell them
              Oh ten cents apiece
              Three for a quarter
              Come and buy now
              'Cause I'm here today
              And tomorrow I'll be gone

GABRIEL enters.

Hey, Rose!

ROSE: How you doing, Gabe?

GABRIEL: There's Troy . . . Hey, Troy!

TROY: Hey, Gabe.

Exit into kitchen.

ROSE [*to GABRIEL*]:   What you got there?

GABRIEL: You know what I got, Rose. I got fruits and vegetables.

ROSE [*looking in basket*]:   Where's all these plums you talking about?

GABRIEL: I ain't got no plums today, Rose. I was just singing that. Have some tomorrow. Put me in a big order for plums. Have enough plums tomorrow for St. Peter and everybody.

TROY *enters from kitchen, crosses to steps.*

[*To* ROSE] Troy's mad at me.

TROY: I ain't mad at you. What I got to be mad at you about? You ain't done nothing to me.

GABRIEL: I just moved over to Miss Pearl's to keep out from in your way. I ain't mean no harm by it.

TROY: Who said anything about that? I ain't said anything about that.

GABRIEL: You ain't mad at me, is you?

TROY: Naw . . . I ain't mad at you, Gabe. If I was mad at you I'd tell you about it.

GABRIEL: Got me two rooms. In the basement. Got my own door too. Wanna see my key?

He holds up a key.

That's my own key! Ain't nobody else got a key like that. That's my key! My two rooms!

TROY: Well, that's good, Gabe. You got your own key . . . that's good.

ROSE: You hungry, Gabe? I was just fixing to cook Troy his breakfast.

GABRIEL: I'll take some biscuits. You got some biscuits? Did you know when I was in heaven . . . every morning me and St. Peter would sit down by the gate and eat some big fat biscuits? Oh, yeah! We had us a good time. We'd sit there and eat us them biscuits and then St. Peter would go off to sleep and tell me to wake him up when it's time to open the gates for the judgment.

ROSE: Well, come on . . . I'll make up a batch of biscuits.

ROSE *exits into the house.*

GABRIEL: Troy . . . St. Peter got your name in the book. I seen it. It say . . . Troy Maxson, I say . . . I know him! He got the same name like what I got. That's my brother!

TROY: How many times you gonna tell me that, Gabe?

GABRIEL: Ain't got my name in the book. Don't have to have my name. I done died and went to heaven. He got your name though. One morning St. Peter was looking at his book . . . marking it up for the judgment . . . and he let me see your name. Got it in there under M. Got Rose's name . . . I ain't seen it like I seen yours . . . but I know it's in there. He got a great big book. Got everybody's name what was ever been born. That's what he told me. But I seen your name. Seen it with my own eyes.

TROY: Go on in the house there. Rose going to fix you something to eat.

GABRIEL: Oh, I ain't hungry. I done had breakfast with Aunt Jemimah. She come by and cooked me up a whole mess of flapjacks. Remember how we used to eat them flapjacks?

TROY: Go on in the house and get you something to eat now.

GABRIEL: I got to go sell my plums. I done sold some tomatoes. Got me two quarters. Wanna see?

He shows TROY *his quarters.*

I'm gonna save them and buy me a new horn so St. Peter can hear me when it's time to open the gates.

GABRIEL *stops suddenly. Listens.*

Hear that? That's the hellhounds. I got to chase them out of here. Go on get out of here! Get out!

GABRIEL *exits singing.*

> Better get ready for the judgment
> Better get ready for the judgment
> My Lord is coming down

ROSE *enters from the house.*

TROY: He gone off somewhere.

GABRIEL [*offstage*]:   Better get ready for the judgment
> Better get ready for the judgment morning
> Better get ready for the judgment
> My God is coming down

ROSE: He ain't eating right. Miss Pearl say she can't get him to eat nothing.

TROY: What you want me to do about it, Rose? I done did everything I can for the man. I can't make him get well. Man got half his head blown away . . . what you expect?

ROSE: Seem like something ought to be done to help him.

TROY: Man don't bother nobody. He just mixed up from that metal plate he got in his head. Ain't no sense for him to go back into the hospital.

ROSE: Least he be eating right. They can help him take care of himself.

TROY: Don't nobody wanna be locked up, Rose. What you wanna lock him up for? Man go over there and fight the war . . . messin' around with them Japs, get half his head blown off . . . and they give him a lousy three thousand dollars. And I had to swoop down on that.

ROSE: Is you fixing to go into that again?

TROY: That's the only way I got a roof over my head . . . cause of that metal plate.

ROSE: Ain't no sense you blaming yourself for nothing. Gabe wasn't in no condition to manage that money. You done what was right by him. Can't nobody say you ain't done what was right by him. Look how long you took care of him . . . till he wanted to have his own place and moved over there with Miss Pearl.

TROY: That ain't what I'm saying, woman! I'm just stating the facts. If my brother didn't have that metal plate in his head . . . I wouldn't have a pot to piss in or a window to throw it out of. And I'm fifty-three years old. Now see if you can understand that!

TROY *gets up from the porch and starts to exit the yard.*

ROSE: Where you going off to? You been running out of here every Saturday for weeks. I thought you was gonna work on this fence?

TROY: I'm gonna walk down to Taylors'. Listen to the ball game. I'll be back in a bit. I'll work on it when I get back.

He exits the yard. The lights go to black.

Scene 3

The lights come up on the yard. It is four hours later. ROSE *is taking down the clothes from the line.* CORY *enters carrying his football equipment.*

ROSE: Your daddy like to had a fit with you running out of here this morning without doing your chores.

CORY: I told you I had to go to practice.

ROSE: He say you were supposed to help him with this fence.

CORY: He been saying that the last four or five Saturdays, and then he don't never do nothing, but go down to Taylors'. Did you tell him about the recruiter?

ROSE: Yeah, I told him.

CORY: What he say?

ROSE: He ain't said nothing too much. You get in there and get started on your chores before he gets back. Go on and scrub down them steps before he gets back here hollering and carrying on.

CORY: I'm hungry. What you got to eat, Mama?

ROSE: Go on and get started on your chores. I got some meat loaf in there. Go on and make you a sandwich . . . and don't leave no mess in there.

CORY *exits into the house.* ROSE *continues to take down the clothes.* TROY *enters the yard and sneaks up and grabs her from behind.*

Troy! Go on, now. You liked to scared me to death. What was the score of the game? Lucille had me on the phone and I couldn't keep up with it.

TROY: What I care about the game? Come here, woman. [*He tries to kiss her.*]

ROSE: I thought you went down Taylors' to listen to the game. Go on, Troy! You supposed to be putting up this fence.

TROY [*attempting to kiss her again*]:   I'll put it up when I finish with what is at hand.

ROSE: Go on, Troy. I ain't studying you.

TROY [*chasing after her*]:   I'm studying you . . . fixing to do my homework!

ROSE: Troy, you better leave me alone.

TROY: Where's Cory? That boy brought his butt home yet?

ROSE: He's in the house doing his chores.

TROY [*calling*]:   Cory! Get your butt out here, boy!

ROSE *exits into the house with the laundry.* TROY *goes over to the pile of wood, picks up a board, and starts sawing.* CORY *enters from the house.*

TROY: You just now coming in here from leaving this morning?

CORY: Yeah, I had to go to football practice.

TROY: Yeah, what?

CORY: Yessir.

TROY: I ain't but two seconds off you noway. The garbage sitting in there over-flowing . . . you ain't done none of your chores . . . and you come in here talking about "Yeah."

CORY: I was just getting ready to do my chores, now, Pop . . .

TROY: Your first chore is to help me with this fence on Saturday. Everything else come after that. Now get that saw and cut them boards.

CORY *takes the saw and begins cutting the boards.* TROY *continues working. There is a long pause.*

CORY: Hey, Pop . . . why don't you buy a TV?

TROY: What I want with a TV? What I want one of them for?

CORY: Everybody got one. Earl, Ba Bra . . . Jesse!

TROY: I ain't asked you who had one. I say what I want with one?

CORY: So you can watch it. They got lots of things on TV. Baseball games and everything. We could watch the World Series.

TROY: Two hundred dollars, huh?

CORY: That ain't that much, Pop.

TROY: Naw, it's just two hundred dollars. See that roof you got over your head at night? Let me tell you something about that roof. It's been over ten years since that roof was last tarred. See now . . . the snow come this winter and sit up there on that roof like it is . . . and it's gonna seep inside. It's just gonna be a little bit . . . ain't gonna hardly notice it. Then the next thing you know, it's gonna be leaking all over the house. Then the wood rot from all that water and you gonna need a whole new roof. Now, how much you think it cost to get that roof tarred?

CORY: I don't know.

TROY: Two hundred and sixty-four dollars . . . cash money. While you thinking about a TV, I got to be thinking about the roof . . . and whatever else go wrong around here. Now if you had two hundred dollars, what would you do . . . fix the roof or buy a TV?

CORY: I'd buy a TV. Then when the roof started to leak . . . when it needed fixing . . . I'd fix it.

TROY: Where you gonna get the money from? You done spent it for a TV. You gonna sit up and watch the water run all over your brand new TV.

CORY: Aw, Pop. You got money, I know you do.

TROY: Where I got it at, huh?

CORY: You got it in the bank.

TROY: You wanna see my bankbook? You wanna see that seventy-three dollars and twenty-two cents I got sitting up in there.

CORY: You ain't got to pay for it all at one time. You can put a down payment on it and carry it on home with you.

TROY: Not me. I ain't gonna owe nobody nothing if I can help it. Miss a payment and they come and snatch it right out your house. Then what you got? Now, soon as I get two hundred dollars clear, then I'll buy a TV. Right now, as soon as I get two hundred and sixty-four dollars, I'm gonna have this roof tarred.

CORY: Aw . . . Pop!

TROY: You go on and get you two hundred dollars and buy one if ya want it. I got better things to do with my money.

CORY: I can't get no two hundred dollars. I ain't never seen two hundred dollars.

TROY: I'll tell you what . . . you get you a hundred dollars and I'll put the other hundred with it.

CORY: All right, I'm gonna show you.

TROY: You gonna show me how you can cut them boards right now.

CORY begins to cut the boards. There is a long pause.

CORY: The Pirates won today. That makes five in a row.

TROY: I ain't thinking about the Pirates. Got an all-white team. Got that boy . . . that Puerto Rican boy . . . Clemente. Don't even half-play him. That boy could be something if they give him a chance. Play him one day and sit him on the bench the next.

CORY: He gets a lot of chances to play.

TROY: I'm talking about playing regular. Playing every day so you can get your timing. That's what I'm talking about.

CORY: They got some white guys on the team that don't play every day. You can't play everybody at the same time.

TROY: If they got a white fellow sitting on the bench . . . you can bet your last dollar he can't play! The colored guy got to be twice as good before he get on the team. That's why I don't want you to get all tied up in them sports. Man on the team and what it get him? They got colored on the team and don't use them. Same as not having them. All them teams the same.

CORY: The Braves got Hank Aaron and Wes Covington. Hank Aaron hit two home runs today. That makes forty-three.

TROY: Hank Aaron ain't nobody. That's what you supposed to do. That's how you supposed to play the game. Ain't nothing to it. It's just a matter of timing . . . getting the right follow-through. Hell, I can hit forty-three home runs right now!

CORY: Not off no major-league pitching, you couldn't.

TROY: We had better pitching in the Negro leagues. I hit seven home runs off of Satchel Paige.* You can't get no better than that!

CORY: Sandy Koufax. He's leading the league in strikeouts.

TROY: I ain't thinking of no Sandy Koufax.

CORY: You got Warren Spahn and Lew Burdette. I bet you couldn't hit no home runs off of Warren Spahn.

TROY: I'm through with it now. You go on and cut them boards.

Pause.

Your mama tell me you done got recruited by a college football team? Is that right?

CORY: Yeah. Coach Zellman say the recruiter gonna be coming by to talk to you. Get you to sign the permission papers.

TROY: I thought you supposed to be working down there at the A&P. Ain't you suppose to be working down there after school?

CORY: Mr. Stawicki say he gonna hold my job for me until after the football season. Say starting next week I can work weekends.

TROY: I thought we had an understanding about this football stuff? You suppose to keep up with your chores and hold that job down at the A&P. Ain't been around here all day on a Saturday. Ain't none of your chores done . . . and now you telling me you done quit your job.

CORY: I'm gonna be working weekends.

TROY: You damn right you are! And ain't no need for nobody coming around here to talk to me about signing nothing.

CORY: Hey, Pop . . . you can't do that. He's coming all the way from North Carolina.

TROY: I don't care where he coming from. The white man ain't gonna let you get nowhere with that football noway. You go on and get your booklearning so you can work yourself up in that A&P or learn how to fix cars or build houses or something, get you a trade. That way you have something can't nobody take away from you. You go on and learn how to put your hands to some good use. Besides hauling people's garbage.

Satchel Paige   *(1960?–1982) legendary black pitcher in the Negro leagues.*

CORY: I get good grades, Pop. That's why the recruiter wants to talk with you. You got to keep your grades to get recruited. This way I'll be going to college. I'll get a chance . . .

TROY: First you gonna get your butt down there to the A&P and get your job back.

CORY: Mr. Stawicki done already hired somebody else 'cause I told him I was playing football.

TROY: You a bigger fool than I thought . . . to let somebody take away your job so you can play some football. Where you gonna get your money to take out your girlfriend and whatnot? What kind of foolishness is that to let somebody take away your job?

CORY: I'm still gonna be working weekends.

TROY: Naw . . . naw. You getting your butt out of here and finding you another job.

CORY: Come on, Pop! I got to practice. I can't work after school and play football too. The team needs me. That's what Coach Zellman say . . .

TROY: I don't care what nobody else say. I'm the boss . . . you understand? I'm the boss around here. I do the only saying what counts.

CORY: Come on, Pop!

TROY: I asked you . . . did you understand?

CORY: Yeah . . .

TROY: What?!

CORY: Yessir.

TROY: You go on down there to that A&P and see if you can get your job back. If you can't do both . . . then you quit the football team. You've got to take the crookeds with the straights.

CORY: Yessir.

Pause.

Can I ask you a question?

TROY: What the hell you wanna ask me? Mr. Stawicki the one you got the questions for.

CORY: How come you ain't never liked me?

TROY: Liked you? Who the hell say I got to like you? What law is there say I got to like you? Wanna stand up in my face and ask a damn fool-ass question like that. Talking about liking somebody. Come here, boy, when I talk to you.

CORY *comes over to where* TROY *is working. He stands slouched over and* TROY *shoves him on his shoulder.*

Straighten up, goddammit! I asked you a question . . . what law is there say I got to like you?

CORY: None.

TROY: Well, all right then! Don't you eat every day?

Pause.

Answer me when I talk to you! Don't you eat every day?

CORY: Yeah.

TROY: Nigger, as long as you in my house, you put that sir on the end of it when you talk to me!

CORY: Yes . . . sir.

TROY: You eat every day.

CORY: Yessir!

TROY: Got a roof over your head.

CORY: Yessir!

TROY: Got clothes on your back.

CORY: Yessir.

TROY: Why you think that is?

CORY: Cause of you.

TROY: Ah, hell I know it's 'cause of me . . . but why do you think that is?

CORY [*hesitant*]: Cause you like me.

TROY: Like you? I go out of here every morning . . . bust my butt . . . putting up with them crackers* every day . . . cause I like you? You about the biggest fool I ever saw.

Pause.

It's my job. It's my responsibility! You understand that? A man got to take care of his family. You live in my house . . . sleep you behind on my bedclothes . . . fill your belly up with my food . . . cause you my son. You my flesh and blood. Not 'cause I like you! Cause it's my duty to take care of you. I owe a responsibility to you! Let's get this straight right here . . . before it go along any further . . . I ain't got to like you. Mr. Rand don't give me my money come payday cause he likes me. He gives me cause he owe me. I gave you your life! Me and your mamma worked that out between us. And liking your black ass wasn't part of the bargain. Don't you try and go through life worrying about if somebody like you or not. You best be making sure they doing right by you. You understand what I'm saying, boy?

CORY: Yessir.

TROY: Then get the hell out of my face, and get on down to that A&P.

ROSE *has been standing behind the screen door for much of the scene. She enters as* CORY *exits.*

ROSE: Why don't you let the boy go ahead and play football, Troy? Ain't no harm in that. He's just trying to be like you with the sports.

TROY: I don't want him to be like me! I want him to move as far away from my life as he can get. You the only decent thing that ever happened to me. I wish him that. But I don't wish him a thing else from my life. I decided seventeen years ago that boy wasn't getting involved in no sports. Not after what they did to me in the sports.

ROSE: Troy, why don't you admit you was too old to play in the major leagues? For once . . . why don't you admit that?

TROY: What do you mean too old? Don't come telling me I was too old. I just wasn't the right color. Hell, I'm fifty-three years old and can do better than Selkirk's .269 right now!

ROSE: How's was you gonna play ball when you were over forty? Sometimes I can't get no sense out of you.

TROY: I got good sense, woman. I got sense enough not to let my boy get hurt over playing no sports. You been mothering that boy too much. Worried about if people like him.

---

crackers   *white people, often used to refer disparagingly to poor whites.*

ROSE: Everything that boy do . . . he do for you. He wants you to say "Good job, son." That's all.

TROY: Rose, I ain't got time for that. He's alive. He's healthy. He's got to make his own way. I made mine. Ain't nobody gonna hold his hand when he get out there in that world.

ROSE: Times have changed from when you was young, Troy. People change. The world's changing around you and you can't even see it.

TROY [*slow, methodical*]:   Woman . . . I do the best I can do. I come in here every Friday. I carry a sack of potatoes and a bucket of lard. You all line up at the door with your hands out. I give you the lint from my pockets. I give you my sweat and my blood. I ain't go no tears, I done spent them. We go upstairs in that room at night . . . and I fall down on you and try to blast a hole into forever. I get up Monday morning . . . find my lunch on the table. I go out. Make my way. Find my strength to carry me through to the next Friday.

Pause.

That's all I got, Rose. That's all I got to give. I can't give nothing else.

TROY *exits into the house. The lights go down to black.*

Scene 4

It is Friday. Two weeks later. CORY *starts out of the house with his football equipment. The phone rings.*

CORY [*calling*]:   I got it!

He answers the phone and stands in the screen door talking.

Hello? Hey, Jesse. Naw . . . I was just getting ready to leave now.

ROSE [*calling*]:   Cory!

CORY: I told you, man, them spikes is all tore up. You can use them if you want, but they ain't no good. Earl got some spikes.

ROSE [*calling*]:   Cory!

CORY [*calling to* ROSE]:   Mam? I'm talking to Jesse.

Into phone.

When she say that? [*Pause.*] Aw, you lying, man. I'm gonna tell her you said that.

ROSE [*calling*]:   Cory, don't you go nowhere!

CORY: I got to go to the game, Ma!

Into the phone.

Yeah, hey, look, I'll talk to you later. Yeah, I'll meet you over Earl's house. Later. Bye, Ma.

CORY *exits the house and starts out the yard.*

ROSE: Cory, where you going off to? You got that stuff all pulled out and thrown all over your room.

CORY [*in the yard*]:   I was looking for my spikes. Jesse wanted to borrow my spikes.

ROSE: Get up there and get that cleaned up before your daddy get back in here.

CORY: I got to go to the game! I'll clean it up *when I get back*.

CORY *exits.*

ROSE: That's all he need to do is see that room all messed up.

ROSE *exits into the house.* TROY *and* BONO *enter the yard.* TROY *is dressed in clothes other than his work clothes.*

BONO: He told them the same thing he told you. Take it to the union.

TROY: Brownie ain't got that much sense. Man wasn't thinking about nothing. He wait until I confront them on it . . . then he wanna come crying seniority.

Calls.

Hey, Rose!

BONO: I wish I could have seen Mr. Rand's face when he told you.

TROY: He couldn't get it out of his mouth! Liked to bit his tongue! When they called me down there to the Commissioner's office . . . he thought they was gonna fire me. Like everybody else.

BONO: I didn't think they was gonna fire you. I thought they was gonna put you on the warning paper.

TROY: Hey, Rose!

To BONO.

Yeah, Mr. Rand like to bit his tongue.

TROY *breaks the seal on the bottle, takes a drink, and hands it to* BONO.

BONO: I see you run right down to Taylors' and told that Alberta gal.

TROY [*calling*]: Hey Rose! [*To* BONO] I told everybody. Hey, Rose! I went down there to cash my check.

ROSE [*entering from the house*]: Hush all that hollering, man! I know you out here. What they say down there at the Commissioner's office?

TROY: You supposed to come when I call you, woman. Bono'll tell you that.

To BONO.

Don't Lucille come when you call her?

ROSE: Man, hush your mouth. I ain't no dog . . . talk about "come when you call me."

TROY [*puts his arm around* ROSE]: You hear this, Bono? I had me an old dog used to get uppity like that. You say, "C'mere, Blue!" . . . and he just lay there and look at you. End up getting a stick and chasing him away trying to make him come.

ROSE: I ain't studying you and your dog. I remember you used to sing that old song.

TROY [*he sings*]: Hear it ring! Hear it ring! I had a dog his name was Blue.

ROSE: Don't nobody wanna hear you sing that old song.

TROY [*sings*]: You know Blue was mighty true.

ROSE: Used to have Cory running around here singing that song.

BONO: Hell, I remember that song myself.

TROY [*sings*]: You know Blue was a good old dog.
Blue treed a possum in a hollow log.

That was my daddy's song. My daddy made up that song.

ROSE: I don't care who made it up. Don't nobody wanna hear you sing it.

TROY [*makes a song like calling a dog*]:   Come here, woman.

ROSE: You come in here carrying on, I reckon they ain't fired you. What they say down there at the Commissioner's office?

TROY: Look here, Rose . . . Mr. Rand called me into his office today when I got back from talking to them people down there . . . it come from up top . . . he called me in and told me they was making me a driver.

ROSE: Troy, you kidding!

TROY: No I ain't. Ask Bono.

ROSE: Well, that's great, Troy. Now you don't have to hassle them people no more.

LYONS *enters from the street.*

TROY: Aw hell, I wasn't looking to see you today. I thought you was in jail. Got it all over the front page of the *Courier* about them raiding Sefus' place . . . where you be hanging out with all them thugs.

LYONS: Hey, Pop . . . that ain't got nothing to do with me. I don't go down there gambling. I go down there to sit in with the band. I ain't got nothing to do with the gambling part. They got some good music down there.

TROY: They got some rogues . . . is what they got.

LYONS: How you been, Mr. Bono? Hi, Rose.

BONO: I see where you playing down at the Crawford Grill tonight.

ROSE: How come you ain't brought Bonnie like I told you. You should have brought Bonnie with you, she ain't been over in a month of Sundays.

LYONS: I was just in the neighborhood . . . thought I'd stop by.

TROY: Here he come . . .

BONO: Your daddy got a promotion on the rubbish. He's gonna be the first colored driver. Ain't got to do nothing but sit up there and read the paper like them white fellows.

LYONS: Hey, Pop . . . if you knew how to read you'd be all right.

BONO: Naw . . . naw . . . you mean if the nigger knew how to *drive* he'd be all right. Been fighting with them people about driving and ain't even got a license. Mr. Rand know you ain't got no driver's license?

TROY: Driving ain't nothing. All you do is point the truck where you want it to go. Driving ain't nothing.

BONO: Do Mr. Rand know you ain't got no driver's license? That's what I'm talking about. I ain't asked if driving was easy. I asked if Mr. Rand know you ain't got no driver's license.

TROY: He ain't got to know. The man ain't got to know my business. Time he find out, I have two or three driver's licenses.

LYONS [*going into his pocket*]:   Say, look here, Pop . . .

TROY: I knew it was coming. Didn't I tell you, Bono? I know what kind of "Look here, Pop" that was. The nigger fixing to ask me for some money. It's Friday night. It's my payday. All them rogues down there on the avenue . . . the ones that ain't in jail . . . and Lyons is hopping in his shoes to get down there with them.

LYONS: See, Pop . . . if you give somebody else a chance to talk sometime, you'd see that I was fixing to pay you back your ten dollars like I told you. Here . . . I told you I'd pay you when Bonnie got paid.

TROY: Naw . . . you go ahead and keep that ten dollars. Put in the bank. The next time you feel like you wanna come by here and ask me for something . . . you go on down there and get that.

LYONS: Here's your ten dollars, Pop. I told you I don't want you to give me nothing. I just wanted to borrow ten dollars.

TROY: Naw . . . you go on and keep that for the next time you want to ask me.

LYONS: Come on, Pop . . . here go your ten dollars.

ROSE: Why don't you go on and let the boy pay you back, Troy?

LYONS: Here you go, Rose. If you don't take it I'm gonna have to hear about it for the next six months.

He hands her the money.

ROSE: You can hand yours over here too, Troy.

TROY: You see this, Bono. You see how they do me.

BONO: Yeah, Lucille do me the same way.

GABRIEL is heard singing offstage. He enters.

GABRIEL: Better get ready for the Judgment! Better get ready for . . . Hey! . . . Hey! . . . There's Troy's boy!

LYONS: How are you doing, Uncle Gabe?

GABRIEL: Lyons . . . The King of the Jungle! Rose . . . hey, Rose. Got a flower for you.

He takes a rose from his pocket.

Picked it myself. That's the same rose like you is!

ROSE: That's right nice of you, Gabe.

LYONS: What you been doing, Uncle Gabe?

GABRIEL: Oh, I been chasing hellhounds and waiting on the time to tell St. Peter to open the gates.

LYONS: You been chasing hellhounds, huh? Well . . . you doing the right thing, Uncle Gabe. Somebody got to chase them.

GABRIEL: Oh, yeah . . . I know it. The devil's strong. The devil ain't no pushover. Hellhounds snipping at everybody's heels. But I got my trumpet waiting on the judgment time.

LYONS: Waiting on the Battle of Armageddon, huh?

GABRIEL: Ain't gonna be too much of a battle when God get to waving that Judgment sword. But the people's gonna have a hell of a time trying to get into heaven if them gates ain't open.

LYONS [*putting his arm around GABRIEL*]:   You hear this, Pop. Uncle Gabe, you all right!

GABRIEL [*laughing with LYONS*]:   Lyons! King of the Jungle.

ROSE: You gonna stay for supper, Gabe. Want me to fix you a plate?

GABRIEL: I'll take a sandwich, Rose. Don't want no plate. Just wanna eat with my hands. I'll take a sandwich.

ROSE: How about you, Lyons? You staying? Got some short ribs cooking.

LYONS: Naw, I won't eat nothing till after we finished playing.

Pause.

You ought to come down and listen to me play, Pop.

TROY: I don't like that Chinese music. All that noise.

ROSE: Go on in the house and wash up, Gabe . . . I'll fix you a sandwich.

GABRIEL [*to* LYONS, *as he exits*]:   Troy's mad at me.

LYONS: What you mad at Uncle Gabe for, Pop.

ROSE: He thinks Troy's mad at him cause he moved over to Miss Pearl's.

TROY: I ain't mad at the man. He can live where he want to live at.

LYONS: What he move over there for? Miss Pearl don't like nobody.

ROSE: She don't mind him none. She treats him real nice. She just don't allow all that singing.

TROY: She don't mind that rent he be paying . . . that's what she don't mind.

ROSE: Troy, I ain't going through that with you no more. He's over there cause he want to have his own place. He can come and go as he please.

TROY: Hell, he could come and go as he please here. I wasn't stopping him. I ain't put no rules on him.

ROSE: It ain't the same thing, Troy. And you know it.

GABRIEL *comes to the door.*

Now, that's the last I wanna hear about that. I don't wanna hear nothing else about Gabe and Miss Pearl. And next week . . .

GABRIEL: I'm ready for my sandwich, Rose.

ROSE: And next week . . . when that recruiter come from that school . . . I want you to sign that paper and go on and let Cory play football. Then that'll be the last I have to hear about that.

TROY [*to* ROSE *as she exits into the house*]:   I ain't thinking about Cory nothing.

LYONS: What . . . Cory got recruited? What school he going to?

TROY: That boy walking around here smelling his piss . . . thinking he's grown. Thinking he's gonna do what he want, irrespective of what I say. Look here, Bono . . . I left the Commissioner's office and went down to the A&P . . . that boy ain't working down there. He lying to me. Telling me he got his job back . . . telling me he working weekends . . . telling me he working after school . . . Mr. Stawicki tell me he ain't working down there at all!

LYONS: Cory just growing up. He's just busting at the seams trying to fill out your shoes.

TROY: I don't care what he's doing. When he get to the point where he wanna disobey me . . . then it's time for him to move on. Bono'll tell you that. I bet he ain't never disobeyed his daddy without paying the consequences.

BONO: I ain't never had a chance. My daddy came on through . . . but I ain't never knew him to see him . . . or what he had on his mind or where he went. Just moving on through. Searching out the New Land. That's what the old folks used to call it. See a fellow moving around from place to place . . . woman to woman . . . called it searching out the New Land. I can't say if he ever found it. I come along, didn't want no kids. Didn't know if I was gonna be in one place long enough to fix on them right as their daddy. I figured I was going searching too. As it turned out I been hooked up with Lucille near about as long as your daddy been with Rose. Going on sixteen years.

TROY: Sometimes I wish I hadn't known my daddy. He ain't cared nothing about no kids. A kid to him wasn't nothing. All he wanted was for you to learn how to walk so he could start you to working. When it come time for eating . . . he ate first. If there was anything left over, that's what you got. Man would sit down and eat two chickens and give you the wing.

LYONS: You ought to stop that, Pop. Everybody feed their kids. No matter how hard times is . . . everybody care about their kids. Make sure they have something to eat.

TROY: The only thing my daddy cared about was getting them bales of cotton in to Mr. Lubin. That's the only thing that mattered to him. Sometimes I used to wonder why he was living. Wonder why the devil hadn't come and got him. "Get them bales of cotton in to Mr. Lubin" and find out he owe him money . . .

LYONS: He should have just went on and left when he saw he couldn't get nowhere. That's what I would have done.

TROY: How he gonna leave with eleven kids? And where he gonna go? He ain't knew how to do nothing but farm. No, he was trapped and I think he knew it. But I'll say this for him . . . he felt a responsibility toward us. Maybe he ain't treated us the way I felt he should have . . . but without that responsibility he could have walked off and left us . . . made his own way.

BONO: A lot of them did. Back in those days what you talking about . . . they walk out their front door and just take on down one road or another and keep on walking.

LYONS: There you go! That's what I'm talking about.

BONO: Just keep on walking till you come to something else. Ain't you never heard of nobody having the walking blues? Well, that's what you call it when you just take off like that.

TROY: My daddy ain't had them walking blues! What you talking about? He stayed right there with his family. But he was just as evil as he could be. My mama couldn't stand him. Couldn't stand that evilness. She run off when I was about eight. She sneaked off one night after he had gone to sleep. Told me she was coming back for me. I ain't never seen her no more. All his women run off and left him. He wasn't good for nobody.

When my turn come to head out, I was fourteen and got to sniffing around Joe Canewell's daughter. Had us an old mule we called Greyboy. My daddy sent me out to do some plowing and I tied up Greyboy and went to fooling around with Joe Canewell's daughter. We done found us a nice little spot, got real cozy with each other. She about thirteen and we done figures we was grown anyway . . . so we down there enjoying ourselves . . . ain't thinking about nothing. We didn't know Greyboy had got loose and wandered back to the house and my daddy was looking for me. We down there by the creek enjoying ourselves when my daddy come up on us. Surprised us. He had them leather straps off the mule and commenced to whupping me like there was no tomorrow. I jumped up, mad and embarrassed. I was scared of my daddy. When he commenced to whupping on me . . . quite naturally I run to get out of the way.

Pause.

Now I thought he was mad cause I ain't done my work. But I see where he was chasing me off so he could have the gal for himself. When I see what the matter of it was, I lost all fear of my daddy. Right there is where I become a man . . . at fourteen years of age.

Pause.

Now it was my turn to run him off. I picked up them same reins that he had used on me. I picked up them reins and commenced to whupping on him. The gal jumped up and run off . . . and when my daddy turned to face me, I could see why the devil had never come to get him . . . cause he was the devil himself. I don't know what happened. When I woke up, I was laying right there by the creek, and Blue . . . this old dog we had . . . was licking my face. I thought I was blind. I couldn't see nothing. Both my eyes were swollen shut. I layed there and cried. I didn't know what I was gonna do. The only thing I knew was the time had come for me to leave my daddy's house. And right there the world suddenly got big. And it was a long time before I could cut it down to where I could handle it.

Part of that cutting down was when I got to the place where I could feel him kicking in my blood and knew that the only thing that separated us was the matter of a few years.

GABRIEL *enters from the house with a sandwich.*

LYONS: What you got there, Uncle Gabe?

GABRIEL: Got me a ham sandwich. Rose gave me a ham sandwich.

TROY: I don't know what happened to him. I done lost touch with everybody except Gabriel. But I hope he's dead. I hope he found some peace.

LYONS: That's a heavy story, Pop. I didn't know you left home when you was fourteen.

TROY: And didn't know nothing. The only part of the world I knew was the forty-two acres of Mr. Lubin's land. That's all I knew about life.

LYONS: Fourteen's kinda young to be out on your own. [*Phone rings.*] I don't even think I was ready to be out on my own at fourteen. I don't know what I would have done.

TROY: I got up from the creek and walked on down to Mobile. I was through with farming. Figured I could do better in the city. So I walked the two hundred miles to Mobile.

LYONS: Wait a minute . . . you ain't walked no two hundred miles, Pop. Ain't nobody gonna walk no two hundred miles. You talking about some walking there.

BONO: That's the only way you got anywhere back in them days.

LYONS: Shhh. Damn if I wouldn't have hitched a ride with somebody!

TROY: Who you gonna hitch it with? They ain't had no cars and things like they got now. We talking about 1918.

ROSE [*entering*]:   What you all out here getting into?

TROY [*to* ROSE]:   I'm telling Lyons how good he got it. He don't know nothing about this I'm talking.

ROSE: Lyons, that was Bonnie on the phone. She say you supposed to pick her up.

LYONS: Yeah, okay, Rose.

TROY: I walked on down to Mobile and hitched up with some of them fellows that was heading this way. Got up here and found out . . . not only couldn't you get a job . . . you couldn't find no place to live. I thought I was in freedom. Shhh. Colored folks living down there on the riverbanks in whatever kind of shelter they could find for themselves. Right down there under the Brady Street Bridge. Living in shacks made of sticks and tarpaper. Messed around there and went from bad to worse. Started stealing. First it was food. Then I figured, hell, if I steal money I can buy me some food. Buy me some shoes too! One thing led to another. Met your mama. I was young and anxious to be a man. Met your mama and had you. What I do that for? Now I got to worry about feeding you and her. Got to steal three times as much. Went out one day looking for somebody to rob . . . that's what I was, a robber. I'll tell you the truth. I'm ashamed of it today. But it's the truth. Went to rob this fellow . . . pulled out my knife . . . and he pulled out a gun. Shot me in the chest. It felt just like somebody had taken a hot branding iron and laid it on me. When he shot me I jumped at him with my knife. They told me I killed him and they put me in the penitentiary and locked me up for fifteen years. That's where I met Bono. That's where I learned how to play baseball. Got out that place and your mama had taken you and went on to make life without me. Fifteen years was a long time for her to wait. But that fifteen years cured me of that robbing stuff. Rose'll tell you. She asked me when I met her if I had gotten all that foolishness out of my system. And I told her, "Baby, it's you and baseball all what count with me." You hear me, Bono? I meant it too. She say, "Which one comes first?" I told her, "Baby, ain't no doubt it's baseball . . . but you stick and get old with me and we'll both outlive this baseball." Am I right, Rose? And it's true.

ROSE: Man, hush your mouth. You ain't said no such thing. Talking about, "Baby, you know you'll always be number one with me." That's what you was talking.

TROY: You hear that, Bono. That's why I love her.

BONO: Rose'll keep you straight. You get off the track, she'll straighten you up.

ROSE: Lyons, you better get on up and get Bonnie. She waiting on you.

LYONS [*gets up to go*]: Hey, Pop, why don't you come on down to the Grill and hear me play?

TROY: I ain't going down there. I'm too old to be sitting around in them clubs.

BONO: You got to be good to play down at the Grill.

LYONS: Come on, Pop . . .

TROY: I got to get up in the morning.

LYONS: You ain't got to stay long.

TROY: Naw, I'm gonna get my supper and go on to bed.

LYONS: Well, I got to go. I'll see you again.

TROY: Don't you come around my house on my payday.

ROSE: Pick up the phone and let somebody know you coming. And bring Bonnie with you. You know I'm always glad to see her.

LYONS: Yeah, I'll do that, Rose. You take care now. See you, Pop. See you, Mr. Bono. See you, Uncle Gabe.

GABRIEL: Lyons! King of the Jungle!

LYONS *exits.*

TROY: Is supper ready, woman? Me and you got some business to take care of. I'm gonna tear it up too.

ROSE: Troy, I done told you now!

TROY [*puts his arm around* BONO]: Aw hell, woman . . . this is Bono. Bono like family. I done known this nigger since . . . how long I done know you?

BONO: It's been a long time.

TROY: I done known this nigger since Skippy was a pup. Me and him done been through some times.

BONO: You sure right about that.

TROY: Hell, I done know him longer than I known you. And we still standing shoulder to shoulder. Hey, look here, Bono . . . a man can't ask for no more than that.

Drinks to him.

I love you, nigger.

BONO: Hell, I love you too . . . but I got to get home see my woman. You got yours in hand. I got to go get mine.

BONO *starts to exit as* CORY *enters the yard, dressed in his football uniform. He gives* TROY *a hard, uncompromising look.*

CORY: What you do that for, Pop?

He throws his helmet down in the direction of TROY.

ROSE: What's the matter? Cory . . . what's the matter?

CORY: Papa done went up to the school and told Coach Zellman I can't play football no more. Wouldn't even let me play the game. Told him to tell the recruiter not to come.

ROSE: Troy . . .

TROY: What you Troying me for. Yeah, I did it. And the boy know why I did it.

CORY: Why you wanna do that to me? That was the one chance I had.

ROSE: Ain't nothing wrong with Cory playing football, Troy.

TROY: The boy lied to me. I told the nigger if he wanna play football . . . to keep up his chores and hold down that job at the A&P. That was the conditions. Stopped down there to see Mr. Stawicki . . .

CORY: I can't work after school during the football season, Pop! I tried to tell you that Mr. Stawicki's holding my job for me. You don't never want to listen to nobody. And then you wanna go and do this to me!

TROY: I ain't done nothing to you. You done it to yourself.

CORY: Just cause you didn't have a chance! You just scared I'm gonna be better than you, that's all.

TROY: Come here.

ROSE: Troy . . .

CORY *reluctantly crosses over to* TROY.

TROY: All right! See. You done made a mistake.

CORY: I didn't even do nothing!

TROY: I'm gonna tell you what your mistake was. See . . . you swung at the ball and didn't hit it. That's strike one. See, you in the batter's box now. You swung and you missed. That's strike one. Don't you strike out!

Lights fade to black.

ACT II

Scene 1

The following morning. CORY *is at the tree hitting the ball with the bat. He tries to mimic* TROY, *but his swing is awkward, less sure.* ROSE *enters from the house.*

ROSE: Cory, I want you to help me with this cupboard.

CORY: I ain't quitting the team. I don't care what Poppa say.

ROSE: I'll talk to him when he gets back. He had to go see about your Uncle Gabe. The police done arrested him. Say he was disturbing the peace. He'll be back directly. Come on in here and help me clean out the top of this cupboard.

CORY *exits into the house.* ROSE *sees* TROY *and* BONO *coming down the alley.*

Troy . . . what they say down there?

TROY: Ain't said nothing. I give them fifty dollars and they let him go. I'll talk to you about it. Where's Cory?

ROSE: He's in there helping me clean out these cupboards.

TROY: Tell him to get his butt out here.

TROY *and* BONO *go over to the pile of wood.* BONO *picks up the saw and begins sawing.*

TROY [*to* BONO]: All they want is the money. That makes six or seven times I done went down there and got him. See me coming they stick out their *hands.*

BONO: Yeah. I know what you mean. That's all they care about . . . that money. They don't care about what's right.

Pause.

Nigger, why you got to go and get some hard wood? You ain't doing nothing but building a little old fence. Get you some soft pine wood. That's all you need.

TROY: I know what I'm doing. This is outside wood. You put pine wood inside the house. Pine wood is inside wood. This here is outside wood. Now you tell me where the fence is gonna be?

BONO: You don't need this wood. You can put it up with pine wood and it'll stand as long as you gonna be here looking at it.

TROY: How you know how long I'm gonna be here, nigger? Hell, I might just live forever. Live longer than old man Horsely.

BONO: That's what Magee used to say.

TROY: Magee's a damn fool. Now you tell me who you ever heard of gonna pull their own teeth with a pair of rusty pliers.

BONO: The old folks . . . my granddaddy used to pull his teeth with pliers. They ain't had no dentists for the colored folks back then.

TROY: Get clean pliers! You understand? Clean pliers! Sterilize them! Besides we ain't living back then. All Magee had to do was walk over to Doc Goldblum's.

BONO: I see where you and that Tallahassee gal . . . that Alberta . . . I see where you all done got tight.

TROY: What you mean "got tight"?

BONO: I see where you be laughing and joking with her all the time.

TROY: I laughs and jokes with all of them, Bono. You know me.

BONO: That ain't the kind of laughing and joking I'm talking about.

CORY enters from the house.

CORY: How you doing, Mr. Bono?

TROY: Cory? Get that saw from Bono and cut some wood. He talking about the wood's too hard to cut. Stand back there, Jim, and let that young boy show you how it's done.

BONO: He's sure welcome to it.

CORY takes the saw and begins to cut the wood.

Whew-e-e! Look at that. Big old strong boy. Look like Joe Louis. Hell, must be getting old the way I'm watching that boy whip through that wood.

CORY: I don't see why Mama want a fence around the yard noways.

TROY: Damn if I know either. What the hell she keeping out with it? She ain't got nothing nobody want.

BONO: Some people build fences to keep people out . . . and other people build fences to keep people in. Rose wants to hold on to you all. She loves you.

TROY: Hell, nigger, I don't need nobody to tell me my wife loves me, Cory . . . go on in the house and see if you can find that other saw.

CORY: Where's it at?

TROY: I said find it! Look for it till you find it!

CORY exits into the house.

What's that supposed to mean? Wanna keep us in?

BONO: Troy . . . I done known you seem like damn near my whole life. You and Rose both. I done know both of you all for a long time. I remember when you met Rose. When you was hitting them baseball out the park. A lot of them old gals was after you then. You had the pick of the litter. When you picked Rose, I was happy for you. That was the first time I knew you had any sense. I said . . . My man Troy knows what he's doing . . . I'm gonna follow this nigger . . . he might take me somewhere. I been following you too. I done learned a whole heap of things about life watching you. I done learned how to tell where the shit lies. How to tell it from the alfalfa. You done learned me a lot of things. You showed me how to not make the same mistakes . . . to take life as it comes along and keep putting one foot in front of the other.

Pause.

Rose a good woman, Troy.

TROY: Hell, nigger, I know she a good woman. I been married to her for eighteen years. What you got on your mind, Bono?

BONO: I just say she a good woman. Just like I say anything. I ain't got to have nothing on my mind.

TROY: You just gonna say she a good woman and leave it hanging out there like that? Why you telling me she a good woman?

BONO: She loves you, Troy. Rose loves you.

TROY: You saying I don't measure up. That's what you trying to say. I don't measure up cause I'm seeing this other gal. I know what you trying to say.

BONO: I know what Rose means to you, Troy. I'm just trying to say I don't want to see you mess up.

TROY: Yeah, I appreciate that, Bono. If you was messing around on Lucille I'd be telling you the same thing.

BONO: Well, that's all I got to say. I just say that because I love you both.

TROY: Hell, you know me . . . I wasn't out there looking for nothing. You can't find a better woman than Rose. I know that. But seems like this woman just stuck onto me where I can't shake her loose. I done wrestled with it, tried to throw her off me . . . but she just stuck on tighter. Now she's stuck on for good.

BONO: You's in control . . . that's what you tell me all the time. You responsible for what you do.

TROY: I ain't ducking the responsibility of it. As long as it sets right in my heart . . . then I'm okay. Cause that's all I listen to. It'll tell me right from wrong every time. And I ain't talking about doing Rose no bad turn. I love Rose. She done carried me a long ways and I love and respect her for that.

BONO: I know you do. That's why I don't want to see you hurt her. But what you gonna do when she find out? What you got then? If you try and juggle both of them . . . sooner or later you gonna drop one of them. That's common sense.

TROY: Yeah, I hear what you saying, Bono. I been trying to figure a way to work it out.

BONO: Work it out right, Troy. I don't want to be getting all up between you and Rose's business . . . but work it so it come out right.

TROY: Ah hell, I get all up between you and Lucille's business. When you gonna get that woman that refrigerator she been wanting? Don't tell me you ain't got no money now. I know who your banker is. Mellon don't need that money bad as Lucille want that refrigerator. I'll tell you that.

BONO: Tell you what I'll do . . . when you finish building this fence for Rose . . . I'll buy Lucille that refrigerator.

TROY: You done stuck your foot in your mouth now!

TROY *grabs up a board and begins to saw.* BONO *starts to walk out the yard.*

Hey, nigger . . . where you going?

BONO: I'm going home. I know you don't expect me to help you now. I'm protecting my money. I wanna see you put that fence up by yourself. That's what I want to see. You'll be here another six months without me.

TROY: Nigger, you ain't right.

BONO: When it comes to my money . . . I'm right as fireworks on the Fourth of July.

TROY: All right, we gonna see now. You better get out your bankbook.

BONO *exits, and* TROY *continues to work.* ROSE *enters from the house.*

ROSE: What they say down there? What's happening with Gabe?

TROY: I went down there and got him out. Cost me fifty dollars. Say he was disturbing the peace. Judge set up a hearing for him in three weeks. Say to show cause why he shouldn't be recommitted.

ROSE: What was he doing that cause them to arrest him?

TROY: Some kids was teasing him and he run them off home. Say he was howling and carrying on. Some folks seen him and called the police. That's all it was.

ROSE: Well, what's you say? What'd you tell the judge?

TROY: Told him I'd look after him. It didn't make no sense to recommit the man. He stuck out his big greasy palm and told me to give him fifty dollars and take him on home.

ROSE: Where's he at now? Where'd he go off to?

TROY: He's gone on about his business. He don't need nobody to hold his hand.

ROSE: Well, I don't know. Seem like that would be the best place for him if they did put him into the hospital. I know what you're gonna say. But that's what I think would be best.

TROY: The man done had his life ruined fighting for what? And they wanna take and lock him up. Let him be free. He don't bother nobody.

ROSE: Well, everybody got their own way of looking at it I guess. Come on and get your lunch. I got a bowl of lima beans and some cornbread in the oven. Come on get something to eat. Ain't no sense you fretting over Gabe.

ROSE turns to go into the house.

TROY: Rose . . . got something to tell you.

ROSE: Well, come on . . . wait till I get this food on the table.

TROY: Rose!

She stops and turns around.

I don't know how to say this.

Pause.

I can't explain it none. It just sort of grows on you till it gets out of hand. It starts out like a little bush . . . and the next thing you know it's a whole forest.

ROSE: Troy . . . what is you talking about?

TROY: I'm talking, woman, let me talk. I'm trying to find a way to tell you . . . I'm gonna be a daddy. I'm gonna be somebody's daddy.

ROSE: Troy . . . you're not telling me this? You're gonna be . . . what?

TROY: Rose . . . now . . . see . . .

ROSE: You telling me you gonna be somebody's daddy? You telling your *wife* this?

GABRIEL enters from the street. He carries a rose in his hand.

GABRIEL: Hey, Troy! Hey, Rose!

ROSE: I have to wait eighteen years to hear something like this.

GABRIEL: Hey, Rose . . . I got a flower for you.

He hands it to her.

That's a rose. Same rose like you is.

ROSE: Thanks, Gabe.

GABRIEL: Troy, you ain't mad at me is you? Them bad mens come and put me away. You ain't mad at me is you?

TROY: Naw, Gabe, I ain't mad at you.

ROSE: Eighteen years and you wanna come with this.

GABRIEL [*takes a quarter out of his pocket*]:   See what I got? Got a brand new quarter.

TROY: Rose . . . it's just . . .

ROSE: Ain't nothing you can say, Troy. Ain't no way of explaining that.

GABRIEL: Fellow that give me this quarter had a whole mess of them. I'm gonna keep this quarter till it stop shining.

ROSE: Gabe, go on in the house there. I got some watermelon in the frigidaire. Go on and get you a piece.

GABRIEL: Say, Rose . . . you know I was chasing hellhounds and them bad mens come and get me and take me away. Troy helped me. He come down there and told them they better let me go before he beat them up. Yeah, he did!

ROSE: You go on and get you a piece of watermelon, Gabe. Them bad mens is gone now.

GABRIEL: Okay, Rose . . . gonna get me some watermelon. The kind with the stripes on it.

GABRIEL *exits into the house.*

ROSE: Why, Troy? Why? After all these years to come dragging this in to me now. It don't make no sense at your age. I could have expected this ten or fifteen years ago, but not now.

TROY: Age ain't got nothing to do with it, Rose.

ROSE: I done tried to be everything a wife should be. Everything a wife could be. Been married eighteen years and I got to live to see the day you tell me you been seeing another woman and done fathered a child by her. And you know I ain't never wanted no half nothing in my family. My whole family is half. Everybody got different fathers and mothers . . . my two sisters and my brother. Can't hardly tell who's who. Can't never sit down and talk about Papa and Mama. It's your papa and your mama and my papa and my mama . . .

TROY: Rose . . . stop it now.

ROSE: I ain't never wanted that for none of my children. And now you wanna drag your behind in here and tell me something like this.

TROY: You ought to know. It's time for you to know.

ROSE: Well, I don't want to know, goddamn it!

TROY: I can't just make it go away. It's done now. I can't wish the circumstance of the thing away.

ROSE: And you don't want to either. Maybe you want to wish me and my boy away. Maybe that's what you want? Well, you can't wish us away. I've got eighteen years of my life invested in you. You ought to have stayed upstairs in my bed where you belong.

TROY: Rose . . . now listen to me . . . we can get a handle on this thing. We can talk this out . . . come to an understanding.

ROSE: All of a sudden it's "we." Where was "we" at when you was down there rolling around with some godforsaken woman? "We" should have come to an understanding before you started making a damn fool of yourself. You're a day late and dollar short when it comes to an understanding with me.

TROY: It's just . . . She gives me a different idea . . . a different understanding about myself. I can step out of this house and get away from the pressures and problems . . . be a different man. I ain't got to wonder how I'm gonna pay the bills or get the roof fixed. I can just be a part of myself that I ain't never been.

ROSE: What I want to know . . . is do you plan to continue seeing her. That's all you can say to me.

TROY: I can sit up in her house and laugh. Do you understand what I'm saying. I can laugh out loud . . . and it feels good. It reaches all the way down to the bottom of my shoes.

Pause.

Rose, I can't give that up.

ROSE: Maybe you ought to go on and stay down there with her . . . if she's a better woman than me.

TROY: It ain't about nobody being a better woman or nothing. Rose, you ain't the blame. A man couldn't ask for no woman to be a better wife than you've been. I'm responsible for it. I done locked myself into a pattern trying to take care of you all that I forgot about myself.

ROSE: What the hell was I there for? That was my job, not somebody else's.

TROY: Rose, I done tried all my life to live decent . . . to live a clean . . . hard . . . useful life. I tried to be a good husband to you. In every way I knew how. Maybe I come into the world backwards, I don't know. But . . . you born with two strikes on you before you come to the plate. You got to guard it closely . . . always looking for the curve ball on the inside corner. You can't afford to let none get past you. You can't afford a call strike. If you going down . . . you going down swinging. Everything lined up against you. What you gonna do. I fooled them, Rose. I bunted. When I found you and Cory and a halfway decent job . . . I was safe. Couldn't nothing touch me. I wasn't going back to the penitentiary. I wasn't gonna lay in the streets with a bottle of wine. I was safe. I had me a family. A job. I wasn't gonna get that last strike. I was on first looking for one of them boys to knock me in. To get me home.

ROSE: You should have stayed in my bed, Troy.

TROY: Then when I saw that gal . . . she firmed up my backbone. And I got to thinking that if I tried . . . I just might be able to steal second. Do you understand after eighteen years I wanted to steal second.

ROSE: You should have held me tight. You should have grabbed me and held on.

TROY: I stood on first base for eighteen years and I thought . . . well, goddamn it . . . go on for it!

ROSE: We're not talking about baseball! We're talking about you going off to lay in bed with another woman . . . and then bring it home to me. That's what we're talking about. We ain't talking about no baseball.

TROY: Rose, you're not listening to me. I'm trying the best I can to explain it to you. It's not easy for me to admit that I been standing in the same place for eighteen years.

ROSE: I been standing with you! I been right here with you, Troy. I got a life too. I gave eighteen years of my life to stand in the same spot with you. Don't you think I ever wanted other things? Don't you think I had dreams and hopes? What about my life? What about me. Don't you think it ever crossed my mind to want to know other men? That I wanted to lay up somewhere and forget about my responsibilities? That I wanted someone to make me laugh so I could feel good? You not the only one who's got wants and needs. But I held on to you, Troy. I took all my feelings, my wants and needs, my dreams . . . and I buried them inside you. I planted a seed and watched and prayed over it. I planted myself inside you and waited to bloom. And it didn't take me no eighteen years to find out the soil was hard and rocky and it wasn't never gonna bloom.

But I held on to you, Troy. I held you tighter. You was my husband. I owed you everything I had. Every part of me I could find to give you. And upstairs in that room . . . with the darkness falling in on me . . . I gave everything I had to try and erase the doubt that you wasn't the finest man in the world. And wherever you was going . . . I wanted to be there with you. Cause you was my husband. Cause that's the only way I was gonna survive as your wife. You always talking about what you give . . . and what you don't have to give. But you take too. You take . . . and don't even know nobody's giving!

> ROSE *turns to exit into the house.* TROY *grabs her arm.*

TROY: You say I take and don't give!
ROSE: Troy! You're hurting me!
TROY: You say I take and don't give.
ROSE: Troy . . . you're hurting my arm! Let go!
TROY: I done give you everything I got. Don't you tell that lie on me.
ROSE: Troy!
TROY: Don't you tell that lie on me!

> CORY *enters from the house.*

CORY: Mama!
ROSE: Troy. You're hurting me.
TROY: Don't you tell me about no taking and giving.

CORY *comes up behind* TROY *and grabs him.* TROY, *surprised, is thrown off balance just as* CORY *throws a glancing blow that catches him in the chest and knocks him down.* TROY *is stunned, as is* CORY.

ROSE: Troy. Troy. No!

> TROY *gets to his feet and starts at* CORY.

Troy . . . no. Please! Troy!

> ROSE *pulls on* TROY *to hold him back.* TROY *stops himself.*

TROY [*to* CORY]:   All right. That's strike two. You stay away from around me, boy. Don't you strike out. You living with a full count. Don't you strike out.

> TROY *exits out the yard as the lights go down.*

Scene 2

It is six months later, early afternoon. TROY *enters from the house and starts to exit the yard.* ROSE *enters from the house.*

ROSE: Troy, I want to talk to you.
TROY: All of a sudden, after all this time, you want to talk to me, huh? You ain't wanted to talk to me for months. You ain't wanted to talk to me last night. You ain't wanted no part of me then. What you wanna talk to me about now?

ROSE: Tomorrow's Friday.

TROY: I know what day tomorrow is. You think I don't know tomorrow's Friday? My whole life I ain't done nothing but look to see Friday coming and you got to tell me it's Friday.

ROSE: I want to know if you're coming home.

TROY: I always come home, Rose. You know that. There ain't never been a night I ain't come home.

ROSE: That ain't what I mean . . . and you know it. I want to know if you're coming straight home after work.

TROY: I figure I'd cash my check . . . hang out at Taylors' with the boys . . . maybe play a game of checkers . . .

ROSE: Troy, I can't live like this. I won't live like this. You livin' on borrowed time with me. It's been going on six months now you ain't been coming home.

TROY: I be here every night. Every night of the year. That's 365 days.

ROSE: I want you to come home tomorrow after work.

TROY: Rose . . . I don't mess up my pay. You know that now. I take my pay and I give it to you. I don't have no money but what you give me back. I just want to have a little time to myself . . . a little time to enjoy life.

ROSE: What about me? When's my time to enjoy life?

TROY: I don't know what to tell you, Rose. I'm doing the best I can.

ROSE: You ain't been home from work but time enough to change your clothes and run out . . . and you wanna call that the best you can do?

TROY: I'm going over to the hospital to see Alberta. She went into the hospital this afternoon. Look like she might have the baby early. I won't be gone long.

ROSE: Well, you ought to know. They went over to Miss Pearl's and got Gabe today. She said you told them to go ahead and lock him up.

TROY: I ain't said no such thing. Whoever told you that is telling a lie. Pearl ain't doing nothing but telling a big fat lie.

ROSE: She ain't had to tell me. I read it on the papers.

TROY: I ain't told them nothing of the kind.

ROSE: I saw it right there on the papers.

TROY: What it say, huh?

ROSE: It said you told them to take him.

TROY: Then they screwed that up, just the way they screw up everything. I ain't worried about what they got on the paper.

ROSE: Say the government send part of his check to the hospital and the other part to you.

TROY: I ain't got nothing to do with that if that's the way it works. I ain't made up the rules about how it work.

ROSE: You did Gabe just like you did Cory. You wouldn't sign the paper for Cory . . . but you signed for Gabe. You signed that paper.

The telephone is heard ringing inside the house.

TROY: I told you I ain't signed nothing, woman! The only thing I signed was the release form. Hell, I can't read, I don't know what they had on that paper! I ain't signed nothing about sending Gabe away.

ROSE: I said send him to the hospital . . . you said let him be free . . . now you done went down there and signed him to the hospital for half his money. You went back on yourself, Troy. You gonna have to answer for that.

TROY: See now . . . you been over there talking to Miss Pearl. She done got mad cause she ain't getting Gabe's rent money. That's all it is. She's liable to say anything.

ROSE: Troy, I seen where you signed the paper.

TROY: You ain't seen nothing I signed. What she doing got papers on my brother anyway? Miss Pearl telling a big fat lie. And I'm gonna tell her about it too! You ain't seen nothing I signed. Say . . . you ain't seen nothing I signed.

ROSE *exits into the house to answer the telephone. Presently she returns.*

ROSE: Troy . . . that was the hospital. Alberta had the baby.

TROY: What she have? What is it?

ROSE: It's a girl.

TROY: I better get on down to the hospital to see her.

ROSE: Troy . . .

TROY: Rose . . . I got to go see her now. That's only right . . . what's the matter . . . the baby's all right, ain't it?

ROSE: Alberta died having the baby.

TROY: Died . . . you say she's dead? Alberta's dead?

ROSE: They said they done all they could. They couldn't do nothing for her.

TROY: The baby? How's the baby?

ROSE: They say it's healthy. I wonder who's gonna bury her.

TROY: She had family, Rose. She wasn't living in the world by herself.

ROSE: I know she wasn't living in the world by herself.

TROY: Next thing you gonna want to know if she had any insurance.

ROSE: Troy, you ain't got to talk like that.

TROY: That's the first thing that jumped out your mouth. "Who's gonna bury her?" Like I'm fixing to take on that task for myself.

ROSE: I am your wife. Don't push me away.

TROY: I ain't pushing nobody away. Just give me some space. That's all. Just give me some room to breathe.

ROSE *exits into the house.* TROY *walks about the yard.*

TROY [*with a quiet rage that threatens to consume him*]: All right . . . Mr. Death. See now . . . I'm gonna tell you what I'm gonna do. I'm gonna take and build me a fence around this yard. See? I'm gonna build me a fence around what belongs to me. And then I want you to stay on the other side. See? You stay over there until you're ready for me. Then you come on. Bring your army. Bring your sickle. Bring your wrestling clothes. I ain't gonna fall down on my vigilance this time. You ain't gonna sneak up on me no more. When you ready for me . . . when the top of your list say Troy Maxson . . . that's when you come around here. You come up and knock on the front door. Ain't nobody else got nothing to do with this. This is between you and me. Man to man. You stay on the other side of that fence until you ready for me. Then you come up and knock on the front door. Anytime you want. I'll be ready for you.

The lights go down to black.

Scene 3

The lights come up on the porch. It is late evening three days later. ROSE *sits listening to the ball game waiting for* TROY. *The final out of the game is made and* ROSE *switches off the radio.* TROY *enters the yard carrying an infant wrapped in blankets. He stands back from the house and calls.*

ROSE *enters and stands on the porch. There is a long, awkward silence, the weight of which grows heavier with each passing second.*

TROY: Rose . . . I'm standing here with my daughter in my arms. She ain't but a wee bittie little old thing. She don't know nothing about grown-ups' business. She innocent . . . and she ain't got no mama.

ROSE: What you telling me for, Troy?

She turns and exits into the house.

TROY: Well . . . I guess we'll just sit out here on the porch.

He sits down on the porch. There is an awkward indelicateness about the way he handles the baby. His largeness engulfs and seems to swallow it. He speaks loud enough for ROSE *to hear.*

A man's got to do what's right for him. I ain't sorry for nothing I done. It felt right in my heart.

To the baby.

What you smiling at? Your daddy's a big man. Got these great big old hands. But sometimes he's scared. And right now your daddy's scared cause we sitting out here and ain't got no home. Oh, I been homeless before. I ain't had no little baby with me. But I been homeless. You just be out on the road by your lonesome and you see one of them trains coming and you just kinda go like this . . .

He sings as a lullaby.

Please, Mr. Engineer let a man ride the line
Please, Mr. Engineer let a man ride the line
I ain't got no ticket please let me ride the blinds

ROSE *enters from the house.* TROY *hearing her steps behind him, stands and faces her.*

She's my daughter, Rose. My own flesh and blood. I can't deny her no more than I can deny them boys.

Pause.

You and them boys is my family. You and them boys and this child is all I got in the world. So I guess what I'm saying is . . . I'd appreciate it if you'd help me take care of her.

ROSE: Okay, Troy . . . you're right. I'll take care of your baby for you . . . cause . . . like you say . . . she's innocent . . . and you can't visit the sins of the father upon the child. A motherless child has got a hard time.

She takes the baby from him.

From right now . . . this child got a mother. But you a womanless man.

ROSE *turns and exits into the house with the baby. Lights go down to black.*

Scene 4

It is two months later. LYONS *enters from the street. He knocks on the door and calls.*

LYONS: Hey, Rose! [*Pause.*] Rose!

ROSE [*from inside the house*]:   Stop that yelling. You gonna wake up Raynell. I just got her to sleep.

LYONS: I just stopped by to pay Papa this twenty dollars I owe him. Where's Papa at?

ROSE: He should be here in a minute. I'm getting ready to go down to the church. Sit down and wait on him.

LYONS: I got to go pick up Bonnie over her mother's house.

ROSE: Well, sit it down there on the table. He'll get it.

LYONS [*enters the house and sets the money on the table*]:   Tell Papa I said thanks. I'll see you again.

ROSE: All right, Lyons. We'll see you.

LYONS *starts to exit as* CORY *enters.*

CORY: Hey, Lyons.

LYONS: What's happening, Cory. Say man, I'm sorry I missed your graduation. You know I had a gig and couldn't get away. Otherwise, I would have been there, man. So what you doing?

CORY: I'm trying to find a job.

LYONS: Yeah I know how that go, man. It's rough out here. Jobs are scarce.

CORY: Yeah, I know.

LYONS: Look here, I got to run. Talk to Papa . . . he know some people. He'll be able to help get you a job. Talk to him . . . see what he say.

CORY: Yeah . . . all right, Lyons.

LYONS: You take care. I'll talk to you soon. We'll find some time to talk.

LYONS *exits the yard.* CORY *wanders over to the tree, picks up the bat, and assumes a batting stance. He studies an imaginary pitcher and swings. Dissatisfied with the result, he tries again.* TROY *enters. They eye each other for a beat.* CORY *puts the bat down and exits the yard.* TROY *starts into the house as* ROSE *exits with* RAYNELL. *She is carrying a cake.*

TROY: I'm coming in and everybody's going out.

ROSE: I'm taking the cake down to the church for the bake sale. Lyons was by to see you. He stopped by to pay you your twenty dollars. It's laying in there on the table.

TROY [*going into his pocket*]:   Well . . . here go this money.

ROSE: Put it in there on the table, Troy. I'll get it.

TROY: What time you coming back?

ROSE: Ain't no use in you studying me. It don't matter what time I come back.

TROY: I just asked you a question, woman. What's the matter . . . can't I ask you a question?

ROSE: Troy, I don't want to go into it. Your dinner's in there on the stove. All you got to do is heat it up. And don't you be eating the rest of them cakes in there. I'm coming back for them. We having a bake sale at the church tomorrow.

ROSE *exits the yard.* TROY *sits down on the steps, takes a pint bottle from his pocket, opens it, and drinks. He begins to sing.*

TROY: Hear it ring! Hear it ring!
      Had an old dog his name was Blue
      You know Blue was a mighty true
      You know Blue was a good old dog
      Blue trees a possum in a hollow log
      You know from that he was a good old dog

BONO *enters the yard.*

BONO: Hey, Troy.

TROY: Hey, what's happening, Bono?

BONO: I just thought I'd stop by to see you.

TROY: What you stop by and see me for? You ain't stopped by in a month of Sundays. Hell, I must owe you money or something.

BONO: Since you got your promotion I can't keep up with you. Used to see you every day. Now I don't even know what route you working.

TROY: They keep switching me around. Got me out in Greentree now . . . hauling white folks' garbage.

BONO: Greentree, huh? You lucky, at least you ain't got to be lifting them barrels. Damn if they ain't getting heavier. I'm gonna put in my two years and call it quits.

TROY: I'm thinking about retiring myself.

BONO: You got it easy. You can *drive* for another five years.

TROY: It ain't the same, Bono. It ain't like working the back of the truck. Ain't got nobody to talk to . . . feel like you working by yourself. Naw, I'm thinking about retiring. How's Lucille?

BONO: She all right. Her arthritis get to acting up on her sometime. Saw Rose on my way in. She going down to the church, huh?

TROY: Yeah, she took up going down there. All them preachers looking for somebody to fatten their pockets.

Pause.

Got some gin here.

BONO: Naw, thanks. I just stopped by to say hello.

TROY: Hell, nigger . . . you can take a drink. I ain't never known you to say no to a drink. You ain't got to work tomorrow.

BONO: I just stopped by. I'm fixing to go over to Skinner's. We got us a domino game going over his house every Friday.

TROY: Nigger, you can't play no dominoes. I used to whup you four games out of five.

BONO: Well, that learned me. I'm getting better.

TROY: Yeah? Well, that's all right.

BONO: Look here . . . I got to be getting on. Stop by sometime, huh?

TROY: Yeah, I'll do that, Bono. Lucille told Rose you bought her a new refrigerator.

BONO: Yeah, Rose told Lucille you had finally built your fence . . . so I figured we'd call it even.

TROY: I knew you would.

BONO: Yeah . . . okay. I'll be talking to you.

TROY: Yeah, take care, Bono. Good to see you. I'm gonna stop over.

BONO: Yeah. Okay, Troy.

BONO *exits.* TROY *drinks from the bottle.*

TROY: Old Blue died and I dig his grave
        Let him down with a golden chain
        Every night when I hear old Blue bark
        I know Blue treed a possum in Noah's Ark.
        Hear it ring! Hear it ring!

CORY *enters the yard. They eye each other for a beat.* TROY *is sitting in the middle of the steps.* CORY *walks over.*

CORY: I got to get by.

TROY: Say what? What's you say?

CORY: You in my way. I got to get by.

TROY: You got to get by where? This is my house. Bought and paid for. In full. Took me fifteen years. And if you wanna go in my house and I'm sitting on the steps . . . you say excuse me. Like your mama taught you.

CORY: Come on, Pop . . . I got to get by.

CORY *starts to maneuver his way past* TROY. TROY *grabs his leg and shoves him back.*

TROY: You just gonna walk over top of me?

CORY: I live here, too!

TROY [*advancing toward him*]:   You just gonna walk over top of me in my own house?

CORY: I ain't scared of you.

TROY: I ain't asked if you was scared of me. I asked you if you was fixing to walk over top of me in my own house? That's the question. You ain't gonna say excuse me? You just gonna walk over top of me?

CORY: If you wanna put it like that.

TROY: How else am I gonna put it?

CORY: I was walking by you to go into the house cause you sitting on the steps drunk, singing to yourself. You can put it like that.

TROY: Without saying excuse me???

CORY *doesn't respond.*

I asked you a question. Without saying excuse me???

CORY: I ain't got to say excuse me to you. You don't count around here no more.

TROY: Oh, I see . . . I don't count around here no more. You ain't got to say excuse me to your daddy. All of a sudden you done got so grown that your daddy don't count around here no more . . . Around here in his own house and yard that he done paid for with the sweat of his brow. You done got so grown to where you gonna take over. You gonna take over my house. Is that right? You gonna wear my pants. You gonna go in there and stretch out on my bed. You ain't got to say excuse me cause I don't count around here no more. Is that right?

CORY: That's right. You always talking this dumb stuff. Now, why don't you just get out my way.

TROY: I guess you got someplace to sleep and something to put in your belly. You got that, huh? You got that? That's what you need. You got that, huh?

CORY: You don't know what I got. You ain't got to worry about what I got.

TROY: You right! You one hundred percent right! I done spent the last seventeen years worrying about what you got. Now it's your turn, see? I'll tell you what to do. You grown . . . we done established that. You a man. Now, let's see you act like one. Turn your behind around and walk out this yard. And when you get out there in the alley . . . you can forget about this house. See? 'Cause this is my house. You go on and be a man and get your own house. You can forget about this. 'Cause this is mine. You go on and get yours 'cause I'm through with doing for you.

CORY: You talking about what you did for me . . . what'd you ever give me?

TROY: Them feet and bones! That pumping heart, nigger! I give you more than anybody else is ever gonna give you.

CORY: You ain't never gave me nothing! You ain't never done anything but hold me back. Afraid I was gonna be better than you. All you ever did was try and make me scared of you. I used to tremble every time you called my name. Every time I heard your footsteps in the house. Wondering all the time . . . what's Papa gonna say if I do this? . . . What's he gonna say if I do that? . . . What's Papa gonna say if I turn on the radio? And Mama, too . . . she tries . . . but she's scared of you.

TROY: You leave your mama out of this. She ain't got nothing to do with this.

CORY: I don't know how she stand you . . . after what you did to her.

TROY: I told you to leave your mama out of this!

He advances toward CORY.

CORY: What you gonna do . . . give me a whupping? You can't whip me no more. You're too old. You just an old man.

TROY [*shoves him on his shoulder*]:   Nigger! That's what you are. You just another nigger on the street to me!

CORY: You crazy! You know that?

TROY: Go on now! You got the devil in you. Get on away from me!

CORY: You just a crazy old man . . . talking about I got the devil in me.

TROY: Yeah, I'm crazy! If you don't get on the other side of that yard . . . I'm gonna show you how crazy I am! Go on . . . get the hell out of my yard.

CORY: It ain't your yard! You took Uncle Gabe's money he got from the army to buy this house and then you put him out.

TROY [TROY *advances on* CORY]:   Get your black ass out of my yard!

TROY*'s advance backs* CORY *up against the tree.* CORY *grabs up the bat.*

CORY: I ain't going nowhere! Come on . . . put me out! I ain't scared of you.

TROY: That's my bat!

CORY: Come on!

TROY: Put my bat down!

CORY: Come on, put me out.

> CORY *swings at* TROY, *who backs across the yard.*

What's the matter? You so bad . . . put me out!

> TROY *advances toward* CORY.

CORY [*backing up*]:   Come on! Come on!

TROY: You're gonna have to use it! You wanna draw that bat back on me . . .
you're gonna have to use it.

CORY: Come on! . . . Come on!

CORY *swings the bat at* TROY *a second time. He misses.* TROY *continues to advance toward him.*

TROY: You're gonna have to kill me! You wanna draw that bat back on me. You're
gonna have to kill me.

CORY, *backed up against the tree, can go no further.* TROY *taunts him. He sticks out his head
and offers him a target.*

Come on! Come on!

> CORY *is unable to swing the bat.* TROY *grabs it.*

TROY: Then I'll show you.

CORY *and* TROY *struggle over the bat. The struggle is fierce and fully engaged.* TROY *ultimately is the stronger and takes the bat from* CORY *and stands over him ready to swing. He
stops himself.*

Go on and get away from around my house.

CORY, *stung by his defeat, picks himself up, walks slowly out of the yard and up the alley.*

CORY: Tell Mama I'll be back for my things.

TROY: They'll be on the other side of that fence.

> CORY *exits.*

TROY: I can't taste nothing. Helluljah! I can't taste nothing no more. [TROY *assumes
a batting posture and begins to taunt Death, the fastball on the outside corner.*] Come on! It's
between you and me now! Come on! Anytime you want! Come on! I be ready for
you . . . but I ain't gonna be easy.

> *The lights go down on the scene.*

Scene 5

The time is 1965. The lights come up in the yard. It is the morning of TROY's *funeral. A funeral
plaque with a light hangs beside the door. There is a small garden plot off to the side. There is
noise and activity in the house as* ROSE, GABRIEL, *and* BONO *have gathered. The door opens and*
RAYNELL, *seven years old, enters dressed in a flannel nightgown. She crosses to the garden and
pokes around with a stick.* ROSE *calls from the house.*

ROSE: Raynell!
RAYNELL: Mam?
ROSE: What you doing out there?
RAYNELL: Nothing.

ROSE comes to the door.

ROSE: Girl, get in here and get dressed. What you doing?
RAYNELL: Seeing if my garden growed.
ROSE: I told you it ain't gonna grow overnight. You got to wait.
RAYNELL: It don't look like it never gonna grow. Dag!
ROSE: I told you a watched pot never boils. Get in here and get dressed.
RAYNELL: This ain't even no pot, Mama.
ROSE: You just have to give it a chance. It'll grow. Now you come on and do what I told you. We got to be getting ready. This ain't no morning to be playing around. You hear me?
RAYNELL: Yes, mam.

ROSE exits into the house. RAYNELL continues to poke at her garden with a stick. CORY enters. He is dressed in a Marine corporal's uniform, and carries a duffel bag. His posture is that of a military man, and his speech has a clipped sternness.

CORY [*to* RAYNELL]:   Hi.

Pause.

I bet your name is Raynell.
RAYNELL: Uh huh.
CORY: Is your mama home?

RAYNELL runs up on the porch and calls through the screendoor.

RAYNELL: Mama . . . there's some man out here. Mama?

ROSE comes to the door.

ROSE: Cory? Lord have mercy! Look here, you all!

ROSE and CORY embrace in a tearful reunion as BONO and LYONS enter from the house dressed in funeral clothes.

BONO: Aw, looka here . . .
ROSE: Done got all grown up!
CORY: Don't cry, Mama. What you crying about?
ROSE: I'm just so glad you made it.
CORY: Hey Lyons. How you doing, Mr. Bono.

LYONS goes to embrace CORY.

LYONS: Look at you, man. Look at you. Don't he look good, Rose. Got them Corporal stripes.
ROSE: What took you so long.
CORY: You know how the Marines are, Mama. They got to get all their paperwork straight before they let you do anything.

ROSE: Well, I'm sure glad you made it. They let Lyons come. Your Uncle Gabe's still in the hospital. They don't know if they gonna let him out or not. I just talked to them a little while ago.

LYONS: A Corporal in the United States Marines.

BONO: Your daddy knew you had it in you. He used to tell me all the time.

LYONS: Don't he look good, Mr. Bono?

BONO: Yeah, he remind me of Troy when I first met him.

Pause.

Say, Rose, Lucille's down at the church with the choir. I'm gonna go down and get the pallbearers lined up. I'll be back to get you all.

ROSE: Thanks, Jim.

CORY: See you, Mr. Bono.

LYONS [*with his arm around* RAYNELL]:   Cory . . . look at Raynell. Ain't she precious? She gonna break a whole lot of hearts.

ROSE: Raynell, come and say hello to your brother. This is your brother, Cory. You remember Cory.

RAYNELL: No, Mam.

CORY: She don't remember me, Mama.

ROSE: Well, we talk about you. She heard us talk about you. [*To* RAYNELL.] This is your brother, Cory. Come on and say hello.

RAYNELL: Hi.

CORY: Hi. So you're Raynell. Mama told me a lot about you.

ROSE: You all come on into the house and let me fix you some breakfast. Keep up your strength.

CORY: I ain't hungry, Mama.

LYONS: You can fix me something, Rose. I'll be in there in a minute.

ROSE: Cory, you sure you don't want nothing. I know they ain't feeding you right.

CORY: No, Mama . . . thanks. I don't feel like eating. I'll get something later.

ROSE: Raynell . . . get on upstairs and get that dress on like I told you.

ROSE *and* RAYNELL *exit into the house.*

LYONS: So . . . I hear you thinking about getting married.

CORY: Yeah, I done found the right one, Lyons. It's about time.

LYONS: Me and Bonnie been split up about four years now. About the time Papa retired. I guess she just got tired of all them changes I was putting her through.

Pause.

I always knew you was gonna make something out yourself. Your head was always in the right direction. So . . . you gonna stay in . . . make it a career . . . put in your twenty years?

CORY: I don't know. I got six already, I think that's enough.

LYONS: Stick with Uncle Sam and retire early. Ain't nothing out here. I guess Rose told you what happened with me. They got me down the workhouse. I thought I was being slick cashing other people's checks.

CORY: How much time you doing?

LYONS: They give me three years. I got that beat now. I ain't got but nine more months. It ain't so bad. You learn to deal with it like anything else. You got to take the crookeds with the straights. That's what Papa used to say. He used to say that when he struck out. I seen him strike out three times in a row . . . and the next time up he hit the ball over the grandstand. Right out there in Homestead Field. He wasn't satisfied hitting in the seats . . . he want to hit it over everything! After the game he had two hundred people standing around waiting to shake his hand. You got to take the crookeds with the straights. Yeah, Papa was something else.

CORY: You still playing?

LYONS: Cory . . . you know I'm gonna do that. There's some fellows down there we got us a band . . . we gonna try and stay together when we get out . . . but yeah, I'm still playing. It still helps me to get out of bed in the morning. As long as it do that I'm gonna be right there playing and trying to make some sense out of it.

ROSE [*calling*]:   Lyons, I got these eggs in the pan.

LYONS: Let me go on and get these eggs, man. Get ready to go bury Papa.

Pause.

How you doing? You doing all right?

CORY *nods.* LYONS *touches him on the shoulder and they share a moment of silent grief.* LYONS *exits into the house.* CORY *wanders about the yard.* RAYNELL *enters.*

RAYNELL: Hi.

CORY: Hi.

RAYNELL: Did you used to sleep in my room?

CORY: Yeah . . . that used to be my room.

RAYNELL: That's what Papa call it. "Cory's room." It got your football in the closet.

ROSE *comes to the door.*

ROSE: Raynell, get in there and get them good shoes on.

RAYNELL: Mama, can't I wear these? Them other one hurt my feet.

ROSE: Well, they just gonna have to hurt your feet for a while. You ain't said they hurt your feet when you went down to the store and got them.

RAYNELL: They didn't hurt then. My feet done got bigger.

ROSE: Don't you give me no backtalk now. You get in there and get them shoes on.

RAYNELL *exits into the house.*

Ain't too much changed. He still got that piece of rag tied to that tree. He was out here swinging that bat. I was just ready to go back in the house. He swung that bat and then he just fell over. Seem like he swung it and stood there with this grin on his face . . . and then he just fell over. They carried him on down to the hospital, but I knew there wasn't no need . . . why don't you come on in the house?

CORY: Mama . . . I got something to tell you. I don't know how to tell you this . . . but I've got to tell you . . . I'm not going to Papa's funeral.

ROSE: Boy, hush your mouth. That's your daddy you talking about. I don't want to hear that kind of talk this morning. I done raised you to come to this? You standing there all healthy and grown talking about you ain't going to your daddy's funeral?

CORY: Mama . . . listen . . .

ROSE: I don't want to hear it, Cory. You just get that thought out of your head.

CORY: I can't drag Papa with me everywhere I go. I've got to say no to him. One time in my life I've got to say no.

ROSE: Don't nobody have to listen to nothing like that. I know you and your daddy ain't seen eye to eye, but I ain't got to listen to that kind of talk this morning. Whatever was between you and your daddy . . . the time has come to put it aside. Just take it and set it over there on the shelf and forget about it. Disrespecting your daddy ain't gonna make you a man, Cory. You got to find a way to come to that on your own. Not going to your daddy's funeral ain't gonna make you a man.

CORY: The whole time I was growing up . . . living in his house . . . Papa was like a shadow that followed you everywhere. It weighed on you and sunk into your flesh. It would wrap around you and lay there until you couldn't tell which one was you anymore. That shadow digging in your flesh. Trying to crawl in. Trying to live through you. Everywhere I looked, Troy Maxson was staring back at me . . . hiding under the bed . . . in the closet. I'm just saying I've got to find a way to get rid of that shadow, Mama.

ROSE: You just like him. You got him in you good.

CORY: Don't tell me that, Mama.

ROSE: You Troy Maxson all over again.

CORY: I don't want to be Troy Maxson. I want to be me.

ROSE: You can't be nobody but who you are, Cory. That shadow wasn't nothing but you growing into yourself. You either got to grow into it or cut it down to fit you. But that's all you got to make life with. That's all you got to measure yourself against that world out there. Your daddy wanted you to be everything he wasn't . . . and at the same time he tried to make you into everything he was. I don't know if he was right or wrong . . . but I do know he meant to do more good than he meant to do harm. He wasn't always right. Sometimes when he touched he bruised. And sometimes when he took me in his arms he cut.

When I first met your daddy I thought . . . Here is a man I can lay down with and make a baby. That's the first thing I thought when I seen him. I was thirty years old and had done seen my share of men. But when he walked up to me and said, "I can dance a waltz that'll make you dizzy," I thought, Rose Lee, here is a man that you can open yourself up to and be filled to bursting. Here is a man that can fill all them empty spaces you been tipping around the edges of. One of them empty spaces was being somebody's mother.

I married your daddy and settled down to cooking his supper and keeping clean sheets on the bed. When your daddy walked through the house he was so big he filled it up. That was my first mistake. Not to make him leave some room for me. For my part in the matter. But at that time I wanted that. I wanted a house that I could sing in. And that's what your daddy gave me. I didn't know to keep up his strength I had to give up little pieces of mine. I did that. I took on his life as mine and mixed up the pieces so that you couldn't hardly tell which was which anymore. It was my choice. It was my life and I didn't have to live it like that. But that's what life offered me in the way of being a woman and I took it. I grabbed hold of it with both hands.

By the time Raynell came into the house, me and your daddy had done lost touch with one another. I didn't want to make my blessing off of nobody's misfortune . . . but I took on to Raynell like she was all them babies I had wanted and never had.

The phone rings.

Like I'd been blessed to relive a part of my life. And if the Lord see fit to keep up my strength . . . I'm gonna do her just like your daddy did you . . . I'm gonna give her the best of what's in me.

RAYNELL [*entering, still with her old shoes*]:   Mama . . . Reverend Tollivier on the phone.

ROSE *exits into the house.*

RAYNELL: Hi.

CORY: Hi.

RAYNELL: You in the Army or the Marines?

CORY: Marines.

RAYNELL: Papa said it was the Army. Did you know Blue?

CORY: Blue? Who's Blue?

RAYNELL: Papa's dog what he sing about all the time.

CORY [*singing*]:   Hear it ring! Hear it ring!
> I had a dog his name was Blue
> You know Blue was mighty true
> You know Blue was a good old dog
> Blue treed a possum in a hollow log
> You know from that he was a good old dog.
> Hear it ring! Hear it ring!

RAYNELL *joins in singing.*

CORY *and* RAYNELL: Blue treed a possum out on a limb
> Blue looked at me and I looked at him
> Grabbed that possum and put him in a sack
> Blue stayed there till I came back
> Old Blue's feets was big and round
> Never allowed a possum to touch the ground.
>
> Old Blue died and I dug his grave
> I dug his grave with a silver spade
> Let him down with a golden chain
> And every night I call his name
> Go on Blue, you good dog you
> Go on Blue, you good dog you

RAYNELL: Blue laid down and died like a man
> Blue laid down and died . . .

BOTH: Blue laid down and died like a man
> Now he's treeing possums in the Promised Land
> I'm gonna tell you this to let you know
> Blue's gone where the good dogs go
> When I hear old Blue bark
> When I hear old Blue bark
> Blue treed a possum in Noah's Ark,
> Blue treed a possum in Noah's Ark.

ROSE *comes to the screen door.*

ROSE: Cory, we gonna be ready to go in a minute.

CORY [*to* RAYNELL]: You go on in the house and change them shoes like Mama told you so we can go to Papa's funeral.

RAYNELL: Okay, I'll be back.

RAYNELL *exits into the house.* CORY *gets up and crosses over to the tree.* ROSE *stands in the screen door watching him.* GABRIEL *enters from the alley.*

GABRIEL [*calling*]: Hey, Rose!

ROSE: Gabe?

GABRIEL: I'm here, Rose. Hey Rose, I'm here!

ROSE *enters from the house.*

ROSE: Lord . . . Look here, Lyons!

LYONS: See, I told you, Rose . . . I told you they'd let him come.

CORY: How you doing, Uncle Gabe?

LYONS: How you doing, Uncle Gabe?

GABRIEL: Hey, Rose. It's time. It's time to tell St. Peter to open the gates. Troy, you ready? You ready, Troy. I'm gonna tell St. Peter to open the gates. You get ready now.

GABRIEL, *with great fanfare, braces himself to blow. The trumpet is without a mouthpiece. He puts the end of it into his mouth and blows with great force, like a man who has been waiting some twenty-odd years for this single moment. No sound comes out of the trumpet. He braces himself and blows again with the same result. A third time he blows. There is a weight of impossible description that falls away and leaves him bare and exposed to a frightful realization. It is a trauma that a sane and normal mind would be unable to withstand. He begins to dance. A slow, strange dance, eerie and life-giving. A dance of atavistic signature and ritual.* LYONS *attempts to embrace him.* GABRIEL *pushes* LYONS *away. He begins to howl in what is an attempt at song, or perhaps a song turning back into itself in an attempt at speech. He finishes his dance and the gates of heaven stand open as wide as God's closet.*

That's the way that go!

(1986)

QUESTIONS FOR REFLECTION

Experience

1. To what extent can you relate to the situations of Wilson's characters? Why or why not?

Interpretation

2. How does Wilson establish the world of his play? What kinds of details help readers and viewers orient themselves?

3. Identify the play's most important references to religion, and explain their function.
4. How does Wilson make his characters believable? Which of them do you understand best? Why?
5. What metaphors do Troy and Rose use to make sense of their lives? How does the playwright use these metaphors for expressive purposes?
6. Identify the various kinds of "fences" the play includes. Explain the significance of the title.
7. Select one longer speech or one important exchange of dialogue, and explain its significance to the play's theme.
8. Select one scene or part of a scene, and explain how you would stage it.

Evaluation

9. Identify the values each of the characters lives by. Whose values does the play seem to endorse?

WENDY WASSERSTEIN

[b. 1950]

Wendy Wasserstein was born and raised in New York City. She was educated at Smith College and at Mount Holyoke College, from which she graduated with a B.A. in 1971. Two years later she earned a master's degree in playwriting from City College of New York. From 1973 until 1976 she studied at the Yale School of Drama, from which she received a master of fine arts. In 1989 she won the Pulitzer Prize and a Tony Award for Best Play for *The Heidi Chronicles,* and in 1993 she won an Outer Circle Critics Award and a Tony nomination for *The Sisters Rosenzweig.* In addition to plays, she has written for public television and film.

    Tender Offer, which was written and produced in 1977, is a one-act play that captures the relationship between a father and his teen-age daughter. The play's economy and its humor belie its underlying seriousness.

WENDY WASSERSTEIN

Tender Offer

A girl of around nine is alone in a dance studio. She is dressed in traditional leotards and tights. She begins singing to herself, "Nothing Could Be Finer Than to Be in Carolina." She maps out a dance routine, including parts for the chorus. She builds to a finale. A man, PAUL, around thirty-five, walks in. He has a sweet, though distant, demeanor. As he walks in, LISA notices him and stops.

PAUL: You don't have to stop, sweetheart.

LISA: That's okay.

PAUL: Looked very good.

LISA: Thanks.

PAUL: Don't I get a kiss hello?

LISA: Sure.

PAUL [*Embraces her.*]:   Hi, Tiger.

LISA: Hi, Dad.

PAUL: I'm sorry I'm late.

LISA: That's okay.

PAUL: How'd it go?

LISA: Good.

PAUL: Just good?

LISA: Pretty good.

PAUL: "Pretty good." You mean you got a lot of applause or "pretty good" you could have done better.

LISA: Well, Courtney Palumbo's mother thought I was pretty good. But you know the part in the middle when everybody's supposed to freeze and the big girl comes out. Well, I think I moved a little bit.

PAUL: I thought what you were doing looked very good.

LISA: Daddy, that's not what I was doing. That was tap-dancing. I made that up.

PAUL: Oh. Well it looked good. Kind of sexy.

LISA: Yuch!

PAUL: What do you mean "yuch"?

LISA: Just yuch!

PAUL: You don't want to be sexy?

LISA: I don't care.

PAUL: Let's go, Tiger. I promised your mother I'd get you home in time for dinner.

LISA: I can't find my leg warmers.

PAUL: You can't find your what?

LISA: Leg warmers. I can't go home till I find my leg warmers.

PAUL: I don't see you looking for them.

LISA: I was waiting for you.

PAUL: Oh.

LISA: Daddy.

PAUL: What?

LISA: Nothing.

PAUL: Where do you think you left them?

LISA: Somewhere around here. I can't remember.

PAUL: Well, try to remember, Lisa. We don't have all night.

LISA: I told you. I think somewhere around here.

PAUL: I don't see them. Let's go home now. You'll call the dancing school tomorrow.

LISA: Daddy, I can't go home till I find them. Miss Judy says it's not professional to leave things.

PAUL: Who's Miss Judy?

LISA: She's my ballet teacher. She once danced the lead in *Swan Lake,* and she was a June Taylor dancer.

PAUL: Well, then, I'm sure she'll understand about the leg warmers.

LISA: Daddy, Miss Judy wanted to know why you were late today.

PAUL: Hmmmmmmmm?

LISA: Why were you late?

PAUL: I was in a meeting. Business. I'm sorry.

LISA: Why did you tell Mommy you'd come instead of her if you knew you had business?

PAUL: Honey, something just came up. I thought I'd be able to be here. I was looking forward to it.

LISA: I wish you wouldn't make appointments to see me.

PAUL: Hmmmmmmmm.

LISA: You shouldn't make appointments to see me unless you know you're going to come.

PAUL: Of course I'm going to come.

LISA: No, you're not. Talia Robbins told me she's much happier living without her father in the house. Her father used to come home late and go to sleep early.

PAUL: Lisa, stop it. Let's go.

LISA: I can't find my leg warmers.

PAUL: Forget your leg warmers.

LISA: Daddy.

PAUL: What is it?

LISA: I saw this show on television, I think it was WPIX Channel 11. Well, the father was crying about his daughter.

PAUL: Why was he crying? Was she sick?

LISA: No. She was at school. And he was at business. And he just missed her, so he started to cry.

PAUL: What was the name of this show?

LISA: I don't know. I came in in the middle.

PAUL: Well, Lisa, I certainly would cry if you were sick or far away, but I know that you're well and you're home. So no reason to get maudlin.

LISA: What's maudlin?

PAUL: Sentimental, soppy. Frequently used by children who make things up to get attention.

LISA: I am sick! I am sick! I have Hodgkin's disease and a bad itch on my leg.

PAUL: What do you mean you have Hodgkin's disease? Don't say things like that.

LISA: Swoosie Kurtz, she had Hodgkin's disease on a TV movie last year, but she got better and now she's on *Love Sidney*.

PAUL: Who is Swoosie Kurtz?

LISA: She's an actress named after an airplane. I saw her on *Live at Five*.

PAUL: You watch too much television; you should do your homework. Now, put your coat on.

LISA: Daddy, I really do have a bad itch on my leg. Would you scratch it?

PAUL: Lisa, you're procrastinating.

LISA: Why do you use words I don't understand? I hate it. You're like Daria Feldman's mother. She always talks in Yiddish to her husband so Daria won't understand.

PAUL: Procrastinating is not Yiddish.

LISA: Well, I don't know what it is.

PAUL: Procrastinating means you don't want to go about your business.

LISA: I don't go to business. I go to school.

PAUL: What I mean is you want to hang around here until you and I are late for dinner and your mother's angry and it's too late for you to do your homework.

LISA: I do not.

PAUL: Well, it sure looks that way. Now put your coat on and let's go.

LISA: Daddy.

PAUL: Honey, I'm tired. Really, later.

LISA: Why don't you want to talk to me?

PAUL: I do want to talk to you. I promise when we get home we'll have a nice talk.

LISA: No, we won't. You'll read the paper and fall asleep in front of the news.

PAUL: Honey, we'll talk on the weekend, I promise. Aren't I taking you to the theater this weekend? Let me look. [*He takes out appointment book.*] Yes. Sunday. *Joseph and the Amazing Technicolor Raincoat* with Lisa. Okay, Tiger?

LISA: Sure. It's Dreamcoat.

PAUL: What?

LISA: Nothing. I think I see my leg warmers. [*She goes to pick them up, and an odd-looking trophy.*]

PAUL: What's that?

LISA: It's stupid. I was second best at the dance recital, so they gave me this thing. It's stupid.

PAUL: Lisa.

LISA: What?

PAUL: What did you want to talk about?

LISA: Nothing.

PAUL: Was it about my missing your recital? I'm really sorry, Tiger, I would have liked to have been here.

LISA: That's okay.

PAUL: Honest?

LISA: Daddy, you're prostrastinating.

PAUL: I'm procrastinating. Sit down. Let's talk. So. How's school?

LISA: Fine.

PAUL: You like it?

LISA: Yup.

PAUL: You looking forward to camp this summer?

LISA: Yup.

PAUL: Is Daria Feldman going back?

LISA: Nope.

PAUL: Why not?

LISA: I don't know. We can go home now. Honest, my foot doesn't itch anymore.

PAUL: Lisa, you know what you do in business when it seems like there's nothing left to say? That's when you really start talking. Put a bid on the table.

LISA: What's a bid?

PAUL: You tell me what you want and I'll tell you what I've got to offer. Like Monopoly. You want Boardwalk, but I'm only willing to give you the Railroads. Now, because you are my daughter I'd throw in Water Works and Electricity. Understand, Tiger?

LISA: No. I don't like board games. You know, Daddy, we could get Space Invaders for our home for thirty-five dollars. In fact, we could get an Osborne System for two thousand. Daria Feldman's parents . . .

PAUL: Daria Feldman's parents refuse to talk to Daria, so they bought a computer to keep Daria busy so they won't have to speak in Yiddish. Daria will probably grow up to be a homicidal maniac lesbian prostitute.

LISA: I know what that word prostitute means.

PAUL: Good. [*Pause.*] You still haven't told me about school. Do you still like your teacher?

LISA: She's okay.

PAUL: Lisa, if we're talking try to answer me.

LISA: I am answering you. Can we go home now, please?

PAUL: Damn it, Lisa, if you want to talk to me . . . Talk to me!

LISA: I can't wait till I'm old enough so I can make my own money and never have to see you again. Maybe I'll become a prostitute.

PAUL: Young lady, that's enough.

LISA: I hate you, Daddy! I hate you! [*She throws her trophy into the trash bin.*]

PAUL: What'd you do that for?

LISA: It's stupid.

PAUL: Maybe I wanted it.

LISA: What for?

PAUL: Maybe I wanted to put it where I keep your dinosaur and the picture you made of Mrs. Kimbel with the chicken pox.

LISA: You got mad at me when I made that picture. You told me I had to respect Mrs. Kimbel because she was my teacher.

PAUL: That's true. But she wasn't my teacher. I liked her better with the chicken pox. [*Pause.*] Lisa, I'm sorry. I was very wrong to miss your recital, and you don't have to become a prostitute. That's not the type of profession Miss Judy has in mind for you.

LISA [*Mumbles.*]:   No.

PAUL: No. [*Pause.*] So Talia Robbins is really happy her father moved out?

LISA: Talia Robbins picks open the eighth-grade lockers during gym period. But she did that before her father moved out.

PAUL: You can't always judge someone by what they do or what they don't do. Sometimes you come home from dancing school and run upstairs and shut the door, and when I finally get to talk to you, everything is "okay" or "fine." Yup or nope?

LISA: Yup.

PAUL: Sometimes, a lot of times, I come home and fall asleep in front of the television. So you and I spend a lot of time being a little scared of each other. Maybe?

LISA: Maybe.

PAUL: Tell you what. I'll make you a tender offer.

LISA: What?

PAUL: I'll make you a tender offer. That's when one company publishes in the newspaper that they want to buy another company. And the company that publishes is called the Black Knight because they want to gobble up the poor little company. So the poor little company needs to be rescued. And then a White Knight comes along and makes a bigger and better offer so the shareholders won't have to tender shares to the Big Black Knight. You with me?

LISA: Sort of.

PAUL: I'll make you a tender offer like the White Knight. But I don't want to own you. I just want to make a much better offer. Okay?

LISA [*Sort of understanding.*]: Okay. [*Pause. They sit for a moment.*] Sort of, Daddy, what do you think about? I mean, like when you're quiet what do you think about?

PAUL: Oh, business usually. If I think I made a mistake or if I think I'm doing okay. Sometimes I think about what I'll be doing five years from now and if it's what I hoped it would be five years ago. Sometimes I think about what your life will be like, if Mount Saint Helen's will erupt again. What you'll become if you'll study penmanship or word processing. If you'll speak kindly of me to your psychiatrist when you are in graduate school. And how the hell I'll pay for your graduate school. And sometimes I try and think what it was I thought about when I was your age.

LISA: Do you ever look out your window at the clouds and try to see which kinds of shapes they are? Like one time, honest, I saw the head of Walter Cronkite in a flower vase. Really! Like look don't those kinda look like if you turn it upside down, two big elbows or two elephant trunks dancing?

PAUL: Actually still looks like Walter Cronkite in a flower vase to me. But look up a little. See the one that's still moving? That sorta looks like a whale on a thimble.

LISA: Where?

PAUL: Look up. To your right.

LISA: I don't see it. Where?

PAUL: The other way.

LISA: Oh, yeah! There's the head and there's the stomach. Yeah! [LISA *picks up her trophy.*] Hey, Daddy.

PAUL: Hey, Lisa.

LISA: You can have this thing if you want it. But you have to put it like this, because if you put it like that it is gross.

PAUL: You know what I'd like? So I can tell people who come into my office why I have this gross stupid thing on my shelf, I'd like it if you could show me your dance recital.

LISA: Now?

PAUL: We've got time. Mother said she won't be home till late.

LISA: Well, Daddy, during a lot of it I freeze and the big girl in front dances.

PAUL: Well, how 'bout the number you were doing when I walked in?

LISA: Well, see, I have parts for a lot of people in that one, too.

PAUL: I'll dance the other parts.

LISA: You can't dance.

PAUL: Young lady, I played Yvette Mimieux in a *Hasty Pudding Show.*

LISA: Who's Yvette Mimieux?

PAUL: Watch more television. You'll find out. [PAUL *stands up.*] So I'm ready. [*He begins singing.*] "Nothing could be finer than to be in Carolina."

LISA: Now I go. In the morning. And now you go. Dum-da.

PAUL [*Obviously not a tap dancer.*]: Da-da-dum.

LISA [*Whines.*]: Daddy!

PAUL [*Mimics her.*]: Lisa! Nothing could be finer . . .

LISA: That looks dumb.

PAUL: Oh, yeah? You think they do this better in *The Amazing Minkcoat?* No way! Now you go—da da da dum.

LISA: Da da da dum.

PAUL: If I had Aladdin's lamp for only a day, I'd make a wish. . . .

LISA: Daddy, that's maudlin!

PAUL: I know it's maudlin. And here's what I'd say:

LISA *and* PAUL: I'd say that "nothing could be finer than to be in Carolina in the moooooooooooornin'."

(*1977*)

QUESTIONS FOR REFLECTION

Experience

1. To what extent can you identify with the situation depicted in Wasserstein's play? Why?

Interpretation

2. How would you characterize the relationship between Lisa and Paul?
3. Examine the play's dialogue for shifts of direction. Account for the conversational logic of these shifts and explain their dramatic effects.
4. Explain the significance of Paul and Lisa's discussion of the meaning of "procrastination" and "maudlin."
5. What is the function of Paul's inaccuracy in naming the title of the Broadway play *Joseph and the Amazing Technicolor Dreamcoat*?
6. Explain the various meanings of the "tender offer" Paul makes Lisa.
7. Consider how you would direct the actors in staging the play's final scene—the father/daughter dance routine.
8. What is the theme of the play?

Evaluation

9. How effectively does Wasserstein characterize a father-daughter relationship? Where is her depiction most convincing, least convincing, and why?

JOSEFINA LÓPEZ

Josefina López wrote her first play at the age of seventeen. *Simply María* was produced in San Diego and later aired on PBS. A surreal exploration of the development of a Mexican woman growing up in the United States, the play's action occurs mostly as a dream sequence. In exploring social and gender values, *Simply María* uses irony and satire to illuminate cultural differences and evaluate cultural mythologies.

J O S E F I N A   L Ó P E Z

Simply María

or

The American Dream

CHARACTERS

Principals:
MARÍA, *daughter of Carmen and Ricardo*
CARMEN, *mother of María*
RICARDO, *father of María*
JOSÉ, *María's husband*
PRIEST

In order of appearance:
GIRL 1
GIRL 2
GIRL 3
MOTHER, *Carmen's mother*
WOMAN
NARRATOR
IMMIGRANT 1
IMMIGRANT 2
IMMIGRANT 3
IMMIGRANT 4
STATUE OF LIBERTY
MEXICAN MAN
MEXICAN WOMAN
POSTMAN
PERSON 1
VENDOR 1
VENDOR 2
BAG LADY
PROTESTOR
MAN 1
DIRTY OLD MAN
CHOLO 2
VALLEY GIRL 1
VALLEY GIRL 2

CHOLO 1
PERSON 2
PERSON 3
PERSON 4
ANGLO BUYER
MYTH
MARY
MARÍA 2
REFEREE
ANNOUNCER
FLOOR MANAGER
HUSBAND
WIFE
SALESMAN
HEAD NURSE
NURSE 2
NURSE 3
NURSE 4
BAILIFF
JUDGE
PROSECUTOR
JUROR 1
JUROR 2

Note: Many of the above characters can be played by the same actor/actress.

Place. The play begins in an unspecified town in Mexico and moves to downtown Los Angeles.
Time. Over a period of years chronicling the growth of María from birth to her womanhood.

SCENE ONE

There is a long thin movie screen on the top and across the stage that will be used to display slides of titles for a couple of seconds each. Lights rise. MARÍA, *a young woman with a suitcase, enters. She goes to the center and remains still.* THREE GIRLS *enter and stand behind her.*

GIRL 3 (*Loud introduction.*):   Romeo and Juliet elope. Or, where's the wedding dress?

(*Lights slowly fade. Then dim lights slowly rise.* RICARDO, *a tall, dark and handsome young Mexican man enters. He tries to hide in the darkness of the night. He whistles carefully, blending the sound with the noises of the night.*)

CARMEN (*From her balcony.*):   Ricardo, ¿eres tú?
RICARDO: Yes! Ready?

CARMEN: Sí. (*She climbs down from her balcony, then runs to* RICARDO, *kissing and consuming him in her embrace.*) Where's the horse?

RICARDO: What horse?

CARMEN: The one we are going to elope on.

RICARDO: You didn't say to bring one. All we agreed on was that I would be here at midnight.

CARMEN: I would have thought that you would have thought to . . .

RICARDO: Shhhh!!! ¡Mira! (*Points to* CARMEN's *room.*)

CARMEN: ¡Mi madre! Let's go! And on what are we going?

RICARDO: On this. (*Brings an old bike.*)

CARMEN: ¡Qué! On that? No! How could . . . Everyone knows that when you elope, you elope on a horse, not on a . . . Ricardo, you promised!

MOTHER (*Discovering* CARMEN *gone.*): ¡Carmencita! Carmen! She's gone!

CARMEN: Oh, no! Hurry! Let's go!

RICARDO (*Hops on the bike.*): Carmen, hurry! Get on!

CARMEN: We won't fit!

MOTHER: ¡M'ija! Where are you?

CARMEN: We better fit! (*Jumps on, and they take off. She falls and then quickly hops back on.*) Ricardo, marry me! (*Crickets are heard, lights dim. Fade out.*)

SCENE TWO

THREE WOMEN *enter a church with candles. A fourth, much older, enters with a lighted candle and lights the other candles. The* THREE WOMEN *then transform into statues of the saints in the church.* PRIEST *comes downstage, waiting for a wedding to begin.* CARMEN *enters, pregnant.*

PRIEST: Will he be here soon?

CARMEN: Soon. He promised.

PRIEST: I was supposed to start half an hour ago.

WOMAN (*Enters with a note.*): Is there anyone here named Carmen?

CARMEN: Yes . . . Is it from Ricardo? (*Reading the note.*) "I haven't been able to get a divorce. It will be some time soon, believe me . . . Just wait. I'm working hard so that I can save money to buy a little house or a ranch for the three of us. If you wait, good things will come." (*To* PRIEST.) There won't be a wedding today.

(*Exits crying with* PRIEST. *The statues become* WOMEN *and they all ad lib malicious gossip about the pregnant bride.* CARMEN *enters again, holding baby.* PRIEST *enters.* WOMEN *become statues again.*)

PRIEST: Will he be here? (RICARDO *enters.*)

CARMEN: He is here.

PRIEST: Good. Now we can start.

CARMEN (*To* RICARDO.): I thought you wouldn't show up.

PRIEST: (*Begins his speech, which is more or less mumbled and not heard except for:*) Do you, Carmen, accept Ricardo as your lawfully wedded husband?

CARMEN: I do.

PRIEST: Do you, Ricardo, accept Carmen as your lawfully wedded wife?

RICARDO: I do.

PRIEST: Under the Catholic Church, in the holy House of God, I pronounce you husband and wife. (*Takes baby from* CARMEN, *and sprinkles holy water on baby.*) Under the Catholic Church, in the holy House of God, this child shall be known as María.

The PRIEST *puts the baby on the center of the stage.* CARMEN, RICARDO *and* PRIEST *exit. On the screen the following title is displayed:* **The Making of a Mexican Girl.**

NARRATOR: The making of a Mexican girl.

(*The statues now transform into* THREE ANGELIC GIRLS *who begin to hum, then sing beautifully with only the word "María." They come center stage and deliver the following, facing the audience:*)

ALL: María.

GIRL 1:   As a girl you are to be

GIRL 2:   Nice,

GIRL 3:   forgiving,

GIRL 1:   considerate,

GIRL 2:   obedient,

GIRL 3:   gentle,

GIRL 1:   hard-working,

GIRL 2:   gracious.

GIRL 3:   You are to like:

GIRL 1:   Dolls,

GIRL 2:   kitchens,

GIRL 3:   houses,

GIRL 1:   cleaning,

GIRL 2:   caring for children,

GIRL 3:   cooking,

GIRL 1:   laundry,

GIRL 2:   dishes.

GIRL 3:   You are not to:

GIRL 1:   Be independent,

GIRL 2:   enjoy sex,

GIRL 3:   but must endure it as your duty to your husband,

GIRL 1:   and bear his children.

GIRL 2:   Do not shame your society!

GIRL 3:   Never,

GIRL 1:   never,

GIRL 2:   never,

ALL: Never!!!!

GIRL 1:   Your goal is to reproduce.

GIRL 2:   And your only purpose in life is to serve three men:

GIRL 3:   Your father,

GIRL 1:   your husband,

GIRL 2:   and your son.

GIRL 3:   Your father. (RICARDO *enters.*)

RICARDO: Carmen, I must go.

CARMEN: Ricardo, don't go. Not after all the time I've waited.

RICARDO: I don't want to leave you, but we need the money. There's no work here. I must go to el norte, so I can find work and send for you.

CARMEN: I don't want to be alone.

RICARDO: You have María. I'm going so that we can have the things we don't have.

CARMEN: I would prefer to have you and not the things I don't have.

RICARDO: I want something else besides a life on this farm.

CARMEN: María will not see you.

RICARDO: She will. When I am on the other side, I will send for you. She will be very proud of me.

CARMEN: You promise?

RICARDO: I promise.

CARMEN: Well, then I will wait; we will wait.

RICARDO: I will write. (*Kisses* CARMEN *on the forehead.*)

CARMEN: Ricardo, remember that I love you. (RICARDO *leaves.*) Don't forget to write.

(*Fade out.*)

SCENE THREE

NARRATOR: Yes, write a lot; they will miss you. All who are in search of opportunity go to the same place: America. And America belongs to those who are willing to risk.

(*A giant sail enters the stage brought on by* FOUR EUROPEAN IMMIGRANTS.)

IMMIGRANT 1:   All for a dream.

IMMIGRANT 2:   Ciao, mia Italia!

IMMIGRANT 3:   Auf Wiedersehen, mein Deutschland!

IMMIGRANT 4:   Au revoir, mon France!

IMMIGRANT 2:   Hello, America!

(*In the background "America the Beautiful" plays, the music growing louder. The* STATUE OF LIBERTY *enters.*)

IMMIGRANT 3:   The Lady!

IMMIGRANT 4:   Up high in the sky, incapable of being brought down.

IMMIGRANT 2:   And like her . . .

IMMIGRANT 3:   . . . we carry . . .

IMMIGRANTS 2 & 4:   . . . a similar torch.

ALL: A torch of hope.

STATUE OF LIBERTY: Give me your tired, your poor, your huddled masses yearning to breathe free . . .

(*At the bottom of the* STATUE OF LIBERTY *are* THREE MEXICAN PEOPLE [RICARDO *is one of them*] *trying to go across the stage as if it is the border. They run around hiding, sneaking, and crawling, trying not to get spotted by the border patrol.*)

RICARDO: ¡Vénganse! ¡Por aquí!
MEXICAN MAN: ¿Y ahora qué hacemos?
MEXICAN WOMAN: What do we do now?
MEXICAN MAN: ¡Vámonos! ¡Por allá!
MEXICAN WOMAN: ¡Nos nortearon!
RICARDO: Let's go back.

(*They go to hide behind the* EUROPEAN IMMIGRANTS. *The* STATUE OF LIBERTY *composes herself and continues.*)

STATUE OF LIBERTY: I give you life, liberty and the pursuit of happiness for the price of your heritage, your roots, your history, your relatives, your language . . . Conform, adapt, bury your past, give up what is yours and I'll give you the opportunity to have what is mine.
MEXICAN MAN: Pues bueno, if we have to.
MEXICAN WOMAN: Sounds good.
IMMIGRANT 4:   Look, fireworks!
RICARDO: ¡Nos hicimos!

(*"America the Beautiful" becomes overwhelming; lights flash, representing the fireworks. A few seconds later the same lights that adorn the celebration for* EUROPEAN IMMIGRANTS *become the lights from the helicopters hunting after the* MEXICAN PEOPLE. *Hound dogs are also heard barking, and the* MEXICAN PEOPLE *scatter and try to hide.*)

RICARDO: ¡La migra!
MEXICAN MAN: The immigration!
MEXICAN WOMAN: ¡Córranle!

(*The* EUROPEAN IMMIGRANTS *and the* STATUE OF LIBERTY *all keep pointing at the* MEXICAN PEOPLE *so that they can be caught. The* MEXICAN PEOPLE *run offstage, and with the sail tilted down, they charge after them. Fade out.*)

SCENE FOUR

POSTMAN (*Throwing in paper airplane.*):   Air mail for Carmen García.
CARMEN (CARMEN *enters and reads letter.*):   "Mi querida Carmen, how are you? How is María? I've sent you some more money. This is the last letter I write to you because I am now sending for you. I fixed my papers with the help of a friend, and I got an apartment where we can live. Tell María I love her, and to you I send all my love . . . " María! . . . "Leave as soon as possible . . . " Leave as soon as possible . . ." María, ¡ven acá!
MARÍA (MARÍA *enters.*):   Yes, Mami.
CARMEN: María get ready; we're going.
MARÍA: Going where?
CARMEN: To join your father in the city of the angels.
MARÍA: Angels?

(MARÍA *puts on her coat for the journey. Fade out.*)

SCENE FIVE

On the screen the following title is displayed: **Los Angelitos Del Norte.** *The following is the making of a city. Actors will take on many roles. It will be organized chaos. Noises of police and firetruck sirens, along with other common city noises are heard. The lights rise on* VENDORS *selling on the streets, and all sorts of unusual and not so unusual* PEOPLE *found in downtown L.A. on Broadway.* CARMEN *and* MARÍA *are engulfed in the scene, appalled to see what they have come to.*

PERSON 1:   Broadway! Downtown L.A.!

VENDOR 1:   Cassettes, ¡cartuchos, dos dólares!

VENDOR 2:   Anillos de oro sólido. Solid gold. Not plated.

CARMEN: Perdone, señora, could you tell me . . .

BAG LADY: Get out of my way!

PROTESTOR: Homosexuality is wrong! No sex! No sex! ¡Se va a acabar el mundo! The world is coming to an end!

(*Separates* CARMEN *from* MARÍA.)

CARMEN: María! María, where are you?! (*Searches frantically.*)

MARÍA: Mami! Mami! (*Cries for* CARMEN.)

WOMAN 1:   Buy this! ¿Sombras para verte como estrella de cine?

WOMAN 2:   Hair brushes, all kinds, a dollar!

WOMAN 3:   You want to buy handbags?

WOMAN 4:   ¡Vámonos! Here comes the police.

(*All the* VENDORS *on the street run away.*)

MAN 1:   Jesus loves you! (*Hands* CARMEN *a pamphlet.*) He died for our sins!

CARMEN: ¿Qué?

WOMAN 1:   That RTD bus is late again!

DIRTY OLD MAN: Hey! Little girl! You want to get married? The world is coming to an end and you don't want to die without having experienced it.

CARMEN: María! María! ¿Dónde estás, hija mia?

CHOLO 2:   East L.A.!

TWO VALLEY GIRLS: We love it!

CHOLO 1:   Hey, bato!

TWO VALLEY GIRLS: Party and let party!

CHOLO 2:   ¡Oye, mi carnal!

PERSON 2:   ¡Viva la huelga! Boycott grapes!

PERSON 3:   Chicano Power!

TWO VALLEY GIRLS: We love it.

PERSON 3:   Chicano Power!

TWO VALLEY GIRLS: We love it.

PERSON 4:   A little culture for the gringuitos. ¡Tostadas, frijoles!

ANGLO BUYER: How much? ¿Cuánto? ¿Salsa? ¿Cerveza?

CARMEN: María!

(MARÍA *runs scared and bumps into* CARMEN. *They hug each other.* RICARDO, *dressed in a charro outfit enters and gives some yells as if ready to sing a corrido. All the chaos of the city stops, and all the city people recoil in fear.* RICARDO *becomes the hero rescuing* CARMEN *and* MARÍA *from their nightmare.*)

TWO VALLEY GIRLS: We love it!

CARMEN: ¡Ayyy! What a crazy city! It's so awful! People here are crazy! (*Almost about to cry, she embraces* RICARDO.) But Ricardo, I'm so happy to be here.

MARÍA (*Trying to get attention.*):   An ugly man chased me!

RICARDO: But you are all right?

MARÍA: Sí. Now that you are here.

RICARDO: Carmen, we are finally together like I promised.

CARMEN: Ricardo, where's our home?

RICARDO: Follow me.

(*They leave the stage. Fade out. Props for next scene are set up quickly.*)

SCENE SIX

NARRATOR: They are going to the housing projects; Pico Aliso, Ramona Gardens, Estrada Courts. No one likes it there, but it's cheap. Es Barato. (*On the screen the following title is displayed:* **Little House in The Ghetto.**) Little house in the ghetto.

RICARDO: Here we are.

CARMEN: ¿Aquí?

RICARDO: Yes, I hope it's all right. It's only for now.

MARÍA (*Smiling.*):   I like it! Look, Mami! There are swings and grass.

RICARDO: There are a lot of kids in the neighborhood you can play with.

MARÍA: Really, Papi? Would they want to play with me?

RICARDO: Sure. (*Noticing* CARMEN'*s displeasure.*) What's wrong? You don't like it?

CARMEN: Oh. No, I'm just tired from the trip.

RICARDO: How was the trip?

MARÍA (*Cutting in.*):   It was great!

CARMEN: Great? You threw up on me the whole way here.

MARÍA: Except, I don't understand why the bus never got off the ground. Where are the angels? And where are the clouds? And the gate? And the music . . . Like in the stories Mami used to tell me. I thought we were going to heaven. I thought you had been called to heaven because you are an angel. Are you an angel?

RICARDO: Yes, I'm your angel always.

MARÍA: So if this isn't heaven and you're an angel, what are we doing here?

RICARDO: María, I brought you to America so that you can have a better life. It wasn't easy for me. I was hiding in a truck with a lot of other people for hours. It was so hot and humid that people preferred to get caught by the migra than die of suffocation. But I was going to make it because I knew that I had a daughter to live for. I did it for you. In America, the education is great! You can take advantage of all the opportunities offered to you. You can work hard to be just as good as anybody. You can be anything you want to be! (*Pause.*) Carmen, let me show you the kitchen. (CARMEN *and* RICARDO *exit.*)

MARÍA: America, I don't even know you yet and I already love you! You're too generous. Thank you. I'll work hard. I can be anything I want to be! (*Starts changing clothes to end up wearing a casual shirt and pants when she finishes the following:*) America, I'm ready to play the game. I'm gonna show those boys in this neighborhood how to really play football!

(*She makes some football moves. Then she runs out.* CARMEN *enters.*)

CARMEN: María, ¡ven aquí! (MARÍA *enters.*)
MARÍA: Yes, Mami.
CARMEN: La señora Martínez told me you were playing football with the boys.
MARÍA: Yes, Mami; I was.
CARMEN: I don't want you playing football with the boys. It's not proper for a lady.
MARÍA: But I'm good at sports. I'm better than some of the boys.
CARMEN: It doesn't look right. ¿Qué van a decir?

(*In the background appear the* THREE GIRLS *who are only seen and heard by* MARÍA. *They whisper to her.*)

GIRL 1: Never shame your society.
GIRL 2: Never,
GIRL 3: never,
GIRL 1: never,
ALL: NEVER!!!
MARÍA: But my Papi said . . .
CARMEN: You are not going to play with boys! (CARMEN *exits.*)
MARÍA: I don't understand. Papi tells me to compete, Mami tells me it doesn't look right. I like to compete, too. (MARÍA *exits to her room.*)
RICARDO (*To* MARÍA.): María, ¡ven aquí! Who were you walking home with today?
MARÍA: A friend.
RICARDO: A boyfriend?
MARÍA: No, just a friend I have in my last class. He lives close by.
RICARDO: I don't want you walking home with or talking to boys. Study!
MARÍA (*Dares to ask.*): Papi, why?
RICARDO: You're thirteen and you are very naïve about boys. The only thing on their minds is of no good for a proper girl. They tell girls that they are "special," sweet things, knowing that girls are stupid enough to believe it. They make pendejas out of them. They get them pregnant, and shame their parents . . . Go to your room!

(*The* THREE GIRLS *appear again and whisper to* MARÍA.)

GIRL 1: Never shame your society!
GIRL 2: Never,
GIRL 3: (*Does not continue, but slowly walks away from the two girls.*)
GIRL 1: Never,
GIRL 1 AND 2: Never!!

(*Spotlight on* MARÍA. MARÍA *goes to the mirror,* GIRL 3 *appears in the mirror.* MARÍA *brushes her hair and so does* GIRL 3. *Then* GIRL 3 *begins to touch herself in intimate ways, discovering the changes through puberty, while* MARÍA *remains still, not daring to touch herself. Finally, when* MARÍA *does dare to touch herself,* CARMEN *comes into the room and discovers her. Lights quickly come back on.*)

CARMEN: María, what are you doing?

MARÍA: Nothing.

CARMEN: María, were you . . . (*Before* MARÍA *can answer.*) It is a sin to do that. Good girls don't do that. (GIRL 3 *goes behind* MARÍA.)

GIRL 3 (*Whispering.*):   Why? Why? Why?

MARÍA: Why?

CARMEN (*Somewhat shocked.*):   Because it is dirty! Sex is dirty.

GIRL 3:   Why is it dirty? What makes it dirty?

MARÍA (*Suppresses and ignores* GIRL 3.):   I'm sorry, I didn't know what I was doing.

CARMEN: María, I'm telling you for your own good. Women should be pure. Men don't marry women who are not unless they have to. Quieren vírgenes. It's best that way, if you save yourself for your wedding night. Be submissive.

GIRL 3:   Why? Why? Why?

MARÍA: Yes, but . . . Why?

CARMEN: That's the way it is. I know it's not fair, but women will always be different from men. Ni modo.

MARÍA AND GIRL 3:   I don't understand. Why must a woman be submissive? Why is sex dirty? (GIRL 1 *appears.*)

GIRL 1:   María, stop questioning and just accept.

GIRL 3:   No, María! God gave you a brain to think and question. Use it!

GIRL 1:   But it is not up to us to decide what is right and what is wrong. Your parents know best, María. They love you and do things for you.

GIRL 3:   María, they are not always right . . .

RICARDO (*Interrupting the argument.*):   María! Come and help your mother with dinner right now!

MARÍA: All right! (*She goes to the table and chairs.*)

RICARDO: What do you do in your room? You spend so much time in there.

MARÍA: I was doing my homework.

RICARDO: It takes you all that time? (RICARDO *has the mail and pulls out a letter from the pile.*)

MARÍA: Yes, I want my work to be perfect so that I can win an award . . .

RICARDO: All for an award? How about if I give you a trophy for washing the dishes when you are supposed to, and for doing the laundry right?

(*He begins to read the letter.* MARÍA *searches through the pile. She finds a letter, reads it and becomes excited.*)

CARMEN (*To* RICARDO.):   Who's the letter from?

RICARDO: My cousin, Pedro.

CARMEN: What are you going to tell him?

RICARDO: The truth. I'm going to tell him his Martita did pendejadita and is due in three months. (*To* MARÍA.) What do I tell you?

CARMEN: Ayy, ¡qué vergüenza!

RICARDO: ¡Tanto estudio y para nada! It's such a waste to educate women. How is all that education helping her now. She's pregnant and on welfare . . . What's that smell? The tortillas are burning!

MARÍA: Ayyy!!!! (MARÍA *runs to the kitchen.*)

CARMEN: When you get married, what is your husband going to say?

MARÍA: I'm sorry; I completely forgot.

CARMEN: You can't cook, you can't clean . . .

MARÍA: I try to do all the chores you ask.

CARMEN: You can't do anything right. Not even the tortillas.

MARÍA: I really try . . .

RICARDO: No Mexican man is going to marry a woman who can't cook.

CARMEN: You're almost eighteen! (*Looks to* RICARDO.) I married your father when I was eighteen and I already knew how to do everything.

MARÍA: Mamá, papá, there are other more important things . . . (*She holds the letter, but decides not to say anything.*) I just don't care for housework.

(MARÍA *goes to her room. Spotlight on* MARÍA. *She looks at the letter and* GIRL 3 *appears. They look at the letter and* GIRL 3 *reads.*)

GIRL 3:   "Congratulations! You are eligible for a four-year scholarship . . . Please respond as soon as possible . . . "

(MARÍA *jumps up in excitement. She then gets a typewriter and begins to type her response. The typewriter is not working. She goes outside to look for her father. Fade out.*)

SCENE SEVEN

RICARDO *and* MARÍA *enter.*

MARÍA: Papá . . . ¿Está ocupado?

RICARDO: I'm reading the paper.

MARÍA: Do you think . . . well . . . maybe when you have finished reading you can fix this for me? Here is the manual.

(*She shows it to him. He pretends to look, but cannot understand it.*)

RICARDO: Go get my tool box. I'll do it my way.

(RICARDO *begins to check the typewriter carefully.* MARÍA *looks attentively and also tries to think of a way to introduce the subject of college.* GIRL 1 *appears.*)

GIRL 1:   There is no one who can take the place of my father, who loves me but cannot show it any other way. If I wasn't scared, I would hold you. I love you.

(RICARDO *finishes fixing the typewriter and hands it to* MARÍA.)

CARMEN: ¡Ayy! ¡Qué huebona! Where is María?

RICARDO: She's in her room typing. I fixed her typewriter.

CARMEN: What is she typing?

RICARDO: I don't know. Ask her.

CARMEN (*She goes to* MARÍA*'s room.*):   María, come help me fold the clothes.

MARÍA: I'm busy!

CARMEN: Busy? Busy! Can't it wait? I have things to do, too.

MARÍA: All right. (*They start folding the clothes.* RICARDO *enters.*)

CARMEN: María, your birthday is almost here. Do you want me to make you a beautiful dress for your birthday? Maybe you can wear it for your graduation? Oh, our neighbor, la señora Martínez, told me today her daughter Rosario is graduating from a good business school. She says she already has a good job as a secretary.

MARÍA: Mamá, Papá, I don't want to be a secretary. (*Pause.*) I want to go to college.

RICARDO: What?

CARMEN: It's too expensive.

MARÍA (*Quickly.*):   I was awarded a big, four-year scholarship!

RICARDO: ¿Que? College? Scholarship?

CARMEN: ¿Para qué?

MARÍA: I want to be educated . . . (*Courageously.*) I want to be an actress.

RICARDO: You want to go to college to study to be an actress? ¿Estás loca?

CARMEN: Ayyy, María, you are crazy! You don't know what you want.

RICARDO: I didn't know you had to study to be a whore.

CARMEN: What have we done to make you want to leave us? We've tried to be good . . .

MARÍA: Nothing. It's not you. I want to be something.

RICARDO: Why don't you just get married like most decent women and be a housewife?

CARMEN: That's something.

RICARDO: That's respectable.

MARÍA: I don't understand what you are so afraid of . . .

RICARDO: I don't want you to forget that you are a Mexican. There are so many people where I work who deny they are Mexican. When their life gets better they stop being Mexican! To deny one's country is to deny one's past, one's parents. How ungrateful!

MARÍA: Papi, I won't. But you said that with an education I could be just as good as anybody. And that's why you brought me to America.

RICARDO: No. Get married!

MARÍA: I will. But I want a career as well. Women can now do both.

RICARDO: Don't tell me about modern women. What kind of wife would that woman make if she's busy with her career and can't tend to her house, children and husband.

MARÍA: And that's all a woman is for? To have children? Clean a house? Tend to her husband like a slave? And heat his tortillas?

RICARDO: ¡Qué atrevida! Why do you make it seem as if it would be some sort of nightmare? (*Sarcastically.*) Women have always gotten married and they have survived.

MARÍA: But surviving is not living.

CARMEN: María, listen to your father.

MARÍA: Papi, I listened to you. That's why! You encouraged me when I was young, but now you tell me I can't. Why?

RICARDO (*Trying to find an answer.*):   Because . . . you are a woman.

MARÍA: Papi, you're not being fair.

RICARDO (*Trying to keep face and control.*):   You ungrateful daughter! I don't want to see you. Get out of my face! (MARÍA *runs to her room, crying.*)

CARMEN: Ricardo, why don't you even let her try, ¿por favor? (*She goes to* MARÍA's *room.* RICARDO *stands, and then exits. Lights change to* MARÍA's *room.*) María, don't cry. Don't be angry at us either, and try to understand us. ¡M'ija! We are doing this for you. We don't want you to get hurt. You want too much; that's not realistic. You are a Mexican woman, and that's that. You can't change that. You are different from other women. Try to accept that. Women need to get married, they are no good without men.

MARÍA: Mami, I consider myself intelligent and ambitious, and what is that worth if I am a woman? Nothing?

CARMEN: You are worth a lot to me. I can't wait for the day when I will see you in a beautiful white wedding dress walking down the aisle with a church full of people. This is the most important event in a woman's life.

MARÍA: Mother, we are in America. Don't you realize you expect me to live in two worlds? How is it done? Can't things be different?

CARMEN: No sé. That's the way your father is. Ni modo.

MARÍA: Ni modo? Ni modo! Is that all you can say? Can't you do anything? (*Gives up on her and just explodes.*) ¡¡Ayy!! Get out! Get out!

(CARMEN *leaves and* MARÍA *continues to pound on her pillow with rage.* MARÍA *slowly begins to fall asleep. Fade out.*)

SCENE EIGHT

On the screen the following title is displayed: **The Dream.** GIRL 2, *who will now portray* MYTH, *appears. She wears a spring dress and looks virginal. She goes to* MARÍA.

MYTH (*Shaking* MARÍA *lightly.*):   María, get up and come see.

MARÍA: Who are you?

MYTH: I'm Myth. María, come see what can be.

MARÍA: What do you mean? What's going on?

MYTH: María, you are dreaming the American Dream. You can be anything you want to be. Follow me.

(*The sound of a horse is heard.*)

MARÍA: Is that a horse I'm hearing?

MYTH: See . . .

(*A* PRINCE *appears and he and* MYTH *begin to dance to a sweet melody. Just as they are about to kiss, the fierce sound of a whip accompanied by loud and wild cries of the horse running off are heard.*)

PRINCE (*In a very wimpy voice.*):   My horse! My horse!

(*Runs off to catch his horse.*)

MARÍA: What happened?

MYTH: I don't know.

(*Another crack of the whip is heard, but now* GIRL 3, *who will portray* "MARY," *appears with the whip.*)

MARY: Sorry to spoil the fairy tale, but Prince Charming was expected at the castle by Cinderella . . . Hello, María.

MARÍA: And who are you?

MARY: My name is Mary. It's my turn now, so get lost Myth!

(*She snaps her finger and a large hook pulls* MYTH *offstage.*)

MYTH: You're such a meanie!

MARY: Control, that's the thing to have. So come along and follow me!

MARÍA: Where are you taking me?

MARY: To liberation! Self independence, economic independence, sexual independence. We are free! María, in America, you can be anything you want to be. A lawyer. A doctor. An astronaut. An actress!!! The Mayor. Maybe even the President . . . of a company. You don't have to be obedient, submissive, gracious. You don't have to like dolls, dishes, cooking, children and laundry. Enjoy life! Enjoy liberation! Enjoy sex! Be free!

(GIRL 1, *who will portray* "MARÍA 2," *appears brandishing a broom.*)

MARÍA 2:   You bad woman! You bitch!

MARY: I'm not!

MARÍA 2:   You American demon. You are. You are. You just want to tempt her, then hurt her.

MARÍA (*Throwing* MARY *her whip.*):   Mary, catch!

MARY: Thanks! Now we will see!

(MARÍA 2 *and* MARY *have a mock sword combat, until a man blows a whistle and becomes a referee for a wrestling match.*)

REFEREE (*Taking away the broom and the whip.*):   All right, c'mon girls. I don't want weapons. Give them. (*The women push him away and charge at each other.* MARY *tries some dirty tricks.*) I told you I wanted this to be a clean fight. What were you using?

MARY: Nothing! I'm so innocent.

REFEREE: Now come over here and shake hands.

MARÍA 2 (*Asking the audience.*):   Should I? Should I?

(*Gets* MARY'S *hand and twists it. They wrestle wildly, with* MARY *winning, then* MARÍA 2. *The* REFEREE *finally steps in.*)

REFEREE: Break! Break! (*He holds* MARY *and pulls her out.*)

MARY (*Barely able to speak.*):   María, before you are a wife, before you are a mother, first you are a woman! I'll be back.

(*She's dragged out.* MARÍA 2, *who won the fight, acknowledges the cheers of the crowd, then gestures for* MARÍA *to kneel and pray.* MARÍA 2 *puts a wedding veil on* MARÍA.)

MARÍA 2:   A woman's only purpose in life is to serve three men. Her father, her husband and her son. Her father.

(RICARDO *appears. He picks up* MARÍA *and escorts her to the church. The bells and the wedding march are heard. The following title is displayed:* **White Wedding.** MARÍA *walks down the aisle; the groom enters.*)

MARÍA 2:   Her husband.

(*The couple kneels and a wedding lasso is put around them.*)

PRIEST (*Same as first* PRIEST.):   Dearly beloved, we are gathered here, under the Catholic Church, in the holy House of God, to unite these two people in holy matrimony. Marriage is sacred. It is the unification of a man and a woman, their love and commitment, forever, and ever, and ever; no matter what! Well, then, let's begin . . . María, do you accept José Juan González García López as your lawfully wedded husband to love, cherish, serve, cook for, clean for, sacrifice for, have his children, keep his house, love him even if he beats you, commits adultery, gets drunk, rapes you lawfully, denies you your identity, money, love his family, serve his family, and in return ask for nothing?

MARÍA (*Thinks about it and turns to her parents.*):   I do.

PRIEST: Very good. Now, José. Do you accept María García González López as your lawfully wedded wife to support?

JOSÉ: I do.

PRIEST: Good. Well, if there is anyone present who is opposed to the union of these two people, speak now, or forever hold your truth. (RICARDO *stands up, takes out a gun and shows it to the audience.*) Do you have the ring? (JOSÉ *takes out a golden dog collar. The* PRIEST *gives it his blessings.*) Five, six, seven, eight. By the power vested in me, under the Catholic Church, in the holy House of God, I pronounce you husband and wife.

(*The* THREE GIRLS *take away* MARÍA*'s veil and bouquet. They place the dog collar around* MARÍA*'s neck. Then they get the lasso and tie it around her to make the collar work like a leash. To* JOSÉ.) You may pet the bride. (*The lasso is given to* JOSÉ. *He pulls* MARÍA, *who gets on her hands and knees. They walk down the aisle like dog and master. The wedding march plays, people begin to leave. Fade out.*)

SCENE NINE

A table and two chairs are placed in the center of the stage. MARÍA, *pregnant, walks in uncomfortably. She turns on the television, then the ensemble creates the television setting, playing roles of T.V. producer, director, make-up people, technicians, as if the actual studio is there. Brief dialogue is improvised to establish on-set frenzy.*

ANNOUNCER: And here is another chapter of your afternoon soap opera, "HAPPILY EVERAFTER." Our sultry Eliza Vázquez decides to leave Devero in search of freedom!

FLOOR MAN: Okay everyone, tape rolling, standby in ten seconds. Five, four, three, two . . .

(*He cues.*)

ACTRESS: Devero, I'm leaving you.
ACTOR: Eliza, why?
ACTRESS: I don't love you anymore. Actually, I never did.
ACTOR: Eliza, but I love you.
ACTRESS: I faked it, all of it. I did it because I had to. But now I must go and be free!

(MARÍA *claps loudly in excitement for her.*)

FLOOR MANAGER: Cut! (*To* MARÍA.) What are you doing here?
MARÍA: This is my living room.
FLOOR MANAGER: Oh, sure it is. Well go into the kitchen, make yourself a snack; we'll have the carpet cleaned in an hour. (*Pushes her aside.*) I know, I'm sorry . . . Standby. Five, four, three, two, one.
ACTRESS: . . . But now I must go and be free!
ACTOR: You can't do this to me!
ACTRESS: Oh, yes I can!
ACTOR: But I've given you everything!
ACTRESS: Everything but an identity! Well, Devero, Devero, Devero, I've discovered I no longer need you. There are unfulfilled dreams I must pursue. I want adventure.
FLOOR MANAGER: And . . . cut! That's a take. Roll commercial. Five seconds. Four, three, two, one.

(*The soap opera ends.* MARÍA *claps approvingly. A commercial quickly begins, with the ensemble creating a similar on-set frenzy. In the commercial a man comes home with a bottle of Ajax as a gift for his wife.*)

HUSBAND: Honey, I'm home! I brought you something. (*Hides the can treating it as if he had flowers.*)
WIFE: Hi, darling! (*They give each other a peck on the mouth from a distance.*) How was work?
HUSBAND: Fine . . . Ta-Dah! (*Presents the can.*)
WIFE: You shouldn't have. Oh, thank you! I need all the cleaning power I can get!
HUSBAND: I can smell you've been cleaning.
WIFE: Yes! I've mopped the floors, done the dishes, the laundry; this house is spotless.
HUSBAND: What a wife! (*They give each other another peck on the mouth from a distance.*) You're a good wife!

(MARÍA *goes to turn off the television. The doorbell rings. She goes to answer the door. It's her husband who grunts at her and comes in, asks for his dinner and sits at the table.*)

JOSÉ: María! María! I'm home. I'm hungry.
MARÍA: José, how was work? Dinner is ready. I made your favorite dish. Do you want to eat now? (JOSÉ *doesn't answer.*) Well, I'll serve you then. (MARÍA *places a plate on the table.*) My mother came to visit today and she asked me what we are going to name the baby. She thought it would be nice to call her Esperanza. (JOSÉ *grunts.*) Of course

it isn't going to be a girl. It's going to be a boy, and we'll name him after you. That would be nice, wouldn't it? (MARÍA *feels pains.*) Ayyy! How it hurts. I hope after the baby is born, I will be better. I've been getting so many pains, and I have a lot of stretchmarks . . . I know you don't like me to ask for money, but I need the money to buy a dress that fits. I have nothing I can wear anymore.

JOSÉ (*After a spoonful.*): My dinner is cold.

MARÍA: Oh, is it cold? Well, I'll heat it up right now. It will only take a minute.

(MARÍA *runs to the kitchen.* JOSÉ *leaves the table and stares at the bed. The following title is displayed:* **The Sex Object.**)

JOSÉ: María! ¡Mi amor! Come here, baby! . . . Come on, m'ijita. I won't hurt you . . .

(*He continues to try to persuade her. Eventually he gets his way. There are sounds of lust and pain. Finally,* MARÍA *gives out a loud scream of pain.*)

JOSÉ: What is it?

MARÍA: The baby!

(*Fade out.*)

SCENE TEN

The lights rise after the scream. MARÍA *spreads her legs wide open, covering herself with a white sheet.* THREE NURSES *run in. On the screen the following title is displayed:* **The Reproducing Machine or Be Fruitful.** *Dolls will be used as babies.*)

SALESMAN: Here we have it. Direct from Mexico. The Reproducing Machine. You can have one by calling our toll-free number. Get your pencil.

HEAD NURSE: Now, relax. Just breathe like this. (*Example.*) Ahhh!! All in good rhythm. Good! Don't worry, millions of women have children, especially Mexican women, they have millions. But you'll get used to it. After your fourth child, they'll just slide right on out.

MARÍA: 'Amá! Mamá!

HEAD NURSE: There's nothing I can do. I went through it myself. Now, isn't the pain great? You're giving birth! Why, it's the most satisfying feeling a woman can feel. Okay, I think it's coming! Push, Push, Push.

(*A baby pops up, flying into the air. It is caught by one of the nurses. She presents the baby to the* HEAD NURSE.)

HEAD NURSE: Oh, it's a girl.

NURSE 2 (*Presenting the baby to* JOSÉ.): Here's your baby daughter.

JOSÉ: A daughter? How could you do this to me? Well, I'll have to call her Sacrifice.

(MARÍA *screams again.*)

HEAD NURSE: What is it?

MARÍA: There's another one inside; I can feel it!

HEAD NURSE: Nahhh! Well, I'll check just in case. (*She peeps under the sheet.*) Well, I'll be! Yeah, there's another one. Push! Push! Push!

(*Another baby pops into the air.* NURSE 3 *catches the baby.*)

NURSE 2 (*Presenting it to* JOSÉ.):   Here's another lovely daughter.

JOSÉ: Another daughter? I'll have to call her Abnegation.

SALESMAN (*Appearing from nowhere.*):   Here we have this amazing machine. The world renowned Reproducing Machine!

(MARÍA *screams again.*)

HEAD NURSE: What is it?

MARÍA: There's another one!

SALESMAN: Ahh, but if you were watching earlier, you saw the other amazing function. It can also be used as a sex object.

HEAD NURSE: Push! Push! Push!

(*Another baby pops up.*)

NURSE 4 (*Catching baby.*):   I got it.

SALESMAN: Yes siree! You can be the boss. It's at your disposal. Hours of pleasure. And if it ever does go out of control, a kick and a few punches will do the job and it will be back to normal.

NURSE 2:   Here's another one.

JOSÉ: Another girl? Why are you doing this to me? I'll call her Obligation.

SALESMAN: It's made in Mexico. It's cheap! It cooks! It cleans!

(MARÍA *screams again.*)

HEAD NURSE: Push! Push! Push!

(THREE BABIES *pop up into the air. Some land in the audience. All the nurses are busy collecting them.*)

SALESMAN: Its stretchmarks can stretch all the way from here to Tijuana. Not even a Japanese model can beat this one.

NURSE 2 (*To* JOSÉ.):   Guess what?

JOSÉ: No, don't tell me; another girl?

NURSE 2:   Surprise!

JOSÉ (*See babies.*):   Three girls! I'll call them Frustration, Regret, and Disappointment.

SALESMAN: It delivers up to twenty-one children. It feeds on beans, chile, and lies.

HEAD NURSE: Are there any more babies in that Mexican oven of yours?

MARÍA: I don't think so.

HEAD NURSE: See you in nine months for your next Mexican litter.

SALESMAN: You can have your own reproducing machine! Call the number on your screen now!

(*Fade out.*)

SCENE ELEVEN

Lights rise after a brief pause. On the stage is a table which serves as a crib for the six crying babies. On the screen the following title is displayed: **The Nightmare.** MARÍA *tries to quiet the babies by holding each one at a time, then by the bunch.* CARMEN, RICARDO *and* JOSÉ *enter. They stand behind her like demons.*

JOSÉ: Shut those babies up!

CARMEN: You're a bad wife!

RICARDO: This house is a mess!

CARMEN: You can't cook, you can't clean!

JOSÉ: Where's my dinner?

RICARDO: The dishes?

JOSÉ: My tortillas?

RICARDO: You're a bad wife!

CARMEN: I did it all my life!

JOSÉ: Bad wife!

MARÍA: No! I'm not! I'm a good wife! I try. I really do!

*(*MARÍA *goes to get the laundry and begins to fold it quickly, but nicely and carefully. Suddenly, the clothes begin to take on a life of their own. There is a giant coat, and a pair of pants surrounding* MARÍA. *They start pushing her around, then her wedding dress appears and heads towards* MARÍA's *neck. They wrestle on the ground.)*

CARMEN: Martyr!

*(*MARÍA *manages to get away, and runs upstage. As she is running, a giant tortilla with the Aztec Calendar emblem falls on her, smashing her to the ground.)*

MARÍA: Help!

RICARDO: Martyr!

*(*MARÍA *manages to get out from under the tortilla; as she escapes, she is attacked by a storm of plates.)*

MARÍA: Help!

RICARDO, CARMEN, *and* JOSÉ: Martyr!!! Martyr!!! Martyr!!!

MARÍA (*Becomes uncontrollably mad.*):   Enough! Do you want your dishes cleaned? I've got the perfect solution for them. (MARÍA *gestures. Sounds of dishes being smashed are heard.*) Now you don't have to worry. I'll buy you a million paper plates! Ohhhh! And the tortillas. Mamá! I'm going to show you how they should be done. (*She gets a bag of tortillas and begins tossing them into the audience like frisbees.*) Are these good enough? I hope so! I tried to get the top side cooked first . . . or was it last? Anyway, who cares! Here are the tortillas! (*Attacks her mother with a couple of tortillas.*) I hate doing the dishes! I hate doing the laundry! I hate cooking and cleaning! And I hate all housework because it offends me as a woman! (*There is a piercing moment of silence.*) That's right. I am a woman . . . a real woman of flesh and blood. This is not the life I want to live; I want more! And from now on I am directing my own life! Action!

(*Lights come fully on.* TWO GIRLS *grab and pull* MARÍA *harshly to take her to another place. The stage now becomes a courtroom.* MARÍA *is sat next to the* JUDGE. *The following title is displayed:* **The Trial.** *The courtroom is filled with people who create a lot of commotion. The* JUDGE, *the* BAILIFF, *and the* PROSECUTOR *enter.*)

BAILIFF: Please rise, the honorable hang-judge presiding.

JUDGE (*Bangs his gavel until everyone quiets down.* JUDGE *will be done by same actor who does* PRIEST.):   Quiet in my courtroom! I am warning you, anyone who causes any such commotion like this again will be thrown out! Is that understood! Let's begin!

BAILIFF: We are here today to give trial to María who is being accused by her husband of rebellion toward her implied duties of marriage.

JUDGE: How do you plead?

MARÍA: Plead? Innocent! Guilty! I don't know!

JUDGE: Are you making a joke out of my question?

MARÍA: No . . . Sir.

JUDGE: It sounds to me like you wish to challenge these laws.

MARÍA: I don't understand why I am on trial. What real laws have I broken?

JUROR 1:   She knows what she's guilty of.

JUROR 2:   She knows what laws not to break!

MARÍA: Who are they?

BAILIFF: Your jury.

MARÍA: But they are women, Mexican, traditional . . . They can't possibly be objective.

BAILIFF: They are a good jury.

MARÍA: This is unjust! I must speak up to this . . .

BAILIFF: You have no voice.

MARÍA: Where's my lawyer? I do get one, don't I?

(*The courtroom fills with cruel laughter, which quickly stops.*)

JUDGE: No, you defend yourself.

MARÍA: How do I defend myself when I can't speak?

PROSECUTOR (*To* MARÍA.):   You're dead meat, shrimp. (*To audience.*) This trial is meant to help preserve the institution of marriage. Ladies and gentlemen of the jury . . . in this case, ladies of the jury. A man's home is his castle. Where he has his foundation. It is the place where he comes home to his family, and he becomes the king of his castle. But this poor man comes home one evening and finds his children unattended, his house a mess, his dinner unprepared and his wife sitting back, watching soap operas!

MARÍA: I object!

JUDGE: You have no voice.

MARÍA: You said I was to defend myself.

JUDGE: Not now!

PROSECUTOR: What we are going to try to do is prove the guilt of this woman . . .

MARÍA: I object!

JUDGE: Shut up!

MARÍA: I won't!

JUDGE: Mister Prosecutor, call your first witness!

PROSECUTOR: I call Ricardo García to the witness stand. (RICARDO *takes the stand.*) Tell us about your daughter.

RICARDO: She was very obedient when she was young, but when she came to the United States she began to think of herself as "American" . . . She studied a lot, which is good, but she almost refused to do her chores because she thought herself above them.

PROSECUTOR: Could you tell us what happened that evening your daughter rebelled?

RICARDO: I'd rather not . . . That evening María was hysterical. She threw dishes, tortillas . . .

PROSECUTOR: Thank you, that will be all. My next witness will be Carmen García. (CARMEN *takes the stand.*) Tell us about your daughter.

CARMEN: She's really a good girl. She's just too dramatic sometimes. She's such a dreamer, forgive her.

PROSECUTOR: Could you tell us what you saw that evening?

CARMEN: Well, she was a little upset, so she did a few things she didn't mean to do.

MARÍA: No, Mamá! I meant it!

JUROR 1:   She admits it!

JUROR 2:   She's guilty!

ALL: Guilty!

CARMEN: No, she's just unrealistic.

MARÍA: I'm guilty then!

(*The whole courtroom becomes chaotic. Everyone yells out "guilty." CARMEN becomes so sad she begins to cry.*)

MARÍA: Mami, don't cry!

(*The lights go on and off and everyone disappears. Fade out.*)

SCENE TWELVE

MARÍA *begins to regain consciousness and wakes up from her dream. She is awakened by* CARMEN's *actual crying, which continues and grows.* MARÍA *gets up and listens to* CARMEN *and* RICARDO *arguing in the kitchen.*

RICARDO: ¡Cállate! Don't yell or María will hear you.

CARMEN: Then tell me, is it true what I am saying?

RICARDO: You're crazy! It wasn't me.

CARMEN: Con mis propios ojos I saw you and la señora Martínez meet in the morning by the park. You have been taking her to work and who knows what! Tell me, is it true? If you don't, I'm going to yell as loud as I can and let this whole neighborhood know what's going on.

RICARDO: Okay. It was me! ¿Estás contenta?

CARMEN: ¿Por qué? Why do you do this to me? And with our neighbor? She lives right in front of us.

RICARDO: Look, every man sooner or later does it.

CARMEN: Do you think I don't know about all of your affairs before la señora Martínez? She is not your first! I never said anything before because I was afraid you would send us back to Mexico. But now I don't care! You break it with that bitch or . . . I'll kill her and you. ¡Ayyy! Ricardo, I've endured so much for you. I knew you were no angel when we ran off together, but I thought you would change. You would change, because you loved me. I love you, Ricardo! But I can no longer go on living like this or I'll be betraying myself and I'll be betraying María.

RICARDO: Carmen, ¡ven aquí! Carmen, wait!

(CARMEN *and* RICARDO *exit. The* THREE GIRLS *enter.* GIRL 3 *hands* MARÍA *a piece of paper and a pen.*)

MARÍA: "Dear Mamá and Papá. Last night I heard everything. Now I know that your idea of life is not for me—so I am leaving. I want to create a world of my own. One that combines the best of me. I won't forget the values of my roots, but I want to get the best from this land of opportunities. I am going to college and I will struggle to do something with my life. You taught me everything I needed to know. Goodbye."

GIRL 1:   Los quiero mucho. Nunca los olvidaré.

GIRL 2:   Mexico is in my blood . . .

GIRL 3:   And America is in my heart.

MARÍA: "Adiós."

(*Fade out.*)

(*1994*)

QUESTIONS FOR REFLECTION

Experience

1. To what extent can you identify with either the minority or gender experience depicted in Lopéz's play?

Interpretation

2. Explain how López distinguishes among her two groups or types of characters.
3. Explain the effect of the play's opening scene. What does the allusion to Shakespeare's *Romeo and Juliet* accomplish?
4. What stereotypes about Mexican men and women does López present in Scene 2? What is her attitude toward these cultural stereotypes?
5. What political ideas emerge from Scene 3? What distinction is made between European and Mexican immigrants in America?
6. What images of America does the play present? How does María see America and her place in it?
7. Identify and explain the function of three types of sound effects included in the play.
8. Explain the relevance of Scene 8—the "dream scene." Comment on the names of the characters who appear in this scene. Compare the marriage vows and ceremony in Scene 8 with those of Scene 2.

9. Explain the function of the screen and the titles projected on it throughout the play.

Evaluation

10. What conflicting values does the play describe? What perspective is offered on the conflict between Mexican and American cultural attitudes toward sex, for example, toward gender roles, and toward self-fulfillment?
11. What images of marriage and motherhood does the play present? What perspectives are offered on them?

CHAPTER NINE

Critical Theory: Approaches to the Analysis and Interpretation of Literature

THE CANON AND THE CURRICULUM

Interpreting literature is an art and a skill that readers develop with experience and practice. Regular reading of stories, poems, plays, and essays will give you opportunities to become a skillful interpreter. Simply reading the literary works, however, is not enough, not if you wish to participate in the invigorating critical conversations teachers and other experienced readers bring to their discussion of literature. To develop a sense of the interpretive possibilities of literary works, you will need to know something of the various critical perspectives that literary critics use to analyze and interpret literature. This chapter introduces you to a number of major critical perspectives, including historical, biographical, psychological, and sociological approaches (among others), each of which approaches the study of literature a different way.

This discussion of critical perspectives aims to provide you with a set of ideas about how literature can be analyzed and interpreted. It is not designed to explain the history of literary criticism. Nor is its goal to convert you to a particular critical approach. Neither has any attempt been made to present the intricacies and variations in interpretive analysis developed by proponents of the various critical perspectives. And although you will find in this chapter discussions of ten critical perspectives, still other approaches to literary interpretation are available, both older ones that have currently declined in use and newer approaches that are still emerging.

Before considering the first of our critical perspectives, that of formalist criticism, we should review some basic questions currently being debated, sometimes heatedly, throughout the educational establishment. You may have already heard about the controversy surrounding the literary "canon" or list of works considered suitable for study in a university curriculum. There is now considerable disagreement about just what books should be read in college courses, why they should be read, and how they should be read. As a way of putting the ten critical perspectives in context, we will take up each of these questions in a brief overview of the current debate about the university literature curriculum.

What We Read

The notion of a literary canon or collection of accepted books derives from the idea of a biblical canon—those books accepted as official scriptures. A scriptural canon contains those works deemed to represent the moral standards and religious beliefs of a particular group, Jews for example, or Muslims, Hindus, or Christians. A canon of accepted works also contains, by implication, its obverse or flip side— that some works are excluded from the canon. Just as certain works, such as the Book of Maccabees, were not accepted into the Hebrew Scriptures and the Gospel of Thomas was denied entry into the Christian New Testament, not every book or literary work written can become part of an officially sanctioned literary canon or a university curriculum. Certain works inevitably will be omitted while others just as necessarily are selected for inclusion. The central question revolves around which works should be included in the canon, and why.

As you may know, certain "classics" for a long time have dominated the canon of literature for study in university courses—epic poems by Homer and Dante, for example, plays by Ibsen and Shakespeare, poems by writers from many countries, but especially those from Europe and America, novels such as Charles Dickens's *Great Expectations,* Jane Austen's *Pride and Prejudice,* Mark Twain's *The Adventures of Huckleberry Finn*, Emily Bronte's *Wuthering Heights,* and many others. In the last two decades, however, there has been a movement to alter the canon of classical works, most of which have been written by white males of European ancestry, in the more or less distant past. Some of the changes in what we read have come from adding works by writers long omitted, such as those by minority writers—African Americans, Native

Americans, Asian Americans, and other writers from around the world beyond Europe, those from Australia, India, and Africa, for example. The works added by minority writers have been largely, though not exclusively, modern and contemporary ones.

Still other changes in the literary canon have come from the rediscovery or recovery of older works, many from the Renaissance and the nineteenth century, especially works by women, which had for a long time been considered unworthy of serious study and of inclusion in college literature curricula. Such works were considered not to have withstood the test of time, lasting decades or centuries, as have the classics. What needs to be remembered, however, is that "time" is an abstraction that itself accomplishes nothing. It is, rather, individuals throughout time who make the choices about which books are to be taught in schools and universities. And it is people today of both genders and of various cultures, races, ethnicities, and sexual dispositions who are debating not only what works should be part of the canon of literature but whether the very idea of a canon is viable at all. In other words, what is a canon for? Is a literary canon inevitable? Is it even necessary?

Why We Read

These changes in what we read are related to a debate about why we read. Classic novels and plays, stories and poems have long been read because the lessons they are presumed to teach are considered valuable. The meanings of certain American canonical works, for example, have been viewed as educationally and morally good for readers to assimilate, largely because the works are believed to reflect values central to the American way of life. They reflect values relating to the importance of friendship, responsible behavior, and hard work, for example, or values relating to decency, justice, and fair play. Of course, other works accepted into the literary canon taught in American colleges and universities do not reflect such views, both works written by American writers and works by writers of other nationalities and literary traditions, many of which are included in this book.

It is certainly the case that regardless of the language(s) and tradition(s) represented by a canon of literary works, those works are often canonized because they are believed to perpetuate a tradition of moral beliefs, cultural attitudes, and social dispositions. What is interesting to note, however, is that canonical literary works of many traditions and genres—Henrik Ibsen's *A Doll House,* for example, or Emily Dickinson's lyric poems—disrupt and run counter to many traditional literary, social, religious, and cultural values. And works such as Shakespeare's tragedies and Keats's and Wordsworth's poetry harbor ideas and attitudes about which common readers and professional critics have long disagreed, a disagreement that derives partly from varying critical perspectives used to interpret the works and partly from their richness and complexity, which makes it impossible to say once and for all just what those enticing and intellectually provocative works mean.

Another reason for the continuity of the traditional canon is that it is easier to preserve the status quo than to initiate change. Change is neither welcomed nor embraced, even when it is inevitable. Moreover, later generations read the books of former ones because earlier generations want their descendants to read and value what they read and valued. Those earlier generations have the power to enforce such a decision since they hold the positions of authority in schools and on councils that design curricula and create reading lists for school programs and university courses.

Today, however, many of these assumptions have been reevaluated by teachers and critics from a wide range of political persuasions. With the demographic changes that have been occurring in educational institutions in the past quarter century have come additional reasons for reading. Minority groups that now form a significant population in university classrooms, minority teachers, younger faculty raised in a much altered political environment, large numbers of women faculty—all insist on the need for multiple perspectives, varying voices, different visions of experience. They argue that literary works should be read to challenge conventional ways of behaving and orthodox ways of thinking. (Some educators say that there is nothing new in this, and that, in fact, traditional canonical works have long been read this way.) For some of these other readers, however, literature exists less for moral instruction or cultural education than to help inaugurate political and social change, a view that is less widely endorsed than the view that literary works should invite critical scrutiny and stimulate questioning and debate.

How We Read

That brings us to the important question of how we read. Just how do we read? Do we simply "just read"? And if we do, then what do we mean by "just reading"? Most often just reading means something on the order of reading for pleasure, without worrying about analysis and interpretation. From the standpoint of more analytical reading, "just reading" refers to interpreting the words on the page, making sense of them in a way that seems reasonable.

But a number of assumptions lie behind this notion. One such assumption is that the meaning of a literary work is available to anyone willing to read it carefully. Another is that literary works contain layers or levels of meaning, that they have to be analyzed to understand their complex meanings. Still another is that although different readers all bring their unique experience as members of particular genders, races, religions, and nationalities to their interpretation of literary works, they finally understand the meaning of those works in the same way. In this view, literary works such as *Hamlet* or *The Scarlet Letter* mean the same thing to every reader.

Each of these assumptions, however, has been challenged by literary theorists in the past two decades, to the extent that many serious readers find them untenable. It doesn't take long, for example, to realize that though we share some understanding of Shakespeare's play or Hawthorne's novel, we invariably see different things in them and see them differently. The differences we make of literary works and the different ways we understand them are related to the varying assumptions about literature and life that we bring to our reading. The different ways these assumptions have been modified and the different emphases and focuses serious readers and literary critics bring to bear on literary works can be categorized according to various approaches or critical perspectives. Ten critical perspectives are here presented, though others could be added. These ten, however, reflect critical positions that many academic readers find useful, whether they are reading works new to the canon or older established ones.

For each critical perspective you will find an overview that introduces the critical approach, an application or two of the critical perspective to a play or plays, and a list of questions you can use to apply the critical perspective to other literary works. A set of selected readings concludes each section.

Think of these ten critical perspectives as a kind of critical smorgasbord, a set of intellectual dishes you can sample and taste. Those you find most appealing you may wish to partake of more heartily, partly by applying them in your own analytical writing, partly by reading from the list of selected books. Or your instructor may encourage you to work with ones he or she believes are especially valuable. The important thing to realize, however, is that you always interpret a literary work from a theoretical standpoint, however hidden or implicit it may be. Understanding the assumptions and procedures of the various theoretical perspectives is crucial for understanding what you are doing when you interpret literature, how you do it, and why you do it that way.

In his lively book introducing college students to literary theory, *Falling Into Theory* (1994), David H. Richter of Queens College CUNY summarizes the important issues concerning literary studies today in a series of provocative questions. Richter organizes his questions according to the categories I have borrowed from him for this introductory overview: *why we read, what we read, how we read.* Keep Richter's guiding questions in mind as you read the discussion of the various critical perspectives.

> *Why we read.* What is the place of the humanities and literary studies in society? Why should we study literature? Why do we read?
> *What we read.* What is literature and who determines what counts as literature? Is there a core of "great books" that every student should read? What is the relationship of literature by women and minority groups to the canon? Are criteria of quality universal, or are literary values essentially political?
> *How we read.* How do we and how should we read texts? Does meaning reside in the author, the text, or the reader? To what degree is the meaning of a text fixed? What ethical concerns do we bring to texts as readers, and how do these concerns reshape the texts we read? What do we owe the text and what does it owe us? How do the politics of race and gender shape our reading of texts? Do political approaches to literature betray or shed light on them?

Canon and Curriculum: Selected Readings

To learn more about the controversy surrounding the literary canon and the college English curriculum, the following books provide a variety of perspectives on the issues.

Alter, Robert. *The Pleasures of Reading in an Ideological Age.* 1989.

Atlas, James. *The Battle of the Books.* 1990.

D'Souza, Dinesh. *Illiberal Education: The Politics of Sex and Race on Campus.* 1991.

Eagleton, Terry. *Literary Theory: An Introduction.* 1983.

Graff, Gerald. *Beyond the Culture Wars.* 1992.

Greenblatt, Stephen, and Giles Gunn. *Redrawing the Boundaries: The Transformation of English and American Literary Studies.* 1992.

Kimball, Roger. *Tenured Radicals: How Politics Has Corrupted Higher Education.* 1990.

Lauter, Paul. *Canons and Contexts.* 1991.

Lentricchia, Frank. *Criticism and Social Change.* 1983.

Levine, George et al. *Speaking for the Humanities.* 1989.

Richter, David. *Falling Into Theory.* 1994.

Scholes, Robert. *Textual Power.* 1985.

FORMALIST PERSPECTIVES

An Overview of Formalist Criticism

Formalist critics view literature as a distinctive art, one that uses the resources of language to shape experience, communicate meaning, and express emotion. Formalists emphasize the form of a literary work to determine its meaning, focusing on literary elements such as plot, character, setting, diction, imagery, structure, and point of view. Approaching literary works as independent systems with interdependent parts, formalists typically subordinate biographical information or historical data in their interpretations. Underlying formalist critical perspectives is the belief that literary works are unified artistic wholes that can be understood by analyzing their parts.

According to the formalist view, the proper concern of literary criticism is with the work itself rather than with literary history, the life of the author, or a work's social and historical contexts. For a formalist, the central meaning of a literary work is discovered through a detailed analysis of the work's formal elements rather than by going outside the work to consider other issues, whether biographical, historical, psychological, social, political, or ideological. Such additional considerations, from the formalist perspective, are extrinsic, or external, and are of secondary importance. What matters most to the formalist critic is how the work comes to mean what it does—how its resources of language are deployed by the writer to convey meaning. Implicit in the formalist perspective, moreover, is that readers can indeed determine the meanings of literary works—that literature can be understood and its meanings clarified.

Two other tenets of formalist criticism deserve mention: (1) that a literary work exists independent of any particular reader—that is, that a literary work exists outside of any reader's re-creation of it in the act of reading; (2) that the greatest literary works are "universal," their wholeness and aesthetic harmony transcending the specific particularities they describe.

The primary method of formalism is a close reading of the literary text, with an emphasis, for example, on a work's use of metaphor or symbol, its deployment of irony, its patterns of image or action. Lyric poetry lends itself especially well to the kinds of close reading favored by formalist critics because its language tends to be more compressed and metaphorical than the language of prose—at least as a general rule. Nonetheless, formal analysis of novels and plays can also focus on close reading of key passages (the opening and closing chapters of a novel, for example, or the first and last scenes of a play, or a climactic moment in the action of drama, poetry, or fiction). In addition, formalist critics analyze the large-scale structures of longer works, looking for patterns and relationships among scenes, actions, and characters.

One consistent feature of formalist criticism is an emphasis on tension and ambiguity. Tension refers to the way elements of a text's language reflect conflict and opposition. Ambiguity refers to the ways texts remain open to more than a single, unified, definitive interpretation. Both tension and ambiguity as elements of formalist critical approaches were picked up and elaborated to serve different interpretive arguments by critics employing the methodologies of structuralism and deconstruction.

Thinking from a Formalist Perspective

A formalist critic reading Ibsen's *A Doll House* might consider how the play begins and ends, contrasting its opening banter with its door-slamming conclusion. A formalist perspective would typically include observations about the relationships among the characters, particularly Torvald and Nora, but also the doctor's relationship with Nora and Krogstad's relationship with Kristine. Character relationships and conflicts are of paramount interest and importance in Ibsen's play and reverberate throughout the play in terms of both plot and theme.

Other aspects of the play of interest from a formalist perspective would include the dramatist's use of stage setting details, especially in their symbolic reverberations. A formalist critic might ask what difference it would make if it were set in a lower-class rather than in a middle-class home, or what effect Nora's dancing the tarantelle would have were she dressed in a housecoat rather than in the costume she wears. The formalist critic would look especially for structural patterns, for recurrent motives of action, for contrasts and shifts of direction. And of course formalist critics would identify the elements of plot that lead toward the play's climax as well as determining the significance of its resolution or denouement.

A CHECKLIST OF FORMALIST CRITICAL QUESTIONS

1. How is the work structured or organized? How does it begin? Where does it go next? How does it end? What is the work's plot? How is its plot related to its structure?
2. What is the relationship of each part of the work to the work as a whole? How are the parts related to one another?
3. Who is narrating or telling what happens in the work? How is the narrator, speaker, or character revealed to readers? How do we come to know and understand this figure?
4. Who are the major and minor characters, what do they represent, and how do they relate to one another?
5. What are the time and place of the work—its setting? How is the setting related to what we know of the characters and their actions? To what extent is the setting symbolic?
6. What kind of language does the author use to describe, narrate, explain, or otherwise create the world of the literary work? More specifically, what images, similes, metaphors, symbols appear in the work? What is their function? What meanings do they convey?

Formalist Criticism: Selected Readings

Burke, Kenneth. *Counterstatement*. 1930.
Eliot, T. S. *Selected Essays*. 1932.
Empson, William. *Seven Types of Ambiguity*. 1930.
Ransom, John Crowe. *The New Criticism*. 1941.
Wellek, Rene, and Austin Warren. *Theory of Literature*. 1949, 1973.
Wimsatt, W. K. *The Verbal Icon*. 1954.

BIOGRAPHICAL PERSPECTIVES

Overview of Biographical Criticism

To what extent a writer's life should be brought to bear on an interpretation of his or her work has long been a matter of controversy. Some critics insist that biographical information at best distracts from and at worst distorts the process of analyzing, appreciating, and understanding literary works. These critics believe that literary works must stand on their own, stripped of the facts of their writers' lives.

Against this view, however, can be placed one that values the information readers gain from knowing about writers' lives. Biographical critics argue that there are essentially three kinds of benefits readers acquire from using biographical evidence for literary interpretation: (1) readers understand literary works better since the facts about authors' experiences can help readers decide how to interpret those works; (2) readers can better appreciate a literary work for knowing the writer's struggles or difficulties in creating it; and (3) readers can better assess writers' preoccupations by studying the ways they modify and adjust their actual experience in their literary works.

Knowing, for example, that Shakespeare and Molière were actors who performed in the plays they wrote provides an added dimension to our appreciation of their genius. It also might invite us to look at their plays from the practical standpoint of a performer rather than merely from the perspective of an armchair reader, a classroom student, or a theatergoer. Considering biographical information and using it to analyze the finished literary work can be illuminating rather than distracting or distorting. Thinking about the different alternative titles a writer may have considered can also lead readers to focus on different aspects of a work, especially to emphasize different incidents and to value the viewpoints of different characters. As with any critical approach, however, a biographical perspective should be used judiciously, keeping the focus on the literary work and using the biographical information to clarify understanding and to develop an interpretation.

Thinking from a Biographical Perspective

A biographical critic can focus on a writer's works not only to enhance understanding of them individually but also to enrich a reader's understanding of the artist. In an essay on the relations between literature and biography, Leon Edel, author of an outstanding biography of Henry James, suggests that what the literary biographer seeks to discover about the subject are his or her characteristic ways of thinking, perceiving, and feeling that may be revealed more honestly and thoroughly in the writer's work than in his or her conscious nonliterary statements. In addition, what we learn about writers from a judicious study of their work can also be linked with an understanding of the writer's world, and thus serve as a bridge to an appreciation of the social and cultural contexts in which the writer lived.

Moreover, whether one focuses on formalist questions to analyze Ibsen's *A Doll House* or whether one considers the psychological factors that motivate the play's characters, biographical information can advance a reader's or viewer's appreciation of the Ibsen play. Knowing, for example, that Ibsen championed women's causes, or that he remarked that *A Doll House* was about human freedom and was not limited to female liberation adds to our depth of understanding of the play without pushing us toward a strictly feminist interpretation. The best way to use a biographical perspective is in conjunction with other critical perspectives, thereby keeping the emphasis on the writer's work rather than on his or her life. It's better to let the life illuminate the work rather than using the work to reveal the life.

A CHECKLIST OF BIOGRAPHICAL CRITICAL QUESTIONS

1. What influences—persons, ideas, movements, events—evident in the writer's life does the work reflect?
2. To what extent are the events described in the work a direct transfer of what happened in the writer's actual life?
3. What modifications of the actual events has the writer made in the literary work? For what possible purposes?
4. Why might the writer have altered his or her actual experience in the literary work?
5. What are the effects of the differences between actual events and their literary transformation in the poem, story, play, or essay?
6. What has the author revealed in the work about his or her characteristic modes of thought, perception, or emotion? What place does this work have in the artist's literary development and career?

Biographical Criticism: Selected Readings

Kohfeldt, Mary Lou. *Lady Gregory: The Woman Behind the Irish Renaissance.* 1985.
Meyer, Michael. *Ibsen: A Biography.* 1971.
Taylor, Gary. *Reinventing Shakespeare.* 1989.
Troyat, Henri. *Chekhov.* 1984.

HISTORICAL PERSPECTIVES

An Overview of Historical Criticism

Historical critics approach literature in two ways: (1) they provide a context of background information necessary for understanding how literary works were perceived in their time; (2) they show how literary works reflect ideas and attitudes of the time in which they were written. These two general approaches to historical criticism represent methods and approaches that might be termed "old historicism" and "new historicism" respectively.

The older form of historical criticism, still in use today, insists that a literary work be read with a sense of the time and place of its creation. This is necessary, insist historical critics, because every literary work is a product of its time and its world. Understanding the social background and the intellectual currents of that time and that world illuminate literary works for later generations of readers.

One potential danger of applying historical perspectives to literature is that historical information and documents may be foregrounded and emphasized so heavily that readers lose sight of the literary work the historical approach is designed to illuminate. When the prism of history is used to clarify and explain elements of the literary work, however, whether in examining intellectual currents, describing social conditions, or presenting cultural attitudes, readers' understanding of literary works can be immeasurably enriched. The challenge for historical understanding, whether one uses the tools of the older historicist tradition or the methods of the new historicism, is to ascertain what the past was truly like, how its values are inscribed in its cultural artifacts, including its literature. Equally challenging is an exploration of the question, What was it possible to think or do at a particular moment of the past, including possibilities that may no longer be available to those living today?

Thinking from a New Historicist Perspective

Like earlier historical approaches, a more contemporary approach identified as "new historicism" considers historical contexts of literary works essential for understanding them. A significant difference, however, between earlier historical criticism and new historicism is the newer variety's emphasis on analyzing historical documents with the same intensity and scrutiny given foregrounded passages in the literary works to be interpreted. For example, historical records and diaries might be read to ascertain prevailing cultural attitudes. New historicist critics might typically compare prevailing cultural attitudes about issues today with those of the times in which a play was written. In fact, one common strategy of new historicist critics is to compare and contrast the language of contemporaneous documents and literary works to reveal hidden assumptions, biases, and cultural attitudes that relate the two kinds of texts, literary and documentary, usually to demonstrate how the literary work shares the cultural assumptions of the document.

An important feature of new historicist criticism is its concern with examining the power relations of rulers and subjects. A guiding assumption among many new historicist critics is that texts, not only literary works but also documents, diaries, records, even institutions such as hospitals and prisons, are ideological products culturally constructed from the prevailing power structures that dominate particular societies. Reading a literary work from a new historicist perspective thus becomes an exercise in uncovering the conflicting and subversive perspectives of the marginalized and suppressed, as, for example, those of Bianca and Emilia in Shakespeare's *Othello.*

While appropriating some of the methods of formalist and deconstructive critics, new historicists differ from them in a number of important ways. Most importantly, unlike critics who limit their analysis of a literary work to its language and structure, new historicists spend more time analyzing nonliterary texts from the same time in which the literary work was written. New historicists, however, do apply the close reading strategies of formalist and deconstructive perspectives, but their goal is not, like the formalists, to show how the literary work manifests universal values or how it is unified. Nor is the new historicist goal to show how the text undermines and contradicts itself, an emphasis of deconstructive perspectives. Instead, new historicists analyze the cultural context embedded in the literary work and explain its relationship with the network of the assumptions and beliefs that inform social institutions and cultural practices prevalent in the historical period when the literary work was written. Finally, it is important to note that for new historicist critics, history does not provide mere "background" against which to study literary works, but is, rather, an equally important "text," one that is ultimately inseparable from the literary work, which inevitably reveals the conflicting power relations that underlie all human interaction, from the small-scale interactions with families to the large-scale interactions of social institutions.

A CHECKLIST OF HISTORICAL AND NEW HISTORICIST CRITICAL QUESTIONS

1. When was the work written? When was it published? How was it received by the critics and the public? Why?
2. What does the work's reception reveal about the standards of taste and value during the time it was published and reviewed?
3. What social attitudes and cultural practices related to the action of the work were prevalent during the time the work was written and published?
4. What kinds of power relations does the work describe, reflect, or embody?
5. How do the power relations reflected in the literary work manifest themselves in the cultural practices and social institutions prevalent during the time the work was written and published?
6. What other types of historical documents, cultural artifacts, or social institutions might be analyzed in conjunction with particular literary works? How might a close reading of such a nonliterary "text" illuminate those literary works?
7. To what extent can we understand the past as it is reflected in the literary work? To what extent does the work reflect differences from the ideas and values of its time?

Historical and New Historicist Criticism: Selected Readings

Dollmore, Jonathan, and Alan Sinfield. *Political Shakespeare.* 1985.
Geertz, Clifford. *The Interpretation of Cultures.* 1973.
Greenblatt, Stephen. *Learning to Curse: Essays in Early Modern Culture.* 1990.
Greenblatt, Stephen. *Marvellous Possessions.* 1991.
Kenner, Hugh. *The Pound Era.* 1971.
Levinson, Marjorie, et al. *Rethinking Historicism.* 1989.
Lindenberger, Herbert. *Historical Drama.* 1975.
Veeser, H. Aram. *The New Historicism.* 1989.
Veeser, H. Aram. *The New Historicism: A Reader.* 1994.

PSYCHOLOGICAL PERSPECTIVES

An Overview of Psychological Criticism

Psychological criticism approaches a work of literature as the revelation of its author's mind and personality. Psychological critics see literary works as intimately linked with their author's mental and emotional characteristics. Critics who employ a psychological perspective do so to explain how a literary work reflects its writer's consciousness and mental world, and they use what they know of writers' lives to explain features of their work. Some psychological critics are more interested in the creative processes of writers than in their literary works; these critics look into literary works for clues to a writer's creative imagination. Other psychological critics wish to study not so much a writer's creative process as his or her motivations and behavior; these critics may study a writer's works along with letters and diaries to better understand not just what a writer has done in life but why the writer behaved in a particular manner. Still other critics employ methods of Freudian psychoanalysis to understand not only the writers themselves such as Shakespeare but the literary characters they create, Iago, for example, or Hamlet.

Psychoanalytic criticism derives from Freud's revolutionary psychology in which he developed the notion of the "unconscious" along with the psychological mechanisms of "displacement," "condensation," "fixation," and "manifest and latent" dream content. Freud posited an unconscious element of the mind below consciousness, just beneath awareness. According to Freud, the unconscious harbors forbidden wishes and desires, often sexual, that are in conflict with an individual's or society's moral standards. Freud explains that although the individual represses or "censors" these unconscious fantasies and desires, they become "displaced" or distorted in dreams and other forms of fantasy, which serve to disguise their real meaning.

The disguised versions that appear in a person's conscious life are considered to be the "manifest" content of the unconscious wishes that are their "latent" content, which psychoanalytic critics attempt to discover and explain. Psychoanalytic critics rely heavily on symbolism to identify and explain the meaning of repressed desires, interpreting ordinary objects such as clocks and towers and natural elements such as fire and water in ways that reveal aspects of a literary character's sexuality. These critics also make use of other psychoanalytic concepts and terms such as "fixation," or "obsessive compulsion," attaching to feelings, behaviors, and fantasies that individuals presumably outgrow yet retain in the form of unconscious attractions.

Among the most important of the categories derived from Freud that psychoanalytic critics employ are those Freud used to describe mental structures and dynamics. Freud recognized three types of mental functions, which he designated the "id," the "ego," and the "superego." Freud saw the id as the storehouse of desires, primarily libidinal or sexual, but also aggressive and possessive. He saw the superego as the representative of societal and parental standards of ethics and morality. And he saw the ego as the negotiator between the desires and demands of the id and the controlling and constraining force of the superego, all influenced further by an individual's relationship with other people in the contexts of actual life.

Thinking from a Psychoanalytic Perspective

These few but important psychoanalytic concepts have been put to varied uses by critics with a wide range of psychological approaches. Freud himself analyzed Sophocles' tragic drama *Oedipus Rex* to explain how Oedipus harbored an unconscious desire to kill his father and marry his mother, events the play accounts for. Other critics have used Freud's insights—which, by the way, Freud himself says he derived from studying literary masters such as Sophocles, Shakespeare, and Kafka—to analyze the hidden motivations of literary characters. One of the most famous of all literary characters, Hamlet, has stimulated psychological critics of all persuasions to explain why he delays killing King Claudius. In his book *Hamlet and Oedipus,* Ernest Jones uses Freud's theory of the "Oedipus complex" to explain Hamlet's delay, which Jones sees, essentially, as Hamlet's inability to punish Claudius for what he, Hamlet, unconsciously wanted to do himself.

For examples of psychoanalytic criticism in practice—as well as some objections to it—in the sections of this text following Sophocles' and Shakespeare's plays, respectively, "Critics on Sophocles" and "Critics on Shakespeare," see Freud, "The Oedipus Complex" and Adrian Poole, "Hamlet and Oedipus."

A CHECKLIST OF PSYCHOLOGICAL CRITICAL QUESTIONS

1. What connections can you make between your knowledge of an author's life and the behavior and motivations of characters in his or her work?
2. How does your understanding of the characters, their relationships, their actions, and their motivations in a literary work help you better understand the mental world and imaginative life, or the actions and motivations, of the author?
3. How does a particular literary work—its images, metaphors, and other linguistic elements—reveal the psychological motivations of its characters or the psychological mindset of its author?
4. To what extent can you employ the concepts of Freudian psychoanalysis to understand the motivations of literary characters?
5. What kinds of literary works and what types of literary characters seem best suited to a critical approach that employs a psychological or psychoanalytical perspective? Why?
6. How can a psychological or psychoanalytic approach to a particular work be combined with an approach from another critical perspective—for example, that of biographical or formalist criticism, or that of feminist or deconstructionist criticism?

Psychological and Psychoanalytic Criticism: Selected Readings

Bloom, Harold. *The Anxiety of Influence.* 1973.
Chodorow, Nancy. *Feminism and Psychoanalytic Theory.* 1990.
Crews, Frederick. *Skeptical Engagements.* 1986.
Felman, Soshana. *Jacques Lacan and the Adventure of Insight.* 1987.
Freud, Sigmund. *The Interpretation of Dreams.* 1900.
Freud, Sigmund. *Introductory Lectures on Psychoanalysis.* 1917–1918.
Freud, Sigmund. *New Introductory Lectures on Psychoanalysis.* 1933.
Hoffman, Frederick J. *Freudianism and the Literary Mind.* 1957.
Holland, Norman. *The Dynamics of Literary Response.* 1968.
Jones, Ernest. *Hamlet and Oedipus.* 1949.
Manheim, Leonard, and Eleanor Manheim, eds. *Hidden Patterns: Studies in Psychoanalytic Literary Criticism.* 1966.
Mitchell, Juliet. *Psychoanalysis and Feminism.* 1975.
Nelson, Benjamin, ed. *Sigmund Freud on Creativity and the Unconscious.* 1958.
Skura, Meredith. *The Literary Use of the Psychoanalytic Process.* 1981.
Wilson, Edmund. *The Wound and the Bow.* 1941.
Wright, Elizabeth, ed. *Psychoanalytic Criticism.* 1984.

SOCIOLOGICAL PERSPECTIVES

An Overview of Sociological Criticism

Like historical and biographical critics, sociological critics argue that literary works should not be isolated from the social contexts in which they are embedded. And also like historical critics, especially those who espouse new historicist perspectives, sociological critics emphasize the ways power relations are played out by varying social forces and institutions. Sociological critics focus on the values of a society and how those values are reflected in literary works. At one end of the sociological critical spectrum, literary works are treated simply as documents that either embody social conditions or are a product of those conditions. Critics employing a sociological perspective study the economic, political, and cultural issues expressed in literary works as those issues are reflected in the societies in which the works were produced.

Two significant trends in sociological criticism have had a decisive impact on critical theory: Marxist criticism and feminist criticism. Proponents of each of these critical perspectives have used some of the tools of other critical approaches such as the close reading of the formalists and deconstructionists and the symbolic analysis of the psychoanalytic critics to espouse their respective ideologies in interpreting literature.

Marxist Critical Perspectives

In the same way that many psychoanalytic critics base their approach to literature on the theoretical works of Sigmund Freud, Marxist critics are indebted to the political theory of Karl Marx and Friedrich Engels. Marxist critics examine literature for its reflection of how dominant elite and middle-class/bourgeois values lead to the control and suppression of the working classes. Marxist critics see literature's value in promoting social and economic revolution, with works that espouse Marxist ideology serving to prompt the kinds of economic and political changes that conform to Marxist principles. Such changes would include the overthrow of the dominant capitalist ideology and the loss of power by those with money and privilege. Marxist criticism is concerned both with understanding the role of politics, money, and power in literary works, and with redefining and reforming the way society distributes its resources among the classes. Fundamentally, the Marxist ideology looks toward a vision of a world not so much where class conflict has been minimized but one in which classes have disappeared altogether.

Marxist critics generally approach literary works as products of their era, especially as influenced, even determined by the economic and political ideologies that prevail at the time of their composition. The literary work is considered a "product" in relation to the actual economic and social conditions that exist at either the time of the work's composition or the time and place of the action it describes.

Marxist analyses of plays focus on the relations among classes to investigate the ways political and economic forces conspire to keep some social, ethnic, and racial groups in power and others out. In fact, Marxist critical perspectives have been brought to bear most often on the novel, next most often on drama, and least often on poetry, where issues of power, money, and political influence are not nearly as pervasive.

Thinking from a Marxist Perspective

A Marxist sociological approach to the study of Shakespeare's *Othello* could focus on the political organization of the Venetian state as depicted in the play and its relation to the play's depiction of authority, perhaps considering as well the breakdown of authority in the scenes set in Cyprus. Another sociological perspective might focus on the play's economic aspects, particularly how money and influence are used to manipulate others. Still other sociological issues that could be addressed include the role of women in the play and the issue of Othello's race. How, for example, does Shakespeare portray the power relations between Othello and Desdemona, Iago and Emilia, Cassio and Bianca? To what extent is each of these women's relationship with men considered from an economic standpoint? Or, to what extent is Othello's blackness a factor in his demise, or is his race a defining characteristic in other characters' perceptions of him? To what extent is his status as a military leader an issue?

A CHECKLIST OF MARXIST CRITICAL QUESTIONS

1. What social forces and institutions are represented in the work? How are these forces portrayed? What is the author's attitude toward them?
2. What political economic elements appear in the work? How important are they in determining or influencing the lives of the characters?
3. What economic issues appear in the course of the work? How important are economic facts in influencing the motivation and behavior of the characters?
4. To what extent are the lives of the characters influenced or determined by social, political, and economic forces? To what extent are the characters aware of these forces?

Marxist Criticism: Selected Readings

Baxandall, Lee, and Stefan Morawski, eds. *Marx and Engels on Literature and Art.* 1973.
Benjamin, Walter. *Illuminations.* 1968.
Eagleton, Terry. *Marxism and Literary Criticism.* 1976.
Jameson, Fredric. *Marxism and Form.* 1971.
Lukacs, George. *Realism in Our Time.* 1972.
Trotsky, Leon. *Literature and the Revolution.* 1924.
Williams, Raymond. *Marxism and Literature.* 1977.

Feminist Critical Perspectives

Feminist criticism, like Marxist and new historicist criticism, examines the social and cultural aspects of literary works, especially for what those works reveal about the role, position, and influence of women. Like other socially minded critics, feminist critics consider literature in relation to its social, economic, and political contexts, and indeed look to analyze its social, economic, and political content. Feminist critics also typically see literature as an arena to contest for power and control, since as sociological critics, feminist critics also see literature as an agent for social transformation.

Moreover, feminist critics seek to redress the imbalance of literary study in which all important books are written by men or the only characters of real interest are male protagonists. Feminist critics have thus begun to study women writers whose works have been previously neglected. They have begun to look at the way feminine consciousness has been portrayed in literature written by both women and men. And they have begun to change the nature of the questions asked about literature that reflect predominantly male experience. In these and other ways feminist critical perspectives have begun to undermine the patriarchal or masculinist assumptions that have dominated critical approaches to literature until relatively recently.

In his influential and widely used *Glossary of Literary Terms,* M. H. Abrams identifies four central tenets of much feminist criticism, summarized in the following list.

1. Western civilization is pervasively patriarchal (ruled by the father)—that is, it is male-centered and controlled, and is organized and conducted in such a way as to subordinate women to
men in all cultural domains: familial, religious, political, economic, social, legal, and artistic.
2. The prevailing concepts of *gender*—of the traits that constitute
what is masculine and what is feminine—are largely, if not entirely, cultural constructs that were generated by the omnipresent
patriarchal biases of our civilization.
3. This patriarchal (or "masculinist," or "androcentric") ideology pervades those writings which have been considered great
literature, and which until recently have been written almost
entirely by men for men.
4. The traditional aesthetic categories and criteria for analyzing
and appraising literary works . . . are in fact infused with masculine assumptions, interests, and ways of reasoning, so that the
standard rankings, and also the critical treatments, of literary
works have in fact been tacitly but thoroughly gender-biased.★

It should be noted, however, that Abrams's list, though helpful, tends to
blur distinctions among the many different varieties of feminist criticism as
currently practiced. Thus the ways these assumptions are reflected in feminist criticism vary enormously from the reader-response approaches used by
feminist critics, such as Judith Fetterley and Elizabeth Flynn, to the cultural
studies approaches used by Jane Tompkins and Eve Kosovsky Sedgwick, to
the Lacanian psychoanalytic approaches employed by Helene Cixous and
Julia Kristeva. It would be better to think of feminist criticism in the plural
as the criticism of feminists rather than to envision it as a singular monolithic entity.

Thinking from a Feminist Perspective

In applying the perspective of feminist criticism to Ibsen's *A Doll House,* we
might consider the way the roles of woman and wife are depicted in the play.
A feminist reading would be alert for signs of power contestation. It would examine Nora's ability to exert her will and control her destiny. Feminist readers
would also ask about Kristine's role in the play.

Feminist readers would interrogate the play to ask why or on whose judgment such a marriage as Nora and Torvald's should seem desirable. Feminist
critics would probe beyond the text to consider whether such differences in
feeling and experience as the play suggests between Nora and Torvald ob-
tained in marriages during Ibsen's lifetime, thus sharing an interest with new
historicist critics in the social and cultural background. These critics might
take a closer look at the play's abrupt ending with its slamming door, and

★M. H. Abrams. *A Glossary of Literary Terms,* 6th ed., 1993, pp. 234–235.

wonder whether it masks an undercurrent of powerlessness and of looking back.

A CHECKLIST OF FEMINIST CRITICAL QUESTIONS

1. To what extent does the representation of women (and men) in the work reflect the place and time in which the work was written?
2. How are the relations between men and women, or those between members of the same sex, presented in the work? What roles do men and women assume and perform and with what consequences?
3. Does the author present the work from within a predominantly male or female sensibility? Why might this have been done, and with what effects?
4. How do the facts of the author's life relate to the presentation of men and women in the work? To their relative degrees of power?
5. How do other works by the author correspond to this one in their depiction of the power relationships between men and women?

Feminist Criticism: Selected Readings

Buck, Claire. *The Bloomsbury Guide to Women's Literature.* 1992.
Cixous, Helene. *The Laugh of the Medusa.* 1976.
Fetterley, Judith. *The Resisting Reader.* 1978.
Gallop, Jane. *The Daughter's Seduction: Feminism and Psychoanalysis.* 1982.
Gates, Henry L., Jr. *Reading Black, Reading Feminist.* 1990.
Gilbert, Sandra, and Susan Gubar. *The Madwoman in the Attic.* 1979.
Heilbrun, Carolyn. *Toward a Recognition of Adrogyny.* 1973.
Moers, Ellen. *Literary Women.* 1976.
Rich, Adrienne. *On Lies, Secrets, and Silence.* 1980.
Ruthven, K. K. *Feminist Literary Studies: An Introduction.* 1984.
Schweickart, Patricinio, and Elizabeth Flynn. *Gender and Reading.* 1986.
Showalter, Elaine. *A Literature of Their Own.* 1977.
Showalter, Elaine. *The New Feminist Criticism.* 1986.
Smith, Barbara. *Toward a Black Feminist Criticism.* 1977.

READER-RESPONSE PERSPECTIVES

An Overview of Reader-Response Criticism

Reader-response criticism raises the question of where literary meaning resides—in the literary text, in the reader, or in the interactive space between text and reader. Reader-response critics differ in the varying degrees of subjectivity they allow into their theories of interpretation. Some, like David Bleich, see the literary text as a kind of mirror in which readers see themselves. In making sense of literature, readers recreate themselves. Other reader-response critics, like Wolfgang Iser, focus on the text rather than on the feelings and reactions of the reader. Text-centered reader-response critics emphasize the temporal aspect of reading, suggesting that readers make sense of texts over time, moving through a text sentence by sentence, line by line, word by word, filling in gaps and making inferences about what is being implied by textual details as they read.

Still other reader-response critics like Norman Holland focus on the psychological dynamics of reading. Holland argues that every reader creates a specific identity theme unique to him or her self in reading any literary work. He suggests that to make sense of a literary work readers must find in it, or create through the process of reading it, their identity themes.

One of the earliest and most influential reader-response critics, Louise Rosenblatt, argues against placing too much emphasis on the reader's imagination, identity, or feelings in literary interpretation. Like Iser, Rosenblatt keeps the focus on the text, though she is more concerned than is Iser with the dynamic relationship between reader and text, since it is in that interrelationship that Rosenblatt believes literary meanings are made.

For Rosenblatt, as for other reader-response critics, the meaning of a literary work cannot exist until it is "performed" by the reader. Until then literary meaning is only potential. It becomes actual when readers realize its potential through their acts of reading, responding, and interpreting.

As you might expect, reader-response critics respect not only the intellectual acts of analysis and comprehension that readers perform but also their subjective responses and their emotional apprehension of literary works.

One benefit of using reader-response perspectives to interpret literary works is that you begin with what is primary and basic—your initial reactions, your primary responses. Of course, as you read, you may change your mind about your reaction to a work. You may experience opposite or different feelings. Or you may make sense of the work differently because of discoveries you make later in the process of reading. What you read in the last chapter of a novel, for example, may change your understanding of what you read in the first chapter or in a middle chapter, which you had interpreted one way until you reached the end. What's important for reader-response critics is just this kind of active reading dynamic, in which a reader's changing ideas and feelings are foregrounded. These critics describe the recursiveness of the reading process, the way in which our minds anticipate what is coming in the text based on what we have already read and, simultaneously, the way we loop back retrospectively to reconsider earlier passages in light of later ones that we read. The literary text does not disappear for reader-response critics. Instead it becomes part of readers' experience as they make their way through it.

Reader-response criticism thus emphasizes process rather than product, an experience rather than an object, a shifting subjectivity rather than a static and objective text and meaning. For reader-response critics the text is not a "thing"; it does not stand still, for it lives only in its readers' imaginations. For these critics, then, literary works do not have an independent objective meaning that is true once and for all and that is identical for all readers. Instead, they argue that readers *make* meaning through their encounters with literary texts. And the meanings they make may be as varied as the individuals who read them.

Reader-response critics emphasize two additional points about the range and variety of readers' interpretations. First, an individual reader's interpretation of a work may change, in fact, probably will change over time. Reading Shakespeare's *Julius Caesar* in high school can be a very different experience from reading it in college or later as an adult. Second, historically, readers from different generations and different centuries interpret books differently. The works say different things to readers of different historical eras based on their particular needs, concerns, and historical circumstances. In both the individual cases and the larger historical occasions, changes occur, changes that affect how individuals perceive, absorb, and understand what they read at different times of their lives.

The crucial thing for readers is to acknowledge their own subjectivity in the act of reading and to be aware that they come to literary works with a set of beliefs, ideas, attitudes, values—with all that makes them who and what they are. Being aware of our predispositions when we read can prevent our biases and prejudices from skewing our interpretations of literary works. At the same time, we need to pay attention to the details of the text. We cannot make words and sentences mean anything at all. There are limits and boundaries to what is acceptable, limits and boundaries that are subject to negotiation and debate. For most reader-response theorists, interpretation has both latitude and limits. Negotiating between them in a delicate balancing act allows readers to exercise their subjectivity while recognizing the significance of the words on the page.

Perhaps an analogy will clarify the double-sided nature of literary interpretation from a reader-response perspective, one that recognizes both the reader's freedom and the text's limits. You might think of a text as a musical score, one that is brought to life in performance. Readers make the potential meanings of a text come to life in much the same way that a musician brings a piece of music to life in performance. When musicians play a score or readers read a literary work, they cannot change the notes of the score or the words of the text. Both readers and musicians are limited by what is on the page. Yet there is room for differing interpretations and varied responses. Two interpretations of a literary work, like two musical performances, are likely to differ, sometimes in significant ways. The varying interpretations will be valid insofar as they respect the words or notes on the page, and insofar as they represent a reasonable and logically defensible approach to the work.

Thinking from a Reader-Response Perspective

In reading Ibsen's *A Doll House,* reader-response critics would consider a reader's emotional reactions to the story's action. They might ask how a reader responds to Torvald, how he or she reacts to Nora's acknowledgment of her feelings, how readers respond to the way she is manipulated by Krogstad. Like feminist critics, they would consider the extent to which female readers might respond differently from males, though the important thing for a reader-response perspective would be the intensity and nature of a particular reader's response. Some reader-response critics would also examine the reader's responses at different points in the text, focusing on particular scenes and dialogue that might signal a shift in the play's tone and hence a change in the reader's response.

Reader-response critics might point to the way the play invites readers to consider the extent to which it reflects their own experience or understanding of marriage. They might ask whether the idea of marriage reflected in the play reminds you of your own relatives' marriages, of the marriage of your parents. If so, why, a reader-response critic might ask, and, if not, why not?

The emphases of reader-response critics essentially, then, would be two: (1) the reader's direct experience of the language and details of the play in the process of reading it; (2) the reader's actual experience outside the play which he or she brings to the reading and which is used to interpret it. Where formalist critics would play down this experiential connection to the play, reader-response critics want to extend the readers' perceptions about the play and deepen their response to it by deliberately evoking actual experiences of readers that they can bring to bear on both their apprehension and their comprehension of the drama.

A CHECKLIST OF READER-RESPONSE CRITICAL QUESTIONS

1. What is your initial emotional response to the work? How did you feel upon first reading it?
2. Did you find yourself responding to it or reacting differently at any point? If so, why? If not, why not?
3. At what places in the text did you have to make inferences, fill in gaps, make interpretive decisions? On what bases did you make these inferential guesses?
4. How do you respond to the characters, the speaker, or the narrator? How do you feel about them? Why?
5. What places in the text caused you to do the most serious thinking? How did you put the pieces, sections, parts of the work together to make sense of it?
6. If you have read a work more than once, how has your second and subsequent readings differed from earlier ones? How do you account for those differences, or for the fact that there are no differences in either your thoughts or your feelings about the work?

Reader-Response Criticism: Selected Readings

Bleich, David. *Readings and Feelings.* 1975.
Bleich, David. *Subjective Criticism.* 1968.
Clifford, John, ed. *The Experience of Reading.* 1991.
Eco, Umberto. *The Open Work.* 1989.

Fish, Stanley. *Is There a Text in This Class?* 1980.
Freund, Elizabeth. *The Return of the Reader.* 1987.
Holland, Norman. *The Dynamics of Literary Response.* 1968.
Iser, Wolfgang. *The Act of Reading.* 1978.
Mailloux, Steven. *Interpretive Conventions.* 1982.
Rabinowitz, Peter. *Before Reading.* 1987.
Rosenblatt, Louise. *Literature as Exploration.* 1939, 1975.
Rosenblatt, Louise. *The Reader, The Text, The Poem: A Transactional Theory of the Literary Work.* 1978.
Steig, Michael. *Stories of Reading.* 1989.
Suleiman, Susan R., and Inge Crosman, eds. *The Reader in the Text.* 1980.
Tompkins, Jane, ed. *Reader-Response Criticism.* 1980.
Wimmers, Inge Crosman. *Poetics of Reading.* 1988.

MYTHOLOGICAL PERSPECTIVES

An Overview of Mythological Criticism

In general terms a "myth" is a story that explains how something came to be. Every culture creates stories to explain what it considers important, valuable, and true. Thus the Greek myth of Persephone, who was kidnapped by Pluto, the god of the underworld, and allowed to return to her mother Demeter every year, explains the changes of the seasons. Or the Biblical story of Eve's temptation by the serpent in the book of Genesis, which concludes with God's curse of the serpent, explains, among other things, why snakes crawl on their bellies.

Myth criticism, however, is not concerned with stories that explain origins so much as those that provide universal story patterns that recur with regularity among many cultures and in many different times and places. The patterns myth critics typically identify and analyze are those that represent common, familiar, even universal human experiences, such as being born and dying, growing up and crossing the threshold into adulthood, going on a journey, engaging in sexual activity. These familiar patterns of human action and experience, however, are of interest to myth critics not primarily in and of themselves, but rather for how they represent religious beliefs, social customs, and cultural attitudes.

Birth, for example, is of interest as a symbolic beginning and death as a symbolic ending. A journey is a symbolic venturing out into the world to explore and experience what it has in store for the traveler. Sleeping and dreaming are not simply states of ordinary experience but symbolic modes of entrance into another realm and an envisioning of unusual and perhaps strange possibilities unimagined in waking life. So too with physical contests, sexual encounters, and other forms of experience, which many times are occasions for individuals to be tested, challenged, and perhaps initiated into an advanced or superior state of being—becoming a warrior, for example, a mother, a prophet, or a king.

Myth critics discover in literature of all times and places stories with basic patterns that can be explained in terms of *archetypes,* or universal symbols, which some mythological critics believe are part of every person's unconscious mind, a kind of a collective unconscious that each of us inherits by virtue of our common humanity. Besides the fundamental facts of human existence, other archetypes include typical literary characters such as the Don Juan or womanizer, the *femme fatale* or dangerous female, the trickster or con artist, the damsel in distress, the rebel, the tyrant, the hero, the betrayer. Creatures real and imaginary can also be archetypal symbols. The lion, for example, can represent strength, the eagle independence, the fox cunning, the unicorn innocence, the dragon destruction, the centaur the union of matter and spirit, animality and humanity, or even humanity and divinity.

It is on plot or the sequence of causally related incidents and actions, however, that myth criticism focuses most heavily. The archetypal images, creatures, and characters exist within stories that themselves exhibit patterns of recurrence. So, for example, there are stories of the arduous quest fraught with perils which a protagonist must survive, perhaps to rescue an innocent victim, perhaps to prove superior courage or morality, perhaps to save others from destruction. There are stories of vengeance, of death and rebirth, of resurrection, of transformation from one state of being into another, stories of enlightenment, of devastation, of lost paradises. Many such stories can be found in the religious literature of cultures around the world. The Bible, for example, contains stories of creation (Adam and Eve), fraternal rivalry and murder (Cain and Abel), destruction (Noah) and forgiveness (the ark and the covenant), wandering and enslavement (the exodus), death and resurrection (Jesus' life and ministry)—and so on. This list can be multiplied by consulting, for example, the Taoist and Confucian religious traditions of China, the Hindu traditions of India, the Buddhist traditions of Japan, and the Islamic tradition of the Middle East.

Myth critics approach the study of literary works and the study of a culture's myths in many ways. The Canadian critic Northrop Frye, for example, explains the traditional literary genres, including the novel, the drama, and epic, with reference to the recurrence in them of mythic patterns such as death and rebirth, departure and return, ignorance and insight. Frye, in fact, associates the genres of comedy, romance, tragedy, and irony or satire with the cycle of the seasons, each genre representing the natural events associated with a particular season (comedy with the fertility of spring, for example, and tragedy with the decline of the year in autumn). The French critic, Claude Lévi-Strauss, who employs the strategies of structuralist and semiotic analysis, treats cultural myths as signs whose meanings are not understood by the cultures that create those myths. His work is grounded in structural anthropology and owes much to the linguistic theory of Ferdinand de Saussure, who had a profound effect on the development of French and American structuralist perspectives on literary analysis and interpretation. And the American critic of popular culture, John Cawelti, to cite still another approach, analyzes the mythic impulse and mythic elements in forms of popular literature such as the western.

Thinking from a Mythological Perspective

What a mythological critic does with archetypal characters, stories, creatures, and even natural elements such as sun and moon, darkness and light, fire and water, is to link them up with one another, to see one literary work in relation to others of a similar type. Thus, for example, Hamlet's revenge of his father's death can be linked with myths from other cultures that include a son's avenging his father. Or the story of Hamlet can be linked with others in which the corruption poisoning a country has been eliminated through some action taken by the hero.

In considering Ibsen's *A Doll House* from a mythological perspective, a myth critic might consider Krogstad as an intruder who comes to menace a happy family. Or he might be seen as a mysterious force that serves as a catalyst for necessary change. A myth critic might also be concerned with Nora's repressed sexuality and the doctor's illness as symptoms of some larger cultural malaise that only some kind of heroic action can make meaningful.

A CHECKLIST OF MYTHOLOGICAL CRITICAL QUESTIONS

1. What incidents in the work seem common or familiar enough as actions that they might be considered symbolic or archetypal? Are there any journeys, battles, falls, reversals of fortune?
2. What kinds of character types appear in the work? How might they be typed or classified?
3. What creatures, elements of nature, or man-made objects play a role in the work? To what extent might they be considered symbolic?
4. What changes do the characters undergo? How can those changes be characterized or named? To what might they be related or compared?
5. What religious or quasi-religious traditions with which you are familiar might the work's story, characters, elements, or objects be compared to or affiliated with? Why?

Mythological Criticism: Selected Readings

Campbell, Joseph. *The Hero with a Thousand Faces.* 1949.
Cawelti, John. *Adventure, Mystery, Romance.* 1976.
Chase, Richard. *Quest for Myth.* 1949.
Frazer, James G. *The Golden Bough,* rev. 1911.
Frye, Northrop. *Anatomy of Criticism.* 1957.
Graves, Robert. *The White Goddess.* 1948.
Jung, Carl Gustav. *Modern Man in Search of a Soul.* 1933.
Lévi-Strauss, Claude. *Structural Anthropology.* 1968.
Vickery, John B., ed. *Myth and Literature,* 1966.

STRUCTURALIST PERSPECTIVES

An Overview of Structuralist Criticism

It is important to distinguish the general meaning of "structure" as used by critics of varying persuasions from its use by adherents of structuralist criticism. In the traditional and most general sense, the word "structure" refers to the organization of a literary work—to its arrangement of incident and action (plot); its division into sections, chapters, parts, stanzas, and other literary units; its employment of repetition and contrast; its patterns of imagery (light and dark images, for example) and sound (its patterns of rhythm and rhyme).

For structuralist critics, however, the notion of "structure" has another meaning, one which derives from linguistics and anthropology and which refers to the systems of signs that designate meaning. To understand the structuralist perspective one needs to understand what structuralists mean by "signs" and how language is an arbitrary system of such signs. We can illustrate with a familiar example—the word "dog," which represents the four-legged animal many of us have as a pet. Why do the letters D-O-G, when put together, signify the creature who barks at the mail carrier and wags its tail while running off with our sneakers? The answer, of course, is because of a particular set of linguistic conventions that operate due to common usage and agreement. Such use and agreement, such a convention, however, is arbitrary. That is, it could have been otherwise. In fact, in languages such as French and Italian, the word "dog" means nothing. In those languages the furry four-footed barker is respectively *chien* (pronounced sheYEN) and *cane* (pronounced CAHnay), a word that looks like the English "cane," or walking stick, but which is a sign, in Italian, for what we call a dog.

But there is one additional linguistic element of importance—that of difference. We have just seen how the English word "cane" differs from the Italian *cane* and the French *chien* and how the two languages designate the faithful canine companion, perhaps named "Fido," in different ways. In both languages (as in all languages) words are differentiated from one another by sound and by spelling. Thus, in English C-A-N-E refers to a walking stick, but C-O-N-E and C-A-P-E to entirely different things. The same is true in Italian, where *cane,* our equivalent of dog, differs from *cani* (CAHknee), the Italian plural, meaning "dogs." This notion of difference is critical to the way structuralism analyzes systems of signs, for it is through differences that languages, literatures, and other social systems convey meaning.

One technique structuralist critics rely on heavily in analyzing difference is "binary opposition," in which a text's contrasting elements are identified and examined. In employing binary opposition as an analytical instrument, structuralist literary critics imitate what structural anthropologists do when they analyze societies to determine which of their social habits and customs are meaningful. The founder of structuralist anthropology, Claude Lévi-Strauss, an important influence on literary structuralism, has explained how a society's most important values can be deciphered by analyzing such binary oppositions as the distinction between "the raw and the cooked," which became a title for one of his books.

Structuralist critics find all kinds of opposition in literature, from small-scale elements, such as letters and syllables; through symbols, such as light and dark; to motions or directions (up and down), times (before and after), places (inside and outside), distances (far and near); to elements of plot and character, such as changes of feeling and reversals of fortune. Such differences are significant structural elements requiring interpretation, whether the differences are explicit or implicit, described or only hinted at.

Semiotics

Semiotics is the study of signs and sign systems; it is, more importantly, the study of codes, or the systems we use to understand the meaning of events and entities, including institutions and cultural happenings as well as verbal and visual texts—from poems to songs to advertisements, and more. Situated on the border between the humanities and the social and behavioral sciences, semiotics is concerned with how the workings of sign systems in various disciplines such as literature and psychology enable us to understand the richly textured significations of all kinds of cultural texts, from action films and television game shows and situation comedies to professional football games to parades and fourth of July celebrations; from religious rituals such as bar mitzvahs and marriage ceremonies to social occasions such as annual company picnics and New Year's parties.

Although semiotic perspectives derive from the theoretical foundations of structuralist and poststructuralist thought, semiotics does not limit itself to the goals and methods of those critical approaches. And though semiotic analysis is sometimes presented in logical symbols and mathematical terminology, it is not restricted to those forms of language. In fact, one of the strengths of a semiotic perspective is its ability to analyze the ways various discourses convey meaning, whether these discourses employ words or communicate, as does fashion, for example, by means of other signs and symbols.

Thinking from a Structuralist Perspective

We can analyze virtually anything from a structuralist perspective—a baseball or football game, an aerobics class, a restaurant menu or a three-course dinner, fashion shows, movies, MTV videos, newspaper cartoons. The possibilities are endless, and, in fact, one critic, Roland Barthes in his book *Mythologies,* has provided a series of brilliant structuralist analyses of foods, fashions, and sports, including wrestling.

Fairy tales and folktales have been a popular source of interpretations for structuralist critics, for such basic stories contain plots and character elements that lend themselves well to binary analysis, and they often reveal much about the values of the cultures that created them. Think of Cinderella, for example, and how she exists in opposition to her stepsisters (she is beautiful while they are ugly; she is poor while they are rich; she is a servant, they her masters). Remember how she loses one slipper while retaining the other, how her coach turns into a pumpkin and her footmen into mice (or is it the other way around)? Difference functions throughout the story on many levels, including the all-important one of the reversal of her fortune with that of her stepsisters and of a prince replacing her nasty stepmother as her future companion. You may also wish to consider books and movies that make use of the "Cinderella plot," where a metaphorical Prince Charming rescues a poor common girl from an oppressive and unhappy life. The films *An Officer and a Gentleman* and *Pretty Woman* provide two examples.

A structuralist perspective on *A Doll House* would consider the difference between Torvald's thoughts about Nora at the beginning of the play and his thoughts about her at the end. It would attend to the difference between his long haranguing speeches when he finds out about Nora's secret and his final plaintive pleas once she announces that she is leaving him. It would also analyze the binary oppositions that exist in the play, including husband/wife, adult/child, sickness/health, helping/hurting, and so on.

A CHECKLIST OF STRUCTURALIST CRITICAL QUESTIONS

1. What are the elements of the work—words, stanzas, chapters, parts, for example— and how can these be seen as revealing "difference"?
2. How do the characters, narrators, speakers, or other voices heard in the work reveal difference?
3. How do the elements of the work's plot or overall action suggest a meaningful pattern? What changes, adjustments, transformations, shifts of tone, attitude, behavior, or feeling do you find?
4. How are the work's primary images and events related to one another? What elements of differentiation exist, and what do they signify?
5. What system of relationships governs the work as a whole?
6. What system of relations could be used to link this work with others of its kind? With different kinds of things with which it shares some similarities?

Structuralist Criticism: Selected Readings

Barthes, Roland. *Elements of Semiology.* 1967.
Culler, Jonathan. *Structuralist Poetics.* 1975.
Genette, Gerard. *Figures.* 1966.
Hawkes, Terence. *Structuralism and Semiotics.* 1977.
Lévi-Strauss, Claude. *The Raw and the Cooked.* 1966.
Macksey, Richard, and Eugenio Donato, eds. *The Structuralist Controversy.* 1970.
Scholes, Robert. *Semiotics and Interpretation.* 1982.
Scholes, Robert. *Structuralism in Literature: An Introduction.* 1974.
Smith, Barbara Herrnstein. *On the Margins of Discourse.* 1978.

DECONSTRUCTIVE PERSPECTIVES

An Overview of Deconstructive Criticism

Deconstruction arose as a further development of structuralism. Like structuralist critics, deconstructive critics look for opposition in literary works (and in other kinds of "texts" such as films, advertisements, and social institutions, including schools and hospitals). Like structuralism, deconstruction emphasizes difference, or the structure of constituent opposition in a text or any signifying system (for example, male/female, black/white, animate/inanimate). For deconstructionist critics, any meaning is constructed as the result of an opposition, which can be read as ideologically grounded. This is the case with the use of language itself, which creates meaning by opposition (the difference in meaning between the English words "cap" and "cup," for example, is based on a difference between their middle letters). The difference is significant as the words refer to different things.

Deconstruction differs from structuralism, however, in describing at once both a pair of equally valid conflicting oppositions, and in identifying a prevailing ideology that needs to be subverted, undermined, challenged, or otherwise called into question—an ideological view, for example, that suggests that one race or gender is superior to another, or a conviction that the poor are happy with their lot. We can distinguish the more explicitly politicized type of deconstruction, "deconstructionist criticism," from a less politically animated type, "deconstructive criticism," in which the ideological impulse is implicit rather than explicit, latent rather than overtly expressed.

Through a careful analysis of a text's language, deconstructive critics unravel the text by pointing to places where it is ambivalent, contradictory, or otherwise ambiguous. Critics who employ deconstruction as a critical method actually would say that the text deconstructs itself, and that critics do not deconstruct the text so much as show how the text contradicts itself and thereby dismantles itself. They would argue that the contradictions found in any verbal text are inherent in the nature of language, which functions as a system of opposition or differences. And since language itself is radically oppositional and thereby inherently ideological, then all discourse is, first, oppositional and hence subject to deconstruction, and, second, ideological, and indicative of power differentiation. In addition, deconstructionist critics also posit the existence of absent textual qualities or characteristics by suggesting that these absent elements have been suppressed by the dominant ideology that controls the apparent meaning of the work.

Deconstructionist critics operate on the premise that language is irretrievably self-contradictory and self-destroying. They argue that since language is unstable, it cannot be controlled by writers. As a result, literary works mean more than their authors are aware of, and their meanings are as unstable as the language of which they are constructed. The aim of deconstructive analysis is to demonstrate the instability of language in texts, thereby revealing how a text's conflicting forces inevitably destroy its apparently logical or meaningful structure and how its apparently clear meaning splits into contradictory, incompatible, and ultimately undecidable possibilities.

Deconstructionist criticism favors terms like "unmasking," "unraveling," "recovering," "suppression," and "contradiction." Unlike formalist criticism, which it resembles in its scrupulous attention to textual detail and its insistence on analyzing the text as a self-contained world, deconstructionist criticism attempts to dismantle the literary work and show that it does not mean what it appears to mean. Deconstructionist criticism includes a penchant for showing how literary texts "subvert" and "betray" themselves, an elevation of criticism to an equal stature with literary creation (so that a deconstructive critical essay on *"Antigonê,"* for example, is as valuable an artistic production as the original story), and its radical skepticism about the ability of language to communicate anything except contradictions.

A crucial notion for deconstructionist criticism is that of difference, or "différence," as the seminal deconstructionist philosopher and critic Jacques Derrida spells it. By différence, Derrida means to suggest both the usual meaning of difference (dissimilarity) and the additional idea of deferral, both derived from the two meanings of the French verb "différer," which means "to differ" and "to defer" or "postpone." The kind of difference meant by Derrida is, specifically, a deferral of meaning that is never completed or finished because a spoken utterance or a written text means whatever it means as a function of differences among its elements. The result is that its meaning cannot be established as single or determinate. Meaning, thus, is indefinitely postponed, endlessly deferred.

This kind of playing with language is further exemplified by Derrida's explanation of the "self-effacing trace," his notion that a network of differences of meaning is implied even though those differences are not actually present in an utterance or a text. The explicit meaning, which is present, carries with it "traces" of the absent implied meanings, which for ideological reasons are suppressed, though other implications are "there" as inescapable alternative possibilities because they can be construed or imagined.

Thinking from a Deconstructive Perspective

A Doll House yields a number of oppositions that deconstructionist critics would describe to unmask a prevailing ideology in need of subversion. Primary in importance among them is the conflict between husband and wife, in which "husband" is the privileged term and "wife" the submissive and submerged one. In this play, however, we find that the wife is not passive or really submissive. She is active behind the scenes, forging signatures and arranging matters her husband has no knowledge of. Other oppositions include those between male and female, older and younger, privileged and unprivileged, all located in the same husband/wife relationship.

A CHECKLIST OF DECONSTRUCTIVE CRITICAL QUESTIONS

1. What oppositions exist in the work? Which of the two opposing terms of each pair is the privileged or more powerful term? How is this shown in the work?

2. What textual elements (descriptive details, images, incidents, passages) suggest a contradiction or alternative to the privileged or more powerful term?
3. What is the prevailing ideology or set of cultural assumptions in the work? Where are these assumptions most evident?
4. What passages of the work most reveal gaps, inconsistencies, or contradictions?
5. How stable is the text? How decidable is its meaning?

Deconstructive Criticism: Selected Readings

Attridge, Derek, ed. *Acts of Literature.* 1992.
Bloom, Harold, ed. *Deconstruction and Criticism.* 1979.
Culler, Jonathan. *On Deconstruction.* 1982.
de Man, Paul. *Allegories of Reading.* 1979.
Derrida, Jacques. *Writing and Difference.* 1978.
Johnson, Barbara. *A World of Difference.* 1987.
Norris, Christopher. *Deconstruction: Theory and Practice.* 1982.
Scholes, Robert. *Protocols of Reading.* 1989.
Taylor, Mark C., ed. *Deconstruction in Context.* 1986.

CULTURAL STUDIES PERSPECTIVES

An Overview of Cultural Studies

The term "cultural studies" indicates a wide range of critical approaches to the study of literature and society. It is a kind of umbrella term that not only includes approaches to the critical analysis of society such as Marxism, feminism, structuralism, deconstruction, and new historicism, but also refers to a wide range of interdisciplinary studies, including women's studies, African-American studies, Asian, Native American, Latino studies, and other types of area studies.

Like deconstruction, feminism, and new historicism, cultural studies perspectives are multidisciplinary. These and other forms of cultural criticism typically include the perspectives of both humanistic disciplines, such as literature and art, and the social and behavioral sciences, such as anthropology, economics, and psychology. The idea of cultural studies, however, is broader than any of the particular critical perspectives described in this chapter. Cultural studies are not restricted, for example, to structuralist or deconstructionist critical procedures, nor are they solely concerned with feminist issues or Marxist causes.

As a critical perspective in the late twentieth century, cultural studies employs a definition of culture that differs from two other common ways of considering it. Traditionally, and especially from the perspective of anthropology, culture has been considered as the way of life of a people, including its customs, beliefs, and attitudes, all of which cohere in a unified and organic way of life. This traditional anthropological notion has coexisted with another idea, one of culture as representing the best that a civilization has produced—in its institutions, its political and philosophical thought, its art, literature, music, architecture and other lasting achievements.

Both of these ways of viewing culture are contested by the newer forms of cultural studies, which look not at the stable coherences of a society or a civilization's history, but at its dissensions and conflicts. For the newer versions of cultural criticism, the unifying concerns and values of older forms of cultural study are suspect, largely because they avoid issues of political and social inequality. In fact, one way of viewing the current debate over the humanities described in an earlier section of this chapter, "The Canon and the Curriculum," is as a conflict between the older view of cultural studies that emphasizes a kind of normative national cultural consensus, and newer versions, which challenge such norms and values and question the very idea of cultural consensus. Moreover, the different goals and procedures of these contrasting cultural studies perspectives, along with the differences among the critical perspectives described earlier, powerfully illustrate how nearly everything now associated with literate culture has become contested. These areas of contestation include not only the meaning of "culture," but the meaning of teaching, learning, reading, and writing, along with notions of text, author, meaning, criticism, discipline, and department. Cultural studies perspectives breach the traditional understanding of these terms, in the process redrawing the boundaries that formerly separated them.

The notion of boundaries, in fact, is one of the more helpful metaphors for thinking about the new cultural studies. That some new emergent critical schools overlap or that critical perspectives may combine forces suggests how disciplinary borders are being crossed and their boundaries reconfigured. In addition to crossing geographical and intellectual boundaries (as well as those between high and popular culture), the new cultural studies also envision a plurality of cultures rather than seeing "Culture" with a capital "C" as singular, monolithic, or universal.

Thinking from a Cultural Studies Perspective

In considering literary works and other kinds of canonical and noncanonical texts from the various standpoints of cultural studies, it is important to note that no single approach, method, or procedure prevails. There is, then, no single "cultural studies" perspective on Shakespeare's *Othello* or Ibsen's *A Doll House*. Rather there are various ways of thinking about the cultural and social issues embedded in these works. Some of these issues have been raised in the explanations of feminist, Marxist, new historicist, structuralist, and deconstructionist critical perspectives.

One additional cultural studies perspective that has recently gained prominence is that of *gender criticism,* more specifically gay and lesbian studies. Gender criticism and studies overlap, to some extent, with feminist critical perspectives. In addition to studying the relations between and among men, gender criticism also explores such intra-gender issues of women as lesbian sexuality and female power relations.

One of the central problems of gender studies is the way gender is defined. To what extent, for example, does gender overlap with sex? To what extent is gender a cultural category and sex a biological one? To what extent do the language of sexuality used in the past and the current uses of both "sex" and "gender" as categories reflect biological, psychological, and socially constructed elements of sexual difference? Related to these overlapping questions are others, especially considerations of what some gender critics see as heterosocial or heterosexist bias in the very concept of gender and gender relations.

Gender critics share with adherents of other socially oriented perspectives a concern for analyzing power relations and for discerning ways in which homophobic discourse and attitudes prevail in society at large. Through analysis of various forms of historical evidence and through acts of political agency, gender critics have challenged perspectives that view homosexual acts and unions as "sinful" or "diseased." They have questioned the way AIDS has been represented in the mainstream media and have opened up discussion about what constitutes such apparently familiar notions as "family," "love," and "sexual identity."

A CHECKLIST OF GENDER STUDIES CRITICAL QUESTIONS

1. What kinds of sexual identity, behavior, and attitudes are reflected in the work? Is there any overtly or covertly expressed view of homosexuality or lesbianism?
2. To what extent does the work accommodate, describe, or exemplify same-sex relationships? To what extent are same-sex sexual relationships either in the foreground or background of the work?
3. With what kinds of social, economic, and cultural privileges (or lack thereof) are same-sex unions or relationships depicted? With what effects and consequences?

Cultural Studies: Selected Readings

Butler, Judith. *Gender Trouble.* 1989.
Comley, Nancy, and Robert Scholes. *Hemingway's Genders.* 1994.
Giroux, Henry. *Border Crossings.* 1992.
Gunn, Giles. *The Culture of Criticism and the Criticism of Culture.* 1987.
Sedgwick, Eve Kosofsky. *Between Men: English Literature and Male Homosexual Desire.* 1985.
Sedgwick, Eve Kosofsky. *Epistemology of the Closet.* 1990.
Tompkins, Jane. *Sensational Designs: The Cultural Work of American Fiction 1790–1860.* 1985.
Torgovnick, Marianna DeMarco. *Crossing Ocean Parkway.* 1994.

USING CRITICAL PERSPECTIVES AS HEURISTICS

One of your more difficult decisions regarding critical theory will be in choosing a critical perspective that is suitable and effective in analyzing a particular literary work. You might be able to offer, for example, a Marxist, deconstructionist, or feminist reading of "Humpty Dumpty" or "Little Bo Peep," even though these nursery rhymes may not be conventionally approached from any of those critical perspectives. You will need to decide whether one of those approaches offers a richer yield than a more traditional approach, such as formalism or myth criticism. The same is true of your approach to such plays as Shakespeare's *Hamlet* or Ibsen's *A Doll House*. Although these works have been discussed in this chapter from ten critical perspectives, you probably found that certain critical perspectives made a better interpretive fit than others.

Another thing to remember is that you can combine critical perspectives. There is no rule of interpretation that says you must limit yourself to the language and method of a single critical approach or method. You may wish, for example, to combine formalist and structural perspectives. Or you may wish to combine new historicist critical concerns with those of a biographical, psychological, or structuralist approach. In some ways, in fact, various concerns of the critical perspectives explained in this chapter overlap. Feminists raise historical questions as well as psychological and biographical ones. Reader-response critics attend to structuralist and formalist issues. And new historicist critics may employ formalist or deconstructionist methods of close reading.

A danger in using any critical approach to literature is that literary texts are read with an eye toward making them conform to a particular critical theory rather than using that critical theory to illuminate the text. In the process, critics may distort the text of a literary work by quoting from it selectively or by ignoring aspects of it that do not fit their theoretical approach or conform to their interpretive perspective. Some critics, moreover, apply their favorite critical perspective in a mechanical way, so that every work of literature is read with an eye toward proving the same ideological point, regardless of how important the issue is in one work as compared with another. Or critics may put all works of literature through an identical ideological meat grinder with every work emerging ground into the same kind of critical hamburger.

The various critical perspectives you have been learning about should be used as ways to think about literary works rather than as formulas for grinding out a particular kind of interpretation. Try to see the various critical perspectives as interpretive possibilities, as intellectual vistas that open up literary works rather than as stultifying formulas that limit what can be seen in them. Try, as well, to experience the element of intellectual playfulness, the imaginative energy and resourcefulness used in thinking with and through these critical perspectives.

Perhaps the best way to consider these and other critical perspectives is as *heuristics,* or methods for generating ideas, in this case, ideas about literature. A heuristic often takes the form of a set of questions. Writers and speakers use a sequence of questions to think through a topic in preparation for writing or speaking about it. Greek and Roman rhetoricians developed heuristics for generating ideas and for developing and organizing their thinking by using sets of questions that would enable them to think through a subject from a variety of perspectives. They used questions that invited comparison and contrast, definition and classification, analysis and division of a topic.

You can do the same with the critical perspectives described in this chapter. Instead of the classical questions that encourage comparison or causal analysis, use the questions that accompany each of the critical perspectives. Rather than deciding at first just which critical perspective is best suited to your chosen literary work, jot down answers to the questions for each of the approaches. As you think and write, you will begin to see which critical perspectives yield the most helpful ideas, which, that is, prompt your best thinking. In the course of using the critical questions to stimulate your thinking, you will also decide whether to use one critical perspective or to combine a few. You will also decide what you wish to say about the work. And you will begin to discover why you see it as you do, what you value in it, and how you can substantiate your way of seeing and experiencing it.

In addition, try to consider these critical perspectives as opportunities to engage in a play of mind. Viewing a literary work (or other cultural artifact) from a variety of critical perspectives will enable you to see more of its possibilities of signification. It will also give you a chance to live inside a variety of critical methods, to put on a number of different critical hats. Try to enjoy the experience.

CHAPTER TEN

Writing with Sources

WHY DO RESEARCH ABOUT LITERATURE?

One reason to do research about the literary works you read and study is to understand them better. Another is to see how they have been interpreted over the years, perhaps even centuries, since they were written. Moreover, scholars who have devoted their lives to the study of particular authors, periods, and genres can provide insights that can enrich your understanding and deepen your appreciation of literature.

Reading and studying literature in an academic environment also often requires research. You may be required to read books and articles about an author or a work, using your research in an essay on a literary topic. This is a fairly standard requirement in both general introductory literature courses and in more specialized courses for literature majors.

Even if research on the literature you read is not a requirement, you may find that what others who have read the same works have to say provides a stimulus for your own ideas. For example, you can use *The Humanities Index,* the *MLA Bibliography,* or your library's computerized catalog (see "Using Computerized Databases" in this chapter) to find articles about many of the selections in this book. You can also use *The New York Times Index* and *Book Review Digest* to find reviews of collections of short stories, essays, poems, or plays.

Locate several articles or reviews on a work you have read and, as you read them, notice when you have a particularly strong reaction. You may disagree with what you read, you may be surprised by a new point of view, or you may find your own opinions reinforced in a way you had not expected. You may find that one or more of the works consulted provides the spark for a fully developed essay of your own.

Research materials consist of two general kinds: primary sources and secondary sources. *Primary sources* are firsthand accounts, such as historical documents, diaries, journals, letters, and original literary works, including novels, stories, poems, plays, and essays. Primary sources constitute raw evidence you can use for your research paper. *Secondary sources* are materials written about primary sources. Secondary sources include critical writing that expresses opinions, draws conclusions, or explains an issue. Secondary sources include books, articles, pamphlets, and reviews.

CLARIFYING THE ASSIGNMENT

It is critical that you understand thoroughly the requirements of the assignment. Does your instructor expect you to write a three-page paper or a twenty-page paper—or, as is more likely, something in between? Are you expected to type your paper double-spaced? Are you required to use primary sources, secondary sources, or both? How many words, how many pages, and how many sources are required?

Are you expected to focus on a single work using only one or two sources, on a single work using multiple sources, on multiple works by an author—or something else? Are you expected to document your sources and to provide a list of works you cite in the paper? Be sure that you clarify the specific requirements of the assignment.

SELECTING A TOPIC

Instructors sometimes provide topics, either by assigning everyone the same topic (or some variation of it) or by giving individual students assigned topics of their own. If that is your situation, you can skip down to the next section on finding and using sources. Most often, however, you will need to choose your own topic for a paper utilizing literary research.

You can do a number of things to simplify the task of finding a topic. First, ask your instructor for suggestions. Second, look over your class notes and your reading notes for key points of emphasis, recurrent concerns, and interesting questions and ideas. Third, talk with other students, both with your classmates and with students who have already written papers for the course you are taking. Fourth, you can consult other sources with information about the author and work (or works) you will be writing about. Any or all of these can provide guidance and suggestions about viable topics for your paper.

A *viable topic* is one you can manage in the allotted number of pages required for the assignment. It should also be a topic you can say something about in detail and with specificity. Once you have settled on a topic, it's a good idea to clear it with your instructor. Once your instructor sees what you're interested in, he or she can help you shape the topic, perhaps by narrowing or broadening it in ways that might make it more manageable or potentially more interesting, or both.

As a general guideline for literary papers, try to turn your topic into a question that your research paper answers. This question need not be explicit in your topic, but it should emerge in the opening paragraphs of your paper, either explicitly or implicitly, as you present your thesis.

FINDING AND USING SOURCES

Researchers have a number of tools available for finding secondary sources—critical studies of authors, analyses of their works, and relevant biographical, social, and historical background material. Your school library's computer databases of books and articles provide comprehensive listings of such sources. But even before tapping into those databases you can consult books in the library reference room as a preliminary step. General reference works about literature can give you an overview of an author's life and work, an introduction to a genre, such as tragedy or epic, or an understanding of a critical approach, such as new historicism, or provide some other kind of generalized prelude to the more focused search you will undertake once you have refined your topic and decided how to proceed with your research.

Works you may find helpful as preliminary guides to literary research include the following:

> *Columbia Literary History of the United States.* Ed. Emory Elliot et al. New York: Columbia University Press, 1988.
>
> *An Encyclopedia of Continental Women Writers.* Ed. Katharina Wilson. 2 vols. New York: Garland, 1991.
>
> *Encyclopedia of World Literature in the Twentieth Century.* Ed. Leonard S. Klein. 5 vols. Rev. ed. New York: Continuum, 1983–1984.
>
> *European Writers.* George Stade and William T. Jackson. 7 vols. New York: Macmillan, 1983–1985.
>
> *Longman Companion to Twentieth-Century Literature.* Ed. A. C. Ward. 3rd ed. New York: Longman, 1981.
>
> *MLA International Bibliography.* Available in print, online, and on CD-ROM. New York: MLA, 1921–.
>
> *The New Cambridge Bibliography of English Literature.* 5 vols. Cambridge: Cambridge UP, 1967–1977.
>
> *The New Guide to Modern World Literature.* Ed. Martin Seymour-Smith. 4 vols. New York: Peter Bedrick Books, 1985.
>
> *The New Princeton Encyclopedia of Poetry and Poetics.* Ed. Alex Preminger and T. V. F. Brogan. Princeton: Princeton UP, 1993.
>
> *The Oxford History of English Literature.* 13 vols. Oxford: Oxford UP, 1945–.
>
> *A Research Guide for Undergraduate Students: English and American Literature.* By Nancy L. Baker. 2nd ed. New York: MLA, 1985.
>
> *Research Guide to Biography and Criticism: Literature.* Ed. Walton Beacham. 2 vols. Osprey, FL: Beacham, 1985.

You can find some or all of these sources in the reference sections of many college libraries.

USING COMPUTERIZED DATABASES

You may have access to your university library with a link from your room, your home, your residence hall, or your school's computer center. You may also be able to access the library's holdings through computer terminals located in the library proper. One of the first things you should do is learn how to use the library's computerized catalog to access bibliographic information. You can get a friend to help you. You can get assistance from the library staff. Your school may even provide formal instructions in use of their online services.

All on-line catalogs are organized in a similar way. The information that is retrieved and displayed on the computer screen depends on the format you use in making your request. Most programs offer at least three search options: author, title, and subject. For example, suppose you know that you want to write about Ernest Hemingway. You don't have a precise topic in mind, and want to consult some books *about* Ernest Hemingway. To find out what books the library has about Hemingway, you would search for "Hemingway, Ernest," as subject. (The program will give you on-screen instructions on how to start the search.) Following is what one university library's online catalog lists for Hemingway as subject:

1. Hemingway, Ernest 1898		1 entry
2. Hemingway, Ernest 1899–1961		52 entries
3. Hemingway, Ernest 1899–1961	Appreciation	1 entry
4. Hemingway, Ernest 1899–1961	Appreciation—Germany	1 entry
5. Hemingway, Ernest 1899–1961	Bibliography	10 entries
6. Hemingway, Ernest 1899–1961	Biography	12 entries
7. Hemingway, Ernest 1899–1961	Juvenile letters	1 entry
8. Hemingway, Ernest 1899–1961	Biography—Marriage	4 entries

Notice that category 2 includes fifty-two items. Since the category has no heading, to determine the kinds of books included within it, you would press 2 and scan the listings. If you press 8, Biography—Marriage, four listings appear:

1. Along with Youth	Griffin, Peter
2. Hadley	Diliberto, Gioia
3. The Hemingway Women	Kert, Bernice
4. How It Was	Hemingway, Mary Welsh

If you want more data on one of these books, press the appropriate number. You will be provided with information about the length and size of the book, its publication date, and location. Most systems also provide information about the book's availability.

In browsing in one of these books about Hemingway's personal life, you might get an idea for a research paper that focuses on the home life depicted in "Soldier's Home." Reading that story in the context of secondary biographical sources would be one way to gain added insight into the story. Another would be to consult critical secondary sources that are less biographical than analytical and interpretive. Here you would return to that large category of 52 items and begin scanning for titles that appeared promising. One such title is Paul Smith's *A Reader's Guide to the Short Stories of Ernest Hemingway* (Boston: G. K. Hall, 1989). After locating a few such sources, you are ready to read and take notes as you work toward refining your topic and developing a thesis for your paper.

USING THE INTERNET FOR RESEARCH

Through the Internet you can connect to the World Wide Web (WWW), a system of linked electronic documents. Navigating the WWW involves connecting to electronic pathways within and between Web pages and Web sites. Accessing various Web sites for information requires either a specific Internet address or use of a search engine, such as YAHOO or InfoSeek, which allows you to enter key words for the topic you wish to research.

To make use of the Internet for your literary research, follow these guidelines:

- Link your computer to the Internet, open your web browser, and call up the browser's home page.
- Go to the browser's search options and select a search engine.
- Enter the words you want to search (key words for your topic).
- Survey the list of "hits" the search engine provides.
- Click on any related hyperlinks that seem interesting.
- Skim each site and download those that appear promising. (Store their addresses for future use.)

Using the Internet for research can be fun. But it can also prove a formidable challenge. One problem you may confront is a large number of hits or potential sources. Deciding which of these are of most value requires careful analysis. This is due largely to the openness of the World Wide Web. Since anyone can put up a Web site and place any information on that site, you cannot be certain that the site's information is accurate, current, or unbiased.

You therefore must evaluate Internet sources for their reliability. You can use the following guidelines to do so.

- Consider the source of the electronic information you discover. Consider the credentials of the source provider. Is the source maintained by a reputable provider, such as a university or corporation?
- Compare your electronic sources with your print sources. Evaluate your electronic sources for range and depth as well as accuracy and currency of information.
- Ask yourself whether you are sufficiently confident of the source's reliability to cite it in your research paper.

For guidance in documenting electronic sources, see p. 669.

DEVELOPING A CRITICAL PERSPECTIVE

How can you use outside critical sources to develop a critical perspective? Let us say, for example, that you are required to write a five- or six-page paper analyzing and interpreting a particular literary work. Let us speculate further that you are required to read and cite in your paper two or three outside sources. And let us also imagine that you have been asked to select critical sources that provide different interpretive perspectives on the work you will be writing about. What will you do? How will you go about writing this paper?

One technique useful for writing critical papers is quoting key passages and commenting on their significance or validity. In writing a paper about Hemingway's "Soldier's Home," for example, you could (and perhaps should) quote a bit of the story directly. Or you might select a few such passages for direct quotation. Of more importance than your apt selection of such passages, however, is the way you relate them in your comments explaining their significance. The way to get a start on this crucial process is to record the relevant passages verbatim and practice commenting on their significance. These comments will provide the germ from which your paper will grow.

In using outside critical sources you will find yourself usually doing one of two things. Either you will agree with the critic and use his or her comments to bolster your interpretation. Or you will disagree and take exception to the critic's ideas by arguing against them in your paper. Both are acceptable ways to proceed. In fact, given a requirement to include more than two sources, it is highly unlikely that you will agree entirely with the positions taken in all of them. Thus even if you agree in part, you will need to make distinctions and to express qualified approval as you modify their viewpoints and express the reservations necessary to make them congruent with your own ideas.

DEVELOPING A THESIS

You should be able to state your thesis in a single direct sentence. Your thesis concentrates in a sentence nutshell what you wish to emphasize—your central idea, the point you wish to make about your topic. Your essay overall elaborates your thesis, providing evidence in the form of textual support.

In general, when you develop your thesis, try to make it as specific as you can. At the same time, try to avoid oversimplifying your idea by setting up mutually exclusive "black and white" categories. Introduce qualifying terms as necessary. Words such as "although," "however," "but," and "rather" suggest an approach that reflects thoughtful consideration of the issues.

Consider Lucienne Retelle's thesis as she analyzes Alice Walker's story "Everyday Use" in the context of a critical article she read about the work. Here is her thesis:

> In relating the story ["Everyday Use"] to the Biblical Prodigal Son, Patricia Kane shows thoughtfulness and insight; however, in her eagerness to expose what she sees as differences in male/female values, she demonstrates a superficial understanding of the Gospel parable and misses the central message: one of repentance and forgiveness.

Notice how Ms. Retelle takes issue with the critical perspective offered by Patricia Kane. She uses the critic's view as a springboard from which to launch her own analysis of the story as one whose central concerns are the prodigal son's repentance and his father's forgiveness. Her thesis is clear, direct, and specific. We know what she thinks. It remains for her to flesh out her interpretation and to refute Patricia Kane's argument.

DRAFTING AND REVISING

In writing your research paper, follow the guidelines for drafting and revising your paper just as you would for an interpretive paper in which you do not use secondary sources. Set aside sufficient time to work out the basic argument of your research paper. This will involve the extra time necessary for tracking down sources, taking notes, and reflecting on their significance for your overall argument.

In your preliminary draft you should try to articulate your argument without your sources. Get your ideas down as clearly as you can. Provide the textual support you need as evidence from the work(s) you are analyzing or otherwise discussing. Then write a second draft in which you incorporate the relevant sources either to support your idea or as representing antithetical views that you attempt to refute.

Leave time for a third draft in which you further refine your thinking, taking into consideration additional evidence you find in the text or in the secondary sources. Use this third draft also to provide precise documentation for your sources—accurate parenthetical citations and precise page references.

In general, approach the drafting of a research essay or paper as you would any other essay or assignment. Make sure you get your own ideas into the initial draft before you begin relying on your secondary sources. This is critical if you want to avoid letting your sources take over the voice and content of your research essay.

CONVENTIONS

In writing about literary works you need to observe a number of conventions, including those regarding quotations, verb tenses, manuscript form, and the strict avoidance of plagiarism.

Using Quotations

In writing about literature you will need to quote lines from poems, dialogue from plays and stories, and descriptive and explanatory passages from prose fiction and nonfiction. For quoted prose passages that exceed four typed lines in your paper, begin a new line and indent ten spaces from the left margin for each line of the quotation. This format, called block quotation, does not require quotation marks because the blocked passage is set off visually from the rest of your text.

When quoting poetry, separate the lines of poetry with slashes. Include a space before and after each slash.

> Lorraine Hansberry derived the title of her best-known play, *A Raisin in the Sun,* from a poem by Langston Hughes. In "Dream Deferred," the speaker asks, "What happens to a dream deferred? / Does it dry up / like a raisin in the sun?"

Verb Tense Conventions in Literary Papers

In writing about literature, you will often need to describe a story, novel, poem, or play. In doing so you will use present tense, past tense, or both. In most instances, it is conventional to use present tense when describing what happens in a literary work. Consider the following examples:

> In Robert Hayden's "Those Winter Sundays," the speaker <u>reflects</u> on his father and <u>realizes</u> how much his father <u>loved</u> the family.

The present tense is used to describe the speaker's actions of reflecting and realizing. The past tense is used to describe the father's action, which occurred in the past, well before the speaker's present acts of reflecting and realizing.

> Ibsen's <u>A Doll House</u> <u>portrays</u> a conventional middle-class environment and a conventional middle-class family. In displaying a strong concern for money and for authority, Ibsen's characters <u>reveal</u> their middle-class values. Ibsen often <u>portrayed</u> characters with everyday problems of the middle class.

The verbs describing what the play does are in the present tense. Those describing what the dramatist did are in past tense.

Manuscript Form

In preparing your paper for submission, observe the following guidelines:

1. Type your essay double-spaced on 8 1/2-inch by 11-inch paper.
2. Leave 1-inch margins at the top and bottom, and on both sides.
3. Beginning in the upper-left corner 1 inch below the top and 1 inch from the left side, type the following on separate lines:
   (a) your name
   (b) your instructor's name
   (c) course title, number, and section
   (d) date

4. Double-space below the date and center your title. It is not necessary to put quotation marks around your title or to underline or italicize it. It is necessary to underline titles of books and plays used in your title. And it is necessary to put quotation marks around the titles of short stories, poems, and essays.
5. Be sure your printer's ink supply or your typewriter ribbon is adequate for clear, readable copy.
6. If your printer feeds connected sheets of paper, be sure to separate them before submitting your essay.
7. Number each page consecutively beginning with the second page, 1/2 inch from the upper-right corner.
8. Clip or staple the paper, making sure the pages are right side up and in the correct numerical order.

Plagiarism

Plagiarism is the act of using someone else's words, ideas, or organizational patterns without crediting the source. Plagiarism may be the result of careless note taking, or may be deliberate. To avoid plagiarism, it is necessary to clearly indicate what you have borrowed so your reader can distinguish your own language and ideas from those of your sources.

Research essays and papers written with little original thought and containing many long passages of quoted and summarized material strung together may include plagiarized words and ideas. Be sure to credit each source you use at the point of borrowing, even in the midst of a paragraph or the middle of a sentence. Be sure not only to acknowledge using the source but also, if you have used exact language from the source, to put quotation marks around the borrowed words and phrases—even if you have separated some of the borrowed material and interspersed your own language.

Plagiarism is a serious offense. A form of academic theft, plagiarism is not tolerated in colleges and universities. Some have stringent policies, including failure for the course in which the plagiarism occurs and even expulsion from school.

To avoid plagiarism observe the following guidelines in writing your research essays and papers.

• Develop your own ideas about the works you read. Keep notes of your ideas separate from the notes you take from sources.
• Jot the title, author, and page number of a source on the page or notecard you use for your notes pertaining to material from that source.
• Put quotation marks around quoted material you copy from sources into your notes.
• When you summarize and paraphrase a source, be sure to use your own words. Avoid having the source open before you when you summarize and paraphrase.

- If you introduce any quotations from a source into your summaries and paraphrases of them, put quotation marks around the quoted words and phrases.
- Make sure that your own ideas and your own voice are the controlling centers in your research essays and papers. Use your sources to support, illustrate, and amplify your own thinking presented in your own words.
- Observe the conventions for documentation provided in the following section of this book, in your college handbook, and in the *MLA Handbook for Writers of Research Papers,* 5th ed. (1999).

DOCUMENTING SOURCES

If you incorporate the work of others into your paper, it will be necessary to credit your sources through documentation. You should always provide source credit when quoting directly, paraphrasing (rewriting a passage in your own words), borrowing ideas, or picking up facts that aren't general knowledge.

By crediting your sources, you are participating honestly and correctly in shared intellectual activity. You are showing your reader that your knowledge of a text includes some insights into what others have thought and said about it. And you are assisting your reader, who may want to consult the sources that you found valuable.

Established conventions for documenting sources vary from one academic discipline to another. For research essays and papers in literature and language the preferred style is that of the Modern Language Association (MLA). MLA documentation style has established conventions for citing sources within the text of research essays, papers, and articles. It also has established conventions for the list of works you use in preparing your research writing—usually called "List of Works Cited" or "Works Cited."

In the current MLA style, parenthetical citations within the text indicate that a source has been used. These citations refer the reader to a reference list, which should start on a new page at the end of the paper. In the "alternate" or "old" MLA style, references are marked by raised numbers in the text that correspond to numbered notes either at the foot of the page (footnotes) or the end of the paper (endnotes). Both the reference list and the endnotes and footnotes contain bibliographic information about the sources; however, the arrangement, punctuation, and capitalization of the sources differs between the two reference styles.

New MLA Style: Parenthetical Citations Paired with a Reference List

When you refer to a specific section of a work in the body of your paper, provide your reader with the author and page numbers of your source. Place the page numbers in parentheses, and add the author's name if it isn't contained in your sentence.

> According to Lawrence Lipking (30–39), a poet's life involves much more than his or her literal biography.

> A recent critic argues that a poet's life involves much more than his or her literal biography (Lipking 30–39).

If your paper includes two or more works by the same author, add the title of the work before the page number(s). The following are examples of other kinds of citations commonly found in literature papers.

A work in an anthology:

> Bacon's "Of Revenge" affords us a glimpse at his view of human nature: "There is no man doth a wrong for the wrong's sake, but thereby to purchase himself profit, or pleasure, or honor, or the like" (1565).

(The author and title of the anthologized selection should be listed in the *Works Cited*.)

A classic verse play or poem:

> "She loved me for the dangers I had passed," recounts Othello, "And I loved her that she did pity them" (I.iii.166–67).

(Act, scene, and line numbers are used instead of page numbers. Arabic numbers may also be used for the act and scene.)

> Tennyson's Ulysses compares a dull existence to a dull sword when he says: "How dull it is to pause, to make an end, / To rust unburnished, not to shine in use!" (22–23).

(Line numbers are used instead of page numbers. Note the use of a slash [/] to indicate the end of a line.)

Styling a Works Cited List

The items in a works cited list should be alphabetically arranged. The following are typical kinds of entries for a literature paper.

A book by a single author:

> Lipking, Lawrence. *The Life of the Poet: Beginning and Ending Poetic Careers.* Chicago: U of Chicago P, 1981.

(The second line is indented five spaces.)

An article in a book:

> Williams, Sherley Anne. "The Black Musician: The Black Hero as Light Bearer." *James Baldwin: A Collection of Critical Essays.* Ed. Kenneth Kinnamon. Englewood Cliffs, NJ: Prentice-Hall, 1974. 147-54.

(The page numbers "147-54" refer to the entire article. References to specific pages would appear in parenthetical citations.)
  A journal article:

> Walker, Janet. "Hardy's Somber Lyrics." *Poetry* 17 (1976): 25-39.

(The article appeared in issue 17 of the journal *Poetry.* The page numbers refer to the entire article.)
  A work in an anthology:

> Bacon, Francis. "Of Revenge." *Literature: Reading Fiction, Poetry, Drama, and the Essay.* 2nd ed. Ed. Robert DiYanni. New York: McGraw-Hill, 1990. 1565-1655.

(The page numbers refer to the entire essay.)
  Cite the anthology itself if you are using more than one selection from it. The selections can simply be cited without repeating the anthology title and publication data.

> DiYanni, Robert, ed. *Literature: Reading Fiction, Poetry, Drama, and the Essay.* 4th ed. New York: McGraw-Hill, 1998.
> Tennyson, Alfred, Lord. "Ulysses." DiYanni. 649-50.

A multivolume work; a second edition:

> Daiches, David. *A Critical History of English Literature.* 2nd ed. 2 vols. New York: Ronald, 1970.

A translation:

> Auerbach, Erich. *Mimesis: The Representation of Reality in Western Literature.* Trans. Willard Trask. Princeton: Princeton UP, 1953.

Alternate MLA Style: Note Numbers Paired with Endnotes / Footnotes

Using Note Numbers

Raised note numbers, in consecutive order, follow the quotation or information being cited. They belong *after* all punctuation, except a dash.

"She loved me for the dangers I had passed," recounts Othello,
"And I loved her that she did pity them."[1]

If you include several quotations from the same text in your paper, you may
switch to parenthetical citations after the first note. This will reduce the number of footnotes or endnotes.

Emilia tells Desdemona that jealousy is "a monster begot upon
itself, born on itself" (III.iv.155-56).

Using Endnotes/Footnotes

Each raised note number corresponds to a footnote or endnote. The only difference between footnotes and endnotes is their placement in the paper. Footnotes appear at the bottom of the page on which the reference occurs:
quadruple-space between the last line of text and the first note. Endnotes are
grouped together on a separate page immediately following the last page of text.
The following are the same sources given above, but now in endnote form.
Note that specific page references are given for each entry; these page references would be contained in parentheses in new MLA style.

[1]Lawrence Lipking, *The Life of the Poet: Beginning and Ending
Poetic Careers* (Chicago: U of Chicago P, 1981) 30-39.
[2]Sherley Anne Williams, "The Black Musician: The Black
Hero as Light Bearer," in *James Baldwin: A Collection of Critical Essays,* ed. Kenneth Kinnamon (Englewood Cliffs, NJ: Prentice-
Hall, 1974) 147.
[3]Janet Walker, "Hardy's Somber Lyrics," *Poetry* 17 (1976): 35.
[4]Francis Bacon, "Of Revenge," *Literature: Reading Fiction, Poetry, Drama, and the Essay,* 2nd ed., ed. Robert DiYanni (New
York: McGraw-Hill, 1990) 1565-66.
[5]David Daiches, *A Critical History of English Literature,* 2nd ed.,
2 vols. (New York: Ronald, 1970) 2: 530.
[6]Erich Auerbach, *Mimesis: The Representation of Reality in Western
Literature,* trans. Willard Trask (Princeton: Princeton UP, 1953) 77.

Noting Subsequent References

It is usually enough simply to list the author's name and the appropriate page(s)
in subsequent references to a source.

[7]Lipking 98.

DOCUMENTING ELECTRONIC SOURCES

The MLA Handbook for writers of Research Papers, 5th ed., distinguishes electronic citation forms according to whether the material is available on a CD-ROM or whether it is available online. Because electronic media are continually changing, the details of citations may evolve even as the basic needs for citing references remain the same.

Source on CD-ROM

Citations for electronic sources are distinguished according to whether the material was published once, like a book, or whether it is published in regularly updated periodical form.

CD Produced as a One-Time Publication

Author's name followed by the title underlined; editor, compiler, or translator if relevant. Publication medium; edition, release, or version if relevant; place of publication; name of publisher; date of publication.

> French, William P., ed. *Database of African-American Poetry, 1760–1900.* CD-ROM. Alexandria, VA: Chadwyck-Healy, 1995.

If you wish to cite part of a work, place quotation marks around the part or section you cite. Underline the title of the work as a whole. If you are not provided with an author, begin your citation with the title.

> "Modernism." *The Oxford English Dictionary.* 2nd ed. CD-ROM. Oxford: Oxford UP, 1992.

CD Updated Periodically

Author or institution name followed by a period. Article's title and original date or inclusive dates in quotation marks. Database name underlined followed by type of source (CD, for example). Locator and provider or the vendor of the database if available; date of publication.

> Smith, Dinitia. "Hollywood Adopts the Canon." *New York Times* 10 Nov. 1996: D4. New York Times Ondisc. CD-ROM. UMI–Proquest. Dec. 1996.

If you cite a CD-ROM multidisk publication, include the total number of disks if you use them all, or the disk number(s) for the one(s) you wish to cite.

> *Patrologia Latina Database.* CD-ROM. 5 discs. Alexandria, VA:
> Chadwyck-Healey, 1995.

Online Sources

When citing Internet sources include the Internet address or URL (uniform resource locator) in brackets < >. Provide the entire address, including the access–mode identifier (http, ftp, gopher, telnet, news).

Online Scholarly Project or Reference Database

Title underlined; editor if given followed by electronic publication information, date or latest update, and name of sponsoring institution if provided. Date of access and electronic address in angle brackets.

> *African American Women Writers of the Nineteenth Century.* Ed.
> Thomas P. Lukas. 1999. Digital Schomburg, New York
> Public Library. 11 May 1999
> <http//digital.nypl.org/schomburg/sriters_aal19/>.

Online Professional or Personal Site

Name of person who created the site, title of site underlined or italicized; if no title is given, provide a title such as Home Page. Name of institution or organization associated with the site, date of access, and electronic address.

> Pace University Home Page. Pace. 3 Dec. 1998
> <http://www.pace.edu/>.

Online Book

Author's name, title underlined or italicized; name of editor, compiler, or translator if relevant. City of publication, publisher, year of publication. Date of access and electronic address.

> Alice Dunbar-Nelson. The Goodness of St. Rocque and Other
> Stories. New York: Dodd, Mead, 1899. African Ameri-
> can Women Writers of the Nineteenth Century. Ed.
> Thomas P. Lukas. 1999. Digital Schomburg, New York
> Public Library. 11 May 1999
> <http://digilib.nypl.org/dynaweb/
> digs-f/wwm976/@Generic_BookView>.

Online Periodical Article

Author, title of article, title of journal or magazine, volume, number, year, and date for scholarly journal; date for magazine; electronic address.

Scholarly Journal

Pereira, Edimilson de Almeida. "Survey of African-Brazilian Literature." *Callaloo* 18.4 (1995): 875–80. 11 Apr. 1997 <http://muse.jhu.edu/journals/callaloo/v0l8/18.4de_almeida_pereira9.html>.

Magazine

Landsburg, Steven E. "Who Shall Inherit the Earth?" *Slate* 1 May 1997. 2 May 1997 <http://slate.com/Economics/97-05-01/Economics.asp>.

A STUDENT PAPER INCORPORATING RESEARCH

The Role of Gender in Communications

Raiza Herrera
Dr. Linda Anstendig
English 102
May 3, 1999

Misperceptions inherent in gender communication create chasms
that divide the sexes and leave them to interpret situations
in incompatible ways. These communication differences form a
basis for their thought and decision making processes which
goes beyond the language. In *Trifles* by Susan Glaspell and in
A Doll's House by Henrik Ibsen, the male characters express
authoritative and controlling characteristics in their
language, reflecting a lack of interest in matters relating to
the female characters. Conversely, in both plays, the females
display indirect and submissive communication styles, which
resonate in their subservient attitude and status. This
communication style, however, ultimately gains them power
beyond that of the male characters.

In *Trifles* the men clearly demonstrate two distinct styles
of communication: a strong, direct style used amongst
themselves for the purpose of investigating the crime, and a
patronizing style reserved for the women for the purpose of
discussing the trifles of the women's lives—housework,
canning preserves, and needlework. Deborah Tannen, a professor
of linguistics at Georgetown University, uses the term
"report-talk" to describe the direct style men use among
themselves (Tanner, *You Just* 77). Report-talk, according to
Tannen, is conversation that relays information. This style of
conversation negotiates the upper hand in a conversation and
protects the speaker from others' perceived attempts to put
him down. When discussing the women's concern for Mrs.
Wright's preserves, the County Attorney remarks in a good-
natured but superior manner, "And yet, for all their worries,
what would we do without the ladies?" (Glaspell 1376). He goes
on to say, "Well, ladies, have you decided whether she was
going to quilt it or just knot it?" (1381). This particular
question—"was [she] going to quilt it or just knot it"—is
asked by the County Attorney multiple times. The irony is that
the answer to that question has the possibility of revealing a
great deal about the crime—but it is a trifle. The County
Attorney's controlling conversation style turns the focus of
the investigation on the things *he* thinks are important—the
barn, the rope and the bedroom—blinding him to the clues that
lie within the cloth of Mrs. Wright's life—the kitchen, the
canning, and the quilting.

When the County Attorney is speaking to Mrs. Hale, she
mentions that Mr. Wright was not well liked. The County
Attorney takes notice of this for a moment and makes a casual
inquiry about it, but never pursues further, possibly thinking
that a clue from the women could not be a clue at all. Yet he
does ask again and again about the knotting versus quilting
dilemma, demonstrating his desire to only pursue a

conversation where he feels he has the upper hand, and one where his authority will not be threatened. The paradox in both *A Doll's House* and *Trifles* is that the men can obtain the truth if they learn how to read and respect the place in which the women's lives are lived.

In *A Doll's House* Torvald's conversation is peppered with strong hints of this petty style, and his fear of not having control. For instance, Torvald tells Nora that the reason Krogstad can no longer work at the bank is because he refers to Torvald by his Christian name: "It's acutely irritating. It would make my position at the bank intolerable" (Ibsen 40). This gesture of familiarity threatens Torvald's sense of authority and reduces his status to at least equal to that of Krogstad. This insecurity is further emphasized by the condescending manner he uses when speaking to Nora. By frequently referring to his wife as "funny little creature," "squanderbird," "little songbird," and "expensive pet," Torvald's language asserts his authority over Nora proclaiming him as the alpha-dog in this verbal battle.

The female equivalent of report-talk is "rapport-talk." This language style, primarily used by women, seeks intimacy and negotiates closeness in which people try to seek and give confirmation and support, and to reach consensus (Tannen, *You Just* 77). A characteristic of this communication style is "indirectness" (77). Indirectness, according to Tannen, is typically perceived as a style which demonstrates powerlessness or subordination of women, but can be quite powerful and, used strategically, can advance one toward achievement of one's goal (Tannen, *Gender & Discourse* 32). Indirectness has the benefits of defensiveness and rapport, which build a bond, "solidarity," among those doing the communicating. Mrs. Peters and Mrs. Hale in *Trifles* through indirect communication develop a rapport of solidarity which ultimately leads them not only to solve the motive of the crime, but to reach an unspoken consensus regarding the fate of Mrs. Wright. The women are able to accomplish this because of the intimate relationship they have formed with each other and the absent Mrs. Wright. Mrs. Hale expresses feelings of cohesion with Mrs. Wright by remarking, "I might have known she needed help[...] We all go through the same things—it's all just a different kind of the same thing" (Glaspell 1382). This relationship is possible because the women are able to view the situation from Mrs. Wright's perspective, and through empathy, validate the surroundings which are the reality of her life.

This perspective of empathy creates a foundation for female values, determining morality based on human justice versus legalities. Psychologist Carol Gilligan learned through psychological testing that men and women use a "different voice" in their thought and language process. Gilligan discovered that there are critical differences in men's and women's approaches to moral problem-solving that are reflected in their "voice." The differences, she stresses, are generated by a combination of the moral dilemma one finds oneself in, the status of those involved, and their gender (Gilligan). According to Gilligan the very traits that have been traditionally associated with women's goodness, their concern for and sensitivity to the needs of others, are the qualities that have led psychologists to describe them as morally inferior to men. Gilligan argues that the issue is not one of moral superiority or inferiority, but rather that men and women have "two disparate modes of experience" that affect their values and views of the world (101).

Women see the world and make decisions based on cultural and relational experiences. They see moral problems in terms of responsibilities, more than abstract principles of justice. These feelings of responsibility are the catalyst for Mrs. Hale and Mrs. Peters's determination that though a man was killed by his wife, the wife's spirit was murdered long before that by the man, and so justice has been done and "emotional" time has been served.

For Nora this principle of moral responsibility becomes a classic case of the ends justifying the means. The act of forgery serves to save Torvald's life, as well as his pride. When rationalizing her heroic decision to save her husband's life, Nora tells Christine, "Then I made up my mind that he had to be saved in spite of himself—and thought of a way" (Ibsen 15). Nora tells her friend Christine, "He's much too strict in matters of that sort. And besides—Torvald could never bear to think of owing anything to me! It would hurt his self-respect—wound his pride" (215). For Nora it is self-evident that the well-being of the one she loves is her responsibility and takes precedence over everything else. It is incomprehensible to her that the world would not use the same moral compass to measure actions that serve a greater good.

Keen awareness of any behavior, but particularly language, can be advantageous toward achieving goals. The women in *Trifles* share a moment of consciousness where they realize that they are underdogs in this language game where straightforwardness will get them nowhere. In the closing of the story the County Attorney takes his final shot at the women by facetiously remarking, "Well, Henry, at least we found out that she was not going to quilt it. She was going to—what is it you call it, ladies?" "We call it—knot it, Mr. Henderson" (Glaspell 1383) replies Mrs. Hale as she puts her hand against the pocket where she is concealing the evidence the men have desperately been searching for. Instead of charging head-on into the offense, the women wisely choose subtlety and indirectness to strategically advance them toward the goal, which they successfully meet, scoring the winning touchdown.

Both *Trifles* and *A Doll's House* reflect the incompatibilities of communications for men and women, which lead to misunderstandings. This is a situation that in spite of our education and sophistication we still struggle with today, and a problem that is responsible for the breakdown of male-female relationships. Men still tend to primarily use communication to report facts, and women use it to express feelings of intimacy. The problem is intensified when a woman expresses a feeling—"I want more romance," and the man interprets it as a fact—"Are you saying I'm not romantic?" The issue is not whether one form of expression is superior to the other, or whether one is right and the other is wrong—it is simply that men and women have different communication styles. It follows that we all need to become not only better communicators, but also better translators.

Works Cited

Gilligan, Carol. *In a Different Voice: Psychological Theory and Women's Development.* Cambridge, MA: Harvard UP, 1993.

Glaspell, Susan. "Trifles." *Literature: Reading Fiction, Poetry, Drama, and the Essay.* Ed. Robert DiYanni. 4th ed. New York: McGraw-Hill, 1998. 1373-83.

Ibsen, Henrik. *A Doll's House. Eight Plays by Henrik Ibsen.* Trans. Eva Le Gallienne. Modern Library College Editions. New York: McGraw-Hill, 1982. 1-77.

Tannen, Deborah. *Gender and Discourse.* New York: Oxford UP, 1994.

--- *You Just Don't Understand: Men and Women in Communication.* New York: William Morrow, 1990.

Glossary

Allegory   A symbolic narrative in which the surface details imply a secondary meaning. Allegory often takes the form of a story in which the characters represent moral qualities.

Antagonist   A character or force against which a main character struggles.

Aside   Words spoken by an actor directly to the audience, which are not "heard" by the other actors on stage.

Blank verse   A line of poetry or prose in unrhymed iambic pentameter.

Caesura   A strong pause within a line of verse.

Catastrophe   The action at the end of a tragedy that initiates the denouement.

Catharsis   The purging of the feelings of pity and fear that, according to Aristotle, occur in the audience of tragic drama.

Character   An imaginary person that lives in a literary work. Literary characters may be major or minor, static or dynamic.

Characterization   The means by which writers present and reveal character.

Chorus   A group of characters in Greek tragedy who comment on the action of a play without participating in it. Their leader is the choragos.

Climax   The turning point of the action in the plot of a play or story. The climax represents the point of greatest tension in the work.

Comedy   A type of drama in which the characters experience reversals of fortune, usually for the better. In comedy things work out happily in the end. Comic drama may be either romantic—characterized by a tone of tolerance and geniality—or satiric. Satiric plays offer a darker vision of human nature, one that ridicules human folly.

Comic relief   The use of a comic scene to interrupt a succession of intensely tragic dramatic moments. The comedy of scenes offering comic relief typically parallels the tragic action the scenes interrupt.

Complication   An intensification of the conflict in a story or play.

Conflict   A struggle between opposing forces in a story or play, usually resolved by the end of the work.

Connotation   The personal and emotional associations called up by a word that go beyond its dictionary meaning.

Convention   A customary feature of a literary work such as the use of a chorus in Greek tragedy or an explicit moral in a fable.

Denotation   The dictionary meaning of a word.

Denouement   The resolution of the plot of a literary work.

Deus ex machina   A god who resolves the entanglements of a play by supernatural intervention (literally, a god from the machine) or any artificial device used to resolve a plot.

Dialogue   The conversation of characters in a literary work.

Diction   The selection of words in a literary work.

Dramatic monologue   A type of poem in which a speaker addresses a silent listener.

Dramatis Personae   The characters or persons of the play.

Exposition   The first stage of a fictional or dramatic plot in which necessary background information is provided.

Fable   A brief story with an explicit moral, often including animals as characters.

Falling action   In the plot of a story or play the action following the climax of the work that moves it towards resolution.

Figurative language   A form of language use in which writers and speakers convey something other than the literal meaning of their words. See *hyperbole, metaphor, metonymy, simile, synecdoche,* and *understatement.*

Flashback   An interruption of a work's chronology to describe or present an incident that occurred prior to the main time frame of the action.

Foil   A character who contrasts and parallels the main character in a play or story.

Foreshadowing   Hints of what is to come in the action of a play or story.

Fourth wall   The imaginary wall of the box theater setting, supposedly removed to allow the audience to see the action.

Gesture   The physical movement of a character during a play.

Hyperbole   A figure of speech involving exaggeration.

Image   A concrete representation of a sense impression, a feeling, or an idea. Imagery refers to the pattern of related details in a work.

Imagery   The pattern of related comparative aspects of language in a literary work.

Irony   A contrast or discrepancy between what is said and what is meant or between what happens and what is expected to happen. In verbal irony characters say the opposite of what they mean. In irony of circumstance or situation the opposite of what is expected happens. In dramatic irony a character speaks in ignorance of a situation or event known to the audience or to other characters.

Literal language   A form of language in which writers and speakers mean exactly what their words denote.

Metaphor   A comparison between essentially unlike things without a word such as *like* or *as*. An example: "My love is a red, red rose."

Meter   The measured pattern of rhythmic accents in poems or verse drama.

Metonymy   A figure of speech in which a closely related term is substituted for an object or idea. An example: "We have always remained loyal to the crown."

Monologue   A speech by one character.

Narrative poem   A poem that tells a story.

Narrator   The voice and implied speaker of a fictional work, to be distinguished from the actual living author.

Parable   A brief story that teaches a lesson often ethical or spiritual.

Parody   A humorous, mocking imitation of a literary work.

Pathos   A quality of a play's action that stimulates the audience to feel pity for a character.

Personification   The endowment of inanimate objects or abstract concepts with animate or living qualities. An example: "The yellow leaves flaunted their color gaily in the wind."

Plot   The unified structure of incidents in a literary work.

Point of view   The angle of vision from which a story is narrated.

Props   Articles or objects that appear on stage during a play.

Protagonist   The main character of a literary work.

Recognition   The point at which a character understands his or her situation as it really is.

Resolution   The sorting out or unraveling of a plot at the end of a drama or narrative.

Reversal   The point at which the action of the plot turns in an unexpected direction for the protagonist.

Rhetorical question   A question to which an overt answer is not expected. Writers use rhetorical questions to set up an explanation they are about to provide and to trigger a reader's mental response.

Rising action   A set of conflicts and crises that constitute that part of a play's plot leading up to the climax.

Romance   A type of narrative fiction or poem in which adventure is a central feature and in which an idealized vision of reality is presented.

Satire   A literary work that criticizes human misconduct and ridicules vices, stupidities, and follies.

Setting   The time and place of a literary work that establish its context.

Simile   A figure of speech involving a comparison between unlike things using *like, as,* or *as though.* An example: "My love is like a red, red rose."

Soliloquy   A speech in a play which is meant to be heard by the audience but not by other characters on the stage. If there are no other characters present the soliloquy represents the character's thinking aloud.

Stage direction   A playwright's descriptive or interpretive comments that provide readers (and actors) with information about the dialogue, setting, and action of a play.

Staging   The spectacle a play presents in performance, including the positions of actors on stage, the scenic background, the props and costumes, and the lighting and sound effects.

Structure   The design or form of a literary work.

Style   The way an author chooses words, arranges them in sentences or in lines of dialogue or verse, and develops ideas and actions *with* description, imagery, and other literary techniques.

Subject   What a story or play is about; to be distinguished from plot and theme.

Subplot   A subsidiary or subordinate or parallel plot in a play or story that coexists with the main plot.

Symbol   An object or action in a literary work that means more than itself, that stands for something beyond itself.

Synecdoche   A figure of speech in which a part is substituted for the whole. An example: "Lend me a hand."

Syntax   The grammatical order of words in a sentence or line of verse or dialogue.

Tempo   The variation in pace in which a scene is acted.

Theme   The idea of a literary work abstracted from its details of language, character, and action, and cast in the form of a generalization.

Tone   The implied attitude of a writer toward the subject and characters of a work.

Tragedy   A type of drama in which the characters experience reversals of fortune, usually for the worse. In tragedy, catastrophe and suffering await many of the characters, especially the hero.

Tragic flaw   A weakness or limitation of character resulting in the fall of the tragic hero.

Tragic hero   A privileged, exalted character of high repute, who by virtue of a tragic flaw and fate suffers a fall from glory into suffering.

Tragicomedy   A type of play that contains elements of both tragedy and comedy.

Understatement   A figure of speech in which a writer or speaker says less than what he or she means; the converse of exaggeration.

Unities   The idea established by Aristotle that a play should be limited to a specific time, place, and story. The events of the plot should occur within a twenty-four-hour period, should occur within a given geographic locale, and should tell a single story.

Acknowledgments

Drama

DAVID BEVINGTON and CRAIG HARDIN "Hamlet, Prince of Denmark" by William Shakespeare, from *Introduction to Shakespeare* edited by Hardin Craig and David Bevington. Reprinted by permission of David M. Bevington.

DUDLEY FITTS and FITZGERALD ROBERT "Oedipus Rex" from *Sophocles: The Oedipus Cycle, an English Version* by Dudley Fitts and Robert Fitzgerald. "The Antigone of Sophocles: An English Version" from *Sophocles: The Oedipus Cycle* by Robert Fitzgerald and Dudley Fitts.

SUSAN GLASPELL *Trifles* from *Plays* by Susan Glaspell. Reprinted by permission of Dodd, Mead & Company.

LORRAINE HANSBERRY *A Raisin in the Sun* by Lorraine Hansberry. Copyright © 1958 by Robert Nemiroff, as an unpublished work. Copyright © 1959, 1966, 1984 by Robert Nemiroff. Reprinted by permission of Random House, Inc.

HENRIK IBSEN "A Doll House," from *The Complete Major Prose Plays of Henrik Ibsen* by Henrik Ibsen, translated by Rolfe Fjelde, translation copyright © 1965, 1970, 1978 by Rolfe Fjelde. Used by permission of Dutton Signet, a division of Penguin Putnam Inc.

JOSEFINA LOPEZ "Simply Maria or The American Dream" by Josefina Lopez is reprinted with permission from the publisher of *Shattering the Myth: Plays by Hispanic Women* (Houston: Arte Publico Press—University of Houston, 1992).

TERENCE MCNALLY *Andre's Mother* by Terence McNally. Copyright © 1994 by Terence McNally. All rights reserved. Reprinted by permission of William Morris Agency Inc. on behalf of the Author. CAUTION: Professionals and amateurs are hereby warned that *Andre's Mother* is subject to royalty. It is fully protected under the copyright laws of the United States of America and of all countries covered by the International Copyright Union (including the Dominion of Canada and the rest of the British Commonwealth), the Berne Convention, the Pan-American Copyright Convention and the Universal Copyright Convention as well as all countries with which the United States has reciprocal copyright relations. All rights, including professional/amateur state rights, motion picture, recitation, lecturing, public reading, radio broadcasting, television, video or sound recording, all other forms of mechanical or electronic reproduction,

Critical Perspective:

ADRIAN POOLE "Sophocles and Athens." "Hamlet and Oedipus" from *Tragedy: Shakespeare and the Greek Example* by Adrian Poole. Reprinted by permission of Blackwell Publishers.

GEORGE STEINER "Principal Constants of Conflict in *Antigone*" from *Antigones*. Oxford UP.

Index

Selection titles appear in italics, and first lines of poems appear in roman type. Page numbers in roman type indicate the opening page of a selection; italic numbers indicate discussion. Bold page numbers indicate complete sections on specific authors.